Research Design and Methods

Research Design and Methods
A Process Approach
SECOND EDITION

Kenneth S. Bordens   Bruce B. Abbott
Indiana University — Purdue University at Fort Wayne

Mayfield Publishing Company
Mountain View, California
London • Toronto

Library of Congress Cataloging-in-Publication Data

Bordens, Kenneth S.
    Research design and methods : a process approach / Kenneth S.
Bordens, Bruce B. Abbott. — 2nd ed.
        p.   cm.
    Includes bibliographical references and index.
    ISBN 1–55934–012–6
    1. Psychology — Research.   2. Psychology — Research — Methodology.
I. Abbott, Bruce B.   II. Title.
BF76.5.B67   1991
150′.72 — dc20   90–47525
                                                                              CIP

Manufactured in the United States of America
10 9 8 7 6 5

Mayfield Publishing Company
1240 Villa Street
Mountain View, California 94041

Sponsoring editor, Franklin C. Graham; managing editor, Linda Toy; production editor, Sondra Glider; manuscript editor, Linda Purrington; text and cover designer, Andrew Ogus; illustrator, Guy Magallanes. The text was set in 10/12 Bembo by Thompson Type and printed on 45# Penntech Penn Plus by R. R. Donnelley & Sons Co.

Cover painting: *Banya* by Victor Vasarely. Tate Gallery, London/Art Resource, N.Y.

Text credits appear on a continuation of the copyright page, p. C-1.

We dedicate this book

to the memory of

Dr. Daniel P. Murphy,

colleague, friend, and teacher.

Contents

Part III   Analyzing and Reporting Results

Part IV   Special Topics

Preface

OUR GOAL WHEN WE WROTE THE FIRST EDITION OF *Research Design and Methods: A Process Approach* was to provide a text that would take students through the whole research process, from its beginning in the formulation of a research question through the publication of the findings. Along the way, we wanted to show students what decisions they would face at each step and indicate the consequences of the choices they would make. In addition, we wanted to give students the tools and skills they would need to conduct their own research projects: how to use library sources to unearth the relevant literature, how to construct questionnaires and conduct surveys, how to select a research design, what issues to consider when choosing subjects, how to treat subjects ethically, how to use descriptive and inferential statistics, how to write a research paper. We therefore organized the text to reflect the sequence of steps usually followed when designing and conducting research. We worked hard to present this information in a friendly, easy-to-read style, with plenty of examples to illustrate and clarify the critical concepts.

A second goal was to provide more advanced material for those classes where such material would be deemed appropriate, and for future reference by students who might later need the information when designing their own research projects. Chapters treating these topics were written in such a way that they could be included or excluded without interrupting the flow of the remaining chapters.

The success of the first edition and encouraging responses from students and instructors suggest that our approach to research methods has been appreciated and accepted. Therefore, in revising the text for the second edition, we have preserved the basic organization and content of the book while taking the opportunity to improve those areas that students and our fellow teachers told us were not as clear or well organized as they might be, and to update some of the material and correct the inevitable errors that somehow crept into the first edition.

This edition preserves the four-part structure of the first. Part I introduces students to general principles of research design, including discussions of why research is important (Chapter 1), how to develop ideas for research (Chapter 2), how to choose an appropriate research method (Chapter 3), how to make systematic observations (Chapter 4), and how to choose an appropriate subject sample (Chapter 5).

Part II introduces various research methods and designs, including both non-experimental techniques (Chapters 6 and 7) and experimental designs (Chapters 8, 9, and 10). These chapters identify the main features of each design and describe the relative advantages and disadvantages of each. After reading these chapters, students should be able to make informed decisions when choosing a research design.

In Part III the chapters focus on analyzing data and reporting research results. Chapters 11 and 12 provide reviews of basic descriptive and inferential statistics, respectively. Chapter 13 introduces students to computer analysis of data, providing an overview of the basic process. Students are shown how to organize data for input into the computer, check for errors, run the appropriate analysis, and interpret the output. Chapter 14 describes how to prepare an APA-style research report. In addition to describing the APA manuscript format, this chapter offers major sections on clarity of expression, organization, and style, including such topics as how to avoid lazy writing and plagiarism.

Part IV comprises three chapters on advanced topics. Chapter 15 gives an overview of multivariate design and analysis, describing the major techniques and indicating their uses. Chapter 16 discusses the uses of theory in science and distinguishes several types. Finally, Chapter 17 takes a look at the effects of publication practices on the validity and reliability of published findings, and discusses meta-analysis, a technique for combining results across studies.

Throughout the text, we have aimed to provide more complete coverage of topics than found in most texts, without becoming overly rigorous. For example, Chapter 2 includes detailed instructions on how to use the *Psychological Abstracts* and *Social Science Citations Index* to locate research literature. A section is also included on how to use PsycLIT (a computer database of the *Psychological Abstracts*) to locate relevant resource materials. Our coverage of ethical issues in Chapter 5 traces the origins of the APA ethical principles to the Nazi war crime trials at Nuremberg at the close of World War II, and in Chapter 10 we trace the history of single-subject research designs. We also provide a balanced coverage of both experimental and nonexperimental techniques, rather than focusing on experimental methods as many texts do.

Several features of the text help students organize and understand the material presented. Each chapter closes with a Summary and a list of Key Terms. We have made liberal use of examples to illustrate many of the concepts and techniques discussed. We have also included numerous figures and tables to help students understand textual material.

In addition to the learning aids included in the text, we have developed an extensive ancillary package. A student workbook includes chapter outlines, key questions to consider, review questions, and "hands-on" exercises for students to do. In addition, an easy-to-use computer statistical program package for use on the personal computer (LabStat) is available at no additional cost to help students analyze their data.

Changes in the Second Edition

The second edition of *Research Design and Methods: A Process Approach* includes changes and additions we believe will make the text clearer for students to read and comprehend. First, we have added a glossary. The glossary terms are bold-faced in the text for added convenience to students.

New examples have been added to Chapter 1 ("Explaining Behavior"), and much of the existing material has been reorganized and rewritten to increase clarity. Chapter 3 ("Choosing a Research Design") now focuses more on distinguishing correlational and experimental research. Two examples of actual research illustrate the difference between these two research methods. The material on special designs has been redistributed to Chapters 6 and 9, where it appears with related material. Chapter 6 ("Using Nonexperimental, Quasi-Experimental, and Developmental Designs") has been revised to include a clearer description of techniques used to evaluate interrater reliability and better computational examples.

Chapter 8 ("Using Between-Subjects Designs") has been reorganized so that the discussion of the limitations of the two-group design clearly applies to both randomized groups and matched pairs designs. Randomized groups and matched pairs designs are now treated in separate sections of the chapter. Chapter 9 ("Using Within-Subjects and Combined Designs") has also been reorganized and rewritten to clarify the advantages and disadvantages of within-subjects designs. Also, the related pretest-posttest design is now discussed in Chapter 9. Chapter 10 more clearly distinguishes between baseline and discrete trials designs by more fully separating their discussion and by summarizing their key features in two tables.

The focus of Chapter 13 ("Using the Computer to Analyze Data") has been shifted from the mainframe computer to the personal computer. We now include an extended example showing how to analyze data using the LabStat package (available to adopters), including how to enter data, select an analysis, and interpret the computer output. The material on data analysis using the mainframe has been shortened. Chapter 15 ("Using Multivariate Design and Analysis") now includes a discussion of loglinear analysis, and Appendix II ("Formulas and Worked Examples") has been expanded to include chi-square and the Mann-Whitney U-test.

Changes to the Ancillaries

The workbook that accompanies this text is very similar to the one that accompanied the first edition. There are still chapter outlines, key terms to define, practice questions, and exercises. However, a few new exercises have been added. We have also added a list of key questions for students to consider while reading the text.

For instructors we have developed an instructor's manual that includes lecture ideas, projects for in-class and out-of-class use, and a list of resource materials. The suggested projects are ones that we (and some of our colleagues) have used. These projects engage the students' interest while showing them the "ins and outs" of research design and methodology. Transparency masters are also available for illustrating concepts from the text.

The test bank has been revised to reflect the changes in the second edition. We have also adopted a new, computerized, test-generating program, Brownstone's *Exam*. One of the most powerful and easy-to-use examination programs available, the program allows instructors to add items directly to chapter item banks, edit existing questions, and generate a wide variety of examinations, including different types of questions.

Acknowledgments

A project such as this requires the help of many people. We thank all those who contributed their time and talents to this text, although we can name only a few. First, we again extend our thanks to those who helped make the first edition a success: Helen J. Crawford (University of Wyoming), Arthur D. Fiske (University of South Carolina), Daniel Leger (University of Nebraska), Beth A. Shapiro (Emory University), Michael S. Wogalter (University of Richmond), Barbara Tabachnick (California State University—Northridge), and Elaine Blakemore (Indiana University-Purdue University at Fort Wayne). They helped lay the foundation on which this second edition was built.

We also extend our thanks to those who contributed to the second edition: Carol Lawton (Indiana University-Purdue University at Fort Wayne), Patricia

Phillips (Illinois State University), Daniel Leger (University of Nebraska), and Lori Temple-Colvet (University of Nevada — Las Vegas) contributed excellent reviews. Thanks also to Franklin Graham, sponsoring editor at Mayfield Publishing for his patient nurturing of both editions of this text, and to the production staff at Mayfield for their expert crafting of the final product.

We extend special thanks to those students of ours who used the first edition and gave us feedback and suggestions on how to make the text better, and to everyone else we neglected to mention by name for their efforts.

Finally, our thanks go to our wives, Ricky Karen Bordens and Stephanie Abbott, and to our families for their support and encouragement. They put up with many a lonely day and night while we hunched over computer screens and manuscript pages, waiting for flashes of insight.

Research Design and Methods

1

Explaining Behavior

ON THE NIGHT OF OCTOBER 23, 1989, Charles Stuart, a handsome 30-year-old businessman, sat slumped behind the wheel of his car with a gunshot wound in his abdomen. His pregnant wife was in the passenger seat dying from a gunshot wound in the head. Stuart desperately called 911 on his cellular car phone. Stuart was unable to tell the police exactly where he was, and it was only by homing in on the sound of their own sirens coming back over Stuart's phone that they were able to locate him and his dying wife. Stuart, after hours of surgery, survived. His wife was not so lucky; her head wound was fatal. Her baby, delivered prematurely via caesarian section, died in the hospital after a nearly three-week struggle for survival.

Although Stuart claimed that he and his wife had been robbed at gunpoint by a black man and then shot, events later proved otherwise. The police, seeing inconsistencies in Stuart's story, began to suspect that Stuart himself was responsible for the whole affair. It turned out that Stuart had contrived the whole robbery scenario to cover up the fact that he himself had shot his wife and himself. Apparently Stuart wanted to avoid the financial obligations of having a child and a wife who was going to leave full-time law practice to become a full-time mother. As police began to close in on him, Stuart leaped to his death from Boston's Tobin Bridge.

What sort of man could commit such a crime? How could he live with himself afterward? Could anyone become such a person, given the right circumstances, or was Stuart just the "type of person" who would do such a thing? All these questions beg for answers. As we attempt to formulate explanations based on the information available and our own experience, we behave much as scientists do.

Kelly (1963) characterizes each person as a scientist who has developed a set of strategies for determining the causes of observed behavior. Nevertheless, the everyday strategies we use to explain what we observe frequently lack the rigor to qualify as truly scientific. In most cases the explanations developed for behaviors observed in everyday life are made on the spot, with little attention to accuracy. We commonly develop an explanation and then, satisfied that the explanation makes sense, simply adopt it. If we *do* give more thought to our explanations, we often base our thinking on hearsay, conjecture, anecdotal evidence, or unverified sources of information. These explanations, even though they reduce transient curiosity about behavior, remain untested conjectures. For example, we might satisfy our curiosity about Charles Stuart by concluding that he was "sick." Satisfied with such a conclusion, we might fail to take into account possible reasons for his behavior derived from his situation and family history.

Unfounded, but commonly accepted, explanations for behavior can have widespread consequences when the explanations become the basis for social policy. For example, segregation of blacks in the South was based on stereotypes of assumed racial differences in intelligence and moral judgment. These beliefs sound ludicrous today and have failed to survive a scientific analysis. Such mistakes might have been avoided if lawmakers of the time had relied on objective information rather than prejudice.

To avoid the trap of easy, untested explanations for behavior, we need to abandon the informal, unsystematic approach to explanation and to adopt an approach that has proven its ability to find explanations of great power and generality. This approach, called the *scientific method,* and how you can apply it to answer questions about behavior are the central topics of this book.

This book is about the research process. In a broader sense, it is about the business of finding unambiguous explanations for behavior. This text describes how to develop scientifically testable research questions about behavior, how to develop and use acceptable methods of observation by using appropriate research designs, how to properly analyze and interpret the resulting data, and how to use these results to arrive at scientifically acceptable explanations.

Whether or not you intend to pursue a career in psychological research, these concepts will be among the more important and useful information that you take with you when you leave college. The complex world of today constantly demands that you evaluate information and draw valid conclusions from it. If you know how to proceed on a scientific basis, you will be in a much better position to deal with such information and to evaluate the conclusions and explanations of others.

Explaining Behavior

Psychology is the science of human and animal behavior. The major goals of any science are to build an organized body of knowledge about its subject matter, and to provide valid and reliable explanations for the phenomena within its domain. Yet the same goals are shared by history, which is not considered a science. What, then, distinguishes a science from nonscience (and from pseudoscience)? The difference lies in the quality of the explanations, and in the methods applied to produce those explanations.

Scientific explanations differ in several fundamental ways from other types of explanations, such as those based on common sense or on faith. The next sections describe the characteristics of scientific explanations and contrast these explanations with those proposed by common sense or by *a priori* belief.

Scientific Explanations

Scientific explanations have a unique blend of characteristics that sets them apart from other types of explanations, as follows:

Scientific Explanations Are Empirical. An explanation is empirical if it is based on the evidence of the senses. To qualify as scientific, an explanation must be based on objective and systematic observation, often carried out under carefully controlled conditions. The observable events and conditions referred to in the explanation must be capable of verification by others.

Scientific Explanations Are Rational. An explanation is rational if it follows the rules of logic and is consistent with known facts. If the explanation makes assumptions that are known to be false, commits logical errors in drawing conclusions from its assumptions, or is inconsistent with established fact, then it does not qualify as scientific.

Scientific Explanations Are Testable. A scientific explanation should either be verifiable through direct observation or lead to specific predictions about what should occur under conditions not yet observed. An explanation is testable if confidence in the explanation could be undermined by a failure to observe the predicted outcome. One should be able to imagine outcomes that would disprove the explanation.

Scientific Explanations Are Parsimonious. Often more than one explanation is offered for an observed behavior. When this occurs, scientists usually prefer the least complex explanation, or the explanation that requires the fewest assumptions. This type of explanation is called a **parsimonious explanation**.

Scientific Explanations Are General. Scientists prefer explanations of broad explanatory power over those that "work" only within a limited set of circumstances.

Such explanations apply well beyond the narrow observations they were originally created to explain.

Scientific Explanations Are Tentative. Scientists may have confidence in their explanations, but they are nevertheless willing to entertain the possibility that the explanation is faulty. This attitude has been strengthened in this century by the realization that even Newton's conception of the universe, one of the most strongly supported views in scientific history, had to be replaced when new evidence showed that some of its predictions were wrong.

Scientific Explanations Are Rigorously Evaluated. This characteristic derives from the other characteristics just mentioned, but it is important enough to deserve its own place in the list. Scientific explanations are constantly evaluated for consistency with the evidence and with known principles, for parsimony, and for generality. Attempts are made to extend the scope of the explanation to cover broader areas and to include more factors. As plausible alternatives appear, these are pitted against the old explanations in a continual battle for the "survival of the fittest." In this way even accepted explanations may be overthrown in favor of views that are more general, more parsimonious, or more consistent with observation.

Commonsense Versus Scientific Explanations

During the course of everyday experience, we develop explanations of the events we see going on around us. Largely, these explanations are based on the limited information available from the observed event and what our previous experience has told us is true. These rather loose explanations can be classified as **commonsense explanations** because they are based on our own sense of what is true about the world around us. Of course, scientific explanations and commonsense explanations share something in common: they both start with an observation of events in the real world. However, the two types of explanations differ in the level of proof required to support the explanation. Commonsense explanations tend to be accepted at face value, whereas scientific explanations are subjected to rigorous research scrutiny.

Take the case of Kitty Genovese, a New York City woman who was stabbed to death over a period of about 40 minutes. During the attack, over thirty of her neighbors listened to her screams, yet not one of them bothered to call the police. The behavior of Kitty Genovese's neighbors begs for an explanation.

At first glance it would appear that Kitty Genovese's neighbors simply did not care about her plight, suffering from "urban apathy." In fact, "urban apathy" was the first explanation (offered mainly by the news media) for the behavior of the witnesses in regard to the murder. Although this explanation seems intuitively compelling, several factors disqualify it as a scientific explanation.

First, the "urban apathy" explanation was not based on careful, systematic observation. Instead, it was based on what some people *believed* to be true of life in a big city. Consequently, the explanation may have been derived from biased, incomplete, or limited evidence. Second, it was not examined to determine if it was consistent with other available observations. For example, does similar "apathy" occur in smaller cities or rural areas? Third, at the time no effort was made to evaluate it against plausible alternative explanations. Fourth, no predictions were derived from the explanation and tested. Finally, no attempt was made to determine how well the explanation accounted for similar behavior in a variety of other circumstances. In short, the explanation was accepted because it appeared to make sense of the murder and was consistent with preexisting beliefs.

For these reasons, the commonsense explanation is likely to be incomplete, inconsistent with other evidence, lacking in generality, and probably wrong. This certainly is the case with the "urban apathy" explanation. Considerable research has shown that bystanders often suffer tremendous guilt and anxiety as they stand and watch and do nothing. Instead, they are paralyzed by conflict, fear, and rationalization.

Although commonsense explanations may "feel right" and give us a sense that we understand a behavior, they may lack the power to apply across a variety of apparently similar situations. To see how commonsense explanations may fail to provide a truly general account of behavior, consider the following event.

Late in December 1903, a fire started in the crowded Iroquois Theater of Chicago and 602 people lost their lives. Of interest to psychologists is not the fact that 602 people died, *per se,* but rather the circumstances that led to many of the deaths. Many of the victims were not directly killed by the fire. Rather, they were trampled to death in the panic that ensued in the first few minutes after the fire started. In his classic book *Social Psychology,* Brown (1965) reproduced an account of the event provided by Eddie Foy, a famous comedian of the time. According to Foy's account,

> . . . it was inside the house that the greatest loss of life occurred, especially on the stairways leading down from the second balcony. Here most of the dead were trampled or smothered. . . . In places on the stairways, particularly where a turn caused a jam, bodies were piled seven or eight deep. (Brown, 1965, p. 715)

As a student of psychology, you may already be formulating ideas to explain why normally rational human beings would behave as a mindless crowd in this situation. Clearly, many lives would have been saved had the patrons of the Iroquois Theater filed out in a more orderly fashion. How would you explain the tragedy?

A logical and "obvious" answer is that the patrons believed their lives to be in danger and wanted to leave the theater as quickly as possible. Hence you may want to explain the panic inside the theater as motivated by a desire to survive.

Notice that the explanation at this point is probably adequate to explain the crowd behavior under the specific conditions inside the theater, and perhaps to explain the same behavior under other life-threatening conditions. However, the explanation is probably too situation-specific to serve as a general scientific explanation of irrational crowd behavior. It cannot explain, for example, the following incident.

On December 10, 1979, a crowd of young people lined up outside a Cincinnati arena to wait for the doors to open for a concert by the popular rock group called the Who. As the time neared for the doors to open, the crowd began to surge ahead. Eleven people were trampled to death even though the conditions were certainly less than life threatening. In fact, the identifiable reward in this situation was obtaining the best seat possible at an open-seating concert.

Clearly, the explanation for irrational crowd behavior at the Chicago theater cannot be applied to the Cincinnati tragedy. People were not going to die if they failed to get desirable seats at the concert. What seemed a reasonable explanation for irrational crowd behavior in the Iroquois Theater case must be discarded here.

You must look for common elements to explain such similar, yet diverse, events. In both situations the available reinforcers were perceived to be limited. A powerful reinforcer (avoiding pain and death) in the Iroquois Theater undoubtedly was perceived as attainable only for a brief time. Similarly, the perceived reinforcer (a seat close to the stage) in Cincinnati, although not essential for survival, was also available for a limited time only. In both cases, apparently irrational behavior resulted as large numbers of people individually attempted to maximize the probability of obtaining the reinforcer.

The new tentative explanation for the irrational behavior now centers around the perceived availability of reinforcers, rather than situation-specific variables. As described later in this chapter, this new tentative explanation has been tested in research and has received some support.

As these examples illustrate, simple commonsense explanations may not apply beyond the specific situations that spawned them. The scientist interested in "irrational crowd behavior" would look for a more general concept (such as perceived availability of reinforcers) to explain observed behavior. That is not to say that simple, obvious explanations are always incorrect. When you are looking for an explanation that transcends situation-specific variables, you must often look beyond simple, commonsense explanations.

Belief-Based Versus Scientific Explanations

Explanations for behavior often arise not from common sense or scientific observation, but from individuals or groups who (through indoctrination, upbringing, or personal need) have accepted on faith the truth of their beliefs. You may agree or disagree with those beliefs, but you should be aware that explanations offered by science and **belief-based explanations** are fundamentally different.

Explanations based on belief are accepted because they come from a trusted source or appear to be consistent with the larger framework of belief. No evidence is required. If evidence suggests that the explanation is incorrect, then the evidence is discarded or reinterpreted to make it appear consistent with the belief. For example, certain religions hold that Earth was created only a few thousand years ago. The discovery of fossilized remains of dinosaurs and other creatures (apparently millions of years old) challenged this belief. To explain the existence of these remains, people defending the belief suggest that fossils are actually natural rock formations that resemble bones, or that the fossils are the remains of the victims of the Great Flood. Thus, rather than calling the belief into question, apparently contrary evidence is interpreted to appear consistent with the belief.

This willingness to apply a different *post hoc* (after-the-fact) explanation to reconcile the observations with belief leads to an unparsimonious patchwork quilt of explanations that lack generality, fail to produce testable predictions about future findings, and often require that one assume the common occurrence of highly unlikely events. Scientific explanations of the same phenomena, in contrast, logically organize the observed facts by means of a few, parsimonious assumptions and lead to testable predictions.

Nowhere is the contrast between these two approaches more striking than in the current debate between evolutionary biologists and the so-called creation scientists, whose explanation for fossils was just described. To take one example, consider the recent discoveries based on gene sequencing, which reveal the degree of genetic similarity among various species. These observations and some simple assumptions about the rate of mutation in the genetic material allowed biologists to develop "family trees" indicating how long ago the various species separated from one another. The trees drawn up from the gene-sequencing data agree amazingly well with, and to a large degree were predicted by, the trees assembled from the fossil record. In contrast, because creationists assume that all animals alive today have always had their current form, and that fossils represent the remains of animals killed in the Great Flood, their view could not have predicted relationships found in the genetic material and must instead invent yet another *post hoc* explanation to make these new findings appear consistent with their beliefs.

In addition to the differences described thus far, scientific and belief-based explanations also differ in tentativeness. Whereas explanations based on belief are assumed to be true, scientific explanations are accepted because they are consistent with existing objective evidence and have survived rigorous testing against plausible alternatives. Scientists accept the possibility that better explanations may turn up or that new tests may show the current explanation is inadequate.

Scientific explanations also differ from belief-based explanations in the subject areas for which explanations are offered. Whereas explanations based on belief may seek to answer virtually any question, scientific explanations are limited to addressing those questions that can be answered by means of objective observations. For example, what happens to a person after death or why suffering exists in the world are explained by religion, but such questions remain outside the realm of scientific explanation. No objective tests or observations can be performed to answer these questions within the confines of the scientific method. Science offers no explanation on questions such as these, and you must rely on faith or belief for answers. However, where questions can be settled on the basis of objective observation, scientific explanations generally have provided more satisfactory and useful accounts of behavior than those provided by *a priori* belief.

When Scientific Explanations Fail

Scientific explanation is preferable to other kinds of explanation when scientific methods can be applied. Using a scientific approach maximizes the chances of discovering the best explanation for an observed behavioral phenomenon. Despite the application of the most rigorous of scientific methods, instances do occur when the explanation offered by a scientist is not valid. Scientific explanations are sometimes flawed. Understanding some of the pitfalls inherent to developing scientific explanations will help you avoid arriving at flawed or incorrect explanations for behavior.

Failures Caused by Faulty Inference

Explanations may fail because developing them involves an inference process. We make observations and then infer the causes for the observed behavior. This inference process always involves the danger of incorrectly inferring the underlying mechanisms that control behavior.

The problem of faulty inference is illustrated in a satirical book by David Macaulay (1979) called *Motel of the Mysteries*. In this book a scientist (Howard Carson) uncovers the remnants of our civilization 5,000 years from now. Carson unearths a motel and begins the task of explaining what our civilization was like, based on the artifacts found in the motel.

Figure 1-1 presents an illustration from Macaulay's book showing three "musical instruments" unearthed at the site. The archeologist describes these instruments as follows:

> The two trumpets on the [bottom] were found attached to the wall of the inner chamber at the end of the sarcophagus. They were both coated with a silver substance similar to that used on the ornamental pieces of the metal animals. Music was played by forcing water from the sacred spring through the trumpets under great pressure. Pitch was controlled by a large silver handle marked HC. . . . The instrument on the [top] is probably of the percussion family, but as yet the method of playing it remains a mystery. It is, however, beautifully crafted of wood and rubber. (p. 68)

In this example the archeologist hypothesized that various plumbing devices served as ceremonial musical instruments. The scientist has reached a number of inaccurate conclusions by basing inferences on available data.

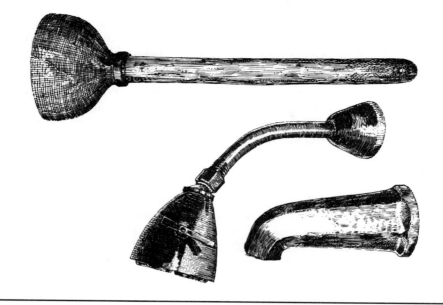

Figure 1-1. Illustration from *Motel of the Mysteries* (Macaulay, 1979) showing common plumbing devices mistakenly believed to be religious artifacts. (Reprinted with permission.)

Although the *Motel of the Mysteries* example is pure fiction, real–life examples of inference gone wrong abound in science, and psychology is no exception. Fancher (1985) describes the following example in his book *The Intelligence Men: Makers of the IQ Controversy*. During World War I, the U.S. Army administered group intelligence tests under the direction of Robert Yerkes. More than 1.75 million men had taken either the Alpha or Beta version of the test by the end of the war and provided an excellent statistical sample from which conclusions could be drawn about the abilities of U.S. men of that era.

The results were shocking. Analysis of the data revealed that the average army recruit had a mental age of 13 years — three years below the "average adult" mental age of 16 and only one year above the upper limit for moronity. Fancher described Yerkes's interpretation as follows:

> Rather than interpreting his results to mean that there was something wrong with the standard, or that the army scores had been artificially depressed by . . . the failure to re-test most low Alpha scorers on Beta, as was supposed to have been the case, Yerkes asserted that the "native intelligence" of the average recruit was shockingly low. The tests, he said, were "originally intended, and now definitely known, to measure native intellectual ability.

They are to some extent influenced by educational requirement, but in the main the soldier's inborn intelligence and not the accidents of environment determined his mental rating or grade." Accordingly, a very substantial proportion of the soldiers in the U.S. Army were actually morons. (p. 127)

In fact, Yerkes's assertions about the tests were not in any sense established, and indeed the data provided evidence against Yerkes's conclusion. For example, poorly educated recruits from rural areas scored lower than their better-educated city cousins. Yerkes's tests had failed to consider the differences in educational opportunities among recruits. As a result, Yerkes and his followers inappropriately concluded that the average intellectual ability of Americans was deteriorating.

In the Yerkes example, faulty conclusions were drawn because the conclusions were based on unfounded assumptions concerning the ability of the tests to unambiguously measure intelligence. The researchers failed to consider possible *alternative explanations* for observed effects. Although the intelligence of U.S. Army recruits may in fact have been distressingly low, an alternative explanation centering around environmental factors such as educational level would have been equally plausible. These two rival explanations (real decline in intelligence versus lack of assumed educational experience) should have been subjected to the proper tests to determine which was more plausible. Later, this book discusses how developing, testing, and eliminating such rival hypotheses are crucial elements of the scientific method.

Pseudoexplanations

Failing to consider alternative explanations is not the only danger waiting to befall the unwary scientist. In formulating valid scientific explanations for behavioral events, it is important to avoid the trap of **pseudoexplanations**. In seeking to provide explanations for behavior, psychologists sometimes offer positions, theories, and explanations that do nothing more than provide an alternative label for the behavioral event. One notorious example was the attempt to explain aggression with the concept of an instinct. According to this position, people (and animals) behave aggressively because of an aggressive instinct. Although this explanation may have intuitive appeal, it does not serve as a valid scientific explanation.

Figure 1-2 illustrates the problem with such an explanation. Notice that the observed behavior (aggression) is used to prove the existence of the aggressive instinct. The concept of instinct is then used to explain the aggressive behavior.

This form of reasoning is called a **circular explanation** or **tautology**. It does not provide a true explanation, but rather merely provides another label (instinct) for a class of observed behavior (aggression). Animals are aggressive because they have aggressive instincts. How do we know they have aggressive instincts? Because they are aggressive! Thus, all we are saying is that animals are aggressive because of a tendency to behave aggressively. Obviously this is not an explanation.

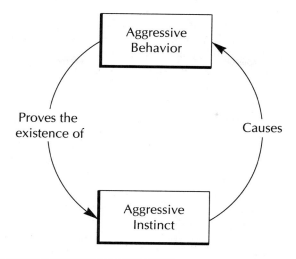

Figure 1-2. A circular explanation. The observed behavior is "explained" by a concept, but the behavior itself is used as proof of the existence of the explanatory concept.

You might expect only novice behavioral scientists to be prone to using pseudoexplanations. However, even professional behavioral scientists have proposed "explanations" for behavioral phenomena that are really pseudoexplanations. In a 1970 article, Martin Seligman proposed a continuum of preparedness to help explain why an animal can learn some associations easily (such as between taste and illness) and other associations only with great difficulty (such as between taste and electric shock).

According to Seligman's analysis, the animal may be biologically prepared to learn some associations (those learned quickly) and contraprepared to learn others (those learned slowly, if at all). Thus, some animals may have difficulty acquiring an association between taste and shock because they are contraprepared by evolution to associate the two.

As with the use of instinct to explain aggression, the continuum of preparedness notion seems intuitively correct. Indeed, it does serve as a potentially valid explanation for the observed differences in learning rates. But, it does not qualify as a true explanation as it is stated. Refer back to Figure 1-2 and substitute "quickly or slowly acquired association" for "aggression," and "continuum of preparedness" for "instinct." As presently stated, the continuum-of-preparedness explanation is circular. Animals learn a particular association with difficulty because they are contraprepared to learn it. How do you know they are contraprepared? You know because they have difficulty learning.

How can you avoid falling into the trap of proposing and accepting pseudoexplanations? When evaluating a proposed explanation, ask yourself whether or not the researcher has provided *independent measures* of the behavior of interest (such as difficulty learning an association) *and* the proposed explanatory concept (such as the continuum of preparedness). For example, if you could find an independent measure of preparedness that does *not* involve the animal's ability to form an association, then the explanation in terms of preparedness would qualify as a true explanation. If you can determine the animal's preparedness only by observing its ability to form a particular association, the proposed explanation is circular. Rather than explaining the differing rates of learning, the statement actually serves only to define the types of preparedness.

Developing independent measures for the explanatory concept and the behavior to be explained may not be easy. For example, in the continuum-of-preparedness case it may take some creative thought to develop a measure of preparedness that is independent of the observed behavior. The same is true for the concept of an instinct.

As these examples have illustrated, even scientific explanations may fail. However, you should not conclude that such explanations are no better than those derived from other sources. Living, behaving organisms are complex systems whose observable workings provide only clues to their inner processes. Given the available evidence, you make your best guess. It should not be surprising that these guesses are often wrong. As these conjectures are evaluated against new evidence, even the failures serve to rule out plausible alternatives and to prepare the way for better guesses. As a result, science has a strong tendency to converge on valid explanations as research progresses. Such progress in understanding is a hallmark of the scientific method.

Methods of Inquiry

Before a scientist can offer valid and general explanations for behavior, information must be gathered about the behavior of interest. Knowledge about behavior can be acquired by several methods, including the method of authority, the rational method, and the scientific method.

The Method of Authority

After reading about the Iroquois Theater tragedy, you might make a trip to your local public or university library, or call your former social psychology professor, in search of information to help explain the irrational behavior inside the theater. When you use expert sources (whether books or people), you are using the **method of authority**. Using the method of authority involves consulting some source you consider authoritative on the issue in question (for example, consulting books, television, religious leaders, scientists).

Although useful in the early stages of acquiring knowledge, the method of authority does not always provide valid answers to questions about behavior, for at least two reasons. First, the source you consult may not be truly authoritative. Some people (such as Lucy in the "Peanuts" comic strip) are more than willing to give you their "expert" opinions on any topic, no matter how little they actually know about it (writers are no exception). Second, sources often are biased by a particular point of view. A sociologist may offer a different explanation for the Iroquois Theater tragedy from the one offered by a behaviorally oriented psychologist. For these reasons, the method of authority by itself is not adequate for producing reliable explanations.

Although the method of authority is not the final word in the search for explanations of behavior, the method does play an important role in the acquisition of scientific knowledge. Information you obtain from authorities on a topic can familiarize you with the problem, the available evidence, and the proposed explanations. With this information you could generate new ideas about causes of behavior. However, these ideas must then be subjected to rigorous scientific scrutiny rather than being accepted at face value.

The Rational Method

René Descartes proposed in the sixteenth century that valid conclusions about the universe could be drawn through the use of pure reason, a doctrine called *rationalism*. This proposal was quite a revolution at the time, because most scholars of the day relied heavily on the method of authority to answer questions. Descartes's method began with skepticism, a willingness to doubt the truth of every belief. Descartes noted, as an example, that it was even possible to doubt the existence of the universe. What you perceive, he reasoned, could be an illusion. Could you prove otherwise?

After establishing doubt, Descartes moved to the next stage of his method: the search for statements, known as "self-evident truths," that must be true because to assume otherwise would contradict logic. Descartes reasoned that if the universe were illusory, then he himself must also be illusory. However, Descartes saw a contradiction: If he was illusory, who was doing all this doubting? Surely, anything that thinks must exist; and anything that exists must have been created.

These two assumptions were held as self-evident truths of Descartes's own existence. Descartes went on to the next step of his method: to draw valid conclusions from the two self-evident assumptions. His reasoning went something like this:

Assumption 1: Something that thinks must exist.

Assumption 2: Something that exists must have been created.

Conclusion: I exist, therefore there must be a creator (God).

Notice that Descartes used deductive logic to arrive at the conclusion that a creator (God) exists. Descartes had proven, to his own satisfaction, the existence of God through purely rational, logical methods. By the way, this example was immortalized by Descartes in the Latin declaration *"Cogito, ergo sum"* ("I think, therefore I am").

Descartes's method came to be called the **rational method,** because it depends on logical reasoning rather than on authority or the evidence of one's senses. Although the method satisfied Descartes, we must approach "knowledge" acquired in this way with caution.

The power of the rational method lies in logically deduced conclusions from self-evident truths. Unfortunately, precious few self-evident truths can serve as assumptions in a logical system. If one (or both) of the assumptions used in the deduction process is incorrect, the logically deduced conclusion will be invalid.

Because of its shortcomings, the rational method is not used to develop scientific explanations. However, it still plays an important role in science. The tentative ideas that we form about the relationship between variables are often deduced from earlier assumptions. For example, having learned that fleeing from a fire or trying to get into a crowded arena causes irrational behavior, we may deduce that "perceived availability of reinforcers" (escaping death or getting a front-row seat) is responsible for such behavior. Rather than accepting our deduction as correct, however, the scientist puts the deduction to empirical test.

The Scientific Method

Braithwaite (1953) proposed that the function of a science is to "establish general laws covering the behavior of the empirical events with which the science in question is concerned" (p. 1). According to Braithwaite, a science should allow us to fuse together information concerning separately occurring events and to make reliable predictions about future, unknown events. One goal of psychology is to establish general laws of behavior that help explain and predict behavioral events that occur in a variety of situations.

Although explanations for behavior and general laws cannot be adequately formulated by relying solely on authoritative sources, and using deductive reasoning, these methods (when combined with other features) form the basis for the most powerful approach to knowledge yet developed: the **scientific method**. This method is made up of a series of four cyclical steps you can repeatedly execute as you pursue the solution to a scientific problem (Yaremko, Harari, Harrison, & Lynn, 1982, p. 212). These steps are (1) observing a phenomenon, (2) forming tentative explanations or statements of cause and effect, (3) further observing or experimenting (or both) to rule out alternative explanations, and (4) revising and refining the explanations.

Observing a Phenomenon. The starting point for using the scientific method in behavioral research is to observe a behavior of interest. Such observations may take a variety of forms. You may want to observe naturally occurring behavior in order to get an idea of the range of possible behaviors in a particular situation. For example, if you were interested in studying how juries judge the guilt or innocence of defendants, you might begin by observing juries under actual trial conditions. Observation can take other forms as well and, as we show in the next chapter, there are many sources of ideas for research.

Through the process of observation, you identify the variables that appear to be important for explaining behavior. A **variable** is any characteristic or quantity that can take on several different values. For example, one variable that might be important to a jury's decision is the number of charges on which the defendant is tried. The number of charges is a variable because it can take on several values; for example, the defendant may face one, two, or seventeen charges.

Formulating Tentative Explanations. After identifying a phenomenon in need of explanation, you then develop one or more tentative explanations that seem consistent with your observations. In science, these tentative explanations often include a statement of the causal relationship between two variables. That is, you tentatively state that changes in the value of one variable cause changes in the value of another.

Up to this point, all you have done is to identify an expected relationship between two variables, based on your initial observations. Your initial observations may lead you to develop a specific **hypothesis** about the variables that control behavior. A hypothesis is a tentative statement about the relationship between variables. It is important that any hypothesis you develop be testable with empirical methods.

For example, imagine that you have observed several criminal trials and you think that jury verdicts are affected by the number of charges included in a trial. You notice that "joined trials" (those in which the defendant was charged with more than one crime) lead to more convictions than "separate trials" (those in which the defendant was charged with a single crime). Consequently, you develop the following hypothesis: "Defendants tried in joined trials are found guilty more often than defendants tried in separate trials." In this hypothesis, one variable (number of charges) is linked with an expected outcome (jury verdicts). Hypotheses are often stated in terms of the variables you expect to affect the behavior of interest.

Further Observing and Experimenting. As described thus far, the scientific method does not differ markedly from the methods of authority and rationalism. All you have done up to this point is develop a hypothesis based on some initial observations. The third step in the scientific method marks the point where the scientific method differs from the other methods of inquiry. Unlike the other methods of inquiry, the scientific method demands that further observations be carried out to test the validity of any hypotheses formulated from your initial observations.

What is meant by "further observation"? The answer to this question is what the scientific method is all about. When you have formulated your hypotheses, you then carry out a more clearly defined and detailed study of the behavior of interest. As an example, return for the moment to our hypothesis about joined trials leading to more convictions than separate trials.

After formulating the hypothesis, Kenneth Bordens and his colleagues (Horowitz, Bordens, & Feldman, 1980) designed an experiment (conducted in a laboratory) to test the hypothesis. Subjects listened to an audiotaped version of the original trial that included either joined charges (that is, subjects heard both charges in one trial) or separate charges (one group of subjects heard only the first charge, whereas a second group heard only the second charge). Comparisons of verdicts were made between subjects hearing the joined and separate trials. The results confirmed the hypothesis. Defendants in the joined trial were more likely to be convicted than were defendants in the separate trials.

Refining and Retesting Explanations. The final step of the scientific method is the process of refinement and retesting. When you have obtained support for an initial hypothesis, you often refine the hypothesis to further explore the behavior of interest. For example, in the Horowitz et al. (1980) study of joinder of offenses, the hypothesis was supported. A follow-up experiment (Bordens & Horowitz, 1983) was then conducted to isolate the cause for the effect of joinder of offenses. The hypothesis in the second study was that joinder of offenses leads to confusion of evidence across charges, which in turn causes elevated conviction rates. That is, evidence from the second charge might be recalled as evidence from the first (or vice versa) and affect verdicts accordingly. The results provided support for the hypothesis.

Generating a new, more specific hypothesis in the light of previous results illustrates the *refinement process*. Often the confirmation of a hypothesis leads to other hypotheses that deal with the limits or causes of the effects observed in the original study. For example, in the Bordens and Horowitz joinder study the original hypothesis was extended, tested, and confirmed. As a result, we now know more about the possible causes of the joinder effect.

In some instances your initial hypothesis may not be confirmed (as the commonsense explanation of the Iroquois Theater situation was not). What do you do then? In some cases you may completely discard the original hypothesis. In other cases you may revise and retest the hypothesis. In this latter case you are using a strategy called *retesting*. Keep in mind that any revised hypothesis must be tested as rigorously as the original hypothesis.

At this point you may be wondering how a method that frequently requires you to spend great amounts of time making careful observations, only to show that your hypothesis is incorrect, can be of any possible value. But this ability to discover error makes the scientific method the powerful tool it is. By repeatedly checking every hypothesis in the ruthless arena of empirical testing, the scientist learns which ideas are worthy and which belong on the trash heap. No other method incorporates such a powerful check on the validity of its conclusions.

Scientific Method at Work: The Iroquois Theater Tragedy

You may be wondering how you could apply the rationale behind the scientific method to finding an explanation for the Iroquois Theater tragedy. This problem, like any other in science, lends itself to scientific scrutiny. Recall the previ-

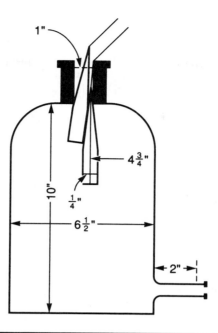

Figure 1-3. The apparatus used in a simulation study of panic behavior. (From Mintz, 1951; reprinted with permission.)

ously developed hypothesis of "panic behavior" being caused by a perception that the availability of reinforcers is limited. It follows that if you limit reinforcers in such a situation you should be able to produce "panic behavior."

To stage panic situations in which you vary the perceived availability of reinforcers would be unethical (ethics are discussed in Chapter 5). However, with a little creativity and ingenuity you could test your hypothesis scientifically without creating actual panic situations.

Researchers often construct "simulations" to study behavior that cannot be studied under naturally occurring conditions. (Simulation methodology is discussed in Chapter 3. For now, it is enough to know that in a simulation you attempt to re-create a real-world situation as closely as possible.) This method was applied by Mintz (1951) to investigate the availability-of-reinforcers hypothesis.

Mintz simulated the crowded theater situation by using a large glass jar (see Figure 1-3). The fire was simulated by filling the jar slowly from the bottom with water. Cones, representing the people in the theater, were suspended by strings in the jar. The cones could be withdrawn one at a time through the neck of the jar. If you tried to withdraw more than one cone at a time, they would jam at the mouth of the jar.

Mintz had subjects try to simultaneously withdraw their cones under several conditions. Some subjects were told that the experiment was designed to test cooperation, and no mention was made of reinforcers for successfully withdrawing cones. Other subjects were told they would receive money if they got their cones out completely dry. In this latter group, subjects were placed in competition for limited reinforcers.

The availability-of-reinforcers hypothesis would predict that subjects vying for rewards would be less successful at withdrawing cones than those not vying for rewards. In fact, this is what happened. Thus, some evidence shows that people do sometimes behave in ways contrary to their best interests when access to reinforcers appears to be limited. By applying the scientific method in this simulation study, you gain a better understanding of the factors that control crowd behavior under conditions of perceived limited availability of reinforcement.

The Scientific Method as an Attitude

The scientific method is not only a means of acquiring knowledge; it is also a way of thinking. An individual who subscribes to the scientific method approaches a problem by carefully defining its parameters, seeking out relevant information, and subjecting proposed solutions to rigorous testing. However, remember that the scientific method is not the only way of approaching a problem. Some problems (philosophical, ethical, or religious) may not lend themselves to exploration with the scientific method. In those cases, other methods of inquiry may be more useful.

Translating the Scientific Method into Practice: The Research Process

The scientific method provides the general framework within which scientists operate. However, to test hypotheses the inherent logic of the scientific method must be translated into a workable research study. It is important to recognize that the scientific method provides the rules within which information is acquired. Working within those rules, you must decide on the particular technique that best tests your hypotheses.

Method Versus Technique

Once you have chosen the scientific method as your means of inquiry, you must make some decisions about how you are going to gather information about the behavior of interest. A variety of techniques is available for any given research hypothesis. For example, if you were interested in studying the relationship between violent television programs and children's violent behavior, you have several techniques at your disposal. You might choose to send parents a questionnaire to indicate how much violent television the children watch and relate that information to observed aggressive behavior. Or you might choose to expose different groups of children to television shows that vary in their levels of violence and then evaluate aggressive behavior in free-play situations. The experiment Mintz conducted used a simulation technique.

Basic and Applied Research

The science of psychology encompasses scientists working in a variety of areas to gain knowledge that helps explain behavior. As a science, psychology systematically approaches the study of behavior by following the scientific method. Observations are carefully planned, with consideration being given to such problems as defining the questions to be answered, specifying what behaviors will be observed and how they will be measured, and determining what steps will be taken to ensure that the observer's expectations do not contaminate the observations.

The science of psychology is highly diverse. Consequently, the goals established by scientists working within the field may vary according to the nature of the research problem being considered. For example, the goal of some scientists is to discover general laws that explain particular classes of behaviors. In the course of the development of those laws, psychologists study behavior in specific situations and attempt to isolate the variables controlling behavior. Other scientists within the field are more interested in tackling practical problems than in finding general laws. For example, they might be interested in determining which of several therapy techniques is best to treat severe phobias.

An important distinction has been made between basic research and applied research along the lines just presented.

Basic Research. **Basic research** is conducted to investigate issues relevant to the confirmation or disconfirmation of theoretical or empirical positions. The major goal of basic research is to acquire general information about a phenomenon with little emphasis placed on applications to real-world examples of the phenomenon (Yaremko et al., 1982). For example, research on the memory process may be conducted to test the efficacy of interference as a viable theory of forgetting. The researcher would be interested in discovering something about the forgetting process while testing the validity of a theoretical position. Of less immediate interest would be the application of results to forgetting in a real-world situation.

Applied Research. The focus of **applied research** is somewhat different. The researcher's concern is to investigate a problem based in the real world. Although the researcher may still work from a theoretical basis in formulating hypotheses, the primary goal of the research is to generate information that can be applied directly to the solution of a real-world problem. A good example of applied research is work in the area of environmental psychology. Researchers in this area are concerned with issues such as how the design of a building can affect the behavior of its inhabitants. Research results can be applied during the process of designing a building (perhaps a mental hospital) to produce a building that is maximally effective.

Overlap Between Basic and Applied Research. In many instances the distinction between applied and basic research is not clear. Some research areas have both an applied and basic flavor. As an example, consider the work of Elizabeth Loftus (1979) on the psychology of the eyewitness. Loftus has extensively studied the factors that affect the ability of an eyewitness to accurately perceive, remember, and recall a criminal event. Her research certainly fits the mold of applied research. Her results have some implications for theory in the psychology of memory, so they also fit the mold of basic research. In fact, many of Loftus's findings can be organized within existing theories of memory.

Even applied research is not independent of theories and other research in psychology. The defining quality of applied research is that the researcher attempts to conduct a study whose results can be applied directly to a real-world event. To accomplish this task, you must choose a research strategy that maximizes the applicability of findings.

The Steps of the Research Process

Scientists in the field of psychology adhere to the scientific method as the principal method for acquiring information about behavior. This is true whether the psychologist is a "clinical psychologist" evaluating the effectiveness of a new therapy technique or an "experimental psychologist" investigating the variables that affect memory. Of course, researchers in psychology adopt a wide variety of techniques in their quests for scientific knowledge.

From the inception of a research idea to the final report of results, the research process has several crucial steps. These steps are outlined in Figure 1-4. At each step you must make one or more important decisions that will influence the direction of your research. Let's explore each of these steps and some of the decisions you must make.

Developing a Research Idea and Hypothesis. The first step in the research process is to identify an issue you want to study. There are many sources of research ideas (observing everyday behavior, reading scientific journals, for example). Once you have identified a behavior to study, you must then state a research question in terms that will allow others to test it empirically. Many students of research have trouble at this point. Students seem to have little trouble identifying interesting, broadly defined, behaviors to study (for example, "I want to study memory"), but they have trouble isolating crucial variables that need to be explored.

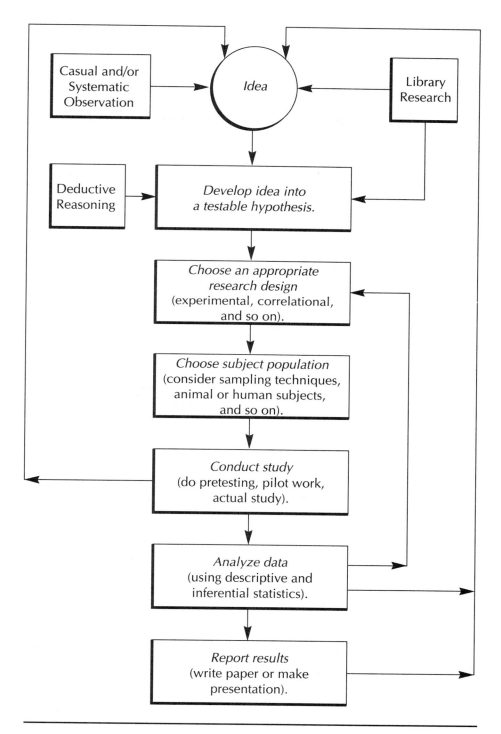

Figure 1-4. The research process. Arrows show the sequence of steps, along with feedback mechanisms.

In order to rationally apply the scientific method, you must be able to state clearly the relationships you expect to emerge in a research study. In other words, you must be able to formulate a precise, testable hypothesis. As noted in Figure 1-4, hypothesis development involves **deductive reasoning,** which involves deriving a specific hypothesis (in this case) from general ideas. For example, during your literature review you may have come across a theory about how memory operates. Using the general ideas developed in a theory, you may logically deduce that one variable (for example, meaningfulness of the information to be learned) causes changes in a second (amount remembered). The specific statement connecting these two variables is your hypothesis.

Choosing a Research Design. Once you have narrowed your research question and developed a testable hypothesis, you must next decide on a design or plan of attack for your research. As discussed in later chapters, a variety of options are available. For example, you must decide whether to do a correlational study (measure two or more variables and look for relationships among them) or an experimental study (manipulate a variable and look for concomitant changes in a second). Other important decisions at this point include where to conduct your study (in the laboratory or in the field), and how you are going to measure the behavior of interest.

With the preliminary decisions out of the way, you must consider a host of practical issues (equipment needs, preparing materials, and so on). You might find it necessary to conduct a miniature version of your study called a *pilot study,* to be sure that your chosen procedures and materials work the way you think they will.

Obtaining Subjects. Once you have designed your study and tested your procedures and materials, you need to obtain subjects. Several important decisions face you at this point. For example, you need to decide whether to use human or animal subjects. You must decide how to obtain your subjects and how they will be handled in your study. You must also be concerned with treating your subjects in an ethical manner.

Conducting Your Study. Now you actually have your subjects participate in your study. You observe and measure their behavior. Data are formally recorded for later analysis.

Analyzing Your Results. After you have collected your data, you must summarize and analyze them. The analysis process involves a number of decisions. You can analyze your data in several ways, and some types of data are better analyzed with one method than another. In most cases, you will probably calculate some descriptive statistics that provide a "nutshell" description of your data (such as averages and standard deviations), and inferential statistics that determine the reliability of your data (such as a *t-test*).

Reporting Your Results. After analyzing your data, you are nearing the final steps in the research process. You are now ready to prepare a report of your research. If your results were statistically reliable and sufficiently important, you may want to publish them. Consequently, you would prepare a formal paper, usually in APA style (APA stands for the American Psychological Association), and submit it to a journal for review. You might also decide to present your paper at a scientific meeting, in which case you prepare a brief abstract of your research for review.

Starting the Whole Process Over Again. Your final report of your research is usually not the final step in your research. You may have achieved closure on (finished and analyzed) one research project. However, the results from your first study may raise more questions. These questions often serve as the seeds for a new study. In fact, you may want to replicate an interesting finding within the context of a new study. This is shown in Figure 1-4 by the arrow connecting "Report Results" with "Idea."

Summary

Although we are constantly trying to explain the behavior we see around us, commonsense explanations of behavior often are too simplistic and situation specific, and frequently are based on hearsay, conjecture, anecdote, or other unreliable sources. Scientific explanations are based on carefully made observations of behavior, rigorously tested against alternative explanations, and developed to provide the most general account that is applicable over a variety of situations. For these reasons, scientific explanations tend to be more valid and general than those provided by common sense.

Explanations for behavior are also provided by beliefs. Explanations provided by belief differ from scientific explanations in that they are considered absolutely true, whereas scientific explanations are always considered tentative. Consequently, when evidence conflicts with an explanation based on belief, the evidence is questioned. When evidence conflicts with a scientific explanation, the explanation is questioned. Although beliefs can provide answers to virtually any question, the scientific method can address only those questions that can be answered through observation.

Even explanations that sound scientific may fail because relationships are often inferred from observable events. The danger always exists that inferences are incorrect, despite being based on empirical data. An explanation may also fail if you do not use independent measures of the explanatory concept and the behavior to be explained. In such cases, you have a pseudoexplanation, which is only a new label for behavior.

There are many ways to acquire knowledge about behavior. With the method of authority, you acquire information from sources that you perceive to be expert on your topic of interest and use the information to develop an explanation for behavior. With the rational method, you deduce explanations from other sources of information. Although the method of authority and the rational method play important roles in the early stages of science, they are not acceptable methods for acquiring scientific knowledge. The scientific method is the only method accepted for the acquisition of scientific knowledge.

The four major steps of the scientific method are observation of a phenomenon; formation of tentative explanations or statements of cause and effect; further observation or experimentation to rule out alternative explanations (or both); and revision and refinement of the explanations. The scientific method is also an attitude or a way of viewing the world. The scientist frames problems in terms of the scientific method.

The scientific method is translated into action by the research process. When performing research, you first choose a technique. Regardless of the technique chosen, research must follow the guidelines of the scientific method. The science of psychology is highly complex and diverse, and the goals of research vary from individual to individual. Some researchers, who are mainly interested in solving real-world problems, conduct applied research. Other scientists, mainly interested in evaluating theoretical problems, conduct basic research. Even though basic and applied research are different to some extent, considerable overlap does exist. Some basic research problems have real-world applications, and some applied problems have some basic research undertones.

The research process involves a sequence of steps. At each step important decisions affect the course of research and how you analyze and interpret data. The steps in the research process are (1) developing a research idea into a testable hypothesis, (2) choosing a research design, (3) obtaining subjects for the study, (4) conducting the study, (5) analyzing results, and (6) reporting results. Often the results from research raise a host of new research ideas. Then the whole process begins anew.

Key Terms

Scientific explanation

Parsimonious explanation

Commonsense explanation

Belief-based explanation

Pseudoexplanation

Circular explanation, or tautology

Method of authority

Rational method

Scientific method

Variable

Hypothesis

Basic research

Applied research

Deductive reasoning

2

Developing Ideas
for Research

To STUDENTS JUST BECOMING ACQUAINTED with the research process, one of the most formidable difficulties is coming up with a good research idea. "OK, class," your instructor may say near the beginning of the research methods course, "we are going to design our first research project. Who has some good research ideas?" Everyone in the class begins turning the pages of the text or stares blankly at the chalkboard. If someone does offer an idea, it may be along the lines of "I want to study stress or memory," with no specific idea in mind. At that point in the class it may seem to you that good research ideas are hard to find. Actually, once you learn how to do it, finding and developing a research topic becomes easy — you just have to know where and how to look. In fact, once you have "narrowed the field" you will be surprised to find that your biggest problem may be deciding which topic to pursue first. This chapter introduces the techniques needed to find and develop a research idea. Typically this is the first step in the research process. You must learn not only how to get the idea, but also how to couch the idea in testable terms. It is not enough to say, "I want to study memory." You must be able to specify exactly what aspects of memory you want to study and what techniques you will use. This chapter explores in some detail how to find and develop testable research questions.

Sources of Research Ideas

Research ideas come from many sources—some that are unsystematic and informal, and others that are systematic and formal. Some ideas derive from theoretical considerations, and others arise from the need to solve practical problems in behavioral prediction or management.

Unsystematic Observation

One of the most potent sources of research ideas is curiosity about the causes or determinants of everyday behavior. You make a helpful suggestion to a friend, and she angrily rebukes you. Why? Perhaps she just found out she did not get the job she was hoping for. Is this the cause, or is it something else? Or, you study all week for an important exam and the test results show you did very well. Although initially you feel good, the emotion soon passes and you find yourself falling into a deep depression. What caused this paradoxical result? Such observations can provide the basis for a research project.

Casual observation of animal behavior can also lead to research ideas. Behaviors such as starlings staging a mass attack on a soaring hawk, a squirrel dropping an acorn on your head, or the antics of a pet all raise questions about the conditions that trigger and direct them—questions that can be the basis of a research idea.

Unsystematic observation sometimes is a good way to discover a general research idea. Given your casual observations, you may decide to study a particular issue. However, remember that such observations (from a scientific perspective) represent only the starting point. You still must transform your casual observations into a form that can be tested empirically. Rarely will you be able to infer the causes of observed behavior from your casual observations. Such inferences can only be derived from a careful and systematic study of the behavior of interest.

Systematic Observation

Ideas for behavioral research can also come from systematic observation. Systematic observation may take a variety of forms. For example, you decide to study a particular behavior, and you choose to observe the behavior under naturally occurring conditions. An example of this, dealing with joinder of criminal offenses, appeared in Chapter 1. You approach the situation with some ideas in mind and, using your observations, you then begin to formulate testable hypotheses.

A second valuable source of systematic observation is published research reports. Instead of observing behavior at first hand, you read about other first-hand observations from researchers. Published research offers an almost limitless source of systematic observations of both human and animal behavior made under well-defined conditions. Although such research answers many questions, it typically raises more than it answers. Are the results reliable? Would the same thing happen if subjects with different characteristics were used? What is the shape of the function relating the variables under study? Would you obtain the same results if the dependent measure were defined differently? These questions and others like them provide a rich source of research ideas.

Another potent source of research ideas is your previous or ongoing research. Unexpected observations made during the course of a project (by a result that contradicts expectations, or the need to test the generality of a finding) can be the basis for further research. As you examine your data, you may see unexpected relationships or trends emerging. These trends may be interesting enough to warrant a new study.

This particular source of research ideas usually is not immediately available to the scientific community. Other researchers may not become aware of these unexpected trends until you publish or present your research findings. Consequently, you and your close colleagues may be the only ones who can benefit from this potentially rich source of research ideas.

Theory. In some cases, enough information is available on a problem to attempt a theoretical solution. A **theory** is a set of assumptions about the causes of a phenomenon and rules that specify how the causes act. Designed to account for known relationships among given variables and behavior, theories generate new research questions through deductive reasoning. They allow the researcher to predict the behavior expected under new combinations of the variables. Testing the theory involves setting up the specified conditions and making the observations.

Sometimes two or more alternative theories account for the same initial observations. This situation may provide a fascinating opportunity to pit the different interpretations against one another. If the alternatives are rigorously specified and mutually exclusive, they may lead to different predictions about what will be observed under a new set of conditions. In this case, a single experiment or observation may be enough to provide strong support for one alternative over another. Such happy situations provide another fruitful source of research ideas.

The Need to Solve Practical Problems. Often research ideas arise from the need to solve practical problems. Chapter 1 distinguished between basic and applied research. Applied research is problem-oriented, whereas basic research is aimed toward building basic knowledge about phenomena. Finding an effective diet that people will follow might require a systematic evaluation of several proposed diets to identify those characteristics of a diet plan that lead to success. Applied research might also identify the most effective therapy for depression, or develop a work environment that leads to the highest levels of productivity and job satisfaction. As with theories, you might find that a single study is not adequate to solve a problem or, during applied research, you might find that new ideas come to mind. Hence, even applied research can raise new questions that suggest more research. In any event, a need to solve a practical problem can be a rich source of research ideas.

Developing Good Research Questions

Having a good idea for research is not enough. You must translate that idea into good research questions. This section describes how to identify good research questions and also suggests what kinds of questions are likely to be important.

Asking Answerable Questions

Whatever the source of your research ideas, you must be able to frame them in terms of specific questions that can be answered through application of the scientific method. After you have decided on a general topic, you must then narrow that topic to a testable hypothesis. This means that you must develop your research idea into a specific set of predictions about the relationships among variables. In addition, your ideas must be testable. This section addresses how to transform your general research idea into a specific, testable hypothesis.

Asking the Right Questions

The first step in developing a workable research project is to ask the kind of question that is answerable through the use of the scientific method. Not all questions are. Here are a few questions that cannot be answered by scientific means: Does God exist? Why is there suffering in the world? Are there human abilities that cannot be measured? How many angels can stand on the head of a pin? Is abortion moral or immoral?

These questions are not answerable by scientific means because the answers cannot be obtained through objective observation. To be objective, an observation must be made under precisely defined conditions, must be reproducible when those same conditions are present again, and must be confirmable by others. Questions that can be answered by objective observation are called **empirical questions**. Here are some examples of empirical questions: Do a criminal defendant's personality characteristics affect a jury's decision? Does a deprived early environment result in lower intelligence? Is punishment an effective tool in socializing children? All these questions can be answered through appropriately designed and executed research. Unlike the first set of questions, the second set identifies variables that can be defined in terms of observable characteristics.

Some questions seem to be empirical but are formulated too broadly to make appropriate observations. Consider the following example of such a question: Do children raised in a permissive atmosphere lack self-discipline as adults?

Before this question can be answered, a number of preliminary questions must be addressed. What exactly is a permissive atmosphere? How is it to be measured? Precisely what does it mean to lack self-discipline, and how do we determine when self-discipline is present or absent? Until you can specify exactly what these terms mean and how to measure the variables they represent, you cannot answer the original question.

Defining variables in terms of the operations required to measure them entails creating **operational definitions** of those variables. Using operational definitions allows you to measure precisely the states of the two variables in question, and thus to determine whether the postulated relationship exists between them. This precision is gained at some cost, however. Operational definitions restrict the generality of answers obtained. Permissive atmospheres are no longer addressed in general, but rather as particular behaviors defined as permissive. Self-discipline is no longer addressed in general, but rather in the context of specific behaviors said to indicate self-discipline. Other ways of measuring the two variables may yield a different answer to the question. Nevertheless, without using operational definitions the question cannot be answered meaningfully.

To summarize, to conduct meaningful research you must choose a question that can be answered through scientific means. You must then operationally define your variables carefully so that you are working with precise definitions. When you have formulated your empirically testable question, you then proceed to the next step in the research process.

Asking Important Questions

Developing answerable questions is not enough. They should also be important questions. Researching a question imposes demands on a researcher's time, financial resources, and the institution's available space. Researching a question makes demands on the available subject population as well, whether it is human or animal. These resources should not be expended to answer trivial questions. Whether a question is important is often difficult to determine. Some valuable information occasionally has been obtained in the course of answering an apparently mundane question. Some questions that at one time seemed terribly important to answer, now appear trivial. However, some rough guidelines will help in identifying important questions.

A question is probably important if answering it will clarify relationships among variables known to affect the behavioral system under study. For example, knowing that memory tends to deteriorate with time since learning, you would want to establish the rate of deterioration as a function of time. You would want to identify how the amount of initial practice, overlearning, previous learning, activity during the retention interval, and other such factors interact to determine the rate of forgetting under specified conditions.

A question is probably important if the answer can support only one of several competing hypotheses or theoretical views. Developing and testing such questions is at the heart of the scientific method. The answers to such questions allow you to "home in" on a proper interpretation of the data. (This technique is discussed in Chapter 16.) On the negative side, if the theories under test are later discarded, research designed to test the theories may become irrelevant, unless the findings demonstrate clearly interpretable empirical relationships that must be accounted for by theory.

A question is probably important if its answer leads to obvious practical application. (However, the lack of obvious practical application does *not* render the question automatically unimportant!) Much research has been conducted to identify working conditions that maximize productivity and job satisfaction, or to screen drugs for potential effectiveness in controlling psychosis. Few would argue that the answers to these problems are unimportant.

In contrast, a question is probably unimportant if its answer is already firmly established. "Firmly established" means that the results have been replicated (duplicated) by different scientists and the scientists agree the finding does occur under the stated conditions. Unless serious deficiencies are identified in the methods used to establish those answers, performing the research again is likely to be a waste of time.

A question is probably unimportant if the variables under scrutiny are known to have small effects on the behavior of interest and these effects are of no theoretical interest.

A question is probably unimportant if there is no *a priori* reason to believe the variables in question are causally related. Research aimed at determining whether the temperature of a room affects memory recall for faces may turn out to have surprising and useful results. But without a reason to expect a relationship, such research would amount to a fishing expedition that would be unlikely to pay off. The time would be better spent pursuing more promising leads.

When you have identified your research idea, the next step is to develop it to the point where you can specify testable hypotheses and define the specific methods used to test the hypotheses. This step is accomplished by familiarizing yourself with research already conducted in your area of interest. To find out about existing research, you must conduct a **literature review**.

Reviewing the Literature

One of the most important preliminary steps in the research process is doing a thorough literature review. Whether you begin with a vague idea of a research project or a well-developed research plan, you must review the literature. There are several important reasons for reviewing the literature before beginning a research endeavor.

No matter what topic you choose, chances are someone has already done research on it. By becoming familiar with that area through a literature review, you can avoid "reinventing the wheel." Your specific research question may have already been addressed and answered. If so, then conducting your research as originally planned would be a waste of time. This does not mean, however, that you must start over from scratch. Quite the contrary, your literature review may reveal other questions (perhaps more interesting) that remain to be answered. By familiarizing yourself with existing research and theory in an area, you can revise your research project to explore some of these newly identified questions.

Another advantage to reviewing the literature applies to the design phase of your research. Designing a study involves several decisions as to what variables to include and how to measure them, what apparatus to use, what procedures to use, and so on. Published research provides you with a rich resource for addressing these important design questions. You may find, for example, that you can use established procedures and existing materials. Or your review of the literature may show that existing methods are inadequate. You may have to develop your own methods to suit your research needs.

Yet another advantage is that a review of the literature keeps you up to date on current empirical or theoretical controversies in a particular research area. As science progresses, new ideas develop concerning age-old behavioral issues. For example, a debate is under way concerning the motives for altruistic behavior. Some argue that altruism is motivated by empathy (a concern for the victim) and others by egoism (self-satisfaction). Such controversies not only provide a rich source of research ideas, but also give direction to specific research hypotheses and designs.

Sources of Research Information

How can you locate this valuable literature? Literally thousands of research papers are published each year in hundreds of scientific journals and books. So attempting to locate relevant materials by grabbing a handful of recent journals and thumbing through them a page at a time is not going to do the job. Fortunately, far more efficient methods are available.

Primary Versus Secondary Sources

Sources containing research information can be classified according to whether a source is primary or secondary. A **primary source** is one containing the full research report, including all details necessary to duplicate the study. A primary source includes descriptions of the rationale of the study, its subjects, apparatus, procedure, results, and references. A **secondary source** is one that summarizes information from primary sources (such as presenting the basic findings). Secondary sources of research include review papers and theoretical articles that briefly describe studies and results, as well as descriptions of research found in textbooks, popular magazines, newspaper articles, television programs, films, or lectures.

The distinction between the primary and secondary sources is important. Students often rely too heavily on secondary sources. They reason, "After all, someone else has already read and summarized the research, so why not save time and use the summary?" Be cautious when using secondary sources. The author of a secondary source may describe or interpret research results incorrectly, or simply view data from a single (and perhaps narrow) theoretical perspective. Also, secondary sources do not usually present detailed descriptions of methods used in the cited studies. You must know the details of the methods used so you can evaluate the quality and the importance of the cited studies. The only way to obtain such detailed information is to read the primary source.

The danger in relying on secondary sources is graphically illustrated in a recent article by Treadway and McCloskey (1987). According to these authors, most scholarly works on the factors that affect eyewitness accuracy incorrectly describe a classic study conducted by Allport and Postman (1945). For example, a widely cited article by Buckhout (1974) gives the following description:

> [Allport] had his subjects take a brief look at a drawing of several people on a subway train, including a seated black man and a white man standing with a razor in his hand . . . after a brief look at the drawing . . . half of the observers report having seen the razor . . . in the black man's hand. (p. 26)

Had you read only Buckhout's article, or another of the secondary sources cited by Treadway and McCloskey, you would come away with the impression that subjects were showing a bias against blacks because they reported seeing the razor in the black man's hand. Unfortunately, Buckhout and many others have dramatically misrepresented Allport and Postman's study. In fact, the study was originally done to study rumor transmission. One subject, while looking at the picture described by Buckhout, whispered a description to another subject who, in turn, whispered a description to another subject, and so on. Allport and Postman actually found that in more than half of the experiments using the infamous picture, someone in the chain of subjects reported the black man was holding the razor (Treadway & McCloskey, 1987).

The moral to this story is that relying heavily on secondary sources is dangerous. The example provided by Treadway and McCloskey clearly shows that secondary sources (sometimes based on secondary sources themselves) may misrepresent an original experiment. Reports of the original study by Allport and Postman misrepresented the methods used, the results obtained, and ultimately led researchers and the courts to draw incorrect inferences about the effects of racial bias on eyewitness accuracy (Treadway & McCloskey, 1987). To avoid this trap, obtain and read the original report of any research that you use in a literature search.

The value of secondary sources lies in their summaries, presentations, and integrations of results from related research studies. The secondary source provides an excellent starting point for your literature search. However, it should not be considered as a substitute for the primary source. An up-to-date review paper will include a reference section from which you can generate a list of primary sources.

An exception to the general rule concerning the use of secondary sources is when the primary source may not be available. In this case you may wish to use

a secondary source. If you must do so, always stay aware of the possible problems. If you use a secondary source, cite only the secondary source in your
research report.

To summarize, use secondary sources as a starting point in your literature
search. Avoid overreliance on secondary sources, and make every effort to obtain
the primary sources of interest to you that have been cited in a secondary source.
Only by reading the primary source can you critically evaluate a study and
determine whether the reported results are reliable and important. Finally, do
not rely on a single secondary source. The author of a review article may not
have completely reviewed the literature. Always augment the information obtained from a secondary source with a thorough literature search of your own.

Where to Find Research

Research findings appear in a variety of sources.

Books. You are probably most familiar with general textbooks (such as those
covering introductory psychology) or texts covering content areas (such as motivation and emotion, abnormal psychology, personality, or human learning and
memory). More specialized professional texts present the results of program-
matic research conducted by the author over a period of years. These specialized
texts may cover research previously published in journals as well as findings not
presented elsewhere. Edited anthologies present a series of articles on related
topics, each written by a different set of authors. Some anthologies are collec-
tions of articles previously published separately; others present articles written
especially for the occasion. Either kind of text may present reviews of the literature, theoretical articles, articles dealing with methodological issues, or original
research.

Anthologies are useful because they collect together papers that the editor
feels are important in a given area. However, be cautious when reading an
anthology. The editor may be biased in judgment on which articles to include.
Also, be sure to check the original publication date of articles in an anthology.
Even if the publication date of the anthology is recent, it may contain outdated
(sometimes classic) articles.

Texts or anthologies are most valuable in the early stages of the literature
search. Often you can use the references from these books to track down relevant
articles. Books (especially textbooks) may have to be treated as secondary
sources. Whenever you use a textbook as a source, make an effort to obtain a
copy of the original report.

The articles in an anthology may be original works and thus can be treated
as primary sources — provided they have been reproduced exactly, not edited for
the anthology. Be careful about relying on a chapter reproduced from a book.
Isolating a single chapter from the original book can be misleading. In other
chapters from the same book, the original author might elaborate on points

made in the reproduced chapter. You could miss important points if you do not read the original work.

Whereas some books may be used as primary sources, others should be used largely as secondary sources. For example, if you were studying the development of intelligence you could use Piaget's book called *The Origins of Intelligence* (1952) as a good primary source. But a book such as *Piaget's Theory of Cognitive Development* by Wadsworth (1971) — a primer on Piaget's theory — should be treated as a secondary source in which you may find references for Piaget's original work.

Whatever route you choose, keep in mind one important factor. Even though you may have used Piaget's original work, problems with using it as a principal source may still exist. Books (especially by noted authors) may not undergo as rigorous a review as works published in scientific journals. You cannot be assured of the quality of the book. Also, you would be well advised to seek out recent research on the issues covered in a book. Was Piaget correct when he speculated in his book about the origins of intelligence? Research published since his book came out may bear on this question. A review of the recent research would help you to evaluate Piaget's theory and contributions.

Scientific Journals. Although textbooks are valuable, the information they contain tends to be old. By the time a scientific finding makes its way into a text, it could already have been around for several years. For current research and theories regarding a subject, researchers turn to scientific journals. Like popular magazines, journals appear periodically over the year in monthly, bimonthly, or quarterly issues (depending on the particular journal). Some journals focus on detailed research reports (although occasionally a theoretical or methodological article may appear). These research reports are the most important primary sources. Other journals deal with reviews of the literature, issues in methodology, or theoretical views.

Table 2-1 provides a list of journals currently published by the American Psychological Association (APA) and by another major publisher of psychology journals, the Psychonomic Society. (The list is not complete. In addition to those listed, many journals are published by major textbook publishers. You become familiar with these by doing reviews of the literature.)

Also, keep in mind that not all journals are created equal. You must consider the source. When you submit your work to a **refereed journal,** it is usually reviewed by two (or more) reviewers. Other, **nonrefereed journals** do not have such a review procedure; the articles may be published in the order in which they were received, or according to some fee that the author must pay.

The review process is intended to ensure that high-quality articles appear in the journal. Although problems do occur with the review procedures (see Chapter 17), you can have greater confidence in an article in a refereed journal than one in a nonrefereed journal.

A problem likely to be encountered more in a nonrefereed journal than in a refereed journal is that the information could be sketchy and incomplete (Mayo & LaFrance, 1977). If information is incomplete, you may not be able to identify

Table 2-1. Journals Published by the American Psychological Association and by the Psychonomic Society

Journals of the American Psychological Association

American Psychologist

Behavioral Neuroscience

Contemporary Psychology

Developmental Psychology

Journal of Abnormal Psychology

Journal of Applied Psychology

Journal of Comparative Psychology

Journal of Consulting and Clinical Psychology

Journal of Counseling Psychology

Journal of Educational Psychology

Journal of Experimental Psychology:

   General

   Learning, Memory and Cognition

   Human Perception and Performance

   Animal Behavior Processes

Journal of Personality and Social Psychology

Professional Psychology

Psychological Abstracts

Psychological Bulletin

Psychological Review

Journals of the Psychonomic Society

Animal Learning & Behavior

Physiological Psychology

Memory & Cognition

Perception & Psychophysics

Behavioral Research Methods, Instruments & Computers

the significance of the article. Rely more heavily on articles published in high-quality, refereed journals than on articles in lower-quality, nonrefereed journals.

Conventions and Professional Meetings. Books and journals are not the only sources of research findings, nor are they necessarily the most current. Behavioral scientists who want the most up-to-date information about research in their areas attend psychological conventions. If you attended one of these conventions, you would confront a number of **paper sessions** covering different areas of research. Paper sessions are usually simultaneously conducted in different rooms and follow one another throughout the day (much as classes do on campus).

When you register at a convention, you receive a program listing the times and places for each session. Figure 2-1 shows an excerpt from a page from the

Fri. Afternoon, April 10: 1:30 PM-3:10 PM

HUMAN FEEDING

REGENCY BALLROOM A

ELIOT STELLAR

University of Pennsylvania Medical School

1:30 PM   87-171

VARIETY STIMULATES CONSUMPTION
FOR OUT-OF-CONTROL EATERS. Jane
M. Conner and Kathryn J. Murphy,
SUNY-Binghamton.
Food consumption was measured
when subjects were presented in
successive courses with either
three different foods or with
their favorite food of the three.
No difference in consumption between the conditions was found
for subjects in different weight
categories. Individuals high on
disinhibition of control (e.g.,
"Sometimes when I started eating,
I just can't seem to stop") ate
more under the varied condition
than under the favorite condition. Individuals low on disinhibition of control ate similar
amounts in each condition.

2:50 PM   87-172

THE EFFECT OF VARIETY ON INTAKE
OF UNDERWEIGHT, NORMAL-WEIGHT,
AND OVERWEIGHT WOMEN.
Theresa A. Spiegel, Rhonda K.
Baumgarten, Sapna Jaiswal &
Eliot Stellar, University of
Pennsylvania.
Nine underweight, nine normal-
weight, and nine overweight women
were given meals with sequential
variety of foods, simultaneous
variety, and no variety. Only
simultaneous variety enhanced intake in normal and overweight subjects, primarily by stimulating
ingestion at the beginning of the
meal. Neither variety condition
enhanced intake of underweight
subjects, who ate more than other
subjects, especially at the beginning of meals. The relationships
between the responses to variety,
within-meal patterns of ingestion, and scores of the three
weight groups on the Three-Factor
Eating Inventory will be
discussed.

Figure 2-1. An excerpt from a page from the program for the 1987 meeting of the Eastern Psychological Association.

program of the 1987 meeting of the Eastern Psychological Association. Listed under the session shown are the titles of the papers, the names of the authors, the times when the papers will be presented, and short abstracts of the papers. You can use the program to identify papers relevant to your research interests. Each participant at a paper session is allotted time (usually ten to twenty minutes) to describe his or her most recent findings, and then usually has about five minutes to answer any questions from the audience.

Attending a paper session has two distinct advantages over reading a journal article. First, the information is from the very frontiers of research. The findings presented may not appear in print for many months (or even years), if ever. Attending a paper session exposes you to newly conducted research that might otherwise be unavailable to you. Second, it provides an opportunity to meet other researchers in your field and to discuss ideas, clarify methodology, or seek assistance. These contacts could prove valuable in the future.

Paper sessions are not the best way to convey details of methodology. The written report is far superior for that purpose. At a convention, the author of a paper is typically given fifteen minutes to describe his or her research. In that short time the author must often omit some details of methodology. The one exception is a poster session where the author presents his or her study in a written format. This form allows the author to provide more details. The poster session also allows you to speak directly to the researcher about the research. Many good research ideas can emerge from such encounters.

Also, a convention can be expensive to attend. In most instances, conventions are located in cities other than where you live. This means you must pay for travel, lodging, and food. Fortunately, you can gain some of the benefits of going to a conference by obtaining a copy of the program. By reading the abstracts of the papers, you can identify those papers of interest and glean something of the findings. If you want more information, you can then write or call the author.

Other Sources of Research Information. Personal replies to your inquiries fall under the heading of **personal communications** and are yet another source of research information. Projects completed under the auspices of a grant or agency often result in the production of a *technical report,* which can be obtained through the agency. In addition, dissertations and theses completed by graduate students as part of their degree requirements are placed on file in the libraries of the university where the work was done. You can find abstracts describing these studies in *Dissertation Abstracts International,* a reference work found in most college libraries. For a fee, the abstracting service will send you a copy of the complete manuscript on paper or microfilm.

Performing Library Research

With so many sources of research information to choose from, you may find yourself quickly overwhelmed if you do not adopt an efficient strategy for separating the wheat from the chaff. You need a method that quickly identifies articles relevant to your topic. Ideally, the method should identify all such articles, because the one you miss may be the one that duplicates exactly what you were planning to do. Fortunately, such a method exists.

The Basic Strategy

Although a number of variations exist, the basic strategy is this: (1) find a relevant research article; (2) use the reference section of the relevant research article to locate other (usually older) articles; (3) repeat steps 1 and 2 for each new relevant article identified until you can find no more; (4) look up the articles in *Science Citations Index* or *Social Science Citations Index* (discussed in the next section) to identify more recent articles citing the articles you already have; and (5) repeat all previous steps until nothing new turns up.

This strategy is discussed in greater detail later in the chapter. First you must become familiar with some of the basic tools needed to conduct an adequate literature search. After you have learned about the tools at your disposal, you can begin to effectively search the literature.

Research Tools

Most college libraries contain several important tools to aid researchers. In addition to the library card catalog used to locate relevant books, the following tools are available: *Psychological Abstracts, Science Citations Index, Social Science Citations Index, Dissertation Abstracts International, Index Medicus,* and *Current Contents.* The sections that follow briefly introduce each of the major tools. Then go to the library to examine each of the them.

Using *Psychological Abstracts*

Each month in the *Psychological Abstracts,* the APA publishes abstracts (summaries) of psychological research papers, theoretical articles, articles on methodology and statistics, literature reviews, and related papers that have appeared in psychology journals within the past few months. Also listed (but not summarized) are psychology theses and dissertations (the abstracts of which have appeared in *Dissertation Abstracts International*), and the titles of professional texts on psychological topics.

The Subject Index. To make it easy to find the kind of information you are looking for, *Psychological Abstracts* includes a listing of articles by subject matter (the Subject Index) and a separate listing by author (the Author Index). Figure 2-2 shows an excerpt from a page from the Subject Index of one issue. Subjects are identified by keywords, much like topics in an encyclopedia. If you were interested in retention of learning, you could begin by looking under "Retention," as shown in Figure 2-2. Under this keyword appear many lines of qualifiers that identify more specifically the topic being covered. The numbers following each qualifier are the abstract numbers of articles relevant to that topic. In this example, if you were interested specifically in the effect of age on retention, you would check abstracts numbered 14647, or 3158, or 11577 (depending on your specific interests). The abstracts themselves are found in another section of this research tool.

▶ Retention [See Also Recall (Learning), Recognition (Learning), Reconstruction (Learning)]
administration of adrenergic blocker DSP4, acquisition vs retention of signaled vs unsignaled avoidance, rats, 791
age differences & number of items learned, long vs short term retention, 3rd vs 10th graders, 14647
age, retention of conditioned taste aversion, weaning vs adult vs old-age rats, 3158.
aging, learning & memory & arousal, aplysia, 11577
apomorphine, acquisition & retention of conditioned avoidance response, male rates, 28125
arecoline & edrophonium & oxotremorine & deanol alone vs in combination, enhancement of memory retention of T maze learning, male mice, 6214
arousal & age & previous experience, retention of preparatory information, 4-17 yr old same-day vs overnight surgery patients, 23999.
biochemical changes in neural mechanisms during acquisition & retention of associative learning, marine snails, 11545
caudate-putamen lesions, acquisition & retention of operant bar-pressing, male rats, 776
classroom activities, mainstreaming & reading instruction & basic skills learning & retention of information, learning disabled primary students, 8057
comprehension & retention of TV programs, 18-24 vs 65-70 yr olds, 28247
computer assisted instruction, academic performance & retention & student attitudes & instructional interaction, college students enrolled in pharmacology course, 7693

Figure 2-2. An example from the Subject Index of *Psychological Abstracts*. The arrow points to the keyword "Retention." If you were interested in the effect of age on retention, you would look up abstracts numbered 14647, 3158, and 11577, found under the listings beginning with "age" or "aging." (Reprinted with permission.)

The *Thesaurus of Psychological Index Terms*. If you have trouble finding the right keyword to use, the *Thesaurus of Psychological Index Terms* steers you to an appropriate one. The *Thesaurus* indexes all the keywords used in the *Psychological Abstracts*. In addition, it contains related words that help you find the keyword actually used to identify a subject. Figure 2-3 shows an example from the *Thesaurus*.

If the keyword you are using in your search is not used by *Psychological Abstracts*, your efforts will fail. At this point you would turn to the *Thesaurus* for help. Looking up your original keyword, you would find several additional

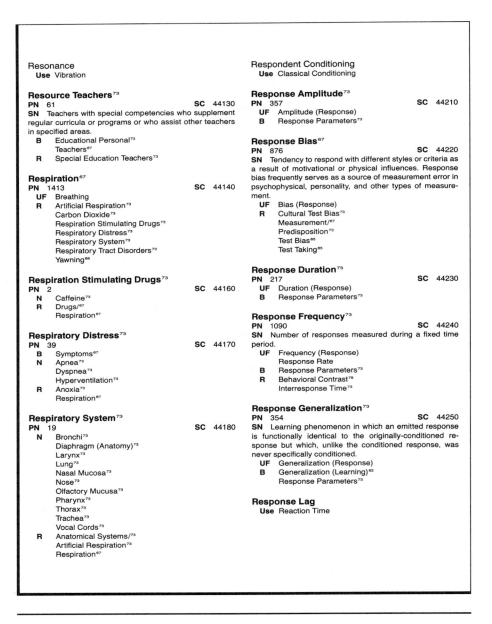

Resonance
Use Vibration

Resource Teachers[73]
PN 61   **SC** 44130
SN Teachers with special competencies who supplement regular curricula or programs or who assist other teachers in specified areas.
  B   Educational Personal[73]
          Teachers[67]
  R   Special Education Teachers[73]

Respiration[67]
PN 1413   **SC** 44140
  UF Breathing
  R   Artificial Respiration[73]
          Carbon Dioxide[73]
          Respiration Stimulating Drugs[73]
          Respiratory Distress[73]
          Respiratory System[73]
          Respiratory Tract Disorders[73]
          Yawning[88]

Respiration Stimulating Drugs[73]
PN 2   **SC** 44160
  N   Caffeine[73]
  R   Drugs/[67]
          Respiration[67]

Respiratory Distress[73]
PN 39   **SC** 44170
  B   Symptoms[67]
  N   Apnea[73]
          Dyspnea[73]
          Hyperventilation[73]
  R   Anoxia[73]
          Respiration[67]

Respiratory System[73]
PN 19   **SC** 44180
  N   Bronchi[73]
          Diaphragm (Anatomy)[73]
          Larynx[73]
          Lung[73]
          Nasal Mucosa[73]
          Nose[73]
          Olfactory Mucusa[73]
          Pharynx[73]
          Thorax[73]
          Trachea[73]
          Vocal Cords[73]
  R   Anatomical Systems/[73]
          Artificial Respiration[73]
          Respiration[67]

Respondent Conditioning
Use Classical Conditioning

Response Amplitude[73]
PN 357   **SC** 44210
  UF Amplitude (Response)
  B   Response Parameters[73]

Response Bias[67]
PN 876   **SC** 44220
SN Tendency to respond with different styles or criteria as a result of motivational or physical influences. Response bias frequently serves as a source of measurement error in psychophysical, personality, and other types of measurement.
  UF Bias (Response)
  R   Cultural Test Bias[73]
          Measurement/[67]
          Predisposition[73]
          Test Bias[85]
          Test Taking[85]

Response Duration[73]
PN 217   **SC** 44230
  UF Duration (Response)
  B   Response Parameters[73]

Response Frequency[73]
PN 1090   **SC** 44240
SN Number of responses measured during a fixed time period.
  UF Frequency (Response)
          Response Rate
  B   Response Parameters[73]
  R   Behavioral Contrast[78]
          Interresponse Time[73]

Response Generalization[73]
PN 354   **SC** 44250
SN Learning phenomenon in which an emitted response is functionally identical to the originally-conditioned response but which, unlike the conditioned response, was never specifically conditioned.
  UF Generalization (Response)
  B   Generalization (Learning)[82]
          Response Parameters[73]

Response Lag
  Use Reaction Time

Figure 2-3. A page from the *Thesaurus of Psychological Index Terms* (fifth edition). The word "Resonance" directs you to use the keyword "Vibration." Looking up the keyword "Vibration" will give you several listings. (Reprinted with permission.)

keywords listed (see Figure 2-3). To help you identify the most appropriate keyword, each keyword is followed by letters indicating the relationship of each keyword to the original topic ("R" for related, "B" for broader, and "N" for narrower). The letters "PN" stand for "posting notes," which indicate the number of times the terms had been used for indexing. The five-digit number opposite "SC" can be used instead of the keyword in online searching. If you find a keyword that seems right, you can go to the Subject Index and use that keyword to locate abstracts.

The Author Index. Most researchers develop a program of research that involves many studies designed to answer related questions within a particular field. This results in finding a string of closely related articles. Therefore, if you have already identified a relevant article, you can use the author's name to search for related material (such as follow-up studies, reviews, or theoretical articles on the same topic). The Author Index identifies the abstract number of each article published by a given author that has been abstracted by *Psychological Abstracts* that month.

The Abstracts. The abstracts occupy the main body of the issue and are numbered consecutively beginning with the first issue of a volume. As a further aid, the abstracts are organized according to the area of psychology in which they fall. You can keep abreast of current research by scanning the abstracts within each area whenever a new issue of the *Psychological Abstracts* comes out. Of course, if you have identified potentially relevant articles by using the Subject Index or Author Index, you can also look up individual abstracts by number. Under that number you will find the names of the authors, title of the article, and a brief abstract of the article's contents. By reading the title and abstract, you can determine whether this particular article is relevant to your topic. Figure 2-4 shows abstract number 14647, one of those listed under "Retention" in the Subject Index example depicted in Figure 2-2.

Bound Volumes and the Cumulative Indexes. Reading the current issue of *Psychological Abstracts* only provides information about abstracts in that issue. To be thorough, you must cover older issues. Reading through *Psychological Abstracts* issue by issue would be extremely tedious. Fortunately, you rarely need to. Issues from previous years are bound together by volume. Each volume has two separately bound parts. One part (the Index) contains the Subject and Author indexes. The other part (the Abstracts) contains the abstracts. Of course, the companion index for a particular volume refers to that volume only.

At intervals of several years, a Cumulative Index is published that pulls together all index information for the years since the previous Cumulative Index. The Cumulative Index is divided into a Subject Index and an Author Index, but does not include any abstracts. Instead, abstract numbers given in the index are preceded by a volume number and a colon. To find the appropriate abstract,

14647. **Dempster, Frank N.** (U Nevada, Las Vegas) **Conditions affecting retention test performance: A developmental study.** *Journal of Experimental Child Psychology*, 1984 (Feb), Vol 37(1), 65–77. —Investigated the conditions that might affect word retention test performance in 54 3rd-graders and 52 10th-graders. Ss were randomly assigned to 1 of 4 trial/retention test conditions. Results show an absence of age differences in proportionalized short-term retention, despite substantial differences in the number of items learned, and significant age differences in long-term retention only between groups that had received a different number of learning trials. Findings suggest that age differences in retention test performance occur only when age is confounded with degree of learning. There do not appear to be any age differences in retention per se. (18 ref.) —*Journal Abstract*

Figure 2-4. A sample abstract from *Psychological Abstracts*, Abstract number 14647, from the Subject Index reference shown in Figure 2-2. (Reprinted with permission.)

locate the volume and look up the abstract number within that volume. Because these cumulative indexes summarize the articles published within a range of years, they can save you time. Instead of leafing through individually bound indexes for individual years, use the Cumulative Index when it is available.

Limitations. Although *Psychological Abstracts* can be useful, it does have a few important limitations. First, although *Psychological Abstracts* covers a large number of journals, it does not cover all of them and does not provide all articles relevant to your topic. Second, it does not contain the most recent articles. By the time an abstract of an article appears, six months or even a year might pass since the article originally appeared. Use other techniques to locate the most recent articles on your topic.

A third possible disadvantage concerns the "disappointment effect." Suppose you have searched the abstracts and have found the "perfect article" containing exactly what you were looking for. When you look to see in what journal it is published, you find that it appeared in a journal your library does not have. Realize that just because you find something in the abstracts it does not necessarily mean that the article is readily available to you. You could obtain the article from your library through interlibrary loan. Typically, however, it can take anywhere from two to six weeks to obtain the article. If you are pressed for time, you will have to do without that "perfect article."

Methods of Searching the Abstracts. The *Psychological Abstracts* can, of course, be searched by going to the library, finding relevant source materials, and perusing those sources. This method of manually searching has several drawbacks. For example, it is tedious. After a few minutes of reading (an index typically is printed in very small type), you may begin to lose concentration and miss some important information. Also, if you are going to search through more than one year, the task becomes overwhelming. Fortunately, technology has provided an alternative to the manual search: the computer search. We discuss this method later in this chapter.

Using *Science Citations Index* and *Social Science Citations Index*

Scientific articles invariably end with a section entitled "References." The reference section identifies by author the articles and books cited by the author of the current article, and includes the author's name, article title, journal or book name, and other such bibliographic information. If you have an older article on your topic, quite possibly authors of newer articles have cited it and listed it in their reference sections. The newer articles are likely to cover the same or closely related topics. If you can identify these more recent articles, you have an efficient way to extend your search closer to the present. The *Science Citations Index* and *Social Science Citations Index* do just that. Published by the same company, these references are organized identically but cover a different range of publications (although with some overlap). Someone performing research on a psychological topic could find useful information in both sources. The examples presented here focus on *Social Science Citations.*

Assume you have located a 1975 article on your research topic. You want to know which articles published since 1975 have cited your article in their reference sections. If you go to the *Social Science Citations Index,* you will find several volumes on the shelf arranged and identified by year. Each year is represented by three types of volumes: the Subject Index, which identifies articles published *that year* by subject; the Source Index, which identifies articles published *that year* by author; and the Citations Index, which identifies articles published *that year or earlier* that have been cited in articles published *that year.* These are listed under the name of the first author of the cited work.

The Citations Index. To find out which articles have cited the one you have, start by looking up the author's name (the name of the first author if there are several authors) in the *Citations Index* for 1975. A page from a Citations Index appears in Figure 2-5. If you cannot find the author's name, then none of the articles he or she has published was cited by another article in 1975. After you find the author's name, you will find under it a list of articles written by the author, arranged from oldest to most recent. Under the bibliographic information for each of these articles will be a list of the authors' names, beside which

CRAIK DM
1858 WOMANS THOUGHTS WOME   174
    VICINUS M   FEMINIST ST   8   603 82

CRAIK F
80 NEW DIRECTIONS MEMOR
    HARKER JO   BK# 26685   1   155 82

CRAIK FI
67 BRIT J PSYCHOL 58 291
    BOURNE B   AGING WORK   5   37 82

CRAIK FIM
65 QUARTERLY J EXPERIME 17 227
    SEKULER R   AVIAT SP EN   R   53   747 82
    SOMBERG BL   J EXP PSY P   8   651 82
    YESAVAGE JA   EXP AGING R   8   195 82
67 BRIT J PSYCHOL 58 291
    FLEISCHM.UM   Z GERONTOL   15   53 82
68 HUMAN AGING BEHAVIOR   131
    BACON LD   PERC MOT SK   55   499 82
68 J VERB LEARN VERB BE 7 996
    CRAIK FIM   BK# 28896   8   191 82
    GLANZER M   BK# 26609   R   1982   63 82
    PARKINSO.SR   J GERONTOL   37   425 82
    WRIGHT RE   "   37   76 82
68 PSYCHON SCI 10 353
    GLANZER M   BK# 26609   R   1982   63 82
69 DEC ANN M AAAS BOST
    ENGLE RW   B PSYCHON S   19   343 82
69 DECISION MAKING AGE
    LARISH DD   J MOTOR BEH   14   322 82
69 J VERB LEARN VERB BE 8 658
    SEE SCI FOR 1 ADDITIONAL CITATION
    MARCELL MM   AM J MENT D   87   86 82
    RONNBERG J   SC J PSYCHO   23   113 82
70 J VERB LEARN VERB BE 9 143
    BUCHANAN JP   MEM COGNIT   9   651 81
    DYDEWALL.G   STUD PSYCHO   24   177 82
    FERRETTI RP   INTELLIGENC   6   69 82
    FRAISSE P   BK# 23697   1981   233 81
    GLANZER M   BK# 26609   R   1982   63 82
    NIXON SJ   B PSYCHON S   18   237 81
    RAAIJMAK.JG   J EXP PSY L   N   8   343 82
    WRIGHT RE   J GERONTOL   37   76 82

→ 75 J EXP PSY G 104 268
    SEE SCI FOR 2 ADDITIONAL CITATIONS
    ACKERMAN BP   J EXP C PSY   33   413 82
    "   "   33   429 82
    BADDELEY A   CAN J PSYCH   36   148 82
    BADDELEY AD   PSYCHOL REV   89   708 82
    BIRD CP   AM J PSYCHO   95   251 82
    BRADSHAW GL   J VERB LEAR   21   165 82
    BRANSFOR.JD   J EXP PSY G   111   390 82
    BURNSTEIE   J EXP S PSY   18   217 82
    CARROLL M   J VERB LEAR   21   55 82
    CHARNESS N   CAN J PSYCH   B   36   537 82
    CLARKE AM   BR J EDUC S   30   43 82
    CRAIK FIM   BK# 28896   8   191 82
    DAW PS   CAN J PSYCH   N   35   351 81
    DIEKHOFF GM   J EXP EDUC   50   180 82
    ERBER JT   BK# 26302   1982   569 82
    ERDELYI M   J VERB LEAR   21   656 82

CRAIK FIM   VOL   PG   YR
    EYSENCK MW   BK# 26609   1982   197   82
    FEGGETTE.AJ   ERGONOMICS   25   1065   82
    FRANKS JJ   BK# 26609   1982   395   82
    GARDINER JM   CAN J PSYCH   N   36   527   82
    GARNHAM A   COGNITION   11   29   82
    GLOVER JA   J EDUC PSYC   74   189   82
    "   "   74   522   82
    GRAF P   CAN J PSYCH   35   293   81
    GREENWAL.AG   BK#23699   15   201   81
    HABER RN   PERCEPTION   11   57   82
    HALL CR   J MOTOR BEH   N   14   91   82
    HARA S   JPN J PSYCH   53   144   82
    HUNT RR   J EXP PSY H   N   8   81   82
    LOVETT MW   BK# 22223   3   1   81
    LUFTIG RL   J PSYCHOLIN   11   127   82
    "   "   11   369   82
    MANDLER G   MEM COGNIT   10   33   82
    MANI K   "   10   181   82
    MARX MH   BK# 23697   R   1981   87   81
    MASON SE   PSYCHOL REP   51   355   82
    MCFARLAN.CE   J EXP C PSY   33   20   82
    MCMURRAY DW   AUST J PSYC   33   197   81
    MECKLENB.S   Z ENTWICK P   14   18   82
    MORGAN SV   PSYCHOL REP   51   675   82
    MORRIS CD   MEM COGNIT   10   188   82
    NAUS MJ   BK# 26572   1982   49   82
    NELSON DL   BK# 23699   15   129   81
    PENROD S   BK# 23054   1982   119   82
    PERLMUTT.M   B PSYCHON S   19   65   82
    PRESSLEY M   CHILD DEV   53   1258   82
    "   CONT ED PSY   7   50   82
    "   J EDUC PSYC   74   693   82
    ROEDIGER HL   J VERB LEAR   21   635   82
    RONNBERG J   SC J PSYCHO   23   113   82
    RUNQUIST WN   J VERB LEAR   21   563   82
    SALTZE P   J EXP C PSY   34   77   82
    SCHMECK RR   HUMAN LEARN   1   95   82
    SIMON EW   J GERONTOL   37   575   82
    SQUIRE LR   ANN R NEUR   R   5   241   82
    "   J EXP PSY L   8   560   82
    TAJIKA H   PSYCHOLOGIA   25   100   82
    TOMLINSO.L   ACT NEUR SC   64   43   81
    WARREN C   BR J PSYCHO   73   117   82
    WATKINS MJ   BK# 26609   1982   173   82
    WEINSTEI.CE   CONT ED PSY   7   107   82
    WESSELLS MG   BEHAVIORISM   R   10   65   82
    WILSON RS   CORTEX   18   329   82
    WINN W   ECTJ   30   3   82
    WOLD AH   SC J PSYCHO   23   267   82
    WOLTERS G   ACT PSYCHOL   51   273   82
    ZEITHAML VA   J CONSUM R   8   357   82
75 RES PSYCHOPHYSIOLOGY
    MACWHINN.B   MEM COGNIT   10   308   82
    PARKIN AJ   BR J PSYCHO   73   389   82
    WILDING J   "   73   479   82

Figure 2-5. Excerpt of entries found in the Citations Index of *Social Science Citations Index* for 1982. The arrow points to the entry for Craik, F. I. M. Craik and Tulving's (1975) article is the "75 J EXP Psy G" (*Journal of Experimental Psychology: General*) entry. (Reprinted with permission.)

appear an abbreviated journal name, volume number, page number, and year. These are the articles that cited the author's article.

In Figure 2-5, a rather famous experiment on memory by Fergus Craik and Endel Tulving, published in 1975, has been looked up in the Citations Index for 1982. Under "Craik, F. I. M." are listed a number of articles, beginning with one published in 1965 in the *Quarterly Journal of Experimental Psychology*. These articles authored by Craik were cited in other articles published in 1982. Each cited article is identified by year of publication, abbreviated journal title, volume, and beginning page number. If you scan down this list, you will find the 1975 article, which appeared in the *Journal of Experimental Psychology: General*, volume 104, beginning on page 268.

Immediately beneath the 1975 reference is the message "SEE SCI FOR 2 ADDITIONAL CITATIONS." This indicates that the 1975 article also appears in *Science Citations Index*, and that two citations not found in the *Social Science Citations Index* list will be found there. The additional citations come from journals indexed in the *Science Citations Index* that are not indexed by *Social Science Citations Index*. The two reference sources have somewhat different data bases.

Immediately beneath the additional citations message is a list of all those articles (in journals surveyed by the *Social Science Citations Index*) that cited the Craik and Tulving (1975) report. They are listed by first author's name (abbreviated if necessary to fit) and initials, abbreviated journal title, volume number, beginning page number, and year of publication. In the example, the first article on the list is by B. P. Ackerman and appeared in 1982 in the *Journal of Experimental Child Psychology*, volume 33, beginning on page 413. It is likely that these articles contain information related to the topic originally pursued by Craik and Tulving, although not all will be directly relevant. At this point it is difficult to tell which articles apply, because neither the titles nor abstracts of the articles are given.

To determine which articles may be relevant, you could look them up individually in the library, but this might entail some work. The journal containing the article may not belong to the library. Or you could look up the articles in *Psychological Abstracts*, using the Author Index as previously described. This would provide the title of the article and the abstract, both of which can help to determine relevance. A more immediate step would be to look up the article in the Source Index of *Social Science Citations Index*.

The Source Index. Sometimes it is necessary to track down an article when you have very little information about it. For example, you may read an article in *Time* magazine that mentions a study of interest to you. Unfortunately, all you have is the name of the person who conducted the study and the year of publication. In other cases you may have only the name of an author you found in the Citations Index. How do you go about tracking down the full reference?

The Source Index of the *Social Science Citations Index* gives you a way to find a complete reference if all you have is the name of the author and date of publication. Each entry in the Source Index is referenced under the name of the first author (as in the Citations Index), but also includes the names of any coauthors. If you looked up the name of the first author of the article, you would find full bibliographic information, including the title of the article, journal in which it was published, volume and issue number of the journal, page numbers, and number of references cited in the article. If you looked up the name of one of the junior authors, you would be referred to the first author's name.

Figure 2-6 shows what you would find if you looked up the Ackerman (1982) article that appeared as the first reference citing the Craik and Tulving (1975) paper located in the Citations Index. The information given in Figure 2-6 is found in the Source Index of the *Social Science Citations Index* for 1982 (the year of publication for the Ackerman article) under "ACKERMAN BP." Several articles by Ackerman are listed, including the *Journal of Experimental Child Psychology* article that begins on page 413, which is the third entry shown in Figure 2-6.

This entry provides a wealth of information, including the full title of the article, the abbreviated name of the journal in which it appears (there is a key provided in the Source Index providing the full name), and complete bibliographic information. For more information on how to use the Source Index, consult your librarian.

The *Permuterm Subject Index*. If you do not have an article in mind (but simply wish to find articles on a specific topic), you can still use the *Social Science Citations Index*. The *Permuterm Subject Index* provides the reference information (first author, journal, volume, page, and year) for articles pertaining to topics it lists and appearing in the journals surveyed. The information provided is thus similar to that found in the Subject Index of *Psychological Abstracts*. An advantage over *Psychological Abstracts* is that more journals are covered. A disadvantage is that no abstracts are provided for the articles.

To continue with the example of the Craik and Tulving (1975) article, imagine that you could not remember the authors' names but did recall that the article was published in 1975. Using the 1975 volume of the Subject Index of the *Social Science Citations Index*, you might try to find the article listed under "memory, episodic." There you would find the name "CRAIK F.I.M." You could then look up the same name under the Source Index to find the relevant article.

Other Research Tools

The three research tools *Psychological Abstracts, Social Science Citations Index,* and *Science Citations Index* are perhaps the most comprehensive indexes relevant to all fields of psychology. But you may want to use others for specialized areas. For example, if you were interested in the medical literature related to psychological topics, you would probably want to consult *Index Medicus*. You can use *Index Medicus* to identify relevant medical articles by looking up your topic under the appropriate keyword heading. Keywords are provided in the first book of each volume under "Medical Subject Headings," and "Tree Structures" are provided to guide you to specific terms under more general headings. Within each volume,

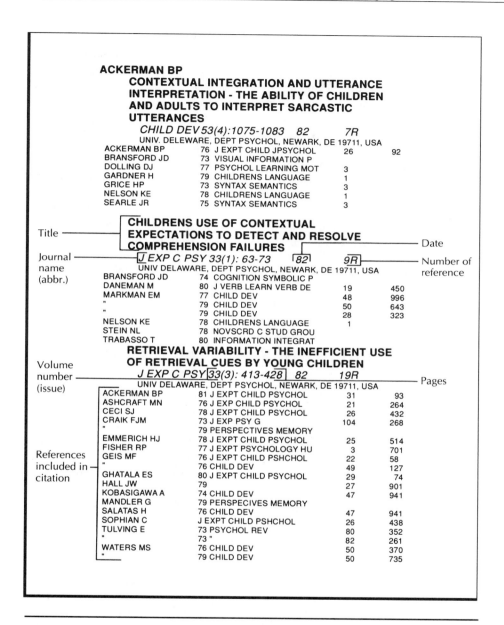

Figure 2-6. Ackerman's (1982) article citing the Craik and Tulving (1975) article (see Figure 2-5) appears in this listing from the Source Index of the *Social Science Citations Index* (1982). The citations listed under Ackerman's article are the references found in the article's reference section. (Reprinted with permission.)

separate sections are provided for empirical articles and reviews. Like the *Social Science Citations Index*, each volume provides access to articles published within a given year. To find articles of different years, you need to check across volumes.

Other indexes you may find useful include *Index to Scientific Reviews* (put out by the publisher of *Social Science Citations Index* and similarly organized, it covers review articles, including those on psychological topics), *Social Sciences Index* (covering sociology), and *Reader's Guide to Periodicals* (listing articles relevant to your topic that have appeared in magazines and other general periodicals). Check with your librarian to determine what indexes are available at your location.

Another helpful research tool is *Current Contents*. This is actually a series of publications. The publication most directly related to psychological topics is *Current Contents: Social & Behavioral Sciences*. Twice each month these publications reproduce the tables of contents for all journals within their spheres that have appeared since the previous issue. If you want to find the most recent articles published on a topic, this is the place to look. However, to use *Current Contents* effectively, you must identify which journals are likely to publish an article relevant to your topic and then read the table of contents for each. No subject index appears in *Current Contents*.

Using a Computer to Search the Literature

In the past the only way to search for relevant resource materials was to do a manual search. Fortunately, advances in both hardware and software have provided an effective alternative: the *computer search*. You can use a computer to locate journal articles or books. The exact method you use, of course, depends on the facilities. Check with your librarian to see what is available.

When conducting a computer search, you usually enter one or more keywords into the computer, which then searches the indexed material for occurrences of those words. When the computer finds your keywords in a reference citation, that citation is added to your reference list.

Computer-Searching the *Psychological Abstracts*

Just a couple of years ago, the only way to conduct a computer search was to give a librarian a list of your keywords and have the librarian use one of the computerized data base systems to do your search for you (for example, BRS Information Services). However, today *Psychological Abstracts* is indexed on a personal computer-based system called *PsycLIT*. *PsycLIT* consists of a data base program that is used to search indexed information stored on and read from a special compact disk system (not unlike the CD player you may have at home). *PsycLIT* currently references over 1,400 journals from fifty countries.

Using *PsycLIT* is relatively simple. You enter keywords and the computer searches its vast pool of indexed material. Let's say you are interested in conducting a research study on short-term memory in elderly adults. You could

TI: Processing resources and age differences in working memory.

AU: Morris, -Robin-G.; Gick, -Mary-L.; Craik, -Fergus-I.

IN: U Newcastle upon Tyne, Royal Victoria Infirmary, England

JN: Memory-and-Cognition; 1988 Jul Vol 16(4) 362-366

AB: Investigated the performance of 24 undergraduates and 24 elderly adults on a modified version of the working memory task developed by A. D. Baddeley and G. J. Hitch (1974). Ss were required to verify a set of sentences of varying complexity while they repeated aloud 0, 2, or 4 words. The older Ss took longer to verify the sentences, especially when the sentences were grammatically complex, but the effect of concurrent memory load on verification latency was the same in both groups. Results cast doubt on the notion that there is an age-related decline in the general pool of processing resources. They also suggest that older people have greater difficulty with the active processing aspects, rather than with the passive holding aspects, of working memory tasks. (PsycLIT Database Copyright 1989 American Psychological Assn, all rights reserved)

KP: task complexity; processing & holding functions of working memory; 19-24 vs 40-80 yr olds

DE: SHORT-TERM-MEMORY; HUMAN-CHANNEL-CAPACITY; AGE-DIFFERENCES; AGED-; YOUNG-ADULTS; TASK-COMPLEXITY; ADULTHOOD-

---

Figure 2-7. Example of a *PsycLIT* reference citation with abstract. (Reprinted with permission.)

---

enter two keywords in the following format: "SHORT TERM MEMORY" and "ELDERLY." *PsycLIT* then searches the titles, abstracts, and descriptor lists for instances of your two keywords. When the search is complete, you can display the contents of the reference list generated. Figure 2-7 illustrates a reference citation generated with these keywords.

The example citation shown in Figure 2-7 includes several important pieces of information: the title (TI), author (AU), journal (JN), the institutional affiliation of the author (IN), abstract (AB), key phrases (KP), and descriptor list (DE). You can tailor the format of the reference citation by specifying exactly what information you want. For example, you may only want to see the title, author, and journal information. Also, you can print out your reference list or save the list on a computer disk for further use.

Data base systems such as *PsycLIT* save a considerable amount of time and effort when doing a literature search. However, keep in mind certain limitations to using computerized search systems. A search is only as good as the keywords you enter. The computer is incredibly fast and obedient—and, unfortunately, pretty stupid. It will only do what you tell it to do; it will not think on its own. So it will find only those references that include your keywords. Sometimes your keywords are used more broadly in the indexed material than you would like. For example, in your search for articles on short-term memory and the elderly, you may have used "aged" (ag-éd) as a keyword. You are initially excited to find over two hundred articles using that keyword. Your excitement wanes, however, when you discover that the computer also found many articles with "aged" referring to an age range (for example, "subjects aged 12–14 years"). Or your chosen keywords may not appear anywhere in an important article, so it will not be included in your reference list. You reduce this problem by using the *Thesaurus of Psychological Index Terms* to help you identify keywords. In fact, *PsycLIT* is keyed to the terms in the *Thesaurus*. Generally, you should use computer search systems only after you have become familiar with a research area so that you will know the relevant keywords.

Another drawback to the computer search is its limited scope. Although the capacity of a compact disk is large, a single disk can only hold indexed material for a limited time period (for example, January 1983 to September 1989). You may have to change disks to get older materials. Also, very old materials may not be available on disk at all, so a manual search will be needed.

Computer-Searching the Card Catalog

Some libraries have installed computer terminals that you can use to search through a data base of books contained in the library's card catalog. Basically, these systems are similar to *PsycLIT*. You can search for authors, titles, subjects, and so on to generate a reference list. Figure 2-8 shows an example of a reference citation from the Indiana University electronic card catalog system.

Computers and Literature Reviews: A Closing Note

It would not be possible to review all the possibilities that currently exist for computer-searching library materials. Availability of computer systems depends on the individual library. If you want to make use of a computerized search system, contact your local librarian. Most libraries with computer systems run special classes on how to do computer searches.

Reading Research Reports

Your search of the literature has identified several potentially useful articles, including reviews, theoretical articles, and research reports. This section describes how to obtain copies of these materials, how to read the materials, and how to critically evaluate the research reports you obtain.

Kelman, Herbert C.
   Crimes of obedience : toward a social psychology of authority and
responsibility / Herbert C. Kelman and V. Lee Hamilton. -- New Haven:Yale
University Press, c1989.
   xiii, 382 p. : ill. ; 24 cm.
   Bibliography: p. 351-367.
   Includes index.
   SUBJECT HEADINGS (Library of Congress; use s =):
      Authority.
      Obedience--Political aspects.
      Political crimes and offenses--Moral and ethical aspects.
      Military discipline--Moral and ethical aspects.

Kelman, Herbert C. Crimes of obedience . . . c1989. (CONTINUED)
   SUBJECT HEADINGS (Library of Congress; use s =):
      Government, Resistance to--United States--Public opinion.
      Military discipline--United States--Public opinion.
      Public opinion--United States.

LOCATION: Indpls UNIV LIB
CALL NUMBER: HM271 .K45 1989
CIRCULATION INFORMATION NOT AVAILABLE IN IO.

Figure 2-8. Example of a citation from the Indiana University On-Line
Card Catalog.

Obtaining a Copy

After identifying relevant research reports, your next step is to obtain copies.
Your library has a list of all periodicals (including scientific journals) found on
its shelves or stored on microfilm. This *Serials Index* includes the call number
assigned to each journal. Use the call number to find the journal just as you
would a book. If your library subscribes to the particular journal you are looking
for, then all you need do is find the article on the shelf. If your library does *not*
subscribe to that journal, you may still be able to obtain a copy of the article
you want by submitting a request for interlibrary loan (see your librarian for
advice on how to do this). The librarian will find a library that does subscribe
to the journal and will have it send a copy of the article for you. However, expect
to wait from two to six weeks before the article arrives.
   If you do find the article in the library, quickly scan it to determine if it is
indeed relevant to your research. If so, copy the article for future reference
(libraries have photocopiers available). Making a copy is legal, even if the article

is copyrighted, as long as the copy is for personal use in your research. Having your own copy will simplify the job of keeping track of important details. You can underline and make marginal notes right on the copy. If you become concerned about some point you had not paid much attention to in your original reading, you can reread your copy.

Reading the Research Report

Assume you have obtained a copy of a research report. Knowing what you will find in it can save you time in locating specific kinds of information. The information contained in the report reflects the purposes for which it was written. These purposes include (1) to argue the need for doing the research, (2) to show how the research addresses that need, (3) to clearly describe the methods used so that others can duplicate them, (4) to present the findings of the research, and (5) to integrate the findings with previous knowledge, including previous research findings and theories. Consider the components of a typical research report and how they fulfill these purposes.

Although the format that an article takes may vary from journal to journal, most research articles include the standard sections shown in Table 2-2. Sometimes sections are combined (results and discussion) or a section added (design). Generally, however, research articles in psychological journals follow the outline shown in Table 2-2.

Abstract. The abstract provides a summary of the question addressed by the research, the method used to answer it, the results, and their implications. It is the abstract that appears in the *Psychological Abstracts* when the article is indexed.

Introduction. Although it is not labeled as such, the introduction follows the abstract and begins the main body of the paper. The introduction establishes the general topic under investigation and reviews the research and theory relevant to the topic. Toward the end of the introduction, specific hypotheses to be tested are usually set out.

When reading the introduction, determine whether the author has reviewed the relevant literature adequately. Were any important articles left out? Also, does the author support any assertions with appropriate reference citations? Learn to distinguish between supported facts and an author's speculation. Also, does the author clearly state the purposes of the study and the nature of the problem under study? Do the hypotheses logically follow from the information provided? Are the hypotheses clearly stated, and more importantly, are they testable?

Method. The method section describes precisely what was done. You might think of this section as a "cookbook," or a set of directions for conducting the study. It usually contains several subsections, including *subjects or participants*

Table 2-2. Parts of an APA-style Article
Abstract
Introduction
Method
Subjects
Apparatus or materials
Procedure
Results
Discussion
References

(where the nature of the subject sample is described fully), *apparatus* (describing the equipment, materials, and measures used), and *procedure* (which describes exactly what was done in the study).

In the method section, you should find enough information concerning the nature of the subject sample (age, sex, race, species, and so on), the apparatus (a description of custom equipment or model numbers of standardized equipment) or materials (for example, questionnaires, rating scales, standardized tests), how variables were manipulated, how behavior was measured, and a discussion of any special steps taken to rule out alternative explanations. All this should be reported in enough detail to allow you to replicate the study if you wish.

Beyond evaluating the specificity of the method section, you should consider a second, more general, question: Does the method used allow for an unambiguous test of the hypotheses stated in the introduction? Carefully read the method, outline the research design, and evaluate it against the purposes of the study. Did the author correctly translate the research problem into an appropriate design?

Results. The results section presents the data, usually in summary form (such as means, standard deviations, correlations, and so on). You will also find the results from any statistical tests reported (such as *t*-tests and analyses of variance) in the results section.

When evaluating the results section, you should note which effects were statistically significant. You might also want to evaluate whether the statistical test used was appropriate (this will require a bit of knowledge about statistics). Check to see that statements made in the text of the results section match what is displayed in any tables or figures.

Discussion. In the discussion section you will find the author's interpretations of the results. Usually the section begins with a summary of the study's major findings. It also includes a synthesis of the findings with previous research and theory, the author's ideas about what the findings mean, and a discussion of any limitations of the study.

Your primary concern with the discussion section is how well the author's conclusions match the data. In a discussion section, the author is permitted to speculate on appplications for the data. However, train yourself to separate the author's speculations from supported fact. Evaluate whether the author oversteps the bounds of the research by making unwarranted speculations that stray too far from the findings. If the author strays too far, be skeptical of the speculations. In addition, determine how well the findings of the study fit previous research and theory. For example, is this the only study that has produced a particular pattern of results? If it is, then be cautious about using the study in your literature review.

References. The final section of an article is usually the reference section (a few articles include appendices as well) in which the author lists all the references cited in the body of the paper. Complete references are provided. You can use these to find other research on your topic.

Developing Hypotheses

All the library research and critical reading you have done has now put you on the threshold of the next major step in the research process: developing your idea into a testable hypothesis. This hypothesis, as we pointed out in Chapter 1, will be a tentative statement relating two (or more) variables that you are interested in studying. Your hypothesis should flow logically from the sources of information used to develop your research question. That is, given what you already know from previous research (either your own or what you read in the journals) you should be able to make a tentative statement about how your variables of interest relate to one another.

Hypothesis development is an important step in the research process because it will drive your later decisions concerning the variables to be manipulated and measured in your study. Because a poorly conceptualized research hypothesis may lead to invalid results, take considerable care when stating your hypothesis.

As an example, imagine that your general research question centers on the relationship between aging and memory. You have spent several hours in the library searching the *Psychological Abstracts* for relevant literature. Given your reading, you have strong reason to believe that aging is related to changes in short-term memory; specifically that older individuals show deficits in processing information in short-term memory compared to younger individuals. Your belief could be stated as the following specific hypothesis: "Processing of information in short-term memory is slower for elderly adults than for younger adults."

Once such a hypothesis has been stated, your next task is to decide how to test it. You must make a variety of important decisions concerning how to design and conduct your study. The next chapter explores some of the major issues you will face during the preliminary stages of planning your study.

Summary

Sources of research ideas include unsystematic observation, systematic observation, theory, and the need to solve a practical problem. Unsystematic observation includes casual observation of both human and animal behavior. Systematic observation includes carefully planned personal observations, published research reports, and your own previous or ongoing research. Theory is a set of assumptions about the causes of a phenomenon and the rules that specify how causes act; predictions made by theory can provide testable research hypotheses.

Developing good research questions begins by asking questions that are answerable through objective observations. Such questions are said to be empirical. Before a question can be answered through objective observation, its terms must be supplied with operational definitions. An operational definition defines a variable in terms of the operations required to measure it. Operationally defined variables can be measured precisely, but may lack generality.

Good research questions should address important issues. A research question is probably important if (1) answering it will clarify relationships among variables known to affect the behavioral system under study, (2) the answer can support only one of several competing hypotheses, or (3) the answer leads to obvious practical applications. A research question is probably unimportant if (1) its answer is already firmly established; (2) the variables under scrutiny are known to have small, theoretically uninteresting effects; or (3) there is no *a priori* reason to believe the variables in question are causally related.

To develop your research idea, you need to conduct a careful review of the literature concerning the topic. A literature review can prevent you from inadvertently conducting a study that has already been done, identify further questions that need to be answered, and help you to design your study.

Sources of research information can be divided into primary sources and secondary sources. Primary sources present original research reports and include scientific journals, some books, and reports presented at scientific conventions. Secondary sources are those that summarize research and include textbooks, other professional books, and reviews found in journals or books. Other sources of research information include personal communication with researchers, technical reports, dissertations, and theses.

The basic strategy to follow in reviewing the literature is (1) find a relevant review article, (2) use the references in the article to find other relevant articles, and (3) use *Science Citations Index* or *Social Science Citations Index* to find more recent articles on the same topic. A number of research tools are available to help you, including *Psychological Abstracts, Science Citations Index, Social Science Citations Index, Dissertation Abstracts International, Current Contents,* and other indexes such as *Index Medicus* and *Social Science Index.*

The *Psychological Abstracts* can be searched manually or via computer. When doing a computer search, you generate a list of keywords and enter them into the computer. The computer then searches the titles and abstracts of articles for instances of those keywords. When found, the reference is included on a reference list. Although the computer can save you time, it may miss important articles if your list of keywords is incomplete.

Research reports follow a standard format that includes an abstract, introduction, method section, results section, discussion section, and references. Each section has a specific purpose. When you read a research report, read it critically, asking questions about the soundness of the reasoning in the introduction, the adequacy of the methods to test the hypothesis, and how well the data were analyzed and interpreted. A good rule of thumb to follow when reading critically is to be skeptical of everything you read.

Once you have done your literature review, you are then ready to formulate your research idea into a testable hypothesis. Using what you have read, you state a research hypothesis, which is a tentative statement concerning the relationship between your variables of interest. The next step is to design a study to test your hypothesis.

Key Terms

Theory

Empirical question

Operational definition

Literature review

Primary source

Secondary source

Refereed journal

Nonrefereed journal

Paper sessions

Personal communications

3

Choosing a Research Design

AFTER SPENDING LONG HOURS READING and digesting the literature in a particular area, you have isolated a behavior that needs further investigation. You have identified some potentially important variables and probably have become familiar with the methods commonly used to measure that behavior. You may even have developed some explanations for the relationships you have identified through your reading and personal experience. You are now ready to choose a research design that will allow you to evaluate the relationships you suspect exist.

Choosing an appropriate research design is crucially important to the success of your project. The decisions you make at this stage of the research process do much to determine the quality of the conclusions you can draw from your research results. This chapter identifies the problems you must face when choosing a research design, introduces the major types of research design, and describes how each type attempts to solve (or at least cope with) these problems.

Functions of a Research Design

Scientific studies tend to focus on one or the other of two major activities. The first activity consists of exploratory data collection and analysis, which is aimed at classifying behaviors within a given area of research, identifying potentially important variables, and identifying relationships between those variables and the behaviors. Such exploration is typical of the early stages of research in an area. The second activity consists of evaluating potential explanations for the observed relationships (hypothesis testing). Testable explanations allow you to predict what relationships should and should not be observed if the explanation is correct. Hypothesis testing usually begins after you have collected enough information about the behavior to begin developing supportable explanations.

Causal Versus Correlational Relationships

The relationships you identify in these activities fall into two broad categories: causal and correlational. In a **causal relationship,** changes in one variable produce changes in another variable. A direct chain of events leads from cause to effect. For example, if you accidentally drop a brick on your toe, the impact of the brick will probably set off a chain of events (stimulation of pain receptors in your toe, avalanche of neural impulses traveling up your leg to the spinal cord and from there to your brain, registration of pain in your brain, involuntary scream) that leads from stimulus to response. You could conclude that dropping a brick on your toe under these conditions *causes* a scream (and probably other things as well!).

Although many variables are related causally, others may be related only correlationally. In a **correlational relationship,** the values of variables are also linked in some way. For example, IQ scores and grade-point averages tend to increase and decrease together. When variables change together in this way, they are said to *covary*. However, such covariation does not imply that changes in the value of one variable actually cause changes in the value of the other. The number of baseball games and the number of mosquitos tend to covary (both increase in the spring and decrease in the fall), yet you would not conclude that mosquitos cause baseball games or vice versa.

When you first begin to develop explanations for a given behavior, knowledge of observed relationships can serve as an important guide, even though you may not yet know which relationships are causal and which are correlational. You simply make your best guess and then develop your explanation based on the causal relationships you think exist. The validity of your explanation will then depend in part on whether the proposed causal relationships turn out, on closer examination, to be in fact causal. Distinguishing between causal and correlational relationships is thus an important part of the research process, particularly in the hypothesis-testing phase.

Your ability to identify relationships and to distinguish causal from correlational relationships varies with the degree of control you have over the variables under study. The next sections describe two broad types of research design: experimental and correlational. Both approaches allow you to identify relationships among variables, but they differ in the degree of control exerted over variables and in the ability to distinguish causal relationships from the merely correlational. We begin with experimental research.

Experimental Research

Experimental research incorporates a high degree of control over the variables of your study. This control, if used properly, permits you to establish causal relationships among your variables. This section describes the defining characteristics of experimental research and how these characteristics enable us to identify causal relationships in data.

Characteristics of Experimental Research

Experimental research has two defining characteristics: manipulation of an independent variable and control over extraneous variables. Be sure you understand these concepts, described as follows, because they are central to understanding experimental research.

Manipulation of Independent Variables. An **independent variable** is a variable whose values are chosen and set by the experimenter. (Another way to look at it is that the value of the independent variable is independent of the subject's behavior.) We call these values the *levels* of the independent variable. For example, imagine you want to determine how sleep deprivation affects a person's ability to recall previously memorized material. To examine this relationship, you might assign subjects to one of three groups defined by the number of hours of sleep deprivation: 0 hours (rested), 24 hours, and 48 hours. These three amounts would constitute the three levels of sleep deprivation, your independent variable.

To manipulate your independent variable, you must expose your subjects to at least two levels of the independent variable. The conditions associated with these different levels are referred to as the *treatments* of the experiment. During the course of an experiment, you expose your subjects to these treatments and record their behavior under each. By manipulating the independent variable in this way, you hope to show that changes in the level of the independent variable cause changes in the behavior being recorded.

The behavior you record is also a variable, and in experimental designs is referred to as the **dependent variable** (or the *dependent measure*). If a causal relationship exists, then the value of the dependent variable depends, at least to some extent, on the level of the independent variable. (Its value also depends on other factors, such as subject characteristics.) Another way to think about the dependent variable is that its value depends on the behavior of the subject, rather than being set by the experimenter.

Manipulating an independent variable can be as simple as exposing one group of subjects to some treatment (distracting noises, for example), and another group of subjects to the absence of the treatment. In this design, the group receiving the treatment is the **experimental group** and the other group is the **control group**. The control group is treated exactly like the experimental group except that it is not exposed to the experimental treatment. The performances of the two groups on the dependent measure are then compared to assess the effect of the independent variable.

More complex experiments can be conducted using more levels of the independent variable, several independent variables, and several dependent variables. You can also choose to expose a single group, or even a single subject, to several levels of an independent variable. (For discussions of specific design options, see Chapters 8, 9, and 10.)

Control over Extraneous Variables. The second characteristic of experimental research is control over extraneous variables. **Extraneous variables** are those that may affect the behavior you wish to investigate, but that for the present experiment are not of interest. For example, you may be interested in determining how well a new anxiety therapy (experimental group), compared to an existing therapy (control group), affects test anxiety in anxious students. If some of your subjects show up for the experiment drunk, their degree of intoxication becomes an extraneous variable. This would be especially problematic if more drunk students ended up in the experimental than in the control group.

If allowed to vary on their own, extraneous variables can produce uncontrolled changes in the value of the dependent variable, with two rather nasty possible consequences. First, uncontrolled variability may make it difficult or impossible to detect any effects of the independent variable. (In our example, the effects of the therapy could be buried under the effects of the alcohol.) Second, uncontrolled variability may produce chance differences in behavior across the levels of the independent variable. These differences could make it appear as though the independent variable produced effects when it did not (the therapy would appear to work when the real effect came from the alcohol). To identify clear causal relationships between your independent and dependent variables, you must control the effects of extraneous variables.

You have two ways to control these effects. The first way is simply to *hold extraneous variables constant*. If these variables do not vary over the course of your experiment, they cannot cause uncontrolled variation in your dependent variable. In the test anxiety experiment, for example, you might want to make sure that all your subjects are sober (or at least intoxicated to the same degree!). In fact, to the degree possible, you would want to make sure that all treatments are *exactly* alike, except for the level of the independent variable.

The second way to deal with extraneous variables is to *randomize their effects across treatments*. This technique deals with the effects of extraneous variables that cannot be held constant, or for reasons that will be explained later, should not be held constant. In an experiment assessing the effect of sleep deprivation on memory, for example, it may not be possible to assure that all your subjects have had identical amounts of sleep deprivation (some may have slept better than others the day before your experiment began) or that their recall abilities are equivalent. The idea is to distribute the effects of these differences across treatments such a way that they tend to even out and thus cannot be mistaken for effects of the independent variable.

For statistical reasons, one of the better ways to accomplish this goal is to assign subjects to treatments at random — by picking their names out of a hat, for example. This technique does not *guarantee* that the effects of extraneous variables will be distributed evenly across treatments, but it usually works reasonably well, and better yet, it allows you to use inferential statistics to evaluate the probability that any observed differences resulted from chance. (For a complete discussion of the logic underlying inferential statistics, see Chapter 12.) Other techniques to deal with uncontrolled extraneous variables are also available. We describe these in later chapters that cover specific design options.

However it is done, control over extraneous variables is crucial to establishing clear causal relationships between your variables. By controlling variables that might affect your dependent variable, you rule them out as possible alternative explanations for your data.

An Example of Experimental Research

As an illustration of experimental research, consider an experiment conducted by Rauh, Achenbach, Nurcomb, Howell, and Teti (1988) on the effects of an early-intervention program on the development of low-birth-weight infants. As you read the description of this study, try to identify the features that qualify the study as a true experiment.

Rauh et al. (1988) obtained a sample of 78 low-birth-weight infants. All the infants were born at the same hospital, had a gestational age of less than 37 weeks, and were hospitalized in an intensive care nursery for at least 10 days. Only infants of married mothers were included in the sample. Infant-mother dyads were randomly assigned to either an experimental or control group.

Mothers of infants in the experimental group were run through a training program designed to help them cope with the special needs of their infants. The training consisted of seven sessions conducted at the hospital before the infant was discharged and four in the infant's home after the infant was discharged. Mothers of infants in the control group were not given the training.

Several dependent variables were measured. Among them were measures of the mother's self-confidence, role satisfaction, and perception of her infant's temperament. Assessments were also done on the infants, using the Bayley Mental Development Indices (MDI) and the McCarthy Scales of Children's Abilities. Rauh et al. found that mothers in the experimental group were more self-confident, had greater role satisfaction, and perceived their infants more favorably than did mothers in the control group. Infants in the experimental group showed greater cognitive development than those in the control group.

Assessing the Rauh et al. Experiment. Have you identified the features of the Rauh et al. (1988) experiment that qualify it as a true experiment? If you have not done so yet, do it now, before you read the next paragraphs.

A crucial element of every true experiment is the manipulation of at least one independent variable. What is the independent variable in the Rauh et al. study? If you said that the intervention manipulation (training versus no training) was the independent variable, you are correct. Note that the value of the independent variable for any mother-infant dyad was assigned to them by the experimenters; it was not chosen by the subjects.

The second crucial element of an experiment is control over extraneous variables. Were extraneous variables controlled in the Rauh et al. (1988) experiment, and if so, how? The answer to the first part of this question is yes, and if you examine the design of the study carefully, you will see that extraneous variables were controlled using both methods described earlier. First, several extraneous variables were held constant across treatments. The infants in both treatments were of low birth weight, had similar gestational ages (under 37 weeks), were hospitalized in intensive care for at least 10 days, and had married mothers. Both groups were treated similarly except that only one group received the training program. Second, the infant-mother dyads were assigned to their treatments at random, and not according to some behavior or characteristic of the subject. This design assured that any remaining uncontrolled differences in the subjects would tend to be distributed evenly between the two treatments. As a result, the investigators could be reasonably sure that any differences found between treatments in the values of the dependent measures were caused by the difference in treatments; that is, by the presence or absence of the training program.

Strengths and Limitations of the Experimental Approach

The great strength of the experimental approach is its ability to identify and describe causal relationships. This ability is not shared by the correlational approach described next. Whereas the correlational approach can tell you only that changes in the value of one variable tend to accompany changes in the value of a second variable, the experimental approach can tell you whether changes in one variable (the independent variable) actually produced changes in the other (the dependent variable).

Despite its power to identify causal relationships, the experimental approach has limitations that restrict its use under certain conditions. The most serious limitation is that you cannot use the experimental method if you cannot manipulate your hypothesized causal variables. For example, studies of personality disorders must use correlational approaches to identify possible causal relationships. Exposing people to various nasty conditions in order to identify which of those conditions cause personality disorders is not ethical.

A second limitation of the experimental approach entails the tight control over extraneous factors required to clearly reveal the effects of the independent variable. Such control tends to reduce the **generality** of the findings, or the degree to which the experimental results apply in situations different from those of the experimental test. A rather unpleasant tradeoff exists in experimental research: as you increase the degree of control you exert over extraneous variables (and thus your ability to establish causal relationships), you decrease your ability to assess the generality of any relationships you uncover. For example, in the Rauh et al. (1988) experiment extraneous variables such as marital status of the mother and gestational age were controlled. However, this control may limit the generality of their results to married mothers with infants fitting into a particular gestational age category.

Experiments Versus Demonstrations

One kind of research design resembles an experiment but lacks one of the crucial features of a true experiment, an independent variable. This design, called a **demonstration,** exposes a group of subjects to one (and only one) treatment condition. In contrast, recall that a true experiment requires exposing subjects to at least two treatments. Whereas a true experiment shows the effect of manipulating an independent variable, a demonstration simply shows what happens under a specified set of conditions. To conduct a demonstration, you simply expose a single group to a particular treatment and measure the resulting behavior.

Demonstrations can be useful because they show that, under such-and-such conditions, *this* happens and not *that*. However, demonstrations are not experiments and thus do not show causal relationships. This fact is sometimes overlooked, as the following example shows.

Wilson Bryan Key, in his book *Subliminal Seduction* (1973), reported a study in which subjects looked at a Gilbey's Gin advertisement that allegedly had sexual subliminal messages embedded within it. The most prominent subliminal message was the word *SEX* spelled out in the bottom three ice cubes in the glass to the right of a bottle of gin (Key, 1973).

Key reported that the ad was tested "with over a thousand subjects" (the details of the study were not given). According to Key, 62 percent of the male and female subjects reported feelings of sexual arousal in response to the ad. Key concluded that the subliminal messages led to sexual arousal. According to Key, advertisers capitalize on these subliminal messages to get you to buy their products.

Now, are you convinced of the power of subliminal messages by this demonstration?

If you said you were not convinced, good for you! The fact that 62 percent of the subjects reported arousal is *not* evidence that the subliminal messages caused the arousal, no matter how many subjects participated. All you know from this demonstration is that under the conditions tested, the advertisement evoked reports of arousal in a fair proportion of the subjects. You do not learn the cause.

In fact, several plausible alternatives can be offered to the explanation that the arousal was caused by subliminal perception. For example, an advertisement for alcohol may lead subjects to recall how they feel when under the influence, or may conjure up images of having fun at a party. As the demonstration was reported, you cannot tell which of the potential explanations is valid. What would you have to do to fully test whether subliminal messages (such as the ones in the Gilbey's Gin ad) actually lead to sexual arousal? Give this question some thought before continuing.

To test whether subliminal messages caused the arousal, you need to add a control group and randomly assign subjects to groups. Subjects in this control group would see the same Gilbey's Gin ad, but without the subliminal message. If 62 percent of the subjects in the "subliminal" group were aroused, but only 10 percent in the other group were aroused, then you could reasonably conclude that the subliminal message caused the arousal. A different conclusion would be drawn if 62 percent of the subjects in *both* groups reported arousal. In this case, you would have to conclude that the subliminal message was ineffective. The fact that the ad leads to reports of sexual arousal (as shown by the demonstration) would have to be explained by some other factor. By the way, most of the controlled, scientific research on subliminal perception shows little or no effect of subliminal messages on behavior.

Although true experiments can effectively identify the factors causing a given behavior, to identify relationships that apply broadly across a variety of situations (that is, relationships with great generality), the correlational approach may be best. We describe correlational research next.

Correlational Research

In **correlational research,** your main interest is to determine whether two variables covary, and if so, to establish the direction of the observed relationship. The strategy involves developing measures of the variables of interest and collecting your data.

Characteristics of Correlational Research

You can grasp the characteristics of correlational research by noting how they differ from those of experimental research. First, you do not manipulate any independent variables. Instead, you simply measure two (or more) dependent variables and then determine whether a correlational relationship exists between them. In keeping with this lack of manipulation of variables, subjects are not randomly assigned to any categorical groups that you may create based on your dependent variable. For example, you might classify your subjects into three groups according to their political affiliation: Democrat, Republican, or Independent. Notice that the subject's response to your question about party affiliation determines the group into which the subject is placed. Political party affiliation does not qualify as an independent variable because the subject, not you, determines inclusion within a group.

Establishing that a correlational relationship exists between two variables makes it possible to predict from the value of one variable the probable value of the other variable. For example, if you know that college grade-point average (GPA) is correlated with Scholastic Aptitude Test (SAT) scores, then you can use a student's SAT score to predict (within limits) the GPA the student is likely to achieve.

When you use correlational relationships for prediction, the variable used to predict is called the *predictor variable* and the variable whose value is being predicted is called the *criterion variable*. Predictor and criterion variables are analogous to the independent and dependent variables of experiments, with one important difference. Whereas you can establish whether an independent variable *causes* changes in a dependent variable, you can only show that predictor variables *predict* changes in criterion variables. Whether the linkage between the latter variables is causal remains open to speculation.

An Example of Correlational Research

Increasingly, mothers are returning to work when their children are still infants, and in many instances parents must then arrange for infant day care for their babies. Is this practice harmful to the infants? For many years, developmental research suggested that high-quality day care has no negative effect on a child's development. However, most of this research studied children who entered day care after their first birthdays. A recent study (Belsky & Rovine, 1988) called into question the benign effect of day care on child development when that care was started during the first year of life.

Belsky and Rovine (1988) decided to investigate the impact of early infant day care on attachment. You can think of attachment as the special relationship that develops between an infant and the parents during the first seven months of life. Belsky and Rovine contacted a group of new mothers and classified them according to the course of infant care chosen (day care versus home care). Mothers choosing early infant day care were subclassified according to the number of hours per week the infant spent in day care: full time (more than 35 hours per week), high part time (20–35 hours per week), low part time (10–20 hours per week), or home reared (0–5 hours per week).

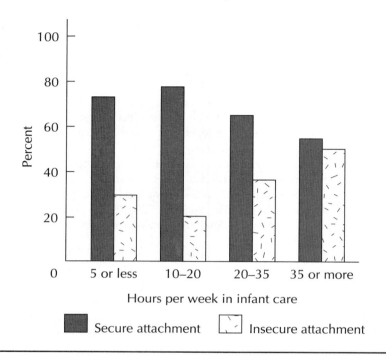

Figure 3-1. Results from a correlational study of early infant day care (drawn from data provided by Belsky & Rovine, 1988).

When the infants were a year old, Belsky and Rovine assessed the quality of attachment to their mothers using a standardized test of attachment security (the Ainsworth Strange Situation Test). Their results are presented in Figure 3-1. These results show that infants placed in day care for more than 20 hours per week during the first six months of life were less securely attached than low part-time or home-reared infants.

Assessing the Belsky and Rovine Study. What qualifies Belsky and Rovine's study as a correlational study? Recall that in correlational research you do not manipulate an independent variable. In Belsky and Rovine's study, no independent variables were manipulated. The two variables examined in the study (hours of infant day care and security of attachment) are *both* dependent variables; their values were simply observed and recorded. Note also that the infants were not randomly assigned to one of the four child care categories, as might have been done in an experiment in order to control the effects of extraneous variables. Rather, Belsky and Rovine simply identified the number of hours per week the infants spent in day care and classified the infants accordingly.

Causation and the Correlational Approach

Given Belsky and Rovine's (1988) results, you might be tempted to conclude that putting an infant into day care for more than 20 hours per week *causes* that child to become insecurely attached to its mother. However, this conclusion that a causal relationship exists is inappropriate, even though the relationship appears compelling. Two obstacles stand in the way of drawing clear causal inferences from correlational data: the third variable problem and the directionality problem.

The Third-Variable Problem. To establish a causal relationship between two variables, you must be able to demonstrate that variation in one of the observed variables could only be due to the influence of the other observed variable. In the example, you want to show that variation in the number of hours an infant spends in day care causes changes in attachment security. However, because the mothers (not the researchers) chose the amount of time the infants spent in day care, possibly other, unmeasured variables were at work. Perhaps mothers who are dissatisfied with their roles as parents choose to place their infants in day care more often and for longer periods than more satisfied mothers. The same dissatisfaction could cause them to remain aloof from their children and thus lead to the child's insecure attachment. Degree of role dissatisfaction, then, and not the number of hours spent in day care, could be the real cause of changes in attachment security.

The possibility that correlational relationships may result from the action of an unobserved "third variable" is called the **third-variable problem**. This unobserved variable may influence both of the observed variables (in this example, hours spent in day care and attachment security), causing them to vary together even though no direct relationship exists between them. The two observed variables thus may be strongly correlated even though neither variable causes changes in the other.

To resolve the third-variable problem, you must examine the effects of each potential third variable to determine whether it does in fact account for the observed relationship. Techniques to evaluate and statistically control the effects of such variables are available (see Chapter 15).

The Directionality Problem. A second reason why it is hazardous to draw causal inferences from correlational data is that, even when a direct causal relationship exists, the direction of causality is sometimes difficult to determine. This difficulty is known as the **directionality problem**.

The directionality problem lurks in Eron's (1963) often-quoted finding of a positive relationship between a child's level of aggression (as rated by classmates) and the amount of violent television the child watches (as measured by a questionnaire completed by the parents). You might be tempted to conclude that children become more aggressive from watching violent television programs, but it seems just as reasonable to turn the causal arrow around. Perhaps aggressive children prefer to watch violent programs.

Why Use Correlational Research?

Given the problems of interpreting the results of correlational research, you may wonder why you would want to use this approach. However, correlational research has a variety of applications, and there are many reasons to consider using it. In this section, we discuss three situations where a correlational approach makes good sense.

Gathering Data in the Early Stages of Research. During the initial, exploratory stage of a research project, the correlational approach's ability to identify potential causal relationships can provide a rich source of hypotheses that later may be tested experimentally. Consider the following example.

Tinbergen (1951) was interested in the behavior of the three-spined stickleback, a fish that inhabits the bottoms of sandy streams in Europe. During the spring, the male stickleback claims a small area of a stream bed and builds a cylindrically shaped nest at its center. At the same time, the male's underbelly changes from the usual dull color to a bright red, and the male begins to drive other males from the territory surrounding the nest. Female sticklebacks lack this coloration and are not driven away by the males.

Put another way, Tinbergen observed that defensive behavior seemed to be positively correlated with the degree of red on the underbelly of the intruding fish. This correlation suggested that the red coloration caused the defensive behavior. But was it color — and color alone — that triggered the response?

Certainly other cues, such as the male's shape or even perhaps his odor, could be responsible. But these cues and the red coloration always appeared and disappeared together (along with the fish to which they belonged). So there was no way, through correlational study alone, to determine whether the red coloration was the actual cause of the defensive behavior or merely an ineffective correlate.

To disentangle these variables, Tinbergen turned to the experimental approach. He set up an artificial "stream" in his laboratory and brought in several male sticklebacks. The fish soon adapted to the new surroundings, setting up territories and building nests. Tinbergen then constructed a number of models designed to mimic several characteristics of male sticklebacks. These models ranged from one that faithfully duplicated the appearance (but not the smell) of a real stickleback, to one that was just a gray disk. Some of the models included red coloration, and some did not (see Figure 3-2).

When the realistic model was waved past a male stickleback in the artificial stream, the male immediately tried to drive it away. Odor obviously was not necessary to elicit defensive behavior. However, Tinbergen was soon amazed to discover that almost any model with red color elicited the response. The only requirements were that the model include an eyespot near the top and that the red color appear below the eyespot.

By manipulating factors such as color and shape, Tinbergen was able to experimentally identify the factors that were necessary to elicit the behavior. The earlier, correlational research conducted in a naturalistic (and therefore poorly

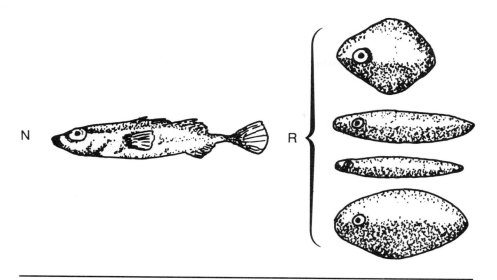

Figure 3-2. Stimuli used by Tinbergen (1951) to follow up on initial observations made in the field: N, neutral underbelly; R, red underbelly. (Reprinted with permission.)

controlled) setting had paved the way for the more definitive research that followed.

Inability to Manipulate Independent Variables. A second reason for choosing a correlational design over an experimental one is that manipulating the variables of interest may be impossible or unethical (see Chapter 5 for a discussion of ethics). The Belsky and Rovine (1988) study of infant day care and attachment security described earlier illustrates this point quite well. In order to establish a clear causal connection between day care and attachment security, you would have to conduct an experiment in which the number of hours of day care was manipulated as an independent variable by assigning infants at random to the various treatment groups. Unfortunately, this experiment would be difficult to carry out. Not many parents who are disinclined toward day care for their infants would agree to put their children into full-time day care for the purpose of an experiment. In such cases a correlational design may be the only practical and ethical option.

Relating Naturally Occurring Variables. A third situation in which a correlational research design may be chosen over an experimental design is when you want to see how naturally occurring variables relate in the "real" world. Such information can be used to make useful predictions, even if the reasons for the discovered relationships are not clear. High school grade-point average, scores on the Scholastic Aptitude Test (SAT), class rank, and scores on the Nelson-Denny reading comprehension test correlate well with each other and with performance in college. Knowledge of these relationships has been used to predict college success. Certain theoretical views may also lead to predictions about which real-world variables should be correlated with which. These predictions can be tested by using a correlational design.

To summarize, correlational designs enable a researcher to identify potential causal relationships among variables and to rule out others. This may be the preferred approach to use during the early stage of a research project when important variables are identified for further study. The correlational approach may also be chosen when the variables of interest cannot be manipulated or should not be manipulated because of ethical considerations. Finally, correlational designs may be chosen when the object of the research is to identify predictor variables or to test the implications of a theory in a real-world setting. However, the correlational approach is weak in its ability to establish causal relationships among variables.

Quasi-Experimental and Combined Designs

Some correlational variables, such as gender, income level, religious preference, or political party affiliation, frequently are treated as though they were independent variables. However, they differ from true independent variables in that the subjects come to the "experiment" already assigned to their treatments by nature (as in the case of gender) or other circumstances of life (as in the case of religion or party affiliation). If you treat a correlational variable as an independent variable and analyze the data accordingly, the correlational variable is called a *quasi-independent variable* and the "experiment" is called a *quasi-experiment*. The prefix "quasi" indicates that the variable or "experiment" only resembles the real thing.

Although quasi-experiments look like real experiments, never forget that they are really correlational studies and that the results you obtain from them must be interpreted accordingly. Showing, for example, that performance on a test of linguistic ability is significantly related to gender (females do better than males, on average) does not prove that the observed differences are caused by one's sex, or genetic gender. Other factors related to gender, such as societal expectations, could mediate the observed relationship. As with more conventional correlational research, correlation does not by itself prove cause.

Quasi-independent variables often are combined with true independent variables in a single design. We refer to such designs as **combined designs**. In combined designs, you can interpret the effects of the independent variable as causal, but not those of the quasi-independent variable.

Specific design options and issues surrounding the use of correlational and quasi-experimental designs are provided in Chapters 6 and 7. You can find more details about combined designs in Chapter 9. At this point, however, we need to provide information on some general problems affecting all research designs.

Internal and External Validity

The goal of research is to establish clear relationships among the variables of interest. This is true whether you choose an experimental or a correlational design. Regardless of your research design, the conclusions you draw from your results depend on how well you construct your study within the bounds of that design. This section examines two important properties of good research design: internal validity and external validity.

Internal Validity

The goal of any research is to test the hypotheses you developed long before you collected any data. To do this, design research that will clearly show the nature of the relationships among your variables of interest. The ability of your research design to adequately test your hypotheses is known as **internal validity** (Campbell & Stanley, 1963). Essentially, internal validity is the ability of your design to test what it was intended to test.

In an experiment, this means showing that variation in the independent variable caused the observed variation in the dependent variable. In a correlational study, it means showing that changes in the value of your criterion variable relate solely to changes in the value of your predictor variable. In both cases, extraneous, uncontrolled variables should neither affect the outcome of your study nor provide alternative explanations for your findings. If such extraneous variables exist, your ability to establish clear and unambiguous relationships among variables is greatly diminished. The design of your study must eliminate (or at least severely limit) the effects of such extraneous variables.

Enhancing Internal Validity. The time to be concerned with internal validity is during the design phase of your study. During this phase, you should carefully plan how your variables are manipulated and measured, with an eye toward eliminating extraneous variables. Discovering problems with internal validity after you have run your study is too late. A poorly designed study cannot be fixed later on.

Threats to Internal Validity. Threats to internal validity come mainly from variables that confound the effects of your independent variable. *Confounding* occurs whenever two variables in a study vary in such a way that the effect of one on the dependent measure cannot be separated from the effect of the other. In other words, the two variables are highly correlated, and ascribing changes in the dependent variable to either one alone is impossible.

Confounding occurs in both correlational and experimental designs, but is particularly damaging to experiments, where the focus is on establishing causal, rather than merely correlational, relationships. **A confounding variable** in an experiment is any uncontrolled variable that systematically varies with your independent variable. When a confounding variable is present, you cannot say unambiguously that the variation in your independent variable caused any changes you observe in your dependent variable.

Confounding and Extraneous Variables. We previously discussed extraneous variables and how they affect the conclusions you draw from your data. Extraneous variables and confounding variables are related in that they both interfere with drawing clear conclusions from your data. They differ, however, in one important respect. In an experiment, an extraneous variable may be the same across your experimental and control groups. For example, if your laboratory room is very humid, all subjects (both experimental and control) are subjected to the high humidity. Performance will be affected for subjects in both groups. Confounding, however, occurs when the extraneous variable varies systematically across conditions along with your independent variable. So if the high humidity in your laboratory was only present for experimental subjects, confounding has occurred.

As an example of confounding, consider the following experiment conducted by McDonnell (1968). McDonnell's experiment was designed to assess whether the price of a product is an important factor determining preference for it. Subjects were given three bottles of beer and were told that each bottle sold for a different price ($.99, $1.20, or $1.30 per sixpack). An experimenter went to the homes of the subjects three times per week for eight weeks and left three bottles of beer on each visit (one from each price level). Each bottle was labeled with a letter, with the $.99 beer labeled as *P,* the $1.20 beer as *L,* and the $1.30 beer as *M.* Subjects were asked to select one of the three beers and drink it at any time before the next visit. Following the last visit, the subjects rated the chosen beers on five-point scales. The higher-priced beer was rated as better than lower-priced beer.

Can you state conclusively from the results of this experiment that the price of beer caused the observed differences in ratings? If you say no, you are correct. There is a confounding variable here. The experimenters attached the same letter to each price level on every visit to the subjects' homes. The observed differences in rating could be due to a preference for one letter over another, rather than to the price of the beer. In fact, this is precisely what happened in the original "Pepsi Challenge." In that comparison, cups containing Pepsi were marked with an *M* and those containing Coke with a *Q.* Although the Pepsi cup was preferred more often than the Coke cup, Coke representatives later showed in a comparison of their own that people tended to choose a cup marked *M* over a cup marked *Q* even when both cups contained the same cola.

Confounding is an extremely serious problem in an experiment, because it makes interpretation of the results ambiguous. You can't say with any certainty that the independent variable, and not the confounding variable, caused any observed effects. Consequently, when designing an experiment you should work hard to avoid confounding.

Confounding is also a problem in correlational research. In correlational research, you hope to identify *potential* causal relationships between predictor and criterion variables. However, you are very likely to find that the predictor variables correlate as much with each other as with the criterion. Using purely correlational techniques in such cases may make it difficult or impossible to determine which of the correlated predictor variables may be causally related to the criterion variable. For example, in Belsky and Rovine's (1988) study on the effects of early infant day care, variables that were correlated with the number of hours an infant was placed in day care (for example, reason for returning to work) might be the actual factors causing changes in attachment.

Confounding arises from many sources, many of which are associated with specific research designs. These sources of confounding and the design types that produce them, are described in Part II of this text ("Research Designs").

External Validity

To be of any value, research must have internal validity; without it, the results simply cannot be trusted. Yet even internally valid research may have limited usefulness if it lacks a second characteristic known as **external validity**. Science is a search for general principles. Given this goal, you want your research findings to apply to a broad range of subjects and situations. In a study of the effect of a new teaching method on children's learning, for example, you want to be able to generalize your findings to children who were not included in your subject sample. In addition, you want to be able to say that your findings are not limited to a particular research setting. The degree to which your findings may be extended beyond the particular research setting and sample is the external validity of your study. Put another way, externally valid research designs produce results that generalize well.

External validity is threatened by using highly controlled laboratory environments (as opposed to naturalistic settings), restricted subject populations (such as college sophomores rather than a cross section of adults), or pretests (used to establish baselines), by demand characteristics of the experiment, experimenter and subject selection biases, and other such factors. We discuss the effect of research setting on external validity later in this chapter, and deal with the problems of demand characteristics and other sources of bias in Chapters 4 and 5. For now we simply note that subtle aspects of your research design can affect how subjects respond to your manipulation, and thus can produce results peculiar to the specific conditions of the study. You must pay careful attention to these problems during the design phase of your study if you want your research to have a reasonable degree of external validity.

Internal Versus External Validity

Although you should strive to achieve a high degree of both internal and external validity in your research, in practice you will find that the steps you take to increase one type of validity tend to decrease the other. For example, a tightly controlled laboratory experiment affords you a relatively high degree of internal validity. Your findings, however, may not generalize to other samples and situations; thus external validity may be reduced. Often the best you can do is reach a compromise on the relative amounts of internal and external validity in your research.

Whether internal or external validity is more important depends on your reasons for conducting the research. If you are most interested in testing a theoretical position (as is often the case in basic research), you might be more concerned with internal than external validity and hence conduct a tightly controlled laboratory experiment. But if you are more concerned with applying your results to a real-world problem (as in applied research), you might take steps to increase the external validity while attempting to maintain a reasonable degree of internal validity. These issues need to be considered at the time you design your study.

As just mentioned, the setting in which you conduct your research strongly influences the internal and external validity of your results. The kinds of setting available and the issues you should consider when choosing a research setting are the topics we take up next.

Research Settings

In addition to deciding on the design of your research, you must also decide on the setting in which you conduct your research. Your choice of setting is affected by the potential costs of the setting, its convenience, ethical considerations, and the research question you are addressing.

The two research settings open for psychological research are the laboratory and the field. For this discussion, the term *laboratory* is used in a broad sense. A laboratory is any research setting that is artificial, relative to the setting in which the behavior naturally occurs. This definition is not limited to a special room with special equipment for research. A laboratory can be a formal lab, but it can also be a classroom, a room in the library, or a room in the student union building. In contrast, the *field* is the setting in which the behavior under study naturally occurs.

Your decision concerning the setting for your research is an important one, so you must be familiar with the relative advantages and disadvantages of each.

The Laboratory Setting

If you choose to conduct your research in a *laboratory setting,* you gain important control over the variables that could affect your results. The degree of control depends on the nature of the laboratory setting. For example, if you are interested in animal learning, you can structure the setting to eliminate virtually all extraneous variables that could affect the course of learning. This is what Ivan Pavlov did in his investigations of classical conditioning. Pavlov exposed dogs to his experimental conditions while the dogs stood in a sound-shielded room. The shielded room permitted Pavlov to investigate the impact of the experimental stimuli free from any interfering sounds. Like Pavlov, you can control important variables within the laboratory that could affect the outcome of your research.

Complete control over extraneous variables may not be possible in all laboratory settings. For example, if you were administering your study to a large group of students in a psychology class, you could not control all the variables as well as you might wish (students may arrive late or disruptions may occur in the hallway). For the most part, the laboratory affords more control over the research situation than does the field.

Simulation: Re-creating the World in the Laboratory. When you choose the laboratory as your research setting, you gain control over extraneous variables that could affect the value of your dependent variable. However, a trade-off is made when choosing the laboratory for your research. Although you gain better control over variables, your results may lose some generality (the ability to apply your results beyond your specific laboratory conditions). If you are concerned with the ability to generalize your results as well as controlling extraneous variables, consider using a **simulation**. In a simulation, you attempt to re-create (as closely as possible) a real-world situation in the laboratory. Carefully designed and executed simulation may increase the generality of results. Because this strategy has been used with increasing frequency lately, a detailed discussion is in order.

Why Simulate? You may decide for a variety of reasons to simulate rather than conduct research in the real world. You may choose simulation because the behavior of interest could not be studied ethically in the real world. For example, Chapter 1 mentioned factors that control panic behavior. Recreating a panic situation in order to study the ensuing behavior is unethical. If you were interested in studying how juries reach a decision, you could not eavesdrop on real juries. But you could conduct a jury simulation study and analyze the deliberations of the simulated juries.

Often researchers choose to simulate for practical reasons. A simulation may be used because studying a behavior under its naturally occurring conditions is expensive and time-consuming. By simulating in the laboratory, the researcher also gains the advantage of retaining control over variables, while studying the behavior under relatively realistic conditions.

Designing a Simulation. For a simulation to improve the generality of laboratory-based research, it must be conducted carefully. Before you design a simulation, you should be intimately familiar with the real-world situation to be simulated. Before you try to construct a simulation, observe the actual situation and study it carefully (Winkel & Sasanoff, 1970). Identify the critical elements inherent in the situation of interest, decide which of them to include in your simulation, and then try to reproduce them in the laboratory.

The more realistic the simulation, the greater are the chances that the results will be applicable to the simulated real-world event. However, as Bray and Kerr (1982) point out, there is no accepted standard against which to judge the realism of a simulation. According to Bray and Kerr, the real-world event to be simulated is often highly diverse and, no matter how realistic, any attempt at simulation may be representative of only a small subset of real-world events.

How might you apply the simulation methodology to study a real-world problem in the laboratory? As an example, suppose you were interested in studying the interpersonal relationships and dynamics that evolve in prisons. It might be difficult to conduct your study in an actual prison, so you might consider a simulation. In fact Haney, Banks, and Zimbardo (1973) did just that.

In their now-famous Stanford prison study, Haney et al. constructed a prison in the basement of the psychology building at Stanford University. Subjects in the study were randomly assigned to be either prisoners or prison guards. Those subjects assigned to be prisoners were "arrested" by the police, fingerprinted, and incarcerated in the simulated prison. Treatment of the prisoner-subjects was like that of actual prisoners: they were issued numbers, bland uniforms, and assigned to cells. Prison guards were issued uniforms, badges, and nightsticks. Their instructions were to maintain order within the simulated prison.

The behavior of the subjects within the simulated prison was observed by a team of social psychologists. Behavior within the simulated prison was similar to (though less extreme than) behavior in a real prison. Guards developed rigid and sometimes demeaning rules, and prisoners banded together in a hunger strike. In fact, the simulation was so real for the subjects that the experiment had to be discontinued after only a few days.

Realism. Most researchers would agree that a simulation should be as realistic as possible (as was the case in the Stanford prison study). The physical reality created in the Stanford prison study probably helped subjects become totally immersed in their roles. However, a simulation may not have to be highly realistic to adequately test a hypothesis. Mintz's (1951) simulation study of panic behavior (see Chapter 1) did not re-create a burning theater. It was nevertheless a highly involving experiment for the subjects.

The importance of the "realism" of a simulation depends in part on the definition of realism you adopt. Aronson and Carlsmith (1968) distinguish between two types of realism: mundane and experimental. *Mundane realism* refers to the degree to which a simulation mirrors the real-world event. In contrast, *experimental realism* refers to the degree to which the simulation psychologically involves the subject in the experiment. Mintz's study might have been low in mundane realism, but was high in experimental realism.

Simulation has become an important issue in the area of social psychology and law. Many researchers have used simulation methods to study issues such as plea bargaining and jury decision making. A simulation in which a courtroom is realistically reconstructed in the laboratory could have high mundane realism. However, such high levels of mundane realism do not guarantee that the results of the study will be any more valid than those of the same study conducted in a more ordinary laboratory setting. Experimental realism is an important factor to be considered. An involving task in a laboratory with low mundane realism may produce more general results than a less-involving task in a laboratory with high mundane realism.

A good illustration of the importance of experimental realism comes from a study by Wilson and Donnerstein (1977). These researchers reported that a crucial factor in the applicability of simulated jury research findings is whether or not the subject believes that his or her decision will have real consequences. As an independent variable, Wilson and Donnerstein varied whether or not subjects believed that their decisions would have consequences. They found that when subjects believed that their judgments had consequences, the defendant's character (a variable previously shown in other research to be an important factor in the decision process) was no longer important.

Leading the subject to believe that his or her decision has consequences beyond the advancement of science increases experimental realism and thus increases the generality of the results. You may be able to increase the generality of your results when designing simulation studies by taking steps to increase not only mundane realism, but also experimental realism.

To summarize, the laboratory approach to research has the advantage of allowing you to control variables and thus isolate the effects of the variables under study. However, in gaining such control over variables, you lose a degree of generality of results. Using simulations that are high in experimental realism may improve the ability to generalize laboratory results in the real world.

The Field Setting

Field research is conducted outside of the laboratory in the natural environment of the subject. Two ways in which field research can be conducted are simply choosing to observe naturally occurring behavior, or choosing to manipulate independent variables and looking for changes in behavior. Chapters 6 and 7 discuss naturalistic observation and field survey methods. This chapter illustrates field research with a discussion of the field experiment.

The Field Experiment. A field experiment is an experiment conducted in the natural environment of the subject. In a field experiment (as in a laboratory experiment), you manipulate independent variables and measure a dependent variable. You decide which variables to manipulate, how to manipulate them, and when to manipulate them. Essentially, the field experiment has all the qualities of the laboratory experiment except that the research is conducted in the real world rather than in the artificial laboratory setting.

As an example, consider a field experiment conducted by Piliavin and Piliavin (1972) on helping behavior. These researchers were interested in the variables that affect the decision to offer help to someone in trouble. They hypothesized that a person's assessment of the costs of providing help would affect the decision to help. Piliavin and Piliavin decided to vary the subject's cost of providing help and measured willingness to offer help.

The experiment was conducted on subway cars in the Philadelphia subway system. In the experimental procedure, a confederate of the researcher (someone who works for the researcher) walked onto the subway car and fell down. The perceived costs to the helper were manipulated by having the confederate either bite on a vial of theatrical blood (bloody victim) or not bite on a vial (nonbloody victim). An observer measured the length of time that elapsed before someone offered help. It turned out that help was faster and more likely to be given when the victim was not bloody.

This field experiment has all the elements of a true experiment. An independent variable was systematically manipulated (bloody versus nonbloody victim) and a dependent variable was measured (latency to help). Hence, causal inferences about helping behavior can be made from the observations.

Advantages and Disadvantages of the Field Experiment. As with the laboratory experiment, the field experiment has its advantages and disadvantages. Because the research is conducted in the real world, one important advantage is that the results can be easily generalized to the real world. An important disadvantage is that you have little control over potential confounding variables. In the Piliavin and Piliavin experiment, for example, the researchers could not control how crowded the subway car was when the experiment was conducted, or who was on the car. These sources of confounding can make interpreting results from field experiments hazardous.

A Look Ahead

At this point you have been introduced to the broad issues you should consider when choosing a research design, the basic design options available to you, and the strengths and weaknesses of each choice. Before you are ready to conduct your first study, you will also need to know how to measure your variables; what methods of observation are available; how to conduct systematic, reliable, and objective observations; how to choose subjects and deal with them ethically; how to minimize subject and experimenter biases; and many other details concerning specific research designs. In the next chapter, we consider how to go about making systematic, scientifically valid observations.

Summary

Some of the most important decisions you will make about your research concern its basic design and the setting in which it will be conducted. Research designs serve one or both of two major functions: (1) exploratory data collection and analysis (to identify new phenomena and relationships) and (2) hypothesis testing (to check the adequacy of proposed explanations). In the latter case, it is particularly important to distinguish causal from correlational relationships between variables. The relationship is causal if one variable directly influences the other. The relationship is correlational if the two variables simply change values together (covary) and may or may not directly influence one another.

Two basic designs are available for determining relationships between variables: experimental designs and correlational designs. Experimental designs provide strong control over variables and allow you to establish whether variables are causally related. The defining characteristics of experimental research are (1) manipulation of an independent variable and (2) control over extraneous variables. Independent variables are manipulated by exposing subjects to different values or levels and then assessing differences in the subjects' behavior across the levels. The observed behavior constitutes the dependent variable of the study. Extraneous variables are controlled by holding them constant, if possible, or by randomizing their effects across the levels of the independent variable.

The simplest experimental designs involve two groups of subjects. The experimental group receives the experimental treatment; the control group is treated identically except that it does not receive the treatment. More complex designs may include more levels of the independent variable, more independent variables, or more dependent variables.

Although experiments can identify causal relationships, there are situations in which they cannot or should not be used. Variables may be impossible to manipulate, or it may not be ethical to do so. In addition, tight control over extraneous variables may limit the generality of the results.

A demonstration is a type of nonexperimental design that resembles an experiment but lacks manipulation of an independent variable. It is useful for showing what sorts of behaviors occur under specific conditions but cannot identify relationships among variables.

Correlational research involves collecting data on two or more variables across subjects or time periods. The states of the variables are simply observed or measured "as is" and not manipulated. Subjects enter a correlational study already "assigned" to values of the variables of interest by nature or circumstances. Correlational designs can establish the existence of relationships between the observed variables and determine the direction of the relationships. However, two problems prevent such designs from determining whether the relationships are causal. The third-variable problem arises because of the possibility that a third, unmeasured variable influences both observed variables in such a way as to produce the correlation between them. The directionality problem arises because even if two variables are causally related, correlational designs cannot determine in which direction the causal arrow points.

Despite its limitations, correlational research is useful on several accounts. It provides a good method for identifying potential causal relationships during the early stages of a research project, can be used to identify relationships when the variables of interest cannot or should not be manipulated, and can show how variables relate to one another in the real world outside the laboratory. Such relationships can be used to make predictions even when the reasons for the correlation are unknown. A variable in a correlational relationship that is used to make predictions is termed a *predictor variable,* whereas a variable whose value is being predicted is termed a *criterion variable.*

Quasi-experimental designs are correlational designs in which the predictor variable has the appearance of an independent variable. Such variables are called *quasi-independent variables.* The value of a quasi-independent variable is a characteristic of the subject and is not assigned to the subject by an experimenter. Quasi-independent variables may be combined with true independent variables in a combined experimental-correlational design. Because quasi-independent variables are actually correlational, results obtained with them in any design cannot be interpreted as establishing a causal relationship between the quasi-independent variable and the dependent variable.

Two important characteristics of any design are its internal and external validity. Internal validity is the ability of a design to test what it was intended to test. Results from designs low in internal validity are likely to be unreliable. A serious threat to internal validity comes from confounding. Confounding exists in a design when two variables are linked in such a way that the effects of one cannot be separated from the effects of the other. External validity is the ability of a design to produce results that apply beyond the sample and situation within which the data were collected. Results from designs low in external validity have little generality.

After deciding on a research design, you must then decide on a setting for your research. You can conduct your research in the laboratory or in the field. The laboratory setting affords you almost total control over your variables. You can tightly control extraneous variables that might confound your results. Laboratory studies, however, tend to have a degree of artificiality. You cannot be sure the results you obtain in the laboratory apply to real-world behavior. Simulation is a technique in which you seek to re-create the setting in which the behavior naturally occurs. The success of your simulation depends on its realism, which is of two types. Mundane realism is the degree to which your simulation re-creates a real-world environment. Experimental realism concerns how involved in your study your subjects become. High levels of mundane realism do not guarantee a valid simulation. Experimental realism is often more important.

Field research is conducted in your subjects' natural environment. Although this setting allows you to generalize your results to the real world, you lose control over extraneous variables. Field experiments therefore tend to have high external validity but relatively low internal validity.

Key Terms

Causal relationship	Independent variable
Correlational relationship	Dependent variable
Experimental research	Experimental group

Control group

Extraneous variable

Generality

Demonstration

Correlational research

Third variable problem

Directionality problem

Combined design

Internal validity

Confounding variable

External validity

Simulation

4

Making Systematic Observations

THE EVERYDAY OBSERVATIONS WE MAKE (the weather is hot and humid today; Martha is unusually grouchy; I'm feeling grouchy, too) are generally unsystematic, informal, and made haphazardly, without a plan. In contrast, scientific observations are systematic: what will be observed, how the observations will be made, and when the observations will be made are all carefully planned in advance of the actual observation.

Information recorded in this systematic way becomes the data of your study. Your conclusions come from these data, so it is important that you understand how your choice of variables to observe, methods of measurement, and conditions of observation affect the conclusions you can legitimately draw. This chapter provides the information you need to make these choices intelligently.

Deciding What to Observe

Chapters 2 and 3 discussed how to obtain and develop a research idea and how to select a general strategy to attack the questions your research idea raises. After you select a specific question to investigate, you must decide exactly what to observe. Most research situations offer many ways to address a single question.

As one example, assume you want to study the relationship between weather and mood. Your general research question involves how the weather affects a person's mood. You must decide what specific observations to make. First, you must specify what you mean by "weather." "Weather" can be defined in terms of a number of specific variables such as barometric pressure, air temperature, humidity, amount of sunlight, and perhaps the type and amount of precipitation. You may want to measure and record all these variables; or you may want to define weather in terms of some combination of these variables. For example, you could dichotomize weather into two general categories: gloomy (cloudy or foggy, humid, low barometric pressure) and zesty (sunny, dry, high barometric pressure).

You must also decide how to index the moods of your subjects. Again a number of possibilities exist. You may choose to have subjects rate their own moods, perhaps by using the Mood Adjective Check List (Nowlis & Green, 1957, cited in Walster, Walster, & Berscheid, 1978); or you may decide to gauge the moods of your subjects through observation of mood-related behaviors.

In this example, you have translated your general research idea into action by selecting particular observations to make. Note that the same general variables (weather, mood) can be defined and measured in a number of ways. As discussed in Chapter 2, the specific way you choose to measure a variable becomes the **operational definition** of that variable within the context of your study. How you choose to operationalize a variable, and thus to observe and measure it, affects how you will later analyze your data and what conclusions you can draw from that analysis. So you should give careful consideration to your choice of what variables to observe and manipulate, and how to operationally define them.

Choosing Specific Variables for Your Study

Assuming you have decided on a general research topic, a number of factors may influence your choice of specific variables to observe and manipulate. Here are some of them:

Research Tradition

If your question follows up on previous research in a particular area, the variables you choose to observe may be the same as those previously studied. In particular, you may choose to study the same dependent variables while manipulating new independent variables. For example, research on operant conditioning typically focuses on how various factors affect the rate of lever pressing (in rats) or key pecking (in pigeons). In experiments on cognitive processing, reaction times are frequently recorded in order to determine how long a hypothesized process requires to complete. Using these traditional measures allows you to compare the results of different manipulations across experiments.

Theory

Your decision about what to observe may depend on a particular theoretical point of view. For example, you may choose to observe behaviors that are seen as important from a certain theoretical perspective. If these behaviors (or other variables) have been used in previous research, you probably should use the measures already developed for them. However, the theory may suggest looking at behaviors not previously observed, in which case you must develop your own measures.

Availability of New Techniques

Sometimes a variable cannot be investigated because there is no suitable way to measure it. In this case, the development of new techniques may open the way to observation and experimentation. You may want to use the new measure simply to explore its potential for answering your research question. As an example, consider the development of positron emission tomography (PET), a technique allowing researchers to visualize the level of activity of parts of a subject's brain. A scanner picks up positrons (positively charged electrical particles) emitted by radioactively labeled glucose, which is being absorbed by neurons of the cortex in order to fuel metabolic activity. More active neurons absorb more glucose and therefore emit more positrons. A computer translates the rates of positron emission in various regions of the cortex into a color-coded image of the cortex on the computer's display screen. By keeping track of changes in the colors, an observer can determine the ongoing pattern of neural activity. This technology has enabled researchers to observe which parts of the cortex are most active during such activities as solving arithmetic problems or analyzing visual patterns.

Availability of Equipment

You are always tempted to adopt measures for which you already are equipped. For example, if you have invested in an operant chamber equipped with a lever and feeder, you may find it easier to continue your studies of operant conditioning by using this equipment rather than starting from scratch. Perhaps this equipment makes it trivially easy to collect data on response frequency (number of lever presses per minute) but does not readily yield information about response duration (amount of time the lever is depressed) or response force (amount of pressure exerted on the lever). You may decide that measuring response frequency will be adequate to answer your research question, particularly if previous research has successfully used this measure.

If the chosen measures provide reasonable answers to your research questions, this decision is not wrong. Problems arise when the measure really is not appropriate or adequate for the question being investigated, but is chosen anyway on the basis of mere convenience. If you have chosen a particular measure simply because it is readily available or convenient, you should ask yourself whether it really *is* the best measure for your question.

The decision of how to observe the behavior and other variables of your study requires that you select appropriate measures of these variables. The next section examines some issues you need to consider when choosing how to measure your variables.

Choosing Your Measures

Several important factors should be considered when choosing your measures, including (1) the reliability and validity of any measures you adopt, (2) whether you can use existing measures or must develop new ones, and (3) the adequacy of the scale of measurement on which the measure rests.

Demonstrating Validity

A **valid measure** is one that measures what you intend it to measure. A measure is not valid if it gauges some dimension other than the one intended. For example, a criticism of IQ scores is that they sometimes lack validity. Critics charge that IQ scores often tap into achievement as well as intelligence.

A number of types of validity exists, each requiring a somewhat different operation to establish. You can establish the *concurrent validity* of a measure by demonstrating a high correlation between your new measure and an established measure. You can establish the *construct validity* of a measure by showing that the data generated from the new measure fit existing research and theory. Two other ways of establishing validity are to demonstrate *predictive validity* or *face validity*. With predictive validity, you determine whether your measure predicts a behavior that it should predict. For example, IQ scores should predict school performance fairly well. If you find a strong correlation between your new measure and a behavior that it should predict, then you have established predictive validity. With face validity, you simply examine your measure. If the measure seems to ascertain what it is supposed to, then it has face validity. For example, a mathematics test has face validity if it requires subjects to perform arithmetic calculations.

Face validity is the least trustworthy of all the measures of validity. Many tests have little face validity and yet, by other criteria, do measure what they are intended to measure. Therefore, it is worth the time and effort required to establish the concurrent, construct, or predictive validity of a new measure rather than simply relying on its face validity.

Demonstrating Reliability and Accuracy

A **reliable measure** produces similar results when measurements are made under identical conditions. An **accurate measure** produces results that agree with a known standard.

A particular measuring instrument can be inaccurate but reliable. For example, a thermometer whose glass has slipped down in its brackets may read 21°F every time it is immersed in ice water. Because it gives the same reading each time it is subjected to the same conditions, the thermometer is reliable. Since ice water should give a reading of 32°F (for reasonably pure water at sea level), the thermometer fails to agree with a known standard and is therefore inaccurate.

Although a thermometer can be inaccurate but reliable, the converse is not true—it cannot be unreliable but accurate. If the thermometer gives a different reading every time it is placed in ice water (the glass keeps moving along the scale), the thermometer reading does not agree with a known standard, except by chance.

In psychological measurement, standards are rare and therefore the accuracy of a measure often cannot be assessed. For example, no standard introvert exists against which to assess the accuracy of a measure of introversion-extraversion (a personality variable). In most research situations, however, you can evaluate reliability. If you are using equipment to record behavior, you can check to be sure that the equipment functions properly and with a minimum of error. Multiple observers are used in some studies to record behavior. Reliability is then established by determining the degree of agreement among observers, a measure called *interrater reliability*. (See Chapter 6 for information on how to assess interrater reliability.)

Reliability and Validity

Just as a measure can be reliable but inaccurate, it can also be reliable but invalid. Consider the work of the phrenologists early in the nineteenth century. The phrenologists were a group of individuals, headed by Franz Gall, who believed that various mental abilities could be assessed by measuring the dimensions of various parts of a person's cranium. To make the task of measurement reliable, they developed special instruments, such as enlarged calipers. By using these instruments properly, the phrenologists were able to collect highly reliable measurements of cranial shapes and sizes.

If the phrenologists had been content to simply state that their measurements indicated something about cranial characteristics *per se,* they would have remained on safe ground. Instead, they asserted that their measurements provided an indirect (but reliable) assessment of such mental characteristics as memory, personality, intelligence, and criminality. Of course, cranial size and shape actually provide no such information. Although highly reliable, the phrenologist's measures were not valid indications of mental characteristics.

Although a measure can be reliable but invalid, the converse is not true. If a measure is unreliable, it is not a valid gauge of anything except the amount of random error in the measuring instrument.

Using Established Measures Versus New Ones

In the weather and mood example we previously presented, the Mood Adjective Check List was one possible measure of subjects' moods. This established measure has been used in previous research. Using established measures is advantageous because the validity of the measure is known.

Although you do not have to spend precious time validating the measure, established measures may not be suitable for addressing your research questions. A case where the established measure was *not* appropriate comes from the literature on jury decision making. Early research on the factors that affect jury decision making required subjects to sentence a defendant (Landy & Aronson, 1969, for example) and several subsequent studies also used this measure. Because jurors are not empowered to sentence a defendant (except in death penalty cases), the established measure lacked realism. Later research attempted to correct this problem by having subjects evaluate the guilt of the defendant either on rating scales or as a dichotomous guilty/not guilty verdict.

An alternative to using established measures is to develop your own. This alternative has the advantage of freeing you from previous dogma and theory. In fact, a successful new measure may shed new light on an old phenomenon. But before you can use your new measure, you must show that it is valid, reliable, and, in some cases, accurate. Unfortunately, demonstrating the validity, reliability, and accuracy of a new measure can be time-consuming and expensive. Consequently, using measures that are already available (especially if you are new to a research area) is advisable.

Scales of Measurement

The following discussion highlights factors you must consider to develop effective measures of behavior. Before addressing this topic, you must become acquainted with the four basic scales of measurement: nominal, ordinal, interval, and ratio.

Nominal Scales. At the lowest level of measurement, a variable may simply define a set of cases or types. For example, sex may be male or female. According to one scheme, a person's personality may be classified as introverted or extraverted. Variables whose values differ by category are said to fall along a **nominal scale**. In a nominal scale, the values have different names, but no ordering of the values is implied. For example, to say that male is higher or lower in value than female makes no sense. They are simply different. It also makes no sense to multiply, divide, add, or subtract nominal values.

Ordinal Scales. At the next level of measurement are variables measured along an **ordinal scale**. The different values of a variable in an ordinal scale not only have different names (as in the nominal scale), but also can be ranked according to quantity. For example, a subject's self-esteem may be scored along an ordinal scale as low, moderate, or high. However, the distance between low and moderate, and between moderate and high, is not known. All you can say for sure is that moderate is greater than low and high is greater than moderate.

Interval and Ratio Scales. If the spacing between values along the scale is known, then the scale is either an **interval scale** or a **ratio scale**. In either case you know that one unit is larger or smaller than another, as well as by how much.

Ratio scales have a zero point that literally indicates the absence of the quantity being measured. Interval scales have a zero point that does not indicate the absence of the quantity. With interval scales the position of the zero point is established on the basis of convenience, but its position is purely arbitrary.

The Celsius scale for temperature is an interval scale. Its zero point does not really indicate the absence of all temperature. Zero on the Celsius scale is the temperature at which ice melts—a convenient, easy-to-determine value. Although this temperature may seem cold to you, things can get much colder. In contrast, the Kelvin scale for temperature is a ratio scale. Its zero point is the temperature at which all heat is absent. You simply can't get any colder.

In psychological research, you measure the number of responses on a lever in an operant chamber by using a ratio scale. Zero responses means literally that there are no responses. Other examples of psychological research data measured on a ratio scale are the number of items recalled in a memory experiment, the numbers of errors made in a signal detection experiment, and the time required to respond in a reaction time experiment. Again, zero on these scales indicates an absence of the quantity measured. On the other hand, if you have subjects rate how much they like something on a scale from zero to 10, you are using an interval scale. In this case a rating of zero does not necessarily mean the total absence of liking.

For practical purposes, an important difference between interval and ratio scales concerns the kinds of mathematical operations you can legitimately apply to the data. Both scales allow you to determine by how much the various data points *differ*. For example, if one subject makes thirty responses and a second makes fifteen responses, you can confidently state that there is a fifteen-response difference between subjects. If the data are measured on a ratio scale (as in this example), you can also correctly state that one subject made half as many responses as the other (that is, you can divide one quantity by the other to form a ratio). Making ratio comparisons makes little sense when data are scaled on an interval scale. Consider the IQ scale of intelligence, which is an interval scale. If one person has an IQ of 70 and another an IQ of 140, saying that the person with the 140 IQ is twice as intelligent as the person with the 70 IQ is nonsense. This is because even a person scoring zero on the test may have some degree of intelligence.

Choosing a Scale of Measurement

You should consider several factors before you decide on a scale of measurement to adopt, including those discussed in this section.

Information Yielded. One way to think about the four scales of measurement described is in terms of the amount of information each provides. The nominal scale provides the least amount of information: All you know is that the values differ in *quality.* The ordinal scale adds crude information about *quantity* (you can rank the order of the values). The interval scale refines the measurement of quantity by indicating how much the values *differ.* Finally, the ratio scale indicates precisely how much of the quantity exists. When possible, you should adopt the scale that provides the most information.

Statistical Tests. An important reason for noting differences among scales of measurement are that the type of scale you use determines the kinds of statistics you can apply to the analysis of your data, and thus affects the conclusions you can draw. Statistics designed for less informative scales make use of less information. These statistics may be less sensitive to the effects of independent variables than statistics designed for use with more informative scales. Try to use a scale that allows you to apply the most sensitive statistical test.

Ecological Validity. The discussion thus far would indicate that you should use ratio or interval scales whenever possible in order to maximize the amount of information contained in the data. However, your research question may limit your choice of a measurement scale. If you are planning to conduct applied research, for example, you may be forced to use a certain scale of measurement, even if that scale is one of the less informative ones. Consider the following example.

One author of this book (Bordens, 1984) conducted a study of the factors that influence the decision to accept a plea bargain, In this study subjects were told to play the role of either an innocent or a guilty defendant. They then were given information concerning the likelihood of conviction at trial and the sentences that would be received on conviction at trial or after the plea bargain.

In this situation the most realistic dependent measure is a simple "acceptance/rejection" of the plea bargain. Real defendants in a plea bargaining situation must make such a choice. Consequently, in this study a dichotomous accept/reject measure was used, even though it employs the least informative scale of measurement (nominal). Sometimes you must compromise your desire for a

sensitive measurement scale (interval or ratio) so that you will have an ecologically valid dependent measure (Neisser, 1976). A dependent measure has *ecological validity* if it reflects what people must do in real-life situations.

As stated, adopting a nominal or ordinal scale for your measure (even if it
results in an ecologically valid measure) has two problems. The amount of information is limited and the statistical tests that can be applied are less powerful. If
you need to adopt a lower-scaled measure to preserve ecological validity, you
may be able to circumvent the limitations of scale by using special techniques.

One technique is to include an interval or ratio scale in your study along
with your nominal or ordinal measure. Before you analyze your data, you can
create a *composite scale* from your measures. A composite scale is one that combines the features of more than one scale. For example, you can include an
interval scale along with your nominal measure.

In the plea-bargaining study, Bordens (1984) included both nominal (dichotomous accept/reject measure) and interval (subjects rated how firm their decisions were on a scale ranging from 0 to 10) scales. A composite scale was created
from these two scales by adding eleven points to the firmness score of subjects
who rejected the plea bargain and subtracting from 10 the firmness scores of
subjects who accepted the plea bargain. The resulting scale (0–21) provided a
continuous measure of degree of firmness of a subject's decision to accept or
reject a plea bargain (0 was firmly accept and 21 was firmly reject the plea
bargain). The composite scale was reported along with the dichotomous accept/
reject measure. The composite scale revealed some subtle effects of the independent variables that were not apparent with the dichotomous measure.

Another strategy you can use when you feel that a nominal scale is important
is to arrange an interval scale so that a dichotomous decision is also required.
For example, Horowitz, Bordens, and Feldman (1980) developed a scale that
preserved some of the qualities of an interval scale while yielding dichotomous
data. To assess the guilt or innocence of a defendant in a simulated criminal trial,
Horowitz et al. used a six-point, bracketed scale illustrated in Figure 4-1. Notice
that points 1 through 3 are bracketed as a not-guilty verdict, whereas points 4
through 6 are bracketed as a guilty verdict. The points on the scale were labeled
so that subjects could also rate the degree to which the evidence proved either
guilt or innocence. This scale forced subjects to decide that the defendant was
either guilty or innocent while yielding a more sensitive measure of the effects
of the independent variables.

Adequacy of a Dependent Measure

You might find that a carefully planned dependent measure looks better on paper
than it works in practice. Two potential problems involve the sensitivity of the
dependent measure and range effects.

Sensitivity of the Dependent Measure. One author of this book (Abbott) recently
conducted an experiment that emphasized the problem of dependent-measure

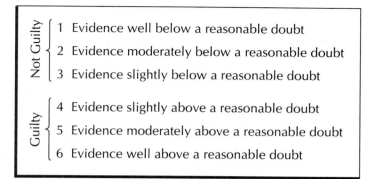

Figure 4-1. A bracketed six-point scale. (Based on Horowitz, Bordens, & Feldman, 1980.)

sensitivity. The goal of the study was to determine whether the cerebral cortex plays a role in modulating certain behaviors seen after giving a few brief, relatively mild shocks to the feet of laboratory rats in an operant chamber. Experiments such as this one are helping us understand how the brain responds to threat and may lead to more effective treatment for anxiety, one of the most common psychological problems. One behavior under study was "freezing," the tendency of rats to become immobile for a period of time following the shocks. Freezing is thought by some to index the level of fear that has been conditioned to the chamber following the shocks (Bolles & Fanselow, 1980).

During the experiment, rats were continuously observed and their behavior was coded as either freezing or showing activity during successive 2-second periods. Note that the basic variable being recorded is dichotomous (two-valued): either the subject is freezing during a given 2-second period or it isn't. What is the scale of measurement being used here? If you say it was ordinal, you are right. (Freezing is greater than no freezing, but you don't know by how much.)

Previous experiments had demonstrated the value of this coding scheme, despite its obvious simplicity. When independent variables (such as the intensity of the shocks) were manipulated, the number of intervals of freezing that occurred following the shocks proved sensitive to those variables (for example, subjects froze more following a strong shock than following a weak shock). There seemed to be no reason to expect that the measure would prove inadequate in the new experiment. Nevertheless, a serious problem did turn up.

It was expected that rats that had their cerebral cortexes removed as newborns would freeze less following the shocks than rats that had not been operated on. This is because the cortex normally acts to inhibit activity in lower brain centers. Without a cortex, the experimental rats would be less able to inhibit their behaviors following shock. In fact, the freezing data confirmed this prediction. The decorticate rats froze very little following shock, whereas the control rats froze a great deal.

If only observations of freezing had been collected, the experimenter would have concluded from these data that the shocks had absolutely *no* effect on the behaviors of the decorticate rats. However, unsystematic observations made during the course of the experiment revealed that, far from being unaffected by the shock, the behaviors of the decorticate rats changed radically. Even with almost no freezing, exploratory activity (which had been going on strongly prior to shock) all but ceased following the shocks and was replaced by a tentative stretch-and-quickly-withdraw behavior. Although frequently observed prior to shock, standing on the hind legs alone was all but absent following shock.

Unfortunately, these behaviors were not carefully defined and systematically recorded. The experimenter could refer only to impressions of behavioral change rather than to hard data. To determine the precise effect of the shocks on decorticate behaviors, the experiment must be run again, with the nominally scaled freezing measure replaced by a ratio-scaled continuous measure of behavioral activity, and the incidence of other behaviors (such as standing) must be recorded.

In this case, the dichotomous ordinal measure of freezing was insensitive to the subtle changes in behavior brought about by the independent variable. This was the case despite the fact that the measure had proven effective in other experiments. Unsystematic observations carried out during the course of the experiment can provide a useful check on the adequacy of your measure and may reveal defects, as they did here. Although you may have to redesign and rerun your study, your understanding of the phenomenon under investigation will benefit.

Range Effects. In addition to worrying about the sensitivity of your dependent variable, you also need to be concerned with what are commonly called **range effects**. Range effects occur when the values of a variable have an upper or lower limit and this limit is encountered during the course of the observation. Two types of range effects are *floor effects* and *ceiling effects*. As you might expect from the names, floor effects occur when the variable reaches its lowest possible value, whereas ceiling effects occur when the variable reaches its highest possible value.

The problems that range effects can cause are subtle and pernicious (harmful). They are subtle in that you don't always know that you have encountered them. Range effects are pernicious in that their consequences are hard to deal with after the fact and may require a redesign of the study. Consider the following example.

Assume you have decided to study the effect of retention interval on memory for fruit and vegetable words (you happen to be fond of salads). You settle on a set of retention intervals that span 10–100 minutes in ten-minute increments, and decide to measure retention by having subjects attempt to pick out the correct word from a list of ten items. The retention score for each subject is the percentage of correct choices in ten trials.

You vary the retention interval across trials and get a retention score for each interval. To your surprise, you find absolutely no effect of retention interval. Averaged across subjects, retention is about 95 percent at each interval!

Fortunately, you are aware of the potential for range effects in your data and stop to examine the scores more closely before concluding that retention interval has no effect on memory for fruit-and-vegetable words. Looking at the scores of each subject, you realize that nineteen out of twenty subjects have scored perfectly at every interval. Could the retention measure be too sensitive?

It is possible that differences in retention might have been detected if the task were more demanding. Perhaps there *is* an effect of retention interval on memory. But in this case, even at the longest interval memory was still good enough to score 100 percent correct on the retention task. Because 100 percent was the upper limit of your measure, showing any better retention at shorter intervals was impossible. You have encountered a ceiling effect.

Range effects affect your data in two distinct ways: First, by limiting the values of your highest data points, the range effect decreases the differences between your treatment means. The apparent effects of your independent variables are lessened, perhaps to the extent that no statistically reliable differences will surface between them. Second, the variability of scores within the affected treatments is reduced. Because many commonly used inferential statistics estimate variability due to random causes from the variability of scores within the treatments, these statistics tend to give misleading results. In this case they will usually underestimate the probability that the observed differences in treatments are caused by chance. (See Chapter 12 for a discussion of inferential statistics and how they work.)

Because range effects distort your data both in central tendency and in variability, do your best to avoid them. Often previous research provides a guide, but on some occasions you may need to determine appropriate methods by trial and error.

Tailoring Your Measures to Your Subjects

As another aspect to designing appropriate measures, you must consider the capabilities of your subjects. If you are working with young children or mentally impaired adults, you must tailor your measure to the level of understanding of your subjects. It makes little sense to use a complicated rating scale with complex instructions if your subjects have limited mental capacities.

One way to tailor the dependent measure to your subjects is to graphically represent your measures. For example, instead of using a rating scale to measure a preference among young children (perhaps for a toy), you could use a more concrete measure. The child could be asked to give you a number of blocks, blow up a balloon, or vary the space between two objects to indicate the degree of preference. Creative measurement techniques may also be needed when dealing with intellectually impaired adults or elderly subjects.

Some good examples of creative measurement techniques are those developed to study infant development. With preverbal infants, you have the problem that the subjects of your study cannot understand verbal instructions or respond to measures as would an older child or an adult. Consequently, researchers of infant behavior have developed techniques to indirectly test the capabilities of the infant.

Three popular techniques that have been used with preverbal infants are habituation, preference testing, and discrimination learning. The *habituation technique* capitalizes on the fact that even infants get bored with repeatedly presented stimuli. For example, in a study of the ability to discriminate shapes, you might repeatedly present the infant with a square until the infant no longer looks at the stimulus. You would then present a new stimulus (a circle). If the infant looked at the circle, you could infer that the infant could tell the difference between the two stimuli.

Alternatively, you could investigate the same problem with the *preference technique*. Here you present the two stimuli simultaneously. If the infant looks at one stimulus more than the other, you can then infer that the infant can distinguish between them.

In *discrimination learning* you attempt to train different behaviors to the different stimuli (for example, suck when a square is present, but not a circle). Differential rates of responding suggest the capacity to discriminate.

Tailoring a measure to your subjects is not limited to children and impaired adults. Even adults of normal intelligence may have difficulty responding to your measures. You must remember that your subjects are probably naïve to the research jargon with which you are familiar. For example, they may not understand what you mean when you say that increasing numbers on a scale represent an increase in whatever is being studied. Whenever you suspect that your subjects may misunderstand how to use the measure, you should make a special effort to clearly describe your measures. For example, Figure 4-2 shows how a scale from 0 to 10 can be graphically presented. Notice how the arrow increases in width as the numbers increase. Such a visual presentation may help subjects understand that a 7 means they feel more strongly and a 4 less so.

Regardless of the measure chosen, pretest your measure to ensure that it is appropriate for your subject population. During the pretest you may find that your measure needs to be modified to fit the needs of your research. Such modifications can be made before investing large amounts of time and effort in your actual study.

Types of Dependent Variables and How to Use Them

Now that we have covered some of the basics of measurement and scaling, we can now discuss the more general issue of how these scales can be placed into action in your study. You must decide what type of dependent measure to use.

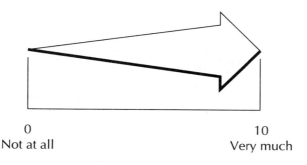

0   10
Not at all   Very much

Figure 4-2. How to format a rating scale to reinforce the idea that increasing numbers represent an increasing amount of some characteristic.

The following sections describe three types of dependent measures: behavioral measures, physiological measures, and self-report measures.

Behavioral Measures. Although the number of dependent variables is potentially vast, those that are used in behavioral research do tend to fall into a few basic categories. One type of dependent measure is a **behavioral measure**. When using a behavioral measure, you record the actual behavior of your subjects. In a study of helping behavior, for example, you might expose subjects to different treatments (such as having a male or female experimenter drop some packages) and then take note of the behavior of your subjects (such as whether or not a subject helps). A count of observed behaviors is the most basic behavioral measure. However, more sophisticated measures exist.

One such measure is the *frequency* of responding. To determine the frequency of a behavior, you count the number of occurrences over some specified period. For example, Goldiamond (1965) calculated the frequency of stuttering in a behavior modification study. Subjects read pages of text, and Goldiamond counted the instances of stuttering across successive pages. Goldiamond found that the rate of stuttering declined during periods when stuttering was punished with bursts of loud noise. Frequency counts can also be made over successive time periods.

Another behavioral measure is *latency*. Here you measure the amount of time it takes for subjects to respond to some stimulus. In the helping experiment just described, you could have measured how long it took subjects to offer help in addition to whether or not subjects helped. Any measure of reaction time is a latency measure.

In some types of research, *number of errors* might be an appropriate behavioral measure. This measure can be used with a well-defined "correct" response.

Learning experiments often record number of errors as a function of the number of learning trials.

Behavioral measures are fine indicators of overt behavior. However, with a behavioral measure you may not be able to collect data dealing with the underlying causes for behavior. In order to gain insight into the factors that underlie behavior, you must often follow up behavioral measures with other measures.

Physiological Measures. A second way to measure your dependent variable is with a **physiological measure**. This type of measure typically requires special equipment designed to monitor the subject's bodily functions. Such measures include heart rate, respiration rate, electrical activity of the brain, galvanic skin resistance, and blood pressure.

A good example of the application of physiological measures is the research on sleep. Typically, subjects come to the sleep laboratory and physiological responses such as brain activity (EEG), heart rate, respiration rate, and eye movements are recorded. This research has shown that the activities of the brain and body change cyclically over the course of a night's sleep.

The physiological measures just described are all noninvasive—the subject is not harmed in any way when they are used. Some measures are invasive and are used with animals. For example, a physiological psychologist may implant an electrode into a rat's brain in order to record the activity of particular brain cells while the animal learns to perform a new behavior. Changes in brain cell activity during learning constitute the dependent variable.

Physiological measures provide you with fairly accurate information about the state of arousal within the subject's body. A drawback to this type of measure is that you must often infer psychological states from physiological states. As noted in Chapter 1, whenever you make inferences you run the risk of drawing incorrect conclusions.

Self-Report Measures. A third method commonly used to assess behavior is the **self-report measure**. Self-report measures take a variety of forms. One common form is the *rating scale*. In a study of jury decision making, for example, subjects could rate the degree of guilt on a scale ranging from 0 to 10. A popular method in attitude assessment is *Likert scaling*. Subjects are provided with statements (for example, "Nuclear power plants are dangerous") and are asked to indicate the degree to which they agree or disagree with the statement (1 = disagree strongly, 5 = agree strongly). (See Chapter 7 for more information on how to use rating scales.)

Self-report measures are highly versatile and relatively easy to use. You can ask subjects to evaluate how they are feeling at the present time. In the jury decision example, subjects would be providing an evaluation of the defendant's guilt immediately after exposure to a trial. In other cases you may ask subjects to reflect on past experiences and evaluate those experiences. This is referred to as a *retrospective verbal report* (Sheridan, 1979). In still other cases you may ask for a *prospective verbal report* (Sheridan, 1979). Here you would ask subjects to speculate on how they would react in a certain future situation.

Although self-reports are relatively easy to use, they do suffer liabilities. When using the retrospective verbal report, you must be aware of the possibility that the measure is somewhat invalid. You cannot really be sure that the subject is giving an accurate assessment of prior behaviors. The subject may be giving you a report or reconstruction of how he or she felt about the behavior you are studying rather than a true account of what happened. The report provided by the subject could be clouded by events that intervened between the original event and the present report. Validity is lowered to the extent that this report is at variance with the actual behavior. Similarly, prospective verbal reports require a subject to speculate about future behavior. In this case, you cannot be sure that what the subject says he or she will do is what he or she actually does.

Another problem with self-report measures is that you cannot be sure that subjects are telling the truth. Subjects have a tendency to project themselves in a socially desirable manner. In a study of racial prejudice using a Likert scaling technique, for example, subjects may not be willing to admit that they have prejudicial attitudes. In fact, research in social psychology has found that self-reports of attitudes (especially on sensitive topics) often do not accurately reflect actual attitudes. You can detect responses that project social desirability by including questions that, if the subject agrees (or disagrees) with them, indicate self-effacement (such as "I have never had a bad thought about a member of a racial minority"). If a subject says that he or she has *never* had such a thought, the subject is probably responding in a socially desirable way.

Choosing When to Observe

After you have chosen what to observe and how to measure it, you need to decide when you will make your observations. If you are performing laboratory research, experimental sessions generally are *when* to observe. However, even within experimental sessions you must still decide when observations are to be made.

As with the other aspects of your design, *when* you observe may be determined by established practices. For example, if previous research has proven the adequacy of a time-sampling procedure (you make observations at 10-minute intervals during the session), then making continuous observations may be safely abandoned in favor of the less demanding technique.

Your decision of when to observe may have to take into account the resources you have at your disposal, particularly if the required observations must be made frequently or over long periods of time. For example, in the previous "freezing" experiment an enormous amount of time would be required to code freezing behavior across consecutive 2-second intervals of time during an experimental session that lasted five hours, especially if a large number of subjects was observed. In such cases, you may be able to adopt a sampling strategy and make occasional observations at randomly chosen intervals during the session. Averaged over a number of subjects, such observations could provide a representative picture of changes across time.

An even better solution than the sampling strategy is to automate the observations. For example, David Leaton and George Borszcz of Dartmouth College recently described a way to automatically record the freezing behavior of rats (Leaton & Borszcz, 1985). Leaton and Borszcz suspended the observation chamber between stiff springs. A bar magnet affixed to the chamber moved slightly up or down whenever the rat made the slightest move, generating an electric current in a coil of wire through which the magnet passed. When the rat froze, movement ceased and the current disappeared. A microcomputer counted the passing intervals of time and scored each interval for the presence or absence of movement. With the apparatus used by Leaton and Borszcz, it was possible to continuously observe the freezing behavior during sessions of any desired length.

Of course, it is important to show that any device provides a good measure of the variable before you adopt the measure. One good measure of success is the degree to which the new measurements agree with measurements done "the old-fashioned way." In the case of the automated freezing measure, Leaton and Borszcz demonstrated that the automatic readings correlate highly with personal observations. Techniques for automating your experiment are discussed in more detail later in the chapter.

The Reactive Nature of Psychological Measurement

One advantage that physicists and chemists have over psychologists when it comes to conducting research is that the "subjects" of physical and chemical experiments (atoms, molecules, electrons, photons, and quarks) pay absolutely no attention to the fact that they are participants in an experiment. They behave as they ordinarily do in nature. The subjects of psychological research (rats, pigeons, and college students) do pay attention to their status as subjects and may modify their behavior as a result of their perceptions. This "reactive" nature of subjects must be considered when designing and assessing psychological research. This section describes the kinds of reactions, the situations that sometimes give rise to them, and the things you can do to minimize (or at least assess) their impacts on your data. A discussion of research with human subjects begins this section, followed by a discussion of research with animal subjects.

Reactivity in Research with Human Subjects

Assume for the moment that you have defined your population of subjects and are now ready to acquire your subjects and to run your experiment. You plan to have volunteers sign up and come to your laboratory for your experiment. What can you expect from these creatures that we call human subjects?

One thing to realize is that the psychological experiment is a social situation. You as the experimenter, by definition, are in a position of power over the subject. Your subject enters this situation with a social history that may affect how he or she responds to your manipulations. Assuming that the subject is a passive recipient of your experimental manipulations is a mistake. The subject is a living, thinking human being who will generate personal interpretations of your experiment and perhaps guide behavior based on these interpretations. In short, the subject is a reactive creature. The behavior you observe in your subjects may not be representative of normal behavior, simply because you are making observations.

To help you understand the reactions of research subjects to your experiment, imagine you have volunteered for a psychological experiment for the first time. You are a first-year student enrolled in introductory psychology who has had a little experience with psychological research. As you sit waiting to be called for the experiment, you imagine what the experiment will be like. Perhaps you have just talked about Milgram's obedience research in your psychology class and are wondering if you are going to be given electric shocks or if the researcher is going to be honest with you. You wonder if you are going to be told the experiment is about one thing when it is actually about something else.

At last the experimenter comes out of the laboratory and says she is ready for you. You are led into a room with a white tile floor, white walls, a stainless steel sink in the corner, some ominous-looking equipment in another corner, and rather harsh fluorescent lighting. The experimenter apologizes for the cold surroundings, and says she is a graduate student and that she had to settle for one of the animal labs to run her master's thesis research. (Do you believe her?) You take a look around the room and muster enough courage to ask if you are going to be shocked. The experimenter chuckles and assures you that the experiment deals with memory for abstract pictures. She then begins to read you the instructions. At that moment some workers begin to hammer out in the hall. (Is this part of the experiment?) Again the experimenter apologizes. She explains that they are installing a new air-conditioning system in that wing of the building. You think you detect a hint of a smile on her face. You don't believe her. You have decided that the experimenter is really trying to test how well you can perform a memory task under distracting conditions. You decide to "show the experimenter" that you can do well despite her obvious attempt to trick you. The experimenter runs you through the experiment. Of course you try your hardest to get all the items right.

After you have completed the memory test, the experimenter asks you if you have any questions. You smugly tell her that you saw through her obvious deception and worked even harder to get the items correct. After all, you weren't born yesterday! To this the experimenter incredulously assures you that the noise was not part of the experiment and tells you that she will have to throw out your data. You have set the experiment back a full day.

Demand Characteristics. Consider the psychological experiment in the light of this example. As stated, the human subject in a psychological experiment does not passively respond to what you may expose him or her to. On entering the laboratory, your subject probably assesses you and the laboratory (Adair, 1973). Given these assessments, the subject begins to draw inferences concerning what the experiment is about.

The cues provided by the researcher and the context that communicate to the subject the purpose of the study (or the expected responses of the subject) are referred to as **demand characteristics**. Subjects gain information about the experiment from these demand characteristics. Unfortunately for you, the subject may be paying attention to cues that are irrelevant to the experiment at hand (as happened in the previous example when you believed that the noise created by the work crew was related to the experiment). With the information obtained from the demand characteristics, the subject begins to formulate hypotheses about the nature of the experiment (such as, the experiment is measuring my ability to perform under adverse conditions) and begins to behave in a manner that is consistent with those hypotheses. Problems occur when the subject's hypotheses are different from the intended purpose of the experiment. Adair (1973) refers to this class of demand characteristic as "performance cues."

A second source of demand characteristics centers around the subject. According to Adair (1973), a class of demand characteristics known as **role attitude cues** may signal the subject that a change in the subject's attitude is needed to conform with his or her new role as a research subject (Adair, 1973, p. 24). Further, Adair points out that subjects enter experiments with preexisting attitudes that dispose them to react either in a positive or negative way to the experimental manipulations. Through various demand characteristics, the experiment can cause the subject to change his or her attitudes (Adair, 1973, p. 26). Adair lists the following three categories of predisposing attitudes of subjects: the cooperative attitude, the defensive or apprehensive attitude, and the negative attitude.

The cooperative attitude is characterized by a strong desire to please the experimenter. According to Adair, volunteering for an experiment "seals a contract between the experimenter and the subject, fostering cooperative behavior" (p. 26). Reasons for the cooperative attitude include a desire to help science, a desire to please the experimenter, a desire to perform as well as possible, and a desire to be positively evaluated by others.

Several demonstrations of the impact of this positive attitude on the outcome of an experiment have been made. For example, Orne (1962) demonstrated that subjects will engage in a boring, repetitive task for hours to please the experimenter. Subjects were provided 2,000 sheets of paper (on which were columns of numbers to add) and a stack of index cards (on which instructions were printed). The subject was instructed to select the first card (which told the subject to add the numbers on the page) and then to select the next card. The next card told the subject to tear the completed sheet into pieces (not less than 32), then select another sheet, and add the numbers. The cycle of adding numbers and tearing sheets continued for as long as the subject was willing to go on.

If you were a subject in this experiment, what would you do? You may have said, "I'd do it for a few times and then quit." In fact, quite the opposite happened! Subjects continued to do the task for hours. Evidently, subjects perceived the test as one of endurance. The subject's cooperative attitude in this example interacted with the demand characteristics to produce some rather bizarre behavior. This "good subject" effect was also shown in an experiment by Goldstein, Rosnow, Goodstadt, and Suls (1972).

Some subjects enter the laboratory worried about what will happen to them. One of the authors of this text was conducting an experiment on jury decision making and several subjects, on entering the lab, asked if they were going to be shocked. This apprehension may stem from the subject's perception of the experimenter as someone who will be evaluating the subject's behavior (Adair, 1973). The apprehensive attitude has also been shown to affect the research outcome, especially in the areas of compliance and attitude change (Adair, 1973).

Some subjects come to the laboratory with a negative attitude. Even though most subjects are either positive or defensive (Adair, 1973), some subjects come to the lab to try to ruin the experiment. This attitude was most prevalent when subjects were *required* to participate in experiments. Required participation made many subjects angry. The present rules against forced participation may reduce the frequency of negative attitudes among subjects. However, you cannot rule out the possibility that some subjects will be highly negative toward the experiment and experimenter.

Other Influences. In addition to demand characteristics and subject attitudes, evidence also indicates that events outside the laboratory can affect research. For example, Greene and Loftus (1984) conducted an experiment on jury decision making in which eyewitness testimony was being studied. Around the time the experiment was conducted and in the same city, a celebrated case of mistaken identification was taking place. Knowledge of that celebrated case was reflected in the data collected from the subjects. Subjects generally were more skeptical of the eyewitness in the study after finding out about the celebrated case than they were before they found out. However, after a while the impact of the case diminished and the responses returned to "normal."

The moral to this story is that subjects are not passive responders to the experiment. The experiment is a social situation in which the interaction between subject attitudes and the experimental context may affect the outcome of the experiment. As a researcher you must be aware of demand characteristics and take steps to avoid them, or at least to assess their impacts. As with other subject-related problems, demand characteristics, subject attitudes, previous research experience, and exposure to everyday life can affect both internal and external validity.

The Role of the Experimenter. The subject is not the only potential source of bias in the psychological experiment. The experimenter can sometimes unintentionally affect the outcome of the experiment. Assume you are running your first experiment, an experiment of your own design. Because you are a student, you will be running your own subjects.

You are sitting alone in your laboratory awaiting the arrival of your first subject. You have butterflies in your stomach and are a bit apprehensive about how you will perform in the experiment. The experiment is important to you as it is required for a class you need for graduation. At last your first subject arrives and you usher him into your laboratory. You begin to read your instructions (which you feel are well written) to your subject and are puzzled to see that your subject is obviously not understanding the instructions. However, you press on.

Your experiment deals with the ability of subjects to recall certain words embedded within the context of other words. You want to show that interference will occur when the words are embedded in a context of other similar words. You are going to read a list of words to your subject and then give a recall test. In the high-similarity condition, you unconsciously read the words at a faster rate than in the low-similarity condition. You notice later that your collected data consistently confirm your preexperimental hypothesis.

Now, analyze what has happened. You wrote your instructions believing that your subjects would be able to understand them. As it turns out, the instructions were less clear than you thought. The problem here was that you assumed too much about the ability of subjects to understand the instructions. This may happen because you are used to talking to other psychology majors or professors familiar with the "jargon" of your discipline. The subject may not have that advantage. One thing that you could do to detect this problem is to pretest the instructions.

A second problem that cropped up in this example was **experimenter bias** (Rosenthal, 1976). Experimenter bias creeps in when the behavior of the experimenter influences the results of the experiment. Experimenter bias flows from at least two sources: expectancy effects and treating various experimental groups differently to produce results consistent with the preexperimental hypotheses.

When an experimenter develops preconceived ideas about the capacities of the subjects, **expectancy effects** emerge. For example, if you believe that your subjects are incapable of learning, you may treat them in such a way as to have that expectation fulfilled. Rosenthal (1976) reports a perception experiment in which the independent variable was the information provided to students acting as experimenters. Some students were told that, according to previous ratings, their subjects should perform well. Others were told that the subjects would probably perform poorly. The student experimenters were also told that they would be paid twice as much if the results confirmed the prior expectations. Rosenthal reports that establishing the expectancy led to different behavior on the part of the subjects in the two experimental groups. Rosenthal points out that such expectancy effects may be a problem, not only in experimental research, but in survey research and clinical studies as well.

In the previous hypothetical example, you (as the experimenter) read the list of words to subjects differently, depending on the condition to which they were assigned. If the experimenter knows what the hypotheses of the experiment are, he or she may possibly behave in a manner that leads subjects into certain behaviors to confirm the hypotheses. Keep in mind that this could be quite unintentional. When running your own research, you may have a vested interest in the outcome of the study, particularly if you have developed a hypothesis that predicts a certain result. Consequently, your expectations may subtly influence the subjects in the different groups.

These two sources of experimenter bias threaten both internal and external validity. If your behavior becomes a source of systematic bias or error, then you cannot be sure the independent variable caused the observed changes in the dependent variable. External validity is threatened because the data obtained may be idiosyncratic to your particular influence.

You can do some things to reduce the possibility of experimenter bias. For example, you could use a *blind technique*. That is, instead of running your own subjects, have someone who does not know the hypotheses run the subjects. In this instance you would be running a *single-blind* experiment. In some research situations, a *double-blind* technique is appropriate.

If you were interested in testing the effects of a particular drug on learning abilities, for example, you would give some subjects the active drug and some a placebo (perhaps an injection of saline solution). The subject would not know which treatment was being administered, thus reducing the possibility that the subject's expectations about the drug would affect the results. Furthermore, you would have an assistant mix the drugs and label them arbitrarily with some code, such as "A" and "B." As the experimenter, you would not be told which was the active drug and which was the placebo until after the experiment was completed and the data analyzed. Thus, neither you nor the subject would know at the time of testing which treatment the subject was receiving. Neither your nor the subject's expectations could systematically bias the results. This is the essence of the double-blind procedure.

Another method for reducing experimenter bias is to automate the experiment as much as possible. In the role-playing example, you could present your stimulus items with a slide projector connected to an electronic timer. The interstimulus interval would be held constant, avoiding the possibility that you might present the stimuli more rapidly to one group than to the other. You could also automate the instructions by having a videotaped version of the instructions that would simply be turned on by the person conducting the experimental session. All subjects would thus be exposed to the same instructions. Automation is more fully discussed later in this chapter.

Perhaps the best preventive medicine for experimenter bias is to know about the bias and its effects. Even if you cannot afford to automate or cannot use a blind technique, you can at least make a special effort to avoid influencing your subjects.

Other potential sources of experimenter bias include the sex, personality, and previous experience of the experimenter. It is beyond the scope of this book to explore all the potential experimenter effects. See *Experimenter Effects in Behavioral Research* (Rosenthal, 1976) for a complete treatment of this topic.

Reactivity in Research with Animal Subjects

The section on using human subjects in research pointed out that the behavior of subjects can be affected by the behavior of the experimenter and by demand characteristics. Similar effects can be found with animal subjects. For example, Rosenthal (1976) reported research in which experimenter expectancy effects influenced the rate of learning of animals in a maze-learning experiment. Subjects serving as experimenters were told that the rats they would be teaching to run a maze were either very bright (would learn the maze quickly with few errors) or very dull (would have trouble learning the maze). The animals were actually assigned at random to the experimenters. Rosenthal found that the animals in the "bright" condition learned more quickly than the animals in the "dull" condition. The differing expectations of the student experimenters led them to treat their rats differently, and these differences in treatment led to changes in the behaviors of the rats.

Use blind techniques to avoid these and other sources of experimenter bias in animal research. For example, in a study in which a drug is to be administered, the person making the observations of the animal's behavior should not know which subjects received the drug and which received the placebo.

Remember that demand characteristics are cues that subjects use to guide behavior within an experiment. Although animals will not be sensitive to "demand characteristics" in the same way as are human subjects, some features of your experiment may inadvertently affect your subject's behavior. For example, you may be interested in how a rat's learning capacity is affected by receiving electric shocks just before the opportunity to work for food. If you do not clean the experimental chamber thoroughly after each animal is tested, the animals may respond to the odor cues from the previous animal. These odor cues may affect the current animal's behavior differently, depending on whether or not the previous animal had received a shock. You must remember that, much like the human subject, the animal subject is an active processor of information. Your animals sense cues that are not intended to be a part of the experiment and may behave accordingly. Ultimately, the internal validity of your experiment may be threatened by the effects of these cues.

Automating Your Experiments

Psychological research presents many opportunities for outside, uncontrolled variables to affect your results. Automation can help to eliminate experimenter effects and increase the precision of your measures.

In addition, automation can save time. Automated equipment allows you to run subjects even if you cannot be present. This is most useful in animal research where subjects can be left unattended in the testing apparatus. In this case, you simply start the testing program and then return at the end of the session to record the data and return the subjects to their home cages.

Automation has other advantages as well. Automated measurements tend to be more accurate and less variable, as they are not subject to the vagaries of human judgment. An automated system is not likely to miss an important event because it was daydreaming at the moment or distracted by an aching back. Nor is such a system likely to misperceive what actually happened because of expectations about what will happen (eliminating this source of experimenter bias).

Conversely, automation can cause you to miss important details. The changes in behavior shown by the nonfreezing decorticate rats might not have been detected had the automated freezing measure of Leaton and Borszcz been in use. Even when all your measurements are automated, you should observe your subjects occasionally. What you learn from these observations may provide fruitful explanations for changes seen in your automated variables and may provide you with new ideas to test.

Techniques for automation include the use of videotaped instructions, timers to control the duration that a stimulus is present and to time interstimulus intervals, and computers to control an experiment. Because the computer has become almost a standard piece of laboratory equipment, a brief discussion of its components and their uses is in order.

Relatively inexpensive personal computers can be programmed and outfitted with the hardware needed to fully automate your experiment. Figure 4-3 illustrates the components of a personal computer needed to automate a learning experiment using animal subjects. The computer acts as the "brain" of your equipment. It controls the presentation of stimuli, establishes the conditions present at any point in the experiment, and keeps track of the responses made by your subjects. The next component, the *interface*, allows your computer to communicate with your equipment (in this case, an operant chamber). The computer sends instructions to the chamber through the interface and receives from the chamber signals that represent the subject's response. Finally, you must have *software* (the program that directs the computer) to run your experiment. It consists of a series of statements written in a language that the computer understands (BASIC or Pascal, for example). Software specifies when and how the computer will operate, records and keeps track of the responses of the subjects.

Experiments can also be controlled by larger "minicomputers" or even by the largest of "mainframe" computers. Also, computers can be used to control research conducted with humans as well as animals. For example, you could program your computer to present stimuli to be used in research areas such as human learning and memory, perception, developmental psychology, and decision making.

If you use computers to conduct your research, remember that the computer performs many of the more tedious tasks involved in your research quickly and accurately, but always does what you tell it to do (even if you make a mistake).

Figure 4-3. Equipment needed to automate a learning experiment. Shown is a personal computer, computer interface, and operant conditioning chamber.

Your automated experiment will only be as good as your program. Before you try to write such programs, you must be intimately familiar with the computer language you will be using and know how to interface your computer with your equipment. For further information on applying computers to experiments, see Deni (1986).

Detecting and Correcting Problems

No matter how carefully you plan your study, problems almost inevitably crop up when you begin to execute it. Two methods you can use to minimize these problems and ensure the usefulness of the data you collect are conducting a pilot study and adding manipulation checks.

Conducting a Pilot Study

A **pilot study** establishes procedures and parameters. Frequently it is a study that began life as a serious piece of research but "went wrong" somewhere along the way. The decorticate rat study became a pilot study for this reason. However, many pilot studies are designed from the ground up as pilot studies, intended to provide useful information that can be used when the "real" study gets under way.

Pilot studies can save tremendous amounts of time and money if done properly. Perhaps you intend to conduct a large study involving several hundred subjects in order to determine which of two methods of teaching works best in introductory psychology. As part of the study, you intend to hand out a large questionnaire to the students in several introductory psychology classes. Conducting a small pilot study (in which you hand out the questionnaire to students in only a couple of classes) may turn up inadequacies in your formulation of questions, inadequacies that lead to confusion or misinterpretation. Finding these problems *before* you train instructors in the two teaching methods, have them teach a full term, and then collect the questionnaires from 2,000 students is certainly preferable to finding the problems afterward.

Pilot studies can help you to clarify instructions, determine appropriate levels of independent variables (to avoid range effects), determine the reliability and validity of your observational methods, and work the bugs out of your procedures. They can also give you practice in conducting your study so that you make fewer mistakes when you "do it for real." For these reasons, pilot studies are often valuable.

You should also be aware of some negative aspects of pilot studies. Pilot studies require time to conduct (even if less than that of the formal study) and may entail some expenditure of supplies. Where animals are involved, their use for pilot work may be questioned by the local animal care and use committee (particularly if the procedures involve surgery, stressful stimulation, or deprivation). In these cases, you may want to use the best available information to determine procedures and to try to "get it right" the first time around. Then only if you guess wrong will the study become a pilot study.

Adding Manipulation Checks

In addition to the dependent measures of the behavior under study, you should include **manipulation checks**. Manipulation checks simply test whether or not your independent variables had the intended effects of your subjects. They allow you to determine if the subjects in your study perceived your experiment in the manner in which you intended. They also provide you with information that may be useful later when attempting to interpret your data. If your experiment yielded results you did not expect, it may be that subjects interpreted your independent variable differently from the way you thought they would. Without manipulation checks, you may not be able to properly interpret surprising effects. Manipulation checks may permit you to determine why an independent variable failed to produce an effect. Perhaps you did not effectively manipulate your independent variable. Again, manipulation checks provide information on this.

A set of measures closely related to manipulation checks are those asking subjects to report their perceptions of the entire experiment. Factors to be evaluated might include their perceptions of the experimenter, what they believed to be the true purpose of the experiment, the impact of any deception, and any other factors you think are important. Like manipulation checks, these measures help you to interpret your results and help you establish the generality of your data. If you find that subjects perceived your experiment as you intended, you are in a better position to argue that your results are valid and perhaps apply beyond the laboratory.

Summary

In contrast to casual, everyday observations, scientific observations are systematic. Systematic observation involves making decisions about what, how, and when to make observations. Observations of behavior are made under controlled conditions using operational definitions of the variables of interest.

One aspect of systematic observation is developing dependent measures. Your data can be scaled along one of four scales of measurement: nominal, ordinal, interval, and ratio. Nominal and ordinal scales provide less information than do interval and ratio scales, so use an interval or ratio scale whenever possible. You will not be able to use an interval or ratio scale in all cases because some research questions demand that a nominal or ordinal scale be used. Your choice of measurement scale should be guided by the needs of your research question. When a less informational scale must be used to preserve ecological validity, you can preserve information by creating a composite scale from a nominal and interval scale. This will help you to "recover" information not yielded by a nominal scale.

Beyond choosing a scale of measurement, you must also decide how to design and collect your dependent measures. Your measures must be appropriate for your subject population. Consequently, you may have to be creative when you design your measures. You may take a count of number of responses, which is a ratio scale. You can use interval scales in a variety of research applications. You must decide how to format these scales, how to present them to subjects, and how to develop clear and concise instructions for their uses.

In some research, your measure of behavior may be limited by range effects. That is, there may be an upper and lower limit imposed on your measure by the behavior of interest. For example, rats can run just so fast in a maze. Range effects become a problem when the behavior quickly reaches its upper or lower limit. In such cases you may not detect a difference between two groups because of ceiling or floor effects. It is a good idea to conduct pilot studies to test your measures before investing the time and energy in your study. During the pilot study, you may find that your measures need to be modified.

Observation in psychological research differs from observation in other sciences because the psychologist deals with living organisms. The subjects in an experiment are reactive; they may respond to more in the experimental situation than the manipulated variables. Subjects bring to the experiment unique histories and attitudes that may affect the outcome of your experiment.

Demand characteristics can be a problem in behavioral research. Subjects pick up on cues from the experimenter and research context. These cues may affect the subject's behavior. Furthermore, the experimenter must be careful not to inadvertently affect the subjects. Experimenter effects can be avoided by using blind tehniques or automating your experiment or both. Automation can be done by videotaping instructions or applying computers to control your experiment or both.

Key Terms

Operational definition

Valid measure

Reliable measure

Accurate measure

Nominal scale

Ordinal scale

Interval scale

Ratio scale

Range effects

Behavioral measure

Physiological measure

Self-report measure

Demand characteristics

Role attitude cues

Experimenter bias

Expectancy effects

Pilot study

Manipulation checks

5

Choosing and Using Subjects

SO FAR IN THE RESEARCH PROCESS, you have made several important decisions. You have decided on a topic for your research, and taken an amorphous, broad idea and honed it into a tight, testable research hypothesis. You have also made some important decisions about the nature of the research design you will use, the variables you want to manipulate and measure, as well as how you will manipulate and measure those variables.

The next major decision you face regards the nature of the subjects to be used in your research. This chapter explores some of the factors you should consider when the time comes to select subjects for your study. This chapter assumes that you have chosen to use an experimental research strategy. Chapter 7 extends the discussion to include the subject-related factors you need to consider if you have to conduct nonexperimental research.

Using Subjects: General Considerations

Choosing and using subjects in psychological research requires you to consider several important issues. You must decide whether to use human or animal subjects. You must also decide how the subjects will be acquired and how the selected subjects will be handled in the experiment.

Your decision concerning human versus animal subjects may be constrained by the nature of your research question. For example, if you are experimentally investigating the effects of brain lesions on learning abilities, you must use animal subjects. If you are interested in why people obey authority figures, then you must use human subjects. However, many research areas can be investigated with either human or animal subjects (such as operant conditioning, memory, perception, and so forth). In these instances, your choice of animals versus humans may depend on special needs of the experiment.

Regardless of whether you choose humans or animals, you must consider certain issues, including ethics, how the subjects will react to the experimental situation, and the degree of generality of your results. Some of these issues may be more important when considering human subjects, but you must also keep them in mind if you choose animal subjects.

Populations and Samples

Imagine that you are interested in investigating the effect of three teaching techniques on how well eighth-graders learn mathematics. Would it be feasible to include *every* eighth-grader in the world in your experiment? Obviously not, but what are the alternatives? You may have thought to yourself, "I will have to choose *some* eighth-graders for the experiment." If this is what you thought, you are considering an important distinction in research methodology: populations versus samples.

In the hypothetical experiment, you could not hope to include all eighth-graders. "All eighth-graders" constitutes the **population** under study. Because it is usually not possible to study an entire population, you must be content to study a **sample** of that population. Figure 5-1 illustrates the relationship between populations and samples. A sample is a small subgroup chosen from the larger population.

Often researchers find it necessary to define a subpopulation for study. In your imaginary study, cost or other factors may limit you to studying a certain region of the country. Your subpopulation might consist of eighth-graders from a particular city, town, or district. Furthermore, you might limit yourself to studying certain eighth-grade classes (especially if the school district is too large to allow you to study every class). In this case you are further dividing your subpopulation. In effect, rather than studying an entire population you are studying a small segment of that population.

A population can be defined in many ways. For example, if you were interested in how prejudiced attitudes develop, you could define the population as those children enrolled in day care centers and early elementary school grades. If you were interested in jury decision making, you could define the population as registered voters who are eligible for jury duty. In any case, you may need to limit the nature of the subject population and sample because of special needs of the research.

Population

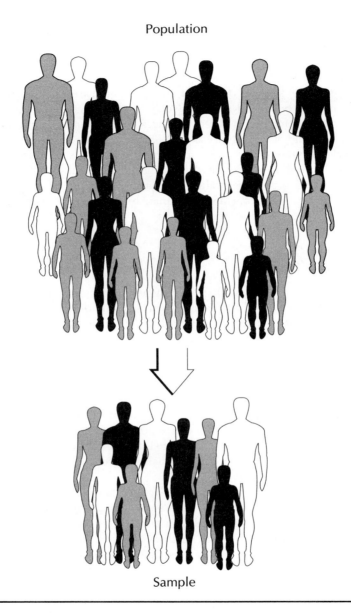

Sample

Figure 5-1. Example of the relationship between population and sample.

Generalization

Your goal as a researcher is to apply the results of your experiment (which are based on a small sample) to the larger population from which the sample was drawn. You do not want the results from your study of the three teaching techniques to apply only to those subjects who participated in the study. Rather, you want to be able to apply your findings to the general population. Applying findings from a sample to a larger population is known as **generalization**.

If the results of an experiment are to generalize to the intended population, you must be careful when you select the sample. The optimal procedure is to identify the population and then draw a **random sample** of individuals for participation in the experiment. In random sampling, every person in the population must be eligible for participation in the experiment. Each person must also have an equal chance of being chosen for the experiment.

True random sampling could be conducted by placing the name of every potential subject in a hat and then drawing out a specified number of names one at a time. The names drawn would constitute the random sample. (In practice, you do not literally pull names out of a hat. Chapter 7 discusses various methods that can be used to acquire a random sample.) A true random sample allows for the highest level of generality from research to real life.

Having a random sample of individuals from the population is an ideal that is rarely met in psychological research. In practice, a large proportion of psychological studies uses individuals from a highly specialized subpopulation as subjects—college students. In fact, McNemar (1946) characterized psychology as "the science of college sophomores." A more recent study (Higbee, Millard, & Folkman, 1982) reported that a majority of studies in social psychology published in the 1970s still relied on college students for subjects.

College students are used so often because they are an easily accessible pool of potential subjects. In the past, participation in research was a requirement of psychology courses. Today, ethical guidelines (described later in this chapter) prohibit required participation. Many institutions offer incentives (such as course credit) to induce students to participate in research. The college student population remains the most important source of research subjects.

If you choose to use college students for the sake of convenience, you may be sacrificing a degree of external validity or generality of your experiment. College students differ in a number of ways from the noncollege population (such as in age or socioeconomic status). These differences may limit your ability to apply your results to the larger population beyond college. You may be limited to generalizing only to other college students.

Research on the issue of student versus nonstudent subjects has produced mixed results. A few studies (such as Feild & Barnett, 1978) have found differences between college and noncollege subjects. In contrast, Tanford (1984) reported a jury simulation study in which student subjects did not differ significantly from "real jurors" on most of the measures included in the study. Given these inconsistent findings, the true impact of using students as subjects is difficult to assess. You should recognize the possible limitations on the generality of results from research using students as subjects.

Other factors that affect the degree of generality of your results beyond the nature of the sample include how realistic the experiment is and how the independent variables are manipulated. More of these factors are discussed in subsequent chapters. Other sampling considerations most relevant to nonexperimental research are discussed in Chapters 6 and 7.

Considerations When Using Human Subjects

Assume for the moment that you have developed a testable hypothesis, selected your population for study, and are now ready to start recruiting subjects. Before you can run your first subject, you should be aware of the ethical guidelines established by the American Psychological Association (APA) and the U.S. Department of Health and Human Services (HHS) that you must follow. The next section addresses these ethical principles.

Ethical Research Practice

In 1954, Vinacke wrote a letter to the editor of the *American Psychologist* (the official journal of the APA) lambasting psychologists for lack of concern over the welfare of their research subjects. In his letter Vinacke pointed out that the psychological researcher frequently misinforms subjects or exposes them to painful or embarrassing conditions, often without telling the subjects the nature and purpose of the study.

Although Vinacke's concerns were well founded and represented some of the earliest criticisms of research practice among psychologists, the concern over ethical treatment of research subjects predates Vinacke's letter by several years. The APA established a committee in 1938 to consider the issue of ethics within psychological research (Schuler, 1982). The current concern over ethical treatment of research participants can be traced to the post–World War II Nuremberg war crimes trials. Many of the ethical principles eventually adopted by the APA in 1951 are rooted in what is now called the Nuremberg Code.

Nazi War Crimes and the Nuremberg Code. In the years before World War II, when the Nazis were first assuming and consolidating power in Germany, several anti-Jewish laws were passed (laws preventing Jews from holding civil service jobs, shopping in non-Jewish stores, and so forth). Through shrewd propaganda, the Nazis were able to identify in the public mind (albeit incorrectly) the Jews with the ills that befell the German people in the post–World War I era. As a consequence of these laws, concentration camps were eventually established to which Jews were deported. Many of these concentration camps served as slave labor camps. Others (Auschwitz, Treblinka, and Sobibor) had another purpose: to carry out Hitler's "final solution of the Jewish problem." The principal reason for the existence of this latter group of concentration camps was the systematic extermination of human beings.

At some of these extermination camps (for example, Auschwitz) a variety of "medical" experiments were conducted on the doomed inmates. For example, an SS doctor at Auschwitz selected inmates for either immediate extermination or incarceration in the camp. Some of those who were spared (most notably twins) served as subjects in a variety of experiments. Some of the experiments were carried out in the name of eugenics and were aimed at proving the existence of a master race or "improving" the genetic stock of such a race. Mass sterilization procedures (without anesthesia) were tried out on inmates in an attempt to find the most efficient way to reduce the population of "inferior races."

Other experiments were carried out for the German military. For example, inmates were placed in decompression chambers to see how long it would take them to die under high-altitude conditions or were immersed in near-freezing water to see how long a pilot could survive in the water before rescue (research carried out for the German Air Force). Bones were broken and rebroken to see how many times they could be broken before healing was not possible. The list of these sadistic "experiments" goes on and on.

In all the experiments conducted at concentration camps, the inmates were unwilling participants. After the war, when the Nazi atrocities came to light, some of those responsible were tried for their crimes at the Nuremberg trials. Out of these trials came the Nuremberg Code, which laid the groundwork for many of the current ethical standards for psychological and medical research. The 10 major principles set forth in the Nuremberg Code (Katz, 1972, pp. 305–306) are listed in Table 5-1.

Note that point 1 requires that participation in research be voluntary and that the subject has the right to know about the nature, purposes, and duration of the research. In addition, points 2 and 3 suggest that frivolous research is unethical. Scientists should not subject people to experimental manipulations if there is another way to acquire the same information, and a firm scientific base must exist for the experiment. Points 4, 5, 6, 7, and 8 place the responsibility on the researcher to ensure that subjects are not exposed to potentially harmful research practices. Finally, points 9 and 10 require that research be terminated by either the subject or experimenter if it becomes obvious to either that continuation of the experiment would be, for any reason, impossible. These factors were embodied in the ethical standards adopted by the APA and the HHS.

APA Ethical Guidelines. The APA began preparing its ethical guidelines in 1947. Complaints from members of the APA served as the impetus for looking into the establishment of ethical guidelines for researchers. The first ethical code of the APA was accepted in 1953 (Schuler, 1982). Since their original publication in 1953, the APA guidelines have been revised several times, most recently in

---

Table 5-1. Ten Points of the Nuremberg Code

1. Participation of subjects must be totally voluntary and the subject should have the capacity to give consent to participate. Further, the subject should be fully informed of the purposes, nature, and duration of the experiment.

2. The research should yield results that are useful to society and that cannot be obtained in any other way.

3. The research should have a sound footing in animal research and be based on the natural history of the problem under study.

4. Steps should be taken in the research to avoid unnecessary physical or psychological harm to subjects.

5. Research should not be conducted if there is reason to believe that death or disability will occur to the subjects.

6. The risk involved in the research should be proportional to the benefits to be obtained from the results.

7. Proper plans should be made and facilities provided to protect the subject against harm.

8. Research should be conducted by highly qualified scientists only.

9. The subject should have the freedom to withdraw from the experiment at any time if he (or she) has reached the conclusion that continuing in the experiment is not possible.

10. The researcher must be prepared to discontinue the experiment if it becomes evident to the researcher that continuing the research will be harmful to the subjects.

1990. The ethical guidelines concerning research using human participants are now grouped together as **Principal 9 of the "Ethical Principles of Psychologists"** (which also specifies ethics for mental health practitioners). Table 5-2 presents the most recent version of the guidelines for using human participants in research. Note the similarities between the Nuremberg Code and the present APA guidelines.

The APA (1973) has also established a set of ethical guidelines for research in which children are used as subjects. If you are going to use children as subjects, you should familiarize yourself with those guidelines.

The period spanning the early 1940s through the late 1950s was one in which researchers became increasingly concerned with the ethical treatment of research subjects. This was true for researchers in psychology as well as in the medical profession. Unfortunately, a greater sensitivity about ethics and the newly drafted guidelines did not ensure that research was carried out in an ethical manner, as the next example clearly shows.

The director of medicine at the Jewish Chronic Disease Hospital in Brooklyn, New York, approved the injection of live cancer cells into two chronically ill patients in July 1963. The patients were unaware of the procedure, which was designed to test the ability of the patients' bodies to reject foreign cells (Katz, 1972). Predictably, the discovery of this ethical violation of the patients' rights raised quite a controversy.

Government Regulations. As a result of abuses similar to the Jewish Chronic Disease Hospital case, the U.S. government was motivated to address the issue of ethical treatment of human subjects in research. The result of this involvement was the establishment of the HHS guidelines for the "protection of human subjects" (1982). These guidelines, which apply to government agencies and any institution receiving government funds, are summarized in Table 5-3.

The guidelines established by the HHS are much more complex than the brief overview presented in Table 5-3. Familiarize yourself with the full set of HHS guidelines and APA code of ethics before you conduct your research.

Ethical Guidelines, Your Research, and the IRB

Now that you are familiar with the ethical principles for research with human subjects, you can begin to think about obtaining and running your subjects. Can you now proceed with your research? In days gone by, you could have done just that. Presently, however, you may be required to have your research reviewed by an **institutional review board** (IRB). If you are affiliated with any institution that receives federal funding, you will be required to have your research screened for ethical treatment of subjects before you can begin to conduct your research. The role of the IRB is to ensure that you adhere to established ethical guidelines.

Submitting your research to the IRB for review involves drafting a proposal. The form of that proposal varies from institution to institution. However, an IRB requires certain items of information to evaluate your proposal. Information will be needed concerning how subjects will be acquired, procedures for obtaining informed consent, experimental procedures, potential risks to the subjects, and plans for following up your research with reports to subjects. Depending on the nature of your research, you may be required to submit a draft of an "informed consent form" outlining to your subjects the nature of the study. A sample informed consent form is provided in Figure 5-2.

One final note on the role of the IRB is in order. You may see these preliminary steps as unnecessary and, at times, a bother. After all, aren't you (the researcher) competent to determine whether subjects are being treated ethically? Although you may be qualified to evaluate the ethics of your experiment, you still have a vested interest in your research. Such a vested interest may blind you to some ethical implications of your research.

The IRB is important because it allows a group of individuals who do not have a vested interest in the research to screen your study. The IRB review and

Table 5-2. Principle 9 of the APA "Ethical Principles of Psychologists": Research with Human Participants

The decision to undertake research rests upon a considered judgment by the individual psychologist about how best to contribute to psychological science and human welfare. Having made the decision to conduct research, the psychologist considers alternative directions in which research energies and resources might be invested. On the basis of this consideration, the psychologist carries out the investigation with respect and concern for the dignity and welfare of the people who participate and with cognizance of federal and state regulations and professional standards governing the conduct of research with human participants.

a. In planning a study, the investigator has the responsibility to make a careful evaluation of its ethical acceptability. To the extent that the weighing of scientific and human values suggests a compromise of any principle, the investigator incurs a correspondingly serious obligation to seek ethical advice and to observe stringent safeguards to protect the rights of human participants.

b. Considering whether a participant in a planned study will be a "subject at risk" or a "subject at minimal risk," according to recognized standards, is of primary ethical concern to the investigator.

c. The investigator always retains the responsibility for ensuring ethical practice in research. The investigator is also responsible for the ethical treatment of research participants by collaborators, assistants, students, and employees, all of whom, however, incur similar obligations.

d. Except in minimal-risk research, the investigator establishes a clear and fair agreement with research participants, prior to their participation, that clarifies the obligations and responsibilities of each. The investigator has the obligation to honor all promises and commitments included in that agreement. The investigator informs the participants of all aspects of the research that might reasonably be expected to influence willingness to participate and explains all other aspects of the research about which the participants inquire. Failure to make full disclosure prior to obtaining informed consent requires additional safeguards to protect the welfare and dignity of the research participants. Research with children or with participants who have impairments that would limit understanding and/or communication requires special safeguarding procedures.

e. Methodological requirements of a study may make the use of concealment or deception necessary. Before conducting such a study, the investigator has a special responsibility to (i) determine whether the use of such techniques is justified by the study's prospective scientific, educational, or applied value; (ii) determine whether alternative procedures are available that do not use concealment or deception; and (iii) ensure that the participants are provided with sufficient explanation as soon as possible.

**Table 5-2. Principle 9 of the APA "Ethical Principles of Psychologists":
Research with Human Participants** (continued)

f. The investigator respects the individual's freedom to decline to participate in or to withdraw from the research at any time. The obligation to protect this freedom requires careful thought and consideration when the investigator is in a position of authority or influence over the participant. Such positions of authority include, but are not limited to, situations in which research participation is required as part of employment or in which the participant is a student, client, or employee of the investigator.

g. The investigator protects the participant from physical and mental discomfort, harm, and danger that may arise from research procedures. If risks of such consequences exist, the investigator informs the participant of that fact. Research procedures likely to cause serious or lasting harm to a participant are not used unless the failure to use these procedures might expose the participant to risk of greater harm, or unless the research has great potential benefit and fully informed and voluntary consent is obtained from each participant. The participant should be informed of procedures for contacting the investigator within a reasonable time period following participation should stress, potential harm, or related questions or concerns arise.

h. After the data are collected, the investigator provides the participant with information about the nature of the study and attempts to remove any misconceptions that may have arisen. Where scientific or humane values justify delaying or withholding this information, the investigator incurs a special responsibility to monitor the research and to ensure that there are no damaging consequences for the participant.

i. Where research procedures result in undesirable consequences for the individual participant, the investigator has the responsibility to detect and remove or correct these consequences, including long-term effects.

j. Information obtained about a research participant during the course of an investigation is confidential unless otherwise agreed upon in advance. When the possibility exists that others may obtain access to such information, this possibility, together with the plans for protecting confidentiality, is explained to the participant as part of the procedure for obtaining informed consent.

SOURCE: American Psychological Association, 1990.

Table 5-3. Summary of the HHS Guidelines for Use of Humans as Research Subjects

1. All research with human subjects is subject to the HHS guidelines except (a) research conducted in established educational settings involving normal educational practices (such as research on the effectiveness of teaching techniques); (b) research using standard educational tests; (c) assuming that the subjects cannot be identified, research involving survey or interview procedures (unless there is a danger that the subject could be identified, harmed by being identified, and the research deals with a sensitive topic); (d) research involving the observation of public behavior (except when the subject's behavior is recorded in such a way to allow the subject to be identified, the observations could compromise the subject if identified, and the research deals with sensitive aspects of the subject's behavior), and (e) research involving the collection or study of preexisting data.

2. Research that will include human subjects and does not fall into one of the categories mentioned above will be reviewed by an institutional review board (IRB). This board will review research proposals to ensure ethical treatment of subjects. The IRB has the power to review and approve, require modifications to, or disapprove proposed research.

3. The IRB is to see that subjects are provided with sufficient information to allow for informed consent. This informed consent shall provide the subjects with the following information: (a) a statement that the study involves research and an explanation of the purposes of the research, the procedures to be followed, an identification of any procedures that are experimental in nature, and a statement of the duration of the study; (b) a description of any reasonably foreseeable risks to the subject; (c) a description of potential benefits to the subject; (d) a description of any appropriate alternative procedures or treatments; (e) a statement about the level of risk involved and an explanation of risk above a minimal risk; (e) an explanation of who should be contacted for questions about the research; and (e) a statement that participation is voluntary and that refusal to participate will result in no negative consequences. There are other elements that the informed consent statement should take under special circumstances (see the actual guidelines for these).

4. Adequate provisions should be made to protect the privacy of subjects and maintain the confidentiality of the data collected. Special attention should be given to situations in which the subjects are especially susceptible to coercion or pressure to participate (such as acutely ill patients, prisoners, mental patients, economically or educationally disadvantaged people, and so forth).

SOURCE: U.S. Department of Health and Human Services, 1982.

INFORMED CONSENT

The experiment in which you are about to participate is designed to investigate the relationship between hypnosis and memory and is being conducted by Dr. James Smith, professor of psychology. This experiment has been approved by the Institutional Review Board of the University of _____.

   In this experiment you will view a film of an automobile accident. Two hours after viewing the film, you will be asked to recall as much as you can about the film. Some participants will be hypnotized prior to the recall test by a licensed psychologist who has been trained in the use of hypnosis. Please be assured that the hypnosis procedure is in no way harmful. Only questions pertaining to the film will be asked. The psychologist will be with you during the entire hypnosis session to ensure your comfort.

   Please be assured that any information that you provide will be held in strict confidence by the researchers. At no time will your name be reported along with your responses. All data will be reported in group form only. At the conclusion of this study, you will receive a report of the results.

   Please understand that your participation in this research is totally voluntary and you are free to withdraw at any time during this study without penalty, and to remove any data that you may have contributed.

   I acknowledge that I have been informed of, and understand, the nature and purpose of this study, and I freely consent to participate. I acknowledge that I am at least 18 years of age.

Signed _____

Date _____

Figure 5-2. Sample informed consent form. The first paragraph explains the purpose of the experiment, who is conducting it, and that it has been approved for ethical considerations. The second paragraph expands on the description of the experiment and outlines the hypnosis procedure and the precautions to be taken. The final paragraphs assure the subject that all data are confidential and will be reported in group form, as well as pointing out that participation is totally voluntary.

approval provides protection for both you and the sponsoring institution. If you choose to ignore the recommendations of the IRB, you may be assuming legal liability for any harm that comes to subjects as a result of participation in your research. In the long run, the extra time and effort needed to prepare the IRB proposal is in the best interests of the sponsoring institution, the subject, and you.

If your proposal is approved by the IRB, you may begin to conduct the study. First on your list of things to do is to acquire subjects.

Acquiring Human Subjects for Research

You must consider two important factors when acquiring subjects for your experiment: the research setting and the policies of the institution or department where the research will be conducted.

The Research Setting

Chapter 3 distinguished between field and laboratory experiments. In a field experiment, you manipulate independent variables in the subject's natural environment, whereas in a laboratory experiment the subject enters an environment created and controlled by you. If you have chosen to conduct a field experiment, your method of subject acquisition will be different from the one used to acquire laboratory subjects.

The Field Experiment. Some field experiments are conducted like laboratory studies. In these cases, the researchers take their equipment to a field setting and conduct their experiments. An example is the field experiment conducted by Friedrich and Stein (1973) at a day care center. In this experiment, the researchers randomly assigned subjects to different television "diets" and then observed the subjects for their aggressiveness during free-play situations. In this type of field experiment, the researchers maintain almost as much control over subject selection and assignment as they would if the study were conducted in a laboratory. However, the researchers are constrained to using only the children who are present on the days of the experiment.

In a second type of field experiment, the researcher sets up a situation and waits for subjects to happen along. In this type of field experiment, you have less control over who will be in the pool of potential subjects than in the day care field experiment. You have little control over recruitment of subjects. If you are running your field experiment in a clearly defined place (such as a library, subway car, or street corner), you must wait until subjects come to you.

Some field situations do permit you to exert greater control over subject selection. These are cases in which your experiment calls for the researcher (or confederate) to approach the subject (rather than having the subject enter the already existing experimental situation). For example, if you are going to study conformity by asking subjects to sign a petition that has 0, 2, 5, or 10 pre-existing signatures, you can control who participates in the research. Say you wanted to include equal numbers of blacks and whites. Although you could do this even if you were not approaching subjects (by simply waiting until enough blacks or whites happen into your experiment), you can more easily control the characteristics of the subject sample if you approach subjects. For a laboratory experiment, you usually acquire subjects from some form of subject pool. A subject pool consists of a group of individuals who are readily available for participation in research. The most common subject pool consists of college students, such as those enrolled in introductory psychology courses. Individuals from that pool are recruited to be subjects in experiments.

Institutional Policies

Institutions have their own rules concerning how human subjects can be recruited and used. For example, it was once fairly common practice among psychology departments to require introductory psychology students to participate in a certain number of experiments in a semester in order to ensure a passing grade. The net effect of such a policy is that some students become unwilling participants in research. Ethical guidelines now prohibit requiring individuals to be subjects in experiments.

Present guidelines may be met by providing some alternative to research participation, such as observing an experiment or writing a paper. Each requirement must involve equivalent time and effort.

Another strategy for acquiring subjects from a pool is to offer them extra course credit or some other reward (money, perhaps) for participation. If this strategy is adopted, you still must offer an alternative to research participation to obtain the reward offered, especially if the reward is extra course credit. In short, you must ensure that potential subjects are in no way coerced or pressured into participating in your research. According to current ethical standards, your subjects must participate voluntarily.

Voluntary Participation and Validity

Ethical treatment of subjects mandates that subjects be informed of the nature, purpose, and requirements of your study, and be given the opportunity to decline participation. There are undoubtedly differences between individuals who choose to participate in research and those who do not. Because a sample made up entirely of volunteers is biased, the validity of your experiment may be affected; this is known as the **volunteer bias**. As Schuler (1982) pointed out, ethical requirements sometimes act in direct opposition to the methodological requirements of good research.

There are two assumptions inherent in the previous discussion: (1) that volunteers differ in meaningful ways from nonvolunteers; (2) that the differences between volunteers and nonvolunteers affect the external validity of your research.

Factors That Affect the Decision to Volunteer

Subject-related Characteristics. Rosenthal and Rosnow (1975) provided the most comprehensive study of the characteristics of the volunteer subject in their book, *The Volunteer Subject.* Table 5-4 lists several characteristics that, according to Rosenthal and Rosnow, distinguish volunteers from nonvolunteers. Associated with each characteristic is the degree of confidence Rosenthal and Rosnow believe you can have in the validity of each attribute.

In some cases, no clear, simple effect of a variable is apparent on whether or not a person will volunteer for behavioral research. For example, Rosenthal and Rosnow pointed out that first-borns may respond more frequently than later-borns to an "intimate" recruitment style for an experiment dealing with group dynamics. Later-borns may respond more frequently than first-borns to a request for subjects for an experiment involving stress. Similarly, a sociable person may be more likely to volunteer for an experiment that is "sociable" in nature and less likely to volunteer for an experiment in which there is little or no contact with others. Also, volunteers may show better adjustment than nonvolunteers in experiments that require self-disclosure.

In addition, other research suggests that volunteer subjects may also be more field-dependent (rely heavily on environmental cues) than are nonvolunteers (Cooperman, 1980) and willing to endure higher levels of stress in an experiment (Saunders, 1980). Thus, subject characteristics separate the person who volunteers from the person who does not.

Situational Factors. In addition to subject characteristics, situational factors may also affect a person's decision to volunteer for behavioral research. According to Rosenthal and Rosnow, you can have "maximum confidence" in the conclusion that people who are more interested in the topic being researched, and who have expectations of being favorably evaluated, will be more likely to volunteer for a particular research study. You can have "considerable confidence" that if potential subjects perceive the research as being important, feel guilty about not participating, and are offered incentives to participate, they will be more likely to volunteer. Other factors that have less impact on the decision include personal characteristics of the person recruiting the subjects, the amount of stress inherent in the experiment, and the degree to which subjects feel that volunteering is the "normative, expected, appropriate thing to do" (Rosenthal & Rosnow, 1975, p. 119). Finally, you can have only "minimum confidence" that a personal acquaintance with the recruiter or public commitment to volunteering will affect the rate of volunteering.

Table 5-4. Characteristics of Individuals Who Volunteer for Research

Maximum Confidence

1. Volunteers tend to be more highly educated than nonvolunteers.
2. Volunteers tend to come from a higher social class than nonvolunteers.
3. Volunteers are of higher intelligence in general, but not when volunteering for atypical research (such as hypnosis, sex research).
4. Volunteers have a higher need for approval than nonvolunteers.
5. Volunteers are more social than nonvolunteers.

Considerable Confidence

1. Volunteers are more "arousal seeking" than nonvolunteers (especially when the research involves stress).
2. Individuals who volunteer for sex research are more unconventional than nonvolunteers.
3. Females are more likely to volunteer than males, except where the research involves physical or emotional stress.
4. Volunteers are less authoritarian than nonvolunteers.
5. Jews are more likely to volunteer than Protestants; however, Protestants are more likely to volunteer than Catholics.
6. Volunteers have a tendency to be less conforming than nonvolunteers, except where the volunteers are female and the research is clinically oriented.

SOURCE: Adapted from Rosenthal & Rosnow, 1975.

As with the subject-related factors, the operation of the situational factors may be complex. For example, people are generally less disposed to volunteer for experiments that involve stress or aversive situations. According to Rosenthal and Rosnow, the personal characteristics of the potential subject and the nature of the incentives offered may mediate the decision to volunteer for this type of research. Also, stable personal characteristics may mediate the impact of offering material rewards for participation in research.

The general conclusion from the research of Rosenthal and Rosnow is that several subject-related and situational characteristics affect the potential subject's decision about volunteering for a particular research study. Such a decision may be influenced by a variety of factors that interact with one another. In any case, it is apparent that volunteering is not a simple random process. Certain types of people are disposed to volunteer generally, and for certain specific types of research. The next question is whether or not this volunteer bias affects the outcome of an experiment.

Volunteerism and Internal Validity

Ideally, you want to establish that variation in your independent variable *causes* observed variation in your dependent variable. However, variables related to voluntary participation may, quite subtly, cause variation in your dependent variable. If you conclude the variation in your independent variable caused the observed effects, you may be mistaken. Thus, volunteerism may affect "inferred causality" (Rosenthal & Rosnow, 1975), which closely relates to internal validity.

Rosenthal and Rosnow conducted a series of experiments investigating the impact of volunteering on inferred causality within the context of an attitude change experiment. In the first experiment, 42 undergraduate women (20 of whom had previously indicated their willingness to volunteer for a study) were given an attitude questionnaire concerning fraternities on college campuses. A week later the experimenters randomly assigned some subjects to a profraternity communication, others to an antifraternity communication, and still others to no persuasive communication. The subjects were then given a measure of their attitudes toward fraternities.

Although the persuasive communication changed attitudes more than the other types, the volunteer subjects were more affected by the antifraternity communication than nonvolunteers, as shown in Figure 5-3. A tentative explanation offered by Rosenthal and Rosnow for this effect centered on the higher need for approval among volunteer than nonvolunteer subjects. Volunteer subjects tended to see the experimenter as being antifraternity (although only slightly). Apparently, the volunteer subjects were more motivated to please the experimenter than were the nonvolunteer subjects. The desire to please the experimenter, not the content of the persuasive measure, may have caused the observed attitude change.

The results of this experiment show that variables relating to voluntary participation may cloud any causal inferences you draw about the relationship between your independent and dependent variables. Rosenthal and Rosnow (1975, p. 155) concluded that "subjects' reactions to a persuasive communication can be largely predicted from their original willingness to participate in the research." According to Rosenthal and Rosnow, the volunteer subject's predisposition to comply with demand characteristics of the experiment indicates that volunteerism serves as a "motivation mediator" and may affect the internal validity of an experiment.

Volunteerism and External Validity

Ideally, we would like the results from any research we conduct to generalize beyond our research sample. Volunteerism may affect our ability to generalize beyond our research sample. It may be that any results you find apply only to

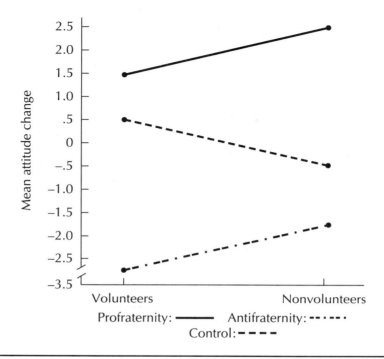

Figure 5-3. Attitude change as a function of type of message and volunteerism. (Based on data from Rosenthal & Rosnow, 1975.)

subjects with the characteristics of the volunteers you used in your research. Thus volunteerism may affect external validity as well as internal validity.

To see how volunteerism affects the external validity of a study, consider an experiment conducted by Horowitz (1969). This study investigated the relationship between the level of fear aroused by a persuasive communication and attitude change. Horowitz examined the impact of fear arousal along with a second variable: whether subjects were volunteers or not. Subjects in a "high-fear" group were exposed to a persuasive communication that pointed out the dangers of drug abuse (subjects read a pamphlet and saw a film). The high-fear communication presented graphic descriptions of drug abuse. Subjects in the low-fear group only read the pamphlet (they did not see the film), and the graphic references to dire consequences of drug abuse were eliminated. Attitudes were measured on a postexperimental questionnaire.

As shown in Figure 5-4, the high-fear communication affected volunteers and nonvolunteers differently. The volunteers showed more attitude change in response to the high-fear communication than did the nonvolunteers. However, little difference emerged between volunteers and nonvolunteers in the low-fear

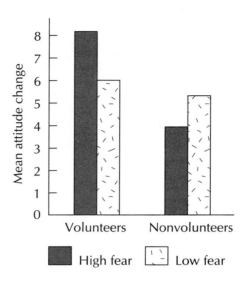

Figure 5-4. Attitude change as a function of fear arousal and volunteerism. (Based on an experiment by Horowitz, 1969.)

condition. Thus, the relationship between fear arousal and attitude change was different for volunteer and nonvolunteer subjects. These results suggest that using volunteer subjects in an attitude change experiment may produce results that do not generalize to the general population. Arnett and Rikli (1981) confirm this problem of external validity in a different research context (motor behavior).

Remedies for Volunteerism

Are there any remedies for the "volunteerism" problem? Rosenthal and Rosnow (1975, pp. 198–199) listed the following things you can do to reduce the bias inherent in the recruitment of volunteers:

1. Make the appeal for subjects as interesting as possible, keeping in mind the nature of the target population.

2. Make the appeal for volunteers as nonthreatening as possible so that potential volunteers will not be "put off" by unwarranted fears of unfavorable evaluation.

3. Explicitly state the theoretical and practical importance of the research for which volunteering is requested.

4. Explicitly state in what way the target population is particularly relevant to the research being conducted and the responsibility of the potential

volunteers to participate in research that has potential for benefiting others.

5. When possible, potential volunteers should be offered not only pay for participation, but also small courtesy gifts simply for taking the time to consider whether they will want to participate.

6. Have the request for volunteering made by a person of status as high as possible, and preferably by a woman.

7. When possible, avoid research tasks that may be psychologically or biologically stressful.

8. When possible, communicate the normative nature of the volunteering response.

9. After a target population has been defined, an effort should be made to have someone known to that population make an appeal for volunteers. The request for volunteers itself may be more successful if a personalized appeal is made.

10. In situations where volunteering is regarded by the target population as normative, conditions of public commitment to volunteer may be more successful. Where nonvolunteering is regarded as normative, conditions of private commitment may be more successful.

Research Using Deception

In most cases, psychological research involves fully informing subjects of the purposes and nature of an experiment. Subjects participating in research on basic processes such as perception and memory are usually informed beforehand what the experiment will involve. However, in some cases full disclosure of the nature and purpose of your study would invalidate your research findings. When you either actively mislead subjects or purposely withhold information from the subject, you are using **deception**.

Deception may take a variety of forms. Arellano–Galdamas (1972, cited in Schuler, 1982) distinguished between active and passive deception. Active deception includes the following behavior (Schuler, 1982, p. 79):

1. Misrepresenting the purposes of the research
2. False statements as to the identity of the researcher
3. False promises made to the subjects
4. Violating a promise to keep the subject anonymous
5. Misleading explanations of equipment and procedures
6. Using pseudosubjects
7. False diagnoses and other reports

8. False interaction

9. Using placebos and secret administration of drugs

10. Misleading settings for the investigations and corresponding behavior by the experimenter

Passive forms of deception include (Schuler, 1982, p. 79):

1. Unrecognized conditioning

2. Provocation and secret recording of negatively evaluated behavior

3. Concealed observation

4. Unrecognized participant observation

5. Use of projective techniques and other personality tests

Although deception is a popular research tactic (especially in social psychology), some researchers consider it inappropriate (Kelman, 1967). In fact, deception does pose a number of problems for both the subject and experimenter. For example, research suggests that once subjects are deceived they may react differently from nondeceived subjects in a subsequent experiment (Silverman, Shulman, & Weisenthal, 1970).

Another problem with deception is that the subject in a deception experiment has been exposed to an elaborate hoax. The subject may feel duped by the experimenter and consequently experience a loss of self-esteem or develop negative attitudes toward research. According to Holmes (1976a), the researcher's responsibility is to "dehoax" the subject after the experiment.

Yet another problem arising from deception research may arise if, during the course of the experiment, subjects find out something disturbing about themselves. Holmes (1976b) maintained that the researcher has the responsibility to desensitize subjects concerning their own behaviors.

Stanley Milgram's (1963, 1974) classic obedience research illustrates these problems of deception research. Briefly, Milgram led subjects to believe they were participating in an experiment investigating the effects of punishment on learning. The subject was told to deliver an electric shock to the "learner" each time the learner made an error. The shock intensity was to be increased following each delivery of shock. In reality, the assignment of individuals to the role of "teacher" or "learner" was prearranged (the "learner" was a confederate of the researcher), and no real shocks were being delivered by the subjects. The true purpose of the research was to test the subject's obedience to an authority figure (the experimenter) who insisted that the subject continue with the procedure whenever the subject protested.

Milgram's research relied heavily on deception. Subjects were deceived into believing that the experiment was about learning and that they were actually delivering painful electric shocks to another person. The problem of hoaxing is evident in this experiment. Subjects also were induced to behave in a highly unacceptable manner. The subject may have found out that he or she was "the type of person who would intentionally hurt another," an obvious threat to the subject's self-concept. To be fair, Milgram did extensively debrief his subjects to help reduce the impact of the experimental manipulations. (Debriefing is discussed later in the chapter.) However, some social psychologists (for example, Baumrind, 1964) maintain that the experiment was still unethical.

Ethical treatment of subjects requires that subjects be informed of the nature and purpose of the research before they participate. Does deception on the part of the researcher constitute unethical behavior? The APA's 1990 revision of ethical principles addresses the issue of deception methodology. According to the APA principles, deception shall only be used if the experimenter can justify the use of deception based on the study's scientific, educational, or applied value; alternative procedures that do not use deception are not available; and if the subjects are provided with an explanation for the deception as soon as possible. The APA code of ethics thus allows researchers to use deception, but only under restricted conditions.

Solutions to the Problem of Deception

Obviously, deception may result in ethical and practical problems for your research. To avoid these problems, researchers have suggested some solutions. These range from eliminating deception completely and substituting an alternative method called *role playing,* to retaining deception but adopting methods to soften its impact.

Role Playing. As an alternative to deception, critics have suggested using **role playing**. In role playing, subjects are fully informed about the nature of the research and are asked to act as though they were subjected to a particular treatment condition. The technique thus relies on a subject's ability to assume and play out a given role.

Some studies demonstrate that subjects *can* become immersed in a role and act accordingly. The famous Stanford prison study is one such example. In that study, subjects were randomly assigned to the role of either prisoners or guards in a simulated prison. Observations were made of the interactions between the "guards" and their "prisoners" (Haney, Banks, & Zimbardo, 1973). Subjects were able to play out their roles even though they were fully aware of the experimental nature of the situation. Similarly, Janis and Mann (1965) directly tested the impact of emotional role playing by having subjects assume the role of a dying cancer patient. Other, non-role-playing subjects did not assume the role, but were exposed to the same information as the role-playing subjects. Subjects in the role-playing condition showed more attitudinal and behavioral changes than subjects in the non-role-playing control group.

Subjects are thus *capable* of assuming a role. The next question is whether the data obtained from role-playing subjects are equivalent to the data generated from deception methods.

Opponents of role playing have likened the practice of role playing to "the days of prescientific techniques when intuition and consensus took the place of data" (Freedman, 1969, p. 100). They contend that subjects fully informed of the nature and purposes of research will produce results qualitatively different from those produced from uninformed subjects.

Resnick and Schwartz (1973) provided support for this view. In a simple verbal conditioning experiment (statements that use "I" or "we" were reinforced), some subjects were fully informed of the reinforcement manipulation whereas others were not. The results showed that the uninformed subjects displayed the usual learning curve (using more "I-we" statements in the reinforcement condition). In contrast, the fully informed volunteers showed a decline in the rate of "I-we" statements. Thus, informed and uninformed subjects behaved differently. Other research (Horowitz & Rothschild, 1970) has provided additional evidence that role-playing techniques are not equivalent to deception methods.

The use of deception raises questions of both ethics and sound methodology. Role playing has not been the panacea for the problems of deception research. For this reason, deception continues to be used in psychological research (most often in social psychological research). Given that you may decide to use deception in your research, are there any steps you can take to deal with the ethical questions about deception and reduce the impact of deception on subjects? The answer to this question is a qualified yes.

Obtaining Prior Consent to Be Deceived. Campbell (1969) suggested that subjects in a subject pool be told at the beginning of the semester that some experiments in which they may participate might involve deception. They could be provided with an explanation of the need for deception at that time. Gamson, Fireman, and Rytina (1982) devised an additional ingenious method for the securing of informed consent to be deceived. Subjects were contacted and asked to indicate the types of research in which they would be willing to participate. Included in the list was research in which the subjects were not fully informed. With this strategy you might choose only those subjects who agree to be deceived. Of course, choosing only the agreeable subjects may contribute to sampling error and affect external validity.

Debriefing. Even if you are able to quell your conscience about the ethical aspects of deception by obtaining prior consent to deceive, you are still obligated to your subjects to inform them of the deception as soon as possible after the research. A technique commonly used to do this is **debriefing**.

During a debriefing session, you inform your subjects about the nature of the deception used and why the deception was necessary. Because knowledge of having been deceived may lead to bad feelings on the part of the subject, one goal of the debriefing session should be to restore the subject's trust and self-esteem. You want the subject to leave the experiment feeling good about the research experience and less suspicious of other research.

Research shows that debriefing has become more frequent in research (Ullman & Jackson, 1982). Ullman and Jackson showed that only 12 percent of studies published in two major social psychology journals reported using debriefing in 1964. In contrast, 47 percent were found to have used debriefing in 1980. Clearly, researchers are becoming sensitive to the problems of deception research and have begun to use debriefing more.

But is debriefing effective? Research on this issue has yielded conflicting results. Walster, Berscheid, Abrahams, and Aronson (1967) found that the effects of deception persisted even after debriefing. In contrast, Smith and Richardson (1983) reported that debriefing was successful in removing negative feelings about deception research. They concluded that effective debriefing can not only reverse the ill effects of deception, but can also help to make subjects who felt harmed by research become more positive about the research experience.

A possible resolution to this conflict in results emerges from an evaluation of different debriefing techniques. Smith and Richardson pointed out that "effective" debriefing can reverse the negative feelings associated with deception. But what constitutes "effective" debriefing?

An answer to this question can be found in a study reported by Ross, Lepper, and Hubbard (1975). This study found that the effects of false feedback about task performance persevered beyond debriefing. When subjects were presented with "outcome" debriefing (which merely pointed out the deception and justified the deception), the effects of deception persevered. In contrast, if subjects were told that sometimes the effects of experimental manipulations persist after the experiment is over, the debriefing was more successful.

Although no easy answers to the problems generated by using deception can be found, some insight on how to soften the effects of deceptive strategies might help solve the problems. First, carefully consider the ethical implications of deception before using it. You, the researcher, are ultimately responsible for treating your subjects ethically. If deception is necessary, you should take steps both to dehoax and to desensitize subjects through debriefing (Holmes, 1976a,b). The debriefing session should be conducted as soon as possible after the experimental manipulations and should include the following:

1. A full disclosure of the purposes of the experiment.
2. A complete description of the deception used and a thorough explanation of why the deception was necessary.
3. A discussion of the problem of perseverance of the effects of the experimental manipulations.
4. A convincing argument for the necessity of the deception. You should also convince the subject that the research is scientifically important and has potential applications.

During debriefing, be as sincere with the subjects as possible. The subject has already been "duped" in your experiment. The last thing the subject needs is an experimenter who behaves in a condescending manner during debriefing (Aronson & Carlsmith, 1968). Despite the deception used, make the subject feel that he or she was an important part of the research.

One final question about debriefing: Will the subject believe your debriefing? That is, will the subject, who has aleady been deceived, believe the experimenter's assertions made during debriefing? Holmes (1976a) pointed out that there is no guarantee that the subjects will believe the experimenter during debriefing. According to Holmes, subjects may feel they are being set up for another deception. The researcher may have to take some drastic measures to ensure that the subject leaves the experiment believing the debriefing. Holmes suggested the following options:

1. Use demonstrations for the subject. For example, the subject could be shown that the experimenter never saw the subject's actual responses (this would be effective when false feedback is given) or that the equipment used to monitor the subject was bogus.

2. Subjects could be allowed to observe a subsequent experimental session showing another subject receiving the deception.

3. Subjects could be made active participants in the research. For example, they could serve as confederates in a subsequent experimental session.

Complete and honest debriefing is designed to make the subject feel more comfortable about deceptive research practices. Whereas this goal may be accomplished to some degree, the integrity of your research may be compromised. If your subjects tell other prospective subjects about your experiment (especially in cases where deception is used), subsequent data may be invalid. Consequently, asking subjects not to discuss with anyone else the nature of your experiment is a good idea. Point out to the subjects that any disclosure of the deception or any other information about your experiment will invalidate your results. Your goal should be to have your subject understand and agree that not disclosing information about your experiment is important.

Note that debriefing is not used exclusively for research using deception. In fact, it is good, ethical research practice to debrief subjects after *any* experiment. During such a debriefing session, the subjects should be given a full explanation of the methods used in the experiment, the purpose of the experiment, and any results available. Of course, subjects should also be given honest answers to any questions they may have.

To summarize, deception raises serious questions about ethical treatment of subjects in psychological research. In the absence of alternative techniques, you may find yourself in the position of having to use deception. You should strive to maintain the dignity of the subject by using effective debriefing techniques. However, you should not be lulled into believing you can use ethically questionable research techniques just because debriefing is used (Schuler, 1982).

Considerations When Using Animals as Subjects in Research

Psychological research is not limited to research with human subjects. The final section of this chapter considers some relevant factors if you decide to use animals as your research subjects.

Contributions of Research Using Animal Subjects

Animal research has played a prominent role in the development of theories in psychology and in the solution of applied problems. For example, Pavlov discovered the principles of classical conditioning by using animal subjects (dogs). Thorndike laid the groundwork for modern operant conditioning by using cats as subjects. B. F. Skinner developed the principles of modern operant conditioning by using rats and pigeons as subjects.

Snowdon (1983) pointed out several areas in which research using animal subjects has contributed significantly to knowledge about behavior. For example, animal research has helped explain the variability in behavior across species. This is important because understanding the variability across animal species may help explain the variability in behavior across humans (Snowdon, 1983). Also, research using animals has led to the development of animal models of human psychopathology. Such models may help explain the causes of human mental illness and facilitate the development of effective treatments (Snowdon, 1983). Animal research also has contributed significantly to explaining how the brain works and how basic psychological processes (such as learning and memory) operate.

Choosing Which Animal to Use

Animals used in psychological research include (but are not limited to) chimpanzees and gorillas (language acquisition research), monkeys (research on attachment formation), cats (learning, memory, physiology), dogs (learning, memory), fish (learning), pigeons (learning), and rats and mice (learning, memory, physiology). Of these, the laboratory rat and the pigeon are by far the most popular. The choice of which animal to use depends on several factors. Certain research questions may mandate the use of a particular species of animal. For example, you would probably use chimpanzees or gorillas if you were interested in investigating the nature of language and cognition in nonhuman subjects. In addition, using the same type of animal used in a previous experiment allows you to relate your findings to those previously obtained without having to worry about generalizing across animals.

Your choice of animals will also depend in part on the facilities at your particular institution. Many institutions are not equipped to handle primates or, for that matter, any large animal. You may be limited to using smaller animals such as rats, mice, or birds. Even if you do have the facilities to support the larger animals your choice may be limited by the availability of certain animals (chimpanzees and monkeys are difficult to obtain). Finally, budgetary constraints may also be a factor. For example, a cat may cost around $125 and a monkey about $600. Contrast that cost to around $10 for a laboratory rat.

Why Use Animals?

You might choose to use animals in your research for many reasons. One reason is that some procedures can be used on animals that cannot be used on humans.

Research investigating how different parts of the brain influence behavior often uses surgical techniques such as lesions, ablation, and cannula surgery. These procedures obviously cannot be conducted on human subjects.

As an example, suppose you were interested in studying how lesions to the hypothalamus affect motivation. You probably would not find many human subjects willing to volunteer for research that involves destroying a part of the brain! Animal subjects are the only available choice for research of this type. Similarly, even if there are areas of research that can be studied with humans (such as examining the effects of stress on learning), you may not be able to expose human subjects to extremely high levels of an independent variable. Again, animals would be the choice for subjects in research where the independent variable cannot be manipulated adequately within the guidelines for the ethical treatment of human subjects.

In addition to these reasons for choosing animals, animals allow you to exert greater control over environmental conditions (both within the experiment and in the living conditions of the animal). Such control may be necessary to ensure internal validity. By controlling the environment, you can eliminate extraneous, possibly confounding, variables. By using animal subjects, you also have control over the genetic or biological characteristics of your subjects. If you wanted to replicate an experiment that used Long-Evans rats, you could acquire your animals from the same source who supplied them to the author of the original study. Finally, animal subjects are convenient. Once you acquire them, they will always be available and ready for you to use.

How to Acquire Animals for Research

After you have decided to use animals and have chosen which animals you are going to use, your next step is to acquire the animals. Two methods for acquiring animals are acceptable. First, your institution may maintain a breeding colony. Second, you may use one of the many reliable and reputable breeding farms that specialize in raising animals for research.

Each method has advantages and disadvantages. The on-site colony is convenient, but the usefulness of these animals may be limited. The conditions under which they were bred and housed may cause them to react in idiosyncratic ways to experimental manipulations. Thus you cannot be sure that the results you produce with on-site animals will be the same as the results that would be obtained had you used animals from a breeding farm.

One advantage to using animals from a breeding farm is that you can be reasonably sure of the history of the animals. These farms specialize in breeding animals for research purposes. The animals are bred and housed under controlled conditions, ensuring a degree of uniformity across the animals. However, animals of the same strain obtained from different breeding farms may differ significantly. For example, Sprague-Dawley rats obtained from different breeders may differ in subtle characteristics such as reactivity to stimuli. These differences may affect the results of some experiments.

Table 5-5. Principle 10 of the APA Code of Ethics: Care and Use of Animals

---

An investigator of animal behavior strives to advance understanding of basic behavioral principles and/or to contribute to the improvement of human health and welfare. In seeking these ends, the investigator ensures the welfare of animals and treats them humanely. Laws and regulations notwithstanding, an animal's immediate protection depends upon the scientist's own conscience.

a. The acquisition, care, use, and disposal of all animals are in compliance with current federal, state or provincial, and local laws and regulations.

b. A psychologist trained in research methods and experienced in the care of laboratory animals closely supervises all procedures involving animals and is responsible for ensuring appropriate consideration of their comfort, health, and humane treatment.

c. Psychologists ensure that all individuals using animals under their supervision have received explicit instruction in experimental methods and in the care, maintenance, and handling of the species being used. Responsibilities and activities of individuals participating in a research project are consistent with their respective competencies.

d. Psychologists make every effort to minimize discomfort, illness, and pain of animals. A procedure subjecting animals to pain, stress, or privation is used only when an alternative procedure is unavailable and the goal is justified by its prospective scientific, educational, or applied value. Surgical procedures are performed under appropriate anesthesia; techniques to avoid infection and minimize pain are followed during and after surgery.

e. When it is appropriate that the animal's life be terminated, it is done rapidly and painlessly.

SOURCE: American Psychological Association, 1990, p. 395.

Ethical Considerations

One advantage of using animals in research is that you can carry out manipulations that are not ethically permissible with human subjects. Does this mean that if you use animals in your research you have a free hand to do anything you please? The answer is no. If you use animals in research, you are bound by a code of ethics, just as when you use human subjects. This ethical code specifies how animals may be treated, housed, and disposed of after use. Table 5-5 presents **Principle 10 of the "Ethical Principles of Psychologists."**

This principle makes it clear that if you use animals in your research you must follow all applicable laws and closely supervise all procedures involving animals, including procedures carried out by laboratory assistants. It also makes clear your responsibility to minimize discomfort, illness, and pain of the animals, and you should use painful procedures only if alternatives are not available.

Finally, keep in mind that ethical treatment of animals is in your best interest as a researcher. Ample evidence shows that mistreatment of animals (such as rough handling or housing them under stressful conditions) leads to physiological changes (for example, housing animals under crowded conditions leads to changes in the adrenal glands). These physiological changes may interact with your experimental manipulations, perhaps damaging the external validity of your results. Proper care and handling of your subjects helps you to obtain reliable and generalizable results. Thus, it is to your benefit to treat animals properly.

Should the Research Be Done?

Even though a study is designed to conform to ethical standards for the use of animal subjects—giving proper care and housing, avoiding unnecessary pain or hardship, and so on—this does not automatically mean that the study should be done. Your decision to go ahead with the study should be based on a critical evaluation of the cost of the study to the subjects weighed against its potential benefits, otherwise known as the *cost-benefit ratio*. Cost to the subjects includes such factors as the stressfulness of the procedures and the likely degree of discomfort or suffering the subjects may experience as a result of the study's procedures. The potential benefits of the study include the study's possible contribution to knowledge about the determinants of behavior, its ability to discriminate among competing theoretical views, or its possible applied value in the real world.

Conducting an unbiased evaluation is not easy. Having designed the study, you have a certain vested interest in carrying it out and must guard against this bias. On the other side of the coin, if you reject a study because its potential findings do not have obvious practical application, you may be tossing out research that would have provided key insights necessary for the development of such applications. The history of science is littered with research findings whose immense value was not recognized at the time they were announced.

Despite these difficulties, in most cases it is possible to come up with a reasonable assessment of the potential cost-benefit ratio of your study. For example, imagine you have designed a study to evaluate the antianxiety effect of a certain drug (para-methyl-doublefloop). You have no particular reason to believe that it has any effect on anxiety; in fact, its chemical structure argues against such an effect. However, you have a sample of the drug, and you're curious. Your subjects (rats) will have to endure a procedure involving water deprivation and exposure to foot shock in order for you to assess the effect of the drug. Given that the cost in stress and discomfort to the rats is not balanced against any credible rationale for conducting the study, you should shelve the study.

Generality of Animal Research Data

One criticism of animal research is that the results may not generalize to humans, or even to other animal species. This criticism has at its core a basic assumption: all psychological research must be applicable to humans. However, psychology is not concerned only with human behavior. Many research psychologists are interested in exploring the parameters of animal behavior, with little or no eye toward making statements about human behavior.

Much animal research does, in fact, generalize to humans. The basic laws of classical and operant conditioning, which were discovered through animal research, have been found to apply to human behavior. Figure 5-5 shows a comparison between two extinction curves. Panel A shows a typical extinction curve generated by an animal in an operant chamber after reinforcement of a response has been withdrawn. Panel B shows the extinction curve generated when a parent stops reinforcing a child's crying at bedtime (Williams, 1959). Notice the similarities. Other examples can also be cited. The effects of alcohol on prenatal development have been studied extensively with rats and mice. The pattern of malformations found in the animal research is highly similar to the pattern observed in the offspring of alcoholic mothers.

Although results from animal studies often do generalize to humans, such generalization should always be done with caution, as the following example illustrates. In the 1950s many pregnant women (mainly in Sweden) took the drug thalidomide to help reduce morning sickness. Some of the mothers who took thalidomide gave birth to children with a gross physical defect called *phocomelia*. A child with this defect might be born without legs and have feet attached directly to the lower body. Tests were conducted on rats to determine whether thalidomide was the cause for the malformations. No abnormalities were found among the rats. However, the malformations were found when animals more closely related to humans (monkeys) were used.

Of course, whether results obtained with animal subjects can be applied to humans is an empirical question that can be answered through further research. If the findings do have relevance to human behavior, then so much the better. Even if they do not, we gain a better understanding of the factors that differentiate humans from other animals and of the limits to our behavioral laws.

The Animal Rights Movement

Concern for how animals are treated is not new. Organizations such as the Humane Society and the Society for the Prevention of Cruelty to Animals (SPCA) have existed for many years. Recently, the concern over treatment of animals in a variety of areas (farming, research, and so forth) has become more visible. People have begun to seriously question the use of animals in research. Many people have taken the position that the role of the animal in research should be reduced. Some have even advocated completely banning the use of animals as subjects in research.

The degree of reduction being advocated varies from a total ban on using animals to simply ensuring that researchers treat their animals ethically. The remainder of this chapter is devoted to exploring the issues surrounding the arguments made against using animals in research. The intention of this discussion is to present the arguments made by both sides and then analyze them critically. The final judgment about the role of animals in research is left to you.

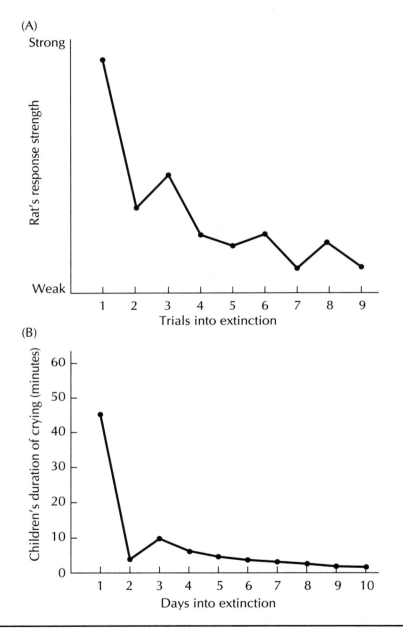

Figure 5-5. Comparison of extinction curves for (A) a rat's lever-pressing behavior and (B) a child's crying at bedtime. (Panel B, from Williams, 1959; reprinted with permission.)

Singer (1975), in a book devoted exclusively to the treatment of animals, raised several objections to using animals in a variety of capacities (from research subject to food). This discussion is limited to the issue of using animals in research. Singer maintained that animals should not be used in research that causes them to suffer. Singer argued that it is "species-ist" (setting our own species above other animal species) to use animals in research that would not be done with human subjects. Singer further argued that "most animal studies published are trivial anyway" (p. 227). To support his point, Singer provided a litany of research examples that subjected animals to sometimes painful procedures. According to Singer, the suffering of the animals was not justified given the trivial nature of the research question and results. Consider an example that Singer provided (a critical analysis of Singer's assertions follows):

> . . . P. [Badia], S. Culbertson, and J. Harsh of Bowling Green State University, Ohio, tested whether a signal warning the rats when they were going to receive an electric shock made a difference to the severity of punishment. They used ten rats. Electric current was again delivered to the rats' feet through a grid on the floor. The test sessions were six hours long and frequent shock was "at all times unavoidable and inescapable." The rats could press either of two levers within the test chamber in order to receive warning of a coming shock. The experimenters concluded that rats preferred to be warned of a shock even when the warning signal led to a longer and stronger punishment. (p. 35)

This and several other summaries like it are included in Singer's book to point out the trivial nature of the research results obtained at the expense of animal suffering. If you had read only Singer's book, you would probably come away with the feeling that "everyone already knows that rats will prefer a warning." Singer can be criticized on at least two grounds concerning the brief research summaries.

First, each of the summaries referred to research that was taken out of the theoretical, empirical, or applied context in which the research was originally conducted. By isolating a study from its scientific context, Singer made the research appear trivial. You could take just about any piece of research and trivialize it by removing it from its context. In fact, Badia's study (summarized in the preceding excerpt) provided important information about how organisms react to stress. To gain a full understanding of the purposes of research, you *must* read the original paper (as pointed out in Chapter 2). In the introduction to the paper, the author will surely provide the theoretical context and potential importance of the research.

Second, Singer's presentation of the research strongly suggested that the research was unnecessary because the findings were already obvious and known. Singer committed what social psychologists call the "I-knew-it-all-along phenomenon" (Myers, 1983). The "I-knew-it-all-along phenomenon" refers to the fact that when you hear about some research results you have the tendency to believe that you already knew that the reported relationship exists. Several researchers (Slovic & Fischoff, 1977; Wood, 1979) have shown that when subjects are asked to predict the outcome of research *before* they hear the results, they fail. However, when the results are known, they are not surprised. You can demonstrate this for yourself with the following experiment suggested by Bolt and Myers (1983).

Choose ten subjects for this demonstration. Provide half of them with the following statement:

> Social psychologists have found that the adage "Out of sight, out of mind" is valid.

Provide the other half with this statement:

> Social psychologists have found that the adage "Absence makes the heart grow fonder" is valid.

Ask subjects to indicate whether they are surprised by the finding. You should find that your subjects are not surprised by the finding reported to them. Next, have subjects write a brief paragraph explaining why they believe the statement to be true. You should find that, in addition to believing that the statement is true, subjects will be able to justify the reported finding.

The point of this exercise is that when you are told about the results of research, they often seem obvious. Singer played on this tendency (probably inadvertently) when he presented results from animal studies and then implied that "we knew it all along." In fact, before the research was done we probably did not know it all along. The research reported by Singer made valuable contributions to science. Taking it out of context and suggesting that the results were obvious leads to the illusion that the research was trivial.

Not all the points made by Singer are invalid. In fact, researchers should treat their animals in a humane fashion. However, you must consider the "cost-benefit" ratio when evaluating animal research. Is the cost to the subject outweighed by the benefits of the research? Some people within the animal rights movement place a high value on the cost factor and a low value on the benefit factor. You must consider the benefits of the research that you plan to do on several levels: theoretical, empirical, and applied. In many cases, the benefits derived from the research outweigh the costs to the subjects.

Alternatives to Animals in Research: *In Vitro* Methods and Computer Simulation

Animal rights activists point out that viable alternatives to using living animals in research (known as *in vivo* methods) exist, two of which are *in vitro* methods and computer simulations. These methods are more applicable to biological and medical research than to behavioral research. *In vitro* (which means "in glass") methods substitute isolated tissue cultures for whole, living animals. Experiments using this method have been performed to test the toxicity and mutagenicity of various chemicals and drugs on living tissue. *Computer simulations* have also been suggested as an alternative to using living organisms in research. In a computer simulation study, a mathematical model of the process to be simulated is programmed into the computer. Parameters and data concerning variables fed into a computer then indicate what patterns of behavior would develop according to the model.

Several problems with *in vitro* and computer simulation methods preclude them from being substitutes for psychological research on living organisms. In drug studies, for example, *in vitro* methods may be adequate in the early stages of testing. However, the only way to determine the drug's effects on behavior is to test the drug on living, behaving animals. At present the behavioral or psychological effects of these chemical agents cannot be predicted by the reactions of tissue samples or the results of computer simulations. Behavioral systems are simply too complex for that. Would you feel confident taking a new tranquilizer that had only been tested on tissues in a petri dish?

The effects of environmental variables and manipulations of the brain also cannot be studied using *in vitro* methods. It is necessary to have a living organism. For example, if you were interested in determining how a particular part of the brain affects aggression, you would not be able to study this problem with an *in vitro* method. You would need an intact organism (such as a rat) to systematically manipulate the brain and observe behavioral changes.

A different problem arises with computer simulation. You need enough information to write the simulation, and this information can only be obtained by observing and testing live, intact animals. Even when a model has been developed, behavioral research on animals is necessary to determine whether the model correctly predicts behavior. Far from eliminating the need for animals in behavioral research, developing and testing computer simulations actually increases this need.

In short, there are really no viable alternatives to using animals in behavioral research. Ultimately, it is up to you to be sure that the techniques you use do not cause the animals undue suffering. Always be aware of your responsibility to treat your animal subjects ethically and humanely. If you treat animals ethically, you are justified in conducting your research, even if it causes the animal a degree of suffering.

Summary

You need to decide on your subject population when you decide to conduct research. Two choices available in behavioral research are human and animal subjects. Your decision about which to use depends on your research question and any special needs of your research.

Using subjects involves selecting an appropriate population of individuals. Because you cannot run every subject in the population (especially when that population is very large), you must select a sample of subjects for inclusion in your study. One goal of your study should be to generalize from your sample to the larger population. This is only possible if the characteristics of your sample match closely the characteristics of the population. Much research in psychology has used college students as the subject sample. Whether the results from such research generalize to the wider population is a subject of debate among researchers.

Precisely how you acquire human subjects for your research depends on two factors: the policies of the institution where the research is being conducted and the nature of the research strategy. Some institutions have subject pools consisting of a population of individuals (such as introductory psychology students) who are available as subjects. Subjects in this pool may be offered extra credit or other incentives for their voluntary participation in research. If no subject pool exists, you will have to recruit subjects on your own. Acquiring subjects for laboratory research can be done through a subject pool. However, subjects for field research cannot be acquired that way.

You must consider the ethics of your research when human subjects are chosen for study. Concern over the ethical treatment of subjects can be traced back to the Nuremberg trials after World War II. During those trials medical experiments conducted on inmates in concentration camps came to light. Because of the treatment of individuals in those experiments, the Nuremberg Code was developed to govern experiments with humans. The APA developed a code of ethics for treatment of human subjects in research that is based on the Nuremberg Code. Ethical treatment of subjects in an experiment requires voluntary participation, informed consent, the right to withdraw, the right to obtain results, and the right to confidentiality (among others).

Sometimes ethical treatment of subjects comes into conflict with research methodology. The requirement of voluntary participation and full disclosure of the methods of your research may lead to problems. For example, individuals who volunteer have been found to differ from nonvolunteers in several ways. This volunteer bias represents a threat to both internal and external validity. It can be counteracted to some extent by careful subject recruitment procedures. In cases where you must use a deceptive technique, take special care to ensure that your subjects leave your experiment in the proper frame of mind. You can accomplish this through effective debriefing techniques. At all times, however, you must remain cognizant of the ethical problems with deception even if debriefing is used.

A large amount of psychological research uses animal subjects. Animals are preferred to humans in situations where experimental manipulations are unethical for use with humans. However, if you use animal subjects, you are still bound by an ethical code. Animals must be treated humanely. It is to your advantage to treat your animals ethically, because research shows that mistreated animals may yield data that is invalid.

Alternatives to using animals in research have been proposed, including the use of *in vitro* testing and computer simulation. These alternatives unfortunately are not viable for behavioral research, where the goal is to understand the influences of variables on the behavior of the intact, living animals.

Key Terms

Population

Sample

Generalization

Random sample

Principle 9 of the "Ethical Principles of Psychologists"

Institutional review board (IRB)

Volunteer bias

Deception

Role playing

Debriefing

Principle 10 of the "Ethical Principles of Psychologists"

6

Using Nonexperimental, Quasi-Experimental, and Developmental Designs

CHAPTER 3 DESCRIBED CORRELATIONAL RESEARCH which involves observation of variables as they exist in nature. This chapter introduces you to research designs that follow the correlational research strategy, including naturalistic observation, participant observation, the case history, archival research, quasi-experimental designs, and developmental designs.

Conducting Observational Research

Although all research is observational (in the sense that variables are observed and recorded), the observational research designs described in this chapter are purely observational in two senses: (1) they are correlational designs and thus do not involve manipulation of variables, and (2) all use trained observers to code subjects' behaviors. This section describes how to make and assess behavioral observations. We begin by showing you how to develop behavioral categories.

Developing Behavioral Categories

The first step when planning a study that includes direct behavioral observations is to develop **behavioral categories** (also referred to as "coding schemes" or in animal research as "ethograms"). Behavioral categories consist of the general and specific classes of behavior you are interested in observing. For example, general behavioral categories in a study of children's free play might include positive social interaction, aggressive behavior, rule-oriented games, same-sex play, and mixed-sex play. Under each general category, you could have specific subcategories. For example, under "mixed-sex" play you might record whether the games are male or female oriented.

Developing behavioral categories can be a simple or formidable task. For example, recording physical characteristics of the subject is a relatively simple affair (Bakeman & Gottman, 1989). However, when recording social behaviors, defining behavioral categories becomes more difficult (Bakeman & Gottman, 1989). This is because coding "socially based" behaviors may involve cultural traditions that are not agreed on (for example, coding vocalizations as "obscene"—Bakeman & Gottman, 1989).

Your behavioral categories define what behaviors should be recorded during observation periods. Make sure your categories are clearly defined. Your observers should not be left wondering what category a particular behavior falls into. Ill-defined and ambiguous categories lead to recording errors and results that are difficult to interpret.

To develop clear, well-defined categories, begin with a clear idea about the goals of your study. Clearly defined hypotheses help narrow your behavioral categories to those that are central to your research questions. Also, keep your behavioral categories as simple as possible (Bakeman & Gottman, 1989), and stay focused on your research objectives. Avoid the temptation to accomplish too much within a single study.

To help clearly define behavioral categories, a good idea is to make some informal, preliminary observations of your subjects under the conditions that will prevail during your study. During these preliminary observation periods, become familiar with the behaviors exhibited by your subjects and construct as complete a list of them as you can. Later you can condense these behaviors into fewer categories, if necessary.

Another way to develop behavioral categories is to conduct a literature search to determine how other researchers in your field define behavioral categories in research situations similar to your own. You might even find an article in which the researchers used categories that are nearly perfect for your study. Adapting someone else's categories for your own use is an acceptable practice. In fact, standardizing on categories used in previous research will enhance the comparability of your data with data previously reported.

Even if you do find an article with what appear to be the "perfect categories," make some preliminary observations to be sure the categories fit your research needs. Take the time necessary to develop your categories carefully. In the long run, it is easier to adjust things before you begin your study than to worry about how to analyze data that were collected using poorly defined categories.

Quantifying Behavior in an Observational Study

As with any other type of measure, direct behavioral observation requires that you develop ways to quantify the behaviors under observation. Methods used to quantify behavior in observational studies include the frequency method, the duration method, and the intervals method (Badia & Runyon, 1982).

Frequency Method. With the *frequency method,* you record the frequency with which a behavior occurs. For example, you can count the number of times a particular behavior occurs within the time period. Instead of just noting that a behavior occurs within a time period, record the number of times it occurs.

Duration Method. With the *duration method,* your interest is in how long a particular behavior lasts. For example, you could record the duration of each aggressive act displayed by children during free play. This method can be used along with the frequency method. In this case, you record both the frequency of occurrence of a behavior and its duration.

Intervals Method. With the *intervals method,* you divide your observation period into discrete time intervals (two-minute intervals, for example) and then record whether a behavior occurs within each interval. For example, you might record whether an aggressive act occurs during successive two-minute time periods. Ideally, your intervals should be short enough that only one instance of a behavior would normally occur during an interval.

Recording Single Events or Behavior Sequences

Researchers doing observational studies have long recorded single events occurring within some identifiable observation period. Recently, however, Bakeman and Gottman (1989) advocated looking at *behavior sequences* rather than at isolated behavioral events. As an example, consider an observational study of language development in which you record the number of times a parent uses language to correct a child's behavior. Although such data may be informative, a better strategy might be to record those same behaviors sequentially, noting which instances of language use normally follow one another. Recording such behavior sequences provides a more complete picture of complex social behaviors and the transitions between them.

Although recording behavior sequences requires more effort than recording single events, the richness of the resulting data may be well worth the effort. You can find more information about this method in Bakeman and Gottman, *Observing Interaction: An Introduction to Sequential Analysis* (1989).

Coping with Complexity

When you have defined your behavioral categories and settled on a method of quantifying behavior, you next must decide how to make your observations. Defining discrete time intervals during which behavior is to be recorded is easy enough, but to actually record the observations is another matter. Take the example of observing the free-play behavior of preschool children.

Assume that you have clearly defined your behavioral categories and have decided to use the frequency method to quantify behavior. On Monday at 8 A.M. you arrive at the preschool classroom where you intend to make your observations. Fourteen children are in the class. You sit in an observation room equipped with a one-way mirror and begin to observe the children in the classroom on the other side of the mirror. It doesn't take you long to realize that something is wrong. Your subjects are running around in small groups, scurrying hither and yon. You cannot possibly observe all the children at once. Dejectedly, you leave the day care center and return to your office to try to work out an effective observation strategy.

This vignette illustrates an important fact about behavioral observation: having clearly defined behavioral categories and adequate quantification methods does not guarantee that your observational techniques will work. Naturally occurring behavior is often complex and fast paced. To make effective observations, you may need to use special techniques to deal with the rate at which the behaviors you wish to observe occur.

One solution to the problem is to sample the behaviors under observation rather than attempting to record every occurrence. Three sampling techniques to choose from are time sampling, individual sampling, and event sampling (Conrad & Maul, 1981).

Time Sampling. With time sampling, you scan the group for a specific period of time (for example, 30 seconds) and then record the observed behaviors for the next period (for example, another 30 seconds). Then alternate between periods of observation and recording as long as necessary. Time sampling is most appropriate when behavior occurs continuously rather than in short bursts spaced over time, and when you are observing large groups of subjects engaged in complex interactions.

Individual Sampling. With individual sampling, you select a single subject for observation over a given time period (for example, 10 minutes) and record his or her behavior. Over successive time periods, you repeat your observations for the other individuals in the observed group. Individual sampling is most appropriate when you want to preserve the organization of an individual's behavior over time rather than simply noting how often particular behaviors occur.

Event Sampling. In event sampling, you observe only one behavior (for example, sharing behavior) and record all instances of that behavior. Event sampling is most useful when you can clearly define one behavior as more important than others and focus on that one behavior.

Recording. You could also use recording devices to make a permanent record of behavior for later analysis. For example, a video recorder could be used to record the free play of children in a day care center. Later you could watch the tape, slowing down the action or backing up the tape where necessary to count specific behaviors.

Recording equipment has several advantages. First, because you have a permanent record you can review your subjects' behavior several times, perhaps picking up nuances of behavior that would have been missed in a single, live observation. Second, you can have multiple observers watch the tape independently and then compare their evaluations of behavior. (Although you can use multiple observers for live observations, it may be disruptive to your subjects to have several observers watching.) Finally, you may be able to hide a camera more easily than you can hide yourself. The hidden camera may be less disruptive to your subjects' behavior than an observer.

Recording behavior on film or tape does not eliminate the need to classify the behaviors and to measure such aspects of the behaviors as frequencies and durations. Whether you perform these activities "live" or work from a recording, you will need a system for coding these characteristics.

One option is to develop a paper-and-pencil coding form similar to the one shown in Figure 6-1. Your observers would then use the form to record the behaviors they see. Another option is to have observers speak into a hand-held tape recorder.

Which of these two options you choose depends on the nature of your study and limitations inherent in the situation. Paper-and-pencil coding sheets can be used in just about any situation. They are quiet and, if properly constructed, efficient. They do have a few drawbacks, however. If you are requiring your observers to make extensive notes (not just checking behavioral categories), the task may become too complex and time-consuming, especially if behaviors occur in rapid succession.

In such cases you might consider having your observers use tape recorders instead of paper-and-pencil coding forms. The main advantage with this technique is that your observers will probably be able to speak into the recorder faster than they could make written notes. They can also keep their eyes on the subjects *while* making their notes. A disadvantage is that observers may disturb your subjects. Consequently, this technique should only be used when your observers are out of earshot of your subjects.

Establishing the Reliability of Your Observations

Assume that by now you have adequately defined the behavior you want to observe, developed a coding sheet, and worked out how you are going to observe behavior. Then you go into the field and begin making your observations. You come back with reams of data-coding sheets in hand and begin to summarize and interpret your data. You have apparently covered every possible base, and your observations accurately portray the observed behavior. But do they? Your observations may not be as accurate as you think. Your personal biases and expectations may have affected how you recorded the behavior observed. As with any measurement technique, when you conduct direct behavioral observations, you should make an effort to establish the reliability of your observations.

If you were the only observer, you could not firmly establish the reliability of your observations. To avoid the problem of single-observer idiosyncrasies,

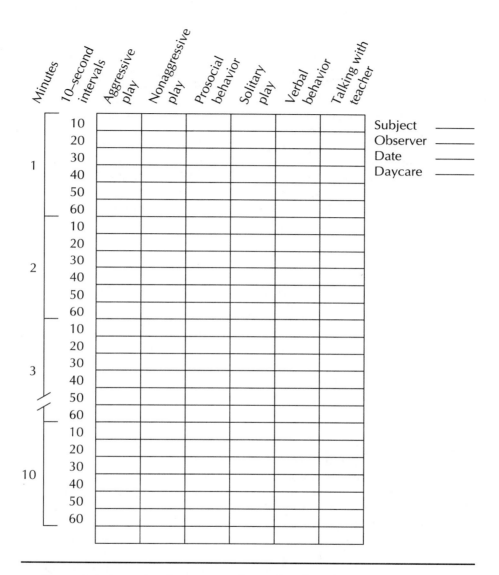

Figure 6-1. Example of a paper-and-pencil coding sheet for an observational study.

you should use multiple observers: two or more trained observers make observations and record behavior. This practice is generally preferred over single-observer methods.

If you decide to use multiple observers, you face the possibility that your observers will not agree on how to code behavior. Theoretically, if you use well-trained observers and well-defined behavior categories there should be a minimum of disagreement. However, disagreement is likely to arise despite your best efforts. Observers invariably differ in how they see and interpret behavior. Disagreement may also arise if your behavioral categories are not clearly defined. Because disagreement is likely to occur to one degree or another, you must establish **interrater reliability,** which provides an empirical index of observer agreement.

Bakeman and Gottman (1989) pointed out that there are three reasons to check for interrater reliability. First, establishing interrater reliability helps ensure that your observers are accurate and that your procedures can be easily reproduced. Second, you can check to see that your observers meet some standard you have established. Third, any problems detected can be corrected with additional training.

Cohen's Kappa

The most commonly used method to establish interrater reliability is to determine the degree to which your observers agree with one another. The preferred statistic is *Cohen's Kappa* (Bakeman & Gottman, 1989). To use this method, you need to determine (1) the proportion of actual agreement between observers (actual agreement) and (2) the proportion of agreement you would expect by chance (expected agreement). These two values are used in the following formula (Bakeman & Gottman, 1989):

$$K = \frac{P_o - P_c}{1 - P_c}$$

where P_o is the observed (o) proportion of actual agreement and P_c is the chance (c) proportion of expected agreement.

Chapter 3 introduced a study done by Belsky and Rovine (1988) on the relationship between (1) the number of hours an infant spent in day care and (2) attachment security. Assume you conducted a similar study. As your measure of attachment security, you have two observers watch a mother and her child for a 20-minute period. The coding scheme here is simple. All your observers are required to do is code the child's behavior as either indicative of a "secure attachment" or an "insecure attachment" within each of twenty 1-minute observation periods. Sample coding sheets are shown in Figure 6-2. A "1" in a cell indicates that the behavior of the subject fell into that category.

The first step in computing Cohen's Kappa is to tabulate the frequencies of agreement and disagreement between observers in a *confusion matrix* (Bakeman & Gottman, 1989). An agreement occurs whenever *both* observers classify behavior in the same way. In this example, we simply count the number of times both observers coded behavior as secure or insecure and the number of times one observer coded behavior one way and the other observer coded it the other way. A confusion matrix for the sample data is shown in Figure 6-3. The numbers on the diagonal (the "diagonal" begins with the upper left cell and ends

Observation period	Observer 1 Secure	Observer 1 Insecure	Observer 2 Secure	Observer 2 Insecure
1	I		I	
2	I		I	
3	I		I	
4	I		I	
5		I		I
6	I		I	
7	I			I
8		I		I
9		I		I
10	I		I	
11	I		I	
12	I		I	
13	I		I	
14	I		I	
15	I		I	
16	I		I	
17	I		I	
18	I		I	
19	I		I	
20	I		I	

Figure 6-2. Sample coding sheets for two observers counting "secure" and "insecure" behavior instances.

with the lower right) represent agreements and the numbers off the diagonal represent disagreements.

The next step is to compute the value of Cohen's Kappa (K). First you determine the proportion of actual agreement by summing the values along the diagonal and dividing by the total number of observations.

$$P_o = \frac{16 + 3}{20} = .95$$

Next you find the proportion of expected agreement by multiplying corresponding row and column totals and dividing by the number of observations squared (Bakeman & Gottman, 1989):

$$P_c = \frac{(17 \times 16) + (3 \times 4)}{20^2} = .71$$

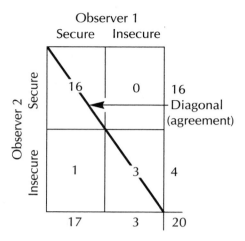

Figure 6-3. Sample confusion matrix.

Finally, enter these numbers into the formula for Cohen's Kappa:

$$K = \frac{.95 - .71}{1 - .71} = .83$$

At this point you have computed a reliability score of .83. What does this number mean? Is this good or bad? Although there is a way to determine the statistical significance of K, the procedure is complicated (see Bakeman & Gottman, 1989, Chapter 4, for a complete discussion). A broad rule of thumb can be used instead: according to Bakeman and Gottman, any value of .7 or greater indicates acceptable reliability.

Pearson's Product Moment Correlation

Pearson's product moment correlation coefficient (Pearson r, see Chapter 11) provides a convenient alternative to Cohen's Kappa for assessing interrater reliability. Pearson r is readily available in virtually all computerized statistical packages and on many scientific calculators. Table 6-1 shows the frequency of aggressive behavior among members of a monkey colony over five 2-minute observation periods, as recorded by two observers (hypothetical data). If the observers agree, then the correlation coefficient will be high. If they disagree, it will be low or possibly negative. For the data in Table 6-1, Pearson r is .90. This is a high correlation (the maximum possible is 1.0), indicating substantial agreement.

Table 6-1. Hypothetical Monkey Aggression Data Collected by Two Observers

OBSERVATION PERIOD	FREQUENCY OF AGGRESSIVE BEHAVIOR	
	Observer 1	Observer 2
One	6	7
Two	2	4
Three	1	0
Four	5	7
Five	3	2

You can easily evaluate Pearson r for statistical significance, an advantage over Cohen's Kappa. However, you must be cautious when using Pearson r to establish interrater reliability. Two sets of numbers can be highly correlated even when observers rarely agree. This situation occurs when the *magnitudes* of the recorded scores increase and decrease similarly across observations by the two observers, but differ in absolute value. For example, assume Observer 1 recorded 1, 2, 3, 4, and 5, and Observer 2 recorded 6, 7, 8, 9, and 10 over the same intervals. These numbers are perfectly correlated ($r = 1.00$), yet the two observers never agreed on the actual numbers to be recorded.

You can check for this problem by conducting a between–subjects t-test on the data (see Chapter 12). If the average frequencies for the two observers does not differ significantly and Pearson r is high, you can safely conclude that your observers agreed.

Dealing with Data from Multiple Observers

It is highly unlikely that your multiple observers will always agree. When they disagree, what do you do? If you have a very high level of agreement, you can average across observers. For example, in Table 6-1 you can average across observers within each observation period to get a mean, or M (for the first period, $M = (6 + 7)/2 = 6.5$) and then obtain an overall average across observation period. This gives you the average aggression shown during the observation period.

Another method commonly used is to designate one of the observers as the "main observer" and the other as the "secondary observer." This designation should be made before beginning your observations. The observations from the "main observer" then serve as the numbers used in any data analyses. The observations from the "secondary observer" are only used to establish reliability.

Sources of Bias in Observational Research

Observational research is a human endeavor. Observers (you included) will be making instantaneous decisions about how to interpret and record observed behaviors. So a degree of bias may contaminate the observations.

One source of bias that can easily be avoided is *observer bias*. Observer bias occurs when your observers know the goals of a study or the hypotheses being tested, and their observations are influenced by this information. For example, suppose you have hypothesized that more interpersonal aggression will be shown by males than females, and that you have told your observers of this hypothesis. Suppose that your observer sees a male child roughly take a toy away from another child and later sees a female child do precisely the same thing. Because of observer bias, your observer may code the male child's behavior, but not the female child's, as aggressive. This is the same problem discussed in Chapter 4 as experimenter bias, and the solution is the same: use a *blind observer*. A blind observer is one who is unaware of the hypotheses under test. (For more details about blind techniques, see Chapter 4.)

Another source of bias in observational research arises when observers interpret what they see rather than simply record behavior. We have all seen nature specials on television where a researcher is observing animals in the wild (chimpanzees, for example). Too often those researchers infer intentions behind the behaviors they observe. When one chimp prods another with a stick, for example, the behavior may be recorded as a "playful, mischievous attack."

The problem with such inferences is that we simply do not know whether they are correct. We tend to read into the behaviors of animals the motivations and emotions we ourselves would likely experience in similar situations. But the animal's motivations and emotions may, in fact, be very different from ours. Stick to what is immediately apparent from the observation. If you have preserved the actual behavior in your records rather than your interpretation of the behavior, you can always provide an interpretation later. If new evidence suggests a new interpretation, you still have the original behavioral observations to reinterpret.

When your subjects are people, you should still do your best to record behaviors rather than your interpretations of those behaviors. Piaget showed that inferences concerning the motivation and knowledge of children are often wrong, and the same is probably true of inferences about adults. Once again, if your data preserve the behavior rather than your interpretations of the behavior, you can always reinterpret your data later if this is required by new evidence.

Now that you know how to go about developing and using direct behavioral measures, it is time to become familiar with nonexperimental and quasi-experimental approaches to data collection.

Naturalistic Observation

Naturalistic observation (also sometimes called *nonparticipant observation*) involves observing your subjects in their natural environments, without making any attempt to control or manipulate variables. For example, you may want to observe chimpanzees in Africa, children in a day care center, Christmas shoppers in a mall, or participants in a court proceeding. In all these cases, you would avoid making any changes in the situation that might affect the natural, ongoing behaviors of your subjects.

Making Unobtrusive Observations

Although you may not intend it, even the act of observing may disturb the behavior of your subjects. Such disturbances may disrupt the external validity of your observations. To prevent this difficulty, you should make *unobtrusive observations,* or observations that do not alter the natural behaviors of your subjects.

Translating this requirement into practice may take considerable effort. If you are interested in studying the nesting habits of a particular species of birds, for example, you may have to build a blind (an enclosure that shields you from the view of your subjects) from which to make your observations. If you are interested in studying social interactions among preschool children in a day care center, you may have to make your observations from behind a one-way mirror. In either case, you want to prevent your subjects from knowing that they are being observed.

Unfortunately, it is not always possible to remain unobtrusive. For example, the day care center at which you will be making your observations may not be equipped with a one-way mirror, or you may need to be closer to your subjects than a blind or observation room allows. In such cases, your presence may disrupt the behavior of your subjects. Fortunately, you can take some steps to soften the impact of your presence.

A widely used technique is to habituate your subjects to your presence (a fancy way of saying "letting your subjects get used to you") before you begin making your observations. Habituating subjects involves gradually introducing yourself to the environment of your subjects. Eventually your subjects will view your presence as normal and ignore you. If you were interested in observing children in a day care center, for example, you might begin by sitting quietly away from the children (perhaps in a far corner of the room) until the children no longer paid attention to you. Gradually you would move closer to the children, allowing them to habituate to your presence at each step before moving closer.

Habituation may be necessary even if you are going to videotape behavior for later analysis. The presence of a television camera in a room will attract attention at first. Allowing your subjects to habituate to the camera before you begin your observations will help reduce the camera's disruptive effects.

Naturalistic Observation: An Example

An excellent example of naturalistic observation was reported by Humphreys and Smith (1987). These researchers were interested in studying positive interpersonal behaviors among school-age children. An important type of positive interpersonal behavior is "rough-and-tumble" play (mock fighting, chasing, and so forth). Such behavior was the focus of their study. Children from three age groups (7, 9, and 11 years old) were observed during periods of free play in a schoolyard across three separate 6-week intervals. Observers were positioned about 200 yards from the subjects, and sometimes they observed through binoculars. A time-sampling procedure was used in which observations of the children were made and recorded every five minutes. Multiple observers were used; the interrater reliability score was 0.70. Observations were verbally recorded on audio tape as they occurred.

Observed behaviors fell into 59 categories, which were eventually condensed into nine major categories for analysis. Panel A of Figure 6-4 shows the proportions of behavior falling into each of the nine categories, plotted against subject age. Younger children seem to distribute their interpersonal behaviors fairly evenly among the nine categories, whereas older children engage more in rule-governed activities. Panel B shows the results from the observations of rough-and-tumble play as a function of subject age and sex. A sex difference was evident for the 7- and 11-year-old children, but not for the 9-year-old children.

The study by Humphreys and Smith (1987) has all the ingredients of good naturalistic observation. Observed behaviors were carefully defined and recorded, an appropriate behavior-sampling technique was used, and observers remained unobtrusive. Because of the care taken in conducting the study, some interesting facts were uncovered about the nature of children's play. (By the way, only a small portion of the results were addressed here. If you are interested in finding out more about this study, read the original article.)

Advantages and Disadvantages of Naturalistic Observation

Naturalistic observation gives you insight into how behavior occurs in the real world. The observations you make are not tainted by an artificial laboratory setting, and you can therefore be reasonably sure your observations are representative of naturally occurring behavior. In other words, properly conducted naturalistic observation has extremely high external validity.

However, because naturalistic observation is a purely descriptive technique, you can only speculate about the causes of behavior. You cannot prove that the observed relationships are causally related. In addition, naturalistic observation can be time-consuming and expensive. Unlike other types of observation in which subjects in effect record their own data, naturalistic observation requires

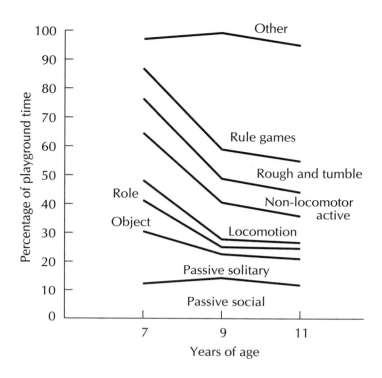

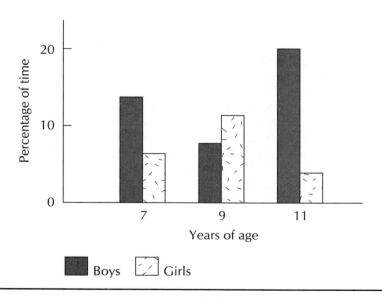

Figure 6-4. Figures showing results from naturalistic observation of child's play. (A) The percent of time spent by children of different age groups in each of the nine major behavioral categories. (B) The frequency of rough-and-tumble play as a function of age and sex of the child. (Humphreys & Smith, 1987, p. 204; reprinted with permission.)

you to be there, engaged in observation, during the entire data-collecting period. Data collection in such studies may last hours, days, or longer. Also, getting to the natural habitat of your subjects may not be easy. In some cases (such as observing chimpanzee behavior in the wild, as Jane Goodall did), naturalistic observation involves traveling great distances to the habitat of your subjects.

Participant Observation

In naturalistic observation, you remain relatively detached from your subjects and record their behaviors without directly interacting with them. In some cases it may be more desirable to interact with your subjects so that you can obtain a better "view" of the behaviors. For example, a social psychologist might join a club in order to study social interactions. This technique is commonly called **participant observation.** Rather than observing behavior from afar, the researcher becomes an integral part of the observed group.

Participant Observation: An Example

An interesting example of participant observation was provided by Festinger, Riecken, and Schachter (1956/1982). Festinger et al. were interested in the dynamics of groups that make predictions about catastrophic events such as the end of the world. Festinger's research team was interested in studying a group whose members believed the world was to end on a certain day. The researchers convinced the group members that they, too, were believers, and they were able to join the group to observe its workings from the inside. The researchers made careful observations of the group's behavior before the day on which the world was to end and then, when the prophecy failed, continued to observe afterward. Contrary to what you might expect, the members' commitments to their beliefs actually *increased* after the prophecy failed. Believing that their prayers had spared the world, the members intensified their efforts to recruit new members to the group.

The study by Festinger et al. could not have obtained the information it did about the dynamics of the group's beliefs if the subjects had been aware they were being observed. By acting as participants in the group, the researchers gained access to information that would not have been volunteered to outsiders.

Advantages and Disadvantages of Participant Observation

An advantage of surreptitious participant observation is that your subjects do not know their behaviors are being observed and recorded. Their behaviors remain natural, and therefore the observations are likely to have considerable external validity. In addition, you may be able to get information you could not obtain by observing "from afar."

Surreptitious participant observation also has a number of disadvantages. Among the more important is the fact that the practice is ethically questionable. Because your subjects are not aware they are part of a research study, they cannot give informed consent to participate. As discussed in Chapter 5, such violations may be acceptable if your results promise to make a significant contribution to the understanding of behavior. Thus, before using participant observation, you need to evaluate the potential benefits of your research against the potential costs to the subjects. If you and the IRB agree that your data would be of significant benefit, then the ethical violation may be allowed.

A general problem with participant observation is that interacting directly with subjects presents the possibility that your behavior will alter the behavior of your subjects. If this happens, the behavior you observe may not accurately reflect the natural behavior of the subjects. You can minimize this problem by using a participant observer who is blind to the purposes of the study. Or, if you must assume the role of the observer, you can become a passive participant. As such you would not contribute significantly to the group, but instead merely observe what goes on.

Like naturalistic observation, participant observation is a descriptive technique. That is, your concern is describing behavior and the conditions under which it occurs. Because no controlled manipulation of variables exists, testing specific hypotheses about the factors that control behavior is impossible. However, from observations made during participant observation you may be able to generate hypotheses about the causes of behavior. Later you can test your hypotheses with an experiment.

The Case History

In some instances your research needs may require you to study in depth a single case or just a few cases. The **case history** is a descriptive technique in which you observe and report on a single case (or a few cases). A case is the object of study and can be just about anything. It can be the life of an important person (such as a study of the life of Jean Piaget) or an event (like the panic in the Iroquois Theater).

There are many ways to use case histories. For example, a clinical psychologist might publish a case history of a patient who shows symptoms of a new disorder. You can also use a case history to highlight and support a theory. Freud's famous case study of "Little Hans" (reprinted in Southwell & Merbaum, 1964) is such an example. Freud observed and reported Hans's symptoms and interpreted them in the light of his psychoanalytic theory. Finally, you can use the case history method to contrast two points of view on a particular issue. For example, two cases (each representing an opposing theory) could be contrasted.

Although a case history can be useful, it does not qualify as an experimental design. In fact, a case history is special application of a demonstration (see

Chapter 3). Because you do not manipulate independent variables, you cannot determine the causes of the behavior observed in your case history. You can, of course, speculate about such causes (as Freud did). You can even compare theories by interpreting cases from different perspectives, but you cannot state with any certainty which perspective is superior.

Archival Research

Archival research is another nonexperimental strategy that involves studying existing records. These records can be historical accounts of events, census data, court records, police crime reports, or any other archived information.

When planning archival research, you should have specific research questions in mind. You may find that the archived material contains an overwhelming amount of information. You need to be able to focus on specific aspects of the material. You can only do so if you know what you are looking for, which depends on having clearly defined and focused research hypotheses. In addition, all the factors pertaining to observational research (developing categories, coding sheets, multiple raters, and so on) apply to archival research.

An important practical matter to consider is your need to gain access to the archived material. This may not be easy. Sometimes the records you are interested in are not available to the general public. You may need to obtain special permission to gain access to the archives. In other cases, archival information may be available in libraries or on a computerized data base (the Prosecutor's Management Information System, or PROMIS, for example). Even in these cases you may have to do some homework to find out how to access them.

Another practical matter is the completeness of the records. After gaining access to the archives, you may find that some of the information you wanted is unavailable. For example, if you were interested in studying court records you might find that some information, such as background information on the defendant, is confidential and unavailable to you. In short, archived material may not be complete enough for your purposes. You may need to use multiple sources.

Like the case history method, archival research is purely descriptive. You may be able to identify some interesting trends or correlations based on your archival research. However, you cannot establish causal relationships.

Content Analysis

Content analysis is used when you want to analyze a written or spoken record for the occurrence of specific categories of events (such as pauses in a speech), items (such as negative comments), or behavior (such as factual information offered during group discussion). For example, content analysis could be used to analyze an interview between a therapist and his clients. Assume you have recorded (with permission) the interactions between the therapist and several of his clients. You then listen to these recordings and categorize the interactions into several response categories (that is, number of times the therapist offers advice, number of times the client mentions a relationship with a loved one).

Content analyses have been conducted on a wide range of materials such as mock juror deliberations (Horowitz, 1985), the content of television dramas (Greenberg, 1980), and the content of children's literature (Davis, 1984). In fact, the possible applications of content analysis are limited only by the imagination of the researcher (Holsti, 1969).

Even though a content analysis seems rather simple to do, it can become as complex as any other research technique. Content analysis should be performed within the context of a clearly developed research idea, including specific hypotheses and a sound research design. All the factors that must be considered for observational research (except that of remaining unobtrusive) apply to a content analysis. Response categories must be clearly defined, and a method for quantifying behavior must be developed. In essence, content analysis is an observational technique. However, in content analysis your unit of analysis is some written, visual, or spoken record rather than the behavior of subjects.

Defining Characteristics of Content Analysis

Holsti (1969) pointed out that proper content analysis entails three defining characteristics. First, your content analysis should be objective. Each step of a content analysis should be guided by an explicit, clear set of rules or procedures. You should decide on the rules by which information will be acquired, categorized, and quantified, and then adhere to those rules. You want to eliminate any subjective influence of the analyst. Second, your content analysis should be systematic. Assign information to categories according to whatever rules you developed, and then include as much information as possible in your analysis. For example, if you are doing a content analysis of a body of literature on a particular issue (such as racial attitudes), include articles that are *not* in favor of your position as well as those that are in favor of your position. A content analysis of literature is only as good as the literature search behind it. Third, your content analysis should have generality. That is, your findings should fit within a theoretical, empirical, or applied context. Disconnected facts generated from a content analysis are of little value (Holsti, 1969).

Performing Content Analysis

To ensure that you acquire valid data for your content analysis, you must carefully define the response categories. According to Holsti (1969, p. 95), your categories should reflect the purposes of the research, be exhaustive, be mutually exclusive, be independent, and be derived from one classification system.

The first requirement is the most important (Holsti, 1969): clear operational definitions of terms. Your categories must be clearly defined and remain focused on the research question outlined in your hypotheses. Unclear or poorly defined categories are difficult to use. The categories should be defined with sufficient precision to allow precise categorization. Yet you do not want your categories to be too narrowly defined. You do not want relevant information to be excluded from a category simply because it does not fit an overly restrictive category definition.

Determining what your categories should be and how you should classify information within them is sometimes difficult. Reviewing related research in which a content analysis was used can help you develop and clearly define your categories. You can then add, delete, or expand categories to fit your specific research needs.

Before you begin to develop categories, read (or listen to) the materials to be analyzed. This will familiarize you with the material, help you develop categories, and help you avoid any surprises. That is, you will be less likely to encounter any information that does not fit into any category. Avoid making up categories as you go along.

After developing your categories, you decide on a unit of analysis. The *recording unit* (Holsti, 1969) is the element of the material that you are going to record. The recording unit can be a word (or words), sentences, phrases, themes, and so on. Your recording unit should be relevant to your research question. Also, Holsti points out that defining a recording unit sometimes may not be enough. For example, if you were analyzing content of a jury deliberation, recording the frequency with which the word *defendant* was used might not be sufficient. You might also have to note the *context unit,* or context within which the word was used (Holsti, 1969). Such a context unit gives meaning to the recording unit and may help later when you interpret the data.

Another factor to consider when performing a content analysis is who will do the analysis. Chapter 4 discussed the concept of experimenter bias. If the person performing the content analysis knows the hypotheses of the study, or has a particular point of view, your results could be biased. Consequently, you should use a blind rater, one who does not know the purpose of your study. Also, avoid using raters who have strong feelings or characteristics that could bias the results. If you use more than one rater (and you should), you must evaluate interrater reliability.

Another important thing to remember about content analysis is that the validity of your results will depend on the materials analyzed. Make every effort to obtain relevant materials, be they books, films, or television shows. In many cases it is not feasible to analyze all materials. For example, a content analysis of all children's books is impossible. In such cases, obtain a sample of materials that is representative of the larger population of materials. A content analysis of a biased sample (for example, only children's books written to be nonsexist) may produce biased results.

The results from a content analysis may be interesting in and of themselves. You may discover something interesting concerning the topic under study. Such was the case with Greenberg's (1980) content analysis of prime time television shows aired during fall 1977. Greenberg found that blacks were portrayed as having low-status jobs and athletic physiques, compared to whites.

Limitations of Content Analysis

Content analysis can be a useful technique to help you understand behavior. However, keep in mind that content analysis is purely descriptive. It cannot establish causal relationships among variables.

Another limitation of content analysis centers on the durability of the findings. In some instances, results from a content analysis are invalidated over time. For example, Greenberg's findings about how blacks are portrayed on television are probably no longer valid. Presently blacks are more likely to be portrayed in higher-status roles (for example, doctors, lawyers, and so on) than in the past. Of course, this prediction could be tested with an updated content analysis!

Content Analysis: An Example

As an example of content analysis, consider Davis's (1984) study of sexism in "nonsexist" children's picture books. Davis wanted to find out whether children's books deliberately written to be nonsexist still contained sexist portrayals of males and females. Davis content-analyzed 96 children's books from three categories: nonsexist, award-winning, and best-selling children's picture books. The recording unit in this study was the frequency with which sexist images were portrayed in these books. Davis developed 15 behavioral categories into which portrayals were classified, including independent (self-initiating or self-sustaining behavior), active (physical activity, work, and play), passively active (fine motor physical behavior such as reading, talking, and thinking), and emotional (affective displays of feelings).

Four graduate students content-analyzed the 96 picture books. Two of the graduate students content-analyzed only the illustrations in the books, whereas the other two content-analyzed only the text. Why do you think two graduate students analyzed the illustrations, and two the text? If you said "to establish interrater reliability," you are right. The mean frequencies for the 15 categories, broken down by book category, are shown in Table 6-2.

Davis found that females tended to be portrayed in less stereotyped ways in the books intended to be nonsexist. However, females in those texts were still found to be more nurturant, less physically active, and more emotional than males. Males were portrayed as less aggressive than in traditional books.

Table 6-2. Mean Frequencies of 15 Categories of Behavior Observed in a Content Analysis

| | BOOK CLASS | | | | | |
| | Nonsexist | | Award Winners | | Best-sellers | |
Behavior	Male	Female	Male	Female	Male	Female
Dependent (DEP)	1.86	1.26	.64	1.05	.72	1.09
Independent (IND)	5.16	11.21	5.23	8.10	4.85	8.95
Competitive (COMP)	.26	.15	.15	.00	.02	.00
Cooperative (COOP)	.59	.53	1.67	.29	.27	.00
Directive (DIR)	1.92	2.38	1.61	1.13	2.32	1.76
Submissive (SUB)	.38	.85	.37	.42	.87	.61
Persistent (PER)	.50	.36	.98	1.74	.67	.57
Explorative (EXP)	1.59	2.79	2.01	1.95	3.05	4.86
Creative (CRE)	2.42	2.25	1.01	1.74	1.45	1.43
Imitative (IMI)	.21	.08	.42	.08	.00	.09
Nurturant (NUR)	1.40	2.25	.71	.94	.92	2.14
Aggressive (AGG)	.37	.23	.34	.58	.60	.24
Emotional (EMO)	6.50	8.23	4.87	5.87	6.70	6.00
Active (ACT)	7.67	10.77	9.14	8.08	8.67	8.86
Passively Active (PACT)	19.35	25.03	16.88	18.87	17.00	18.14

SOURCE: Davis, 1984; reprinted with permission.

Quasi-Experimental Designs

A quasi-experimental design is a form of correlational research that resembles an experiment. Despite this resemblance, like all correlational designs, the quasi-experiment does not allow you to draw firm causal inferences from the data.

The main feature of *quasi-experimental research* is that subjects come into the research preassigned to treatments. They may belong to preformed groups of subjects (such as first-shift versus second-shift factory workers) or to groups determined by subject characteristics (such as schizophrenic versus nonschizophrenic hospital patients).

Because you are using naturally occurring groups, you do not randomly assign subjects to treatment conditions as you would in a true experiment. Recall that random assignment of subjects is a major feature of an experiment. Hence, the main difference between the true experiment and quasi-experiment is in the area of subject selection and assignment.

Quasi-experimental research is used when the random assignment of subjects to treatment conditions is not possible. In other respects, the quasi-experiment is identical to a true experiment. In both you observe changes in a dependent variable as a function of changes in an independent variable. The next two sections discuss two related types of quasi-experimental designs: the time series design and the equivalent time samples design.

Time Series Designs

In the **time series design** (Campbell & Stanley, 1963), you make several observations (O) of behavior over time prior to (O1 to O4) and immediately after (O6 to O8) introducing your independent variable. For example, you might measure children's school performance on a weekly basis and then introduce a new teaching technique. Following the introduction of the new teaching technique, you again measure school performance on a weekly basis. A contrast is then made between preintervention and postintervention performance. The basic time series design is shown in Figure 6-5.

Interrupted Time Series Design. A variation on the basic time series design is the **interrupted time series design,** in which you chart changes in behavior as a function of some naturally occurring event (such as introduction of a new law or a natural disaster) rather than manipulate an independent variable. In this design the naturally occurring event is called a **quasi-independent variable**. (Since "quasi" means "resembling," a "quasi-independent variable" is a variable that resembles a true independent variable.) As with the other time series designs, you make comparisons of behavior prior to and after your subjects were exposed to the quasi-independent variable.

A study conducted by Berkowitz (1970) provides a good illustration of an interrupted time series design. Berkowitz examined the frequency of violent crime before and after the assassination of President Kennedy. Statistics on the rates of violent crimes for the years preceding and following President Kennedy's assassination were obtained from FBI crime records. Figure 6-6 shows the results from Berkowitz's study. Berkowitz's data showed an increase in the rate of violent crime after the assassination.

Basic Data for Time Series Studies. This chapter previously defined archival research as research where you search existing records for your data. Archival data can be used in a time series design. The Berkowitz study used crime statistics made available through the FBI. In Berkowitz's study, the inclusion of the quasi-independent variable defined the study as a time series study. Hence, in some cases you may be able to use archival data to investigate possible causal relationships among variables.

O1 O2 O3 O4 Treatment O5 O6 O7 O8

Figure 6-5. Basic time series design.

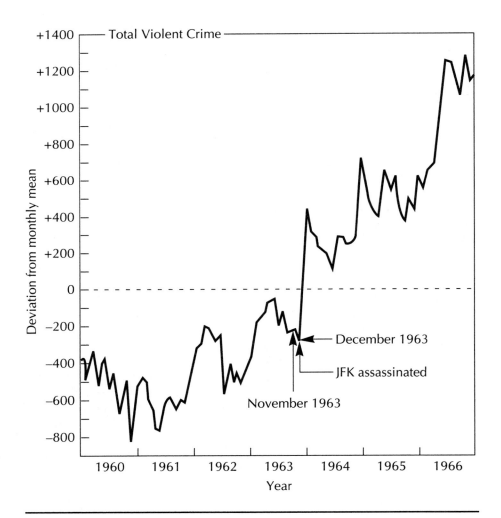

Figure 6-6. Graph showing data on the impact of John F. Kennedy's assassination on the rate of violent crime. (From Berkowitz, 1970, p. 101; reprinted with permission.)

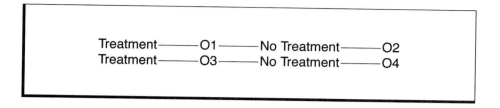

Figure 6-7. Equivalent time samples design.

You are not limited to archival data when conducting a time series or interrupted time series study. In the example of the impact of a new teaching method on school performance, you could measure ongoing behavior (students' exam scores). In an interrupted time series design, if you know that an event is going to happen (such as the introduction of television to an area where television is presently unavailable), you can make your observations prior to the introduction of the quasi-independent variable and continue observations afterward.

Equivalent Time Samples Design

A quasi-experimental strategy related to the time series design is the **equivalent time samples design** (Campbell & Stanley, 1963). In this design the independent variable is administered repeatedly. Figure 6-7 shows this design. Note that the treatment is introduced and then observations (O) are made. Next, observations are made without the treatment, followed by a repeat of this sequence. You could repeat the sequence (in any order appropriate to the research question) as many times as necessary. This design is most appropriate when the effects of the independent variable are temporary or transient (Campbell & Stanley, 1963).

Advantages and Disadvantages of Quasi-Experiments

One advantage of quasi-experimental designs is that they allow you to evaluate the impact of a quasi-independent variable under naturally occurring conditions. In those cases where you manipulate the independent variable, or even simply take advantage of a naturally occurring event, you may be able to establish clear causal relationships among variables. However, quasi-experimental research does have drawbacks that affect the internal and external validity of your research.

One drawback is that you do not have control over the variables influencing behavior. Another variable that changed along with the variable of interest actually may have caused the observed effect. For example, when the speed limit was reduced to 55 miles per hour, the accident and death rate on the nation's highways noticeably decreased. The temptation is to conclude that driving more slowly caused a reduction in the accident rate.

Although this conclusion is the one that was drawn (and is probably true), other events occurred at the same time. The 55-mph speed limit was instituted during a gasoline shortage. In fact, people drove less and some states instituted "gasless Sundays" when gasoline was not sold at all. The accident rate could have been reduced because fewer people were on the roads and those who *were* on the roads drove less after the speed limit reduction than before. Exercise caution when interpreting results from quasi-experiments. Be careful to take into account any changes that may have accompanied changes in the variable of interest.

A second drawback to the quasi-experimental strategy also relates to your degree of control over variables. When you are using naturally occurring events as quasi-independent variables, you have little or no control over when the event will occur. For example, you have no control over when a law is changed or a new service is introduced. An experiment of any kind requires significant preparation. In the absence of forewarning about an event, you may be caught off guard and not be able to adequately study the behaviors of interest. In the case of a change in a law or introduction of a new service, keeping in touch with current events will provide you with enough advanced warning to design a reasonably good quasi-experiment. However, in other cases you may not have such advanced warning.

As an example, if you were interested in studying the impact of the eruption of Mount St. Helens on the nearby residents, you probably would have had a problem conducting your research. You would have had to predict when the volcano was going to erupt and taken behavioral measures prior to and after the eruption. Unless you were extremely lucky (or knew more about volcanos than the experts), you probably would not have been prepared to study the impact of such a natural disaster on human behavior with a quasi-experiment.

The major problems with the quasi-experiment obviously are related to issues of internal validity. Because the researcher does not completely control the quasi-independent variable and other related variables, confounding variables will probably cloud any causal inferences drawn from the data collected. A partial solution to these problems is to include appropriate control groups in your quasi-experiment. Campbell and Stanley (1963) suggest some quasi-experimental designs that include such control groups to evaluate the internal validity of your study.

Nonequivalent Control Group Design

One such design is the **nonequivalent control group design**. In this design you include a time series component (that is, O1 O2 O3 Treatment O4 O5 O6) along with a "control group" that is not exposed to the treatment (O1 O2 O3 O4 O5 O6). The essence of the nonequivalent control group design is that a comparable group of subjects is chosen and observed for the same period as the group for which the treatment is introduced. The control group is nonequivalent because it comes from a different community.

A study reported by Fiedler, Bell, Chemers, and Patrick (1984) illustrates a multiple time series design with a nonequivalent control group. Fiedler et al. investigated the impact of a training program on productivity and safety in the silver mining industry. Records of mine safety were examined for three years (1978–1980) prior to the introduction of an "organization development" program at the Lucky Friday mine. The organization development program helped the mining company develop evaluation procedures and promoted mine safety workers to the rank of foreman. Also a $25,000 bonus was developed to be distributed to the members of mining shifts with the best safety records. Data on mine safety were collected after the intervention with the organization development program.

The Fiedler et al. study also included a second mine as a nonequivalent control group. Data were collected on mine safety at the Star mine for the same period during which data were collected at the Lucky Friday mine. The difference between the two mines was that the organization development program was instituted only at the Lucky Friday mine.

Figure 6-8 shows the results from this study. Notice that the frequency of mine accidents at the Lucky Friday mine was consistently above the frequency for the Star mine before the training program. After intervention, the two mines reversed positions with respect to mine accidents: the Lucky Friday mine now showed fewer accidents than the Star mine.

Developmental Designs

If you are interested in evaluating changes in behavior that relate to changes in a person's chronological age, you need to use one of the *developmental designs*. The principal aim of developmental psychology is to chart the changes in behavior that occur with chronological age.

Age cannot be assigned at random to subjects and therefore must be used as either a purely correlational variable or a quasi-independent variable. The developmental designs we explore in this section (the cross-sectional design, the longitudinal design, and the cohort-sequential design) are special cases of quasi-experimental research.

Even though research in developmental psychology is often experimental in nature (see the example of an experiment in Chapter 3 for an illustration), much of it involves age as a variable. For example, you may want to know whether intelligence varies with age. Assessing such questions requires using one of three major developmental designs: the cross-sectional design, the longitudinal design, or the cohort-sequential design. We explore each of these next.

The Cross-Sectional Design

Suppose you were interested in evaluating the changes in intelligence with age. One way to approach the problem is to use a cross-sectional design. In the

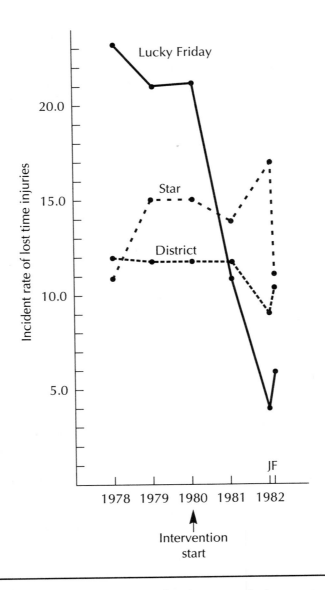

Figure 6-8. Graph showing the results of a nonequivalent control group study of mine safety. (From Fiedler et al., 1984, p. 13; reprinted with permission.)

cross-sectional design, you select several subjects from each of a number of age groups. Figure 6-9 illustrates the general strategy of the cross-sectional design.

In essence, you are creating groups based on the chronological ages of your subjects *at the time of the study*. Different subjects form each of the age groups. In a cross-sectional study, you do not measure the same subject at different ages.

Assume that you are interested in investigating the developmental changes in intelligence across the life span (birth to death). Your hypothesis is that intelligence increases steadily during childhood and adolescence, levels off during early and middle adulthood, and declines in late adulthood. To evaluate this hypothesis with a cross-sectional design, you would obtain subjects representing the different age groups elaborated in your hypothesis. You would then administer a standardized intelligence test to each group (for example, the Stanford–Binet) and compare results across age groups.

An advantage of the cross-sectional design is that it permits you to obtain useful developmental data in a relatively short period of time. You do not have to follow the same subject for ten years in order to assess age-related changes in behavior. If you found data consistent with your hypothesis, for example, what would you conclude? The purpose of the study was to draw conclusions about changes in intelligence across the life span. The observed decline in intelligence test scores would seem to indicate that intelligence deteriorates with age after middle adulthood.

Yet a serious problem exists with cross-sectional design that may preclude drawing clear conclusions from the observed differences among intelligence test scores: generation effects. The term *generation effect* refers to the influence of generational differences in experience, which become confounded with the effects of age *per se*. This confounding threatens the internal validity of cross-sectional studies. Let's say that the subjects in your "late adulthood" group were 70 years old and subjects in your "early adulthood" group were 20 years old. Assume that your study was done in 1990. Simple subtraction shows that subjects in the different groups were not only of different ages, but also were born in different decades. The 70-year-olds were born in 1920, and 20-year-olds in 1970.

The fact that subjects in different age groups were born in different decades may provide an alternative explanation for the observed differences in intelligence scores, and thus the internal validity of your study. The educational opportunities available in 1920 could have differed markedly from those available to subjects born in 1970. The observed reduction in intelligence test scores for older subjects may be due to poorer educational opportunity rather than chronological age. Recent research indicates that the reduced intelligence test scores shown by older subjects in cross-sectional studies were indeed caused in part by a generation effect (Anastasi, 1976).

Generation effects are a major problem when you use a cross-sectional design to evaluate age-related changes in behavior of subjects of quite disparate ages. The design may be more appropriate when the subjects are closer in age. For example, you could use the design to evaluate the changes in the ability to solve verbal problems in children ranging in age from 2 to 6. These children would

Age Group

Five years
old

Ten years
old

Fifteen years
old

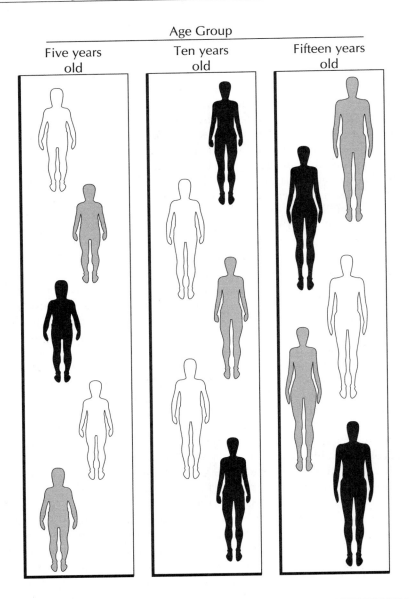

Figure 6-9. Cross-sectional developmental design.

all be of the same generation. In this case, the problem of generation effects may be reduced.

The Longitudinal Design

An alternative to the cross-sectional design, the **longitudinal design,** is illustrated in Figure 6-10. In this design, a single group of subjects is followed over some time period. For example, you could obtain a group of subjects and give them intelligence tests at five-year intervals over a 30-year span.

Generation Effects in Longitudinal Designs. In one respect, the longitudinal design circumvents the problem of generation effects that plagues cross-sectional designs. Because you are studying people from the same age group, you need not worry about generational effects when drawing conclusions about *that group*. Even so, generation effects may still be of concern in the longitudinal design. Shaffer (1985) points out that longitudinal research has the problem of *cross-generational effects*. That is, the conclusion drawn from the longitudinal study of a particular generation may not apply to another generation.

Suppose a longitudinal study was begun in 1910 and carried out through 1940. Data were collected on attachment (the special bond between parent and child) and other developmental events. Would the conclusions derived from these data apply to the generation you begin to study in 1990? You cannot be sure. Changing attitudes toward child rearing, day care, breastfeeding, and so forth could invalidate the conclusions drawn from data accumulated during the period from 1910 to 1940. Thus, even though the longitudinal design provides important information about developmental trends, you must be careful when attempting to generalize from one generation to another.

Other problems you should consider when choosing a longitudinal design include subject mortality, testing effects, and the time needed to collect even small amounts of data.

Subject Mortality. The term *subject mortality* refers to the loss of subjects from the research. Subjects may not complete a longitudinal study because they have moved (and don't notify you of their new address), lost interest in the study, find the study offensive, or have died.

The problem of subject mortality relates directly to the external validity of a longitudinal study. If subject mortality is related to factors such as moving or loss of interest, mortality is less problematic than if it is related to the research. Loss of subjects due to factors such as changes in address can be considered random in the sense that moving is as likely to happen to one subject as another. If subjects drop out of a study because of the nature of the research (for example, the methods are stressful, or boring), a biased sample results. Those subjects who remain in the study (despite finding it offensive) may have special qualities that differentiate them from subjects who quit for this reason. Because the loss

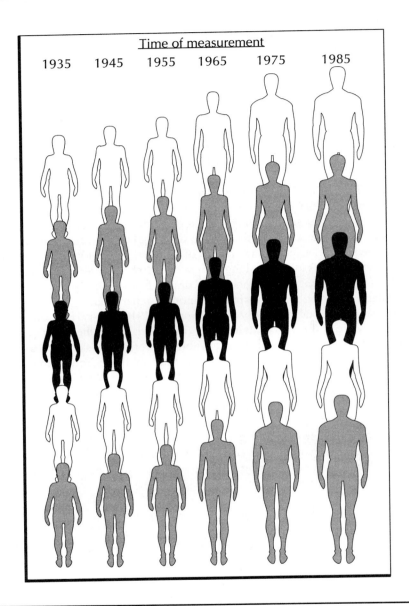

Figure 6-10. Longitudinal developmental design.

of those subjects biases the sample, the results may not apply to the general population.

Because subject mortality can bias the results of a longitudinal study, you should make every effort to evaluate why subjects do not complete the study. Subject mortality may be more problematic with longitudinal research that spans a long period of time. The longer the time period, the more difficult it is to keep track of subjects.

Multiple-Observation Effects. In a longitudinal design, you make multiple observations of the same subjects across time. This very procedure raises problems that may threaten the internal validity of your longitudinal research. Two factors related to multiple observations threaten internal validity.

First, improved performance on the tests over time may be related more to the subjects' increasing experience with taking the tests, than to changes related to age *per se*. For example, increases in intelligence scores with age may stem from the fact that subjects develop a strategy for taking your test, not from age-related changes in cognitive abilities. Changes in performance due to the effects of repeated testing are referred to as *carryover* (see Chapter 9 for additional information on carryover). The solution to the problem of carryover is relatively simple: (1) use multiple forms of a test to evaluate behavior at different times or (2) use different tests that measure the same behavior at different times.

The second problem that results from observing the same subjects over time is that other factors tend to arise and become confounded with age (Applebaum & McCall, 1983). For example, if evaluations of behavior are made at five-year intervals, it is not possible to say conclusively whether the changes observed were due to increased age or to some other factor not related to age. Campbell and Stanley (1963) call this a *history effect* that affects internal validity. An example may help to clarify this point.

Suppose you were interested in evaluating the strength of attachment between a parent and child. You choose a longitudinal design and evaluate attachment behaviors at two-year intervals. You notice a change in attachment. Is the change caused by the fact that the child has grown older or by other factors, such as a shift in attitudes toward children or increased use of day care (Applebaum & McCall, 1983)? It is difficult to know.

The longitudinal design suffers from a problem in which the prevailing attitudes at the time of behavior assessment may influence behavior as much as the change in chronological age. This problem is not as easily handled as is the problem of carryover. You might try to deal with it by including a large-enough sample so that any effects of attitudes could be statistically controlled while you are evaluating age-related changes in behavior. However, such large samples of people who are willing to make a long-term commitment to a research project may be hard to find. Once found, those people may constitute a biased sample.

Advantages of the Longitudinal Design. Despite its disadvantages, the longitudinal design has an attractive quality. It permits you to see developmental changes clearly. You can witness the development of a behavior. This advantage may make the longitudinal design worth the rather large investment of time it takes to collect data.

Returning for the moment to the issue of changes in intelligence with age, longitudinal research indicates that intelligence for the most part changes very little with age. A few areas of intelligence, such as measures requiring reaction time or perceptual skills, do seem to decline with age. However, the large declines seen with the cross-sectional design do not emerge in the longitudinal data.

The Cohort-Sequential Design

A disadvantage of the cross-sectional and longitudinal designs is their relative inability to determine whether factors other than age are influencing the observed changes in behavior. The **cohort-sequential design,** described by Schaie (1965), combines the two developmental designs and lets you *evaluate* the degree of contribution made by factors such as generation effects. However, the cohort-sequential design does not *eliminate* generation effects. It simply lets you detect them and consider them in interpreting your data.

Figure 6-11 illustrates a cohort-sequential design. Notice that the design embodies the features of both the cross-sectional and longitudinal designs. Along the vertical edge of Figure 6-11 is listed the "year of birth." The subjects making up one level of this variable (for example, 1980) constitute a *cohort group.* Specifically, a cohort group consists of subjects born at a specified time. In our example there are three cohort groups: subjects born in 1960 (Group A), 1970 (Group B), or 1980 (Group C). These three cohort groups constitute the cross-sectional component when comparisons are made across cohort groups. Along the horizontal edge of the figure is "time of measurement." The different measurement times constitute the longitudinal component when we look at a single cohort group across different times of measurement.

By comparing subjects from different cohort groups of the same age (for example, comparing the data from 5-year-olds across cohort groups), we can identify potential generation or cohort group effects. This design is thus useful for evaluating developmental changes in behavior while affording the capability to detect potentially important cohort effects. For a more detailed discussion of this and the other developmental research designs, see Applebaum and McCall (1983).

Summary

In some situations, conducting an experiment may not be possible or desirable. In the early stages of research, or where you are interested in studying naturally occurring behaviors of your subjects, a nonexperimental or quasi-experimental approach may be best.

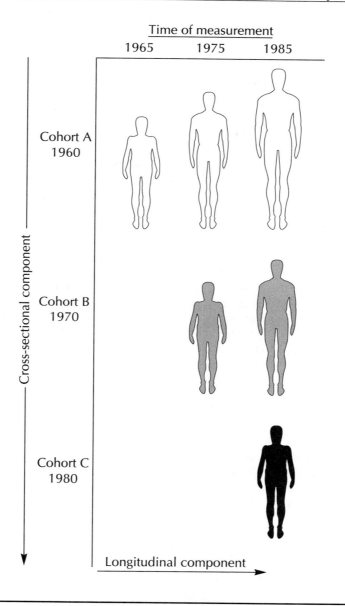

Figure 6-11. Example of cohort-sequential developmental design. Comparisons across time of measurement represent the longitudinal component, whereas comparisons across cohort groups represent the cross-sectional component of the design.

Observational research involves observing and recording the behaviors of your subjects. This can be accomplished either in the field or in the lab and can use human or animal subjects. Although observational research sounds easy to conduct, as much preparation goes into an observational study as any other study. Before making observations of behavior, clearly define the behaviors to be observed, develop observation techniques that do not interfere with the behaviors of your subjects, and work out a method of quantifying and recording behavior.

The frequency, duration, and intervals methods are three widely accepted ways to quantify behavior in an observational study. In the frequency method, you count the number of occurrences of a behavior within a specified period of time. In the duration method, you measure how long a behavior lasted. In the intervals method, you break your observation period into small time intervals and record whether or not a behavior occurred within each.

After you have decided how to quantify behavior, you must make some decisions about how to record your observations. Paper-and-pencil data-recording sheets provide a simple and, in most cases, adequate means of recording behavior. In some situations (such as when the behavior being observed is fast paced), you should consider using tape recorders rather than a paper-and-pencil method. Using a tape recorder allows observers to keep their eyes on subjects while making notes about behavior.

In addition to developing a method for quantifying behavior, you must also decide on how and when to make observations. Sometimes it is not possible to watch and record behaviors simultaneously because behavior may occur quickly and be highly complex. In such situations, you could use time sampling or individual sampling, or automate your observations by using a video recorder.

In observational research, you should use multiple observers. When multiple observers are used, you must evaluate the amount of interrater reliability. This can be done using either Cohen's Kappa or Pearson r. A Cohen's Kappa of .70 or greater or a statistically significant Pearson r suggests an acceptable level of interrater reliability.

Although useful, naturalistic observation, participant observation, case histories, archival research, and content analysis are purely descriptive techniques and do not allow you to firmly establish whether the observed relationships are causally connected. The best way to establish such causal connections is by conducting experiments. However, if a true experiment cannot be conducted, a quasi-experimental study may provide a partial solution. This type of study makes use of naturally occurring groups or events. You do not randomly assign subjects to conditions and, in some cases, may not have the proper control groups. Consequently, the quasi-experiment lacks both internal and external validity. You might consider conducting a quasi-experiment using the nonequivalent control group design to combat the problems of internal and external validity.

The basic developmental designs are the longitudinal and cross-sectional designs. In a longitudinal study a group of subjects is followed over a period of time (weeks, months, or years). This design allows you to see subtle changes in behavior, but suffers from cross-generational problems, subject mortality, and high cost. In cross-sectional research you study subjects of different ages at the same time. This approach is less costly than the longitudinal design, but conceptual problems arise when a wide range exists between the youngest and oldest subjects in your study. Generation effects may be a problem in this case. The cohort-sequential design, which combines elements of the longitudinal and cross-sectional designs, has been developed to test for generation effects.

Key Terms

Behavioral categories

Interrater reliability

Naturalistic observation

Participant observation

Case history

Archival research

Content analysis

Time series design

Interrupted time series design

Quasi–independent variable

Equivalent time samples design

Nonequivalent control group design

Cross-sectional design

Longitudinal design

Cohort-sequential design

7

Using Survey Research

THIS CHAPTER CONTINUES THE DISCUSSION of nonexperimental research with a detailed account of survey research. An expanded discussion of survey research appears in a separate chapter because survey research is so common in science and in everyday life. We have all been exposed to surveys in one way or another. That questionnaire you receive in the mail asking you about which brand of soap you use is a survey. The telephone caller who asks you a few questions about where you do your banking is conducting a survey. When television commercials claim that "four out of five dentists recommend sugarless gum to their patients who chew gum," they are basing the claim on data collected in a survey. During political campaigns, we are flooded with polls about candidate popularity.

Because survey research is highly visible, you should understand the "ins and outs" of this important research technique. If you plan to use a survey technique in your own research, you should know about proper questionnaire construction, administration techniques, sampling techniques, and how to analyze data from a survey. Even if you never use survey techniques, understanding something about them will help you make sense out of the surveys you are exposed to every day.

Survey Research

Before we discuss survey techniques, note the difference between the *field survey* and the observational techniques outlined in Chapter 6. In naturalistic observation and participant observation, you do not administer any measures to your subjects. Instead, you observe behavior and make copious notes about the observed behaviors. Consequently, you may only speculate about the motives, attitudes, and beliefs underlying the observed behaviors. In a field survey, you directly question your subjects about behavior (past, present, or future), their underlying attitudes, beliefs, and intentions. From the data collected, you can draw more accurate inferences about the factors underlying behavior.

However, remember that you do not manipulate independent variables in a field survey. Instead, you acquire several (perhaps hundreds) of measures about the behaviors of interest. Hence, the survey follows a correlational research strategy. As such, you usually cannot draw causal inferences from your data. For example, finding that political conservatism is a good predictor of voter choices does not justify concluding that political conservatism *causes* voter choices. If you need a refresher on this issue, reread the section on correlational research and causality in Chapter 3.

The field survey is used to evaluate specific attitudes or behaviors. Questions concerning attitudes about issues such as nuclear disarmament, political candidates, or foreign imports can be evaluated with a field survey. You can also evaluate behaviors. For example, you could design a questionnaire to determine which household products people use.

Surveys have another important use: predicting behavior. Political polls often seek to predict behavior. Attitudes about political candidates are assessed, and then projections are made about subsequent voter behavior.

Survey methodology typically involves designing and administering a questionnaire. The following sections explore the issues relevant to proper survey design and administration. The three major areas discussed are how to design the questionnaire, how to write effective questions, and how to obtain and contact your subject sample.

Designing a Questionnaire

Designing a questionnaire is as much art as science. A properly designed questionnaire elicits precisely the information you want. A poorly designed questionnaire yields data that are confusing, difficult to analyze, and of little value.

The first step in designing a questionnaire is to clearly define the topic of your study. Having a clearly defined topic keeps your questionnaire focused on the chosen behavior or attitude (Moser & Kalton, 1972). Avoid the temptation to do too much in a single questionnaire. Trying to tackle too much leads to an inordinately long questionnaire that may confuse or burden your subjects. It may also confuse or burden you when you summarize and analyze the data (Moser & Kalton, 1972). In other words, the topic of your questionnaire should be broad enough to thoroughly assess behavior, but not so broad as to lose focus and become confusing. Your questionnaire should elicit the responses you are most interested in, without much extraneous information.

The type of information gathered in a questionnaire depends on its purpose. However, most questionnaires include questions designed to assess the characteristics of the subjects, such as age, sex, marital status, occupation, income, and education. Such characteristics are called *demographics*. Demographics are often used as *predictor variables* during analysis of the data to determine whether subject characteristics correlate with, or predict responses to, other questions in the survey. Other nondemographic questions can also be included to provide predictor variables. For example, attitude toward abortion might be used to predict voter preference. In this case, attitude toward abortion would be used as a predictor variable.

In addition to demographics and predictor variables, you will also have questions designed to assess the behavior of interest. For example, if you were interested in predicting voter preference, you would include an item on your questionnaire to specifically measure that variable. That item, or a combination of several items, would constitute the *criterion variable*.

Developing Questionnaire Items

The questions to which your subjects will respond are the heart of your questionnaire. Take great care to develop questions that are clear, to the point, and relevant to the aims of your research. And take the necessary time to develop good items. The time spent in this early phase of your research will pay dividends later. Well-constructed items are easier to summarize, analyze, and interpret than poorly constructed ones. The sections that follow present some information on how to develop good questionnaire items.

Types of Questionnaire Items. Items on your questionnaire can be of several types. Two types that you might consider are the **open-ended item** and **restricted item** (or close-ended item). Open-ended questions allow the subject to provide a response in his or her own words. Such information may be more complete and accurate than the information obtained with a more restricted question format. A drawback to the open-ended question is that subjects may not understand exactly what you are looking for, or may inadvertently omit some answers. Thus the subjects might give an answer that does not provide the needed information. Another drawback to the open-ended question is that summarizing your data can be difficult. You must decide how to classify different answers. When you must interpret what the subject says, you run the risk of misclassifying answers.

A restricted item asks subjects to respond by choosing an answer from a set of alternatives. Dillman (1978) distinguished among three types of restricted questions: close-ended with ordered alternatives, close-ended with unordered alternatives, and partially open-ended.

A restricted question with ordered alternatives provides alternatives in a logical order:

How many times in the last year have you eaten in a restaurant?

___ NONE

___ 1 TO 5 TIMES

___ 6 TO 10 TIMES

___ MORE THAN 10 TIMES

Ordered alternatives are used whenever alternatives lend themselves to such ordering. When they don't, close-ended questions with unordered alternatives are used:

Which of the following candidates do you prefer?

___ SMITH

___ JONES

___ HERMANN

Restricted items provide control over the subject's range of responses by providing specific response alternatives. These responses are, therefore, easier to summarize and analyze than the responses to open-ended items. However, the information you obtain from a restricted item is not as rich as the information from an open-ended question. Subjects cannot be specific or elaborate on their responses. Also, you may fail to include an alternative that correctly describes the subject's opinion. So the subject may choose an alternative that does not really fit.

The **partially open-ended item** is designed to deal with these problems, by providing an "other" category and an opportunity to specify an answer:

Which fast-food restaurant do you prefer?

___ MCDONALD'S

___ BURGER KING

___ WENDY'S

___ TACO BELL

___ OTHER (specify _____)

The partially open-ended question controls the response categories while giving the subject the opportunity to provide an alternative that you missed. Carefully wording your questions can minimize the disadvantages of restricted-item questions.

Dillman (1978) has several suggestions for formatting questions. He suggests using lowercase and uppercase letters for the stem of your questions and upper-case letters for response categories, as we have done in the previous examples. This helps set your response categories apart from the question stem. Also, response categories should be identified by blank spaces or numbers to the left of each response. A few other suggestions are

1. Clearly specify what you are asking for.
2. Provide alternatives that cover as wide a range as possible. It is helpful to see what other researchers have included.
3. Make your alternatives as specific as possible.
4. Include an "other" category, and provide a space for the subject to spec-ify what the "other" is.
5. Provide a blank space in which subjects can elaborate on or qualify an answer.

Rating Scales. A variation on the restricted question uses a rating scale rather than response alternatives. A rating scale provides a graded response to a question:

How well do you think the president is dealing with the threat of nuclear war?

1	2	3	4	5	6	7	8	9	10

Very
Poorly   Very
                                                                Well

There is no set number of points that a rating scale must have. A rating scale can have as few as 3 and as many as 100 points. However, rating scales com-monly do not exceed 10 points. A 10-point scale has enough points to allow a wide range of choice while not overburdening the subject. Scales smaller than 10 points are also used frequently, but you should not go below 5 points. Many subjects may not want to use the extreme values on a scale. Consequently, if you have a 5-point scale and the subject excludes the endpoints, you really have only 3 usable points. Scales ranging from 7 to 10 points leave several points for the subjects, even if subjects do avoid the extreme values.

You must also decide how to label your scale. Figure 7-1 shows three ways you might do this. In the first example, only the endpoints are labeled. In this case the subject is told what are the upper and lower limits of the scale. Such labeled points are called *anchors* because they keep the subject's interpretation of the scale values from drifting.

With only the endpoints anchored, the subject must interpret the meaning of the rest of the points. In the second example, all the points are labeled. In this case the subject knows exactly what each point means and may consequently provide more accurate information.

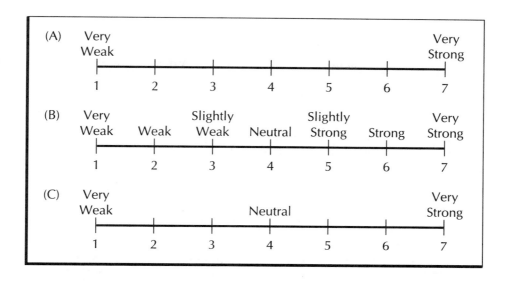

Figure 7-1. Three ways of labeling a rating scale: (A) endpoints only, (B) each point labeled, (C) endpoints and midpoint labeled.

You may be wondering whether labeling each point changes the way the subject responds on the scale. The answer seems to be a qualified no. When you develop a measurement scale, you are dealing with (1) the psychological phenomenon underlying the scale and (2) the scale itself. Labeling each point does not change the nature of the psychological phenomenon underlying the scale. You can assume that your scale, labeled at each point, still represents the phenomenon underlying the scale. In fact, researchers have sometimes expressed a misguided concern about such scale transformations (Nunnally, 1967). Minor transformations of a measurement scale (such as labeling each point) probably do not affect its measurement properties or how well it represents the underlying psychological phenomenon being studied.

The third example in Figure 7-1 shows a scale labeled at the endpoints and at the midpoint. This scale provides three anchors for the subject. This scale is a reasonable compromise between labeling only the endpoints and labeling all the points.

In the previous examples, subjects respond by checking or circling the scale value that best represents their judgments. Alternative ways to format your scale provide subjects with more flexibility in their responses. Figure 7-2 shows an example where the endpoints are anchored and the subjects are instructed to place a check or perpendicular line on the scale to indicate how they feel. This method allows subjects to choose intermediate values along the scale. Hence the information obtained from the second example may be more precise. To interpret

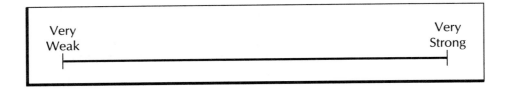

Figure 7-2. Rating scale formatted with no numbers. Endpoints are labeled, and subjects place marks on the line to indicate their responses.

the responses, you simply use a ruler to measure from an endpoint to the subject's mark. Your scale is then expressed in terms of inches or centimeters, and the resulting numbers are treated just like the numbers on a numbered scale.

Another variation on the rating scale is the *Likert scale,* which is widely used in attitude measurement research. A Likert scale provides a series of statements to which subjects can indicate degrees of agreement or disagreement. Figure 7-3 shows two examples of formatting a Likert item. In the first example the attitude statement is followed by five blank spaces labeled from "strongly agree" to "strongly disagree." The subject simply checks the space that best reflects the degree of agreement or disagreement with each statement. The second example shows a Likert item using a continuous rating scale rather than blank spaces. In this case subjects are instructed to circle the number that best reflects how much they agree or disagree with each statement. For further information on Likert scaling, see Edwards (1953).

A final note on rating scales is in order. Although rating scales have been presented in the context of survey research, be aware that rating scales are widely used in experimental research as well. Adapting rating scales to your particular research needs is a relatively simple affair. Anytime your research calls for the use of rating scales, you can apply the suggestions presented here.

Writing Questionnaire Items. Writing effective questionnaire items that elicit the information you want requires care and skill. You cannot simply sit down, write several questions, and use those first-draft questions on your final questionnaire. Writing questionnaire items involves writing and rewriting items until they are clear and succinct. In fact, once you have written your items and assembled your questionnaire, it should be administered to a pilot group of subjects matching your main sample to ensure that the items are reliable and valid. After establishing reliability and validity on the small sample, you then administer your questionnaire to your main sample. Here are a few things to keep in mind when writing questionnaire items.

First, keep the wording of your items simple. Questions with complex words may not be understood by all subjects, especially if the subjects are poorly

---

(A) The president is doing all he can to reduce the threat of nuclear war.

Strongly Agree	Agree	Neutral	Disagree	Strongly Disagree
_____	_____	_____	_____	_____

(B) The president is doing all he can to reduce the threat of nuclear war.

Strongly Agree				Strongly Disagree
1	2	3	4	5

Figure 7-3. Samples showing Likert scales: (A) a standard Likert item where the subject places a check in the blank under the statement that best reflects how he or she feels; (B) Likert-type scale using a five-point rating scale.

---

educated (Dillman, 1978; Moser & Kalton, 1972). If a word you are considering has more than six or seven letters, a simpler alternative is probably available. Table 7-1 presents some of the simpler substitutions suggested by Moser and Kalton (1972) and by Dillman (1978).

However, you need not always use a simpler substitution. If the complex word conveys your meaning better than a simpler one, use the complex word — especially if doing so simplifies the sentence.

Second, strive to make your questions precise, but not overly precise. A precise question elicits only the information in which you are interested. Consider the following examples:

Vague: "What should Congress do about the budget deficit?"

Precise: "What should Congress do in the areas of tax reform and budget cutting to reduce the deficit?"

Too Precise: "How much should Congress cut taxes to reduce the budget deficit?"

The first example allows too much latitude in the response, as subjects could say just about anything in response to the question. The third example limits

---

Table 7-1. Making Simpler Substitutions for Complex Words — Examples

Complex Word	Simpler Substitution
Acquaint	*Inform* or *tell*
Assist	*Help*
Candid	*Honest*
Consider	*Think*
Courageous	*Brave*
Employment	*Work*
Exhausted	*Tired*
Initiate	*Begin, start*
Leisure	*Free time*
Major	*Important, chief, main*
Purchase	*Buy*
Preserve	*Protect*
Require	*Need, want*
Reside	*Live*
Sufficient	*Enough*
Terminate	*End*
Virtually	*Nearly*

SOURCE: After Moser & Kalton, 1972, and Dillman, 1978.

---

your subjects to recommending a specific amount of tax reduction, which may not be what you want. The "precise" example asks subjects to comment on specific ways to cut the deficit, but does not overly restrict their responses.

Third, avoid biased wording. Your wording should not communicate a point of view to your subjects:

Biased: "Do you think that pornography is vile and disgusting?"

Unbiased: "What do you think about pornography?"

The first example leads the subject to an answer, whereas the second does not. In addition, subjects may refuse to answer objectionable questions. Compare these two questions:

Objectionable: "How many times per week do you drink alcohol?"

Unobjectionable: "Which of the following best describes how many alcoholic beverages you drink per week?"

___ none   ___ 1 to 2   ___ 3 to 5   ___ more than 5

The first question puts the subject on the spot. The subject may be a heavy drinker and not want to admit it. The second question allows the subject to give you fairly precise information without forcing the issue. Dillman (1978) suggests that when you are dealing with a particularly sensitive topic (such as sexual preferences or theft), you may have to use a series of questions. (See Dillman, 1978, p. 107, for an example.)

Dillman (1978) discusses several guidelines for item construction. First, do not use uncommon abbreviations or phrases in your questions. For example, many subjects may not know that APA stands for the American Psychological Association. Second, questions that are too demanding may confuse your subjects. For example, it may just be too much to ask subjects to rank–order 50 universities. Third, your questions should have a precise time referent so that responses given by subjects at different times of the year (July versus December, for example) will be equivalent. For example,

Poor Referent: How many times this year did you play golf?

Better Referent: How many times did you play golf in 1989?

Fourth, items should ask for only one thing at a time, especially when you are using restricted items. Avoid double questions; for example,

Double Question: Should the president support an income tax increase or a gasoline tax increase?

___ YES

___ NO

Better: Should the president support an income tax increase?

___ YES

___ NO

Finally (fifth), avoid questions that include a negative, because they are confusing:

Negative: Should the president not nominate a conservative for a federal judge position?

___ YES

___ NO

Better: Should the president nominate a conservative for a federal judge position?

___ YES

___ NO

For more suggestions on phrasing questionnaire items properly, see Dillman (1978) and Moser and Kalton (1972).

Assembling the Questionnaire

A collection of questions does not make a questionnaire. The questions must be organized into a coherent, visually pleasing format. This process involves paying attention to the order in which the questions are included and to the way in which they are presented.

Dillman (1978) and Moser and Kalton (1972) agree that demographic items should not be presented first on the questionnaire. These questions, although easy to complete, may lead subjects to believe the questionnaire is boring. Instead, Dillman suggests leading with questions that have social importance. These questions capture the interest of the subjects and may induce a high completion rate.

Your questionnaire should have continuity; that is, related items should be presented together. This keeps your subject's attention on one issue at a time, rather than jumping from issue to issue. Your questionnaire will have greater continuity if related items are grouped. An organized questionnaire is much easier and more enjoyable for the subject to complete, factors that may increase completion rate (Dillman, 1978).

Continuity also means that groups of related questions should be logically ordered (Dillman, 1978). Your questionnaire should read like a book. Avoid the temptation to skip around from topic to topic in an attempt to hold the attention of the subject. Rather, strive to build "cognitive ties" between related groups of items (Dillman, 1978).

The order in which questions are included on a questionnaire has been shown to affect the responses of subjects. For example, McFarland (1981) presented questions on a questionnaire ordered in two ways. Some subjects answered a general question before specific questions, whereas others answered the specific questions first. McFarland found that subjects expressed more interest in politics and religion when the specific questions were asked first than when the general questions were asked first. Sigelman (1981) found that question order affected whether or not subjects expressed an opinion (about the popularity of the president) but only if the subjects were poorly educated. Hence, question order may play a greater role for some subjects than for others. Carefully consider your sample and the chosen topic when deciding on the order in which questions are asked.

The placement of items asking for sensitive information (such as sexual preferences or illegal behavior) is an important factor. Dillman suggests placing objectionable questions after less objectionable ones. Once your subjects are committed to answering your questions, they may be more willing to answer some sensitive questions. You need not save all the objectionable questions for the end. Instead, try to salt the objectionable questions through the rest of your questionnaire while adhering to the previous principles of order (Dillman, 1978).

In addition to order, pay attention to the format of your questionnaire. Avoid visually confusing your subjects. The questions should be carefully and logically laid out on your questionnaire. It is a good idea to establish a "vertical flow" to your questionnaire (Dillman, 1978); that is, have the blanks preceding response categories of a restricted item line up in a vertical line down the page. This format helps reduce the chance that a subject will inadvertently skip a question. Subjects should not have to skip all over a page to answer questions. Provide concise instructions on how to answer your items. For example, tell subjects to check a box, place a check on a line, or circle a number. Finally, include a short transition statement between groups of related questions to introduce the topic of the next group of questions. Such transition statements help establish a flow for your questionnaire and hold your subjects' interest (Dillman, 1978).

Administering Your Questionnaire

After you develop your questionnaire, you must decide how to administer it. You could mail your questionnaire to your subjects, telephone subjects to ask the questions directly, conduct face-to-face interviews, or administer your questionnaire to a large group at once. Each method has advantages and disadvantages, and makes its own special demands. The remainder of this section reviews each of these methods and then finishes with a discussion of sampling procedures.

Mail Surveys

In a **mail survey,** you mail your questionnaire directly to your subjects. The subjects then complete and return the questionnaire at their leisure. This is a rather convenient method. All you need to do is put your questionnaires into addressed envelopes and mail them. However, a serious problem called **nonresponse bias** occurs when a large proportion of subjects fails to complete and return your questionnaire. If the subjects who fail to return the questionnaire differ in significant ways from those who do return it, your survey may yield answers that do not represent the opinions of the intended population.

Combating Nonresponse Bias. To avoid nonresponse bias, you should develop strategies to increase your return rate. Dillman (1978) offered several suggestions for obtaining a high return rate. One factor, the cover letter, introduces your survey to your subjects and explains its purpose. It is probably the first thing that subjects will read when they open your survey. Avoid using phrases such as "enclosed is a questionnaire," "this is a survey" (Dillman says the words *questionnaire* and *survey* should be avoided), "Your help is needed," and any pleas indicating that the survey is a requirement for your degree (Dillman, 1978). Instead, Dillman suggests the following information in your cover letter (in the following order): your institutional affiliation; the date, name, and address of the respondent; a statement about why the subject is important and who should complete the questionnaire; a promise that all responses will be confidential, the usefulness of the study; a token reward for participating; where to address questions or comments; a statement of appreciation; your signature (in ink); and your title. Figure 7-4 depicts a short cover letter that follows Dillman's suggestions.

You may be able to increase your return rate somewhat by including a small token of your appreciation, such as a pen or pencil that the subject can keep. Some researchers include a small amount of money as an incentive to complete the questionnaire. Research has shown that as little as 10¢ will increase return rates (Pressley & Tullar, 1977). Such small rewards make the subject feel obligated to complete and return your questionnaire. Ironically, if the reward is too large it may not increase return rate (Kanuk & Berensen, 1975; Warner, Berman, Weyant, & Ciarlo, 1983). According to these researchers, the added expense of a monetary reward exceeding 25¢ does not pay off in terms of a proportional increase in the number of subjects who return the questionnaire. Note that the actual inclusion of the monetary reward is much more effective than the promise of such a reward (Kanuk & Berensen, 1975).

Two other strategies can be used to increase response rate. One is to precontact subjects about the questionnaire that will be mailed. Precontact is most effective when done by telephone. Research reported by Hornik (1982) suggested that a female caller is more effective than a male caller (especially with male subjects) in obtaining a good response rate. Also, Hornik reported that an ingratiating plea ("We are earnestly asking for your generous help . . .") or a polite plea ("We would appreciate it if you would complete . . .") is more effective than more curt pleas.

One of the most effective ways to increase return rates is to send follow-up letters (Kanuk & Berensen, 1975). Dillman suggested sending out a reminder (a postcard will suffice) to all subjects one week after sending out the questionnaire. This first reminder could include a paragraph thanking those who returned the questionnaire and a nice reminder for those who did not. Three weeks after sending out the questionnaire, a letter and replacement questionnaire might be sent. A short cover letter might point out that the original questionnaire was not received. Finally, another reminder (similar to the second) would be sent to the subjects after seven weeks, this time by certified mail (to underscore the importance of the survey). Of course, do not coerce or badger subjects, but merely remind them courteously of the survey.

The type of follow-up may have to be matched to the subject sample. Anderson and Berdie (1975) found that humorous, less formal follow-up techniques are most effective when your sample consists of undergraduate students. Graduate students and professionals seem to respond more to a formal follow-up.

A few factors that do *not* significantly affect response rate include questionnaire length, personalization, promising anonymity, and including a deadline (Kanuk & Berensen, 1975). (For a complete review of the research supporting these findings, see Kanuk & Berensen, 1975, and Warner et al., 1983.)

Citizen's State University
Washington, D.C.

5/23/86
Susan Smith
123 Main Street
Union, NJ 07083

Dear Ms. Smith,

Recently, the congress of the United States introduced a
bill on tax reform. This bill could affect how much of
your pay you keep and how much the government keeps. It
could also affect the budget deficit and social services.
The congress, however, does not know how people in the
general population feel about the new tax proposal.

You are one of a small group of people that I have
contacted to find out about your views on the current tax
laws and potential changes in those laws. Since I have
only sent out a few questionnaires it is important that
they all be completed and returned. A good return rate
will ensure that the results that I report to your
congressman are accurate. I would like you to take some
time and complete this questionnaire.

Please be assured that all of your responses will remain
confidential. Also, at no time will your name be reported
along with any of your responses. In fact, do not even
put your name on the questionnaire. If you want a copy of
the summarized results complete and mail separately the
postcard that is included with the questionnaire.

The results of this survey will be provided to congress
so that it may have an indication about how the people
affected by this bill feel about it. We have included a
pen for you to use to fill out the questionnaire. You may
keep the pen as a token of our appreciation for your time
and effort.

If you have any questions feel free to call me at
(999) 555-5555 during regular business hours.

Your assistance is greatly appreciated.

Sincerely,

Henry Baker

Henry Baker
Survey Director

Figure 7-4. Sample cover letter for a mail survey. (Adapted from Dillman, 1978.)

Group Administration

Sometimes you may have at your disposal a large group of individuals to whom you can administer your questionnaire. In such a case you design your questionnaire as you would for a mail survey, but administer it to the assembled group. For example, you might distribute to a first-year college class a questionnaire on attitudes toward premarital sex. Using such a captive audience permits you to collect large amounts of data in a relatively short time. You do not have to worry about subjects misplacing or forgetting about your questionnaire. You may also be able to reduce any volunteer bias, especially if you administer your questionnaire during a class period. People may participate because very little effort is required.

As usual, this method has some drawbacks. Subjects may not treat the questionnaire as seriously when they fill it out as a group rather than alone. Also, you may not be able to ensure anonymity in the large group if you are asking for sensitive information. Subjects may feel that other subjects are looking at their answers. You may be able to overcome this problem by giving adjacently seated subjects alternate forms of the questionnaire. Another drawback to group administration is that a few subjects may express hostility about the questionnaire by purposely providing false information.

A final drawback to group administration concerns the subject's right to decline participation (which is the subject's right under ethical research practice). A subject may feel pressure to participate in your survey. This pressure arises from the subject's observation that just about everyone else is participating. In essence, a conformity effect occurs because completing your survey becomes the norm defined by the behavior of your other subjects. Make special efforts to reinforce the understanding that subjects should not feel compelled to participate.

Telephone Surveys

In a **telephone survey,** you contact subjects by telephone rather than by mail. You can ask some questions more easily over the telephone than you can in written form. However, because you will be asking questions verbally, the questions must be worded differently from those in a mail survey to ensure that they are comprehended and remembered. Questions that are too long or complex may not be answered truthfully. By the time your subject gets to the end of your question, he or she may not recall the first part. This could lead the subject to choose any answer so as not to appear foolish. To avoid these problems, keep your questions short (Dillman, 1978).

Also, limit the number of response categories on restricted items (Dillman, 1978). If your list of alternatives is too long, subjects may forget the first few alternatives by the time they get to the last ones. Try to consolidate response categories as much as possible.

Be careful when asking subjects to respond to a question in which the responses are ordered along some continuum or are organized in a series. Because subjects do not have the questionnaire physically in front of them, such questions can be difficult to deal with (Dillman, 1978).

Word your questions so that they can be read accurately. If you constantly stumble over questions, the subject may not be able to understand them clearly. Consequently, subjects may give inappropriate answers, or they may become impatient with the interviewer and break off participation. To detect these problems, read your questions aloud several times before you contact your subjects.

Unlike the mail survey, the telephone survey requires an interviewer. The behavior of your interviewer may affect whether subjects agree to complete your survey. If your interviewer believes it will be difficult to convince subjects to cooperate, a low cooperation rate may result (Singer, Frankel, & Glassman, 1983). Factors such as the interviewer's age and degree of experience may also affect response rates (Singer et al., 1983).

The interviewer's clarity of speech can affect how well your subjects understand and answer your questions (Dillman, 1978). Keep in mind that your subjects are not familiar with any of the questions before they are read on the telephone and do not have a copy of the questionnaire. You might want to pretest your interviewer to ensure that he or she can be understood by potential subjects.

Several problems are unique to the telephone survey. Subjects may be suspicious about the legitimacy of your survey. Well-publicized cases of obscene phone callers posing as researchers may contribute to this problem. A recent trend in telemarketing in which "subjects" are solicited to answer a few questions also may cause problems. In one case, "subjects" were asked to answer a few questions about their knowledge of cancer treatments. As it turned out, the final questions asked subjects if they were aware of a new service available from a particular company and asked if they would like more information about the service.

The suspicions engendered by these experiences and the plethora of "junk calls" to which the population is exposed may make subjects less willing to participate in a legitimate survey. However, you can take steps to reduce this problem. First, clearly identify yourself and your affiliation. If the subject still is suspicious, provide your telephone number and have the subject call you back. Your willingness to provide a genuine number at which you can be reached should help to dispel any mistrust.

Another step toward improving participation is to develop a good opening statement. As in the mail survey, your opening statement can be crucial. Make the subject feel important. Indicate to the subject that the information gathered is important and, if possible, offer some small token for participation.

Another problem with the telephone survey concerns the subject's reaction to being called. Imagine for the moment that you are at home watching your favorite television program. The telephone rings and you rush to pick it up. To your dismay the caller states that she is conducting a telephone survey. Angry at the interruption, you may decline to participate, or perhaps vent your anger by giving false answers to the questions. Even if not angered, you may attempt to continue watching the show while answering the questions. Because your full attention is not on the survey, your answers may be inaccurate. To combat these problems, you must try to make the questionnaire as interesting as possible. Catch and keep the subject's attention.

Finally, keep the interview short. Unlike the mail survey, the length of your questionnaire may affect the responses of your subjects. Research suggests that subjects exposed to a long telephone interview (say 75 minutes) are more likely to be preoccupied, less willing to be reinterviewed a year later, and more likely to view the interview as time poorly spent than subjects exposed to a short (25-minute) interview (Sharp & Frankel, 1983).

The Interview

Still another method for obtaining survey data is the face-to-face **interview**. In this method you talk to your subject directly. This can be done in the subject's home or place of employment, in your office, or in any other suitable place. If you decide to use a face-to-face interview, keep several things in mind. First, decide whether or not to use a structured interview or unstructured interview. In a structured interview, you ask prepared questions. This is similar to the telephone survey in that you prepare a questionnaire in advance and simply read the ordered questions to your subjects. In the unstructured interview, you have a general idea about the issues to discuss. However, you do not have a predetermined sequence of questions.

An advantage of the structured interview is that you know all subjects are asked the same questions in the same order. This eliminates fluctuations in the data that result from differences in when and how questions are asked. Responses from a structured interview are therefore easier to summarize and analyze.

However, the structured interview tends to be inflexible. You may miss some important information by having a highly structured interview. The unstructured interview is superior in this respect. By asking general questions and having subjects provide answers in their own words, you may gain more complete (although perhaps less accurate) information. However, responses from an unstructured interview may be more difficult to code and analyze later on. You can gain some advantages of each method by combining them in one interview. For example, begin the interview with a structured format by asking prepared questions; later in the interview, switch to an unstructured format.

Using the face-to-face interview strategy leads to a problem that is not present in mail surveys, but is present to some extent in telephone surveys: the appearance and demeanor of the interviewer may affect the responses of the subjects. Experimenter bias and demand characteristics become a problem. Subtle changes in the way in which an interviewer asks a question may elicit different answers. Also, your interviewer may not respond similarly to all subjects (for example, an interviewer may react differently to an attractive subject and an unattractive one). This, too, can affect the results.

The best way to combat this problem is to use interviewers who have received extensive training in interview techniques. Interviewers must be trained to ask questions in the same way for each subject. They must also be trained not to emphasize any particular words in the stem of a question or in the response list. The questions should be read in a neutral manner. Also, try to anticipate any questions that subjects may have and provide your interviewers with standardized responses. This can be accomplished by running a small pilot version of your survey before running the actual survey. During this pilot study, try out the interview procedure on a small sample of subjects. (This can be done with just about anyone, such as friends, colleagues, or students.) Correct any problems that arise.

A final note on survey technique is in order. Although each of the discussed techniques has advantages, the mail survey has been the most popular. The mail survey is able to reach large numbers of subjects at a lower cost than either the telephone survey or face-to-face interview (Warner, Berman, Weyant, & Ciarlo, 1983), and produces data that are less affected by the social desirability of response options. For these reasons, give mail surveys first consideration.

Once you have designed your questionnaire and chosen a method of administration, you must then select your subjects. The next section addresses how to acquire subjects for your survey.

Acquiring a Sample for Your Survey

Chapter 5 distinguished between a population and a sample. Recall that a population includes all people in a definable group. A sample consists of a smaller number of people selected from the population. Once you have designed and pretested your questionnaire, you then administer it to a group of subjects. It is usually impractical to have everyone in the population (however that may be defined) complete your survey. Instead, you administer your questionnaire to a small sample of that population.

Proper sampling is a crucial aspect of sound survey research methodology. Without proper sampling, you can't generalize your results to your target population (for example, accurately predict voter behavior in an election). Three sampling-related issues you must consider are representativeness, sampling technique, and sample size.

Representativeness

Regardless of the technique you use to acquire your sample, your sample should be representative of the population of interest. A **representative sample** closely matches the characteristics of the population. Imagine that you have a bag containing 300 golf balls: 100 are white, 100 are orange, and 100 are yellow. Assume you select a sample of 30 golf balls. A representative sample would have 10 balls of each color. A sample having 25 white and 5 orange would not be representative (the ratio of colors does not approximate that of the population). Such a sample is said to be nonrepresentative or a **biased sample**.

The importance of representative sampling is shown by the failure of a political poll taken during the 1936 presidential election. In that election Alf Landon was opposing Franklin Roosevelt. The editors of the *Literary Digest* (a now-defunct magazine) conducted a poll by using telephone directories and vehicle registration lists to draw their sample. The final sample consisted of nearly 10 million people! The results showed that Landon would beat Roosevelt by a landslide. Quite to the contrary, Roosevelt soundly defeated Landon. Why was the poll so wrong?

The problem stemmed from the method used to obtain the sample. Fewer people owned a car or telephone in the 1930s than do today. In fact, very few owned either. Those who did own a telephone or car tended to be relatively wealthy and Republican. Consequently, most of the subjects polled favored the Republican candidate. Unfortunately for the *Literary Digest,* this sample was not representative of the population of voters, and the prediction failed. How could the editors have been so stupid? In fact, they weren't stupid. Such sampling techniques had been used before and worked. It was only in that particular election (in which people were clearly split along party lines) that the problem emerged (Hooke, 1983).

The *Literary Digest* poll failed because it used a biased source (car registration and telephone listings). Whatever source you choose, you should make an effort to determine whether it includes members from all segments of the population in which you have an interest. A good way to overcome the problem of biased source lists is to use multiple lists. For example, you could use the telephone book, *and* vehicle registration, *and* voter registration lists to select your sample.

Sampling Techniques

At the heart of all sampling techniques is the concept of *random sampling*. In random sampling, every member of the population has an *equal chance* of appearing in your sample. Whether or not a subject is included in your sample is based on chance alone. Sampling is typically done *without replacement*. Once an individual is chosen for your sample, he or she cannot be chosen a second time for that sample.

Random sampling eliminates the possibility that the sample is biased by the preferences of the person selecting the sample. In addition, random sampling affords some assurance that the sample does not bias itself. As an example of self-biasing, consider the following case. In 1976 Shere Hite published *The Hite Report: A Nationwide Study on Female Sexuality,* which was a survey of women's sexual attitudes and behaviors. Hite's sample was obtained by initially distributing questionnaires through national mailings to women's groups (the National Organization for Women, abortion rights groups, university women's centers, and others). Later, advertisements were placed in several magazines (the *Village Voice, Mademoiselle, Brides,* and *Ms.*) informing women where they could write for a copy of the questionnaire. Finally, the questionnaire was reprinted in *Oui* magazine in its entirety (253 women returned the questionnaire from *Oui*).

The question you should ask yourself at this point is "Did Hite obtain a random sample of the population of women?" The answer is no. Hite's method had several problems. First, the memberships of the organizations Hite contacted may not be representative of the population of women. For example, you cannot assume that members of NOW hold similar views, on the average, to those of the population of all women. Second, asking people through magazine ads to write in for questionnaires further biases the sample. Can you figure out why?

If you said that the people who write in for the questionnaires may be somehow different from those who do not, you were correct. Who would write in to obtain a questionnaire on sexuality? Obviously, women who have an interest in such an issue. In fact, Hite indicates that many of her subjects expressed such an interest. One woman wrote, "I answered this questionnaire because I think the time is long overdue for women to speak out about their feelings about sex" (Hite, 1976, p. xxxii). As with the members of the women's organizations, you could question whether the women who wrote in for questionnaires are representative of all women. They probably are not.

When a sample is biased, the data obtained may not be indicative of the attitudes of the population as a whole. Hite concluded from her sample that women in this country were experiencing a "new sexuality." However, that new sexuality was limited to those women whose attitudes were similar to those who answered her questionnaires.

In 1983 Hite published the *Hite Report on Male Sexuality*. The method she used to gather data was similar to the one used in her earlier study of women. In this book Hite responded to the criticisms of her method. She presented evidence that her sample of men was similar in age, religion, and education to the most recent census data. What was not clear, however, was whether or not the attitudes of the men who responded to her questionnaire were similar to those of the general population. As in the survey of women, the data obtained may not be representative of the population of men. Some evidence suggests they were not. Hite said that 72 percent of married men reported having had an extramarital affair. Is this an accurate estimate of the population or an estimate of a special subsection of the population? Apparently it is the latter. Other surveys have found that about 25 percent of men report having had extramarital affairs.

The lesson of the Hite example is that you should make every effort to obtain a random sample. This may be difficult, especially if you are dealing with a sensitive topic. You could use some of the strategies previously suggested for reducing nonresponse bias (such as including a small reward or using follow-ups). If your sample turns out to be nonrandom and nonrepresentative, temper any conclusions you draw.

Using the proper sampling technique is one way to obtain a representative sample. Several techniques are available to you. Four of them (simple random sampling, stratified sampling, systematic sampling, and cluster sampling) are discussed next. These techniques are not mutually exclusive. Often researchers combine them to help ensure a representative sample of the population.

Simple Random Sampling. Randomly selecting a certain number of individuals from the population is a technique called **simple random sampling.** Remember the golf ball example? A simple random sample of 50 would involve dipping your hand into the bag 50 times, each time withdrawing a single ball. Figure 7-5 illustrates the simple random sampling strategy. From the population illustrated at the top of the figure, 10 subjects are selected at random for inclusion in your survey.

In practice, selecting a random sample for a survey is more involved than pulling golf balls from a bag. Often it involves consulting a *table of random numbers.* The numbers in such a table have been chosen at random and then subjected to a number of statistical tests to ensure they have the expected properties of random numbers. You can find a table of random numbers in Appendix I (Table I-A).

As an example of how to use the table of random numbers to select a random sample, imagine you are using the telephone book as a source list. Starting on any page of the random number table, close your eyes and drop your finger on the page. Open your eyes and read the number under your finger. Assume that the number was 235,035. Then go to page 235 in the telephone book and select the thirty-fifth name on that page. Repeat this process until you select all the subjects constituting the sample.

A variant of random sampling that can be used when conducting a telephone survey is *random-digit dialing* (Dillman, 1978). List all the exchanges in a particular area (the first three digits of the phone numbers, not including the area code). You then use the table of random numbers to select four-digit numbers (for example, 5,891). The exchange plus the four-digit number provides the number to be called. (Any nonworking numbers are discarded.) This technique allows you to reach unlisted as well as listed numbers.

Even though random sampling reduces the possibility of systematic bias in your sample, it does not guarantee a representative sample. You could, quite at random, select subjects who represent only a small segment of the population. In the golf ball example, you might select 50 orange golf balls. White and yellow golf balls, even though represented in the population, are not in your sample. One way to combat this problem is to select a large sample (such as 200 rather than just 50 balls). A large sample is more likely to represent all segments of the population than a small one. However, it does not *guarantee* that representation in your sample will be proportionate to representation in the population. You may end up with 90 white, 90 orange, and only 20 yellow golf balls in a sample of 200, although such a result is highly unlikely. In addition, as you increase sample size you also increase the cost and time needed to complete the survey. Fortunately, more sophisticated techniques provide a random, yet representative, sample without requiring a large number of subjects.

Stratified Sampling. **Stratified sampling** provides one way to obtain a representative sample. You begin by dividing the population into segments, or *strata* (Kish, 1965). For example, you could divide the population of a particular town

Population

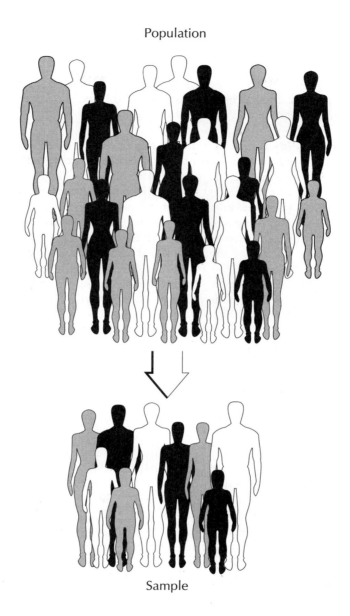

Sample

Figure 7-5. Example of simple random sampling. The people at the top of the figure represent the population, and the people at the bottom represent the randomly selected sample.

into whites, blacks, and Hispanics. Next, you select a separate random sample of equal size from each stratum. Because individuals are selected from each stratum, you guarantee that each segment of the population is represented in your sample. Figure 7-6 shows the stratified sampling strategy. Notice that the population has been divided into two segments (black and white figures). A random sample is then selected from each segment.

Proportionate Sampling. Simple stratified sampling ensures a degree of representativeness, but it may lead to a segment of the population being overrepresented in your sample. For example, consider a community of 5,000 that has 500 Hispanics, 1,500 blacks, and 3,000 whites. If you used a simple stratification technique in which you randomly selected 400 people from each stratum, Hispanics would be overrepresented in your sample relative to blacks and whites, and blacks would be overrepresented relative to whites. You could avoid this problem by using a variant of simple stratified sampling called **proportionate sampling**.

In proportionate sampling, the proportions of people in the population are reflected in your sample. In the population example, your sample would consist of 10 percent Hispanics (500/5,000 = 10%), 30 percent blacks (1,500/5,000 = 30%), and 60 percent whites (3,000/5,000 = 60%). So, if you draw a sample of 1,200, you would have 120 Hispanics, 360 blacks, and 720 whites. According to Kish (1965), this technique is the most popular method of sampling.

By the way, stratification and proportionate sampling can be done after a sample has been obtained (Kish, 1965). You randomly select from the subjects who responded the number from each stratum needed to match the characteristics of the population.

Systematic Sampling. **Systematic sampling** is a popular technique that is often used in conjunction with stratified sampling (Kish, 1965). Figure 7-7 illustrates the systematic sampling technique.

According to Kish, this technique involves sampling every kth element after a random start. For example, once you have randomly chosen the page of the telephone book from which you are going to sample, you then might pick every fourth item (where $k = 4$). Systematic sampling is much less time-consuming and more cost-effective than simple random sampling. For example, it is much easier to select every fourth item from a page than to select randomly from an entire list.

Cluster Sampling. In some cases, populations may be too large to allow cost-effective random sampling — or even systematic sampling. You might be interested in surveying children in a large school district. To make sampling more manageable, you could identify naturally occurring groups of subjects (clusters) and randomly select certain clusters. For example, you could randomly select certain departments or classes from which to sample. Once the clusters had been

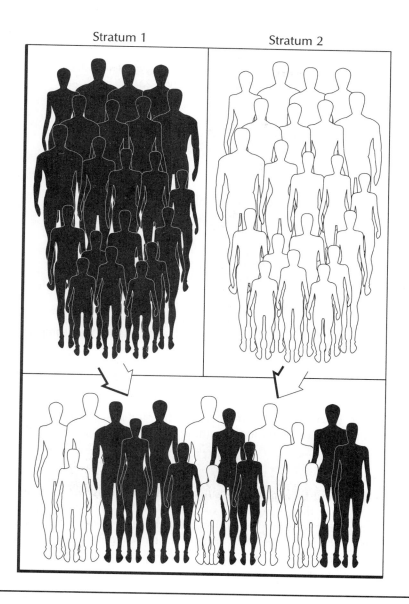

Figure 7-6. Example of stratified sampling. The population is divided into two strata from which independent random samples are drawn.

Richardson, E.   555-6396*
Richardson, J. B.   555-6789
Richardson, L. R.   555-2311
Richardson, M.   555-9902
Richardson, V.   555-7822*
Richeson, A. P.   555-8211
Richeson, T.   555-3762
Richey, B. B.   555-9943
Richey, C. L.   555-1470*
Richey, G. J.   555-8218
Richhart, W.   555-6539
Richman, A.   555-8902
Richman, B. I.   555-0076*
Richman, H. H.   555-9215
Richman, Z. L.   555-1093
Richmond, A.   555-7634
Richmond, B. B.   555-7890*
Richmond, C.   555-2609
Rideman, L.   555-7245
Ritchey, A. K.   555-6790

Each of the names with a star (*) would be included in your sample.

Figure 7-7. Example of systematic sampling. After a random start, every selected name is included in the sample (indicated with an asterisk).

selected, you would then survey all subjects within the clusters. **Cluster sampling** differs from the other forms of sampling already discussed in that the basic sampling unit is a group of subjects (the cluster) rather than the individual subject (Kish, 1965). Figure 7–8 illustrates cluster sampling. This figure shows how you select four groups from a larger pool of groups. Those subgroups are then sampled randomly.

An obvious advantage to cluster sampling is that it saves time. It is not always feasible to select random samples that focus on single elements (that is, individuals, families, and so forth). Cluster sampling provides an acceptable, cost-effective method of acquiring a sample. On the negative side, cluster sampling does limit your sample to those subjects found in the chosen clusters. If subjects within clusters are fairly similar to one another, but differ from those in other clusters, the sample will leave out important elements of the population. For example, clusters consisting of geographical areas of the United States (East, Midwest, South, Southwest, West) may differ widely in political opinion. If

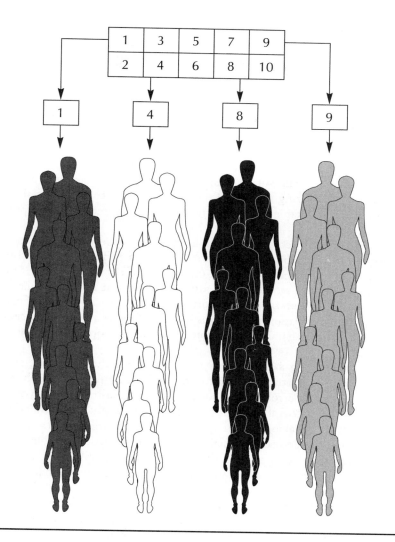

Figure 7-8. Example of cluster sampling. After selecting subgroups of the population, you randomly sample.

only East and Midwest are selected for the sample, the opinions collected may not reflect the opinions of the country as a whole. Thus, cluster sampling does have drawbacks.

One way to circumvent this problem is to use **multistage sampling**. You begin by identifying large clusters and randomly select from among them (first stage). From the selected clusters, you then randomly select individual elements (rather than selecting all elements in the cluster). This method can be combined with stratification procedures to ensure a representative sample.

Other sophisticated sampling techniques are available to the survey researcher, but to explore them all would require a whole book. If you are interested in learning about these techniques, read Kish (1965).

Sample Size

One factor you must contend with if you perform a survey is the size of your sample. You should try to select an *economic sample* — one that includes enough subjects to ensure a valid survey, and no more. You must take into account two factors when considering the size of the sample needed to ensure a valid survey: the amount of acceptable error and the expected magnitude of the population proportions.

The question of acceptable error arises because most samples deviate to some degree from the population. If you conduct a political poll on a sample of 1,500 registered voters and find that 62 percent of the sample favor Smith and 38 percent Jones, you would like to say that 62 percent of the population favor Smith. However, these sample proportions do not exactly match those of the population (the population proportions may be 59 percent and 41 percent). This deviation of sample characteristics from those of the population is called **sampling error**.

When determining sample size, you must decide the acceptable amount of sampling error. Unfortunately, there are no broad rules of thumb as to the acceptable margin of error. It depends in part on the use to which you will put your results (Moser & Kalton, 1972). If you plan to apply your results to implement changes in behavior, you may want a small margin of error. If you are interested simply in describing a set of characteristics, you may tolerate a larger margin of error. A good way to determine the acceptable margin of error is to look at literature describing similar surveys to see what margin of error was used.

The second component you need to consider when determining sample size is the magnitude of the differences you expect to find. Here again, there is no broad rule of thumb to guide you. Again, you can make use of previous surveys to get an estimate of the magnitude of the differences. Or you can conduct a small pilot survey to gain some insight into the magnitudes. Once you have settled on this component, you can then determine the size of the sample needed to be representative of the population.

Once you have determined the acceptable error and the expected magnitude of differences, you can calculate the size of the sample needed. The calculation is relatively easy for simple random sampling. Moser and Kalton suggested the following formula:

$$n' = \frac{P'\,(1 - P')}{[S.E._{\mathrm{p}}]^2}$$

where P' is the estimate of the proportion of the population that has a particular characteristic, and $S.E._p$ is the acceptable margin of error. For example, if you expect 62 percent of the population to favor Smith in an election and your acceptable level of error is 2 percent (0.02), then the formula gives $n' = 589$. Thus, you should have 589 subjects in your sample.

When the size of the population is large, you do not need to consider population size when calculating sample size. If the population is small, however, then you must use the *finite population correction* (*f.p.c.*) when calculating sample size. Crano and Brewer (1986) suggested using the following formula when the sample size is more than 10 percent of the population size.

$$n = N \times n'/(N + n')$$

where n = the corrected sample size, n' = the sample size calculated with the previous formula, and N = the size of the population from which the sample is to be drawn. For example, using the previous numbers and $N = 2,000$, you have

$$n = 2000 \times 589/(2000 + 589) = 455$$

Thus, if the population from which your sample will be drawn consists of only 2,000 subjects, you would use a sample size of 455 rather than of 589.

For stratified sampling, determining sample size is more difficult than for simple random sampling. You must take into account the between–strata error (the variability in the scores of subjects in different strata) and the within–strata error (the variability in the scores of subjects within the same stratum). The formulas for computing sample size with the more sophisticated sampling techniques are complex. If you pursue survey research using these techniques, consult Moser and Kalton (1972) and Kish (1965) for more information.

Summary

Survey research is used to evaluate the behavior (past, present, and future) and attitudes of your subjects. Survey research falls into the category of correlational research. Therefore, you cannot draw causal inferences about behavior from your survey data, no matter how compelling the data look. Surveys are used in a wide variety of situations. They can be used to research the marketability of a new product, to predict voter behavior, or to measure existing attitudes on a variety of issues.

The first step in a survey is to clearly define the goals of your research. Your questionnaire is then designed around those goals. You should have a reasonably focused goal for your survey. A questionnaire that tries to do too much may be confusing and burdensome to your subjects. Keep your questionnaire focused on the central issues of your research.

Often a questionnaire is organized so that questions about your subjects' characteristics (demographic items) and questions about the behavior or attitude of interest are included. The demographic items can later be used as predictor variables when you look for relationships among the variables that you measured.

Questionnaire items can be of several types. Open-ended questions allow your subjects to answer in their own words. A major advantage of this type of question is the richness of the information obtained. A drawback is that responses are difficult to summarize and analyze. A restricted question provides response categories for subjects. A variation on the restricted item is a rating scale where subjects circle a number reflecting how they feel. This type of item yields data that are easier to summarize and analyze. However, the responses made to restricted items are not as rich as those obtained with an open-ended item. A partially open-ended item not only provides subjects with clearly defined response alternatives, but also provides a space for subjects to write in their own response category.

Once you have decided what types of items to include on your questionnaire, you must then actually write your questions. When writing items, you should avoid using overly complex words where more simple words will suffice. Your questions should be precise. Vague or overly precise wording yields inconsistent data. In addition, avoid question wording that is biased or judgmental.

A questionnaire is more than just a collection of questions. Questions should be presented in a logical order so that your questionnaire has continuity. Also, it is a good idea to place demographic items at the end. These questions tend to be boring, and subjects may be turned off if you have demographic items at the beginning of your questionnaire. Sensitive questions should be placed toward the middle. Your subjects may be more willing to answer such questions after answering several other, more innocuous questions. Sensitive items should be carefully worded.

Three ways to administer your questionnaire are the mail survey, telephone survey, and interview. The mail survey is easiest. You simply mail your questionnaires and wait for a response. However, this method is plagued by nonresponse bias. Return rates can be increased with effective cover letters, follow-up reminders tailored to the nature of your subject population, and small rewards. In group administration you give your survey to a large number of subjects at once. The advantage of group administration is that you can collect large amounts of data quickly. Surveys can also be conducted over the telephone. Questionnaires designed for telephone surveys should be relatively short, with clearly worded, short questions. Because your questions will be read to your subjects, make sure that the person reading questions speaks clearly and slowly. In an interview, you ask your questions to your subjects in a face-to-face session. Interviews can be either structured (questions asked from a prepared questionnaire in a fixed order) or unstructured (each interview is different).

One of the most crucial stages of survey research is acquiring a sample of subjects. Because you want to make statements about how people think on an issue, be sure your sample represents the population. Biased samples lead to invalid data and ultimately incorrect conclusions. Sampling techniques include simple random sampling (where every subject has an equal chance of being in your survey) and stratified sampling (where your population is broken into smaller segments and random samples are then drawn from those smaller segments). Other sampling techniques are proportionate sampling, multistage sampling, and cluster sampling. The sampling technique you use depends on the needs of your survey.

Whichever sampling technique you choose, you must consider the issue of sample size. Your sample should be large enough to be representative of the population, yet not too large. Try to acquire an economic sample that has just enough subjects to adequately assess behavior or attitudes. The size of the most economic sample is determined with a special formula.

Key Terms

Open-ended item

Restricted item

Partially open-ended item

Mail survey

Nonresponse bias

Telephone survey

Interview

Representative sample

Biased sample

Simple random sampling

Stratified sampling

Proportionate sampling

Systematic sampling

Cluster sampling

Multistage sampling

Sampling error

8

Using Between-
Subjects Designs

As we pointed out in Chapter 1, a major goal of research is to establish clear, causal relationships between variables. The correlational research designs discussed in Chapters 6 and 7 may help to identify potential causal relationships and are often used when causal variables cannot or should not be manipulated directly. But correlational designs are simply not adequate for establishing causal relationships between variables.

When your goal is to establish causal relationships, and you can manipulate variables, an experimental research design is used. By manipulating an independent variable while rigidly controlling extraneous factors, you can determine whether this manipulation causes changes in the value of the dependent variable.

Types of Experimental Design

In Chapter 3 we noted that every true experiment contains two fundamental elements: an independent variable, which the experimenter manipulates, and a dependent variable, which the experimenter observes and records. To manipulate the independent variable, you set its value to at least two different values or "levels" during the course of the experiment and observe your subjects' performances under each level. You then compare these performances. If you can show that performance differed across the levels of the independent variable and that these differences are reliable, you can conclude that a change in the level of the independent variable *causes* a change in the value of the dependent variable.

This simple logic is at the heart of every experimental design. However, to deal with the complexities of real-world research problems, researchers have developed a large variety of designs. We can simplify the situation somewhat by noting that all these designs can be categorized into three basic types: between-subjects, within-subjects, and single-subject designs. Before we deal with the between-subjects designs that are the main subject of this chapter, let's briefly examine the main features of each type.

Between-Subjects Designs

In the **between-subjects design,** different groups of subjects are randomly assigned to the levels of the independent variable. For example, consider an experiment designed to determine the effect of tetrahydrocannabinol, or THC (the main psychoactive ingredient in marijuana) on the number of errors in a simulated air traffic controller task. To conduct this experiment as a between-subjects design, you assign some subjects to a group (the experimental group) that will receive, say, a 1-mg dose of the drug. You assign other subjects to a group that does not receive the drug (the control group). After testing your two groups on the simulation, you average the scores for each group and compare the two means to see which group performed better. You then submit your results to a statistical analysis to determine the reliability of any difference be-tween the performances of the two groups (see Chapter 12).

The experiment described represents the simplest between-subjects design, with only one independent variable manipulated. The basic design can be ex-tended in several ways to meet the requirements of your research questions. You can provide additional groups, include more factors (independent variables), or measure additional dependent variables. Regardless of the number of groups, factors, or dependent variables, the basic method remains the same: assign dif-ferent subjects to the different experimental conditions.

Within-Subjects Designs

Within-subjects designs differ from between-subjects designs in that only one group of subjects is included. This single group receives all the levels of the independent variable. Of course, you must apply the different levels of the independent variable to the same subjects at different times. If you wanted to conduct your drug study using a within-subjects design, you might first test subjects without administering the drug and subsequently test the same subjects after administering the drug. You would then average the subjects' performances across each treatment condition and compare the two resulting means. Finally, submit any apparent effect of the independent variable to a statistical analysis to evaluate its reliability.

As with the between-subjects design, your experimental design may include as many levels of the independent variable as needed to evaluate your research question (within limits!) or more than one factor. However, as you add factors and levels of the independent variables, the logistics involved in this design become more complicated. Chapter 9 discusses the special requirements of the within-subjects design.

Single-Subject Designs

Single-subject designs use the same method of varying the level of the independent variable used by the within-subjects design. That is, you expose the same subjects to all the levels at different times. The major difference from the within-subjects design is that you do not evaluate averaged data from groups of subjects. Instead, you focus on changes in the behavior of the individual subject under the different treatment conditions. Reliability is assessed by immediate replication rather than by applying a statistical analysis. To assess whether the resulting data are typical or aberrant for the type of subject being tested, you administer the same treatments to several subjects (usually somewhere between three and six).

Given the number of subjects usually included, the name "single-subject" may seem a misnomer for this type of design, but it really is not. The name refers to the fact that the design is capable of detecting the effect of an independent variable on a single subject's behavior.

Now that you can distinguish the basic types of experimental design, it is time to more closely examine the characteristics of between-subjects designs and the various design options available to you within that category. We begin by examining how between-subjects designs deal with a serious problem for all experimental designs: error variance.

Between–Subjects Designs and the Problem of Error Variance

Error variance is the statistical variability between scores caused by the influence of variables other than your independent variable, known as *extraneous variables* (see Chapter 12 for a discussion of why scores may vary within a distribution). The problems posed by error variance are common to all three experimental designs. Each design, however, has its own way of dealing with error variance. In this chapter, we focus on how we deal with error variance in between-subjects designs. In the next two chapters, we explore how within-subjects and single-subject designs handle the problem.

Sources of Error Variance

In the real world, it is rarely possible to hold constant all the extraneous variables that could affect the value of your dependent variable. For example, subjects in

Table 8-1. Scores from Hypothetical THC Experiment

Performance on Dependent Measure	
Control Group	*Experimental Group*
25	13
24	19
18	22
29	18
19	23
Mean 23	19

your experiment differ from one another in innumerable ways that could individually or collectively affect their scores on the dependent measure, the environmental conditions are not absolutely constant, and even the same subject will not be exactly the same from moment to moment. To the extent that these variations affect your dependent variable, they induce fluctuations in scores that have nothing to do with your intended manipulation. That is, they produce error variance.

An example may help to clarify this concept. In the THC experiment described earlier, you had two groups of subjects. One group was exposed to the dose of THC (the experimental group), and one was not (the control group). Within each group, all subjects would have been exposed to the same level of the independent variable. Yet it is unlikely that all subjects in a group would turn in the same scores on the dependent measure (number of errors on the simulated air traffic controller task). Subjects differ from one another in many ways that affect their performances. Some may be more resistant to fatigue, have better attention skills, or perceptual abilities than others, for example. The variation in scores produced by the uncontrolled variables is the error variance we are discussing.

Table 8-1 shows the scores turned in by subjects in this hypothetical experiment. The scores for each group have been averaged and the means presented at the bottom of the table. Judging from the means, it appears that THC reduced the subjects' scores on the dependent variable. However, given the variability in scores evident within each group, it seems plausible to suggest that the difference in the means may reflect nothing more than pre-existing subject differences that did not quite balance out across the two conditions of the experiment. The problem is that you cannot tell, simply by looking at the means, which explanation is correct. The problem of error variance is therefore serious. It affects your ability to determine the effectiveness of your independent variable.

Handling Error Variance in Between-Subjects Designs

Fortunately, there are ways you can cope with the problem of error variance. You can take steps to reduce error variance, you can take steps to increase the effect of your independent variable, and you can randomize error variance across groups. Let's look at each of these strategies in more detail.

Reducing Error Variance. Error variance is a bit like static on the telephone line. As the static becomes louder, it becomes more difficult to hear the conversation. In the same way, as error variance increases, it becomes more difficult to detect any effect of your independent variable. Anything you can do to reduce these irrelevant differences in subject performance will increase your ability to establish the effectiveness of your independent variable.

A prime way to reduce error variance is to hold extraneous variables constant. Treat all subjects within a particular group as similarly as possible. For example, by testing subjects in a relatively isolated room, you can remove temporary distractions that may cause performance to vary. Present any instructions in the same way to each subject (for example, by putting the instructions on tape), and follow a standard protocol when conducting your experimental procedure.

Another way to reduce error variance is to select subjects who are similar in certain characteristics that you believe contribute to error variance in your dependent measure (for example, you could use rats that are all 90 days old, female, and of the Sprague-Dawley strain). Although such restrictions tend to reduce the external validity of your results, you can always relax these restrictions in a later experiment. The first priority is to demonstrate that you can obtain reliable results. A similar tactic is to match subjects across groups on certain potentially important characteristics. We discuss this option more fully later in this chapter (see the section on matched groups designs).

Increasing the Effectiveness of Your Independent Variable. Another way to increase your ability to detect the effect of your independent variable (assuming it has one) is to select the right levels for your experiment. A weak manipulation may have relatively little influence on your dependent variable, leaving the effect of your independent variable buried in whatever amount of error variance is present. Unfortunately, finding an effective manipulation may be difficult. Usually you will not know what level (if any) is effective until you perform the experiment. If the effect of the variable has been examined before, the literature may provide a guide to selecting an effective level. Also, if there are several ways to operationally define your dependent variable, one measure may prove more sensitive than another. Again, you may be able to find some clues in the literature.

Randomizing Error Variance Across Groups. No matter how much attention you pay to reducing error variance, you will never be able to eliminate it. The final strategy for dealing with whatever error variance remains is to randomize error variance across groups. This is accomplished by the simple method known as *random assignment*. You might, for example, put slips of paper with the names of all your subjects into a hat and draw names one at time to determine to which condition the subjects would be assigned. This results in groups of subjects that have been equalized, over the long run, on individual difference factors (for example, intelligence and socioeconomic status). Random assignment is characteristic of randomized groups designs, which are discussed later in this chapter.

Although random assignment of subjects to conditions by pulling names out of a hat is a good metaphor for the process, in reality you usually use a different method when actually doing research. One technique involves assigning each subject a number (1 through 8, for example) and then using a table of random numbers (such as Table I-1B in Appendix I) to make your assignments. Using Table I-1B, read down a column for the subject's number. The first four numbers encountered, for example, would be assigned to the experimental group and the rest to the control group.

By randomly assigning subjects to their respective groups, you tend to distribute error variance evenly among the groups. As a result, any differences in group performance tend to reflect the effect of the independent variable rather than the effect of error variance.

Statistical Analysis. Although random assignment *tends* to even out the effects of error variance across groups, there is no guarantee that it *will* do so. In addition, no matter how hard you try to eliminate error variance, some will always appear in your data. How can you determine whether a given effect in your data was caused by your manipulation and not by error variance? The answer is that you can never be sure. Nevertheless, it is possible to evaluate the *probability* that error variance is responsible for your obtained differences in group performance. If this probability is low enough, you may conclude with reasonable confidence that the observed effect is due to your independent variable.

The techniques that allow you to perform this evaluation are called *inferential statistics*. If you have not yet had a class in statistics or wish to brush up on the logic underlying them, you might wish to read the introduction to statistical concepts we provide in Chapters 11 ("Descriptive Statistics") and 12 ("Inferential Statistics"). If a given result is not likely to have arisen by chance, the result is said to be *statistically significant*. This is just another way of saying that the results are probably due to the effect of the independent variable rather than to error variance. Another way of putting it is that the result is probably *reliable*.

Inferential statistics have been developed for specific designs and types of data, so it is important to know which inferential statistic to use. When we discuss specific types of between-subjects design later in the chapter, we indicate some of the inferential statistics that would be appropriate to each type.

The statistical tests mentioned with each design may include both parametric and nonparametric types. Parametric inferential statistics require that your data represent samples from populations with certain well-defined properties. For example, such populations should have an approximately normal distribution. Use nonparametric statistics when your data do not meet these assumptions. In general, parametric statistics make better use of the information contained in the data and therefore are usually preferred if the conditions for their use are met. For more information on the distinction between parametric and nonparametric statistics, see Chapter 12 or any good introductory statistics text.

The time has come to examine the types of between-subjects designs available to you. These designs differ along several dimensions, including the number of levels of the independent variable, whether only one independent variable is included or more than one, whether subjects are randomly assigned to groups or matched, and whether one or more than one dependent variable is included. Treating each combination as a different design can get repetitious, so let's simplify things a bit by presenting single-factor randomized groups designs as the basic theme. We will then explore the variations on this theme produced by varying the number of factors, method of subject assignment, and number of dependent measures.

Single-Factor Randomized Groups Designs

Single-factor designs include only one independent variable (factor) in the design. When using a *randomized groups design,* you randomly assign subjects to the levels of your independent variable to form "groups" of subjects. We have already explored the randomized groups design in our general discussion of between-subjects designs. However, a couple of points must be added to that general discussion.

The Randomized Two-Group Design

If you randomly assign your subjects to two groups, expose the two groups to different levels of the independent variable, and take steps to hold extraneous variables constant, you are using a **randomized two-group design**. Figure 8-1 illustrates the basic steps to follow when conducting a randomized two-group experiment. Begin by sampling a group of subjects from the general population (top rectangle). Then randomly assign the subjects from this group into your two treatment groups. Next expose the subjects in each group to the appropriate treatment condition and record the resulting data. Finally, compare the two means to determine whether they differ. Any difference you find is submitted to a statistical analysis to assess its reliability.

The randomized two-group design is one of the simplest available, yet it has several advantages over other, more complex designs. First, it is simple to carry out. Usually you need only to select a small group of subjects (often you can get by with fewer than 20) and randomly assign them to the two groups of the experiment. An experiment with this few subjects is relatively economical in

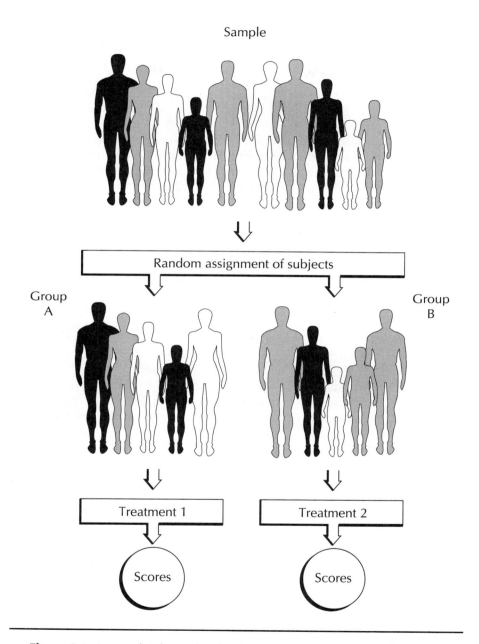

Figure 8-1. A completely randomized two-group experimental design.

terms of time and materials. Second, no pretesting or categorization of subjects is necessary. The randomized group strategy often is more than adequate to test your hypothesis, obviating the need for more complex matching strategy (see section on matched groups designs later in this chapter). Finally, statistical analysis of the resulting data is relatively simple. Indeed, some electronic calculators have the required statistics built into them, so you need only enter the data and press the appropriate button.

A disadvantage of the randomized two-group design is that it provides a limited amount of information about the effect of the independent variable. You learn only a few things, such as whether the two groups differed (on the average) in their responses to the independent variable under the two levels tested, in what direction, and by how much. You do not learn much about the function relating the independent and dependent variable.

This point can be illustrated with an experiment by Gold (1987). Gold was interested in determining whether glucose (blood sugar) affects memory. In Gold's experiment, rats were individually placed on the white side of a rectangular box that was divided into a well-lit white compartment and a dimly lit black compartment. Because rats tend to prefer darkness over light, they quickly crossed into the black compartment, where they received a mild foot shock. Immediately after this experience, the rats were each injected with glucose. Different groups received different amounts of the glucose. The rats were then returned to their home cages. Twenty-four hours later, the animals were again placed in the white compartment, and the amount of time they took to re-enter the black compartment was recorded. The rats should have been hesitant to re-enter to the extent that they remembered the shock they had received on the previous day. Thus, greater amounts of time to re-enter should have reflected better memory for the shock.

Figure 8-2 shows, in idealized form, the results of Gold's experiment. In Panel A, the mean number of seconds to re-enter the black compartment is plotted against glucose dose. Glucose did affect memory, and in a dose-dependent manner. The function relating glucose dose to re-entry time is shaped somewhat like an inverted *U*, with intermediate doses being more effective than higher or lower doses. Gold concluded that sugar can be used in some cases to improve memory (if it's not overdone).

Although Gold's experiment used several groups, imagine that Gold had used only two. Panel B shows what Gold's results would have looked like had he chosen to use glucose doses of 10 and 100 mg/kg of body weight. What would Gold have concluded?

Panel C shows what Gold's results would have looked like had he chosen to use 100 and 1,000 mg/kg doses. What would Gold's conclusion have been in this case?

Finally, Panel D shows Gold's results had he chosen 10 and 100 mg/kg doses. What would the conclusion have been now?

If you were unaware of the inverted U-shaped function relating memory to glucose level, it might seem that these three experiments had yielded contradictory results. Furthermore, if you attempted to extrapolate the function beyond

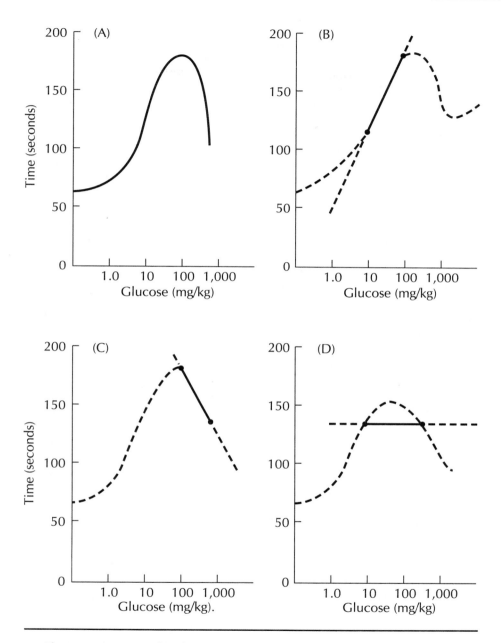

Figure 8-2. (A) Results of experiment relating glucose dosage to memory (as measured by the time required to enter a dark compartment). (B, C, and D) Three functions based on Gold's data, showing lines estimated from various pairs of points. (Panel A reprinted from Gold, 1987, with permission.)

the two data points collected in a given experiment (dotted lines in Panels B, C, and D), you would form an erroneous picture of the relationship.

This problem can be solved by conducting a series of two-group experiments in which different levels of the independent variable are chosen for each experiment. However, more efficient designs for sweeping out a functional relationship are available and will be examined later.

A second limitation of the randomized two-group design concerns its sensitivity to the effect (if any) of the independent variable. Where subjects differ greatly from one another on characteristics that influence their performances on the dependent measure, these variations may make it difficult to detect the effect of the independent variable. In such cases, the randomized groups design may indicate no effect of the independent variable, although one was actually present. (If you have taken a course in statistics, you might recognize this as a type II error. See Chapter 12.)

Finally, when you are interested in investigating the limits of an effect, two groups are rarely enough. You must include several levels of an independent variable to adequately test the more subtle effects of your independent variable.

Statistical Analysis. After you have run your randomized two-group experiment and summarized your data, the next step is to apply an inferential statistic in order to assess the reliability of your findings. Most likely you would use the *t*-test for independent samples for this evaluation. You can use the *t*-test if your dependent variable were measured on at least an interval scale. (For other assumptions that must be met before a *t*-test can be applied, see Chapter 12.) In cases where your dependent variable is measured along an ordinal scale, or your interval or ratio data fail to meet the assumptions of the *t*-test, you can use a *Mann-Whitney U-test* (Siegel & Castellan, 1988). For nominal data, an appropriate test would be the *chi-square test*.

Single-Factor Multigroup Designs

One way to expand the simple two-group design is to add additional groups in order to assess the independent variable at more than two levels. The different levels of the independent variable may represent different *categories* (nominal scale), or they may represent different *amounts* of the independent variable (ordinal, interval, or ratio scale). Such designs are forms of the *single-factor multigroup design*. Variations on this theme are described in the following sections.

Single-Factor Parametric Design. If different levels of the independent variable represent quantitative differences, the design is sometimes referred to as a **parametric design**. The term *parametric* refers to the systematic variation of the amount of an independent variable. (This use of the term must be distinguished from the use of *parametric* to denote a class of inferential statistic.) This discussion deals with a between-subjects design that includes only one such independent variable. Strictly speaking, the term *parametric* can be applied to a number of

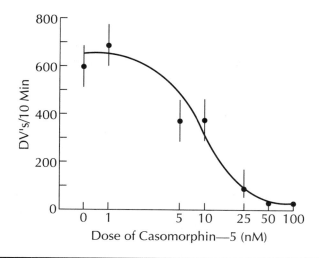

Figure 8-3. Graph illustrating results from a parametric, multigroup experiment. (From Panksepp et al., 1984; reprinted with permission.)

designs, including those that have multiple independent variables and those of the within-subject design (see Chapter 9).

An example of a single-factor parametric design was conducted by Panksepp, Normansell, Siviy, Rossi, and Zolovick (1984). Panksepp et al. investigated the effect of casomorphin-5 (a peptide found in milk) on the amount of distress calling produced by chicks when separated from their broodmates. Different groups of chicks received doses of 0, 1, 5, 10, 25, 50, or 100 nM (nanomoles). Each chick was then placed in an isolation chamber for ten minutes and the number of distress peeps was recorded.

Figure 8-3 shows the results of the experiment. The number of distress vocalizations (DV/10 min) is plotted as a function of the amount of drug. Each point on the graph represents the average performance of a different group of chicks (the vertical lines indicate the variation of scores within each group). The data depicted in Figure 8-3 can be analyzed several ways, depending on the questions you want to answer. For example, you could ask whether the performance of any of the experimental groups (nonzero nM dose) differs reliably from that of the control group (zero nM dose). Answering this question requires comparing each experimental group mean to the control group mean. Another question you could ask is whether the data show a *trend* and, if so, what is the nature of the trend. A trend is a uniform pattern of change. Trends can be linear (straight-line), quadratic (U-shaped), cubic (S-shaped), or higher-order. In addition, one set of points may show two or more trends combined. Appropriate statistics are available to determine whether apparent trends in the data are likely to be real trends, or simply the result of random fluctuations among the points. What trend appears to be represented in Figure 8-3? The S-shaped trend is cubic.

Single-Factor Nonparametric Design. If your independent variable falls on a nominal scale (the various levels represent different categories rather than amounts), and you assign each level of the independent variable to a different group, then the design you are using is called a single-factor **nonparametric design**. Because of the nominal character of the independent variable, the order in which the group means are plotted on a graph is arbitrary and looking for trends makes no sense. Such data are represented better by histograms (bar graphs) than by line graphs.

An experiment illustrating this type (entitled "How deep is the meaning of life?") was conducted by Loftus, Greene, and Smith (1980). After receiving different instructions, three groups of subjects viewed several color slides showing pictures of scenery. An "Intention to Learn" group was instructed to carefully study the slides for later identification. A "Percentage of Sky" group was instructed to estimate the percentage of each slide taken up by the sky. Finally, a "Meaning of Life" group was instructed to use each slide as a starting point for contemplating the meaning of life. All subjects saw each slide for five seconds. Forty-five minutes later, they were shown a series of slides and asked to identify which slides they had seen before.

Figure 8-4 shows the number of errors made by each group. The greatest number of errors was made by the "Percentage of Sky" group; the least by the "Meaning of Life" group. Because, in information-processing terms, errors should be fewer with increased "depth" of processing, the investigators concluded that the meaning of life is very deep.

Note that the bars representing the errors made by each group could be displayed in a different order from the one used in Figure 8-4, without changing the information communicated by the graph.

Multiple Control Group Design. Still another variation on the single-factor multigroup design is one that includes multiple control groups. This design is used when a single control group is not adequate to rule out alternative explanations of your results and is known as the **multiple control group design**.

A good illustration is provided by an experiment conducted to test the effect of a drug. It is well known that if a person believes that he or she is under the influence of a drug, then that person's behavior changes even if the drug was not administered. For example, Abrams and Wilson (1983) showed that subjects who *believed* they had consumed an alcoholic beverage reported greater sexual arousal and less embarrassment in response to erotic stimuli than if they did not believe they had consumed alcohol. This effect occurred even if the beverage they had consumed was actually nonalcoholic. Subjects in this study showed modifications in behavior simply because they believed they were under the influence.

You should include a *placebo control group* to detect such effects. This group receives the same treatment as the subjects who receive the drug. The only difference is that the "drug" they are administered is a *placebo,* or treatment

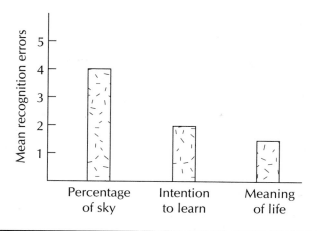

Figure 8-4. Graph illustrating results from a nonparametric, multigroup experiment. (From data provided by Loftus et al., 1980.)

lacking active ingredients. This control group allows you to determine the effect of the drug over and above the effect of the beliefs surrounding the drug.

Although the multiple control group design has been illustrated with a drug study, keep in mind that multiple control group designs are not limited to drug studies. In any experiment where the potential exists for confounding from several variables, the multiple control group design is indicated. The additional control groups allow you to evaluate the impact of each potentially confounding factor on the dependent variable.

Statistical Analysis of Single-Factor Multigroup Designs

When you move beyond the simple two-group design into designs with multiple groups, statistical analysis of the data resulting from these designs becomes more complex. One reason for this increased complexity is that you have more comparisons to make. As an example, consider a three-group design that includes a control group and two experimental groups. You may want to determine not only whether each experimental group mean differs from the control, but also whether the two experimental groups differ from each other. In this situation, you might think you could simply do a *t*-test for independent samples on each pair of groups to be compared, but you would be wrong. Because each *t*-test has a specified probability of finding a significant difference *by chance* (the alpha level), conducting multiple *t*-tests on the same data provides several opportunities for such a chance difference to occur. This problem is termed *probability pyramiding*. The result is that you are likely to find at least one significant difference by chance more often than the stated alpha level would suggest.

To combat probability pyramiding, investigators usually employ a statistical analysis that simultaneously considers all the data. The most popular parametric statistic used for this purpose is analysis of variance (ANOVA). Chapter 12 describes the use of ANOVA. For now, simply note that for multigroup studies with one independent variable, you would use a form of ANOVA called a *one-way ANOVA*. For ordinal data, the Kruskal-Wallis one-way analysis of variance would be appropriate. For nominal data, you would use chi-square for multiple independent samples.

Designs with Two
or More Independent Variables

Thus far, the discussion has assumed that only one independent variable is being manipulated across groups in a given experiment. If you wanted to assess the effects of several independent variables on a given dependent variable, one solution would be to conduct a separate experiment for each independent variable of interest. Although this approach is frequently used, you may be able to gain more information at less expense by using a design that incorporates two or more independent variables. The most common such design is the **factorial design**. In addition, you may be able to develop special designs where the factorial design is not practical.

Factorial Designs

A study that illustrates the factorial design was reported by Glass, Singer, and Friedman (1969, Experiment 1). Glass et al. examined the aftereffects of exposure to an irritating noise on several behavioral measures. Of interest here was the tolerance for frustration by the subjects, which was assessed by giving subjects the opportunity to solve several puzzles. Although the subjects did not know it at the time, two of the puzzles were, in fact, insoluble. The dependent measure was the number of attempts the subjects made to solve the insoluble puzzles before they became frustrated and gave up.

Glass et al. wanted to test the effect of two noise-related variables: noise intensity and noise predictability. Subjects were to be exposed to one of two levels of noise intensity (loud and soft) and one of two levels of noise predictability (unpredictable and predictable). (There was also a no-noise condition, but it is not included in this illustration.) They wanted to vary these two independent variables in such a way as to identify the separate effects of each variable on tolerance for frustration. That is, they wanted to avoid confounding the two variables. Glass et al. achieved this goal by using a factorial design.

In a factorial design, you include a separate group for each possible combination of the levels of the independent variables. Figure 8-5 shows the resulting

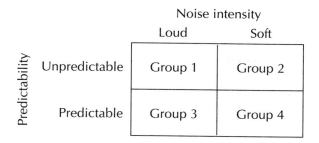

Figure 8-5. A 2 × 2 factorial design investigating noise intensity and noise predictability. (Based on data provided by Glass et al., 1969.)

	Noise intensity	
	Loud	Soft
Unpredictable	6.33	12.00
Predictable	26.78	25.80

Figure 8-6. Organization of a simple two-factor (2 × 2) experimental design with cell means filled in. (Based on data provided by Glass et al., 1969.)

groups for the tolerance for frustration study. The two levels of noise intensity are represented by the two columns (labeled across the top). The two levels of predictability are represented by the two rows (labeled along the side). The four boxes represent the four groups that result from each combination of complexity and intensity: Group 1 receives a loud, unpredictable noise; Group 2, a soft, unpredictable noise; Group 3, a loud, predictable noise; and Group 4, a soft, predictable noise.

Subjects were assigned at random to the different groups. Subjects in this experiment were exposed to the noise while they worked at several tasks. Immediately after this exposure, they were given the puzzles to solve. Figure 8-6 presents the group means for the insoluble-puzzles task (the results are for the second insoluble puzzle). On the surface, the experiment appears horribly confounded, since two independent variables have been allowed to vary at once.

Predictability	Noise intensity: Loud	Noise intensity: Soft	
Unpredictable	6.33	12.00	9.17
Predictable	26.78	25.80	26.29
	16.56	18.90	

Figure 8-7. Two-factor design showing cell means, and row and column means. (Based on data provided by Glass et al., 1969.)

This is not the case, however. Because all possible combinations of the levels of the independent variables are represented, you can statistically separate the effects of the independent variables.

Main Effects. The separate effects of each independent variable are termed **main effects**. Here's how you calculate the main effects of your independent variables. First, average the group means in the first column and write the result under the first column. Then do the same for the group means in the second column. These two numbers are your *column* means. Now average the group means across the first row and write the result to the right of the first row. Then do the same for the second row. These two numbers are your *row means*. The result should look like Figure 8-7.

Compare the column means. These represent the main effect of noise intensity, averaged over the two values of noise predictability. They are directly analogous to the two means you would get in a simple two-group design employing these two levels of noise intensity. Now compare the row means. These represent the main effect of noise predictability, averaged over the two values of noise intensity. They are directly analogous to the means of a simple two-group experiment varying noise predictability.

A reliable difference in the column means would indicate an effect of noise intensity, *independent of noise predictability*. Similarly, a reliable difference in the row means would indicate an effect of noise predictability, *independent of noise intensity*.

Interactions. Although the main effects of the independent variables are of considerable interest, they are not the only information you can extract from a factorial experiment. You can also test for the presence of interactions among your independent variables. An **interaction** is present when the effect of one

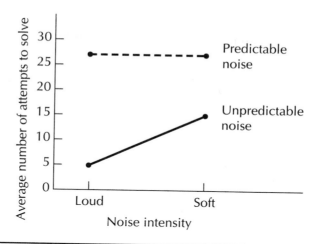

Figure 8-8. Graph showing interactions between variables. (Data from Glass et al., 1969.)

independent variable changes across the levels of another independent variable. For example, Glass et al. found that the number of attempts to solve the insoluble puzzle was greater when the noise was soft than when it was loud. But this relationship held only when the noise was unpredictable. When the noise was predictable, the number of attempts was about 26 *regardless* of noise intensity. Here, changing the noise predictability alters the relationship between noise intensity and attempts to solve. Under these conditions, the noise intensity and noise predictability interact.

Figure 8-8 shows how this relationship looks when graphed. The dashed and solid lines indicate the groups for which noise predictability was the same: unpredictable for the solid line, predictable for the dashed line. Note that, for the groups receiving the unpredictable noise, the number of attempts to solve the puzzles increases from loud noise to soft noise. In contrast, for the groups receiving the predictable noise, the number of attempts to solve the puzzles remains high at both levels of noise intensity.

Interactions can take a variety of forms when graphed. In general, if the lines of the graph representing different levels of an independent variable are *not parallel,* an interaction *may* be present.

The "may" in the preceding statement results from the fact that the lines drawn on the graph may appear to be nonparallel because of random variability in the data. To determine that an interaction exists, you must establish that the apparent nonparallelism of the lines is not likely to have resulted simply from sampling error. Fortunately, statistical tests are available that simultaneously determine the probable reliability of both the main effects and interactions of a particular experiment. (These tests are discussed in Chapter 12.) Incidentally, if the lines on the graph *are* parallel, no interaction exists, and no statistical test will find one.

Higher-Order Factorial Designs. The simple two-factor four-group design can be extended to include any number of levels of a given factor, and any number of factors. These are **higher-order factorial designs**. However, practical considerations limit the usefulness of these designs if you try to extend them too far. Two important problems concern the number of subjects required for the design and the complexity of potential interactions.

You should probably use at least five subjects per group for a reasonable ability to detect the effects of the independent variables. The number of required groups can be calculated by multiplying together the number of levels of each factor in the design. In the noise experiment, the two levels of noise intensity and two levels of noise predictability yield four (2×2) groups. If you were to repeat this study using five subjects per group, you would need to recruit twenty subjects. Adding a third two-level factor would produce a design that required eight ($2 \times 2 \times 2$) groups, or forty (5×8) subjects. If each factor had three levels instead of two, you would need twenty-seven ($3 \times 3 \times 3$) groups multiplied by 5, or 135 subjects! And this estimate uses a *minimum* number of subjects per group. It would be preferable to use more subjects for statistical reliability, but could you afford the time and money required to run such an experiment? As you can see, extended factorial experiments get out of hand quickly.

The second problem with extended factorial designs concerns the number and complexity of the resulting interactions. With three factors, you get three main effects (one for each factor), three *two-way interactions* (Factor A versus Factor B, Factor A versus Factor C, and Factor B versus Factor C) and a *three-way interaction* (Factor A versus Factor B versus Factor C). The two-way interactions are each similar to the simple interaction found in the two-factor design. For example, the A $\times$ B interaction represents the interaction of Factors A and B, averaged over the levels of Factor C. But what is the A $\times$ B $\times$ C interaction? This interaction occurs when the A $\times$ B *interaction* changes depending on the level of Factor C! (Other interpretations are also possible.) Adding a fourth variable to your design adds further interactions, including the dreaded A $\times$ B $\times$ C $\times$ D four-way interaction, which requires five years of training in a Tibetan monastery simply to comprehend! Because data resulting from such designs are difficult to analyze and interpret (not to mention expensive because of the large subject requirement), most investigators limit factorial designs to no more than three factors.

If you are willing to give up information about some of the higher-order interactions, you can include a relatively large number of factors and levels within factors while keeping the requirement for subjects within reasonable bounds. To describe the logic behind these designs and the analyses appropriate to them is beyond the scope of this book. If you are interested in looking into such designs, see the discussion of fractional replications of factorial designs in Edwards (1985, pp. 243–245) or Chapter 8 in Winer (1971).

Statistical Analysis of Factorial Designs

If your data meet the usual parametric assumptions, you would typically apply an appropriate version of ANOVA. ANOVA was briefly mentioned during the discussion of using a "one-way" ANOVA to analyze the data from a single-factor multigroup experiment. ANOVA is actually a family of analyses that can be configured to suit the particular experimental design. Statistical packages such as SPSS, SAS, and BMD (discussed in Chapter 13) offer specific programs that can provide an appropriate ANOVA for a large number of multifactor factorial designs. These analyses can provide information on the reliability of main effects and interactions, on specific comparisons, or (for parametric data) on trend analyses.

If your data do not meet the assumptions required for ANOVA, you may be able to use a nonparametric test. For example, the chi-square test for contingency tables can be used for analyzing data from a two-factor experiment in which the data consist of choices along a nominal scale (yes/no, for example). Unfortunately, suitable nonparametric statistics are not available for many factorial designs. Some possible options are discussed in Siegel and Castellan (1988).

Other Between-Subjects Designs

This chapter has presented a logical progression from the two-group design through the single-factor multi-group design, and finally to the factorial design. This progression might lead you to believe that these are the only ways to conduct experiments. This is far from the truth.

Chapter 3 indicated that you should first develop your research questions and then choose your design. This rule applies when you are deciding how to conduct a between-subjects experiment. Situations occur in which a full factorial design is not the best design to test your hypotheses. After all, in a full factorial design you examine every possible combination of the levels of your independent variables. In some research situations, this may be neither necessary nor desirable. For example, to address specific questions you may need to add control groups to the basic factorial plan. (The Glass et al. 1969 study in fact included such an additional control group — one receiving no noise.) Alternatively, some groups may not be possible (you may not be able to combine certain drugs, for example).

Designs such as these that do not follow one of the more standard design formats can help you to address special questions or deal with unusual circumstances. However, the data they provide sometimes require special statistical techniques to interpret properly. For example, if you have a full factorial design with a single "dangling control group," you must use a special ANOVA to analyze your data. This may mean extra work in identifying the appropriate techniques and learning to apply them. In other cases (where you simply cannot run a full factorial design), analysis may simply involve using multiple *t*-tests to contrast crucial groups. You then must be concerned with probability pyramiding across comparisons.

In short, the special versions of between-subjects designs may pose special problems for you. Nevertheless, you should make the effort. Choose the design that best addresses the questions you want to answer. If your design does not address these questions, you may save some effort, but what effort you do make will be wasted.

Matched Groups Designs

In some cases you know or suspect that some subject characteristics correlate significantly with the dependent variable. For example, subjects often differ considerably in their reaction times to simple stimuli. If you were interested in studying the effect of stimulus complexity on reaction time, this large inherent variation in reaction time already present in your subjects could pose a problem. By creating large amounts of error variance, it could swamp any effect of stimulus complexity, making even large differences in group means statistically unreliable. One way to deal with this problem is to use a matched groups design.

A **matched groups design** is one in which matched sets of subjects are distributed at random, one per group, into the groups of the experiment. Figure 8-9 illustrates this process. You begin by obtaining a sample of subjects (rectangle at the top of the figure) from the larger population. Next, you assess the subjects on one or more characteristics you believe exert an influence on the dependent measure, and then group the subjects whose characteristics match. In the reaction time experiment, for example, subjects could be pretested for their simple reaction times and then grouped into pairs whose reaction times were similar. These pairs of subjects are shown in the middle rectangles of Figure 8-9.

Having matched your subjects, you then distribute them randomly across the experimental groups. In the reaction time experiment, for example, one subject of each pair would be randomly assigned to one of the treatments (perhaps to the high-stimulus-complexity condition); the other subject would then automatically go into the other treatment (in this case the low-stimulus-complexity condition). This assignment to treatments is shown in the bottom rectangles of Figure 8-9.

From here on, the experiment is conducted as in the randomized groups design. Expose your subjects to their respective levels of the independent variable and record the resulting data. Then compare the data from the different groups to determine the effect of the independent variable.

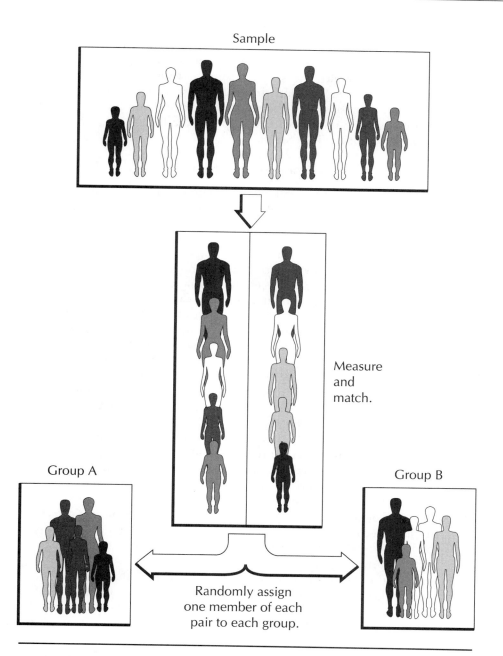

Figure 8-9. Matched subjects, two-group experimental design.

Logic of the Matched Groups Design

Because each of the matched subjects goes into a different group, the effect of the characteristic on which the subjects were matched is distributed evenly across the treatments. As a result, this characteristic contributes little to the differences in group means. The effect of the error variance contributed by the characteristic has been minimized, making it more likely that any effect of the independent variable will be detected.

Advantages and Disadvantages of the Matched Groups Design

The advantage of matching over random assignment is that it allows you to control subject variables that may otherwise obscure the effect of the independent variable under investigation. Where such variables exist, matching can increase the experiment's sensitivity to the effect of the independent variable (if such an effect is present). This is a potent advantage. You may be able to discover effects that you would otherwise miss. In addition, you may be able to demonstrate a given effect with fewer subjects, thus saving time and money. However, using a matched design is not without risks and disadvantages.

One risk involved in using a matched design concerns what happens if the matched characteristic does *not* have much effect on the dependent variable under the conditions of the study. Matched designs require you to use somewhat modified versions of the inferential statistics you would use in an unmatched, completely randomized design (see below). These statistics for matched groups are somewhat less powerful than their unmatched equivalents. This means that they are less able to discriminate any effect of the independent variable from the effect of uncontrolled, extraneous variables.

If the matched characteristic has a *large* effect on the dependent variable, eliminating this effect from group differences will more than compensate for the reduced sensitivity of the statistic, resulting in a more sensitive experiment. However (and this is an important "however"), if the matched characteristic has *little or no effect* on the dependent variable, then matching will do no good. Worse, the loss of statistical power will result in a *reduced* ability to detect the effect of the independent variable. For this reason, use matching only when you have good reason to believe that the matched variable has a relatively strong effect on the dependent measure.

When using a matched design, you must also be sure that the instrument used to determine the match is valid and reliable. If you want to match on IQ, for example, be sure that the test you use to measure IQ is valid and reliable. Of course, for some characteristics such as race, age, or sex, this is usually not a problem.

In other respects, matched groups designs have the same advantages and disadvantages as randomized groups designs. However, the requirement for pretesting and matching makes the matched design more demanding and time-consuming than the randomized design. In addition, you may require a larger subject pool if you cannot find a match for certain subjects and must discard them from the study. This may be particularly troublesome if you are attempting to match subjects on more than one variable or if the subject pool is limited.

Any of the randomized groups designs described in the previous sections of this chapter could be modified into a matched groups design. The simplest case, described next, involves the two-group design.

The Matched Pairs Design

The **matched pairs design** is the matched groups equivalent to the randomized two-group design. The hypothetical reaction time experiment described above uses a matched pairs design. As with the randomized two-group design, the need for only two groups makes this approach relatively economical of time and subjects, but does limit the amount of information you can obtain from the experiment.

Statistical Analysis. Data from the matched pairs design require a statistical analysis that is somewhat different from that used for data from the randomized two-groups design. This analysis, called the t-*test for correlated samples,* uses the difference in performance between each matched pair of subjects to estimate the amount of error variance, rather than the differences among subjects within each group. Matched subjects should perform more similarly than unmatched subjects, giving rise to a correlation between their scores. The t-test for correlated samples takes advantage of this correlation to improve the sensitivity of the test. Using the t-test for independent samples on these data would eliminate this advantage and remove any benefit to be derived from the matched pairs design.

Matched Multigroup Designs

The same approach used in the matched pairs design can be extended to other, more complex designs involving multiple levels of a single factor (single-factor, multigroup designs) or multiple factors (factorial designs). You use these matched groups designs to gain control over subject-related variables that affect your dependent variable and thus tend to obscure any effects of your independent variable.

Using the matching strategy on these multigroup designs requires you to find a matched subject for every treatment group in your experiment. Thus, if your experiment included four treatment groups, you would need to find quadruplets of subjects having similar characteristics on the variables being matched. After matching subjects, you would distribute the subjects from each quadruplet randomly across your experimental groups.

As you might guess, matching becomes unwieldy if your design has more than about three groups, as it becomes increasingly difficult to find three, four, or more subjects with equivalent scores on the variable or variables to be matched. In this case, a better approach might be to use a within-subjects design. The within-subjects design eliminates the need for measuring and matching subject variables, reduces the number of subjects required for the experiment, and yet provides the ultimate degree of matching — in effect, each subject is matched with himself or herself. Unfortunately, situations occur where the within-subjects design cannot or should not be used. In such cases, matching may be your best alternative. Chapter 9 describes within-subjects designs and indicates when they should or should not be used.

Statistical Analysis. As with the matched two-group design, the more complex matched multigroup designs require statistical analyses that take advantage of the correlations between subject performances to reduced error variance. Where assumptions are met for a parametric statistic, you would probably use a *one-way within-subjects ANOVA.* For a two-factor factorial design yielding ordinal data, you would use the Friedman two-way analysis of variance. For nominal data, you would use the Cochran Q-test (Siegel & Castellan, 1988).

Designs with Two or More Dependent Variables

Just as it is possible to include more than one independent variable in a design, it is also possible to include more than one dependent variable. Indeed, all the designs discussed thus far could be modified to include multiple dependent variables, without changing their essential characters. Designs that include multiple dependent variables are termed *multivariate designs.* Those with single dependent variables (such as previously discussed) are termed *univariate designs.* However, multivariate designs are not limited to experiments. Correlational research that simultaneously measures three or more variables is also termed *multivariate.* Chapter 15 covers multivariate designs in some detail, including experimental, correlational, and mixed strategies. However, the next section provides a brief look at multivariate experimental designs, emphasizing their advantages and disadvantages.

Multivariate Experimental Designs

Any univariate design can be made into the equivalent multivariate design simply by adding one or more additional dependent variables. For example, in the choice reaction time experiment described previously, you may want to record not only the reaction time to each stimulus, but also whether the selected choice was correct or incorrect. When averaged across subjects, these measures would provide the mean reaction time and percentage of correct responses at each stimulus value.

Statistical Analysis of Multivariate Designs

It is generally inappropriate to apply multiple *t*-tests to evaluate the results of multigroup experiments. Similarly, applying a separate analysis of variance to the data for each dependent variable in a multivariate experiment is inappropriate for two major reasons. First, because the scores on each dependent variable were obtained from the same subjects, it is possible, even likely, that the scores will be correlated. This correlation needs to be taken into account when you analyze your data. Second, separate analyses will not identify composite dependent variables and show their relationship to the dependent variable. A composite dependent variable is a weighted composite of the original dependent variables measured in your study. See Chapter 15 for a more complete discussion of the nature of this composite dependent variable. In a particular case, a composite variable could be reliably affected by your independent variables, whereas none of the individual dependent variables shows a significant effect of the independent variables. Thus, the multivariate analysis can provide information that separate, univariate analyses of variance cannot.

For parametric data, you would probably use an appropriate version of a *multivariate analysis of variance (MANOVA)*. Such programs are readily available as part of statistical computer packages such as SPSS, SAS, and BMD-P (see Chapter 13).

The review of between-subjects designs is now complete. At this point you should have a clear idea of the varieties of designs available, their uses, their advantages, their disadvantages, and their appropriate statistical analyses. However, one aspect of design is yet to be covered, one that remains a central concern no matter which approach you choose. This is the problem of confounding and how to deal with it.

The Problem of Confounding

Chapter 3 defined a confounding variable as one that varies along with your independent variable. The presence of a confounding variable damages the internal validity of your experiment. Consequently, you may not be able to establish a causal relationship between your independent variable (or variables) and your dependent variable. One of the most important aspects of research design is to develop an experiment that is free of confounding variables.

Assume that you are ready to conduct an experiment on the effects of drugs on discrimination capabilities. You have decided to use laboratory rats as subjects because of their availability and because testing the drug on human subjects would be risky. You order your rats and place them in individual cages in the department's colony room. You then decide to place all the rats in the top row of cages into the experimental group and all those in the second row into the control group. You run your experiment and find that the experimental group performs better on the discrimination task than the control group.

Apparently you could conclude from this evidence that the drug improves discrimination. But you cannot because you have no way of knowing whether the two groups would have performed differently even *without* the drug. The two groups contain different rats. Perhaps the rats that were assigned to the experimental group (the top row) were better at discrimination to begin with than those that were assigned to the control group (the second row).

If this seems unlikely to you, consider the following. The rats are shipped from the supplier in large crates. To place the rats in their individual cages, you have to catch them as they scurry around in the crate. The slower rats will be easier to catch. If the rats are placed in their cages in the order in which they are caught, then the slower rats will wind up in the top row and the faster rats in the second row. What if running speed is related to excitability? Your experimental rats could be calmer, less excitable animals than your control rats, and thus able to learn the discrimination faster.

Randomly assigning subjects to conditions is the way to deal with such sources of confounding. In random assignment, each subject has an equal chance of being assigned to any particular group. Random assignment minimizes the possibility that all subjects in a group will be similar in terms of a particular characteristic. In short, random assignment reduces one source of systematic bias.

If your experiment will take an extended period of time to complete (several weeks or months), you should also be sure that your experimental conditions are spread out over the entire span of time. This problem is graphically illustrated in a study reported by Bouchard (1972). In this study, traditional group "brainstorming" (group members produce as many novel ideas as possible) and "synectics" (a method in which subjects are instructed to role-play while coming up with ideas) were compared. Subjects in the brainstorming group were recruited from introductory psychology classes at the beginning of the course. Subjects assigned to the synectics group were recruited "much later during the course" (Bouchard, 1972, p. 419). The results of the study showed that synectics was superior to brainstorming in generating ideas.

The problem with this conclusion is that the two groups differed on more than one dimension. For example, suppose that subjects recruited later in the semester differed from those recruited earlier (Huck & Sandler, 1979). Subjects received course credit for participation in the experiment, so subjects recruited later may have been desperate for extra credit. They may also have received information about the experiment from other subjects. These differences could have led to the superior performance of the synectics group.

An obvious way to avoid this source of confounding is to spread experimental conditions out over the course of the study. Subjects could have been randomly assigned to different groups in Bouchard's study such that some brainstorming and synectics groups were run both early and late in the semester. Similarly, in your own research you want to assign subjects to groups and test the groups in such a way that the order in which subjects are tested will not become a source of systematic bias.

Another source of confounding is *experimenter bias,* as discussed in Chapter 4. For example, if you assigned your subjects to groups because you thought particular subjects would perform better in one group than in the other, you would be introducing this bias into your experiment as a confounding factor. In this case (as discussed in Chapter 4), using a blind or double-blind method reduces the impact of experimenter bias.

Confounding can also occur if your independent variables are not carefully conceived and executed. A classic example of this problem, also noted earlier, was provided by the original "Pepsi Challenge." The Pepsi Challenge was a simple demonstration designed to test for a preference of one cola over another. In the original version of this study, glasses of Pepsi were *always* marked with the letter *M,* whereas glasses of Coke were always marked with the letter Q. The data from the challenge suggested that there was a clear preference for Pepsi over Coke. However, when researchers from Coca-Cola tried to replicate this study, they found that choices by subjects were based on the letter (*M* versus Q) rather than taste. In Coca-Cola's experiment, both glasses contained Coke, but one glass was marked with an *M* and one with a Q. The results showed that subjects preferred the cola marked *M* (Huck & Sandler, 1979).

Avoiding this source of confounding may require little more than some attention to detail. In the Pepsi Challenge, for example, the glasses could have been left unmarked. Or the use of the letters could have been *counterbalanced.* That is, Pepsi could have been poured into the containers marked Q (and the Coke in the containers marked *M*) on half the trials, and vice versa on the other half. Counterbalancing is discussed in more detail in Chapter 9.

As a final example, consider an experiment conducted by Wexley and Thornton (1972). The purpose of this experiment was to test the impact of immediate feedback on test performance. Four quizzes were given to introductory psychology students. The questions for each quiz (35 per quiz) were projected on a screen for forty-five seconds each. After each quiz the students were reshown 18 of the questions (feedback questions), then given the correct answer and a brief explanation for why the answer was correct. The remaining 17 questions (nonfeedback questions) were not reshown (subjects were told that there was not enough time). A final exam was given at the end of the term. On this final was a set of 38 feedback questions (some questions from each of the four quizzes) and 38 nonfeedback questions. The subjects' performances on the feedback and nonfeedback items were compared.

The subjects performed better on the feedback questions than on the nonfeedback questions. The authors concluded that giving immediate feedback facilitates learning. Do you agree with this conclusion?

Unfortunately, the conclusion is not justified. The subjects saw feedback items twice, nonfeedback items only once. Greater exposure and not the feedback possibly led to the improved performance. Being more familiar with the feedback items, subjects may have remembered them better than the nonfeedback items. As a consequence, they may have performed better on the feedback items than on the nonfeedback items.

Sometimes a simple counterbalancing strategy is not sufficient to ensure an unconfounded experiment. The best way to avoid confounding is to carefully plan how your independent variables are to be executed. Ask yourself whether or not there are potential alternative explanations for the effects that you find. Is your independent variable the only factor that could affect the value of the dependent variable? Careful evaluation of your experimental conditions and a good knowledge of the literature in your area will help you avoid confounding.

Although we have discussed confounding in our chapter on between-subjects designs, it is important to understand that confounding is not a problem unique to between-subjects designs. Confounding can also occur in within-subjects and single-subject designs as well.

Summary

Experimental designs can be classified as between-subjects, within-subjects, or single-subject designs. Between-subjects designs manipulate the independent variable by administering the different levels of the independent variable to different groups of subjects. Within-subjects designs administer the different levels of the independent variable at different times to a single group of subjects. Single-subject designs manipulate the independent variable as the within-subjects designs do, but focus on the performances of single subjects rather than the average performances of a group of subjects.

A key problem for any experimental design is the problem of error variance. Error variance consists of fluctuations in scores that have nothing to do with the effect of the independent variable. Error variance tends to obscure any causal relationship that may exist between your independent and dependent variables.

Three steps can be taken to reduce error variance: you can hold extraneous variables constant, manipulate your independent variable more strongly, and randomize the effects of error variance across groups. You can then use inferential statistics to assess the probability that your observed effects were due to error variance rather than to your independent variable. If this probability is small, you can be reasonably confident that your independent variable is effective.

Between-subjects designs can be classified according to the number of groups required (two-group versus multigroup), the number of independent variables manipulated (single-factor versus multifactor), the way in which subjects are assigned to groups (random assignment or matching), and the number of dependent variables (univariate or multivariate). If the independent variable takes on three or more quantitative values, the design is said to be *parametric;* otherwise it is said to be *nonparametric.*

Multigroup designs can include multiple control groups to assess the impacts of several potentially confounding factors. Multiple control groups can be included in both parametric and nonparametric designs.

If two or more independent variables are manipulated and one group in the design accounts for each possible combination of the levels of the independent variables, the design is called a *factorial design.* Factorial designs make it possible to assess in one experiment the main effect of each independent variable and any interactions among the variables. The number of groups required for a factorial design can be computed by multiplying the number of levels of each factor manipulated.

Some questions are best addressed using designs other than the standard ones. For example, a basic factorial design might be expanded to include control groups in order to make comparisons beyond those involving main effects and interactions. Although the statistical analyses required for these designs may be more difficult to define, do not let this difficulty prevent you from choosing the best design for the questions you want to address.

When subjects are assigned to groups at random, the design is termed a *randomized groups design*. Such designs are best when subject characteristics do not contribute greatly to error variance. However, when subject characteristics strongly influence the dependent variable of your study, you can reduce the error variance created by these characteristics by using a matched groups design. This control over error variance can improve your chances of detecting any effects of your independent variable. However, compared to randomized groups designs, matched groups designs require the extra steps of testing and matching subjects, use somewhat different inferential statistics to evaluate the data, and may actually be less sensitive to the effects of the independent variable if the matching does not succeed in reducing error variance. In addition, it may be difficult to find enough matching subjects if the design includes several groups.

Multivariate experimental designs include two or more dependent variables. These designs provide information about the effect of the independent variable on each dependent variable and on a composite dependent variable formed from a weighted combination of the individual dependent variables.

Confounding in between-subjects designs emerges from a variety of sources. Nonrandom assignment, experimenter bias, and ill-conceived experimental conditions are all sources of confounding. Steps such as random assignment, blind techniques, and careful assessment of experimental conditions and of potential alternative explanations should be taken to avoid potential confounding.

Key Terms

Between-subjects design	Multiple control group design
Within-subjects design	Factorial design
Single-subject design	Main effects
Error variance	Interaction
Randomized two-group design	Higher-order factorial design
Parametric design	Matched groups design
Nonparametric design	Matched pairs design

9

Using Within-Subjects and Combined Designs

THE BETWEEN-SUBJECTS DESIGNS DISCUSSED in Chapter 8 are by no means the only experimental designs available. This chapter introduces several additional designs, including within-subjects designs, mixed designs (which combine aspects of the within-subjects and between-subjects designs), nested designs, and combined experimental/correlational designs.

Within-Subjects Designs

Chapter 8 described a number of between-subjects experimental designs. In these designs, you randomly assign subjects to groups and then expose each group to a single experimental treatment. You measure each subject's performance on the dependent variable, calculate the average score for each group, and then compare the means to determine whether the independent variable or variables had any apparent influence on the dependent variable. You then subject the data to a statistical analysis to assess the reliability of your conclusions.

Within-subjects designs follow a logic similar to that of between-subjects designs. As in between-subjects designs, you expose subjects to different experimental treatments. You average the scores within each treatment, compare the means to determine the influence of the independent variable on performance, and statistically evaluate the differences in performance for reliability. The two types of design differ in the way you expose subjects to the experimental treatments. Instead of exposing different groups of subjects each to a different treatment, you expose a single group of subjects to all the treatments. Figure 9-1 illustrates this approach with a simple two-treatment experiment. Note that each subject's performance is measured under Treatment A. Subjects then move into Treatment B (as indicated in the figure by the arrows) and performance is measured again. The design is called "within-subjects" because the comparison of treatment effects involves looking at changes in performance within each subject across treatments. Each subject's performance is repeatedly measured, and within-subjects designs therefore are sometimes called "repeated measures" designs.

Within-subjects designs offer some powerful advantages over the equivalent between-subjects designs if certain conditions can be met. They also introduce problems whose solution adds complexity to the basic designs, and offer other disadvantages as well. We begin by examining the advantages.

Advantages of the Within-Subjects Design

Chapter 8 introduced the concept of error variance: differences in subject scores that have nothing to do with the effect of the independent variable. You can see error variance most clearly by comparing the scores of subjects within a particular treatment. Because all subjects are exposed to supposedly identical conditions, their performances ideally should be identical. Yet scores do differ. These differences arise from the effects of extraneous variables, which include relatively stable subject-related factors as well as momentary fluctuations that change each subject's performance from moment to moment.

Error variance can be a serious problem, as it tends to mask any effect of your independent variable and can also make it appear that your independent variable had an effect when it did not. Between-subjects designs, by assigning subjects at random to treatment groups, attempt to spread error variance evenly across the treatments. This approach does not reduce error variance but does make it possible to assess the likelihood that these randomized effects would by chance produce the observed differences in treatment means. If this likelihood is small enough (as determined by the appropriate statistical test), you conclude that the differences did not result from error variance and therefore that they must have resulted from the effect of your independent variable.

Unfortunately, when subject-related factors exert a large influence on performance, error variance may be large enough to obscure any effect of your independent variable. In Chapter 8, we described one approach for dealing with this problem, namely matching subjects on variables thought to have a strong influence on their performances. Matched groups designs help to control error variance by directly comparing the differences in performance among the matched subjects. If matching has been successful, these subjects will perform similarly except for any effect of the independent variable. In other words, there will be

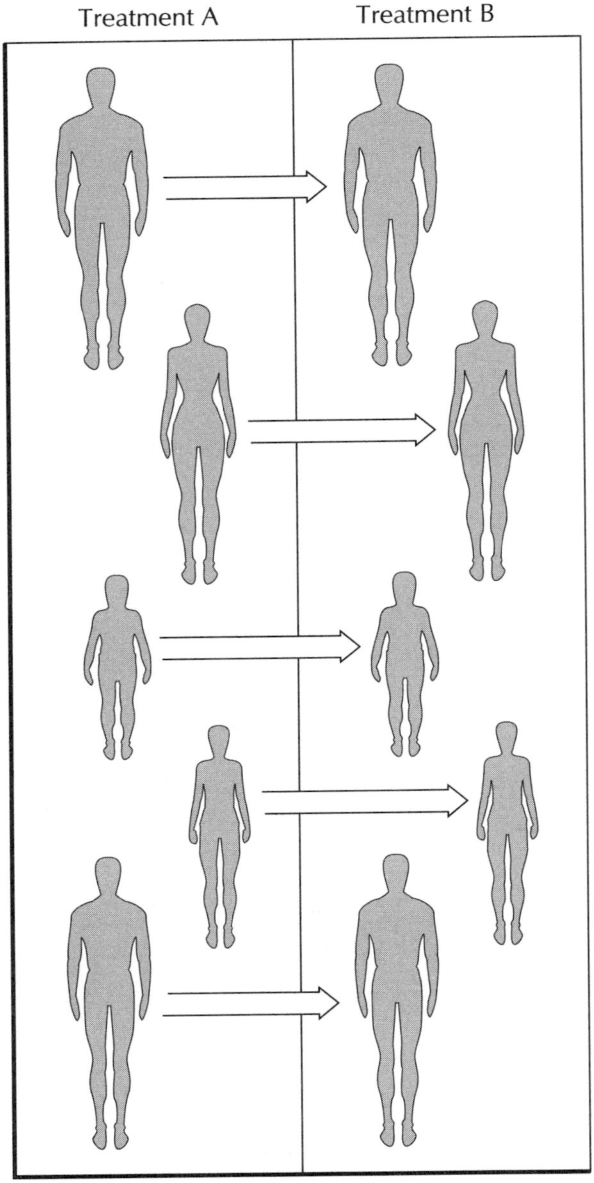

Figure 9-1. Simple two-treatment within-subjects design.

less error variance to contribute to performance differences, and the effect of the independent variable will be easier to detect.

Within-subjects designs push the logic of the matched groups design to the limit. Each subject is "matched" with other subjects who are virtual clones of each other, because they are all the same subject! This is the ultimate in matching. All subject-related factors (such as age, weight, IQ, personality, religion, and sex) are literally identical across treatments. It is as though you had been able to measure and match subjects on every subject factor that could affect the dependent variable. Any performance differences observed between the treatments therefore cannot be due to error variance arising from such differences.

Because of this ideal matching of subject factors, the within-subject design tends to be more powerful than an equivalent between-subjects design. A powerful design is one that does a good job of detecting real effects of the independent variables. The increased power of the within-subjects design may allow you to use fewer subjects than you would otherwise need to obtain statistically reliable differences among your treatments. For example, a four-group between-subjects design with 10 subjects per condition requires 40 subjects. In contrast, the same four-group experiment run as a within-subjects design requires only 10 subjects. As the number of treatments increases, the savings in number of subjects required can result in significant savings of materials and money, and in the time required to debrief subjects following the experimental manipulations. The savings can be especially important if your subject pool is limited.

Alternatively, by using the same number of subjects as in an equivalent between-subjects design you may be able to detect effects of your independent variable that in the between-subjects design would be obscured by subject-related error variance. Thus, for the same cost in subjects, you may be able to obtain more reliable data.

Disadvantages of the Within-Subjects Design

Although increased power and reduced subject numbers are strong advantages, the within-subjects design also carries some potentially serious disadvantages, some of which may even preclude its use in certain cases. One disadvantage is that within-subjects designs require each subject to spend more time in the experiment than would the equivalent between-subjects design. This is because each subject must participate in every experimental treatment. A complex design involving nine treatments could require a great deal of time to complete. If you find it difficult to get subjects to spend half an hour participating in your experiments, imagine what will happen when you ask them to spend 4½ hours!

You can decrease the potential for fatigue and boredom by administering only one or two treatments per session and spreading sessions over the week, but if you take this approach you are likely to experience subject attrition. If the subject fails to show up for Session 4, you will have to discard that subject's data and much time will have been wasted.

Subject attrition can also occur if you make a mistake while administering one of your treatments, if you experience apparatus failure, or (in long-term experiments with animals) if your subject dies. In each case you may have to throw out the data collected from the lost subject and start over with a new one.

A second, and potentially far more serious, disadvantage of within-subjects designs is their ability to produce carryover effects. **Carryover effects** occur when a previous treatment alters the observed behavior in a subsequent treatment. The previous treatment changes the subject, and these changes "carry over" into subsequent treatment where they alter how the subject performs. By changing the subject, earlier treatments upset the perfect match of subject characteristics that the within-subjects design is supposed to provide.

As an illustration of carryover effects, imagine that you are conducting an experiment to assess the effect of two kinds of practice (simple rehearsal and rehearsal plus imagery) on memory for lists of concrete nouns. Your subjects first learn a list of nouns using simple rehearsal and then are tested for retention. Next the subjects learn a second list of nouns, using rehearsal plus imagery, and are again tested. You find that subjects correctly recall more nouns when they used a rehearsal-plus-imagery technique than when they used rehearsal alone. However, you cannot confidently conclude that the former technique is superior to the latter.

The problem is that the rehearsal-alone treatment gave subjects practice memorizing nouns. They may have done better in the rehearsal-plus-imagery treatment simply because they were more practiced at the task, rather than because of any effect of imagery. The previous exposure to the rehearsal-alone treatment may have changed the way subjects performed in the subsequent treatment.

Carryover effects can be a serious problem in any within-subjects design. Between-subjects designs do not suffer from carryover effects, simply because there are no previous conditions from which effects can carry over.

The problem of carryover in within-subjects design has received plenty of attention from researchers, who have developed strategies to deal with it. The next section identifies potential sources of carryover. After that, we describe several design options that can help you deal with potential carryover effects.

Sources of Carryover

Carryover effects can arise from a number of sources, including the following:

- *Learning.* If a subject learns how to perform a task in the first treatment, performance is likely to be better if the same or similar tasks are used in subsequent treatments. For example, rats given alternate sessions of reinforcement and extinction show faster acquisition of lever pressing across successive reinforcement sessions, and more rapid return to baseline rates of responding across successive extinction sessions.

- *Fatigue.* If performance in earlier treatments leads to fatigue, then performance in later treatments may deteriorate, regardless of any effect of the independent variable. If measuring your dependent variable involves having subjects squeeze against a strong spring device to determine their strength of grip, for example, the subjects are likely to tire if repeated testing takes place over a short period of time.

- *Habituation.* Under some conditions, repeated exposure to a stimulus leads to reduced responsiveness to that stimulus. This reduction is termed *habituation.* Your subjects may jump the first time you surprise them with a sudden loud noise, but may not do so after repeated presentations of the noise.

- *Sensitization.* Sometimes exposure to one stimulus can cause subjects to respond more strongly to another stimulus. In a phenomenon called "potentiated startle," for example, a rat will show an exaggerated startle response to a sudden noise if the rat has recently received a brief foot shock in the same situation.

- *Contrast.* Because of contrast, exposure to one condition may alter the responses of subjects in other conditions. If you pay your subjects a relatively large amount for successful performance on one task, and then pay them less (or make them work harder for the same amount) in a subsequent task, they may feel underpaid. Consequently, they may work less than they otherwise might have. This change occurs because subjects can compare (contrast) the treatments.

- *Adaptation.* If subjects go through a period of adaptation (becoming adjusted to the dark, for example), then earlier results may differ from later results because of the adaptive changes. Adaptation to a drug schedule is a common example. If adaptation to the drug causes reduced response, the change is called *tolerance.*

Dealing with Carryover Effects

You can deal with carryover effects in three ways: (1) you can use counterbalancing to even out carryover effects across treatments, (2) you can take steps to minimize carryover, and (3) you can separate carryover effects from treatment effects by making treatment order an independent variable.

Counterbalancing. In **counterbalancing,** you assign the various treatments of the experiment in a different order for different subjects. The goal is to distribute any carryover equally across treatments so that it does not produce differences in treatment means that could be mistaken for an effect of the independent variable. Two counterbalancing options are complete counterbalancing and partial counterbalancing.

Complete counterbalancing provides every possible ordering of treatments and assigns at least one subject to each ordering. Table 9-1 shows an example of a completely counterbalanced single-factor design that includes three treatments. Six subjects are to be tested (identified as subjects S_1 through S_6), one for each

Table 9-1. Counterbalanced Single-Factor Design with Three Treatments

SUBJECTS	TREATMENTS		
	T_1	T_2	T_3
S_1	1	2	3
S_2	1	3	2
S_3	2	1	3
S_4	2	3	1
S_5	3	1	2
S_6	3	2	1

possible ordering of Treatments T_1, T_2, and T_3. Note that in a completely counterbalanced design, every treatment follows every other treatment equally often across subjects, and every treatment appears equally often in each position (first, second, and so on).

The minimum number of subjects required for complete counterbalancing is equal to the number of different orderings of the treatments. N treatments have exactly $N!$ (N factorial) orders, where $N! = (N) (N-1) (N-2) . . . (1)$. For example, with three treatments (as in our example), the number of treatment orders is $(3) (2) (1) = 6$. If you need to increase the number of subjects in order to improve statistical power, add the same number of additional subjects to each order, so that the number of subjects receiving each order remains equal.

Complete counterbalancing is practical for experiments with a small number of treatments, but this approach becomes increasingly burdensome as the number of treatments grows. For an experiment using only four treatments, the $4 \times 3 \times 2 \times 1 = 24$ possible treatment orders require at least 24 subjects to complete the counterbalancing. The economy of subjects that makes a within-subjects approach attractive erodes rapidly.

Fortunately, you can recover some of this economy by switching to partial counterbalancing. *Partial counterbalancing* includes only some of the possible treatment orders. The orders to be retained are chosen randomly from the total set, with the restriction that each treatment appear equally often in each position. Table 9-2 displays all 24 possible orders for a four-treatment experiment, followed by a subset of 8 randomly selected orders that meet this criterion.

When you use partial counterbalancing, you assume that randomly chosen orders will randomly distribute carryover effects among the treatments. Although carryover effects may not balance out under such conditions, they usually will come close to doing so. Furthermore, the likelihood that treatments will differ because of carryover can be evaluated statistically and held to an acceptable level.

Table 9-2. Twenty-four Possible Treatment Orders for a Four-Treatment Within-Subjects Design, and a Randomly Selected Subset in Which Each Treatment Appears Equally Often in Each Position

Entire Set of Treatment Orders		Selected Subset	
1.	ABCD	1.	DABC
2.	ABDC	2.	ABCD
3.	ACBD	3.	CDAB
4.	ACDB	4.	BCDA
5.	ADBC	5.	DCBA
6.	ADCB	6.	ADCB
7.	BACD	7.	BADC
8.	BADC	8.	CBAD
9.	BCAD		
10.	BCDA		
11.	BDAC		
12.	BDCA		
13.	CABD		
14.	CADB		
15.	CBAD		
16.	CBDA		
17.	CDAB		
18.	CDBA		
19.	DABC		
20.	DACB		
21.	DBAC		
22.	DBCA		
23.	DCAB		
24.	DCBA		

If you choose to make the number of treatment orders in your partially counterbalanced design equal to the number of treatments, you can use a **Latin square design** to assure that each treatment appears an equal number of times at each ordinal position. A Latin square is an $N \times N$ table of items in which each item appears exactly once in each column and row, where N is the number of different items. In this case the items are treatments. Table 9–3 shows a Latin

Table 9-3. A Fourth-Order Latin Square			
	1	2	3	4
1	B	A	C	D
2	C	D	A	B
3	A	B	D	C
4	D	C	B	A

square for four treatments (A, B, C, and D). Each row of the Latin square provides a different treatment order. This restriction on randomization might be desirable if, for example, you wanted practice effects across treatments to be equal.

You can construct a Latin square of order N by following these four steps (Edwards, 1985). Refer to Figure 9-2 to see the results of each step.

1. Arrange the first N letters of the alphabet in alphabetical order (*A, B, C,* and *D* for a four-treatment experiment). Then repeatedly rotate the first letter into last position until the next rotation would bring you back to the starting order (Panel A). The result is a particular Latin square of order N (in this case, order 4).

2. Randomly rearrange the order in which the columns appear by using a table of random numbers (Panel B).

3. Randomly rearrange the order in which the rows appear (Panel C).

4. Randomly assign treatments to the letters (Panel D).

Counterbalancing (whether complete or partial) can be counted on to control order effects only if the order effects induced by different orders are of the same approximate magnitude. Consider the case of a simple two-treatment experiment shown in Table 9-4. This case has only two possible orders: 1-2 and 2-1. Assume that carryover from Treatment 1 to Treatment 2 increases the mean score of Treatment 2 by 10 points, and that carryover from Treatment 2 to Treatment 1 has a similar effect on the mean score of Treatment 1. Table 9-4 shows the result for a completely counterbalanced design. Note that the two carryover effects, being equal, cancel out each other. When carryover effects are equivalent across orders, counterbalancing is effective.

In contrast, when the magnitude of the carryover effect differs for different orders of treatment presentation, counterbalancing may be ineffective. Table 9-5 illustrates this problem, known as *differential carryover effects* (Keppel, 1982). In this example the carryover from Treatment 2 to Treatment 1 averages 20 points — twice the carryover from Treatment 1 to Treatment 2. Thus, you have a treat-

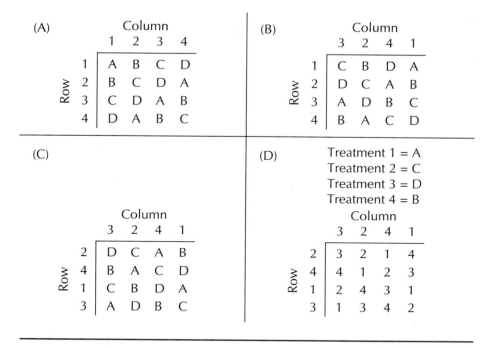

Figure 9-2. Steps followed to construct a Latin square.

ment by position interaction. When this occurs, no amount of counterbalancing will eliminate the carryover effects (Keppel, 1982).

The most serious asymmetry in carryover effects occurs when a treatment produces *irreversible changes*. The classic type of irreversible change is that produced by a treatment such as brain lesioning. The effects of the operation, once present, cannot be undone. A somewhat less serious change may occur if subjects learn to perform a task in one treatment, and this learning then alters the way in which they perform in a subsequent treatment. It may not be possible to restore subjects to the "naïve" state once they have learned the task. In either case, you would want to choose a between-subjects approach.

Taking Steps to Minimize Carryover. The second way to deal with carryover effects is to try to minimize or eliminate them. Of course, you would want to do this only if the carryover effects were not themselves the object of study. Minimizing carryover effects reduces error variance and increases the power of the design.

Not all sources of carryover can be minimized. For example, permanent changes produced by learning inevitably carry over into subsequent treatments and affect behavior. You cannot return your subjects to the naïve state in

Table 9-4. Balancing of Order Effects in a Counterbalanced Two-Treatment Design

	TREATMENT		
	1	2	
Actual treatment effect	40	30	(Difference = 10)
Carryover effect (1-2)		10	
Carryover effect (2-1)	10	—	
Observed treatment effect	50	40	(Difference = 10)

Table 9-5. Failure of Order Effects to Balance Out in a Counterbalanced Two-Treatment Design

	TREATMENT		
	1	2	
Actual treatment effect	40	30	(Difference = 10)
Carryover effect (1-2)		10	
Carryover effect (2-1)	20	—	
Observed treatment effect	60	40	(Difference = 20)

preparation for a second treatment. However, if you are not interested in the effect of learning *per se,* you may be able to pretrain your subjects before introducing your experimental treatments. Psychophysical experiments (testing such things as sensory thresholds) and experiments on human decision making often make use of such "practice sessions" to familiarize subjects with the experimental tasks. The practice brings their performances up to desired levels, where they stabilize, and effectively eliminates changes caused by practice as a source of carryover.

Adaptation and habituation changes can be dealt with similarly. Before introducing the treatments, allowing time for subjects to adapt or habituate to the experimental conditions can eliminate carryover from these sources.

Another way to deal with habituation (if habituation is short term), adaptation, and fatigue is to allow breaks between the treatments. If sufficiently long, the breaks allow subjects to recover from any habituation, adaptation, or fatigue induced by the previous treatment.

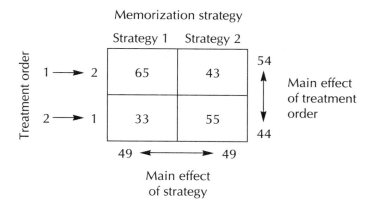

Figure 9-3. A design in which order of treatments is made an independent variable.

You can take steps to minimize carryover effects in combination with either of the other two strategies. If you simply want to control carryover, you could take these steps and then use counterbalancing to distribute whatever carryover remains across treatments. Similarly, if you want to determine whether certain variables contribute to carryover, you could take steps to minimize other potential sources of carryover and then treat the variables of interest as independent variables as described in the following section.

Making Treatment Order an Independent Variable. A third way to deal with the problem of carryover is to make treatment order an independent variable. For example, if you were going to conduct a one-factor experiment to compare the effect of two memorization strategies on recall, you could design the experiment to include the order of testing as a second independent variable. Figure 9-3 illustrates the resulting two-factor factorial design.

In the figure, the two memorization strategies (Strategy 1 and Strategy 2) are factorially combined with the two possible treatment orders (Strategy 1 then Strategy 2, and Strategy 2 then Strategy 1) to produce four cells. Subjects are randomly assigned to two groups. Group 1 receives *both* memorization strategy treatments in 1-2 order (top row of cells in Figure 9-3). Group 2 receives both memorization strategy treatments in 2-1 order (bottom row of cells).

You may have noticed that treatment order varies between subjects (different subjects in the two orders of treatment), whereas memorization strategy varies within subjects (same subjects in the two treatments). This type of design is referred to as a *mixed design,* which is discussed in more detail later in this chapter.

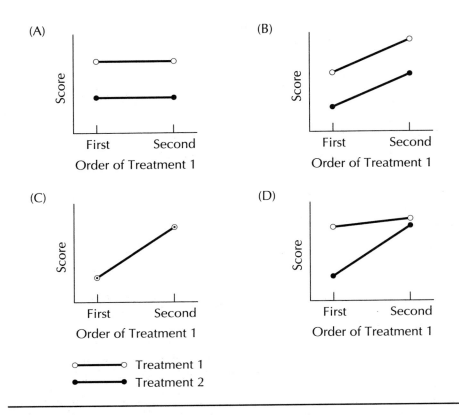

Figure 9.4. Four possible outcomes of a two-treatment within-subjects experiment in which treatment order is an independent variable.
(A) treatment effect but no order effect, (B) treatment effect and order effect; (C) no treatment effect but order effect; (D) treatment by order interaction.

The main advantage of making order of treatments an independent variable is that you can measure the size of any present carryover effects. You can then take these effects into account in future experiments. If you find that carryover is about equal in magnitude regardless of the order of treatments, for example, then you can be confident that counterbalancing will eliminate any carryover-induced bias.

How you identify carryover is best shown by example. Figure 9-4 shows four possible outcomes of a two-treatment experiment. Each panel displays the scores obtained in each of the treatments when the treatment was given first and when it was given second. Panel A shows the pattern obtained with a treatment effect (Treatment 1 produces higher scores than Treatment 2) and no order effect (in other words, no carryover). Note that Treatment 1 scores are superior to Treatment 2 scores by the same amount, regardless of the order in which the treatments were given.

Panel B depicts the outcome when both treatment and order have an effect on the cell means and these effects are purely additive (no interaction). In this example, Treatment 1 is superior to Treatment 2, whether Treatment 1 is experienced first (leftmost circles) or second (rightmost circles). In addition, *both* treatments produce higher scores if they have first been preceded by the other treatment (compare data points at left to those at right). In other words, there is carryover from the first treatment experienced to the second one experienced, and this carryover has the same effect on both treatments.

Panel C indicates a situation in which carryover is present similar to that found in Panel B, but in which a treatment effect is absent. Subjects perform better in the second treatment administered (rightmost circles), no matter which treatment that is.

Finally, Panel D shows one example of the case where the magnitude of carryover depends on which treatment is given first. In this example, Treatment 1 produces the same scores whether it is given first (circle to left) or second (circle to right). In contrast, Treatment 2 produces low scores when given first (solid circle to left), but high scores when given second (solid circle to right). The pattern shown in Panel D indicates that Treatment 2 produces no carryover to Treatment 1, whereas Treatment 1 does produce carryover to Treatment 2.

In addition to identifying carryover effects, the strategy of making treatment order an independent variable provides a direct comparison of results obtained in the within-subjects design with those obtained in the logically equivalent between-subjects design. This comparison can be made because every treatment occurs first in at least one of the treatment orders. These "first exposures" provide the data for a purely between-subjects comparison in the absence of carryover effects.

Grice (1966) noted that between-subjects and within-subjects designs applied to the same variables do not always produce the same functional relationships. A case in point was provided by an investigation of the effect of motivation on the running speed of rats down a straight alley (Crespi, 1942).

Three groups of rats were timed as they ran down an alley toward a bit of food reward. Two groups received a large reward at the end of the alley (16 or 256 pellets) whereas the other group received a small reward (1 pellet). The running speed was recorded across a series of trials until the speeds appeared to level off.

When running speeds had stabilized, the 1-pellet and 256-pellet groups were shifted to a 16-pellet reward. Figure 9-5 shows the results of the experiment.

First consider the data from the group that did *not* receive a shift in the size of the reward. The running speed of subjects in this group remained fairly stable. Now look at the data from the two groups that received the shift. Prior to the

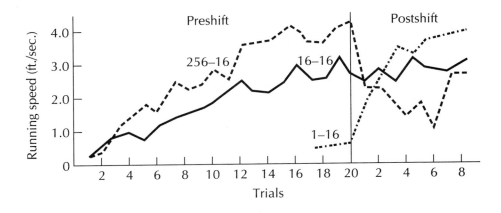

Figure 9-5. The effect of motivation on running speed of rats, before and after a shift in reward. (Data from Crespi, 1942; reprinted with permission.)

shift, subjects in the 256-pellet group ran faster than subjects in the 16-pellet group (comparable preshift data are not shown for the 1-pellet group in Figure 9-5). Following the shift, the performance of the 256-pellet group dropped below that of the unshifted 16-pellet group, and the performance of the 1-pellet group exceeded the performance of the unshifted group. Rather than simply matching performance after a reward shift, the shifted group performance actually *overshot* that of the unshifted group!

One explanation offered for this phenomenon was that the change in reward size produced an "elation effect" in the rats whose reward size had been increased and a "disappointment effect" is those whose reward size had been decreased. You might recognize these as forms of the contrast effect previously discussed. Whether the cognitive explanation in terms of elation and disappointment actually contributes to the understanding of the phenomenon has been debated, but there is no question as to the reality of contrast effects.

The carryover effects produced by contrast were possible in the shifted groups (which in effect each received a within-subjects manipulation) but not in the unshifted group. Together the three groups constitute (prior to shifting) a between-subjects manipulation. The presence of such effects in some designs, but not in others, can often explain why studies manipulating the same variables sometimes yield different results.

Although making treatment order a factor in your experiment can provide important information about the size of carryover effects and can pinpoint the source of differences between findings obtained from within-subjects versus between-subjects experiments, the technique does have disadvantages. Every treatment order requires a separate group of subjects. These subjects must be tested under every treatment condition. The result is a complex, demanding experiment that is costly in terms of numbers of subjects and time to test them. Furthermore, these demands escalate rapidly as the number of treatments (and therefore number of treatment orders) increases. This latter problem is the same one encountered when using completely counterbalanced designs. For these reasons, the approach is practical only with a small number of treatments.

When to Use a Within-Subjects Design

Given the problems created by the potential for carryover effects, the best strategy may be to altogether avoid within-subjects designs. If you decide to do this, you have a lot of company. However, you should not let these difficulties prevent you from adopting the within-subjects design when it is clearly the best approach. There are several situations in which the within-subjects design is best, and others in which it is the *only* approach.

Subject Variables Correlated with the Dependent Variable. You should strongly consider using a within-subjects design when subject differences contribute heavily to variation in the dependent variable. As an example, assume you want to assess the effect of display complexity on target detection in a simulated air traffic controller task. Your display simulates the computerized radar screen display seen in actual air traffic control situations, with aircraft (the targets) appearing as blips in motion across the screen. Your independent variable is the amount of information being displayed (the dots alone, or dots plus transponder codes, altitude readings, and so on). Because this is a pilot study (no pun intended), you are using college sophomores as subjects rather than real air traffic controllers.

Your student subjects are likely to differ widely in their native ability to detect targets, regardless of the display complexity. If you were to conduct the experiment using a between-subjects design, this large variation in ability would contribute greatly to within-group error variance. As a consequence, the between-group differences would probably be obscured by these uncontrolled variations.

In this case, you could effectively eliminate the impact of subject differences by adopting a within-subjects design. Each subject is exposed to every level of display complexity. Because each subject's native ability at target detection remains essentially the same across all the treatment levels, the changes (if any) in target detection across treatments would clearly stand out.

Of course, you would have to be reasonably sure that practice at the task does not contribute to success at target detection (or at least that the effect of such practice could be distributed evenly across treatments by using counterbalancing) before you decided to adopt the within-subjects approach. One way to eliminate practice as a source of confounding would be to include several practice sessions in which your subjects became proficient enough at the task that little further improvement would be expected.

Economizing on Subjects. You should also consider using a within-subjects design when the number of available subjects is limited and carryover effects are absent (or can be minimized). If you were to use actual air traffic controllers in the previous study, for example, you probably would not have a large available group from which to sample. You probably would not be able to obtain enough subjects for your study to achieve statistically reliable results using a between-subjects design. Using a within-subjects design would reduce the number of subjects required for the study while preserving an acceptable degree of reliability.

Assessing the Effects of Increasing Exposure on Behavior. In cases where you wish to assess changes in performance as a function of increasing exposure to the treatment conditions (measured as number of trials, passage of time, and so on), the within-subjects design is the only option (unless you have sufficient control to use a single-subject design—see Chapter 10). Designs that repeatedly sample the dependent variable across time or trials are frequently used in psychological research to examine the course of processes such as reinforcement, extinction, fatigue, and habituation. These changes occur as a function of earlier exposure to the experimental conditions and thus represent carryover effects. However, the carryover effects in these designs are the object of study rather than something to be eliminated by measures such as counterbalancing.

Be aware, however, that not all carryover effects can or should be studied within the framework of a within-subjects design. For example, transfer-of-training studies (in which the effects of previous training on later performance of another task are assessed) are not good candidates for a within-subjects approach. This is because the earlier training may have effects on later performance that cannot easily be reversed. For example, if you wanted to compare performance on a mirror-tracing task with and without previous training, subjects first receiving the "previous training" condition probably could not be brought back to the "naïve" state prior to being given the "no previous training" condition. In this case you would have to use separate groups for the training and no-training conditions.

Statistical Analysis of Within-Subjects Designs

Using the same subjects in every treatment of an experiment poses special problems not only for design (the need for counterbalancing and irreversible effects) but also for statistical analysis. The statistical tests used to analyze data from between-subjects designs are not appropriate for data from within-subjects designs. Specialized tests are required, to take advantage of certain statistical properties that arise from using the same subjects in all the experimental conditions.

These tests include the *t*-test for correlated samples (used for data from single-factor, two-level within-subjects designs) and several versions of within-subjects analysis of variance (ANOVA). Use a repeated-measures ANOVA to analyze data from single-factor within-subjects experiments. Factorial within-subjects designs require a multifactor within-subjects ANOVA. Before you can use these tests, however, the data must meet several restrictive assumptions, including normality, homogeneity of variance, and homogeneity of covariance. (See Chapter 12 for a discussion of these tests and their assumptions.)

For experiments that yield nominal or ordinal data, nonparametric tests are available (for example, the Wilcoxon matched pairs Sign test; the McNemar test; and the Friedman two-way analysis of variance. See Siegel and Castellan (1988) for a complete discussion of these tests.

Types of Within-Subjects Designs

Just as with the between-subjects design, the within-subjects design is really a family of designs that incorporate the same basic structure. This section discusses several variations on the within-subjects design. These variations include the single-factor, multilevel within-subjects design (in both parametric and non-parametric versions); the multifactor within-subjects design; and multivariate within-subjects designs.

The Single-Factor Two-Level Design

The *single-factor two-level design* is the simplest form of within-subjects design and includes just two levels of a single independent variable. All subjects receive both levels of the variable, but half the subjects receive the treatments in one order and half in the opposite order. The scores within each treatment are then averaged (ignoring the order in which the treatments were given) and the two treatment means are compared.

This design is directly comparable to the two-group between-subjects design, including the general advantages and disadvantages of the within-subjects approach. If order effects are not severe and are approximately equal for both orders, then counterbalancing will control the order effects without introducing excessive error variance. If the dependent variable is strongly affected by subject-related variables, then the two-factor within-subjects design will control this source of variance and the experiment will more likely detect the effect (if any) of the independent variable. However, if the dependent variable is not strongly affected by subject-related variables, this design will be less effective in detecting the effect of the independent variable than will its two-group between-subjects equivalent.

Statistical Analysis. Data resulting from a two-treatment within-subjects design can be analyzed by means of the *t*-test for correlated samples if the data meet the assumptions of a parametric test and are scaled on at least an interval scale. This is the same version of the *t*-test that is used for the matched two-group design (see Chapter 8), and is used here for the same reason. Because the same subject participates in both treatments of the experiment, the scores from the two treatments are very likely to be correlated. The *t*-test for correlated samples takes account of the correlation, in effect removing average differences (across treatments) among subjects from the analysis and focusing instead on between-treatment differences within each subject.

Note that the degrees of freedom on which the critical value of *t* is calculated is equal to the total number of subjects in the experiment (not in each treatment) minus 1. This is less than the degrees of freedom used for the same number of data points from a two-group analysis.

If you have a computer program that performs a single-factor within-subjects ANOVA, you can substitute this ANOVA for the *t*-test with equivalent results. If you are performing the calculations by hand, however, the *t*-test is easier to conduct.

When your data do not meet the assumptions of a parametric statistic, or your data are scaled on a nominal scale, you can use the McNemar test for the significance of changes to analyze data from this design (Siegel & Castellan, 1988). For data that fall on an ordinal scale, the Sign test or the Wilcoxon matched pairs, signed ranks test is appropriate.

Single-Factor Multilevel Designs

Just as with the between-subjects design, the within-subjects design can include more than two levels of the independent variable. In the *single-factor, multilevel within-subjects design,* a single group of subjects is exposed to three or more levels of a single independent variable. If the independent variable is not a cumulative factor (such as practice), then the order of treatments is counterbalanced to prevent any carryover effects from confounding the effects of the treatments.

Table 9-6 shows the organization of a single-factor within-subjects design with four levels or treatments and eight subjects. In this example, subjects have been randomly assigned to eight different treatment orders, with the restriction that each treatment appears equally often in each ordinal position. Each row indicates the ordinal position of each treatment for a given subject. Treatment orders were determined by constructing two Latin squares, one for each batch of four subjects.

Chapter 8 distinguished among several types of single-factor between-subjects design, including parametric, nonparametric, and multiple control group versions. The same distinctions can be applied to within-subjects designs. Because the basic features of these designs have been described before, a separate section is not provided here for each type. Instead, a parametric within-subjects experiment will illustrate the single-factor multilevel within-subjects design.

Peterson and Peterson (1959) conducted a now-classic study of memory processes. This study was designed to determine the effect of retention interval on memory for three-consonant trigrams (such as JHK). Retention intervals of 3, 6, 9, 12, 15, and 18 seconds were tested, with each subject receiving all the retention intervals and with order of intervals counterbalanced across subjects.

Table 9-6. Structure of a Counterbalanced Single-Factor Within-Subjects Design with Four Treatments

SUBJECTS	TREATMENTS			
	T_1	T_2	T_3	T_4
S_1	4	1	2	3
S_2	1	2	3	4
S_3	3	4	1	2
S_4	2	3	4	1
S_5	4	3	2	1
S_6	1	4	3	2
S_7	2	1	4	3
S_8	3	2	1	4

To prevent them from rehearsing the trigram during the retention intervals, the subjects were kept busy doing a demanding mental arithmetic task. Figure 9-6 shows the results. Probability of correct recall was found to decline sharply as the retention interval increased. This evidence provided strong support for the existence of short-term memory as a separate entity from long-term memory.

The Petersons' experiment could have been conducted using a between-subjects design. In this case, however, the use of the within-subjects design reduced the time and the number of subjects required to complete the study. At the same time, this design prevented the sometimes large individual differences in recall performance from obscuring the effect of retention interval.

The results from a multigroup within-subjects design are interpreted much like the results from a multigroup between-subjects design. If the independent variable is quantitative (that is, measured along an interval or ratio scale) as in the Peterson and Peterson (1959) study or in designs where trials or time is the independent variable, then the design is said to be *parametric* (just as with between-subjects designs). In that case, your primary interest in conducting the study may be to determine the form of the function relating the independent and dependent variable. (The term *parametric* as used here has nothing to do with statistics. But if your independent variable represented different categories (such as different types of drugs), then talking about functional relationships would be meaningless. In that case, you would want to compare the effects of the different treatments with each other and with those of any control conditions included in the design.

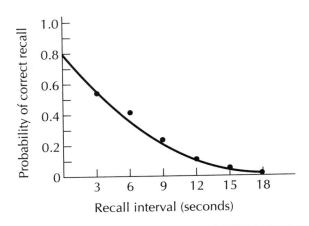

Figure 9-6. Probability of correct recall as a function of retention interval. (Peterson & Peterson, 1959; reprinted with permission.)

Statistical Analysis. If your data meet the requirements of a parametric statistic, then the statistical analysis of choice is the *single-factor within-subjects ANOVA*. This analysis differs from the equivalent between-subjects ANOVA in that it effectively ignores the average differences in scores among subjects and focuses instead on the change in scores within each subject across treatments.

If your ANOVA indicates that significant differences exist among your treatment means, then you can conduct various subsequent analyses to determine which means differ significantly from which. Chapter 12 describes some of these options.

In the case of a parametric design, you may want to determine the functional relationship between your independent and dependent variable. This determination is usually accomplished by first graphing the results and then submitting the data to a trend analysis, which assesses the reliability of various "trends" in the data. Trends take the form of straight lines (linear), or various shapes of curve, such as U-shaped (quadratic) or S-shaped (cubic). Trend analysis in the within-subjects designs imposes restrictions on the form of the variance-covariance matrix, just as it does for the general analysis of variance. See Chapter 15 for a discussion of these restrictions and ways to deal with them.

Multifactor Within-Subjects Designs

The basic multitreatment within-subjects design can be expanded to include two or more independent variables, just as described in Chapter 8 for between-subjects designs. Both factorial and nonfactorial options are available, depending on the goals of the research and the resources available to conduct it. These options are discussed next.

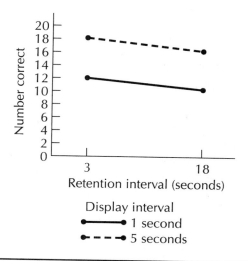

Figure 9-7. Results of class experiment using a factorial design. (From Peterson & Peterson, 1959.)

Factorial Designs. In the factorial within-subjects design, each subject is exposed to every combination of levels of all the factors (independent variables). You may recall from the discussion of factorial designs in Chapter 8 that such designs allow you to identify the independent effects (called the *main effects*) of each factor and to determine whether the relationship between each factor and the dependent variable changes with the levels of the remaining factors (the *interactions*).

An example of the factorial design was recently conducted by a research methods class. This experiment was a variant of the Peterson and Peterson (1959) study described previously. In the class's version, the consonant trigrams were presented on the screen of a computer, rather than being given verbally as in the original experiment. The students wanted to know whether the display duration of the trigram affected retention and, if so, whether it affected retention more after long retention intervals than after short ones.

To answer these questions, the class decided to test retention after display intervals of 1 second or 5 seconds, and retention intervals of 3 seconds or 18 seconds. Combining each display interval with each retention interval resulted in four treatments. Each subject was exposed to each of these treatments in random order until he or she had completed 20 trials at each combination of display interval and retention interval. Figure 9-7 shows the mean number of correct recollections.

As you can see in the figure, the number of correct recalls was lower when the retention interval was 18 seconds than when it was 3 seconds, regardless of the display interval. Also, the number of correct recalls was lower when the display interval was 1 second (lower line) than when it was 5 seconds (upper line), regardless of retention interval. The lines connecting treatments having the same display interval appear to be parallel, indicating that the two factors did not interact. A statistical analysis showed a significant effect of display interval, a significant effect of retention interval, and no significant interaction.

The research methods class experiment was conducted using just 20 subjects (the entire class). To conduct this experiment using a between-subjects design with ten subjects per treatment combination would have required 40 subjects to complete. (Each subject in a group would have received 20 retention trials.) As the number of levels of each factor and/or the number of factors increases, the savings in number of subjects, time to deliver instructions, materials, and so on, that were achieved by adopting the within-subjects approach becomes considerable.

There is also a dark side to this scenario, however. As the number of levels of each factor and/or number of factors increases, so also does the time required to run each subject through all the required treatments. The number of possible orderings of treatments becomes astronomical with only a few levels per factor and a few factors, thus making complete counterbalancing impractical. And unless care is taken, the large demands on subjects may lead to fatigue, boredom, inattention, and perhaps outright hostility toward you and your experiment. In other words, the practical limits to the size of a factorial within-subjects experiment are reached more rapidly than with the equivalent between-subjects design.

To provide a graphic example of how rapidly practical limits can be exceeded, imagine that the class experiment on memory was expanded to include each of Peterson and Peterson's original retention intervals (3, 6, 9, 12, 15, and 18 seconds). With two display intervals, the experiment would have required twelve (6 × 2) treatments, which at 20 trials per treatment would have required each subject to complete 240 trials. If a third variable with two levels were added (say, meaningfulness of the trigram), this number would double to 480 trials.

At an average rate of one trial every 15 seconds, each subject would require two hours to complete the experiment, assuming no breaks. Would the results be comparable to those obtained in the equivalent between-groups experiment, where each subject would have received only 20 trials, or five minutes of participation?

Despite this limitation, factorial within-subjects designs are often used, especially in areas such as sensory threshold testing, decision making, and perceptual processing. In these areas, the large amount of practice subjects get across treatments confers a desirable stability on their performances. To determine whether your research question can best be answered by using a within-subjects design, you need to carefully consider how multiple treatment exposures will affect your subjects' responses to the treatments and willingness to cooperate.

Statistical Analysis. If your data meet the assumptions required for parametric statistics as applied to within-subject designs, you would probably want to select a multifactor within-subjects (or repeated measures) analysis of variance to determine whether any reliable differences exist among the treatments. The two-factor extension of the Peterson and Peterson study employed the two-factor version of this analysis.

The multifactor within-subjects ANOVA assumes that both factors were manipulated within subjects. This type of analysis is said to be "completely within." This description distinguishes this type of analysis from analyses intended for data from mixed designs, in which one or more factors are manipulated between subjects. Mixed-design experiments are described later in this chapter.

If assumptions of a parametric test are violated, there are no easy solutions. Unfortunately, no readily available nonparametric tests can be used in place of the analysis of variance. Other possible solutions are corrections such as the Geisser-Greenhouse correction, the Box correction (see Keppel, 1982), and data transformations (see Chapter 12 for more information about data transformations). Finally, you might consider using a multivariate analysis when assumptions are violated. Chapter 15 discusses this option in more detail.

Other Within-Subjects Designs

Chapter 8 described research situations in which two independent variables do not cross completely. For various reasons, certain combinations of levels of your independent variable may not be possible or may not make logical sense. In these situations, you might consider using a nonfactorial design that includes treatment groups representing theoretically or empirically important combinations of your independent variables. Of course, this logic can be extended to the within-subjects design. Within practical limits, subjects can be run through as many treatments as necessary to test your hypotheses.

Multivariate Within-Subjects Designs

As was the case with between-subjects designs, within-subjects designs can be extended to include two or more dependent variables. As indicated in Chapter 8, designs that make use of more than one dependent variable are called *multivariate designs*. Data from such *multivariate within-subjects designs* require special statistical tests. See Chapter 15 for an introduction to statistics used for multivariate designs.

Combining Between-Subjects and Within-Subjects Designs

When deciding how to conduct a study, you may be able to find a suitable design from among the experimental and nonexperimental designs described in this chapter and in Chapters 6, 7, and 8. However, don't limit yourself to these designs. Some research questions can be better answered with an approach that

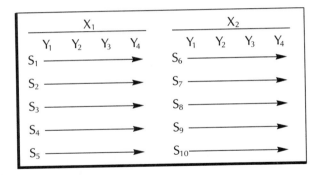

Figure 9-8. Mixed between-within design. Factor *X* has two levels that are manipulated between subjects. Factor *Y* has four levels that are manipulated within subjects.

combines elements of these different design options. This section discusses two designs that combine between-subjects and within-subjects manipulations: the mixed design and the nested design. The section following then introduces some designs that combine experimental and correlational variables.

The Mixed Design

A **mixed design** is sometimes also called a *split plot design*. The term comes from agricultural research, where the design was first developed (it referred to a plot of land). In the split plot design, a field was divided into several plots. Different plots received different levels of a given treatment (different pesticides). Each plot was then split into subplots, and each subplot received a different level of a second treatment (different fertilizers). Thus each plot received all the levels of fertilizer, but only one level of pesticide. In psychological research, each "plot" is a group of subjects who receive the same level of the between-subjects variable, whereas each "subplot" is an individual subject within the group who receives all the levels of the within-subjects variable.

Figure 9-8 depicts a mixed design with one between-subjects variable (Factor X) and one within-subjects variable (Factor Y). Two different groups of subjects are assigned to the two levels of Factor X. Within each group, all subjects receive all four levels of Factor Y.

A mixed design allows you to assess the effects of variables that, because of irreversible effects or carryover, cannot be manipulated effectively within subjects. A mixed design maintains the advantages of the within-subjects design for the remaining variables. An example of this design is provided by a classic experiment on motor learning conducted by I. Lorge (1930).

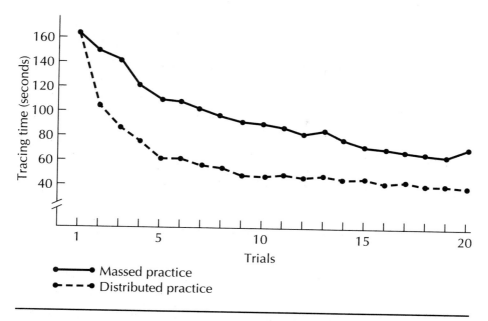

Figure 9-9. A mixed design combining within-subjects and between-subjects design. (Graph drawn from data provided in Lorge, 1930.)

Lorge (1930) was interested in determining whether massed practice ("cramming") or distributed practice (spacing the learning out over several sessions) produced faster learning in a mirror-tracing task. Subjects learned to trace around a simple geometric figure (such as a star) while looking at the figure through a mirror. Two groups received 20 tracing trials, and the time required to complete the tracing was recorded after each trial. One group completed all 20 trials in one sitting (massed practice), whereas the other group completed its 20 trials at the rate of one trial per day (distributed practice).

Figure 9-9 shows the results of Lorge's (1930) experiment. The upper and lower curves represent the tracing time (in seconds) as a function of trials for the groups receiving massed practice and distributed practice, respectively. What is the within-subjects variable in this study? What is the between-subjects variable? "Trials," of course, is the variable manipulated within subjects, and type of practice ("massed" or "distributed") is the variable manipulated between subjects.

This mixed design included one factor that was manipulated between subjects and one that was manipulated within. More complex mixed designs are possible. Factorial mixed designs with three, four, or more factors in any combination of within-subjects and between-subjects manipulations can be conducted. For designs with up to three factors, parametric statistical analyses based on the ANOVA model are readily available (see Keppel, 1982; Winer, 1971).

Statistical Analysis. For data that fit a parametric model, a *split plot* or *mixed analysis of variance* would be the appropriate analytic tool for data from a mixed design. For the between-subjects factor or factors, this analysis produces the identical result as a complete between-subjects analysis. Analysis of the within-subjects factors and of their interactions with the between-subjects factors takes into account the correlations among treatment scores.

Two major disadvantages to using a mixed design are both related to statistical analysis of your data. As you move from a completely within-subjects or completely between-subjects design to a mixed design, analyzing your data becomes more complex. In the mixed ANOVA, for example, you must calculate separate error terms to test the between-subjects effects and within-subjects effects. As you go from a two-factor to a multifactor mixed design, the analyses become even more complex, since you must calculate appropriate error terms for several (rather than one) interactions.

A second problem surrounds the assumptions of the mixed ANOVA, which are much more restrictive than those for a simple between-subjects design. (See Chapter 15 for a discussion of this topic.) Suffice it to say, at this point, it is more difficult to meet the assumptions required for a mixed ANOVA than for a between-subjects ANOVA. Unfortunately, if your data do not meet the assumptions, there are no nonparametric alternatives.

The Nested Design

Another design that combines within-subjects and between-subjects components is the **nested design**. Figure 9-10 shows an example of a nested design. This example includes three levels of a between-subjects factor (A_1, A_2, and A_3). Under each of the levels of A are "nested" three levels of B. Notice that the levels of B found under different levels of A are not the same. For example, B_1, B_2, and B_3 appear under A_1, whereas B_4, B_5, and B_6 appear under A_2. Each level of Factor A thus includes a within-subjects manipulation of Factor B, although the levels of B included in the manipulation differ with the A level.

Nesting Tasks. Nested designs are useful when you want to include more than one task under a level of an independent variable. For example, imagine that you were conducting an experiment on the ability to solve anagrams (unscrambling letters to form words). The between-subjects factor might be anagram difficulty (low, moderate, and high). Under each level of anagram difficulty, you might want to include two sets of anagrams, with all subjects in each level of difficulty completing both sets of anagrams. Figure 9-11 shows this design.

The major advantage of a nested design like the one shown in Figure 9-11 is that you increase the generality of your results. By demonstrating the effect of item difficulty with several different tasks, you can be more certain that your effect is not limited to a particular type of problem.

Nesting Groups of Subjects. A nested design can also be useful when you must test subjects in large groups, rather than individually. For example, you may

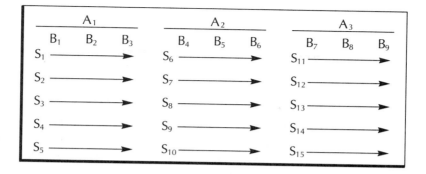

Figure 9-10. A nested design that has a within-subjects component.

	Low			Moderate			High	
	Set 1	Set 2		Set 3	Set 4		Set 5	Set 6
S_1 ⟶			S_6 ⟶			S_{11} ⟶		
S_2 ⟶			S_7 ⟶			S_{12} ⟶		
S_3 ⟶			S_8 ⟶			S_{13} ⟶		
S_4 ⟶			S_9 ⟶			S_{14} ⟶		
S_5 ⟶			S_{10} ⟶			S_{15} ⟶		

Figure 9-11. A design with two tasks nested under each level of the independent variable.

find it necessary to test subjects during their regularly scheduled class hours. If you tested three classes under each of your experimental conditions, you would then have a class nested under each level of your independent variable. Figure 9–12 illustrates this situation.

Nesting groups of subjects within levels of the independent variable should not be done if you can nest only one group under each level of your independent variable. In this case, your experiment is hopelessly confounded since you have no way of knowing whether the differences between groups of subjects across treatment levels occur because of your independent variable or because of something relating to the nested groups (Keppel, 1982).

Nesting several independent groups under each level of your independent variable is analogous to running individual subjects. When you randomly assign

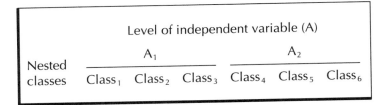

Figure 9-12. Groups of subjects nested under levels of the independent variable.

individual subjects to conditions in a between-subjects design, you are essentially nesting subjects within treatments. Each group in a nested design can be viewed as a "subject" nested under a level of your independent variable. As long as you randomly assign groups of subjects to experimental conditions, nesting groups of subjects is legitimate.

Statistical Analysis. The appropriate analysis for a nested design is a *nested analysis of variance*. When you have only one independent variable, the analysis includes an effect of your treatment and an effect of your repeated task (or subjects) nested within the independent variable. The analysis is a bit more complex than the simple within-subjects or between-subjects ANOVA. A complete discussion of nested designs and nested ANOVAs can be found in Keppel (1982, chapter 12).

Combining Experimental and Correlational Designs

Experimental designs such as those described in this chapter and in Chapter 8 have the strong advantage of allowing you not only to identify whether relationships exist between variables, but also to determine whether the relationships so identified are causal ones. The strategy requires that you be able to manipulate the suspected causal variable, hold constant as many extraneous variables as possible, and randomize the effects of any remaining extraneous variables across treatments. Unfortunately, holding variables constant can reduce the generality of your findings (using all males, for example, may yield results that do not generalize to females), whereas randomizing their effects across treatments can produce error variance that obscures the effects of your independent variables.

Fortunately, you can often deal with such problems effectively by using designs that combine both experimental and correlational variables. This section examines two such design options: including quasi-independent variables in your experiment, and including a correlational variable as a covariate.

Including Quasi-Independent Variables in an Experiment

A quasi-independent variable, as you may recall from Chapter 6, is a correlational variable that resembles an independent variable in an experiment. It is created by assigning subjects to groups according to some characteristic they possess (such as age, gender, or IQ), rather than using random assignment. Because subjects come into the "experiment" already "assigned" to their treatment levels, it is always possible that any relationship discovered may be due to the action of some third, unmeasured variable that happens to correlate well with the quasi-independent variable. Even so, the knowledge that a relationship exists may be important. This is especially true when quasi-experimental variables are added to an experimental design.

Such combinations of both experimental and quasi-experimental variables often resemble the factorial designs described earlier in this chapter and in Chapter 8. These combinations yield a main effect for each independent variable, a main effect for each quasi-independent variable, and one or more interactions. The interactions in such designs can be especially illuminating. An example where this was the case is provided by Schachter (1971) in a study of obesity.

Schachter brought his subjects (college students) into a "waiting room" that was equipped with a large wall clock and told the subjects that they should wait there until called to participate in an experiment. Actually they were already in the experiment. Bowls of crackers were placed in the room, and subjects were invited to help themselves to some crackers if they wished.

The experimental manipulation of Schachter's study concerned the clock on the wall. For one group of subjects, the clock ran fast, and soon it seemed that it was nearly dinnertime. For another group, the clock ran slow. For this group, dinnertime really was approaching, but this was not indicated by the clock.

Schachter combined this experimental variable with a correlational one: the weight of the subjects. Subjects were divided into two groups, one consisting of participants whose weights were considered "normal," the other consisting of participants who were considered "overweight." The dependent variable of the study was the number of crackers eaten.

Subject weight is a correlational variable because subjects came to the experiment already having a given weight. They were not assigned randomly to the "normal" or "overweight" conditions. If Schachter had created his two weight classes by force-feeding a randomly chosen half of the subjects, then subject weight would have been an experimental variable.

Schachter found that the "normal" subjects essentially ignored the clock and consumed more crackers when it was nearly dinnertime than when it was not. "Overweight" subjects, in contrast, used the clock to regulate their behavior, eating more crackers when the clock said it was near dinnertime than when the clock said dinnertime was still distant. These findings can be summarized by saying that subject weight *interacted* with indicated time.

If you ignore the fact that subject weight is a correlational variable, then Schachter's design looks exactly like a 2 × 2 factorial between–subjects design. This similarity extends even further, as the results of the study would be analyzed exactly as those from the equivalent factorial design, as well. What differs is the interpretation.

Any significant effect of the experimental variables in the combined design can be interpreted to mean that the independent variable *caused* changes in the dependent variable. In the Schachter study, the effect of indicated time on cracker consumption would be interpreted in this way. Any significant effect of the correlational variables in the study *cannot* be legitimately interpreted to indicate a causal relationship. Any correlation between two variables could result from the effect of a third, unmeasured variable that influences both variables. A significant effect of subject weight on cracker consumption would indicate only that consumption is related to weight.

In the case of Schachter's (1971) experiment, the presence of an interaction between indicated time and subject weight complicates the interpretation of the effect of both variables on subject weight. The main effect of indicated time lumps together the very different behaviors of "normal" and "overweight" subjects. Similarly, the main effect of subject weight combines the very different effects of early time and late time. Indeed, the suspicion that "overweight" subjects would react differently to indicated time was what prompted the study in the first place.

To understand what went on in the study, you need to look at the simple effect of indicated time at each level of subject weight. This analysis would show that indicated time affected cracker consumption for "overweight" subjects, but not "normal" subjects. (See Chapter 12 for a discussion of the analysis of simple effects.)

Advantages of Including a Quasi-Independent Variable. Experimental designs that include a quasi–independent variable allow you to test the generality of your findings across the levels of the quasi–independent variable. In the example, Schachter was able to show that altering the clock reading had effects on the subjects' eating behavior that did not generalize from normal-weight to overweight individuals. In fact, the effect was reversed across the two groups. Had Schachter analyzed the data without regard to the subject's weight, these two effects might have canceled each other out, leading to the false conclusion that clock time had no effect on eating.

Disadvantages of Including a Quasi-Independent Variable. The main disadvantage of including a quasi-independent variable in your design is that the results are frequently misinterpreted. Although paying lip service to the dictum "Cause cannot be inferred from correlation," researchers too often discuss their results as if they had established causal links between their quasi-independent and dependent variables. This mistake is encouraged by the fact that the correlational variables look exactly like experimental variables in the statistical analysis of the data. In Schachter's experiment, you may wish to conclude that being over-weight causes people's eating behavior to be governed more by the clock than is the case with people of normal weight. However, one could just as well argue that being more sensitive to external cues leads to being overweight. Because weight was not experimentally manipulated, the causal status of this variable remains ambiguous.

Another disadvantage of these designs (although a minor one) is the extra effort sometimes required to obtain subjects differing in the required character-istics. Some quasi-experimental variables (such as anxiety level or IQ) require administration of a questionnaire or test before subjects can be classified. Add-ing quasi-experimental variables to an experimental design also increases the number of groups of subjects required and adds complexity to the analysis of the data.

Statistical Analysis. Data from experimental designs that include quasi-experi-mental variables are analyzed exactly as you would if all the variables were experimental. For example, for data from a factorial between-subjects design that included one independent variable and one quasi-independent variable, you would normally use a two-factor between-subjects ANOVA.

Including a Covariate in Your Experimental Design

Where subjects differ on some continuous variable (such as IQ or simple reaction time), you can statistically control the effects of this variable by simply measur-ing its value in each subject along with the value of the dependent variable. This additional variable is referred to as a **covariate**. The name derives from the fact that you expect the covariate to *covary* with the dependent variable. This will be the case if the covariate has a direct influence on the dependent variable or if it correlates with some unmeasured variable that does have such an influence.

Advantages of Including a Covariate. By including a covariate in your experi-mental design, you can effectively "subtract out" the influence of the covariate (or any variable correlated with it) on the dependent variable, thus reducing error variance and improving the sensitivity of your experiment to the effects of the independent variable.

These designs are also relatively easy to implement. By simply collecting additional data on potentially relevant correlational variables, you can convert a standard experimental design into one that examines the impact of those vari-ables on the relationship between the study's independent and dependent variables.

Disadvantages of Including a Covariate. Including a covariate in your experimen-tal design adds the time and effort required to measure these additional variables, and increases the complexity of the statistical analysis.

Statistical Analysis. Analysis of data from designs that include a covariate is accomplished with an *analysis of covariance* (*ANCOVA*). The analysis statistically controls error variance in order to increase the sensitivity of the statistical test. Error variance is controlled statistically by reducing the differences between subjects within a treatment group (error variance) before evaluating the differences between treatment means (Keppel, 1982). The ANCOVA is too complex to discuss in detail here. See Keppel (1982, chapter 20) for a detailed account of ANCOVA.

Pretest–Posttest Designs

As the name suggests, **pretest-posttest designs** include a pretest of subjects on the dependent measure before the introduction of the treatment conditions, followed by a posttest after the treatment conditions have been introduced. These are not really new designs, but because they share a common feature (the pretest), we have given them their own section in which we can explore their uses.

Pretest-posttest designs are used to evaluate the effects of some change in the environment on subsequent performance. You might employ a pretest-posttest design to assess the effect of changes in an educational environment (for example, introduction of a new teaching method) or in the work environment (for example, using work teams on an assembly line). By using a pretest-posttest design, you can compare levels of performance before the introduction of your change, to levels of performance after the introduction of the change.

Evaluating changes in performance after some change would seem simple: just measure a behavior, introduce the change, and then measure the behavior again. You should recognize this design as a simple within-subjects experiment with two levels: pretreatment and posttreatment. As with any within-subjects design, carryover effects may confound the effect of the manipulation. Giving your subjects the pretest may change the way they perform after you introduce your manipulation; for example, by drawing their attention to the behaviors you are assessing, providing practice on the test, introducing fatigue, and so on. Normally you would control such carryover effects through counterbalancing. Unfortunately, you cannot counterbalance the pretest and posttest administrations (think about it!). Thus, a simple pretest-posttest design leads to problems with internal validity.

To ensure internal validity, you must include control groups. Campbell and Stanley (1963) discuss pretest-posttest designs extensively. According to Campbell and Stanley, the simplest practical pretest-posttest design should take the form of the diagram shown in Figure 9-13.

As shown in Figure 9-13, the design includes two independent groups of subjects. Group 1 (the experimental group) receives your treatment (for exam-

Group 1: Pretest-Treatment-Posttest
Group 2: Pretest   Posttest

Figure 9-13. The simplest practical pretest-posttest design: a mixed design with pretest-posttest as the within-subjects factor and with treatment versus no treatment as the between-subjects factor.

ple, a new teaching method) between the pretest and posttest. Group 2 (the control group) also receives the pretest and posttest but does not receive the treatment. The pretest and posttest are given to the subjects in the experimental and control groups at the same time intervals.

You may have recognized this design from earlier in this chapter: it is simply a mixed design with pretest-posttest as the within-subjects factor and with treatment versus no treatment as the between-subjects factor. As such, you can use the design to determine the main effect of each factor and the interaction between them.

If the pretest affected the performances of subjects in the posttest, you would expect to find a difference between pretest and posttest scores *in both groups*. The same could be said for the effects of any other events, unrelated to your treatment, that might occur between the pretest and posttest administrations: they would be expected to affect the two groups similarly. In contrast, if you found a difference between the pretest and posttest scores in the experimental group only, then you would be justified in concluding that your treatment, and not some other factor, produced the observed changes in performance.

An example follows. Imagine you are interested in whether using computers in a second-grade class affects the children's knowledge of scientific principles. You obtain a sample of 100 second-graders. You randomly assign 50 of them to a new teaching method involving computer-aided instruction. These subjects constitute your experimental group; the remaining subjects are your control group. You give a pretest of scientific principles to all 100 students and then provide computer-aided instruction to your experimental group (the control group continues to get the usual instruction). Finally, you give both groups your posttest.

Imagine you find that your experimental subjects show an average gain of 20 points from pretest to posttest, whereas your control subjects show an average gain of only 2 points. You could then conclude that your new teaching method was responsible for the observed change and not some other factor. Now imagine that both groups had shown the same 20-point gain. Would you reach the same conclusion? Of course not. Now you would have to conclude that the students showed the same rate of improvement regardless of the teaching method used.

Campbell and Stanley (1963) pointed out that in order for this design to qualify as a true experiment, subjects must be randomly assigned to your groups. You *could* use naturally formed groups in a pretest-posttest format, but then the between-subjects component would involve a quasi-independent variable, and your conclusions regarding the effect of this variable would be weaker. For example, if you used different classes in your study of computer-aided instruction and found that the class receiving the computers showed a greater increase in performance from pretest to posttest, you could not conclude with any confidence that the computers caused the difference. Perhaps they did, but it is also possible that the teacher of the experimental class simply did a better job of teaching.

Campbell and Stanley also pointed out that although the two-group pretest-posttest design ensures a degree of internal validity, it does not preclude potential problems with external validity. Your results may not generalize beyond the immediate research setting. Although this problem can affect any experiment, a particular problem of this design is that subjects may be sensitized by the pretest. Having had the pretest, subjects may now perform differently than they would have without the pretest. For example, the experimental group may do better than the control group when both groups receive a pretest, but not when the pretests are omitted. Campbell and Stanley suggest two remedies to the problem.

The first remedy is to use a design called the **Solomon four-group** design. This design is illustrated in Figure 9-14. Note that four groups are included in this design. Groups 1 and 2 are identical to those in the two-group design. The additional groups allow you to test for any possible sensitization effects of the pretest. Groups 3 (treatment and then posttest) and 4 (posttest alone) allow you to evaluate the impact of your treatment in the absence of a pretest. By comparing this effect with the impact of your treatment when a pretest is included, you can determine whether inclusion of the pretest alters the effect of your treatment.

Campbell and Stanley's second remedy to the pretest sensitization problem is to entirely eliminate the pretest. Minus the pretest, this design represents a simple two-group experiment. The decision to eliminate the pretest depends on the question being asked. Situations may exist in which the pretest is needed to completely answer a research question.

Summary

There are several alternatives to the between-subjects approach to experimental design. These alternatives include within-subjects designs, mixed designs, and designs that combine the experimental and correlational strategies. Special variants of these designs include a pretest: these are called pretest-posttest designs.

```
Group 1:  Pretest-Treatment-Posttest
Group 2:  Pretest           Posttest
Group 3:           Treatment-Posttest
Group 4:                    Posttest
```

Figure 9-14. A Solomon four-group design.

Within-subjects designs expose every subject in the experiment to all the treatment conditions. This strategy reduces the number of subjects required for an experiment compared to the number required for the equivalent between-subjects design. In a sense, the ultimate form of matching (each subject is matched to him- or herself), the within-subjects design excludes error variance caused by subject differences from the analysis of the data. If subject differences strongly influence the value of the dependent variable, the analysis will have more power (ability to detect the effect of the independent variable) than the equivalent analysis performed on between-subjects data.

On the negative side, within-subjects designs will have less power than equivalent between-subjects designs if the dependent variable is only weakly related to subject differences. In that case, any decrease in error variance is offset by the reduced degrees of freedom obtained from the within-subjects design. In addition, within-subjects designs suffer from the possibility of damaging carryover effects. Carryover effects occur when exposure to one treatment alters the behavior of subjects in a subsequent treatment.

Carryover effects can be dealt with by counterbalancing or by making treatment order an independent variable. Counterbalancing involves exposing different subjects to the treatments in different orders. Complete counterbalancing provides at least one subject for every possible ordering of treatments. With a large number of treatments, complete counterbalancing becomes impractical. In that case, partial counterbalancing (in which subjects receive a randomly selected subset of possible orderings) is used instead. The number of times each treatment appears in each ordinal position can be kept in balance by using a Latin square.

Counterbalancing will be effective only if carryover between treatments is approximately equivalent no matter which treatment comes first. Counterbalancing will not work if a treatment produces irreversible changes that affect performance in subsequent treatments.

Making treatment order an independent variable allows you to determine whether carryover effects are present and, if so, their magnitude and direction. This strategy may be useful in the beginning stages of research in order to assess whether counterbalancing will be effective in later experiments. However, such designs quickly become impractical as the number of treatments expands.

You should consider using a within-subjects design when the number of available subjects is limited and carryover is likely to be minimal, when the dependent variable is strongly affected by subject characteristics, or when the variable of interest is inherently a within-subject change (such as the effects of practice, reinforcement, habituation, or adaptation).

Statistical analysis of within-subjects designs is similar to that of between-subjects designs, with the difference that the analysis takes into account the correlations among treatment scores across subjects. In addition, univariate analyses assume that both the variances and the correlations between treatments are identical to one another except for random fluctuations. Violations of this compound symmetry assumption may lead to highly biased estimates of statistical significance. If compound symmetry is violated, it is possible to correct for those violations or to use a multivariate analytic approach that makes no assumptions about the correlation matrix.

Within-subjects designs come in the same variations previously discussed for between-subjects designs. These include two-treatment, single-factor multilevel, factorial, multiple control group, and multivariate designs.

Mixed designs combine aspects of the within-subjects and between-subjects designs. Such designs, also called split plot designs, are often used to investigate the effects of treatments for which carryover effects would be a problem while repeatedly sampling behavior across time or trials. Nested designs include different levels of the nested factor under each level of the between-groups variable. These designs are useful when you cannot use the same levels of the nested variable under each level of the between-groups variable. Statistical analyses are available for these designs to take advantage of the reduction of error term possible for the within-subjects variables, while properly analyzing the effect of the between-subjects variables.

Another way to combine designs is to include both experimental and correlational variables. Such designs are frequently used when it is suspected that subject-related variables (such as sex, IQ, or anxiety level) may interact with the experimental variables of the study to alter their effects. The failure to find such interactions can help to establish the generality of experimental relationships.

A problem with combined experimental designs is the temptation to over-interpret the data as if the correlational variable were an experimental one. In such designs, cause-effect conclusions can only be drawn for the experimental variables.

The pretest-posttest design is used when you want to evaluate the impact of some environmental change on naturally occurring behavior (such as the introduction of a new policy in a factory). Behavior is measured before and after the introduction of the change. A major problem with this design is that subjects may be sensitized by your pretest. Special designs (such as the Solomon four-group design) have been developed to circumvent the problems inherent in this design.

Key Terms

Carryover effects

Counterbalancing

Latin square design

Mixed design

Nested design

Covariate

Pretest–posttest design

Solomon four-group design

10

Using Single-Subject Designs

THE EXPERIMENTAL DESIGNS DESCRIBED in the last two chapters require that one or more groups of subjects be exposed to the various treatments of the experiment. The data from each treatment are then averaged. The differences among the means are tested statistically to determine the probability that the observed differences could have arisen by chance through the operation of uncontrolled random factors. If this probability is acceptably low, the investigator concludes that the differences are reliable and attributes these differences to the effect of the independent variable.

This chapter presents a very different approach to conducting experimental research, one that focuses on the behavior of individual subjects. It does not depend on averaging across subjects to control the effects of random factors and, therefore, can be used with few or even only one subject. For this reason, the approach is often called the *single-subject* or *small-n* approach. If you have trouble with inferential statistics, you will be pleased to learn that this approach generally avoids them. This chapter describes the logic of the single-subject approach, indicates conditions under which the single-subject approach is appropriate or inappropriate, and identifies specific single-subject designs.

A Little History

A major goal of psychology is to understand human and animal behavior. Understanding a particular behavior means knowing what variables control the behavior and what functional relationships exist between these variables and the behavior. To be useful to psychologists, this understanding must be applicable to individuals.

This emphasis on developing laws that can be applied to individuals dates back to psychology's beginnings as an experimental discipline in the latter half of the nineteenth century. The psychophysics of Weber and Fechner, the memory experiments of Ebbinghaus, the investigations of perceptual processes by the early Gestalt psychologists, Wundt's examinations of "mental chronography," as well as the learning experiments of Thorndike and Pavlov all focused on the behaviors of individual subjects in an effort to understand psychological processes. An extreme example is provided by Ebbinghaus's research, which employed but a single subject — Ebbinghaus himself.

The pioneering experimentalists managed to identify important psychological phenomena, and the functional relationships they uncovered, by and large, have withstood later scrutiny. This was all accomplished without the benefit of inferential statistics, which had not yet been developed.

From the beginning, these early researchers recognized the problems created by apparently random variations in the behaviors of their subjects. One solution to these problems was to repeat the observations many times under a given set of conditions and then average across observations to provide a stable estimate of the "true" values. Although inferential statistics had not yet been developed, researchers knew that estimates based on means become more stable with increasing numbers of observations.

The focus on individual behavior naturally led investigators to adopt a type of within-subjects approach that differs from that described in Chapter 9. In the traditional within-subjects design outlined in Chapter 9, each subject is exposed once to each level of the independent variable, and then scores are averaged across subjects. The method adopted by the early investigators exposed each subject repeatedly to the different treatments, and then averaged across exposures within each treatment. The result was a functional relationship between independent and dependent variables that applied (strictly speaking) to the one individual from whom the data were collected. Functional relationships from different individuals were then compared to determine the generality of the relationships.

Despite intersubject variability, the approach worked because of three factors. First, a very large number of observations were collected from a single subject, thus allowing momentary fluctuations to average out. Second, to the extent possible, incidental factors that might contribute unwanted variability were rigidly controlled. For example, Ebbinghaus ate the same meal at the same time each day during the years he studied his own memory processes (Fancher,

1979). Third, the investigators focused their attentions on powerful variables whose effects could easily be detected against the remaining background of uncontrolled variability.

Of course, certain problems could not be attacked with this approach. These problems involved independent variables that produced irreversible changes in subject behavior, or that exerted very weak effects on the dependent variable, or dependent variables that could not be stabilized through rigid control of experimental conditions. Such problems required an approach that could extract the relatively weak signal of the independent variable from the noisy background of random variation. Inferential statistics were developed for these cases.

The application of statistical techniques to the study of individual differences was pioneered by Sir Frances Galton (a cousin of Charles Darwin) in the late 1800s. The first correlational statistic was developed by Karl Pearson under the guidance of Galton and laid the groundwork for the application of statistical techniques to other problems in psychology.

The next major step in the evolution of the statistical revolution came in the 1920s and 1930s when Sir Ronald Fisher and other statisticians developed the rationale of inferential statistics to provide some of the first statistical tests. Soon researchers in psychology recognized that these statistical techniques provided powerful tools for dealing with uncontrolled variability. Inferential statistics were adopted, and the single-subject approach waned in popularity. By 1950 it was virtually impossible to publish research in a respectable psychological journal unless the data had been subjected to an appropriate statistical test and were judged to be reliable.

Meanwhile, some die-hard researchers persisted in using the old nonstatistical, single-subject approach. Most prominent among these was B. F. Skinner. Focusing his efforts on the effects of environmental stimuli on the motor behavior of rats, Skinner developed a highly controlled laboratory environment to observe and record selected behaviors of his subjects. Electromechanical equipment (such as clocks, relays, and switches) was used to gain precise control of environmental stimuli, to program the experimental contingencies, and to define and record the behavioral responses. Skinner and his students continued the tradition of observing and analyzing the behavior of individual subjects. In the process, they developed several methodological refinements that extended the power and usefulness of the single-subject approach.

Unfortunately for Skinner and his followers, their unwillingness to use inferential statistics to establish the reliability of their findings made it increasingly difficult for them to get their results published. In 1958 they attacked this problem by establishing their own journal, the *Journal of the Experimental Analysis of Behavior,* or *JEAB.* Eventually researchers using the single-subject approach were able to convince others of the validity of the method. Today the approach is widely accepted, and experiments using it can be published in most reputable psychology journals. Because the method specifically focuses on changes in the behavior of the single subject, it has gained widespread acceptance in applied situations, where it has been used to assess the effectiveness of behavioral change programs and therapies in the treatment of individuals.

As this brief review indicates, single-subject designs have a long and respectable history, and have emerged again into acceptance after being temporarily eclipsed by group-based designs.

Baseline Versus Discrete Trials Designs

Although single-subject designs come in a variety of forms, all these forms can be categorized into one of two basic types: baseline designs (developed primarily by B. F. Skinner and his followers) and discrete trials designs (the type used most often by early researchers). Today when researchers refer to "single-subject designs," they usually mean baseline designs. However, discrete trials designs are still in use, especially in areas, such as psychophysics, where the emphasis continues to be on the performances of individual subjects.

The baseline and discrete trials designs are sufficiently different from one another enough to require separate treatment. The next sections describe the logic of baseline designs and indicate how to analyze and interpret the results obtained from such designs. The remainder of the chapter then describes the discrete trials approach and examines the issues surrounding the use of statistical techniques with single-subject designs.

Baseline Designs

The essential feature of the **baseline design** is the establishment of a behavioral baseline during the **baseline phase** of the experiment. This baseline establishes the level of performance on the dependent measure before introduction of the experimental treatment. Following the baseline phase, the subject is exposed to the experimental treatment and behavior is again measured. This second phase is called the **intervention phase**.

To illustrate the baseline approach to single-subject design, we begin by describing a typical example, part of a larger experiment that investigated whether rats prefer a schedule of signaled shocks over an equivalent schedule of unsignaled shocks (Badia & Culbertson, 1972). The subjects were tested individually in a small operant conditioning chamber equipped with a response lever, a houselight, and a floor of metal rods that could be electrified to deliver a brief shock to the rat's feet. (The shocks are similar to static electric pokes and do not harm the rat.)

In the baseline phase, each subject received a series of "training" sessions to familiarize the rat with the characteristics of each shock schedule and to establish a behavioral baseline. At times the chamber houselight was off, and at other times it was on. When the light was off, shocks occurred unpredictably according to a random schedule at an average rate of one shock every two minutes (unsignaled schedule). When the light was on, shocks continued to occur on the same schedule, but each shock was immediately preceded by a five-second warning tone (signaled schedule). Each session provided equal experience with the two schedules.

During the baseline phase, responses on the lever had no effect on conditions, but the number of responses during each session was recorded. At the end of each session, the percentage of responses out of the total possible was calculated and plotted to provide the behavioral baseline. The investigators continued to train each rat until three successive points on the baseline remained within a 10 percent range. The subject was then placed in the intervention phase of the experiment.

During the intervention phase, the rat was placed on the unsignaled schedule (identified by darkness). Pressing the lever now "bought" the rat one minute of time on the signaled schedule. The houselight turned on to indicate that the signaled schedule was now in effect, and any shocks that happened to be programmed during the minute were preceded by the warning tone. When this one-minute "changeover period" ended, the houselight extinguished and the unsignaled schedule was automatically reinstated. At this time the rat could buy another minute in the signaled schedule by again pressing the lever. The number of "changeover responses" on the lever was recorded and, as in the baseline phase, the percentage of responses out of the total possible was calculated and plotted. Intervention-phase sessions continued until three successive points on the baseline again remained within a 10 percent range. The intervention phase was then repeated, followed by a second exposure to the intervention phase.

Note that the two shock schedules were identical except for the signal and that the rat could neither avoid nor escape the shocks. Would the rats nevertheless press the lever to get into the signaled schedule during the intervention phases? The answer to this question can be found in Figure 10-1, which shows the level of responding during the final three sessions in each phase for each rat.

During the initial baseline phase (during which responses had no programmed consequences), the level of responding of each rat remained low, typically around 10 percent. However, note the dramatic changes that occurred when subjects were placed in the intervention phase: response rates zoomed up to over 85 percent of possible. The subsequent return to baseline conditions produced an equally dramatic effect as response rates fell back to the low levels obtained during the first baseline phase. Finally, response rates jumped back to high levels when subjects were returned to the intervention phase.

The fact that response rates were high in the intervention phases would mean little without the comparison provided by responding in the baseline phase, when responses did not produce the signaled schedule. This comparison shows that response rates were high *only* when responses did produce the signaled schedule.

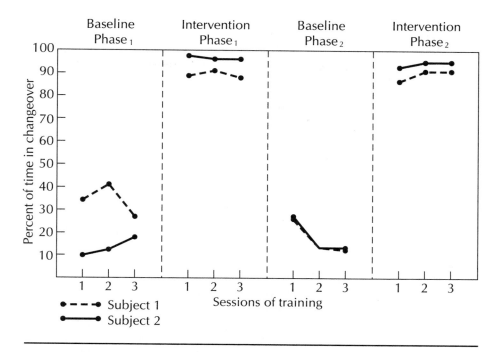

Figure 10-1. Results of a single-subject experiment on rat preference for scheduled shock over unscheduled shock. (Data from Badia & Culbertson, 1972, table 3.)

Badia and Culbertson (1972) concluded from this experiment that rats strongly prefer the signaled shock schedule over an equivalent unsignaled schedule, although it was unclear why. Evidently the signaled schedule contains a powerful source of reinforcement that was capable of generating high rates of responding during the intervention phase. The findings, which could not be explained adequately by known principles of conditioning, led to an extensive series of follow-up studies that sought to clarify the sources of reinforcement and their impact on preference responding (reviewed in Badia, Harsh, & Abbott, 1979).

Features of the Baseline Design

The Badia and Culbertson (1972) experiment illustrates all the basic features of a typical baseline design, as described next. Become thoroughly familiar with them.

The Behavioral Baseline. A characteristic feature of the baseline design is its use of a **behavioral baseline**, a record of a subject's performance across time within a phase. The behavioral baseline has two important functions: (1) to establish the level of the dependent variable under each phase (baseline and intervention), and (2) to assess the amount of uncontrolled variability. To establish the behavioral baseline, you repeatedly assess the subject's behavior within a phase and maintain an up-to-date plot of the behavior as a function of time or sessions. In the Badia and Culbertson (1972) example, the percentage of responses made during each session was plotted immediately after the session to provide the baseline.

Stability Criterion. Systematic changes such as those due to learning or habituation show up in the behavioral baseline as trends toward increasing or decreasing values. Such trends usually occur immediately after a change to a new phase, when behavior is in transition from one stable level to another. To ensure that the baseline accurately represents the level of behavior produced by a given treatment, researchers usually define a **stability criterion** to identify when the baseline no longer shows any systematic trends. When the baseline meets the stability criterion, the subject is moved into the next phase.

The only way to determine whether your baseline has met the stability criterion is to update your plot after each session and then examine it. If you fail to keep your plot current, you may discover, much to your surprise, that you have run your subject through another session under the previous phase when you should have changed to a new phase. As this is both a waste of time and a violation of experimental procedure, you can appreciate how important it is, when using a baseline design, to keep the baseline up to date.

Choosing a good stability criterion is something of an art. If your stability criterion is too stringent, your baseline may never achieve it and you will not be able to proceed to the next phase. Yet if your stability criterion is too lax, you may proceed to the next phase before your subject's performance has actually stabilized. As a result, your "stable" baseline values will not accurately reflect the effects of your independent variable. Developing a good stability criterion may require some pilot work in which you observe your baseline until it shows no long-term trends. You then attempt to identify a stability criterion that would have allowed you to stop sooner without including transitional data. In the example experiment, experience with the percentage measure used indicated that the baseline was likely to remain stable if the data remained within 10 percent across three successive sessions.

Because only the stable performances truly represent the long-term effect of an independent variable on the dependent variable, you usually report only the data that meet the stability criterion. This was done in the example: Figure 10-1 omits the transitional data from the plot.

Intrasubject Replication. If you look again at Figure 10-1, you will note that the baseline and intervention phases were repeated. Each subject's performance thus

---

Table 10-1. Characteristics of the Single-Subject Baseline

1. Individual subjects are observed under each of several phases. Multiple responses are recorded in a phase before the next phase begins.

2. Extensive observations are made during the baseline phase to establish a *behavioral baseline* against which any changes due to the independent variable are compared. A behavioral baseline will also be established during the intervention phase.

3. Each subject is observed under all phases, with each treatment phase repeated at least twice. This repetition, or *intrasubject replication,* establishes the reliability of the findings.

4. Subjects usually remain in each phase until a *stability criterion* is met.

5. Multiple subjects may be included in the experiment. This *intersubject replication* helps establish the generality of the findings across subjects.

---

was assessed twice under each phase, a procedure called **intrasubject replication** ("intra" means "within"). You can now compare the same subject's performance during the original assessment and during replication to determine whether the levels of performance obtained within the baseline and intervention phases were repeatable or *replicable*. The ability to replicate the initial finding indicates that the data are reliable and thus most likely the result of the treatment conditions rather than chance fluctuations in behavior.

Intersubject Replication. Although the Badia and Culbertson (1972) experiment followed a classic single-subject baseline design, you may have noticed that it included more than one subject. The inclusion of extra subjects in the design is called **intersubject replication** ("inter" means "between"). Each subject represents an independent replication of the entire experiment. These extra subjects may give the experiment the appearance of a group-based design, but the similarity is superficial. In baseline designs, you present the data individually for each subject, never as averages across subjects.

We have summarized the characteristics of the single-subject baseline design in Table 10-1.

Rationale of the Baseline Design

At the outset of this chapter, we pointed out that the single-subject approach differs from the group approaches that characterize the designs covered in Chapters 8 and 9. There are four areas in which the baseline design and group-based designs differ: dealing with random variability, handling error variance (see

Chapter 12), assessing the reliability of findings, and determining the generality of results.

Dealing with Random Variability. As discussed in Chapters 8 and 9, when you manipulate an independent variable you hope to show that this manipulation causes changes in behavior. Such changes vary systematically with the level of the independent variable and are, therefore, called **systematic variance**. Other changes in behavior that are not related to variation in the independent variable may also be present. Produced by uncontrolled factors within the experiment, such changes are termed *unsystematic variance* or **error variance**. Error variance is seen in unsystematic fluctuations of a baseline within a phase or of scores across repeated application of a treatment. It also occurs between subjects undergoing the same treatment. Error variance obscures the systematic variance produced by the independent variable.

How you view and choose to deal with error variance depends on the research strategy you adopt. A basic philosophical difference between the single-subject and group approaches concerns how to deal with error variance.

The group approach deals with random variability with two methods: control over extraneous variables likely to influence the dependent variable and averaging data across subjects. Control over extraneous variables can be achieved by exerting tight experimental control over the conditions of your experiment and by using statistical techniques.

With the group approach, you seek to control potential sources of variability through design and procedural measures. During the design phase, for example, you try to identify and control variables that could adversely affect your results. Nevertheless, you will not be able to identify or control all sources of error variance. This remaining error variance becomes part of the error term in the subsequent statistical analysis.

The unit of analysis in the group approach is the group average. Scores from subjects within a group are mathematically combined to arrive at a score intended to represent the performance of the subjects within the group. The difference between means is evaluated against the amount of error variance in the data. If the observed difference between means is sufficiently large, and error variance is relatively low, then the observed difference will be statistically significant.

Given a statistically significant effect, you will probably interpret the observed difference between means and pay little or no attention to the error variance. Another experiment may be designed and conducted with the same sources of error variance. In short, when significant effects are found in group research, usually little effort is made to identify the sources of error variance.

More attention may be paid to error variance when an expected, statistically significant effect does *not* emerge. For example, the difference between group means may have been obscured by too much error variance. If this occurs, you may try to bring the error variance under control by redesigning some aspects of your experiment. For example, you might rework materials and procedure to reduce error variance. Or, if you believe that the error variance was related to subject variables (such as personality or intelligence), you may choose to measure these variables in a subsequent experiment. The subject variables are then used in an effort to statistically control error variance.

Within the single-subject approach, error variance is handled by tight experimental control. Statistical control measures are avoided. Error variance can only be controlled if you can identify its source. Consequently, the single-subject researcher makes an effort to identify the possible sources of variance. The first step in this process is to graph the data from each subject and look for error variance. Error variance will be evident when the data points on your graph show moderate to high levels of instability across observation periods or subjects.

Of course, it is unreasonable to expect a given subject to show exactly the same pattern of behavior across observational periods, or to expect different subjects to display identical patterns of behavior in a given phase. You must decide how much error variance is acceptable. If the observed error variance is within acceptable limits, then you (much like the group researcher) consider the observed effects to be reliable. Unlike the group researcher, however, you may still be concerned with error variance, despite the emergence of a clear relationship between the independent and dependent variables. In your next experiment, you would then take steps to bring error variance under control.

The difference between the single-subject and group approach is a philosophical one. The group approach assumes that if experimental controls fail to reduce error variance, then statistical methods should be used. The single-subject approach assumes that the relevant sources of the variation have simply not been identified and properly controlled. The search then continues for ways to control sources of error variance.

Because these sources contribute strongly to variation in the dependent variable, identifying them should help you to understand the behavior in question. The single-subject approach strongly encourages you to identify these important sources of behavioral control. The group approach does not, as the effects of the sources are hidden from view during the averaging process.

Handling Error Variance. Taking repeated measurements of the dependent variable within a treatment allows you to determine how successful you have been at controlling extraneous sources of variation. If the measurements vary wildly from one measurement to the next, or if they drift systematically up or down, uncontrolled factors are producing these changes. For example, response rates of rats in an operant conditioning experiment may vary from session to session under seemingly identical conditions. These variations occur because of uncontrolled fluctuations in the degree of food deprivation, amount of exercise, quality and duration of sleep, time of day, and health of the subject. Some of these may not be controllable, yet others are. To increase the stability of the dependent measure, you might carefully adjust the amount of food given between sessions, ensure against unnecessary intrusions into the room where the animals are kept, conduct your tests at the same time each day, and monitor the health of your subjects.

A second way to reduce the variability of data collected within a phase is to impose a stability criterion on the data, as described earlier. This approach helps if the behavior requires time to "settle down" following transition from one phase to the next. Behavior may change slowly as the subject adapts to the new test conditions. In some cases, behavior changes as subjects become more practiced at the tasks provided by the treatment. As learning progresses, discriminations may sharpen and behavior may come under the control of new contingencies. Imposing a stability criterion ensures that the next phase is not introduced until stable behavior has been achieved in the current condition.

By imposing a stability criterion, the single-subject baseline approach removes transitional data from the analysis and eliminates unnecessary time spent collecting data after stability has been achieved. Of course, if the focus of the experiment is on transitional behavior, then using a stability criterion will not reduce the variability of the data. However, it still may indicate that the transition is over and you can stop collecting data.

The group approach encourages you to design experiments in which all subjects receive the same amount of exposure to each treatment. If some subjects reach stable levels of performance in the allotted time and others do not, then the data from each treatment will reflect varying mixtures of average transition rates and average levels of steady-state performance. Such differences between treatments may turn out to be statistically significant, yet misleading.

Assessing the Reliability of Findings. The group approach establishes the reliability of its findings through a complex chain of logical inferences from the data of a single experiment. The means and variances obtained in each phase are used to estimate population characteristics. These characteristics are used to determine the probability that data like those obtained in the phases could have been sampled from a single population. (See Chapter 12 for a more complete explanation.) All this is intended to give you an index of the likelihood that differences in your treatment means could have arisen by chance rather than by the action of your independent variable. If chance is deemed to be an unlikely cause of these differences, it is assumed that the differences were caused by the independent variable. If the independent variable caused the differences, then similar results would likely occur if the experiment were repeated. That is, the results are probably reliable.

The single-subject approach assesses reliability more directly through actual replication. Each subject experiences each phase two or more times, and performances across these multiple exposures are compared. If the data replicate from one exposure of a given phase to another, then the data are deemed reliable.

Of course, data collected across replications of a given phase usually will be similar, not identical. How similar do they have to be, and in what ways, before you can say that the results have been replicated? The answer depends on the degree of control you have over the dependent variable within a treatment condition (its stability) and on the questions the experiment was designed to answer.

If you have a relatively high degree of control over your dependent variable within a phase, variation in the baseline across successive observations will be minimal. Any effect of the independent variable will be clearly visible as a shift in performance upward or downward relative to this baseline. If each replication of a given condition produces levels of performance that overlap the levels observed in previous administrations of the same conditions, then the reliability of the data is unquestionable.

If your degree of control over the dependent variable is relatively low, the baseline will be variable, and the effect of the independent variable will be more difficult to detect. Variation in baseline levels may occur both within and between replications of the same conditions. Variations between replications can occur both as a result of chance (the data points are varying and happen to be higher or lower during replication) and as a result of carryover. Nevertheless, changes in behavior induced by a particular treatment may be consistent in direction and approximate size.

Figure 10-2 shows an example of such a case. The graph indicates the percentage of study behavior during class for Robbie, a disruptive third-grader (Hall, Lund, & Jackson, 1968). During the baseline phase, Robbie's study behavior fluctuated a fair amount, but never exceeded 45 percent. When the teacher began to give Robbie special attention for studying (intervention phase), Robbie's study behavior increased dramatically. Withdrawal of the special attention (reversal phase) was accompanied by a reduction in studying, but the original baseline was not recovered. The return to the intervention phase brought a gradual return to previous reinforcement levels.

In this example, the baseline obtained during the original baseline phase was not recovered during replication. Nevertheless the change in response rates from the baseline phase to the reinforcement phase is similar on both occasions and there is little doubt that this change is reliable, even if the amount of change is not.

Whether you would consider the intrasubject replication shown in Figure 10-2 successful would depend on your experimental question. If your question asked whether reinforcement increases the rate of studying, then the answer is yes and the replication was successful. Studying increased relative to the baseline phase on both occasions. If your question asked by what amount studying increases, however, then the answer differs from first to second administration, and the replication was not successful.

Determining the Generality of Findings. The group approach establishes generality of findings across subjects by averaging over a large number of subjects. The group approach assumes that the average performance will be "representative" of the population from which the subjects of the experiment were sampled.

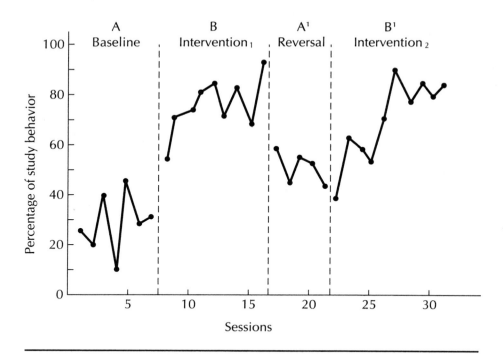

Figure 10-2. Percentage of study behavior during baseline and reinforcement showing intrasubject replication. (Hall et al., 1968; reprinted with permission.)

Although this assumption usually holds, it may not. Behavior of different subjects may develop differently under the same experimental treatment, perhaps because of uncontrolled subject variables. When this occurs, the average performance of the group represents a blend of these different patterns into an average that is unrepresentative of the individual behavior underlying that average. For example, if half the subjects learn a response completely and half do not, the average will suggest that the average subject performed at a 50 percent level. In fact, no subject behaved this way.

The single-subject approach avoids this problem by using intersubject replication instead of averaging over subjects. Direct comparisons of the behavior of different subjects provides a measure of intersubject replicability. Assume for the moment that all subjects were exposed to the treatment conditions in the same order (which may not be the case because of possible carryover effects). If the subjects show different patterns of behavioral change across treatments, then your findings (though replicable within a given subject) may be specific to that subject rather than general. In such a case, you would then attempt to identify the source of intersubject variability and deal with it. However, if all subjects

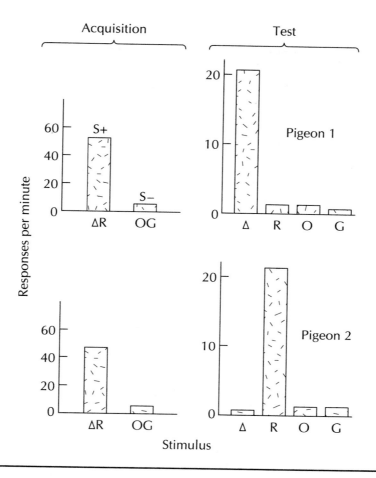

Figure 10-3. A classic example of intersubject replication failure. (Reynolds, 1961; reprinted with permission.)

show similar patterns, you can be fairly confident that similar results would be obtained with most subjects from the same population.

A classic example of a failure of intersubject replication was provided by Reynolds (1961). In this experiment, pigeons were trained to peck at a translucent disk on which was projected a triangle against a red background. Pecking was extinguished when the disk showed a circle on a green background.

Two pigeons were trained until they had sufficiently learned the discrimination. They were then tested, first with the shapes present but with the colors removed from the disks, and then with the colors present but the shapes removed. Figure 10-3 shows the results.

In the figure, the upper and lower panels indicate the response rates of Pigeon 1 and Pigeon 2, respectively. The left graph in each case shows the average rate of key pecking to the reinforced (S+) and nonreinforced (S−) compound stimulus. These graphs show that responses occurred almost exclusively to the reinforced compound. The right panel for each bird shows the response rates during presentation of each simple stimulus: triangle alone, red alone, circle alone, and green alone. In the first test (triangle alone), one bird responded at high rates, but the other bird hardly responded at all. The reverse pattern developed in the second test (red alone). Neither bird responded to either simple stimulus in the compound that had been paired with nonreinforcement. Simply stated, the response of each bird was controlled by a different stimulus from the original reinforced compound.

To explain this failure to obtain intersubject replication, several theorists have suggested that each bird must have attended to different aspects of the original stimuli on which they had been trained. Apparently, one pigeon must have focused on the shapes and the other on the colors. The phenomenon has been termed "overshadowing" and has been used to support theories of selective attention.

Note that although the intersubject replication failed in the Reynolds (1961) experiment, the failure itself revealed a general principle: learning to discriminate a complex stimulus on the basis of one aspect blocks learning about other, equally predictive aspects. The fact that the two birds' key-pecking behaviors came under the control of different stimuli within the compound stimulus suggests that uncontrolled determining factors were at work. These factors could be the subject of further research. Such factors tend to be hidden by the averaging process when a group approach is used.

In addition to intersubject replication, the generality of results in single-subject research is evaluated in another way. Results are usually double-checked in new experiments. These experiments build on the original findings while extending the range of assessed variables, the types of variables manipulated, and/or the kinds of subjects tested. For example, the patterns of responding generated under various schedules of reinforcement have been replicated by using such varied reinforcers as food, water, chocolate milk, and cigarettes, with such diverse subjects as goldfish, rats, pigeons, cats, dogs, monkeys, dolphins, and humans. Such extensions that incorporate aspects of the original experiment while adding new wrinkles are termed **systematic replications** to distinguish them from exact or **direct replications** (Sidman, 1960).

You now should have a grasp of the general features of single-subject designs, the logic behind this approach, and the differences between single-subject and group designs in how they deal with variability and establish generality. The next section describes the steps taken to implement such designs, practical problems that sometimes arise, and solutions to those problems.

Implementing a Single-Subject Baseline Design

Imagine you are conducting an experiment to assess the impact of a particular form of behavior modification on disruptive behavior in a high school classroom. The particular class consists of tenth-graders who are taking remedial math. These students have a history of failure, and many of them have developed an uncooperative attitude. You are attempting to identify an approach that will eliminate the disruptive behavior and replace it with cooperation and successful completion of assignments.

Your first step would be to identify and operationally define the specific behaviors to be eliminated or encouraged. Having done so, you would then establish a baseline for each of these behaviors for each student. Such a baseline might consist of observations sampled at regular intervals during the class period. Such a *time-sampling* procedure would allow you to collect data on each student by observing a different student in each interval. (Observers often use a timing device that delivers beeps through an ear plug to determine when to shift to the next student.) At the end of the period, each student's behavior would have been sampled many times to provide a frequency count of each type of behavior being coded.

Each class period would thus provide one data point (the frequency count) for each coded behavior for each student. The baselines would consist of the series of these points across class periods. You would maintain a running plot of each student's behaviors until you had enough points to determine the baseline frequencies of each behavior coded. The baselines would tell you the typical frequencies of each behavior and their stability across time.

Assume that you have decided to target one particular behavior for treatment at this time: paying attention to the teacher. *How* you get them to pay attention is, of course, the central question. You decide to try rewarding attentive behavior. You tell the students that you will be recording the amount of time they pay attention to the teacher while in class. Each instance of attention will earn them a point. At the end of each week, each student will be able to turn in the points for money.

You begin the intervention phase the next day. Each class period you observe the students and record their behaviors just as in the baseline phase. You continue long enough to give the treatment a fair chance to work and then wait until the frequencies of attentive behavior show no systematic changes across periods (that is, stabilize). Figure 10-4 shows the hypothetical results of your experiment to date for two of the students. Although you have collected data on several behaviors, Figure 10-4 shows only the frequency of attentive behavior across class periods.

Note that during the baseline phase both of these students showed relatively low levels of attentive behavior. This behavior fluctuated somewhat from period to period, but appeared to be stable in the sense that no systematic trends were evident. The beginning of the intervention phase is indicated by the vertical line in the middle of the graph. During intervention, the frequencies of attentive behavior remained low for the first week and then on the average began to slowly rise (fluctuations indicate good days and bad days). Eventually the rate of paying attention showed no further systematic change.

Comparing the frequencies of attentive behavior during baseline against those during the final periods of intervention, you can see that both students

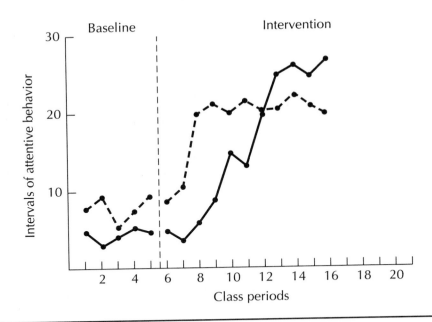

Figure 10-4. Results of a hypothetical behavior modification study showing intervals of attentive behavior for two students during baseline and intervention phases.

showed an increase in attentive behavior following introduction of the treatment. This increase *may* have been caused by the treatment. However, your ability to draw this conclusion is hampered by the presence of a confounding variable: time. It may be that changes associated with the passage of time are responsible for the improvement, changes such as maturation of the students, outside factors such as parental pressure to do better, or a change in the weather. Given the history of problems shown by these students, these are not likely explanations, but you cannot rule them out.

To determine whether your intervention caused the changes, you need to continue your experiment by returning to the baseline phase. This is termed a **reversal strategy**. You announce to the class that the reward system is being discontinued, and then continue to collect behavioral data as before. You continue until the baselines again appear to stabilize.

If attentive behavior deteriorates to its original, preintervention levels, then you can conclude that the intervention caused the original changes. It is unlikely that, merely by coincidence, attentive behavior would increase following initiation of the treatment and then decrease the moment the treatment is withdrawn. It is even more unlikely that such coincidental changes would occur in a like fashion across several students.

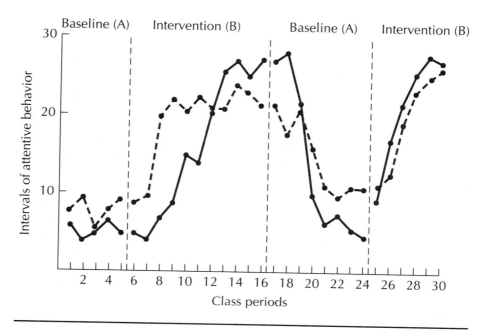

Figure 10-5. Results of hypothetical behavior modification study following an ABAB design.

The single–subject design outlined thus far is a form of baseline experiment called the **ABA design**. "A" represents the baseline phase, "B" the intervention phase. ABA designs include a baseline phase, an intervention phase, and a reversal phase that returns subjects to baseline conditions.

In this example, ending the experiment with the students back to their old inattentive selves would be undesirable. To add confidence to your results, extend the design to include a second reversal that would put the students back into the treatment condition for a second time. The resulting extended design is called, logically enough, an **ABAB design**.

The ABAB design provides a complete intrasubject replication of the experiment. If the behavior returns to baseline levels during the second baseline phase (reversal), and then returns to the previous treatment levels during the second intervention phase (second reversal), you can be confident that the treatment (and not some incidental time-correlated variable) caused the observed changes.

Figure 10-5 shows how the data from the hypothetical behavior modification experiment might look following inclusion of a second baseline phase and a second intervention. Because the initial levels of behavior in both phases were recovered in replication, the treatment was deemed effective in modifying the attentional behaviors of the two students.

Dealing with Problem Baselines

In this behavior modification example, the baselines obtained during the baseline and intervention phases were reasonably stable. The baselines showed neither a great deal of unsystematic variation nor any apparent systematic changes with time once stable levels of performance were reached. Furthermore, the levels of performance within each phase were recovered during replication.

Although this degree of stability is desirable, it is not always achieved. However, if you encounter problems with your baselines, you can take steps to overcome them. What steps are appropriate depends on the nature of the problem.

Unsystematic Within-Phase Baseline Variability. If your baseline within a phase is highly variable, uncontrolled factors are causing this variability. You need to identify these factors and, if possible, control them. For example, in a laboratory setting you can rigidly control outside disturbances, arrange for testing at the same time each day, allow plenty of time for behavior to "settle down" after a phase has been started, and so on. If the baseline continued to fluctuate after steps had been taken to control these variables, you would continue to look for the sources of the variation and attempt to bring them under control.

In a situation such as the classroom, you may have little control over factors that have a strong effect on behavior. Disputes between students, a fight with parents, closeness to a holiday, drug use, and other such influences can conspire to cause large daily swings in many behavioral measures. If stabilizing the baseline by bringing these factors under control is impossible, you can deal with the variability by extending the number of observations you make within a phase. This is logically similar to increasing the number of subjects in group experiments. The larger number of observations provides a better estimate of the "true" baseline. Thus, the increased observations make it easier to detect any change in the level of performance when the treatment is introduced or removed.

Drifting Baselines. In some cases, it may prove impossible to stabilize a baseline against slow, systematic changes (drift). For example, during an experiment in which the dependent measure is basal skin conductance (a psychophysiological measure of arousal), conductance may gradually drift upward or downward as time passes during the experiment. If attempts fail to control this drift, you may be able to deal with the drift by effectively subtracting it out.

Figure 10-6 shows the results from a hypothetical ABAB experiment in which the baseline drifted systematically. Note that the baseline drifted gradually upward within each phase. Because the drift was consistent, it is possible to estimate the position (dotted lines) the baseline would have reached at any point during the experiment had the treatment not been introduced. The effect of the treatment is clearly discernible after allowing for the drift.

Unrecoverable Baselines. Another, potentially serious problem arises if baseline levels of performance cannot be recovered during reversal. Such changes are

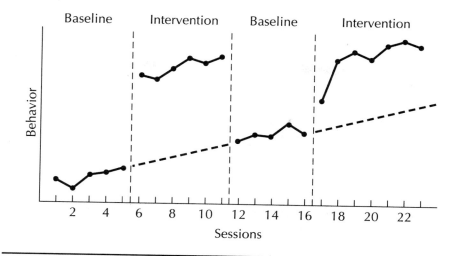

Figure 10-6. Hypothetical single-subject data showing a drifting baseline.

considered carryover effects, the familiar problem discussed in Chapter 9 that plagues within–subjects designs. Some carryover effects render the baseline completely unrecoverable (in which case it becomes impossible to conduct a successful intrasubject replication). Special designs are required to deal with such completely irreversible changes. A discussion of these special designs appears later in the chapter. Other carryover effects are less of a problem because they render the baseline at least partially recoverable.

Such partially recoverable baselines frequently occur when learning develops during a treatment condition. In a simple operant conditioning experiment, for example, rats may rarely press a lever during the initial baseline phase (before reinforcement is introduced). During the reinforcement phase, subjects learn that pressing the lever produces food, and the reinforcing effect of this contingency generates high response rates. Return to baseline conditions at this point often fails to produce a return to baseline levels of responding.

Despite the lack of reinforcement for lever pressing, the rats repeatedly approach the lever and press it in a series of widely spaced "bursts" of responding that are characteristic of extinction conditions. As a result, the rate of responding (although considerably lower that than obtained during reinforcement) remains somewhat elevated relative to the initial baseline rate. The rats are no longer naïve concerning the potential result of lever pressing.

Partial reversals such as this present few problems for analysis as long as a clear, replicable change remains in the levels of performance across treatments. You may be even able to remove some such carryover effects by taking appropriate steps. For example, if partial reversal results from fatigue or adaptation, you can minimize the effects of these variables by providing rest periods between your experimental treatments.

Unequal Baselines Between Subjects. In some cases, the baselines of different subjects in an experiment level off at very different values, even though the conditions imposed on the subjects are nominally identical. For example, after the same number of hours of deprivation, one rat may press a lever vigorously to earn a food reward, whereas another may respond in a lackluster fashion. These initial differences in response rates may then produce different rates of learning in the treatment condition and result in apparently different functional relationships. In this case, intrasubject replication may be successful but intersubject replication may not.

In this case, apparently identical levels of deprivation generate different levels of motivation because physiological differences exist between the subjects. To reduce the difference in motivation, you may increase the level of deprivation of the rat with the lower response rate. A little experimentation may provide a level that produces response rates similar to those of the first rat. With the baseline rates equated, the two subjects may now perform similarly across treatments.

Because the dependent variable is repeatedly measured during the baseline conditions, such steps may be taken to "fine-tune" the baseline to meet desired characteristics of stability and comparability. If comparable baselines are established across subjects, achieving intersubject replication may become more likely.

Inappropriate Baseline Levels. Even if all subjects show similar baseline levels during the baseline phase, the particular levels obtained may not be useful for evaluating the effect of subsequent manipulations. A low baseline is desirable if you expect the treatment to increase the level of responding, but is clearly undesirable if you expect the treatment to *decrease* the level of responding. Studies of the effects of punishment on behavior fall into the latter category. Detecting any suppressive effect of punishment would be difficult if the dependent variable were already near zero before the punishment contingency was introduced. Similarly, you will not be able to detect a facilitating effect of a treatment on behavior if the baseline starts at a value near its ceiling.

The solution to these problems is usually obtained by adjusting the experimental conditions to produce the desired baseline levels. In the punishment experiment, for example, you might increase the baseline response rates by reinforcing responses according to a variable interval schedule. The schedule could then be adjusted to produce any desired level of responding. The same schedule would be maintained in the punishment condition. Thus, you could attribute any changes in the rate of responding to the punishment contingency.

Types of Single-Subject Baseline Design

As yet, no widely accepted nomenclature exists to describe the wide variety of single-subject designs, although a few descriptive terms have emerged. This section differentiates among designs that manipulate a single independent variable (single-factor designs), those that manipulate two or more independent variables (multifactor designs), and those that measure several dependent variables (multiple baseline designs).

Single-Factor Designs. The basic single-factor baseline designs include a baseline condition (A), during which the baseline is established, and an intervention condition (B), in which the effect of the treatment (independent variable) is observed. These are the AB, ABA, and ABAB designs.

The AB design presents only a single administration of each condition and thus lacks intrasubject replication. Confounding by time-related factors is a serious problem with this design. The ABA design includes a reversal phase in which baseline conditions are re-established after exposure to the treatment. This baseline reassessment allows you to determine whether the observed changes in behavior after treatment introduction were caused by the treatment. The ABAB design adds a second reversal to provide a complete replication of the AB design.

These basic procedures can be extended to include multiple levels of the independent variable. As in group designs, if these levels represent quantitative differences, the design is said to be *parametric*.

Using multiple levels of the independent variable presents certain problems for single-subject designs. Because only one or a few subjects are tested, completely counterbalancing the order of treatments across subjects is not usually possible. Instead, each subject may be exposed to the same order of treatments, but treatments will be presented repeatedly in different orders to assess the degree of carryover.

As an example of this counterbalancing strategy, consider a parametric single-factor experiment in which the three levels of the independent variable are A, B, and C. A single subject might be exposed to these treatments in the following order: A, B, A, C, B, C. This order provides transitions between close values of the independent variable (A-B, B-C, C-B), as well as a transition between distant values (A-C). Additional subjects might be tested with different orders. Note that this design provides a single replication of each treatment, and thus represents a logical extension of the ABAB design.

If you must test a number of levels of your independent variable, and are concerned about possible drift in your baseline, you may want to include a return to the baseline phase after each exposure to a treatment phase. Abbott and Badia (1979) used this technique with rat subjects. The experiment assessed the preference for signaled over unsignaled foot shocks. Signaled shocks were preceded by a warning tone, whereas unsignaled shocks were not. Subjects could choose to receive signaled shocks by pressing a lever. Each response produced one minute in the signaled-shock schedule, identified by illumination of a houselight. At other times, unsignaled shocks were delivered.

The independent variable was the length of the signal, which was systematically varied across treatments from 0.5 second to 2.0 seconds (in half-second steps). Baseline response levels were collected during training phases, which also

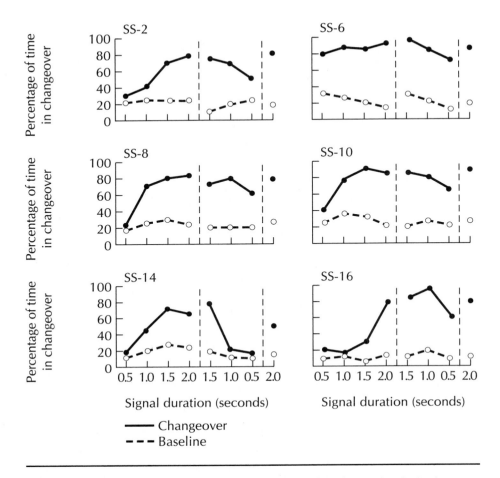

Figure 10-7. Results of an experiment in which baselines (the dashed lines) were repeatedly assessed. Each graph represents the performances of a single subject. (From Abbott & Badia, 1979.)

familiarized subjects with the signaled and unsignaled schedules prior to each test phase. Each training phase provided a given signal length and was followed by a test phase at the same length.

Figure 10-7 shows the results of the Abbott and Badia (1979) experiment. The dependent variable (percent time in changeover) reflects the number of minutes in the signaled condition "bought" by responses as a percentage of total session time. During training, the responses actually had no effect, but the number of minutes that would have been bought by these responses served to provide the baseline. The average percent time in changeover is shown across the final three stable sessions in each condition during the baseline (the dashed line) and testing (the solid line) phases as a function of signal length. Each graph represents the performance of a different subject.

The levels of changeover responding during testing were low (with the exception of one subject) during initial testing at a signal length of 0.5 second. These levels increased as the signals were lengthened across treatments until they reached nearly maximum values. When signals were then shortened, responding tended to decline. These changes were not caused simply by baseline drift. This is shown by the fact that the baselines collected during training phases remained relatively low throughout the experiment.

Also note the failure to recover the original levels of responding on the final return to the 0.5-second signal length in four subjects (all but SS-6 and SS-14). This indicates that some carryover effects were present. Even so, the effect of signal length on changeover responding is clear. Shorter signals supported weaker responding than did longer signals.

Multifactor Designs. Single-subject designs can include more than one independent variable. As in factorial group designs, you can assess the effects of independent variables and their interactions. Sidman (1953) provided an example of this design during an investigation of responding on the free operant avoidance schedule that bears his name. The Sidman avoidance schedule delivers a brief shock at regular intervals (for example, every five seconds) during the shock-shock (or S–S interval). A response, usually a lever press, terminates the S–S interval and starts another interval, the response-shock (or R–S interval). If the subject fails to respond during the R–S interval, a shock occurs and a new S–S interval begins. If the subject responds during the R–S interval, no shock is delivered and the subject is returned to the beginning of the R–S interval. Thus, if the subject responds during the R–S interval all scheduled shocks can be avoided.

Sidman investigated the effect of varying both the length of the S–S and R–S interval. Thus, this experiment had two factors: length of the S–S interval and length of the R–S interval. Rats were exposed to several levels of each independent variable in every combination.

Figure 10-8 shows the results from this two-factor single-subject experiment. The figure shows the rates of lever pressing generated under each combination of S–S and R–S intervals. The graph shows portions of each condition in which the stability criterion was met. As you can see, the number of responses per minute was affected by the lengths of both intervals.

Because the data from multifactor single-subject experiments are not submitted to a statistical analysis, omitting some cells of the factorial matrix presents no special analytical problems. If the functional relationships between independent and dependent variables follow regular patterns (as is usually the case), then it is possible to "sweep out" the functions. You can do this by providing data points at well-placed intervals rather than at every possible combination of levels.

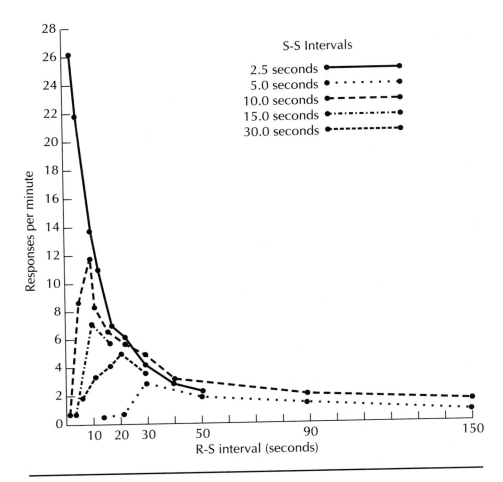

Figure 10-8. Performance of a single subject in a two-factor design in which both R-S and S-S intervals were manipulated. (Sidman, 1953; reprinted with permission.)

Each subject must be exposed to every combination of levels for which a point is required. Using less than the full factorial number of combinations can result in considerable savings in the time required to complete the experiment.

Multiple-Baseline Designs. Some variables cause irreversible changes in behavior and a special approach is required to deal with this problem. **Multiple-baseline designs** provide one solution. These designs simultaneously sample several behaviors within the experimental context to provide multiple behavioral baselines.

As an example, imagine you have developed a new technique for eliminating undesirable habits. You expect the changes it produces to be relatively permanent, so a reversal design is clearly inappropriate. You decide to use a multiple baseline design.

To test your technique, you identify a few individuals who have at least two undesirable habits they wish to kick: smoking and excessive coffee drinking. You begin your study by simply observing and recording the frequencies of these two behaviors across a number of days to establish a baseline for each behavior. You then introduce your treatment, but apply it to only *one* of the behaviors. For one subject you choose to attack smoking; for the other, coffee drinking.

The treatment appears to be successful. The treated behavior soon declines to levels well below baseline. At the same time, however, the untreated behavior remains at its previous baseline levels. When the new levels of the treated behaviors stabilize, you begin to apply the treatment to the remaining behaviors. These, too, now decline to low levels.

Figure 10-9 shows the data from the hypothetical multiple baseline study. Note that each behavior changes only after the treatment is introduced for that behavior. Which behavior is treated first apparently makes little difference.

The multiple baseline design uses the untreated behavior as a partial control for time-correlated changes that may confound the effect of the independent variable. It is possible that the change in the treated behavior would have happened when it did even if the treatment had not been introduced. However, if this change was not caused by the treatment, the untreated behavior likely would have changed as well. In addition, the untreated behavior most likely would not subsequently change as soon as the treatment was applied to it.

For the multiple baseline design to be effective, the behaviors chosen for observation should be relatively independent of one another. If the behaviors are correlated, then applying the treatment to one of the behaviors will affect both. Your ability to discriminate treatment-induced changes from changes induced by time-correlated confounding factors will be seriously hampered.

A real-life example of a multiple baseline design was provided by Liberman and Smith (1972). Liberman and Smith tested the effect of systematic desensitization on the multiple phobias (fears) of a 28-year-old woman. Four phobias were identified, and the systematic desensitization treatment was applied to each in turn. Figure 10-10 shows the results.

Each panel of Figure 10-10 shows the level of fear (as measured by self-report) for a single phobia across successive weeks. The dotted vertical line indicates introduction of the treatment. Treatment for fear of being alone was introduced first, then fear of menstruation, fear of chewing hard foods, and finally fear of dental work.

Note that self-reports of fear in each case declined after the treatment was introduced, but not before. From these data you can confidently conclude that the treatment's effect was specific to the targeted phobia (that is, the phobias responded independently to the treatment), and that the observed reductions in self-reported fear were due to the treatment, not to some time-correlated factor.

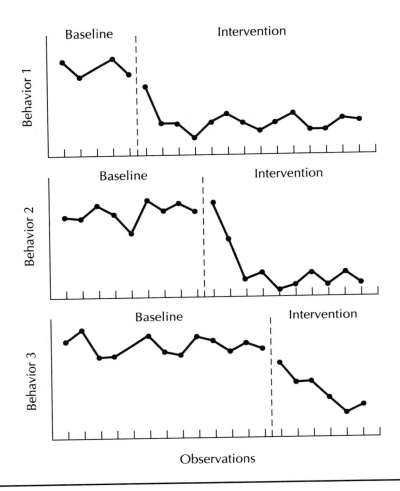

Figure 10-9. Results of the hypothetical multiple-baseline study. All three behaviors are collected simultaneously from a single subject.

Discrete Trials Designs

Although the baseline designs can be powerful tools for discovering causal relationships in the single subject, they will not work in every experimental situation. Imagine, for example, that you are interested in studying the ability of an air traffic controller to detect a radar signal representing a single airplane in trouble (the "signal") against a radar screen full of radar signals from other airplanes (the "noise"). In one condition of your experiment, you present the

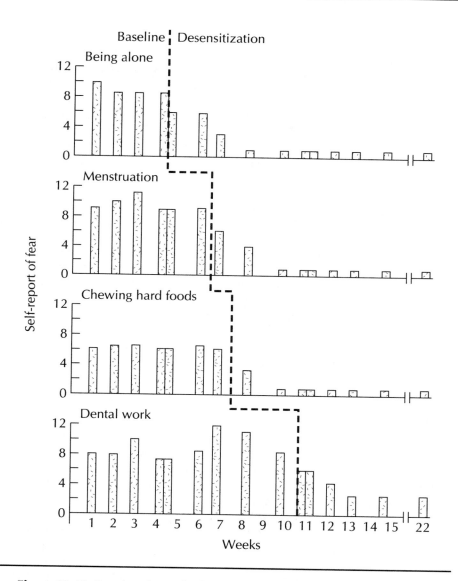

Figure 10-10. Results of a multiple-baseline study on self-reports of fear. (Liberman & Smith, 1972; reprinted with permission.)

target radar "blip" embedded within other radar blips ("signal plus noise," in signal detection theory terms). In the second condition, the target blip is absent (only the other radar blips are present—"noise only"). After each trial, your subject indicates whether the target blip was present on the radar screen.

Using the baseline approach, you should first expose all your subjects to a series of signal-plus-noise trials. After every 50 trials, you calculate the number of "yes" responses and plot these numbers to provide the behavioral baseline. You then continue the signal-plus-noise treatment until the baseline stabilizes and then switch over to the noise-only treatment. Can you see any problem with this design?

If you said yes, you're right! During the signal-plus-noise treatment, your subject would soon begin to suspect that the target radar blip (the signal) was present on every trial. Before long you would discover that your baseline had jumped to 100 percent "yes" responses and would stay there, inducing a ceiling effect. The baseline would not provide a true reflection of your subject's ability to detect the target blip, because on many of the trials the subject would respond yes simply out of habit and not because the signal had actually been detected.

In such cases, the baseline approach must be abandoned in favor of a design that will discourage the subject from establishing a response set, as was the case in the previous example. Fortunately, such a design exists: the **discrete trials design**. Like baseline designs, discrete trials designs use the individual subject (for example, your air traffic controller) as the basic unit of analysis.

Characteristics of the Discrete Trials Design

Both the baseline and discrete trials designs seek to rigidly control extraneous sources of variance, to make the effect of the independent variable readily visible. Unlike the baseline design, however, the discrete trials design does not produce a continuous within-treatment baseline that can be adjusted and fine-tuned. Instead, behavior measured over a series of discrete trials must be averaged to provide relatively stable indices of behavior under the various treatment conditions. The major characteristics of the discrete trials design are shown in Table 10-2.

The single-subject designs commonly used in experimental psychology prior to the 1920s were generally discrete trials. They continue to be used today, especially in psychophysics (which studies the relationship between physical stimuli and the sensations they generate), as well as in some areas of human judgment and decision making.

An example of such a design is provided by an experiment on signal detection reported by Tanner, Swets, and Green (1956). In this experiment, two subjects were exposed to a series of trials in which an auditory signal was either present or absent against a background of noise. On each trial, the subjects were required to respond yes if they thought they heard the signal, and no if they did not. The probability of the signal being present on a trial was systematically varied across

---

Table 10-2. Characteristics of the Discrete Trials Design

1. Individual subjects receive each treatment condition of the experiment dozens (perhaps hundreds) of times. Each exposure to a treatment or *trial,* produces one data point for each dependent variable measured.

2. Extraneous variables that might introduce unwanted variability in the dependent variable are tightly controlled.

3. If feasible, the order of presenting the treatments is randomized or counterbalanced to control order effects.

4. The behavior of individual subjects undergoing the same treatment may be compared to provide intersubject replication.

---

days from 0.1 to 0.9 in steps of 0.2. Subjects received 300 trials per day and spent two days at each probability level.

Figure 10-11 shows the results for each subject. The figure depicts the "hit" rate (probability of saying yes when the signal was present) plotted against the "false alarm" rate (probability of saying yes when the signal was absent). The diagonal line represents the case where hits equal false alarms, a situation that indicates no ability to detect the signal. The points actually obtained under the different signal probabilities fell above this diagonal line, indicating that the subjects had some sensitivity to the signal.

Analysis of data from discrete trials single-subject experiments usually begins by averaging the responses across the repeated presentations of a particular treatment. A large number of presentations helps to ensure that the resulting mean provides a stable and representative estimate of the population mean (that is, of the mean that would be obtained if an infinite number of trials could be given to the same subject under the treatment conditions). The means obtained from the different treatment conditions may then be compared to determine whether they appear to differ. This comparison may or may not include assessment through inferential statistics to determine whether the observed differences are reliable.

The analysis applied to the data of discrete trials single-subject experiments is usually determined by a theory or model of the behavior being examined. For example, in the area of human judgment and decision making, a lens model analysis has often been applied to data collected from single subjects. Another example is provided by the theory of signal detectability that provided the analytical model for the signal detection experiment previously described. Often these analyses yield a small number of descriptive statistics, such as the d' (a measure of sensitivity) and B (a measure of response bias) in signal detection. If a relatively large number of subjects have been tested, these descriptive measures

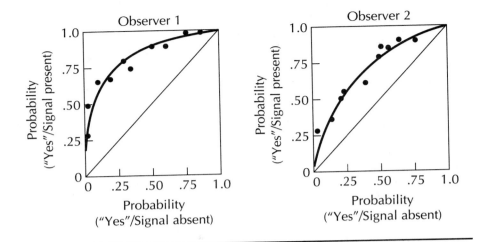

Figure 10-11. Results for two observers in a signal detection study. (Tanner, Swets, & Green, 1956.)

(although derived from a single-subject analysis) may be used as data for a between-subjects analysis.

Used in this way, inferential statistics are not applied to analyze the data of an individual subject, but rather groups of subjects. Recently some investigators have argued for the application of inferential statistics to single-subject data.

Inferential Statistics and Single-Subject Designs

Those who advocate the application of inferential statistics to data from single-subject designs would not want to use them as a substitute for control over variables and replication. However, in some cases, they argue that the desired level of control is difficult to achieve (in some clinical situations, for example). For these cases in which the necessary control cannot be obtained, they suggest that inferential statistics may provide a solution.

If you choose to take this route, be aware that the usual statistical procedures developed for group designs cannot be applied to data from single-subject designs without modification, and even then problems may exist (Kazdin, 1976).

The most straightforward approach is to use the multiple observations taken within a treatment to provide an estimate of uncontrolled error variance (in group designs this estimate is provided by within-treatment observations of multiple subjects). This estimate is then compared to the variance of scores between treatments to give an estimate of the probability that the treatment deviations were the product of chance (Chassan, 1967).

Unfortunately, this approach is upset by the serial dependency across data points. That is, scores from adjacent observations within a treatment are more likely to be similar to each other than to scores from more widely separated observations. This is similar to the problem of correlated scores that appears in within-subjects designs (see Chapter 9). For reasons not discussed here, it is a more serious problem for single-subjects designs. Several ways to deal with serial dependency have been proposed, but none is entirely satisfactory. For a discussion of the general problem and a review and assessment of the available options, see Kazdin (1976).

Advantages and Disadvantages of the Single-Subject Approach

A design that affords advantages in one arena often carries disadvantages in another. This section of the chapter explores some of the major advantages and disadvantages of the single-subject approach.

The main advantage of the single-subject approach is its focus on controlling error variance. By focusing on behavior of individual subjects (as opposed to looking at group means), you may better identify potential sources of error and control them. On a related note, focusing on individual subjects may lead to a truer estimation of the impact of your independent variable. Individual patterns of behavior often reveal nuances obscured by averaging used in the group approach. (This issue is discussed again in more detail in Chapter 11.)

Single-subject designs in general (and baseline designs in particular) require that a single subject's behavior be followed over a relatively large number of observations. A perhaps extreme example was provided by an experiment conducted by one of the authors of this text (Abbott) in which the same rat subjects were tested in various conditions of the experiment for more than a year. This experiment included two independent variables. Each assessment phase was preceded by a training phase in which baselines were established. About nine days, on the average, were required to reach the stability criterion for the behavior, and each phase had to be replicated.

Of course, not many single-subject designs require this much time to test a subject, but most do require much more time than the equivalent group design would. This intensive investigation of the behavior of a single subject is both a strength and a weakness of the single-subject approach. It is a strength in that the long observational period often reveals nuances of behavior that might be missed in a short-term design. The ability to adjust and fine-tune the baseline over time provides an extended opportunity to identify previously unsuspected important variables. The intensive investigation is a weakness in that the strategy commits the investigator to a relatively long-term project that may be disrupted by uncontrolled factors such as illness or breakdowns of equipment.

On the bright side, even the breakdown of equipment can sometimes lead to new discoveries. Sidman (1960) documented how a sticking relay in his operant conditioning equipment resulted in the accidental delivery of unavoidable shocks to a rat that had been successfully responding to an avoidance schedule. The baseline of responding had been stable, but now began to climb to high rates. The finding was unexpected and generated a whole new direction of research.

Another advantage of single-subject designs is the fact that causal relationships can be established by using as few as one subject. This is particularly important in clinical settings where the objective of the research may be to identify an effective treatment for the behavioral disorder of a specific client. Where more than one subject is used, the single-subject design permits the investigator to compare individual responses to the independent variable. Each subject may be found to exhibit reliable, yet idiosyncratic, responses to the same variable. Comparing subject-related variables may then suggest which differences between the subjects might be responsible for the differential responses. A design with only one subject may provide a good demonstration that a variable has an effect on behavior. However, in order to elevate the demonstration to the status of a general finding, the results should be replicated with additional subjects.

Another disadvantage of single-subject designs is that the design is inappropriate for many research applications. For example, potential carryover effects may confound the effects of the independent variable. If carryover effects are severe enough to cause irreversible changes, then the single-subject approach may have to be abandoned in favor of the between-groups approach. In addition, some research questions simply do not lend themselves to a single-subject design. Much of the research in social and developmental psychology could not be run as single-subject designs.

Moreover, the results from single-subject designs sometimes are of limited generality. By tightly controlling the experimental situation to reduce error variance, you may be creating a highly artificial environment within which the behavior of interest is observed. For example, if you study the effects of positive reinforcement on the behavior of autistic children in a tightly controlled laboratory, you cannot be sure that your results will apply to autistic children in a hospital setting. In short, tight experimental control of extraneous variables increases internal validity. However, remember that when you increase internal validity you often reduce external validity.

A final disadvantage of the single-subject approach is that despite all attempts to control extraneous variables, some variables cannot be easily controlled. Subject variables such as personality and intelligence cannot be controlled by tight experimental design. In research where a homogeneous strain of rats serves as the subject population, this problem may not be important. However, when you apply single-subject research design to humans (such as in a clinical setting), these variables may come into play, and there is no easy way to eliminate their effects. The only option may be to measure those variables and statistically control their effects.

Consider single-subject research as an alternative to group-based research when appropriate. You should not try to fit every research question into a single-subject design. However, keep this option open when your research question could be best answered with a single-subject approach. Finally, even if you use a group design, you can apply some of the logic of the single-subject approach. Do not ignore individual subject behavior and look only at average performance. In many cases, looking at the scores of individual subjects within your experiment can help you to interpret your data.

Summary

Single-subject (or small-*n*) designs allow you to establish causal relationships among independent and dependent variables while focusing on the behavior of one or a few subjects. These designs work by collecting large numbers of observations of a subject's behavior within each treatment condition; rigidly controlling extraneous variables that might contribute to unwanted variability in the dependent measure; focusing primarily on relatively powerful independent variables whose effects (given the small amount of uncontrolled variation in the dependent measure) are easily detected by inspection of graphs; and repeating each treatment condition to establish reliability through intrasubject replication.

Single-subject designs dominated psychological research prior to the 1920s but were overshadowed by group-based designs following the development of inferential statistics. Experiments based on single-subject designs were difficult to publish in the past, but today the single-subject approach has regained wide acceptance. This acceptance has arisen especially in applied areas such as clinical psychology where the primary interest is in assessing the effectiveness of therapeutic procedures on individual clients.

Single-subject designs fall into two broad categories: discrete trials designs and baseline designs. Discrete trials designs expose subjects to a series of trials, with each trial providing one exposure to a given treatment and yielding one score for each dependent measure. Each treatment is repeated a large number of times to provide stability to the treatment means. The resulting means may or may not be submitted to an inferential statistical analysis.

Baseline designs repeatedly record the subject's score on the dependent measure within each treatment exposure to plot a baseline for the behavior. Steps are taken to identify and control extraneous variables so that the variability and drift of the baseline are reduced to the minimum level. Usually the baseline must meet a stability criterion before the next treatment condition can be introduced. Each treatment is repeated at least once (intrasubject replication) to determine the reliability of the findings. If more than one subject is tested (intersubject replication), comparison across subjects is performed to establish the generality of results. Generality and reliability are also assessed through systematic replication. This replication examines the same independent and dependent variables under conditions somewhat different from those of the original experiment (for example, different species of subject or different reinforcer).

Baseline designs include single-factor designs (which include one independent variable), multifactor designs (two or more independent variables), and multiple-baseline designs (more than one dependent variable). Single-factor designs may be of the AB, ABA, or ABAB type. The AB type evalutes behavior during a baseline (A) condition and then in a treatment (B) condition. The lack of intrasubject replication makes this design subject to confounding by time-related factors and, therefore, undesirable. The ABA design controls time-related factors by adding a second baseline evaluation after the treatment evaluation. The ABAB design provides a complete intrasubject replication of the experiment. The ABAB design is preferable to the ABA design, especially if it would be unethical to end the experiment after returning the subject's behavior to an undesirable state in the second baseline evaluation. The ABAB design format can be extended for multilevel variables. When such variables are quantitative, the design is said to be parametric.

Multifactor baseline designs require that different combinations of the independent variables be tested across the study. A factorial design may be used (in which every combination is evaluated) or specific combinations of interest may be tested. In either case, each treatment is evaluated at least twice to provide intrasubject replication. These designs can become extremely time consuming to conduct if the number of variable combinations to be tested is large.

Multiple-baseline designs provide a partial solution to the problem of irreversible treatment effects. Different behaviors are observed and a baseline established for each. The treatment is then introduced separately for each behavior in staggered fashion across time. The treatment is judged effective if the level of each behavior changes only after the treatment is applied to it. The multiple-baseline approach requires that each behavior be relatively independent of the others.

Discrete trials designs are used in areas such as psychophysics, human judgment, and decision making, where the interest focuses on the perceptual or decision-making abilities of individuals. Such designs often follow from a theoretical analysis of the behavior and yield descriptive statistics that are then evaluated in the light of the theory. If a relatively large number of subjects are thus tested, the summary statistics from each subject may provide the data for a group-based inferential statistical analysis.

Some interest has recently been expressed in developing inferential statistics that can be applied to single-subject data. These statistics would be employed when the data cannot be stabilized or the independent variables are too weak to produce results that can be visually analyzed. A problem with such analyses is the serial dependency (or correlation) between successive observations of a single subject. Serial dependency seriously biases the traditional statistical tests (such as the *t*-test or ANOVA). Despite attempts to deal with serial dependency, the various proposed solutions are controversial and not yet widely accepted.

Single-subject designs have both advantages and disadvantages. Advantages include the ability to obtain functional relationships that apply to a single subject; avoidance of artifacts that may emerge in group studies because of averaging data across subjects with differing behaviors; potential identification of new important variables while attempting to stabilize baselines; and ability to conduct experiments with an extremely limited number of available subjects. Disadvantages include the length of time required to test each subject through all the conditions of the experiment (increasing the possibility of subject loss because of attrition or equipment failure); inability to detect the effects of weak variables when behavior is not well controlled; difficulty in assessing the effects of variables that cause irreversible changes; and possibly limited external validity.

Key Terms

Baseline design

Baseline phase

Intervention phase

Behavioral baseline

Stability criterion

Intrasubject replication

Intersubject replication

Systematic variance

Error variance

Systematic replications

Direct replications

Reversal strategy

ABA design

ABAB design

Multiple-baseline design

Discrete trials design

11

Describing Data

CHAPTERS 1–10 HAVE EXPLORED HOW TO design and conduct research. Once you have conducted your research, the next step is to organize, summarize, and describe your data. This chapter reviews strategies you can use to effectively organize, summarize, and describe data. The sections on descriptive statistics are intended to provide a brief review of these statistics. If you need more information on these statistics, see one of the many introductory statistics texts available (such as Gravetter & Wallnau, 1990, or Jaccard & Becker, 1990). Also, computation is only addressed in this chapter where necessary to explain a particular statistic. The formulas and some worked examples of the descriptive statistics discussed in this chapter can be found in Appendix II.

Organizing Your Data

Before you can interpret your data, you must first organize and summarize them. This section shows how to organize unanalyzed data, using as an example data from an experiment published by Bordens and Horowitz (1986) on joinder of multiple criminal offenses (see Chapter 1). Bordens and Horowitz conducted a two-factor between-subjects experiment. The first factor, "charges filed," was the number of charges initially filed against the defendant (one, two, three,

Table 11-1. Data Summary Sheet for a 2 × 4 Between-Subjects Design from Bordens and Horowitz (1986)

Number of Charges Filed	One Charge Judged				Two Charges Judged			
	1	2	3	4	1	2	3	4
Subject								
1	3	5	6	2	6	3	4	5
2	3	4	3	4	4	5	6	5
3	3	4	4	5	4	5	4	5
4	4	4	4	5	5	5	5	6
5	4	5	5	5	4	4	5	5
6	3	3	5	5	5	5	4	4
7	2	3	4	5	5	4	4	5
8	5	4	5	4	3	5	5	5
9	6	4	3	6	3	5	5	6
10	5	5	4	6	5	3	6	6
Mean	3.8	4.1	4.3	4.7	4.4	4.4	4.8	5.2
Standard Deviation	1.23	.74	.95	1.16	.97	.84	.79	.63

four). The second factor, "charges judged," was the number of charges actually judged (one or two). The dependent variable was a six-point scale on which subjects rated the degree of guilt of the defendant, with higher numbers indicating a greater belief in the defendant's guilt (the actual scale is shown in Chapter 4 in Figure 4-1).

Organizing and summarizing your data begins by grouping on a *data summary sheet* the data from all subjects receiving the same treatments. If you planned ahead, you probably were doing this as you collected your data. If not, you must first organize your data before any analysis. Table 11-1 shows a data summary sheet for the Bordens and Horowitz (1986) data.

A useful data summary sheet must be clearly labeled. Note that the columns of data in Table 11-1 are clearly labeled with the levels of the independent variable in effect for each group. The top headings indicate the two levels of charges judged. The second level of headings indicates the level of charges filed as appropriate to each group. Located under each heading are the scores for each subject who received the combination of levels of the independent variables. The left-hand column identifies by number the subject from whom the scores were collected. The scores from each subject appear in the same row. Finally, at the bottom of the table are listed some summary statistics (mean and standard deviation).

The organization just described works well for a 2 × 4 factorial experiment and can be expanded to handle more levels of each factor or more factors. Other designs may require a different organization. Again, always display the data clearly.

Distributions of Scores

A collection of scores generated in a study is called a **distribution**. Table 11-1 organizes the data into eight distributions, one for each group. Other distributions are also possible. For example, you could form two distributions (each with 40 scores) by collecting all the scores under "One Charge Judged" and "Two Charges Judged" across the levels of "Number of Charges Filed." One large distribution could be formed by collecting all 80 scores (10 from each level of "Number of Charges Filed") over both levels of the number of charges judged independent variable.

Grouped Versus Individual Data

After you have organized your data into a coherent format, you must decide on a basic descriptive strategy. In some cases you may want to summarize your data by averaging scores for each group. In other cases you may want to focus on the scores of individual subjects. Either strategy is valid, but each has different advantages and disadvantages.

Grouped Data. The major advantage of grouped data is convenience. When you calculate an average, you have one score that characterizes an entire distribution. You can then refer to the performance of subjects in a group by citing the average performance. If your data will be submitted to a statistical analysis based on treatment means, you will be treating your data in this way.

Although convenient, the grouped method does have two important limitations. First, the average score may not represent the performance of individual subjects in a group. An average score of 5 can result if all ten subjects in a group scored 5, or if half had high scores (all 10) and half low scores (all 0). In the former case, the average accurately reflects the individual performance of each subject. In the latter case, however, it does not. This idea is examined in more detail during the discussion of the mean.

The second limitation of using grouped data is that a curve resulting from plotting averaged data may not reflect the true nature of the psychological phenomenon being studied. For example, you might conduct a memory experiment in which subjects attempt to recall a list of words until they achieve two errorless trials in a row. If you averaged for each trial the number of subjects who reached your learning criterion, you might produce a graph like the one shown in the

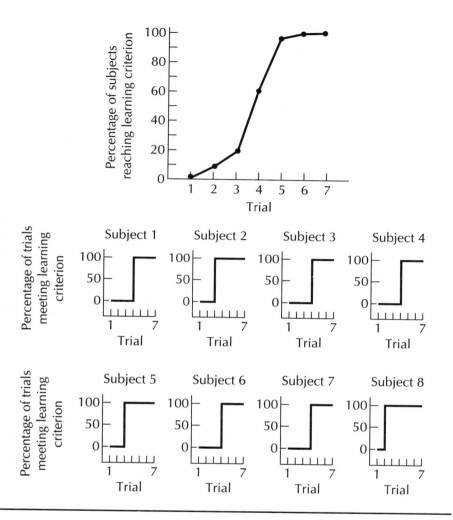

Figure 11-1. Comparison of grouped versus single-subject data from a hypothetical learning experiment.

top part of Figure 11-1. The shape of the curve suggests that learning is a gradual process.

The remaining graphs show the data cast in a different way, with each graph showing the course of one individual's performance. Here, learning is defined in terms of whether or not the list was perfectly recalled on any given trial. Casting the data in this way suggests that learning may be an all-or-none proposition. That is, once a subject learns the list to criterion, he or she never again makes a mistake. In contrast, the grouped data suggested that learning is a gradual process.

Individual Data. Examining individual scores makes the most sense when you have repeated measures of the same behavior. Inspecting individual data can also be useful when the phenomenon under study is an either-or proposition (for example, something was learned or not, or a stimulus was detected or not). In some cases the individual data may reflect the effect of the independent variable more accurately than data averaged over the group.

Using Grouped and Individual Data. Researchers too often fall into the pattern of collecting data and then calculating an average without considering the individual scores constituting the average. A good strategy to adopt is to look at both the grouped and individual data. When you have repeated measures of the same behavior, examining individual data shows how each subject performed in your study. This may provide insights into the psychological process being studied that are not afforded by grouping data.

When you collect only a single score for each subject, you should still examine the distribution of individual scores. This usually entails plotting the individual scores on a graph and carefully inspecting the graph.

Graphing Your Data

Whether you have chosen a grouped or individual strategy for dealing with your data, you will often find it beneficial to plot your data on a graph. Graphing helps you make sense out of your data by representing it visually. The next sections describe the various types of graphs and indicate their uses. For details on drawing graphs, see Chapter 14.

Elements of a Graph

A graph represents your data in a two-dimensional space. The two dimensions (horizontal and vertical) are defined by two lines intersecting at right angles, called the *axes* of the graph. The horizontal axis is called the *abscissa* or *x-axis* of the graph, and the vertical axis is called the *ordinate* or *y-axis*. (The terms "*x*-axis" and "*y*-axis" are used in this discussion.)

When graphing data from an experiment, you normally represent levels of your independent variable along the *x*-axis and values of the dependent variable along the *y*-axis. A pair of values (one for the *x*-axis and one for the *y*-axis) defines a single *point* within the graph. This point could represent an individual score or a group mean at a particular value of the independent variable.

Data within the two-dimensional space of a graph can be presented as histograms (or bar graphs), line graphs, scattergrams, or (abandoning the Cartesian *x*-axis, *y*-axis geometry) pie charts.

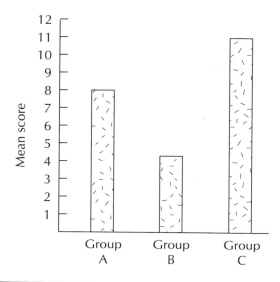

Figure 11-2. Histogram of means from a hypothetical one-factor design.

Histograms

A **histogram** (or **bar graph**) presents your data as bars extending away from the axis representing your independent variable (usually the x-axis, although this convention is not always followed). The length of each bar is determined by the value of the dependent variable. Figure 11-2 shows group means from a one-factor, three-group experiment plotted as a histogram.

The three bars in Figure 11-2 represent the three levels of the independent variable for which data were collected. The length of each bar along the y-axis represents the score obtained on the dependent variable. Note that each bar straddles the x-axis value it represents. The width of each bar has no meaning and is chosen to provide a pleasing appearance.

You can also use a histogram to represent data from a multifactor design. Figure 11-3 shows a histogram of the data from the two-factor joinder experiment discussed earlier. Notice that the four levels of number of charges filed (one to four) are placed along the x-axis. The two levels of charges judged (the second independent variable) are represented within the graph itself. The shaded bars represent the data from the one-charge judged group, whereas the white bars represent the data from the two-charges judged group.

A histogram is the best method of graphing when your independent variable is categorical (such as the type of drug administered). In this case, the distance along the x-axis has no real meaning. A line graph (which visually emphasizes that distance) would be misleading. The histogram makes the arbitrary ordering

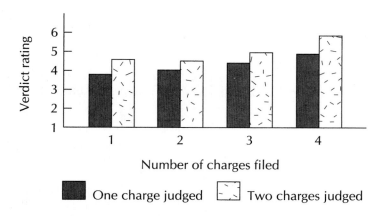

Figure 11-3. Histogram of means from a two-factor design.

of categories apparent, whereas a line graph would inappropriately suggest the presence of trends in these data.

Line Graphs

Although histograms can be used to represent the data from multifactor experiments, they become confusing when too many factors are represented. In this case a **line graph** is more appropriate. The line graph presents data as a series of points connected by a line and is appropriate when the independent variable is quantitatively manipulated (such as for the number of milligrams of a drug administered).

The line graph is the most widely used method to illustrate functional relationships among variables. A *functional relationship* is one in which the value of the dependent variable varies as a function of the value of the independent variable. Usually the depicted functional relationship is causal.

An illustration of a line graph is shown in Figure 11-4, which depicts the means from the single-factor experiment whose data were shown in Figure 11-2 in histogram form. Notice the difference in how the two types of graphs visually represent the means.

A line graph can also be used to depict the means from multifactor experiments. Figure 11-5 shows such a line graph for the two-factor experiment on joinder of offenses cited earlier. The levels of one factor are represented along the x-axis, just as in a single-factor experiment. The levels of the other factor are represented by using different symbols for the data points. All points collected under the same value of the second factor have the same symbol and are connected by the same line. Chapter 14 discusses how to draw line graphs.

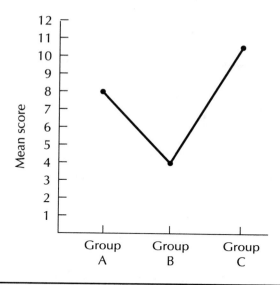

Figure 11-4. Line graph of means from a one-factor design.

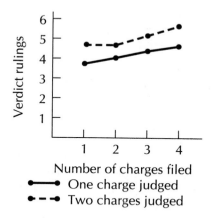

Figure 11-5. Line graph of means from a two-factor design.

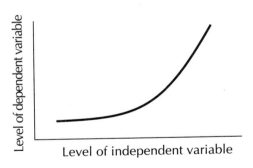

Figure 11-6. Line graph of positively accelerated functional relationship.

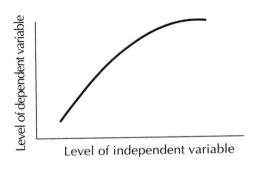

Figure 11-7. Line graph of negatively accelerated functional relationship.

Shapes of Line Graphs. Relationships represented on a line graph can take a variety of shapes. Figure 11-6 shows a graph on which the curve is *positively accelerated*. A positively accelerated curve is relatively flat at first and becomes progressively steeper as it moves along the *x*-axis. Positive acceleration can occur both in the upward and downward directions along the *y*-axis.

A curve may also be *negatively accelerated*, as shown in Figure 11-7. Here the curve is steep at first but becomes progressively flatter as it moves along the *x*-axis. Eventually the curve "levels off" at some maximum or minimum value. The function is said to be *asymptotic* at this value. The *asymptote* of a curve is its theoretical upper limit, or the point after which no further increase in the value of the dependent variable is expected. In Figure 11-7 the relationship is asymptotic.

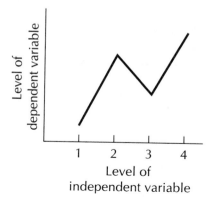

Figure 11-8. Line graph of nonmonotonic functional relationship.

Whether positively or negatively accelerated, any curve may also be characterized as *increasing* or *decreasing*, which refers to whether the values along the *y*-axis increase or decrease, respectively, as the value along the *x*-axis increases. For example, a negatively accelerated, increasing function would approach a ceiling value at asymptote, whereas a negatively accelerated, decreasing function would approach a floor value.

A graph may also vary in complexity. The curves depicted in Figures 11-6 and 11-7 are both *monotonic*. That is, the curve represents a uniformly increasing or decreasing function. A *nonmonotonic* function contains reversals in direction, as illustrated in Figure 11-8. Notice how the curve changes direction twice by starting off low, rising, falling off, and then rising again.

Scattergrams

In research using a correlational strategy, the data from the two dependent measures are often plotted as a **scattergram**. On a scattergram, each pair of scores is represented as a point on the graph.

For example, consider the data shown in Table 11-2. To make a scattergram of these data, you plot the values of Variable A along the *x*-axis and the values of Variable B along the *y*-axis (or vice versa, it really does not matter). Then each pair of values is represented by a point within the graph. Figure 11-9 shows a scattergram of the data in Table 11-2.

Pie Charts

If your data are in the form of proportions or percentages, then you might find a **pie chart** the best way to represent the value of each category in the analysis.

Table 11-2. Bivariate Data for a Scattergram

Subject Number	Variable A	Variable B
1	5	7
2	4	2
3	9	8
4	2	7
5	6	8
6	3	9

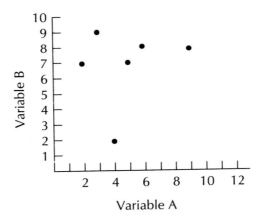

Figure 11-9. Scattergram of the bivariate data presented in Table 11-2.

In a pie chart, the data are represented as slices of a circular pie. Figure 11-10 shows two representative pie charts. The pie to the left indicates the proportion of various behaviors observed in rat subjects during a half-hour coding period. The pie to the right displays the same proportions while emphasizing the proportion of time devoted to grooming. This type of display is called an "exploded" pie.

The Importance of Graphing Data

You can use either tables or graphs to summarize your data. If you organize data in tables, you present the numbers themselves (averages and/or raw score distri-

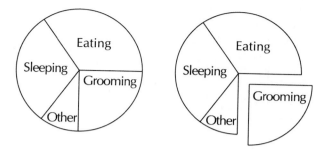

Figure 11-10. Pie chart and exploded pie chart.

Table 11-3. Means from the 2 × 4 Joinder Experiment, in Tabular Format				
NUMBER OF CHARGES JUDGED	**NUMBER OF CHARGES FILED**			
	One	Two	Three	Four
One	3.80	4.10	4.30	4.70
Two	4.40	4.40	4.80	5.20

butions). If you display the data in a graphical format, you lose some of this numerical precision. The value of a point usually can only be approximated by its position along the y-axis of the graph. However, graphing data is important for two major reasons, discussed in the next sections.

Showing Relationships Clearly. An old saying, "one picture is worth a thousand words," applies to graphing data from your research. Although summarizing data in a table is fine, proper graphing adds a degree of clarity no table can provide. Consider the data presented in Table 11-3 and the same data graphically presented in Figure 11-5. Whereas both formats present the data accurately, the graph makes the relationships between the independent variables and dependent variable clearer. The graph brings out subtleties in the relationships that may not be apparent from inspecting a table.

Deciding on a Statistic to Use. In addition to making it easier to see relationships in your data, graphs allow you to evaluate your data for the application of an appropriate statistic. Before you apply any statistic to your data, graph your sample distributions and examine their shapes. Your choice of statistic will be affected by the manner in which scores are distributed, as described in the next section.

Graphing your data on a scattergram is helpful when you intend to calculate a measure of correlation. Inspecting a scattergram of your data can help you to determine which measure of correlation is appropriate for your data. What you would look for and how your findings would affect your decision are taken up during the discussion of correlation measures later in the chapter.

The Frequency Distribution

Before you can decide which statistic to apply to your data, you must generate a **frequency distribution**. This consists of a count of the number of scores falling into a response category. A frequency distribution is the collection of these frequencies across all the response categories. Consider an example.

Suppose the scores in one condition of your experiment are 1, 2, 2, 3, 3, 3, 4, 4, 4, 4, 5, 5, 5, 6, 6, and 7. To generate a frequency distribution for these scores, simply count the number of subjects who scored a 2, 3, and so on. The frequency distribution resulting from these data is shown in Table 11-4.

If most of the categories in your frequency distribution contain frequencies of only one or two cases, or if you wind up with more than about eleven to fifteen categories, then your categories are too narrow and should be broadened. The broadened categories each would span a particular range of scores rather than a specific score.

Frequency distributions are usually represented graphically as a histogram. The response categories (in this case, 1, 2, 3, 4, 5, 6, and 7) are placed along the x-axis and the frequency along the y-axis. The bars are then drawn to a height representing the appropriate frequency. Figure 11-11 shows a histogram of the data from the frequency distribution of scores.

The Normal Distribution

The frequency distribution shown in Figure 11-11 approximates a theoretical model known as a **normal distribution**. The normal distribution, a mathematical entity rarely seen in real life, has useful properties for the statistical evaluation of data. Real frequency distributions often approximate the normal distribution and have a shape resembling a symmetrical hill (the scores bulge at the center and trail off into two long "tails" as one moves outward).

Skewed Distributions

Figure 11-12 illustrates two **skewed distributions** where the center bulge seems to be pushed to one side of the distribution, leaving a long tail streaming off in

Table 11-4. Frequency Distribution

Score	Frequency
1	1
2	2
3	3
4	4
5	3
6	2
7	1

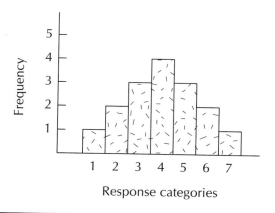

Figure 11-11. Histogram of the frequency distribution given in Table 11-4.

the other direction. The graph in Panel A of Figure 11-12 shows *positive skewness*, where most of the scores are located at the low end of the distribution and the long tail extends to the right, in the positive direction along the *x*-axis. Conversely, Panel B shows a distribution with *negative skewness*, where most of the scores are located at the high end of the distribution and the long tail extends toward the left, in the negative direction.

Determining Whether Your Distribution Is Skewed. Determining whether your frequency distribution is skewed can be accomplished in two ways. First, you

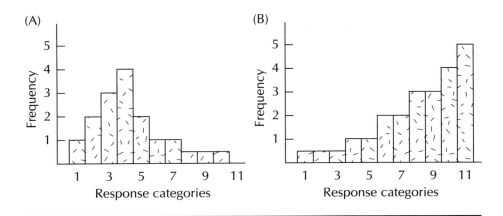

Figure 11-12. Two types of frequency distribution: (A) positively skewed frequency distribution; (B) negatively skewed frequency distribution.

can construct histograms to represent your frequency distributions and visually inspect them. If your distribution is seriously skewed, you can easily see it. If your distribution is more moderately skewed, however, such a visual inspection may not be sensitive enough to detect it.

Skewness that cannot be detected by inspection of a graph may be detected by means of a statistic called the *Pearson coefficient of skewness*. The formula for the coefficient is as follows (Runyon & Haber, 1984):

$$P_{cs} = \frac{3\,(\text{average} - \text{median})}{\text{standard deviation}}$$

The coefficient of skewness tells you the direction (according to the sign of the number) and the degree of skewness (according to the magnitude of the number). For example, if you find the average of your distribution is 50, the median is 60, and the standard deviation is 10, then the coefficient of skewness is -3.

The sign of the coefficient indicates that your distribution is negatively skewed. But how high can the coefficient be before the skewness is serious? Generally, a coefficient of skewness between plus or minus 0.50 indicates a nonsignificant deviation from normality (Runyon & Haber, 1984). Values outside this range indicate more serious skewness. If you want a more exact test of skewness, a z-test is available to determine the significance of skewness (see Tabachnick & Fidell, 1989, p. 73). If your distribution is moderately or seriously skewed, you can take steps to correct the problem. These steps are discussed in Chapter 15.

Descriptive Statistics: Central Tendency and Variability

In many research situations, it is convenient to summarize your data by applying *descriptive statistics*. Descriptive statistics allow you to summarize the properties of an entire distribution of scores with just a few numbers, and are used when you have decided to evaluate grouped data. This section reviews two categories of descriptive statistics: measures of central tendency and measures of variability. The next section describes another category of descriptive statistics, measures of correlation.

Measures of Central Tendency

A *measure of central tendency* gives you a single score that represents the general magnitude of scores in a distribution. This score characterizes your distribution by providing information about the score at or near the middle of the distribution. The most common measures of central tendency are the mode, the median, and the mean (also called the *average*). Each measure of central tendency has strengths and weaknesses. Also, situations exist in which a given measure of central tendency cannot be used.

The Mode. The **mode** is simply the most frequent score in a distribution. To obtain the mode, count the number of scores falling into each response category. The response category with the highest frequency is the mode. The mode of the distribution 1, 2, 4, 6, 4, 3, 4 is 4.

No mode exists for a distribution where all the scores are different. Some distributions, called *bimodal distributions,* have two modes. Figure 11-13 shows a bimodal distribution.

Although the mode is simple to calculate, it is limited because the values of scores outside of the most frequent score are not represented. The only information yielded by the mode is the most frequent score. The values of other data in the distribution are not taken into account. Under most conditions, take into account the other scores to get an accurate characterization of your data. To illustrate this point, consider the following two distributions of scores: 2, 2, 6, 3, 7, 2, 2, 5, 3, 1 and 2, 2, 21, 43, 78, 22, 33, 72, 12, 8.

In both these distributions, the mode is 2. Looking only at the mode, you might conclude that the two distributions are similar. Obviously, this conclusion is incorrect. It is clear that the second distribution is very different from the first. The mode may not represent a distribution very well and may not be the best measure to use when comparing distributions.

The Median. A second measure of central tendency is the **median**. The median is the middle score in an ordered distribution. To calculate the median, follow these steps:

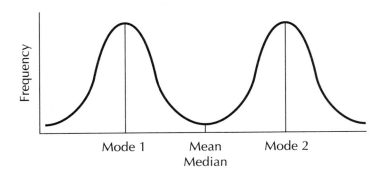

Figure 11-13. Graph of bimodal distribution showing location of modes, median, and mean.

1. Order the scores in your distribution from lowest to highest (or highest to lowest, it does not matter).
2. Count down through the distribution and find the score in the middle of the distribution. This score is the median of the distribution.

What is the median of the following distribution: 7, 5, 2, 9, 4, 8, 1? The correct answer is 5. The ordered distribution is 1, 2, 4, 5, 7, 8, 9, and 5 is the middle score.

You may be wondering what to do if you have an even number of scores in your distribution. In this case, there is no middle score. To calculate a median with an even number of scores, you order the distribution as before, then identify the *two* middle scores. The median is the average of these two scores. For example, with the ordered distribution of 1, 3, 6, 7, 8, 9, the median is 6.5 (6 + 7 = 13; 13/2 = 6.5).

The median takes more information into account than the mode. However, it is still a rather insensitive measure of central tendency because it does not take into account the magnitude of the scores above and below the median. As with the mode, two distributions can have the same median and yet be very different in character. For this reason, the median is used primarily when the mean is not a good choice.

The Mean. The **mean** (denoted as M) is the most sensitive and widely used measure of central tendency. The computational formula for the mean is

$$\text{Mean} = \frac{\Sigma X}{N}$$

where ΣX is the sum of the scores and N is the number of scores in the distribution. To obtain the mean, simply add together all the scores in the distribution and then divide by the total number of scores.

The major advantage of the mean is that, unlike the mode and the median, its value is directly affected by the magnitude of each score in the distribution. However, this sensitivity to individual score values also makes the mean susceptible to the influence of extreme scores, or *outliers*. One or two such outliers may cause the mean to be artificially high or low. The following two distributions illustrate this point. Assume that Distribution A contains the scores 4, 6, 3, 8, 9, 2, and 3, and Distribution B contains the scores 4, 6, 3, 8, 9, 2, and 43. Although the two distributions differ by only a single score (3 versus 43), they differ greatly in their means (5 versus 10.7, respectively).

The mean of 5 appears to be more representative of the first distribution than the mean of 10.7 is of the second. The median is a better measure of central tendency for the second distribution. The medians of the two distributions are 4 and 6, respectively—not nearly as different from one another as the means.

Before you choose a measure of central tendency, carefully evaluate your data for skewness and the presence of deviant, outlying scores. Do not blindly apply the mean just because it is the most sensitive measure of central tendency.

Choosing a Measure of Central Tendency. Which of the three measures of central tendency you choose depends on two factors: the scale of measurement and the shape of the distribution of the scores. Before you use any measure of central tendency, evaluate these two factors.

Chapter 4 described four measurement scales: nominal (categories), ordinal (rank orderings), interval (quantities measured from an arbitrary zero point) and ratio (quantities measured from a true zero point). The measurement scale you chose when you designed your experiment will now determine which measure of central tendency you can use.

If your data were measured on a nominal scale, you are limited to using the mode. It makes no sense to calculate a median or mean sex, even if the sex of subjects has been coded as zeros (males) and ones (females). What would it mean to say that the mean sex of the subjects was 0.4?

If your data were measured on an ordinal scale, you could properly use either the mode or the median, but it would be misleading to use the mean as your measure of central tendency. This is because the mean is sensitive to the distance between scores. With an ordinal scale, the actual distance between points is unknown. You cannot assume that scores equally distant in terms of rank order are equally far apart, but you do assume this (in effect) if you use the mean.

The mean can be used if your data are scaled on an interval or ratio scale. Numbers on these two scales can be added, subtracted, multiplied, or divided— operations that must be performed to calculate the mean.

Even if your dependent measure was scaled on an interval or ratio scale the mean may be inappropriate. One of the first things you should do when summarizing your data is to generate a frequency distribution of the scores. Next, plot the frequency distribution as a histogram and examine its shape. If your scores are normally distributed (or at least nearly normally distributed), then the mean, median, and mode will fall at the same point in the middle of the distribution, as shown in Figure 11-14. When your scores are normally distributed,

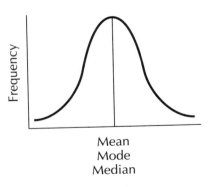

Figure 11-14. Line graph of normal frequency distribution, showing location of mean, mode, and median.

use the mean as your measure of central tendency because it provides the most information.

As your distribution deviates from normality, the mean becomes a less representative measure of central tendency. The two graphs in Figure 11-15 show the relationship between the three measures of central tendency with a positively skewed distribution and a negatively skewed distribution. Notice the relationship between the mean and median for these skewed distributions. In a negatively skewed distribution, the mean underestimates the central tendency. Conversely, in a positively skewed distribution the mean overestimates the central tendency. When your distribution is skewed, the median is a better estimate of central tendency than the mean.

Deviations from normality also create problems when deciding on an inferential statistic. Chapter 12 discusses inferential statistics and ways to deal with data that are not normally distributed.

The mean also will not accurately represent the central tendency if your distribution is bimodal. With a bimodal distribution, the mean underrepresents one large cluster of scores and overrepresents the other. Look at Figure 11-13 to see how the mean represents the central tendency of a bimodal distribution.

To summarize the discussion to this point, the three measures of central tendency are the mean, the median, and the mode. The mean is the most sensitive measure of central tendency because it takes into account the magnitude of each score in the distribution. The mean is also the preferred measure of central tendency. The median is less sensitive to the distribution of scores than the mean, but is preferred when your distribution is skewed or the distribution contains a couple of highly deviant scores. Which measure of central tendency you can legitimately use depends on the scale on which the dependent variable was measured and on the manner in which the scores are distributed.

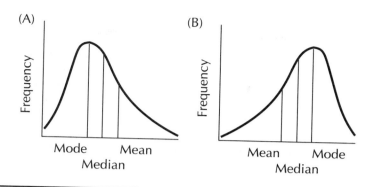

Figure 11-15. Line graph of positively and negatively skewed distributions, showing relationship between mean, mode, and median.

Measures of Variability

Another important descriptive statistic you should apply to your data is a *measure of variability*. If you look again at some of the sample distributions described thus far (or the data presented in Table 11-1), you will notice that the scores in the distributions differ from each other. This difference in scores is called *variability*. When you conduct an experiment, all your subjects most probably will not provide the same score on your dependent measure. A measure of variability provides information that helps you to interpret your data. Two sets of scores may have highly similar means, yet very different distributions, as the following example illustrates.

Imagine you are a scout for a professional baseball team and are considering one of two players for your team. Each player has a .263 batting average over his four years of college. The distributions of the two players' averages are as follows: Player 1—.260, .397, .200, .195; Player 2—.263, .267, .259, .263.

Which of these two players would you prefer to have on your team? Most likely, you would pick Player 2 because he is more "consistent" than Player 1. This simple example illustrates an important point about descriptive statistics. When you are evaluating your data, you should take into account both the central tendency *and* the amount of variability among the scores. This section reviews four measures of variability: the range, the semi-interquartile range, the variance, and the standard deviation.

The Range. The **range** is the simplest and least informative measure of variability. To calculate the range, you simply subtract the lowest score from the highest score. In the baseball example, the range for Player 1 is .202, whereas the range for Player 2 is .008.

Two problems with the range are that it does not take into account the magnitude of the scores between the extremes, and it is very sensitive to extreme scores in the distribution. Compare the following two distributions of scores: 1, 2, 3, 4, 5, 6; and 1, 2, 3, 4, 5, 31. The range for the first distribution is 5, whereas the range for the second is 30. The two ranges are highly discrepant despite the fact that the two distributions are nearly identical. For these reasons, the range is rarely used as a measure of variability.

The Semi-Interquartile Range. The **semi-interquartile range** is another measure of variability that is easy to calculate. To obtain the semi-interquartile range, follow these steps:

1. Order the scores in your distribution.
2. Divide the distribution into four equal parts (quartiles).
3. Find the score separating the lower 25 percent of the distribution (Quartile 1 or Q_1) and the score separating the top 25 percent from the rest of the distribution (Q_3). The interquartile range is equal to Q_3 minus Q_1.
4. Divide the interquartile range by 2.

The semi-interquartile range is less sensitive than the range to the effects of extreme scores. It also takes into account more information, because more than just the highest and lowest scores are used for its calculation. Thus, the semi-interquartile range may be preferred over the range in situations where you want a relatively simple, rough measure of variability.

The Variance. The **variance** is the average squared deviation from the mean. The defining formula is

$$\text{Variance } (s^2) = \frac{\Sigma(X - M)^2}{N - 1}$$

where X is each individual score making up the distribution, M is the mean of the distribution, and N is the number of scores. Table 11-5 shows how to use this formula by means of an example worked out for one distribution of scores.

Notice in this example that the mean for the distribution was obtained and then subtracted from each score in the distribution. Each deviation score was squared and a sum of the deviation scores was obtained. Finally, the variance was obtained by dividing the sum of the squared deviation scores by $N - 1$. Using this formula can be somewhat inconvenient. In practice, you would probably want to use a simpler "computational" formula to derive the variance. This formula and a worked example can be found in Appendix II.

The Standard Deviation. Although the variance is frequently used as a measure of variability in certain statistical calculations, it does have the disadvantage of being expressed in units different from those of the summarized data. However, the variance can be easily converted into a measure of variability expressed in the *same* unit of measurement as the original scores: the **standard deviation**. To

Table 11-5. Calculation of a Variance

	X	X^2	$(X - M)$	$(X - M)^2$
	3	9	-2	4
	5	25	0	0
	2	4	-3	9
	7	49	2	4
	9	81	4	16
	4	16	-1	1
Sum	30	184		34

$M = 30/6 = 5.0$

Variance $(s^2) = 34/5 = 6.8$

convert from the variance to the standard deviation, simply take the square root of the variance. The standard deviation of the data in Table 11-5 is 2.61 ($\sqrt{6.8}$). The standard deviation is the most popular measure of variability.

Choosing a Measure of Variability. The choice of a measure of central tendency is affected by the distribution of the scores and the same is true for the choice of a measure of variability. Like the mean, the range and standard deviation are sensitive to extreme scores. In cases where your distribution has one or more extreme scores, the semi-interquartile range may provide a better measure of variability.

In addition to noting the presence of extreme scores, you should note the shape of the distribution (normal or skewed) when selecting a measure of variability. Remember that the mean is not a representative measure of central tendency when your distribution of scores is skewed, and that the mean is used to calculate the standard deviation. Consequently, with a skewed distribution, the standard deviation does not provide a representative measure of variability. If your distribution is seriously skewed, use the semi-interquartile range instead.

Measures of Correlation, Regression, and Related Topics

In some cases you may want to evaluate the direction and degree of relationship (correlation) between the scores in two distributions. For this purpose you must use a *measure of correlation*. This section discusses several measures of correlation,

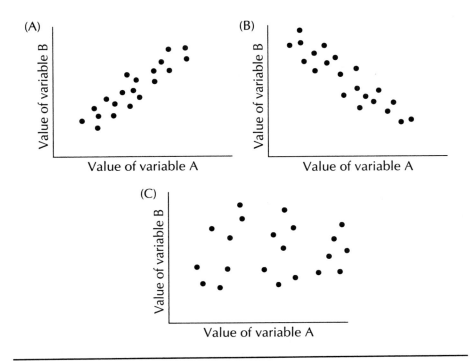

Figure 11-16. Scattergrams showing positive (A), negative (B), and no correlation (C).

along with the related topics of linear regression, the correlation matrix, and the coefficient of determination.

The Pearson Product Moment Correlation Coefficient

The most widely used measure of correlation is the *Pearson product moment correlation coefficient*, or **Pearson r**. It can be used when your dependent measures are scaled on an interval or a ratio scale. The Pearson correlation coefficient provides an index of the direction of the relationship between two sets of scores.

The value of the Pearson *r* can range from +1 through zero to −1. The sign of the coefficient tells you the direction of the relationship. A positive correlation indicates a *direct relationship* (as the value of the scores in one distribution increase, so do the values in the second). A negative correlation indicates an *inverse relationship* (as the value of one score increases, the value of the second decreases). Figure 11-16 illustrates scattergrams of data showing a positive, negative, and no correlation.

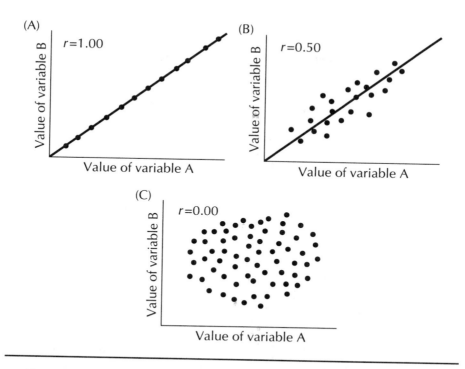

Figure 11-17. Scattergrams showing correlations of differing strengths:
(A) perfect positive correlation, (B) moderate positive correlation,
(C) zero correlation.

The magnitude of the correlation coefficient tells you the degree of *linear relationship* (straight line) between your two variables. A correlation of zero indicates that no relationship exists. As the strength of the relationship increases, the value of the correlation coefficient increases toward either $+1$ or -1. Both $+1$ and -1 indicate a perfect linear relationship. The sign is unrelated to the magnitude of the relationship, but simply indicates the direction of the relationship. Figure 11-17 shows three correlations of differing strengths. Panel A shows a correlation of $+1$, Panel B a correlation of about $+0.5$, and Panel C a correlation of zero.

Factors That Affect the Pearson Correlation Coefficient. Before you use the Pearson correlation coefficient, examine your data much as you do when deciding on a measure of central tendency. Several factors affect the magnitude and sign of the Pearson correlation coefficient.

One factor that affects the Pearson correlation coefficient is the presence of outliers. An outlier can drastically change your correlation coefficient and affect

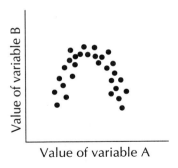

Figure 11-18. Scattergram showing a curvilinear relationship.

the magnitude of your correlation, its sign, or both. This is especially true if the correlation coefficient is based on a small number of pairs of scores.

A second factor that affects the Pearson correlation coefficient is the variability in scores within each of the two measures. When the range of scores in one distribution is restricted (for example, if the scores were all 1's and 2's), the Pearson correlation coefficient underestimates the magnitude of the relationship between the variables. Inspect the standard deviations of the two distributions (they should be similar).

The Pearson correlation coefficient is sensitive not only to the range of the scores, but also to the shapes of the score distributions. The formula used to calculate the coefficient uses the standard deviation for each set of scores. Recall that the mean is used to calculate the standard deviation. If the scores are not normally distributed, the mean does not represent the distribution well. Consequently, the standard deviations will not accurately reflect the variability of the distributions, and the correlation coefficient will not provide an accurate index of the relationship between your two sets of scores. Hence, you should inspect the frequency distributions of each set of scores to ensure that they are normal (or nearly normal) before using the Pearson coefficient.

Finally, the Pearson coefficient reflects the degree to which the relationship between two variables is linear. Because of this assumption, take steps to determine whether the relationship appears to be linear. You can do this by constructing a scattergram and then determining whether the points appear to scatter symmetrically around a straight line. Figure 11-18 shows a scattergram in which the measures have a *curvilinear relationship* (rather than a linear relationship).

When the relationship between variables is nonlinear, the Pearson correlation coefficient underestimates the degree of relationship between the variables. For example, the Pearson correlation between the variables illustrated in Figure 11-18 is zero. However, the two variables are obviously systematically related.

There are special correlation techniques for nonlinear data, which are not discussed here.

To summarize, the Pearson correlation coefficient is an index of the direction and degree of linear relationship between two variables. It can be used when data are scaled on at least an interval scale. This measure of correlation should be used only if the two sets of scores have similar levels of variability, the scores are normally distributed, and the relationship between the two sets of scores is essentially linear.

The Pearson correlation coefficient is used when both of your variables are measured along a continuous scale (interval or ratio). You may need to correlate variables when one (or both) of them is not measured along a continuous scale. Special correlation coefficients are designed for these purposes, three of which are discussed in the next sections.

The Point-Biserial Correlation

You may have one variable measured on an interval scale and the other measured on a nominal scale. For example, perhaps you want to investigate the relationship between self-rated political conservatism (measured on a ten-point scale) and whether or not a referendum was voted for (yes or no). Because one variable is continuous and the other dichotomous (able to take on one of only two values), you would apply the **point-biserial correlation**.

Although there is a special formula for the point-biserial correlation (see Appendix II), in practice the formula for the Pearson r is used to compute it. The dichotomous variable is dummy-coded as 0 for one response and 1 for the other. It is easier to use the Pearson formula, especially if you are using a computer program to evaluate your data (assuming the program cannot compute a point-biserial correlation).

Factors That Affect the Point-Biserial Correlation. You should know a couple of things about the point-biserial correlation. First, its magnitude partly depends on the proportion of subjects falling into each of the dichotomous categories. If the number of subjects in each category is equal, then the maximum value the point-biserial can attain is plus or minus 1.0 (just as with the Pearson r). However, if the number of subjects in each category is *not* equal, then the maximum attainable value for the point-biserial correlation is less than plus or minus 1.0. As a consequence, the degree of relationship between the two variables may be underestimated. You should examine the proportion of subjects using each category of the dichotomous variable and, if the proportions differ greatly, temper your conclusions accordingly.

The magnitude of the point-biserial correlation is also affected by the restriction of range on the dichotomous variable. A dichotomous variable is by definition measured on a two-point scale. A restriction on the range of values a variable can attain leads to an underestimation of the strength of relationship between two variables. Consequently the point-biserial correlation may underestimate the true degree of relationship.

The Spearman Rank Order Correlation

The **Spearman rank order correlation**, or *rho* (ρ), is used either when your data are scaled on an ordinal scale (or greater), or when you want to determine whether the relationship between variables is monotonic (Gravetter & Wallnau, 1990). The rank order correlation is relatively easy to calculate and can be interpreted in much the same way as a Pearson correlation.

The *Phi* Coefficient

The *phi* coefficient (ϕ) is used when *both* of the variables being correlated are measured on a dichotomous scale. The phi coefficient can be calculated by means of its own formula. However, like the point-biserial, phi is usually calculated by dummy-coding the responses as 1's and 0's, and then plugging the resulting scores into the formula for the Pearson *r*. The same arguments concerning restriction of range that apply to the point-biserial also apply to phi—only doubly so.

Linear Regression and Prediction

A topic closely related to correlation is **linear regression**. With simple correlational techniques, you can establish the direction and degree of relationship between two variables. With linear regression, you can estimate values of variables based on knowledge of the value of another. The following section introduces you to simple bivariate (two-variable) regression (also included are some calculations to help you understand regression). Chapter 15 extends bivariate regression to the case where you want to consider multiple variables together in a single analysis.

Bivariate Regression. The idea behind **bivariate linear regression** is to find the straight line that best fits the data plotted on a scattergram. Consider an example using the data presented in Table 11-6, which shows the scores for each of 10 subjects on two measures (*X* and *Y*). Figure 11-19 shows a scattergram of these data. You want to find the straight line that best describes the linear relationship between *X* and *Y*.

The best-fitting straight line is the one that minimizes the sum of the squared distances between each data point and the line, as measured along the *y*-axis (least squares criterion). This line is called the **least squares regression line**. At any given value for *X* found in the data, the position of the line indicates the

Table 11-6. Data for Linear Regression Example

X	Y	$(X - M_x)$	$(Y - M_y)$	SP	SS_x
7	8	1.40	1.30	1.82	1.96
3	4	−2.60	−2.70	7.02	6.76
2	4	−3.60	−2.70	9.72	12.96
10	9	4.40	2.30	10.12	19.36
8	9	2.40	2.30	5.52	5.76
7	7	1.40	0.30	0.42	1.96
9	8	3.40	1.30	4.42	11.56
6	8	0.40	1.30	0.52	0.16
3	4	−2.60	−2.70	7.02	6.76
1	6	−4.60	−0.70	3.22	21.16
M = 5.6	6.7			Sum = 49.80	88.4

value of Y predicted from the linear relationship between X and Y. You can then compare these predicted values to the values actually obtained. The best-fitting straight line minimizes the difference between the predicted and obtained values.

The regression line is described mathematically by the following formula:

$$Y' = bX + constant$$

where Y' is the predicted Y score, b is the slope of the regression line (also called the *regression weight*), X is the value of the X-variable, and *constant* is the y-intercept (Pagano, 1986). The constants, b and *constant*, define a particular regression line. You can use the following formula to determine the value of b for a given set of data points (Gravetter & Wallnau, 1990):

$$b = \frac{SP}{SS_x}$$

where $SP = \Sigma(X - M_x)(Y - M_y)$ and $SS_x = \Sigma(X - M_x)^2$.

Using the numbers from Table 11-6, we have

$$b = \frac{49.8}{88.4} = 0.56$$

The formula for the y-intercept (*constant*) is

$$constant = M_y - b(M_x)$$

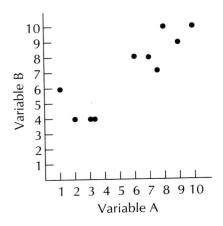

Figure 11-19. Scattergram of data from Table 11-6.

For this example,

$$constant = 6.7 - .56(5.6) = 3.56$$

Substituting these values for *b* and *constant* in the regression equation gives

$$Y' = 0.56x + 3.56$$

This equation allows you to predict the value of Y for any given value of X. For example, if $X = 6$, then $Y' = 0.56(6) + 3.56 = 6.92$.

This regression equation was based on raw scores. Its **regression weight** (*b*) is known as a *raw score regression weight*. If you plug standardized scores rather than raw scores into these equations, you will obtain a different regression equation with a different value for the weight and a zero value for the intercept. The regression weight you obtain from this analysis is called the *standardized regression weight*, or the *beta weight* (β). You would want to use the standardized regression weights when interpreting a regression equation. Chapter 15 discusses how to interpret standardized regression weights.

Residuals and Errors in Prediction. After you have computed a regression analysis, you will have a score on one variable (Y) predicted from another variable (X). Because you have the actual values of a variable (Y) as well as the values predicted from the regression equation (Y') you are in a position to see how accurately your regression equation predicts scores on Y. The difference between the values of Y and Y' ($Y - Y'$) is called a *residual*. Residuals will be low when the regression equation generates values of Y' that are close to the actual values of Y.

When your variables are perfectly correlated, there is no error in prediction (the predicted and actual values of Y will always agree). However, when your correlation is less than perfect, there will be error in predicting Y from X. You can estimate the amount of error in prediction by calculating the **standard error of estimate**, which is a measure of the distance between your data points and your computed regression line (Gravetter & Wallnau, 1990). The following formula is used to compute the standard error of estimate (Gravetter & Wallnau, 1990, df stands for degrees of freedom):

$$ SE = \sqrt{\frac{SS_{error}}{df}} = \sqrt{\frac{\Sigma(Y - Y')^2}{n - 2}} $$

In the current example, SE = 1.008.

A close relationship exists between the magnitude of SE and the magnitude of the correlation between X and Y. If X and Y are highly correlated, the data points will be clustered tightly around the regression line and SE will be small. As the strength of the relationship between X and Y decreases, SE increases.

The Coefficient of Determination

The square of the correlation coefficient (whether Pearson r, point-biserial, Spearman's rho, or phi) is called the *coefficient of determination*. The coefficient of determination provides a measure of the amount of variance shared by the two variables being tested. It indicates how much of the variability in one of the scores can be "explained" by the variability in the other score. For example, if variation in Score X actually *caused* variations to occur in Score Y, the coefficient of determination would indicate what proportion of the total variation in Score Y was caused by variation in Score X.

As an example, assume you investigated the relationship between intelligence and school performance and found a correlation of 0.60. Then the coefficient of determination is 0.60×0.60, or 0.36. This means that 36 percent of the variation in school performance can be accounted for by the variation in intelligence.

Of course, you usually don't know if the relationship is truly a causal one, or in which direction the causal arrow points. Consequently you should interpret this statistic with caution. Perhaps the most enlightening use of this statistic is to subtract it from 1.0. The resulting number, called the *coefficient of nondetermination*, gives the proportion of variance in one variable *not accounted for* by variance in the other variable. This is, in effect, *unexplained* variance caused by unmeasured factors. If the coefficient of nondetermination is large, then your measured variables are having little impact on each other relative to these unmeasured factors. If this happens, then perhaps you should try to identify these unmeasured variables and either hold them constant or measure them.

The Correlation Matrix

If you have computed all the possible correlations among a number of variables, you can make the relationships among the variables easier to comprehend by

Table 11-7. A Correlation Matrix

	VARIABLES				
VARIABLES	1	2	3	4	5
2	.54				
3	.43	.87			
4	.52	.31	.88		
5	.77	.44	.06	.39	

displaying the correlation coefficients in a table called a *correlation matrix*. Table 11-7 shows a hypothetical correlation matrix for five variables (1–5). The headings along the top and left side of the matrix indicate the variables being correlated. Each number within the matrix is the correlation between the two variables whose row and column intersect at the position of the number. For example, the correlation between Variables 5 and 3 can be found by reading across the row labeled "Variable 5" to the column labeled "Variable 3." The correlation found at that intersection is 0.06.

Note that the numbers along the diagonal have been omitted from the table. This is because the diagonal positions represent the correlations of each variable with itself, which are necessarily 1.0. The correlations above the diagonal are omitted because they simply duplicate the correlations already given below the diagonal. For example, the correlation of Variable 5 with Variable 3 (below the diagonal) is the same as the correlation of Variable 3 with Variable 5 (which would appear above the diagonal).

Multivariate Correlational Techniques

The measures of correlation and linear regression discussed in this chapter are all bivariate. Even if you calculate several bivariate correlations and arrange them in a matrix, your conclusions are limited to the relationship between pairs of variables. Bivariate correlation techniques are certainly useful and powerful tools. In many cases, however, you may want to look at three or more variables simultaneously. For example, you might want to know what the relationship between two variables is with the effect of a third held constant. Or, you might want to know how a set of predictor variables relates to a criterion variable. In these cases and related others, the statistical technique of choice is *multivariate analysis*.

Multivariate analysis is a family of statistical techniques that allow you to evaluate complex relationships among three or more variables. Multivariate analyses include multiple regression, discriminant analysis, part and partial correlation, and canonical correlation. Chapter 15 provides an overview of these and other multivariate techniques.

Summary

When you have finished conducting your research, you begin the task of organizing, summarizing, and describing your data. The first step is to organize your data so you can more easily conduct the relevant analyses. A good way to gain some understanding of your data is to graph the observed relationships. You can do this with a histogram, line graph, scattergram, or pie chart, whichever is most appropriate for your data.

Descriptive statistics are methods for summarizing your data. Descriptive statistics include measures of central tendency, measures of variability, and measures of correlation.

The mode, median, and mean are the three measures of central tendency. The mode is the most frequent score in your distribution. The median is the middle score in an ordered distribution. The mean is the arithmetic average of the scores, obtained by summing the scores and dividing the sum by the total number of scores.

Which of the three measures of central tendency you should use depends both on the scale on which the data were measured and on the shape of the distribution of scores. The mean can be used only with data that are scaled on either a ratio or an interval scale and are normally distributed. In cases where the data are skewed or bimodal, then the mean does not provide a representative measure of central tendency, and the median or mode should be considered. Ordinally scaled data are best described with the median, whereas nominally scaled data are best described with the mode.

Measures of variability include the range, semi-interquartile range, variance, and standard deviation. The range is simply the difference between the highest and lowest score in your distribution. Although simple to calculate, the range is rarely used. Serious limitations of the range are that it is strongly affected by extreme scores and takes into account only the highest and lowest scores (thus ignoring the remaining scores in the distribution). The semi-interquartile range takes into account more of the scores in the distribution and is less sensitive than the range to extreme scores. The variance uses all the scores in its calculation, but has the disadvantage that its unit of measurement differs from that of the scores from which it derives. This problem can be overcome by taking the square root of the variance. The resulting statistic, the standard deviation, is the most commonly used measure of variability.

Your decision about which of the measures of variability to use is affected by the same two factors that affect your decision about central tendency (scale of measurement and distribution of scores). The standard deviation is a good measure of variability when your scores are normally distributed. As scores deviate from normality, the standard deviation becomes a less representative measure of variability. When your data are skewed, use the semi–interquartile range.

Measures of correlation provide an index of the direction and degree of relationship between two variables. The most popular measure of correlation is the Pearson product moment correlation coefficient (r). This coefficient can range from -1 through zero to $+1$. A stronger relationship is indicated as the coefficient approaches plus or minus 1. A negative correlation indicates that an increase in the value of one variable is associated with a decrease in the value of the second (inverse relationship). A positive correlation indicates that the two measures increase or decrease together (direct relationship).

The Pearson r is applied to data scaled on either an interval or ratio scale. Other measures of correlation are available for data measured along other scales. The point-biserial correlation is used if one variable is measured on an interval or ratio scale, and the other on a dichotomous nominal scale. Spearman's rho is used if both variables are measured on at least an ordinal scale. The phi coefficient is used if both variables are dichotomous.

Linear regression is a statistical procedure closely related to correlation. With linear regression, you can estimate the value of a criterion variable given the value of a predictor. In linear regression, you calculate a least squares regression line, which is the straight line that best fits the data on a scattergram. This line minimizes the sum of the squared distances between each data point and the line, as measured along the y-axis (least squares criterion), and minimizes the difference between predicted and obtained values of y. The amount of discrepancy between the values of y predicted with the regression equation and the actual values is provided by the standard error of estimate. The magnitude of the standard error is related to the magnitude of the correlation between your variables. The higher the correlation, the lower the standard error.

By squaring the correlation coefficient, you obtain the coefficient of determination, an index of the amount of variation in one variable that can be accounted for by variation in the other. Subtracting the coefficient of determination from 1.0 gives you the coefficient of indetermination, the proportion of variance *not* shared by the two variables. The larger this number is, the larger the effect of unmeasured sources of variance relative to that of the measured variables.

Multivariate statistical techniques are used to evaluate more complex relationships than simple bivariate statistics. With multivariate statistics you can analyze the degree of relationship between a set of predictor variables and a criterion variable, or look at the correlation between two variables with the effect of a third held constant.

Key Terms

Distribution

Histogram *or* bar graph

Line graph

Scattergram

Pie chart

Frequency distribution

Normal distribution

Skewed distribution

Mode

Median

Mean

Range

Semi-interquartile range

Variance

Standard deviation

Pearson *r*

Point-biserial correlation

Spearman rank order correlation (*rho*)

Linear regression

Bivariate linear regression

Least squares regression line

Regression weight

Standard error of estimate

12

Using Inferential Statistics

CHAPTER 11 REVIEWED DESCRIPTIVE STATISTICS that help you characterize and describe your data. However, they do not help you assess the reliability of your findings. A reliable finding is repeatable, whereas an unreliable one may not be. Statistics that assess the reliability of your findings are called **inferential statistics** because they allow you to infer the characteristics of a population from the characteristics of the samples comprising your data.

This chapter reviews the most widely used inferential statistics. Rather than focusing on how to calculate these statistics, this discussion focuses on issues of application and interpretation. Consequently, computational formulas or worked examples are not presented in this chapter. However, some computational formulas and worked examples do appear in Appendix II. More complete information on the computation of these statistics can be found in statistics texts such as Gravetter and Wallnau (1990), Keppel (1982), Winer (1971), and Bruning and Kintz (1987).

Inferential Statistics: Basic Concepts

Before exploring some of the more popular inferential statistics, consider some of the basic concepts underlying these statistics. You should understand these concepts before tackling the discussion on inferential statistics that follows. If you need a more comprehensive refresher on these concepts, consult a good introductory statistics text (such as Gravetter & Wallnau, 1990).

Sampling Distribution

Chapter 11 introduced the notion of a distribution of scores. Such a distribution results from collecting data across a series of observations and then plotting the frequency of each score or range of scores. You can think of this distribution as a sample from a larger set of scores that constitute the population. Descriptive statistics calculated on your sample distribution (such as the mean and standard deviation) characterize the sample distribution. However, because of sampling error, descriptive statistics may or may not agree with the population values. For example, the mean of your sample distribution may or may not agree with the mean of the population distribution.

Imagine you made your observations enough times to obtain every possible sample of a given size from the population. You then calculate a mean for each of the samples. Because of sampling error, the means will vary. The distribution of these means is called the *sampling distribution of the mean.*

The sampling distribution of the mean has well-defined characteristics. It follows a normal distribution, and the mean of the sampling distribution is the same as the mean of the population from which the samples were drawn. In fact, according to the *central limit theorem*, the distribution of sample means will tend to be normal even if the distribution of population scores (from which the samples were drawn) deviates wildly from normality. You can therefore often make statements about population values (statements depending on an assumption of normality) even though the population scores are not themselves normally distributed.

Each sample statistic has its own theoretical sampling distribution that you can use to estimate the population value of that statistic from sample values. For example, the tabled values for the z statistic, Student's t, the F-ratio, and chi-square represent the sampling distributions of those statistics. Using these sampling distributions, you can determine the probability that an obtained value of a statistic occurred by chance. (To determine statistical significance, compare an obtained value of a statistic with the tabled value.)

Sampling Error

When you draw a sample from a population of scores, the mean of the sample will probably differ from the population mean (denoted as μ). An estimate of the amount of variability in the expected sample means across a series of such samples is provided by the **standard error of the mean** (or *standard error* for short). It may be calculated from the standard deviation of the sample as follows:

$$S_{M} = \frac{s}{\sqrt{n}}$$

where s is the standard deviation of the sample and n is the number of scores in the sample. The standard error is used to estimate the standard deviation of the sampling distribution of the mean for the population from which the sample was drawn.

Degrees of Freedom

In any distribution of scores with a known mean, a limited number of data points yields independent information. For example, if you have a sample of 10 scores and a known mean (for example, 6.5), only 9 scores are free to vary. That is, once you have selected 9 scores from the population, the value of the tenth one cannot vary. Thus, the **degrees of freedom** (df) for a single sample are $n - 1$ (where n is the total number of scores in the sample).

Degrees of freedom come into play when you use any inferential statistic. You can extend this logic to the analysis of an experiment. If you have three groups in your experiment with means of 2, 5, and 10, the grand mean (the sum of all the scores divided by n) is then 5.7. If you know the grand mean and you know the means from two of your groups, the final mean is set. Hence, the degrees of freedom for a three-group experiment are $A - 1$ (where A is the number of levels of the independent variable). The degrees of freedom are then used to find the appropriate tabled value of a statistic against which the computed value is compared.

Parametric Versus Nonparametric Statistics

Inferential statistics can be classified as either *parametric* or *nonparametric*. A *parameter* is a characteristic of a population, whereas a *statistic* is a characteristic of your sample (Gravetter & Wallnau, 1990). A *parametric statistic* estimates the value of a population parameter from the characteristics of a sample. When you use a parametric statistic, you are making certain assumptions about the population from which your sample was drawn. A key assumption of a parametric test is that your sample was drawn from a normally distributed population. Moreover, parametric tests assume your data were measured on an interval or a ratio scale.

In contrast to parametric statistics, nonparametric statistics make no assumptions about the distribution of scores underlying your sample. Nonparametric statistics are used if your data do not meet the assumptions of a parametric test, or if your data are scaled on an ordinal or nominal scale.

The Logic Behind Inferential Statistics

Whenever you conduct an experiment, you expose subjects to different levels of your independent variable. Although a given experiment may contain several groups, assume for the present discussion that the experiment in question included only two.

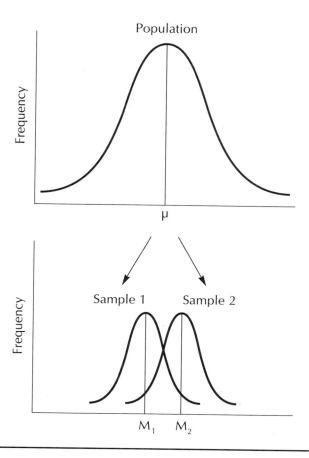

Figure 12-1. Line graphs showing the relationship between samples and population, assuming the null hypothesis is true. (M_1, mean of sample 1; M_2, mean of sample 2.)

The data from each group can be viewed as a sample of the scores obtained if all subjects in the target population were tested under the conditions to which the group was exposed. For example, the treatment group mean represents a population of subjects exposed to your experimental treatment. Each mean is assumed to represent the mean of the underlying population.

In all respects except for treatment, the treatment and control groups were exposed to equivalent conditions. Assume that the treatment had *no effect* on the scores. In that case, each group's scores could be viewed as an independent sample taken from the *same* population. Figure 12-1 illustrates this situation.

Each sample mean provides an independent estimate of the population mean. Each sample standard error provides an independent estimate of the standard deviation of sample means in the sampling distribution of means. Because the two means were drawn from the same population, you would expect them to differ only because of sampling error. You can assume the distribution of these means is normal (central limit theorem), and you have two estimates of the standard deviation of this distribution (the standard errors). From this information, you can calculate the probability that the two sample means would differ as much as they do, simply because of chance factors.

Let's review these points. If the treatment had no effect on the scores, then you would expect the scores from the two groups to provide independent samples from the same population. From these samples you can estimate the characteristics of that population, and from this estimate you can determine the probability that sampling error would produce the observed difference between the two means.

Consider the case where the treatment *does* affect the scores, perhaps by shifting them upward. Figure 12-2 illustrates this situation. In the upper part of the figure is a population underlying the control group sample distribution, and another one underlying the treatment group sample distribution. Notice the population distribution underlying the treatment group is shifted upward and away from the control group population distribution. This shift could be obtained by simply adding a constant to each value in the control group distribution. This new shifted distribution resembles the old, unshifted distribution in standard deviation, but its mean is higher.

The bottom part of the figure shows two possible sample distributions — one for the control group and one for the treatment group. The scores from the control group still constitute a sample from the unshifted distribution (left-hand upper curve in Figure 12-2), but the scores from the treatment group now constitute a sample from the shifted distribution (right-hand upper curve in Figure 12-2). The two sample means provide estimates of two *different* population means. Because of sampling error, the two sample means might or might not differ, even though a difference exists between the underlying population means.

Your problem (as a researcher) is that you do not know whether the treatment really had an effect on the scores. You must decide this based on your observed sample means (which may differ by a certain amount), and the sample standard deviations. From this information, you must decide whether the two sample means were drawn from the same population (the treatment had no effect on the sample scores) or from two different populations (the treatment shifted the scores relative to scores from the control group). Inferential statistics help you make this decision.

These two possibilities (different or the same populations) can be viewed as statistical hypotheses to be tested. The hypothesis that the means were drawn from the same population (that is, $\mu_1 = \mu_2$) is referred to as the *null hypothesis* (H_0). The hypothesis that the means were drawn from different populations ($\mu_1 \neq \mu_2$) is called the *alternative hypothesis* (H_1).

Inferential statistics use the characteristics of the two samples to evaluate the validity of the null hypothesis. Put another way, they assess the probability that the means of the two samples would differ by the observed amount or more, if

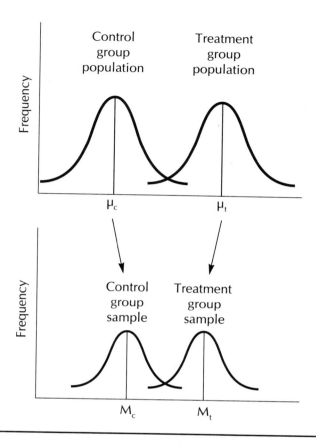

Figure 12-2. Line graphs showing the relationship between samples and population, assuming the null hypothesis is false.

they had been drawn from the same population of scores. If this probability is sufficiently small (that is, if it is very unlikely that two samples this different would be drawn by chance from the same population), then the difference between the sample means is said to be *statistically significant*, and the null hypothesis is rejected.

Statistical Errors

When making a comparison between two sample means, there are two possible states of affairs (the null hypothesis is true, or it is false) and two possible decisions you can make (to not reject the null hypothesis or to reject it). These conditions lead to four possible outcomes, as shown in Table 12-1. The labels

Table 12-1. Statistical Errors			
		TRUE STATE OF AFFAIRS	
		H_0 True	H_0 False
DECISION	Reject H_0	Type I Error	Correct Decision
	Do Not Reject H_0	Correct Decision	Type II Error

across the top of Table 12-1 indicate the two states of affairs, whereas those in the left-hand column indicate the two possible decisions. Each box represents a different combination of the two conditions.

The lower left-hand box represents the situation where the null hypothesis is true (the independent variable had no effect), and you correctly decide not to reject the null hypothesis. This is a disappointing outcome, but at least you made the right decision.

The upper left-hand box represents a more disturbing outcome. Here the null hypothesis is again true, but you have incorrectly decided to reject the null hypothesis. In other words, you decided that your independent variable had an effect when, in fact, it did not. In statistics this mistake is called a **type I error** or *alpha error*. In signal detection experiments, the same kind of mistake is called a "false alarm" (saying a stimulus was present when actually it was not).

The lower right-hand box in Table 12-1 represents a second kind of error. In this case, the null hypothesis is false (the independent variable did have an effect) but you have incorrectly decided not to reject the null hypothesis. This is called a **type II error** or *beta error*, and represents the case where you concluded your independent variable had no effect when it really did have one. In signal detection experiments, such an outcome is called a "miss" (not detecting a stimulus that was present).

Ideally, you would like to minimize the probability of making either a type I or a type II error. Unfortunately, some of the things you can do to minimize a type I error actually increase the probability of a type II error, and vice versa.

Statistical Significance

An inferential statistic can be used to determine the probability that your observed means came from one or two underlying populations. Based on your sample data, you calculate an *observed value of a statistic*. This observed value is compared to a *critical value* of that statistic (normally found in a statistical table such as those in Appendix I). Ultimately, you will make your decision about rejecting the null hypothesis based on whether or not the observed value of the statistic meets or exceeds the critical value. As stated, you want to be able to reduce the probability of committing a type I error.

The probability of committing a type I error depends on the criterion you use to accept or reject the null hypothesis. This criterion, known as the **alpha level** (α), represents the probability that the observed difference between your sample means could have occurred purely through sampling error. The alpha level you adopt (along with the degrees of freedom) also determines the critical value of the statistic you are using. The smaller the value of alpha, the larger the critical value.

Alpha represents the probability of a type I error. Thus, the smaller you make alpha, the less likely you are to make a type I error. In theory you can reduce the probability of making a type I error to any desired level. For example, you could average less than one type I error in 1 million experiments by choosing an alpha value of 0.000001. There are good reasons, discussed later, why you do not ordinarily adopt such a conservative alpha level.

By convention, alpha has been set at 0.05 (5 chances in 100 that a difference was caused by sampling error). The particular level of alpha you adopt is called the *significance level*. A difference between means yielding an observed value of a statistic meeting or exceeding the critical value of your inferential statistic is said to be *statistically significant*.

One-Tailed Versus Two-Tailed Tests

The critical values of a statistic depend on such factors as the number of observations per treatment, the number of treatments, and the desired alpha level. They also depend on whether the test is one-tailed or two-tailed.

Figure 12-3 shows two examples of the sampling distribution for the z statistic. This distribution is normal and, therefore, symmetrical about the mean. The left distribution shows the **critical region** (hatched area) for a *one-tailed test*, assuming alpha has been set to 0.05. This region contains 5 percent of the total area under the curve, representing the 5 percent of cases whose z-scores occur by chance with a probability of 0.05 or less. The z values falling into this critical region are judged to be statistically significant.

The right distribution in Figure 12-3 shows the *two* critical regions for the *two-tailed test*, using the same 0.05 alpha value. To keep the probability at 0.05, the total percentage of cases found in the two tails of the distribution must equal 5 percent. Thus, each critical region must contain 2.5 percent of the cases. Consequently the z-scores required to reach statistical significance must be more extreme than was the case for the one-tailed test.

A one-tailed test is conducted if you are interested only in whether the obtained value of the statistic falls in one tail of the sampling distribution for that statistic. This is usually the case when your research hypotheses are directional. For example, you may want to know whether a new therapy is measurably *better*

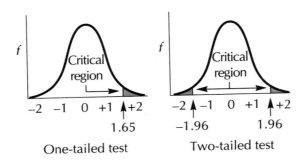

Figure 12-3. Graphs showing critical regions for one-tailed and two-tailed tests of statistical significance.

than the standard one. However, if the new therapy is not better, then you really do not care whether it is simply as good as the standard method or is actually worse. You would not use it in either case.

In contrast, you would conduct a two-tailed test if you wanted to know whether the new therapy was either better *or* worse than the standard method. In that case, you need to check whether your obtained statistic falls into either tail of the distribution.

The major implication of all this is that for a given alpha level, you must obtain a greater difference between the means of your two treatment groups to reach statistical significance if you use a two-tailed test than if you use a one-tailed test. The one-tailed test is, therefore, more likely to detect a real difference if one is present (that is, it is more powerful). However, using the one-tailed test means giving up any information about the reliability of a difference in the other, untested direction.

The use of one-tailed versus two-tailed tests has been a controversial topic among statisticians. Strictly speaking, you must choose which version you will use *before* you see the data. You must base your decision on such factors as practical considerations (as in the therapy example), your hypothesis, or previous knowledge. If you wait until after you have seen the data and then base your decision on the direction of the obtained outcome, your actual probability of falsely rejecting the null hypothesis will be greater than the stated alpha value. You have used information contained in the data to make your decision, but that information may itself be the result of chance processes and unreliable.

If you conduct a two-tailed test and then fail to obtain a statistically significant result, the temptation is to find some excuse why you "should have done" a one-tailed test. You can avoid this temptation if you adopt the following rule of thumb: always use a two-tailed test unless there are compelling *a priori* reasons not to.

Parametric Statistics

Two types of inferential statistics are parametric and nonparametric. The type you apply to your data depends on the scale of measurement used and how your data are distributed. This section discusses parametric inferential statistics.

Assumptions Underlying a Parametric Statistic

Three assumptions underlie parametric inferential tests (Gravetter & Wallnau, 1990): (1) the scores have been sampled randomly from the population; (2) the sampling distribution of the mean is normal; and (3) the within-groups variances are homogeneous. Assumption 3 means the variances of the different groups are highly similar. In statistical inference, the independent variable is assumed to affect the mean but not the variance.

Serious violation of one or more of these assumptions may bias the statistical test. Such bias will lead you to commit a type I error either more or less often than the stated alpha probability, and thus undermine the value of the statistic as a guide to decision making. The effects of violations of these assumptions are examined later in more detail during a discussion of the statistical technique known as the *analysis of variance*.

Inferential Statistics with Two Groups

Imagine you have conducted a two-group experiment on whether "death-quali-fying" a jury (that is, removing any jurors who could not vote for the death penalty) affects how simulated jurors perceive a criminal defendant. Subjects in your experimental group were death qualified, whereas subjects in your control group were not. Subjects then rated on a scale from zero to 10 the likelihood that the defendant was guilty as charged of the crime. You run your experiment and then compute a mean for each group. You find the two means differ from one another (the experimental group mean is 7.2, and the control group mean is 4.9).

Your means may represent a single population and differ only because of sampling error. Or, your means may reliably represent two different populations. Your task is to determine which of these two conditions is true. Is the observed difference between means reliable, or is it merely caused by sampling error? This question can be answered by applying the appropriate statistical test, which in this case is a *t*-test.

The *t*-Test

The *t*-test is used when your experiment includes only two groups (as in the jury example), or if you want to make comparisons between pairs of groups in a more complex experiment. Special versions of the *t*-test are designed for between-subjects and within-subjects designs.

The t-Test for Independent Samples. You use the ***t*-test for independent samples** when you have data from two groups to contrast *and* you have randomly assigned independent samples of subjects to your groups. Also, the *t*-test can be used if you have an unequal number of subjects in each of your groups (for example, 12 in the control group and 10 in the experimental group). However, because the *t*-test uses an error term that is a composite of the variances from both groups, the difference in sample size between the groups should be kept as small as possible. With highly dissimilar sample sizes, the variances of the two groups are likely to be heterogeneous. In such a case, the composite error term may not provide an adequate test of the difference between your means.

The t-Test for Correlated Samples. When the two means being tested come from samples that are not independent of one another, the formula for the *t*-test must be adjusted to take into account any correlation between scores. This case arises when the means derive from a matched groups between-subjects design, a within-subjects design, or a correlational study. The adjusted *t*-test is called the ***t*-test for correlated samples** (or alternatively, the *t*-test for dependent samples).

Contrasting Two Groups: An Example from the Literature. Return to the example of a two-group experiment on jury death qualification. Although experiments employing only two groups are rare in the literature, they do sometimes appear. One such experiment was conducted by Haney (1984) on the impact of "death-qualifying" jurors.

Subjects in the control group viewed a videotape of jury selection in which no death qualification took place, whereas subjects in the experimental group saw the same tape but with death qualification added. Subjects were told that they would view a videotape of a jury selection procedure and were told to imagine that they were part of the jury. After viewing the videotape, subjects completed fourteen measures, including an estimation of the likelihood of the defendant's guilt and the likelihood that the defendant would be convicted.

Because Haney used a two-group, between-subjects design, the appropriate statistical test is the *t*-test for independent samples. Each of the 14 measures was analyzed with a separate *t*-test. Data from 3 of Haney's measures are shown in Table 12-2. Columns 1 and 2 present the means from the experimental and control groups, respectively. The third column shows the calculated results from the *t*-tests.

As presented, the data in Table 12-2 do not make much sense. All that you have are means and a *t*-value for each measure. Next you must decide if the *t*-values are large enough to warrant a conclusion that the observed differences are statistically significant.

After calculating a *t*-score, you compare its value to a critical value of *t* found in Table I-2 of Appendix I. Before you can evaluate your obtained *t*-value,

Table 12-2. Means and *t*-Values from Three of Haney's (1984) Measures

MEASURE	MEANS		
	Experimental	Control	*t*
Likelihood defendant found guilty of first-degree murder	46.7	36.2	2.12
Likelihood defendant will be convicted of first-degree murder and sentenced to death	39.6	24.5	3.00
Estimated percentage of first-degree murder convictions in which defendants are given the death sentence	23.5	17.9	1.32

however, you must obtain the degrees of freedom (df) (for the between-subjects *t*-test, df is $N - 2$, where N is the total number of subjects in the experiment).

Once you have obtained the degrees of freedom, you compare the obtained *t*-score with the tabled critical value, a process requiring two steps. First, read down the column labeled "Degrees of Freedom" and find the number matching your degrees of freedom. Second, find the column corresponding to the desired alpha level (labeled "Alpha Level"). The critical value of *t* is found at the intersection of the degrees of freedom (row) and alpha level (column) of your test. If your observed *t*-score is equal to or greater than the tabled *t*-score, then the difference between your sample means is statistically significant at the stated alpha level.

In some instances you may find that the table you have does not include the degrees of freedom you have calculated (for example, 65). If this occurs you can use a statistical calculator (such as the Texas Instruments 58 or 59) to evaluate your obtained *t*-value, find a table with the degrees of freedom you need, or use the next *lowest* degrees of freedom in the table that you have. In the latter case, if your degrees of freedom are 65, you would use 60 degrees of freedom in the table. This strategy is most appropriate if your *t*-value exceeds the tabled value by quite a bit. If you just miss statistical significance using the lesser degrees of freedom, you must use one of the other two methods for evaluating your *t*-value.

Examine the data in Table 12-2. Since Haney had a total of 67 subjects in his experiment, the degrees of freedom are 65 (67 − 2). If you consult Table I-2 in Appendix I, you find the first two *t*-values in Table 12-2 exceed the tabled critical value (using df = 60) at $p = 0.05$. The third *t*-value does not exceed the tabled critical value. You can then conclude that for the first two measures in Table 12-2 (likelihood that the defendant will be found guilty of first-degree murder, and likelihood of being convicted and sentenced to death) the experimental and control group means differ significantly.

The z-Test for the Difference Between Two Proportions. In some research, you may have to determine whether two proportions are significantly different. In a jury simulation where subjects return verdicts of guilty or not guilty, for example, your dependent variable might be expressed as the proportion of subjects who voted guilty. A relatively easy way to analyze data of this type is to use a **z-test for the difference between two proportions**. The logic behind this test is essentially the same as for the *t*-tests. The difference between the two proportions is evaluated against an estimate of error variance. The formula for this test (with an example) is in Appendix II.

Beyond Two Groups: Analysis of Variance (ANOVA)

When your experiment includes more than two groups, the statistical test of choice is **analysis of variance** (ANOVA). As the name implies, ANOVA is based on the concept of analyzing the variance that appears in the data. For this analysis, the variance is divided, or *partitioned*, according to the factors assumed to be responsible for producing variance. These factors are referred to as *sources of variance*. The next sections describe how variance is partitioned into sources and how the resulting source variances are used to calculate a statistic called the *F*-ratio. The *F*-ratio is ultimately checked to determine whether the variation among means is statistically significant.

Partitioning Variance. The value of any particular score obtained in a between-subjects experiment is determined by three factors: (1) characteristics of the subject at the time the score was measured; (2) measurement or recording errors (together called *experimental error*); and (3) the value of the independent variable (assuming the independent variable is effective). Because subjects differ from one another (factor 1), and because measurement error fluctuates (factor 2), scores will vary from one another even when all subjects are exposed to the same treatment conditions. Scores will vary even more if subjects are exposed to different treatment conditions and the independent variable is effective.

Figure 12-4 shows how the total variance in the scores from a given experiment can be partitioned into two sources of variability ("between–groups" variability and "within–groups" variability). Notice that the example begins with a total amount of variability among scores. Again, this total amount of variability may be attributable to one or more of three factors: your independent variable, individual differences, and experimental error (Gravetter & Wallnau, 1990).

The first component resulting from the partition is the *between-groups variability*. The between-groups variability may be caused by the variation in your independent variable, individual differences among the different subjects in your groups, experimental error, or a combination of these (Gravetter & Wallnau, 1990). The second component, the *within-groups variability*, may be attributed to

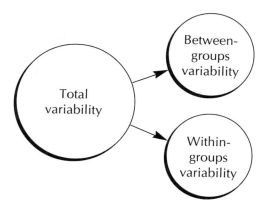

Figure 12-4. Partitioning total variability into between-groups and within-groups sources.

error. This error can arise from either or both of two sources: individual differences between subjects treated alike within groups and experimental error (Gravetter & Wallnau, 1990). Take note that variability caused by your treatment effects is unique to the between-groups variability.

The F-ratio. The statistic used in ANOVA to determine statistical significance is the **F-ratio**. The F-ratio is simply the ratio of between-groups variability to within-groups variability. Both types of variability constituting the ratio are expressed as variances. (Chapter 11 described the variance as a measure of variability.) However, statisticians perversely insist on calling the variance the *mean square*, perhaps because the term is more descriptive. Just as with the t statistic, once you have obtained your F-ratio, you compare it against a table of critical values to determine whether your results are statistically significant.

The One-Factor Between-Subjects ANOVA

The one-factor between-subjects ANOVA is used when your experiment includes only one factor (with more than two levels) and has different subjects in each experimental condition. As an example, imagine you have conducted an experiment on how well subjects can detect a signal against a background of noise. Subjects were exposed to different levels of background noise (no noise, 20 decibels, or 40 decibels) and asked to indicate whether or not they heard a tone. The number of times the subject correctly stated that a tone was present represented your dependent variable. You found subjects in the no-noise group detected more of the tones (36.4) than subjects in either the 20-decibel (23.8) or 40-decibel (16.0) groups. Table 12-3 shows the distributions for the three groups.

Table 12-3. Data from Hypothetical Signal Detection Study

	No Noise	20 Decibels	40 Decibels
	33	22	17
	39	24	14
	41	25	19
	32	21	11
	37	27	19
ΣX	182	119	80
ΣX^2	6,684	2,855	1,328
M	36.4	23.8	16.0

Submitting your data to a one-factor between-subjects ANOVA, you obtain an F-ratio of 48.91 (the computational formulas and calculations for this example are found in Appendix II). This F-ratio is now compared to the appropriate critical value of F in Tables I-3A and B in Appendix I. To find the critical value, you need to use the degrees of freedom for both the numerator ($a - 1$, where a is the number of groups) *and* denominator ($a[s - 1]$), where s is the number of subjects in each group) of your F-ratio. In this case the degrees of freedom for the numerator and denominator are 2 and 12, respectively.

To identify the appropriate critical value for F (at $p = 0.05$), first locate the appropriate degrees of freedom for the numerator across the top of Table I-3A. Then read down the left-hand column to find the degrees of freedom for the denominator. In this example, the critical value for $F(2,12)$, at $p = 0.05$ is 3.89. Since your obtained F-ratio is greater than the tabled value, you have an effect significant at $p = 0.05$. In fact, if you look at the critical value for $F(2,12)$ at $p = 0.01$ (found in Table I-3B) you will find your obtained F-ratio is also significant at $p = 0.01$.

When you report a significant effect, typically you express it in terms of a **p-value**. *Alpha* refers to the cutoff point you adopt. In contrast, the p-value refers to the actual probability of making a type I error. Hence, for this example you would report that your finding was significant at $p < 0.05$ or $p < 0.01$. The discussion in the following sections assumes the "$p <$" notation.

Sometimes the table of the critical values of F does not list the exact degrees of freedom for your denominator. If this happens, you find a table that does. If this is not possible, you may use a statistical calculator to compute the critical value of F with given degrees of freedom. Failing that, you can approximate the critical value of F by choosing the next lowest degrees of freedom for denominator in the table. Choosing this lower value provides a more conservative test of your *F*-ratio.

Interpreting Your F-ratio. A significant *F*-ratio tells you that at least some of the differences among your means are probably not caused by chance, but rather by variation in your independent variable. The only problem, at this point, is that the *F*-ratio fails to tell you where among the possible comparisons the reliable differences actually occur. To isolate which means differ significantly, you must conduct specific comparisons between pairs of means. These comparisons can be either planned or unplanned.

Planned Comparisons. **Planned comparisons** are used when you have specific pre-experimental hypotheses. For example, you may have hypothesized that the no-noise group would differ from the 40-decibel group, but not from the 20-decibel group. In this case, you would compare the no-noise and 40-decibel groups, and then the no-noise and 20-decibel groups. These comparisons are made using information from your overall ANOVA (see Keppel, 1982). Separate *F*-ratios (each having one degree of freedom) or *t*-tests are computed for each pair of means. The resulting *F*-ratios are then compared to the critical values of *F* in Tables I-3A and B.

You can conduct as many of these planned comparisons as necessary. However, a limited number of such comparisons yield unique information. For example, if you found that the no-noise and 20-decibel groups did not differ significantly and that the 40- and 20-decibel groups did, you have no reason to compare the no-noise and 40-decibel groups. You can logically infer that the no-noise and 40-decibel groups differ significantly. Those comparisons that yield new information are known as *orthogonal comparisons*. Any set of means has $(a - 1)$ orthogonal comparisons, where *a* is the number of treatments.

Planned comparisons can be used in lieu of an overall ANOVA if you have highly specific pre-experimental hypotheses. In this case you would not have the information required to use the given formula for planned comparisons. A simple alternative is to conduct multiple *t*-tests. You should not perform too many of these comparisons, even if the relationships were predicted before you conducted your experiment. Performing multiple tests on the same data increases the probability of making a type I error across comparisons through a process called *probability pyramiding* (discussed later in this chapter).

Unplanned Comparisons. If you do not have a specific pre-experimental hypothesis concerning your results, you must conduct **unplanned comparisons**. Unplanned comparisons are often "fishing expeditions" in which you are simply looking for any differences that might emerge. In experiments with many levels of an independent variable, you may be required to perform a fairly large number of unplanned comparisons to fully analyze the data.

Two types of error must be considered when many comparisons are made: **per-comparison error** and **familywise error**. Per-comparison error is the alpha for each comparison between means. If you set an alpha level of $p = 0.05$, the per-comparison error rate is 0.05. Familywise error rate (Keppel, 1982) takes into account the increasing probability of making at least one type I error as the number of comparisons increases (that is, probability pyramiding). Familywise error can be approximated with the following formula:

$$\alpha_{FW} = c(\alpha)$$

where c is the number of comparisons made and α is your per-comparison error rate (Keppel, 1982).

Special tests can be applied to control familywise error, but it is beyond the scope of this chapter to discuss each of them individually. Table 12-4 lists the tests most often used to control familywise error and gives a brief description of each. For more information about these tests, see Keppel (1982, Chapter 8).

Sample Size

You can still use an ANOVA if your groups contain unequal numbers of subjects, but you must use adjusted computational formulas. The adjustments can take one of two forms, depending on the reasons for unequal within-cell sample sizes.

Unequal sample sizes may simply be a by-product of the way you conducted your experiment. If you conducted your experiment by randomly distributing your materials to a large group, for example, you would not be able to keep the sample sizes equal. In such cases, unequal sample sizes do not result from the properties of your treatment conditions.

Unequal sample sizes may also result from the effects of your treatments. If one of your treatments is painful or stressful, subjects may drop out of your experiment because of the aversive nature of that treatment. Death of animals in a group receiving highly stressful conditions is another example of subject loss related to the experimental manipulations that result in unequal sample sizes.

Unweighted Means Analysis. If you end up with unequal sample sizes for reasons *not* related to the effects of your treatments, one solution is to equalize the groups by randomly discarding the excess data from the larger groups. Even then, discarding data may not be a good idea, especially if the sample sizes are small to begin with. The loss of data inevitably reduces the power of your statistical tests. Rather than dropping data, you could use an unweighted means analysis that involves a minor correction to the ANOVA. This analysis gives each group in your design equal weight in the analysis, despite unequal group sizes.

Weighted Means Analysis. If the inequality in sample sizes was planned or if it resulted as a consequence of your treatments, you should use a *weighted means analysis* (Keppel, 1973). In a weighted means analysis, each group mean is weighted according to the number of subjects in the group. As a result, means

Table 12-4. Comparison of *Post Hoc* Tests

Test	Use	Comments[a]
Scheffe test	To keep familywise error rate constant regardless of the number of comparisons to be made	Very conservative test; Scheffe correction factor corrects for all possible comparisons, even if not all are made
Dunnett test	To contrast several experimental groups with a single control group	Not as conservative as the Scheffe test because only the number of comparisons made is considered in the familywise error rate correction
Tukey test	To hold the familywise error rate constant over an entire set of two-group comparisons	Not as conservative as the Scheffe test for comparisons between pairs of means; less powerful than the Scheffe for more complex comparisons
Newman-Keuls test	To compare all possible pairs of means and control per-comparison error rate	Less conservative than the Tukey test; critical value varies according to the number of comparisons made
Duncan test	To compare all possible pairs of means	Computed in the same way as the Newman-Keuls test; with more than two means to be compared, it is less conservative than the Newman-Keuls
Fisher test	To compare all possible combinations of means	Powerful test that does not overcompensate to control familywise error rate; no special correction factor used; significant overall *F*-ratio justifies comparisons

[a]A conservative test is one with which it is more difficult to achieve statistical significance than with a less conservative test. *Power* refers to the ability of a test to reject the null hypothesis when the null hypothesis is false.

SOURCE: Information in this table was summarized from Keppel (1982, pp. 153–159), Winer (1971), and Pagano (1986).

with higher weightings (those from larger groups) contribute more to the analysis than do means with lower weights. See Keppel (1973, 1982) or Gravetter and Wallnau (1990) for more information about unequal sample size in ANOVA.

The One-Factor Within-Subjects ANOVA

If you used a multilevel within-subjects design in your experiment, the statistical test to use is the *one-factor within-subjects ANOVA*. As in a between-subjects analysis, the between-treatments sum of squares can be affected by the level of the independent variable and by experimental error (Gravetter & Wallnau, 1990). However, unlike the between-subjects case, individual differences no longer contribute to the between-treatments sum of squares since the same subjects are in each experimental treatment group. The within-subjects source of variance(s) can also be partitioned into two factors: variability within a particular treatment (that is, different subjects reacting differently to the same treatment) and experimental error.

The contribution of individual differences is estimated by treating subjects as a factor in the analysis (S). You then subtract S from the usual within-groups variance. This subtraction reduces the amount of error in the denominator of the F-ratio, thus making the F-ratio more sensitive to the effects of the independent variable — a major advantage.

The Latin Square ANOVA. Latin square designs are used to counterbalance the order in which subjects receive treatments in within-subjects experiments (see Chapter 9). The carryover effects contained in the Latin square design tend to inflate the error term used to calculate your F-ratio (Keppel, 1982). Consequently, they must be removed before you calculate F. This is done by treating practice effects as a factor in the analysis and removing their effects from the error term. For more information on the Latin square ANOVA, see Keppel (1982, pp. 385–391).

Interpreting Your F-ratio. A significant overall F-ratio tells you that significant differences exist among your means, but, as usual, it does not tell you where these significant differences occur. To determine which means differ, you must further analyze your data. The tests used to compare your means are similar to those used in the between-subjects analysis. Once again, they can be either planned or unplanned.

The Two-Factor Between-Subjects ANOVA

Chapter 8 discussed the two-factor between-subjects design. In this design, you include two independent variables and randomly assign different subjects to each condition. In addition, you combine independent variables across groups so that you can extract the independent effect of each factor (the main effects) and the combined effect of the two factors (interaction) on the dependent variable. (If

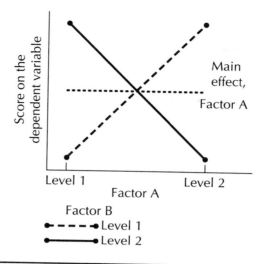

Figure 12-5. Graph showing a two-way interaction that masks main effects.

you are unclear about the meanings of these terms, review Chapter 8.) The analysis appropriate to data from this design is the *two-factor between-subjects ANOVA*. This ANOVA is necessarily more complicated than a one–factor ANOVA because it must determine the statistical significance of both main effects and of their interaction as well.

Main Effects and Interactions. If you find both significant main effects and inter-actions in your experiment, you must be careful about interpreting the main effects. When you interpret a main effect, you are suggesting that your inde-pendent variable has an effect on the dependent variable, regardless of the level of your other independent variable. The presence of an interaction provides evidence to the contrary. The interaction shows that neither of your independent variables has a simple, independent effect. Consequently, you should avoid in-terpreting main effects when an interaction is present.

Another fact to be aware of when dealing with interactions is that certain kinds of interaction can cancel out the main effects. The independent variables may have been effective, and yet the statistical analysis will fail to reveal statis-tically significant main effects for these factors. To see how this can happen, imagine you have conducted a two-factor experiment with two levels of each factor. Figure 12-5 shows the cell means for this hypothetical experiment.

The solid and dashed lines depict the functional relationship between Factor A and the dependent variable at the two levels of Factor B. The fact that the lines form an X indicates the presence of an interaction. Notice, Factor A strongly affects the level of the dependent variable at *both* levels of Factor B, but these effects run in opposite directions.

The dotted line in Figure 12-5 represents the main effect of Factor A, computed by averaging the upper and lower points to collapse across the levels of Factor B. This dotted line is horizontal, indicating that there is no change in the dependent variable across the two levels of Factor A (collapsed over Factor B). Although Factor A has strong effects on the dependent variable at each level of Factor B, its average (main) effect is zero.

Logically, if the interaction of two variables is significant, then the two variables themselves have reliable effects. Consequently, if you have a significant interaction, ignore the main effects. The factors involved in the interaction are reliable whether or not the main effects are statistically significant.

Finally, most of the time you are more interested in the significant interaction than main effects, even before your experiment is conducted. Hypothesized relationships among variables are often stated in terms of interactions. Interactions tend to be inherently more interesting than main effects. They show how changes in one variable alter the effects on behavior of other variables.

Sample Size. Just as with a one-factor ANOVA, you can compute a multifactor ANOVA with unequal sample sizes. The unweighted means analysis can be conducted on a design with two or more factors (the logic is the same). For details on modifications to the basic two-factor ANOVA formulas for weighted means and unweighted means analyses, see Keppel (1973, 1982).

ANOVA for a Two-Factor Between-Subjects Design: An Example. An experiment conducted by Donnerstein and Donnerstein (1973) provided an excellent example of the application of the ANOVA to the analysis of data from a two-factor experiment. Donnerstein and Donnerstein were interested in studying some of the variables mediating interracial aggression. Subjects (all whites) were told that they would be participating in an experiment on learning. They were told that they would have to administer a mild reward each time the "learner" made a correct response and administer punishment (electric shock) each time the learner made a mistake.

In the first of two experiments, Donnerstein and Donnerstein manipulated the race of the learner (black or white). They also manipulated the extent to which subjects believed that their behavior would be censured. In a high-censure condition, subjects were told that their responses were being recorded on videotape. In a low-censure condition, no mention was made of videotaping the responses. The dependent variable analyzed with a 2×2 ANOVA was a composite of shock intensity, shock duration, and the sum of the high-shock intensities. The results of the ANOVA revealed a main effect of potential censure, $F(1,32) = 10.49$, $p < 0.01$, and a significant interaction between the race of the learner and potential censure, $F(1,32) = 6.81$, $p < 0.05$.

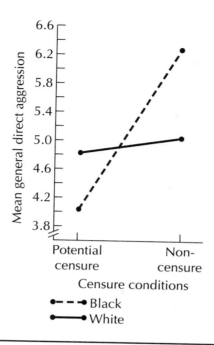

Figure 12-6 Graph showing interaction between race of learner and censure condition (Donnerstein & Donnerstein, 1973). Reprinted with permission.

Interpreting the Results. This example shows how to interpret the results from a two-factor ANOVA. First, consider the two main effects. There was a significant effect of potential censure on aggression. Subjects in the censure condition were more aggressive than subjects in the noncensure condition. If this were the only significant effect, you could then conclude that race of the learner had no effect on aggression because the main effect of race was not statistically significant. However, this conclusion is not warranted, because of the presence of a significant interaction between race of learner and censure.

The presence of a significant interaction suggests that the relationship between your independent variables and your dependent variable is complex. Figure 12-6 shows the data contributing to the significant interaction in the Donnerstein and Donnerstein experiment. Analyzing a significant interaction like this one involves making comparisons among the means involved.

Because Donnerstein and Donnerstein predicted the interaction, they used planned comparisons (*t*-tests) to contrast the relevant means. The results showed a black learner received significantly *less* punishment than a white learner when the potential for censure existed, $t(32) = 5.92$, $p < 0.01$. Conversely, when no potential for censure existed, the black learner received *more* punishment than the white learner, $t(32) = 2.38$, $p < 0.05$. The conclusion that race did not affect aggression must be discarded. In fact, race does affect aggression, but only when the other independent variable is considered.

The Two-Factor Within-Subjects ANOVA

All subjects in a within-subjects design with two factors are exposed to every possible combination of levels of your two independent variables. These designs are analyzed using a *two-factor within-subjects ANOVA*. This analysis applies the same logic developed for the one-factor within-subjects ANOVA. As in the one-factor case, subjects are treated as a factor along with your manipulated independent variables.

The major difference between the one-factor and two-factor within-subject ANOVA is that you must consider the interaction between each of your independent variables and the subjects factor (A × S and B × S) in addition to the interaction between your independent variables (A × B). Because the basic logic and interpretation of results from a within-subjects ANOVA are essentially the same as for the between-subjects ANOVA, a complete example is not given here. A complete example of the two-factor within-subjects ANOVA can be found in Keppel (1973).

Mixed Designs

In some situations, your research may call for a design mixing between-subjects and within-subjects components. This design was discussed briefly in Chapter 8. If you use such a design (known as a *mixed* or *split plot* design) you can analyze your data with an ANOVA. The computations involve calculating sums of squares for the between factor and for the within factor.

The most complex part of the analysis is the selection of an error term to calculate the *F*-ratios. The within-groups mean square is used to calculate the between-subjects *F*, whereas the interaction of the within factor with the within-groups variance is used to evaluate both the within-subjects factor and the interaction between the within-subject and between-subject factors. Keppel (1973, 1982) provides an excellent discussion of this analysis and a complete worked example.

Higher-Order and Special Case ANOVAs

There are variations of ANOVA for just about any design used in research. For example, you can include three or four factors in a single experiment and analyze the data with a *higher-order ANOVA*. In a three-factor ANOVA, for example, you are able to test three main effects (A, B, and C), three two-way interactions

(AB, AC, and BC), and a three-way interaction (ABC). As you add factors, however, the computations become more complex and probably should not be done by hand. In addition, as discussed in Chapter 8, it may be difficult to interpret the higher-order interactions with more than four factors.

A special ANOVA is used when you have included a correlational variable in your experiment (such as age, sex, or a personality factor). This type of ANOVA, called the *analysis of covariance (ANCOVA),* allows you to examine the relationship between experimentally manipulated variables while controlling another variable that may be correlated with them. Keppel (1973, 1982) provides clear discussions of these analyses and other issues relating to ANCOVA.

To summarize, ANOVA is a powerful parametric statistic used to analyze one-factor experiments (either within subjects or between subjects) with more than two treatments, and to analyze multifactor experiments. It is intended for use when your dependent variable is scaled on at least an interval scale. The assumptions that apply to the use of parametric statistics in general (such as homogeneity of variance and normally distributed sampling distribution) apply to ANOVA.

ANOVA involves forming a ratio between the variance (mean square) caused by your independent variable and the variance (mean square) caused by experimental error. The resulting score is called an *F*-ratio. A significant *F*-ratio tells you that at least one of your means differs from the other means. Once a significant effect is found, you then perform more detailed analyses of the means contributing to the significant effect in order to determine where the significant differences occur. These tests become more complicated as the design of your experiment becomes more complex.

Nonparametric Statistics

Thus far, this discussion has centered on parametric statistical tests. In some situations, however, you may not be able to use a parametric test. When your data do not meet the assumptions of a parametric test, or when your dependent variable was scaled on a nominal or ordinal scale, consider a nonparametric test. This section discusses two nonparametric tests: chi-square and the Mann–Whitney *U*-test. You might consider using many other nonparametric tests. For a complete description of these, see Siegel and Castellan (1988). Table 12-5 summarizes some information on these and other nonparametric tests.

Chi-Square

When your dependent variable is a dichotomous decision (such as yes/no or guilty/not guilty) or a frequency count (such as how many people voted for Candidate A and how many for Candidate B), the statistic of choice is **chi-square** (χ^2). Versions of chi-square exist for studies with one and two variables.

Table 12-5. Nonparametric Tests

Test	Minimum Scale of Measurement	Comments
One-Sample Tests		
Binomial	Nominal	
Chi–square	Nominal	
Kolmogorov-Smirnov	Ordinal	Can be used as a more powerful alternative to chi-square
Two Independent Samples		
Chi–square	Nominal	
Fisher exact probability	Nominal	Alternative to chi-square when expected frequencies are small
Kolmogorov-Smirnov	Ordinal	More powerful than the Mann-Whitney U-test
Wald-Wolfowitz runs	Ordinal	
Moses test of extreme reactions	Ordinal	Less powerful than Mann-Whitney U-test
Randomization test	Interval	Tests the difference between means without assuming normality of data or homogeneity of variance
Two Related Samples		
McNemar	Nominal	Good test when you have a before-after hypothesis
Sign	Ordinal	Good when quantitative measures are not possible, but you can rank data
Wilcoxon matched pairs	Ordinal	Good alternative to t-test when normality assumption is violated
Walsh test	Interval	Good nonparametric alternative to the t-test; data must be distributed symmetrically
Randomization test for matched pairs	Interval	

Table 12-5. Nonparametric Tests *(Continued)*

Test	Minimum Scale of Measurement	Comments
More Than Two Related Samples		
Cochran Q-test	Nominal	Most useful when data fall into natural dichotomous categories
Friedman two-way ANOVA	Ordinal	
More Than Two Independent Samples		
Chi-square	Nominal	
Kruskal-Wallis one-way ANOVA	Ordinal	Good alternative to a one-factor ANOVA when assumptions are violated

SOURCE: Data from Siegel & Castellan, 1988, and Roscoe, 1975.

This discussion is limited to the two-variable case. For further information on the one-variable analysis, see either Siegel and Castellan (1988) or Roscoe (1975).

Chi-Square for Contingency Tables. Chi-square for contingency tables is designed for frequency data in which the relationship, or contingency, between two variables is to be determined. In a voter preference study, for example, you might have measured sex of respondent in addition to candidate preference. You may want to know whether the two variables are related or independent. The chi-square test for contingency tables compares your *observed cell frequencies* (those you obtained in your study) with the *expected cell frequencies* (those you would expect to find if chance alone were operating).

A study reported by Harari, Harari, and White (1985) provided an excellent example of the application of the chi-square test to the analysis of frequency data. Harari et al. investigated whether male subjects would help the victim of a simulated rape. Previous research on helping behavior suggested individuals are less likely to help someone in distress if they are with others than if they are alone. Harari et al. conducted a field investigation of this effect. Subjects (either walking alone or in noninteracting groups) were exposed to a mock rape (a male confederate of the experimenters grabs a female confederate and drags her into some bushes). Observers recorded how many subjects helped the female rape victim. Table 12-6 shows the frequencies of subjects helping under the two conditions. The results from a chi-square test performed on these data showed a significant relationship between the decision to offer help and whether subjects

Table 12-6. Number of Subjects Helping Mock Rape Victim, in Two Conditions

	Intervened	Did Not Intervene	
Subjects in Groups	34	6	40
Subjects Alone	26	14	50
	60	20	

SOURCE: Data from Harari, Harari, & White, 1985.

were alone or in groups. Subjects in groups were actually more likely to help than subjects who were alone.

Limitations of Chi-Square. A problem arises if any of your expected cell frequencies is less than five. In such cases the value of chi-square may be artificially inflated (Gravetter & Wallnau, 1990). You have three options to deal with this problem. First, you could include more subjects to increase your sample size. Second, you could combine cells (if it is logical to do so). For example, you could categorize subjects into three categories rather than five. Third, you could consider a different test. The Fisher Exact Probability Test (see Roscoe, 1975, or Siegel & Castellan, 1988) is an alternative to chi-square when you have small expected frequencies and a 2×2 contingency table (Roscoe, 1975).

A significant chi-square tells you that your two variables are significantly related. In the previous example, all you know is that group size and helping are related. As with ANOVA, however, chi-square does not tell you where the significant differences occur when more than two categories of each variable exist. To determine the locus of the significant effects, you can conduct separate chi-square tests on specific cells of the contingency table.

The Mann-Whitney U-Test

Another powerful nonparametric test is the **Mann-Whitney U-test**. The Mann-Whitney U-test can be used when your dependent variable is scaled on at least an ordinal scale. It is also a good alternative to the *t*-test when your data do not meet the assumptions of the *t*-test (such as when the scores are not normally distributed, when the variances are heterogeneous, or when you have small sample sizes).

Calculation of the Mann-Whitney U-test is fairly simple. The first step is to combine the data from your two groups. Scores are ranked (from highest to lowest) and labeled according to the group to which they belong. If there is a difference between your groups, then the ranks for the scores in one group should be consistently above the ranks from the other group, rather than being randomly distributed. A U-score is calculated for each group in your experiment. The lower of the two U-scores obtained is then evaluated against critical values of U. If the lower of the two U-scores is *smaller* than the tabled U-value, you then conclude your two groups differ significantly.

Parametric Versus Nonparametric Statistics

Nonparametric statistics are useful when your data do not meet the assumptions of parametric statistics. If you have a choice, choose a parametric statistic over a nonparametric one because parametric statistics are generally more powerful. That is, the parametric statistic usually provides a more sensitive test of the null hypothesis than does an equivalent nonparametric statistic.

A second problem with nonparametric statistics is they are not easily applied to complex experiments. For example, although it is possible to calculate a chi-square in a three-factor design, it is difficult. The analysis of variance is much more easily applied to higher-order factorial designs. Consequently, when designing your study you should try to scale your dependent measures so an ANOVA or other suitable parametric statistic can be used.

Special Topics in Inferential Statistics

The application of the appropriate inferential statistic may appear simple and straightforward. However, several factors must be considered, beyond whether to apply a parametric or nonparametric statistic, when using any inferential statistic. This section discusses some special topics to consider when deciding on a strategy to statistically evaluate data.

Power of a Statistical Test

Inferential statistics are designed to help you determine the validity of the null hypothesis. Consequently, you want your statistics to detect differences in your data that are inconsistent with the null hypothesis. The **power** of a statistical test is its ability to detect these differences. Put in statistical terms, power is a statistic's ability to correctly reject the null hypothesis (Gravetter & Wallnau, 1990). A powerful statistic is more sensitive than a less powerful one to differences in your data.

The issue of the power of your statistical test is an important one. Rejection of the null hypothesis implies that your independent variable affected your dependent variable. Failure to reject the null hypothesis may lead you to abandon a potentially fruitful line of research. Consequently, you want to be reasonably sure your failure to reject the null hypothesis is not caused by a lack of power in your statistical test.

The power of your statistical test is affected by your chosen alpha level, the size of your sample, and whether you use a one-tailed or two-tailed test (Gravetter & Wallnau, 1990).

Alpha Level. As you reduce your alpha level (for example, from 0.05 to 0.01), you reduce the probability of making a type I error. Adopting a more conservative alpha level makes it more difficult to reject the null hypothesis. Unfortunately, it also reduces power. Given a constant error variance, a larger difference between means is required to obtain statistical significance with a more conservative alpha level.

Sample Size. The power of your statistical test increases with the size of your sample because larger samples provide more stable estimates of population parameters. In particular, the standard error of the means from your treatments will be lower, so the likely positions of the population means fall within narrower bounds. Consequently it is easier to detect small differences in population means and thus to reject the null hypothesis when it is false.

One-Tailed Versus Two-Tailed Tests. A two-tailed test is less powerful than a one-tailed test. This can be easily demonstrated by looking at the critical values of t found in Table I-2. At 20 degrees of freedom, the critical value at $p = 0.05$ for a one-tailed test is 1.73. For a two-tailed test, the critical value is 2.09. It is thus easier to reject the null hypothesis with the one-tailed test than with the two-tailed test.

Because the business of inferential statistics is to allow you to decide whether or not to reject the null hypothesis, the issue of power is important. You want to be reasonably sure that your decision is correct. Failure to achieve statistical significance in your experiment (thus not rejecting the null hypothesis) can be caused by many factors. Your independent variable actually may have no effect, or your experiment may have been carried out so poorly that the effect was buried in error variance. Or maybe your statistic simply was not powerful enough to detect the difference, or you did not use enough subjects.

Although alpha (the probability of rejecting the null hypothesis when it is true) can be set directly, it is not so easy to determine what the power of your analysis will be. However, you can work backward from a desired amount of power to estimate the sample sizes required for a study. To calculate these estimates, you must be willing to state the amount of power required, the magnitude of the difference you expect to find in your experiment, and the expected error variance.

The expected difference between means and the expected error variance can be estimated from pilot research, from theory, or from previous research in your area. For example, if previous research has found a small effect of your independent variable (for example, two points) you can use this as an estimate of the size of your effect.

Unfortunately, the proper amount of power is not easy to establish. There is no agreed-on acceptable or desirable level of power (Keppel, 1982). If you are willing and able to specify the values mentioned, however, you can estimate the size of the sample needed to detect differences of a given magnitude in your research. (See Gravetter & Wallnau, 1990, or Keppel, 1982, for a discussion on how to calculate sample size.)

Too much power can be as bad as too little. If you ran enough subjects, you could conceivably find statistical significance in even the most minute and trivial of differences. Similarly, when you use a correlation you can achieve statistical significance if you include enough subjects. Consequently, your sample should be large enough to be sensitive to differences between treatments, but not so large as to produce significant but trivial results.

The possibility of your results being statistically significant and yet trivial may seem strange to you. If so, the next section may clarify this concept.

Statistical Versus Practical Significance

To say results are significant (statistically speaking) merely indicates that the observed differences between sample means are probably reliable, not the result of chance. Confusion arises when you give the word *significant* its more common meaning. Something "significant" in this more common sense is important or worthy of note.

The fact that the treatment means of your experiment differ significantly may or may not be important. If the difference is predicted by a particular theory and not by others, then the finding may be important because it supports the theory over the others. The finding may also be important if it shows one variable strongly affects another. Such findings may have practical implications by demonstrating, for example, the superiority of a new therapeutic technique. In such cases, a statistically significant (that is, reliable) finding may also have *practical significance*.

Advertisers sometimes purposely blur the distinction between statistical and practical significance. A few years ago, Bayer Aspirin announced the results of a "hospital study on pain other than headache." Evidently groups of hospital patients were treated with Bayer Aspirin and with several other brands. The advertisement glossed over the details of the study, but apparently the patients were asked to rate the severity of their pain at some point after taking Bayer or Brand X (the identities of both brands were probably concealed). According to the ad, "the results were significant — Bayer was better."

But the ad did not say in what way the results were significant. Evidently the results were statistically significant, and thus probably not caused by chance. But without any information about the pain ratings, you do not know if this finding has any practical significance. It may be that the Bayer and Brand X group ratings differed by less than one point on a ten-point scale. Although this average difference may have been reliable, it may also be the case that no individual could tell the difference between two pains so close together on the scale. In that case, the statistically significant difference would have no practical significance, and would provide no reason for choosing Bayer over other brands of aspirin.

The Meaning of the Level of Significance

In the behavioral sciences, an alpha level of 0.05 (or 1 chance in 20), is usually considered the maximum acceptable rate for type I errors. This level provides reasonable protection against type I errors while also maintaining a reasonable level of power for most analyses. Of course, if you want to guard more strongly against type I errors, you can adopt a more stringent alpha level, such as the 0.01 level (1 chance in 100).

Whatever alpha level you determine is reasonable for your purposes, remember this number does nothing more than provide a criterion for deciding whether the differences you have obtained are reliable. A difference is either reliable or it is not. If your results are significant at the 0.0001 level, they are not any more reliable than if they were significant at the 0.05 level. It does not mean your results are "more significant" or "more reliable" than significant results obtained at the 0.05 level. If the results are statistically significant at your chosen alpha level, it simply means you are willing to believe that the differences are real. However, lower alpha levels (moving from 0.05 to 0.01) allow you to have greater confidence in your decision about your results.

The importance of type I errors may vary depending on the type of research and the purposes to which the information may be put. For example, applied research may be better evaluated at a less conservative alpha level (for example, $p < 0.10$). If you were testing the effectiveness of a new form of judicial instructions on the reduction of bias against black defendants, a type II error might be more serious than a type I error. If you retain the null hypothesis when it is false, more black defendants may be convicted as a result.

Ultimately, it is up to you to decide on an appropriate balance between type I and type II errors. Unfortunately, most journals will not publish a finding unless it is significant at least at the $p < 0.05$ level. Chapter 17 examines this issue during the discussion of publication practices.

Data Transformations

Sometimes you may find it necessary to transform your data with the appropriate **data transformation**. Transforming data means converting your original data to a new scale. For example, a simple transformation can be accomplished by adding or subtracting a constant to or from your data. You might do this if the original numbers are very large. When you compute some statistics, large numbers make the computations difficult. Subtracting a constant from each

Table 12-7. Data Transformations and Uses

Transformation	Formula	Use
Square Root	$X' = \sqrt{X}$ or $X' = \sqrt{X + 1}$ [a]	When cell means and variances are related, this transformation makes variances more homogeneous; also, if data show a moderate positive skew
Arcsin	$X' = 2\,\text{arcsin}\,\sqrt{X}$ or $X' = 2\,\text{arcsin}\,\sqrt{X \pm (1/2n)}$ [b]	When basic observations are proportions and have a binomial distribution
Log	$X' = \text{Log}\,X$ or $X' = \text{Log}\,(X + 1)$ [c]	Normalizes data with severe positive skew

[a] Formula used if basic observations are frequencies or if values of X are small.
[b] Formula used if values of X are close to 0 or 1.
[c] Formula used if value of X is equal to or near 0.

SOURCE: Information summarized from Winer, 1971, and Tabachnick & Fidell, 1989.

score can make the numbers manageable without affecting the relationships within the data. Conversely, adding a constant to each score might remove negative numbers.

When you add or subtract a constant (or multiply or divide by a constant), the shape of the original frequency distribution does not change. The value of the mean of the distribution changes, but its standard deviation does not. Such transformations are called *linear transformations*. A linear transformation simply changes the magnitude of the numbers representing your data, but does not change the scale of measurement.

Certain statistics can only be used if your data meet certain assumptions. If your data do not meet these assumptions, you could choose a different statistic. Unfortunately, this is not always desirable or possible. A nonparametric statistic that can be substituted for a parametric statistic may not exist for your experimental situation. Another solution is to consider using a data transformation that will tend to correct the problem (for example, by changing a skewed distribution of scores into a normal one or by removing inhomogeneities in variance). Different problems with the data require different transformations to correct them. Table 12-7 lists some of the more popular data transformations and the conditions under which each might be used.

Data transformations to make data conform to the assumptions of a statistic are being used less and less frequently (Keppel, 1973). ANOVA, perhaps the most commonly used inferential statistic, appears to be very robust against even moderately serious violations of its assumptions underlying the test. For example, Winer (1971) has demonstrated that even if the within-cell variances vary by a 3:1 ratio, the F-test is not seriously biased. Transformations of the data may not be necessary in these cases.

Also, when you transform your data, your conclusions must be based on the transformed scale and not the original. In most cases, this is not a problem. However, Keppel (1973) provides an example in which a square-root transformation changed significantly the relationship between two means. Prior to transformation, the mean for group 1 was lower than the mean for group 2. The opposite was true after transformation.

Use data transformations only when absolutely necessary, because they can be tricky. Sometimes transformations of data correct one aspect of the data (such as restoring normality) but induce new violations of assumptions (such as heterogeneity of variance). If you must use a data transformation, before going forward with your analysis check to be sure that the transformation had the intended effect.

Alternatives to Inferential Statistics

Inferential statistics are tools to help you make a decision about the null hypothesis. Essentially, inferential statistics provide you with a way to test the reliability of a single experiment. When you reject the null hypothesis at $p < 0.05$, it means a difference (as large as or larger than the one obtained) caused by chance would occur only once (on the average) in 20 replications of the experiment.

Because such chance differences are relatively rare, you conclude that the difference you obtained was probably not caused by chance, but rather by the effect of the independent variable. If, in fact, the independent variable was the cause of the observed differences, then you would expect to obtain similar results on replication of the experiment. In other words, you would expect your findings to be reliable.

Inferential statistics cannot always be applied to assess the reliability of your results. You may have too few subjects (such as in single-subject or small-n research designs). Or you may have data that badly violate the assumptions of parametric tests with no appropriate nonparametric statistic to use instead. In these cases you may test the reliability of your data by replication.

Replication means that you repeat your experiment. If your data are reliable, you should find a highly similar pattern of results after each replication. Replication does not mean that you have to conduct exactly the same experiment each time. Often a subsequent experiment in a series will include conditions that replicate those of the original experiment. The subsequent experiment may include conditions designed to test the effects of changing some parameters within the original context. The new experiment will provide a check on the original findings while providing new information.

Keep in mind that replication is not limited to small-n designs or situations in which violations of assumptions occur. You can include an element of replication in just about any study. Moreover, you need not limit yourself to replicating your own findings. If you are conducting research where previous research shows a certain effect, you may wish to replicate the original finding before extending your observations to new situations. Indeed, such replications are the heart of the scientific method. When successful, they demonstrate the reliability of findings both within the original context and across experimenters, subjects, and laboratories. When unsuccessful, they point to potentially important variables that may limit the generality of findings to particular situations and parameters. Either result can be important for the advancement of scientific knowledge.

Inferential statistics were developed to assess the reliability of findings within the confines of a single set of observations. By providing an index of probable reliability, they reduce the need for direct replication and thus save time and money by reducing the requirement for subjects. Nevertheless, they should not be viewed as a substitute for replication. Probably no finding in psychology has been accepted on the basis of a single experiment that was statistically significant at some alpha level. The value of inferential statistics is found not so much in the elimination of replication as in their warning that the effects apparent in research data may result from nothing more than random factors. Human beings are extremely good at recognizing patterns, even when such patterns are simply the result of "noise." Inferential statistics can control the human tendency to interpret every apparent trend or difference in the data as if it were meaningful.

Inferential statistics may sometimes lack sufficient power, and may therefore fail to detect effects that are clearly shown by replication. A case in point is provided by a series of experiments conducted by one of the authors of this text (Abbott) to test the effect of predictable versus unpredictable stress schedules on pain sensitivity. In each experiment, three groups of eight rats were exposed to a schedule of predictable stress, unpredictable stress, or no stress. The subjects were then tested in the same apparatus for pain sensitivity by means of the "tail flick" test. In the tail flick test, a hot beam of light was focused on the rat's tail. The length of time elapsing until the rat flicked its tail out of the beam (a protective reflex) indicated the degree of pain sensitivity.

The results of the first experiment indicated that the two groups exposed to stress were less sensitive to the heat than the group exposed to no stress, replicating a well-established finding. In addition, the group exposed to unpredictable stress seemed to be less sensitive than the group exposed to predictable stress. However, this effect was not statistically significant ($p > 0.05$).

Parameters of the experiment were twice altered in ways that were expected to increase the size of the predictability effect (if it existed) and the experiment was replicated. But each replication produced virtually the identical result. On each occasion, the unpredictable stress group demonstrated less sensitivity to pain than the predictable stress group, and each time this difference was not statistically significant.

The problem could be dealt with by taking measures to increase the power of the statistical test (such as increasing sample sizes or going to a matched groups design). However, to do so would appear to be a waste of resources. In this case the reliability of the finding was already established through replication, even though the statistical analysis itself indicated that the results were probably not reliable.

Inferential statistics are simply a guide to decision making and are not the goal of the research project. As such, you should not design and conduct your research in a particular way simply because a particular inferential statistic is available to analyze such a design. Much like designing your experiment before developing hypotheses, choosing a statistical test before designing a study can place unwanted restrictions on your research. For example, you may not be able to manipulate your independent variable the way you would like and may miss some important relationships. Instead, design your study to answer your research questions in the clearest way possible, and then select the method of analysis (whether inferential statistic or replication) that works best for that design.

Summary

This chapter has reviewed some of the basics of inferential statistics. Inferential statistics go beyond simple description of results. They allow you to determine whether the differences observed in your sample are reliable. Inferential statistics allow you to make a decision about the viability of the null hypothesis (which states that there is no difference among treatments) while controlling the probability of rejecting the null hypothesis when it is, in fact, true (type I error). The two types of inferential statistics are parametric and nonparametric. Parametric tests (such as the t-test and ANOVA) make assumptions about the populations underlying your samples. For example, these tests assume that the sampling distribution of means is normal and that there is homogeneity of within-cell variances. Parametric statistics are designed for use when your data are scaled on at least an interval scale. If your data seriously violate the assumptions of a parametric test, or your data are scaled on a nominal or ordinal scale, a nonparametric statistic can be used (such as chi-square or the Mann-Whitney U-test). These tests are usually easier to compute than parametric tests. However, they are less powerful and more limited in application. Nonparametric statistics may not be available for higher-order factorial designs.

Statistical significance indicates that the difference between your means was probably not caused by chance. It suggests that your independent variable had an effect. Two factors contribute to a statistically significant effect: the size of the difference between means and the variability among the scores. You can have a large difference between means, but if the variability is high, you may not find statistical significance. Conversely, you may have a very small difference and find a significant effect if the variability is low.

Consider the power of your statistical test when evaluating your results. If you do not find statistical significance, perhaps no differences exist. Or it could mean that your test was not sensitive enough to pick up small differences that do exist. Sample size is an important contributor to power. Generally, the larger the sample the more powerful the statistic. This is because larger samples are more representative of the underlying populations than are small samples. Use a sample that is large enough to be sensitive to differences, but not so large as to be oversensitive. There are methods for determining optimal sample sizes for a given level of power. However, you must be willing and able to specify an expected magnitude of the treatment effect, an estimate of error variance, and the desired power. The first two can be estimated from pilot data or previous research. Unfortunately, there is no agreed-on acceptable level of power.

An alpha level of 0.05 is the largest generally acceptable level for type I errors. This value has been chosen because it represents a reasonable compromise between type I and type II errors. In some cases (such as in applied research), the 0.05 level may be too conservative. However, journals probably will not publish results that fail to reach the conventional level of significance.

Data transformations are available for those situations in which your data are in some way abnormal. You may transform data if the numbers are large and unmanageable, or if your data do not meet the assumptions of a statistical test. The transformation of data to meet assumptions of a test, however, is being done less frequently because inferential statistics tend to be robust against the effects of even moderately severe violations of assumptions. Transformations should be used sparingly, because they may change the conclusions of your study.

Key Terms

Inferential statistics

Standard error of the mean

Degrees of freedom

Type I error

Type II error

Alpha level

Critical region

t-test for independent samples

t-test for correlated samples

z-test for the difference between two proportions

Analysis of variance (ANOVA)

F-ratio

p-value

Planned comparisons

Unplanned comparisons

Per-comparison error

Familywise error

Chi-square

Mann-Whitney U-test

Power

Data transformation

13

Using the Computer to Analyze Data

ANALYZING YOUR DATA BY HAND CAN BE tedious and difficult work. Even a simple analysis for a two-group design may require you to calculate the means, standard deviations, and standard errors of the mean for the two groups, the difference between the two means, the standard error of the difference, and Student's t. The calculations required for more complex designs can be truly mind-boggling. Worse, a small error early in the calculations can invalidate the whole analysis. Stuck with the task of performing a three-factor analysis of variance, complete with orthogonal comparisons and *post hoc* tests, even the most dedicated researcher would begin to dream wistfully about a change of career. Then came salvation, in the form of the digital computer and statistical software.

This chapter describes using the computer to analyze your data: the advantages and disadvantages of computer data analysis, the general steps to follow, and examples of computer data analysis using several popular statistical analysis software packages running on personal computers or on the larger, more powerful minicomputers and mainframes. Our aim is not to make you a proficient user of a particular statistical package, but rather to show you how you might go about doing an analysis by computer. Once familiar with the general steps involved, you will be in a better position to learn to use the specific packages available to you.

Statistical Analysis on Computers

Doing your statistical analysis on the computer can make complex analyses relatively easy to perform, but it can also make simple analyses difficult to perform (especially compared to doing them on some of the current hand-held calculators with built-in statistical functions). In addition, personal and mainframe computers offer different sets of advantages and disadvantages for conducting your analysis.

Advantages of Computerized Data Analysis

Tireless, accurate, lightning fast, and incapable of boredom, computers are perfectly suited to doing statistical analysis of your research data. In a matter of seconds or minutes, they can perform complex statistical computations that would have taken you several hours to compute by hand. The calculations are carried out to more decimal places than you would probably use (generally eight or more), yielding greater accuracy in the results. Finally, the flexibility of the computer allows you to rapidly analyze your data in several ways. You do so simply by including new commands or modifying old ones between each analysis. For example, you might initially analyze data from a two-factor, between-subjects experiment using a two-factor, between-subjects ANOVA. On finding no significant main effect for one factor, you might decide to collapse the data across the nonsignificant factor and reanalyze the data using a one-way (single-factor) ANOVA. Try doing *that* by hand!

Disadvantages of Computerized Data Analysis

As wonderful as computers can be for data analysis, they are not without their disadvantages and limitations. First, the statistical package you choose may not provide the specific analysis you need. If the package does not include a certain analysis, you may have to forgo the analysis, look for a package that has the desired analysis, write your own program to conduct the analysis, or (heaven forbid!) perform the analysis by hand. For example, Version 9 of SPSS (one of the more popular programs) used a weighted means analysis when conducting an ANOVA with unequal sample sizes. If you wanted to perform an unweighted means analysis, you had to use a different package, requiring you to learn a new set of commands and reenter your data. This could be frustrating and time-consuming.

The ease with which a computer performs analyses leads to a second potential problem. Although this ease is an advantage, it may tempt you to use a statistic you do not fully understand. If you simply enter numbers blindly and obtain your output, you may lose sight of what the statistic does. Consequently, you may misinterpret your results. Become thoroughly familiar with a statistical analysis before you attempt to interpret the results provided by the computer.

A third problem with computer data analysis is that the computer will perform all the calculations you specify, whether suited to your data or not. It will analyze garbage if you ask it to. You must ensure that your data are correctly entered, that they meet the underlying assumptions and requirements of the tests you are planning to request, and that you are requesting the proper tests.

Another problem has to do with the quality of the software you are using. A recent review of several commercial statistical packages found errors in some of the programs. Programmers are human; like the rest of us, they sometimes make mistakes. Because of the large number of users, errors in the more popular packages are usually discovered quickly and corrected. Errors in less popular packages may not be noticed for years. Do not automatically assume that the software you are using gives accurate results. A good idea is to test new software with a set of data for which you have known results. For example, LabStat (the statistical package provided to instructors who adopt this text) was checked by comparing its results against those provided by SPSS-X.

Finally, learning to use a computer and the statistical programs needed to analyze your data may be time-consuming. If you need only a simple analysis, you may find that using a computer is overkill. However, for more complex analyses it can be invaluable. In the long run, learning to use a statistical package, even for relatively simple analyses, will be worth the time you invest.

Personal Computers Versus Minicomputers and Mainframes

Until recently, statistical analysis could be done only on minicomputers and mainframe computers, which had the memory capacity and processing speeds necessary to compute complex statistics rapidly. Small, powerful personal computers, such as the Apple Macintosh and the IBM PC and PS-2, are now also able to handle complex statistical analyses with reasonable speed, and statistical software has been developed to take advantage of this capability. However, personal computers and their larger cousins offer a somewhat different mix of abilities and liabilities.

Statistical Analysis on the Personal Computer. A wide range of statistical packages is available for the personal computer (PC), including versions of several popular mainframe packages (for example, SPSS, BMD-P, and SAS). However, these PC-based packages process data more slowly than their mainframe parents and do not offer all the options available on the mainframe. They also tend to be expensive — some cost almost $1,500 for full versions, although less capable student versions may be available at a reduced price.

Other packages have been designed specifically for the PC. CSS-Statsoft, for example, offers all the popular basic statistics (such as *t*-test, ANOVA, and chi-square) as well as advanced statistics (MANOVA, loglinear analysis, and multiple regression). These packages are usually less expensive than those adapted from mainframe packages.

The primary advantage of PC-based programs is convenience. If you have a PC, you can conduct your analyses at your leisure. You do not have to wait for the computer center to open or for a terminal to become available. However, there are tradeoffs. PC-based packages process data more slowly and may not be able to handle large sets of data. For sophisticated analyses of large data bases, the mainframe or minicomputer packages may be better choices. In addition, PC-based packages usually offer a narrower range of data analysis options.

Statistical Analysis on the Minicomputer and Mainframe. The most sophisticated and powerful statistical analysis packages remain those available for the mainframe and minicomputers, including SPSS-X, BMD-P, and SAS. The primary advantages of these packages are speed of processing data, flexibility, and the range of statistical tests available. On the negative side, these programs are complex and often require you to familiarize yourself with special programming languages and procedures. They can be difficult to master, especially if you want to make use of specialized functions. Also, access to a mainframe or minicomputer may be limited and cumbersome. Computer centers that house such computers may have limited hours or terminals.

Steps Involved in Computer Data Analysis

Whether you choose a PC or a mainframe to analyze your data, four steps are involved in computer data analysis:

1. Preparing your data for computer input
2. Entering your data into the computer and checking for errors
3. Selecting and running the appropriate statistical test
4. Interpreting the output

The rest of this chapter is organized around these four steps. These steps apply equally to PC-based and mainframe computer data analysis.

One final note before we begin: We cannot hope to teach you how to use any particular package in any depth. Nor can we cover all the statistical packages available. We can, however, introduce you to the general idea behind computer data analysis and get you started in the right direction.

Step 1: Preparing Data for Input

Before you sit down in front of a computer or terminal, you must prepare your data for input. This means taking your raw data and organizing them along the lines we discussed in Chapter 11. You may want to use a *computer coding sheet*. Special coding sheets are available for a variety of applications. For example, you should use an 80-column coding sheet when you use SPSS-X, because SPSS-X allows you only 80 characters per line.

Coding Independent and Dependent Variables. Before transferring your data to computer coding sheets, you must decide how to code your variables. Most computer programs look for a numeric or alphabetic code to determine the levels or values of your independent and dependent variables. You must decide how to code these variables.

Coding independent variables involves assigning values to corresponding levels. For a quantitative independent variable (for example, number of milligrams of a drug), simply record the number of milligrams administered to subjects in each treatment group (for example, 10, 20, or 30) on your coding sheet. For qualitative independent variables, you must assign an arbitrary number to each level. For example, if your independent variable were the loudness of a tone in an auditory discrimination experiment (low, moderate, and high) you might code the levels as 1 = low, 2 = moderate, 3 = high). This assignment of numbers to qualitative independent variables is called **dummy-coding**.

For quantitative data (for example, if your subjects rated the intensity of a sound on a scale ranging from zero to 10), simply transfer each subject's score to your coding sheet. If, however, your dependent measure were qualitative (yes/no, for example), you must dummy-code your dependent variable. For example, you could code all "yes" responses as 1, and all "no" responses as 2.

When coding your dependent variables, transfer the data (numeric or dummy-coded) to your coding sheet exactly as they were. Don't be concerned with creating new variables (for example, by adding together existing ones) or with making special categories. Most computer programs have special commands that let you manipulate data in a variety of ways (for example, adding numbers, doing data transformations such as a log transformation, and so on). So don't waste time creating new variables when preparing your data for input.

Step 2: Entering Your Data

PC-based statistical programs usually contain their own data entry and editing facilities, whereas most mainframe or minicomputer programs require you to enter your data using a separate editor program supplied with the computer. Either way, you will have to become familiar with the keyboard and learn how the editor makes use of special keys such as the cursor keys and the Backspace, Delete, Enter, and Function keys. Learn how to use the editor to enter data, to correct faulty entries, to save and retrieve data, and to perform any special functions such as data transformations.

Entering your data into the computer can be one of the most tedious tasks in the whole research process. Boredom, fatigue, and general frustration can lead to inaccurately entered data and consequently to invalid statistical results. Fortunately, there are a few things you can do to reduce the tedium, errors, and frustration.

You can make data entry easier by organizing your data-coding sheet the way your data editor expects the data to be entered. For example, if your data will be entered a column at a time, organize the data into columns on the sheet. Then simply read down the columns while entering your data.

Some statistical packages require you to allot blocks of columns to each variable. Unfortunately, keeping data aligned in the appropriate columns can be difficult when the numbers vary in length, especially if you will be entering the numbers one row at a time. You can solve this problem by entering leading zeros as necessary, so that each number fills the block allotted to it. Not only does this keep the numbers in their proper columns, but also the constant pattern of numbers gives a rhythm to your typing. When the rhythm breaks, you know you've made a mistake.

Errors climb when fatigue sets in, so if you are entering a large amount of data, take frequent breaks. Be sure to save any data you have entered before you leave the keyboard.

Speaking of saving data, nothing can be more frustrating than spending half an afternoon entering data, only to have them obliterated by an unexpected power failure. You can minimize your losses on such occasions by frequently saving your data to disk. Also, don't forget to save your data before you turn off the computer or exit from the data editor. Any data you fail to save will be lost. At this time you should also make a backup copy of your data on another disk. Then if your original disk fails, you will still be able to retrieve your data from the backup.

When you save your data to disk, you create a **data file** from which the data will be read when the computer conducts your analysis. When you save the file, the computer will ask you to type in a file name (usually a single word of eight characters or less) under which the data will be saved. Try to think of a descriptive file name that will uniquely identify the data. When you have several data files on the same disk, using descriptive file names makes it easier to find the correct file.

After you have entered your data, check for errors. Because the computer cannot detect incorrectly entered data, it is up to you to catch any mistakes if you are to avoid invalid results. If you have had someone else enter the data for you, don't assume that the other person has already done the checking.

There are two types of errors to look for: transcription errors and misplaced data errors. **Transcription errors** are errors in copying data from one place to another. These errors can occur first when you copy your data from the original data sheets to your computer coding sheet and again when you copy them from the coding sheet into the computer. To avoid transcription errors, carefully check your transcriptions at each step. The easiest way to check for transcription errors is to have someone read aloud the data from the original while you check the copy.

Misplaced data errors occur when numbers are entered in the wrong columns of a data file. Getting your data where they belong is important when using any computer program, but it becomes crucial when using a program (SPSS-X, for example) that you instruct to look in specific columns for specific data. If for some subjects the data are accidentally placed in the wrong columns, the computer will not read your data correctly and invalid results will occur.

A good way to detect misplaced data errors is to have the computer print out a copy of the data file. Then look carefully at the pattern of numbers. Misplaced data errors will usually produce misaligned columns.

Step 3: Conducting the Analysis

The third step in using the computer to analyze your data is to select and conduct the appropriate analysis. How you specify the analysis depends on the statistical analysis program. For some programs, you simply choose the desired analysis from a menu. For others, you need to write a series of commands specifying the analyses desired and save these as a file. (Examples of each approach are provided later in the chapter.)

Once you have specified your analysis, the computer does the rest. It performs all the necessary calculations and produces an output. You can have your output displayed on the computer screen or request a printout or "hard copy" from the printer.

Step 4: Interpreting the Output

The final step in the analysis process is to interpret, or make sense of, the output produced by the computer. With the more sophisticated packages, you will usually be given more information than you know what to do with, so that simply finding the statistics of interest becomes something of a treasure hunt. The other statistics are there to provide a more detailed picture of the data or to evaluate whether your data appear to meet the assumptions of the statistical analysis you selected.

Of course, before you can properly interpret the output, you need to know what information is being presented and how that information bears on the conclusions you can draw from your data. The computer can conduct the analysis for you, but it cannot interpret the results for you. Some programs come with a manual that explains what statistics are produced in a given analysis and shows where they appear in the printout. To be able to interpret these numbers properly, however, you may have to consult a statistics text or ask someone with a good background in statistics to help you.

Doing Statistical Analyses on the PC

To illustrate statistical analysis of data on the personal computer, we take you through the four steps using data from an experiment conducted by some of our students in the research methods class. To perform the analysis, we used LabStat, a statistical analysis package developed by one of us (Abbott) for the IBM PC and compatibles. You can obtain a copy of LabStat from your instructor. If you have access to an IBM PC or compatible, you can try the example analysis yourself.

The experiment replicated and extended the classic experiment by Peterson and Peterson (1959) on short-term memory. Subjects were given either a three-letter word or a consonant trigram (three consonants, such as *CJK*) and then had to remember the stimulus for a retention interval of 3 or 18 seconds while simultaneously performing difficult mental arithmetic. The purpose of the arithmetic task was to prevent the subjects from rehearsing the stimulus. The two independent variables (stimulus type and retention interval) were manipulated in a factorial design, so there were four treatments representing all possible combinations of stimulus type and retention interval. Each combination was presented twenty times in randomized order, for a total of 80 trials. The dependent variable was the number of stimuli correctly recalled.

Step 1: Preparing the Data for Input

The raw data provided by the subjects were transferred to a computer coding sheet, which in this case was simply a sheet of paper from an ordinary columnar pad. Figure 13-1 shows the data organized on this sheet. The numbers in the left-hand column represent the 34 subjects. The next two columns show the data for the two retention intervals when the stimuli were words. The last two columns show the data for the retention intervals when the stimuli were consonant trigrams, or CCCs. Each row gives the number of stimuli correctly recalled by a single subject under the four treatments.

Note the descriptive labels written at the top of each column, indicating the treatment given, and the label across the top of the sheet identifying the dependent variable. To avoid confusion later, you should always label your data sheets in this way.

Step 2: Entering the Data

LabStat uses a spreadsheet format to enter and edit data. After loading the program, you see a menu of options along the bottom of the screen. To enter the data, we selected the "Data Entry/Correction" option by pressing the F2 function key as indicated on the menu. This brought up the data editor, which presented an empty set of rows and columns to be filled in with data. The top row of each column is reserved for an identifying name. Into this row, beginning with the first column, we typed the four descriptive labels from the data-coding sheet.

Having entered the labels, we then began typing in the data. LabStat allows you to enter the data across the rows or down the columns, as you prefer. To enter a number, simply type it and press the Enter key. The cursor then moves automatically to the next row or column, depending on the entry mode you

Subject number	Words/3 sec	Words/18 sec	CCCs/3 sec	CCCs/18 sec
1	19	19	16	16
2	18	17	16	06
3	19	14	20	14
4	19	16	15	14
5	19	15	19	13
6	19	17	13	07
7	20	20	18	13
8	19	19	14	06
9	20	19	17	14
10	18	13	05	02
11	19	16	14	11
12	18	17	08	02
13	18	13	11	00
14	16	06	11	03
15	20	16	13	15
16	20	17	15	12
17	20	16	16	10
18	20	17	14	07
19	18	15	12	08
20	20	19	16	07
21	20	20	18	15
22	20	16	19	15
23	19	20	18	19
24	20	20	19	18
25	16	10	07	03
26	20	19	16	06
27	19	17	18	14
28	17	19	17	11
29	19	17	17	11
30	20	15	14	13
31	19	19	14	08
32	20	17	19	17
33	19	14	07	00
34	20	14	16	10

Figure 13-1. Sample data for the LabStat example.

selected. When you reach the end of a row or column, simply press the Home key to move to the beginning of the next.

Figure 13-2 shows the LabStat data entry screen after all the data were entered. (Only 15 rows can be displayed at a time; to see the rest of the data, you would use the PgDn key.)

Saving the Data. Having entered the data, we then saved them to disk. As indicated in the menu at the bottom of the LabStat data entry screen (see Figure 13-2), we pressed the F3 function key. The computer then requested the file name under which the data would be stored (a single word up to eight characters

Entry by Column	LABSTAT: Data Entry			Entry: 1 1
Column:	1	2	3	4
Name:	Words/3sec	Words/18sec	CCCs/3sec	CCCs/18sec
Row: 1	19.00000	19.00000	16.00000	16.00000
2	18.00000	17.00000	16.00000	6.00000
3	19.00000	14.00000	20.00000	14.00000
4	19.00000	16.00000	15.00000	14.00000
5	19.00000	15.00000	19.00000	13.00000
6	19.00000	17.00000	13.00000	7.00000
7	20.00000	20.00000	18.00000	13.00000
8	19.00000	19.00000	14.00000	6.00000
9	20.00000	19.00000	17.00000	14.00000
10	18.00000	13.00000	5.00000	2.00000
11	19.00000	16.00000	14.00000	11.00000
12	18.00000	17.00000	8.00000	2.00000
13	18.00000	13.00000	11.00000	0.00000
14	16.00000	6.00000	11.00000	3.00000
15	20.00000	16.00000	13.00000	15.00000

F1: Directory	F2: Retrieve	F3: Save	F4: Delete	F5: Column/Row
F6: Print	F7: Transform	F8: Help	F10: Exit	

Figure 13-2. LabStat data entry screen showing data for the first fifteen subjects of the short-term memory experiment (see text).

long). We typed in "peter" and pressed the Enter key. The computer added the file name extension "dat" (for "data file") and saved the data as "peter.dat."

Checking for Errors. To check for errors, we had LabStat make a printout of the data (requested by pressing the F7 function key). We could have simply scrolled through the data file on screen, but it is usually easier to work from a printed copy. We found a couple of errors and corrected them by moving the cursor to the location of the error (using the cursor keys), then simply retyping the number and pressing the Enter key. We then saved the data again to the same file. (If you forget this step, your corrections will be lost.) Having completed our data entry and correction, we then exited from the data entry and correction program and returned to the Opening Menu by pressing the F10 key.

Step 3: Selecting an Analysis

Because our experiment used a two-factor, within-subjects design, the appropriate statistical analysis was, logically enough, a two-factor, within-subjects analysis of variance (ANOVA). To conduct the ANOVA, we began by selecting ANOVA from the opening menu. This brought up the ANOVA program, which presented its main menu. The first task was to retrieve the data from disk, accomplished by pressing the F2 function key, typing the file name of the data file, and pressing the Enter key. The computer loaded the data into memory and indicated on the screen that our data file contained four treatments with 20 scores per treatment and no missing numbers. (This information confirms that we loaded the correct file and provides another check on the integrity of the data.)

To conduct an ANOVA using LabStat, you specify the type of ANOVA (we selected the two-factor, within-subjects ANOVA) and then fill in an on-screen "form" identifying the name and number of levels of each factor and indicating which columns of your data represent which combinations of factor levels. You then select "Conduct Analysis" from the menu, and the computer goes to work. (We provide a detailed example of these steps in the student workbook that accompanies this text.) Our analysis took the computer about five seconds to complete.

Step 4: Interpreting the Output

Figure 13-3 shows the printout from LabStat for the preceding analysis. The top portion shows the name of the data file (upper left), the analysis performed, the title, and the names of the dependent and independent variables. Underneath are three tables showing the results. The first table provides descriptive statistics for each treatment (cell): the mean, standard deviation, and standard error. The second table provides the same statistics for each main effect (stimulus type and retention interval). The third table provides the results of the ANOVA. The columns give sums of squares (SS), degrees of freedom (df), mean square (MS), and F-ratio (F).

What do all these numbers mean? To interpret these data, we began by looking at the F-ratios in the ANOVA table. These values had to be compared to the critical values of F given in Table I-3 in Appendix I to determine whether the F's were statistically significant. This comparison showed that all three F's were statistically significant. Thus there was a reliable effect of stimulus type, a reliable effect of retention interval, and a reliable interaction between the two.

We then examined the middle table to determine the nature of the two significant main effects. For stimulus type, the mean for words (17.721) is higher than the mean for CCCs (12.382), indicating that, on average across the two retention intervals, words are easier to remember than CCCs. For retention interval, the mean for 3 seconds (16.897) is higher than the mean for 18 seconds (13.206), indicating that, on average across stimulus types, it is easier to recall a stimulus after a 3-second retention interval than after an 18-second interval.

The best way to understand the significant interaction is to graph the effect of retention interval on number correct using separate lines to connect the means of the "word" treatments and those of the "CCC" treatments. The interaction

Treatment Descriptives

Title: Short-Term Memory Experiment

Dependent Variable: Recall

Factor A = Stimulus Type
Factor B = Interval

Factor A	Factor B	Cell	N	Mean	Std Dev	Std Err
Words	3 Seconds	1	34	19.029	1.114	0.191
Words	18 Seconds	2	34	16.412	3.006	0.516
CCCs	3 Seconds	3	34	14.765	3.782	0.649
CCCs	18 Seconds	4	34	10.000	5.257	0.902

Main Effects

Factor	Level	N	Mean	Std Dev	Std Err
Stimulus Type	Words	68	17.721	2.608	0.316
	CCCs	68	12.382	5.140	0.623
Interval	3 Seconds	68	16.897	3.503	0.425
	18 Seconds	68	13.206	5.338	0.647

Title: Short-Term Memory Experiment

Dependent Variable: Recall

Source	SS	df	MS	F
Total	3194.640	135		
Subjects	1052.890	33		
Stimulus Type	968.890	1	968.890	78.876
Error A	405.360	33	12.284	
Interval	463.243	1	463.243	103.285
Error B	148.007	33	4.485	
A X B Inter	39.184	1	39.184	11.046
Error A X B	117.066	33	3.547	

Figure 13-3. A printout of a two-factor within-subjects ANOVA produced by the LabStat program.

will show up as nonparallel lines (see the discussion of factorial designs in Chapter 8). However, you can visualize the interaction in this case by comparing the difference in number correct between the 3-second and 18-second retention intervals under the two stimulus types (upper table). Retention dropped by 2.6 when the stimuli were words and by about 4.8 when the stimuli were CCCs. Thus the effect of retention interval on recall was somewhat more severe for CCCs than for words. Note, however, that the score for the words/3-second treatment (19.029) was near the ceiling of the measure (20). The interaction thus may have been produced by a ceiling effect on the scores in this treatment.

Data Analysis Using Other PC-Based Programs

Although the details vary, the same basic steps illustrated in the LabStat example would be followed with any PC-based statistical analysis. Other PC-based packages (CSS-Statsoft or SPSS-PC, for example) provide a wider range of options and statistics than LabStat. For example, with CSS-Statsoft you can generate graphs illustrating important relationships. The more sophisticated PC packages also include a wider range of statistical analysis options such as factor analysis, multivariate analysis of variance, loglinear analysis, and multiple regression (see Chapter 15 for an introduction to these analyses). If your data analysis calls for a complex, sophisticated analysis, you might consider one of the more advanced PC packages.

Statistical Analysis on the Mainframe

To illustrate how to use a statistical package designed for the mainframe, we reanalyzed the data from the LabStat example using SPSS-X. Next, we outline the steps involved in using SPSS-X to analyze these data.

Step 1: Preparing the Data for Input

SPSS-X can read data in a variety of formats, but the most common format arranges data in specific columns, with a maximum of 80 columns. Figure 13-4 shows the data for the first 24 subjects arranged on a computer coding sheet originally intended for coding FORTRAN statements. It happens to provide the correct number of columns for SPSS-X and conveniently gives the column numbers along the top of the entry field.

Notice that the numbers have been placed into fields (pairs of columns, in this case) representing each treatment. To facilitate data entry, we placed a blank column between each field and added leading zeros to each single-digit number.

Step 2: Entering the Data

When using SPSS-X, you must write a series of commands to execute your analysis. You have the option of creating either a single SPSS-X file containing

FORTRAN CODING FORM

PROGRAM SPSS-X Peterson Example – Sample Data

PROGRAMMER

DATE 1/30/90

PUNCHING INSTRUCTIONS | GRAPHIC | PUNCH

PAGE 1 OF 2

CARD ELECTRO NUMBER

COMM. | STATEMENT NUMBER | CONT. | FORTRAN STATEMENT | IDENTIFICATION SEQUENCE

```
19 19 16 16
18 17 16 06
19 14 20 14
19 16 15 14
19 15 19 13
19 17 13 07
20 20 18 13
19 19 14 06
20 19 17 14
18 13 05 02
19 16 14 11
18 17 08 02
18 13 11 00
16 06 11 03
20 16 13 15
.           .
.           .
.           .
.           .
.           .
.           .
.           .
19 14 07 00
20 14 16 10
```

Figure 13-4.
Coding form for SPSS.

both your data and these commands, or two separate files, one for data and one for commands. We recommend using separate files because they are easier to manage. When you read through your data in a separate file, there is no need to read through a long list of commands before getting to your data. To analyze the LabStat example data, we used separate data and command files.

To create your SPSS-X data file, you need to gain access to the data editor provided as part of the computer system software. (SPSS-X does not have its own editor. Have someone show you how to use the editor provided with the computer system.) In our computer center, SPSS-X resides on the VAX computer, and we used the EDT editor provided with the VAX to enter our data, correct the errors, and save the data to disk.

Step 3: Conducting the Analysis

To analyze the data using SPSS-X, we had to create a command file. A **command file** contains several commands (the number varies with the analysis) that tell the computer where data will be found, what form they will take, any data transformations to apply, and which analyses to conduct. A command file is needed if you use any of the major packages (SPSS-X, BMD-P, or SAS).

Figure 13-5 shows the SPSS-X command file we created for analyzing the short-term memory data. Each of the commands has a specific purpose, as we explain next.

Unnumbered. Beginning at the top, the "unnumbered" command tells SPSS-X not to look for a line number preceding each command. (Earlier versions of SPSS-X required line numbers, but you can now leave them out.)

Title. You can give your SPSS-X run a title that will be printed at the top of each page of your printout. This is handy because each run is then clearly labeled. We gave our run the title "Short-Term Memory Experiment."

Set Width. You can tell SPSS-X how wide you want your printout to be. The default is a 132-column format, which is appropriate for wide computer forms. However, we wanted to have our printout printed on standard-width paper, which uses 80 columns. The Set Width command instructed the computer to format the output for an 80-column width.

File Handle. This SPSS-X run was accomplished with separate data and command files. The File Handle command tells the computer the actual name of the data file (Peter.dat) and assigns a dummy file name for use by SPSS-X (Peterdat).

Data List. The Data List command tells the computer the location of the scores for each variable or treatment within the data file and assigns a brief name (up to eight characters) to each. The "file = peterdat" tells the computer that the data are found in the file whose dummy file name is "peterdat" (assigned in the File Handle command). "Records = 1" indicates that a "record" consists of one line of data. That is, each line provides one score

```
unnumbered
title Short-Term Memory Experiment
set width = 80
file handle    peterdat name = 'peter.dat'
data list      file = peterdat records = 1
               /1 w3 1-2,w18 4-5,ccc3 7-8,ccc18
               10-11
variable labels w3 'Words/3 Seconds'/w18
'Words/18 Seconds'/ccc3 'CCCs/3 Seconds'/
ccc18 'CCCs/18 Seconds'
manova          w3 to ccc18/
wsfactors = Stimulus(2),Interval(2)/
wsdesign = Stimulus,Interval,Stimulus by
               Interval/
                  print = cellinfo/
```

Figure 13-5. SPSS-X command file for repeated-measures ANOVA example.

for each of the variables or treatments included in the data file. (When a large number of variables are included, a single record may require several lines.) The "/1" indicates the start of the field assignment on the first (and in this case only) line of the record. After this come the names assigned to the first treatment (w3 for "word/3-seconds") and the column numbers in which the data for this treatment appear (1 and 2). The remainder of the command gives equivalent information for the other treatments.

Variable Labels. The Variable Labels command assigns extended labels to the variables to facilitate reading and interpreting the SPSS-X printout.

Manova. The Manova command specifies the statistical procedure to be applied to your data. This is actually the last command in the command file; the two "commands" appearing below the Manova command are actually subcommands of Manova. The Manova command calls the MANOVA (multivariate analysis of variance) subprogram, which SPSS-X uses to conduct a repeated-measures analysis of variance.

The "w3 to ccc18" found to the right of the Manova command specifies the treatments you want to include in the analysis. We wanted to include the data from all four treatments of the experiment, and the "to" in the command tells the computer to include all treatments in the range listed. The "to" convention allows you to specify large numbers of variables or treatments without having to list each.

The subcommand, Wsfactors, tells the computer the names of your factors and how many levels of each factor exists. We assigned the names *Stimulus* and

Interval to the two factors in the design. These names are used on the printout to identify the cells in your design. The numbers in parentheses tell the computer how many levels of each factor there are.

The Wsdesign subcommand specifies how to conduct the analysis. For this example, we wanted to analyze the two main effects (stimulus and retention interval) as well as the interaction (stimulus × retention interval). Consequently, we listed those effects on the design subcommand.

The final subcommand, "print = cellinfo," requests that SPSS-X provide the means and standard deviations for each cell of the design.

In addition to creating and saving both your data and command files, you may also have to create and submit a "job file" that tells the computer to run SPSS-X and specifies the command file to use for the run. Your "job" will then be assigned a priority and placed in line with everyone else's jobs. Eventually your analysis will be conducted and the results printed.

Step 4: Interpreting the Output

The SPSS-X printout includes much more information than just the results of the statistical analysis. Probably the first information you see will include a listing of the computer used, the amount of computer time used, and a few other messages in "computerese." These messages vary from computer center to computer center. After the messages, you will find a summary of the SPSS-X commands you specified, the data format table, and, finally, the analyses you requested. Each of these areas requires a bit of explanation.

Summary of SPSS-X Commands. The first information directly relevant to your SPSS-X analysis is a list of the commands you entered. If there were any errors in your commands, they will be flagged for you. For each error, SPSS-X indicates that an error has occurred and prints a brief error message pointing out possible causes for the error. With a little practice, you should be able to decipher the error messages, correct the problem, and rerun your analysis.

There are two things to remember about errors. First, errors on required commands (for example, the Data List command) will cause SPSS-X to stop the analysis but continue an error scan. Your command file is scanned for further errors and any other errors are noted, but your data are not analyzed. In contrast, errors on nonrequired commands (for example, "variable labels") will be flagged, but your data will be processed and analyzed. However, the erroneous command will not be executed. In this case, the extended labels you wanted to use will not be used.

Second, errors flagged on commands appearing late in your file may be caused by an error made on an earlier command. For example, assume that you inadvertently left a variable off your Data List command and then asked the computer to assign an extended name to it on a subsequent Variable Labels com-

Variable	Rec	Start	End	Format
W3	1	1	2	F2.0
W18	1	4	5	F2.0
CCC3	1	7	8	F2.0
CCC18	1	10	11	F2.0

Figure 13-6. SPSS-X data format table.

mand. The computer will flag the error when reading the Variable Labels command, even though that command is not in error. With a little practice, you will be able to recognize the crucial errors in your run and effectively correct them.

The Data Format Table. Next is the *data format table*, which shows where the computer expects to find your variables. A data format table is shown in Figure 13-6. The first column ("Variable") lists the names of your variables using the short names given to them on the Data List command. The next column lists the record numbers ("Rec"). In some cases, you may need more than one line to hold all your data. Each line becomes a record in your analysis. On the Data List command, you would specify how many records exist for each subject. The next two columns ("Start" and "End") tell you in which columns the computer expects to find your data. Check the tabled values against the columns where the data are actually found, to ensure that they match up. The final column ("Format") tells you how the computer expects your data to be formatted. The "F2.0" shown in our example means that the computer expects to find each variable to be two columns wide (or two *Fields* wide), and to be two-digit numbers (the "2" indicates this), with no decimal values (the ".0" indicates this). Check this last column carefully as well.

Data Analysis Information. After the format table, you will find the start of the data analyses you requested. SPSS-X prints out the commands you included before the analysis. These commands will be followed by the analysis tables themselves. In our example, we requested a within-subjects ANOVA using the MANOVA subprogram, with tables listing the cell descriptive statistics.

Descriptive Statistics. Figure 13-7 shows part of the printout (edited for our presentation) from the MANOVA run requested. This figure shows how the cell means, standard deviations, and N's are displayed. Look at the top portion of the figure. First you see the name of the cell being displayed. Both the short variable name provided on the Data List command ("w3") and longer variable name assigned with the Variable Labels command ("words/3 seconds") are displayed. Next the mean (in the column marked "Mean"), standard deviation ("Std.

Cell Means and Standard Deviations

Variable . . W3   Words/3 Seconds

	Mean	Std. Dev.	N
For entire sample	19.029	1.114	34

Variable . . W18   Words/18 Seconds

	Mean	Std. Dev.	N
For entire sample	16.412	3.006	34

Variable . . CCC3   CCCs/3 Seconds

	Mean	Std. Dev.	N
For entire sample	14.765	3.782	34

Variable . . CCC18   CCCs/18 Seconds

	Mean	Std. Dev.	N
	10.00	5.257	34

Figure 13-7. Descriptive statistics table produced by the SPSS-X MANOVA example.

Dev."), and number of subjects in the cell ("N") are all shown. This is repeated four times, once for each cell (labeled "Variable" on the printout) of your design.

Analysis of Variance. Figure 13-8 shows the results of the within-subjects analysis of variance requested. Interpreting this figure is relatively simple. First look at the portion labeled "Tests involving 'STIMULUS' Within-Subject Effect." This table shows the significance test for the main effect of the type of stimulus presented (word or CCC). The table shows the sums of squares (SS), degrees of freedom (df), mean square (MS), F, and the p-value ("Sig of F"). The first row of the table, labeled "WITHIN CELLS," provides you the SS, df, and MS; whereas the row labeled "STIMULUS" provides the SS, df, MS, F, and p for the stimulus main effect. The next portions of the table provide the same information for the "INTERVAL" main effect and the "STIMULUS BY INTERVAL" interaction.

BMD-P and SAS

Two packages mentioned at the outset of this section (BMD-P and SAS) are powerful programs that you can use to analyze your data. Although the syntax of the commands for these two packages differs from the syntax used in SPSS-X, the basic logic behind the programs is the same. Both BMD-P and SAS include command statements that define your data for the computer, that tell the

****** ANALYSIS OF VARIANCE -- DESIGN 1 *****

Tests of Between-Subjects Effects.

Tests of Significance for T1 using UNIQUE sums of squares

Source of Variation	SS	df	MS	F	Sig of F
WITHIN CELLS	1052.89	33	31.91		
CONSTANT	30810.36	1	30810.36	965.67	.000

****** ANALYSIS OF VARIANCE -- DESIGN 1 *****

Tests involving 'STIMULUS' Within-Subject Effect.

Tests of Significance for T2 using UNIQUE sums of squares

Source of Variation	SS	df	MS	F	Sig of F
WITHIN CELLS	405.36	33	12.28		
STIMULUS	968.89	1	968.89	78.88	.000

****** ANALYSIS OF VARIANCE -- DESIGN 1 *****

Tests involving 'INTERVAL' Within-Subject Effect.

Tests of Significance for T3 using UNIQUE sums of squares

Source of Variation	SS	df	MS	F	Sig of F
WITHIN CELLS	148.01	33	4.49		
INTERVAL	463.24	1	463.24	103.29	.000

****** ANALYSIS OF VARIANCE -- DESIGN 1 *****

Tests involving 'STIMULUS BY INTERVAL' Within-Subject Effect.

Tests of Significance for T4 using UNIQUE sums of squares

Source of Variation	SS	df	MS	F	Sig of F
WITHIN CELLS	117.07	33	3.55		
STIMULUS BY INTERVAL	39.18	1	39.18	11.05	.002

Figure 13-8. ANOVA table for SPSS-X within-subject design example.

computer where to look for data, to perform special functions (select certain variables), and tell the computer which analyses to perform.

BMD-P. BMD-P consists of several programs that perform a wide range of statistical analyses (for example, BMD-P 2V performs a wide variety of ANO-VAs and BMD-P 1R performs a multiple linear regression analysis). The programs are accessed with a command statement that appears at the beginning of your program (the exact format of this statement may vary according to the computer system you use).

```
{Command lines to access BMBD-P 2V}
/Problem    Title = 'One Factor Anova Example'.
/Input      Variables = 2.
            Format = (F1.0,1x,f1.0).
/Variable   Names = IV,DV.
/Design     Depend = DV.
            Group = IV.
/Group      Codes (IV) = 1,2,3.
            Names (IV) = G1,G2,G3.

/End
1 6
1 9
1 8
1 9
1 9
2 3
2 4
2 2
2 1
2 5
3 6
3 7
3 8
3 5
3 4
```

Figure 13-9. Sample BMD-P command and data file.

After entering the preliminary system commands, you include commands that direct the computer to carry out a given analysis. In BMD-P, commands are arranged in *paragraphs* that begin with a keyword. Keywords always begin with a "/" followed by a command (/Procedure, /Input, and so on). Within the paragraphs you include whatever *sentences* are necessary to define, manipulate, and analyze your data. Sentences follow keywords and end with a period(.). Figure 13-9 illustrates a BMD-P 2V program to perform a one-factor 3-group ANOVA.

The title of your computer run is defined in the /Problem paragraph. In the /Input paragraph, you tell the computer how many variables you have in your data file and how the data are formatted. The "Format = " sentence in BMD-P is similar to the Data List command in SPSS-X. The /Variable paragraph allows you to assign names to your variables (analogous to the Variable List in SPSS-X). The /Design paragraph tells the computer which variable to use as the independent variable and which to use as the dependent variable in the requested ANOVA. The dependent variable is specified in the "Depend = " sentence and the independent variable in the "Group = " sentence. In the /Group paragraph you inform the computer how the independent variable is coded in the "Codes = " sentence and the names to be attached to the independent variable in the "Names = " sentence. Finally the /End paragraph tells the computer that the end of the command file has been reached. You place your data file following the /End command.

The output resulting from the program in Figure 13-9 yields several pieces of important information. First, you would receive the means for each of your three groups. Second, you would receive the ANOVA table (including the sum of squares, degrees of freedom, mean squares, F-ratios, and p-values). Finally, you would receive t-tests contrasting each pair of groups in your experiment along with the associated p-values.

The program shown in Figure 13-9 is a very simple one. Other paragraphs and sentences could be included if you wanted to perform some more sophisticated functions. For example, a /Transform paragraph could be included if you wanted to create a new variable by adding two existing ones (such as Newvar = DV1 + DV2), or to create new variables conditioned on the value of a variable (such as, if (DV1 = 1) then Newvar = 100), or select specific variables for inclusion in your analysis. Exploring all the functions of BMD-P is beyond the scope of this chapter. For more information on these functions and how to use BMD-P, you should consult the BMD-P manual.

SAS. SAS is yet another powerful statistical package. Like SPSS-X and BMD-P it performs a wide variety of statistical functions on request. The available functions range from computing simple means to analyzing your data with the most sophisticated multivariate statistics available.

The logic behind SAS is the same as the logic behind SPSS-X and BMD-P. That is, you have a set of commands that define, manipulate, and analyze your data. Figure 13-10 shows a simple SAS program that performs a one-factor 3-group ANOVA, provides you with group means, and contrasts the group means with a *post hoc* test (Scheffe). The program begins with the system commands needed to access SAS (as with the previous two packages, the format of these commands is determined by your computer).

In SAS (as was the case in BMD-P), you arrange commands into paragraphs beginning with a keyword. Statements to perform specific functions are then contained in the paragraphs. The statements in the DATA paragraph define your variables for the computer (IV and DV) and tell the computer to read the data. After the data are the statements needed to actually perform the ANOVA. Data manipulation and analysis functions are called with *PROC statements* ("PROC" is short for procedure). The PROC SORT paragraph tells the computer to group (sort) your groups according to the value of the variable called IV. In the PROC ANOVA paragraph, you specify which variable is noncontinuous (in this example, the groups in your analysis are classified according to IV) and the design of your analysis. The design is specified in the MODEL statement in which you specify the dependent variable (DV) and the independent variable (IV). The

```
{Commands to call SAS}
Data;
        Input IV,DV;
        Cards;
        1       6
        1       9
        1       8
        1       9
        1       9
        2       3
        2       4
        2       2
        2       1
        2       5
        3       6
        3       7
        3       8
        3       5
        3       4
Proc Sort;
        By IV;
Proc Anova;
        Class IV;
        Model DV = IV;
        Means DV/Scheffe;
        Title = 'One-Factor ANOVA Example';
```

Figure 13-10. Sample SAS command and data file.

"means" statement will produce the mean for each group. The statement following the "/" will result in the groups in your experiment being contrasted with a *post hoc* test (in this case a Scheffe test, but others are available).

Choosing a Statistical Package

Your decision about which package to use will depend on at least three factors. First, which package you use depends on what your computer center has available. Because the major statistical packages cost thousands of dollars to install and maintain each year, your computer center may offer only one of them. Second, one package may do a better job than another on a particular analysis. Consequently, one package may better meet your needs than the others. For example, BMD-P is preferred over SPSS-X for such multivariate statistics as multiple regression and discriminant analysis (see Chapter 15). This is because BMD-P allows you to more easily determine if your data meet the assumptions of these statistical tests than SPSS-X does. Before choosing a package to learn, determine what each is capable of doing and then choose the one that best meets your research needs.

A third factor that might affect your decision is closely related to the second. For some analyses, some packages offer more flexibility and ease of use than others. If you wanted to perform a two-factor within-subjects ANOVA, consider using SAS or BMD-P over SPSS-X. To perform such an analysis with SPSS-X requires using the MANOVA subprogram and yields a printout that is difficult to read and interpret.

Writing Your Own Statistical Programs

If you know how to program a computer, and have the time to devote, you can write your own programs to statistically analyze data in one of the popular PC programming languages (for example, BASIC or Pascal). Your programs can be as simple or complex as you want. For example, a program to perform a single *t*-test might only include a provision for data input, calculation of the test, and display of the results on the computer screen. A more complex program might include a data editor, the ability to customize output, and the ability to print the results on a printer. A still more complex program might include the ability to store data to disk and retrieve it from disk and to transform data. Of course, the more you want the program to do, the more time it will take to write and debug the program.

With the availability of commercially available, powerful packages for the PC, writing programs for doing most analyses is unnecessary. However, knowing how to write your own program may be an important advantage when your research design calls for an analysis not commonly available on the popular commercial programs. For example, one of us (Bordens) conducted an experiment that included a factorial component (a 3 × 2 between-subjects design) and a "dangling control group." The dangling control group is simply a group of subjects run to provide baseline data. The dangling control group is then compared to the other cells in the design. Unfortunately, none of the commercially available programs provides such an analysis. However, Winer (1971) provides the formulas needed to perform the required analysis. A previously written ANOVA program was easily modified to conduct this unique analysis.

Computer Data Analysis: A Final Note

If you are interested in learning about these statistical packages, obtain the manual (for the mainframe packages) or the program (for the PC) and learn the package on your own. If you want to learn to use a package designed for the mainframe, the first thing to do is to contact your computer center. Some computer centers run seminars and classes on how to use SPSS-X, BMD-P, or SAS. If such classes are not offered, you can find someone who is familiar with the package and ask for help. Keep in mind, however, that the only way to learn these packages effectively is to use them.

Also keep in mind that the computer will perform any and all of the calculations you ask for. You must ensure that your data meet the assumptions underlying the test you will be using. For example, the computer will not magically transform skewed data into normal data. The numbers the computer produces are based on what you enter. The "garbage in, garbage out" (GIGO) computer adage certainly applies to statistical analysis on the computer. If you enter garbage into SPSS-X, for example, you will ultimately get garbage out.

Because of the GIGO principle, you might consider learning more than one of the mainframe packages. Situations may arise in which you need to use more than one package to effectively analyze your data. For example, if you wanted to use multivariate statistics, the BMD-P has programs that allow you to test whether your data meet the assumptions of the statistics. SPSS-X, on the other hand, does not have these programs. In many cases, however, the SPSS-X programs are much more powerful than BMD-P programs for conducting the statistical analysis. Consequently, you may have to use BMD-P to check to see that your data conform to the assumptions of the statistical analysis you are planning to use, and then use SPSS-X to conduct the analyses.

Finally, remember that learning to use a computer and later one of the statistical packages can be a frustrating experience. The computer, although fast, is not very smart. If an SPSS-X command calls for a comma and you entered a period, for example, this may be enough to abort your entire run. The computer will provide you with error messages that may help you isolate your error. Too often, however, these error messages are too vague and cryptic to be of much help. For example, what does "ERROR NUMBER 8988" mean? Have patience and stick with it. If you need to analyze data in the future, you will not regret having learned how to use the computer.

Summary

An alternative to calculating statistical analyses by hand is to use a computer. Computers have a wide range of applications, one of which is data analysis. The computer can compute complex statistics in a matter of seconds that might require several hours to compute by hand, and do it more accurately than those done by hand.

Although there are many advantages to using computers to analyze data, there are also drawbacks. The ease of analysis of the computer may encourage you to use statistics that you are not entirely familiar with, resulting in misinterpretations of data. Also, you are limited to those analyses offered by the program you are using. And the computer will perform only the calculations you ask for, even if those calculations produce nonsensical results.

Statistical packages are available for both PCs and mainframes. Many of the programs originally written for mainframes are now available for PCs, usually in scaled-down forms. There are also packages written specifically for PCs. The PC packages are usually easier to learn than mainframe packages, but run slower and offer a narrower range of options.

Whether you choose a PC or a mainframe package, there are four steps to analyzing data on the computer: (1) preparing your data for input, (2) entering your data, (3) selecting the desired analysis, and (4) interpreting the output. Methods for entering data, selecting analysis, and specifying output vary from program to program. When preparing data for input, you must transcribe your data from your original data sheets to a computer coding sheet. Your independent and dependent variables have to be coded. Coding may simply involve transcribing a number to your coding sheet. In cases of qualitative variables, they may have to be dummy-coded with numbers.

Data entry can be done by you or by someone you hire. If you enter your data yourself, you can facilitate the process by doing a few simple things (for example, by organizing your data on the coding sheet in such a way that they are easily read, and by taking frequent breaks). It is important to check your data for errors after they have been entered, even if you had your data professionally entered.

Program packages designed for the PC usually include a data editor. After entering and correcting your data, you then select the desired analysis, usually from some type of menu. The data are then analyzed and displayed on the computer screen or printed out. Analyzing data with one of the mainframe packages usually involves writing a series of commands to define your data and to specify the analyses to be done. A second file is also needed for your data (if you choose to use separate command and data files).

You may elect to write your own statistical package. With some knowledge of a programming language, such as BASIC or Pascal, you can write your own programs. Writing programs for popular analyses may not be worth your time, because powerful commercial PC packages are available. However, in some cases you may need to conduct an analysis not included in one of the commercial packages. In this case you could write your own program for your special analysis needs.

Finally, keep in mind that the computer simply performs the calculations you specify. It cannot, on its own, correct errors in your data. You must carefully transcribe your data from the raw data sheets onto your computer coding sheet, and then correctly enter your data. You must ensure that your data meet any assumptions of the statistic you are using so that your data analysis will be valid. Remember the GIGO adage: Garbage in, garbage out.

Key Terms

| Dummy-coding | Transcription error | Command file |
| Data file | Misplaced data error | |

14

Reporting Your Research Results

YOUR JOURNEY THROUGH THE WORLD OF RESEARCH thus far has taken you through the steps involved in choosing a research question, developing hypotheses, choosing a general strategy and specific design to test your hypotheses, and describing and analyzing your data. The final step in this process is to report your research results.

Reporting your research results is perhaps the most important step because it is only by this reporting that science progresses. Other scientists working in the field need to know what you have done: the questions you have asked, the methods you have used to address them, and the answers you have found. Not only is this step essential for progress, it is required to assess the reliability of your findings and the soundness of your conclusions. Only when your research has been reported can others attempt to replicate and extend your findings.

To effectively communicate the results of your research, you need to know what must be said and how to communicate it clearly and in the proper format. This chapter discusses how to organize and present your research findings.

Even if you are not planning to pursue a career in psychological research, you will find that much of the information contained in this chapter is valuable. Many occupations — especially those at a managerial or technical level — require you to organize facts, to draw conclusions, and to present the facts and conclusions clearly and logically in a written report. Although the format and contents of your reports are likely to differ from those of the scientific report described here, the general principles of organization and composition will be the same.

APA Writing Style

Scientific journals in all disciplines specify the format, or *writing style*, that articles submitted to the journal are to follow. This writing style determines what subsections will be present in the report, how figures and tables will be presented, what rules are to be followed in typing the manuscript, and other such details.

In psychology, most journals follow the style established by the American Psychological Association (APA) in the *Publication Manual of the American Psychological Association* (third edition, 1983). We refer to this manual simply as the APA style manual. When you follow the manual, your manuscript conforms to APA style.

Sometimes you may come across a journal that does not completely follow APA style. For example, *Animal Learning & Behavior* follows the style of the American Institute of Physics in abbreviating physical units, rather than the style specified by the APA. Nevertheless, these journals usually follow APA style closely, with only a few minor exceptions. (These exceptions are usually indicated on or near an inside cover of each journal issue under a heading such as "Notes to Authors.") Therefore, most of what you learn about APA style will apply even to non-APA psychology journals.

The discussion that follows briefly describes how to write a research report in APA style. A comprehensive review cannot be presented in the space available here. (For additional details, consult the APA style manual.) In this chapter we also discuss how to avoid some common errors of composition and grammar and a discussion on how to prepare a paper presentation.

Throughout the section on the contents and style of the various sections of an APA-style paper, illustrations are used to reinforce the text. The material in the illustrations was drawn from several articles published in the *Bulletin of the Psychonomic Society*. The published articles have been put into manuscript form for the sake of illustration. To see the original published papers, go to the library and look them up. The full references for these papers are given in the reference section of this text.

Writing an APA-Style Paper

There are seven sections in an APA-style manuscript: the title page, abstract, introduction, method, results, discussion, and references. When you are preparing an APA-style manuscript, many guidelines must be followed. For example, specific instructions govern setting up margins, line spacing, what to cover in each section, and how to present information in tables and figures. In this section, we discuss some of the basic guidelines for preparing an APA-style manuscript.

Getting Ready to Type

To create an APA-style manuscript, use standard 8.5- × 11-inch white typing paper (no onion skin or erasable bond). If you are writing the manuscript on a computer or word processor, you can use white computer paper with perforations that allow you to tear the paper into 8.5- × 11-inch sheets after printing. Set your left margin at 1.5 inches and your right margin to give room for a 5.5-inch line of text (1.5-inch right margin). Leave 1.5 inches for the top and bottom margins as well. Double-space all text. Finally, type no more than 25 double-spaced lines of text on each page.

Each page of an APA manuscript (excluding figures) includes a short title and a page number typed flush against the right margin in the upper right corner. The short title consists of the first two or three words of the title of your manuscript. It is used by the editorial staff of a journal to identify pages that may become separated from your manuscript. Figure 14-1 shows the proper placement of the short title and page number.

The Title Page

The title page includes (in order) the title of your paper, author name(s) and affiliation(s), and a running head. Figure 14-1 shows an example title page.

Title. When researchers looking for relevant articles on a particular topic scan the table of contents of a journal, or peruse the pages of *Psychological Abstracts*, the title of an article first captures attention. If the title fails to communicate clearly what the paper is about, readers may skip the paper.

A paper that isn't read is useless. To avoid this fate for your paper, make your title concise, yet informative. Avoid using words that add little to the meaningfulness of your title (for example, "An Experimental Investigation of," "A Correlational Field Study of"). Keep your title short enough to avoid confusion about your research (12 to 15 words at most), but not so short that it fails to convey the topic of your paper.

The following examples show a title that is too long, a title that is too short, and one that is just right:

Too Long: "An Experimental Study of the Effect of Delay of Reinforcement on Discrimination Learning in White Rats"

Too Short: "The Effect of Reinforcement on Learning"

Just Right: "The Effect of Delay of Reinforcement on Discrimination Learning in Rats"

In the first example, the words "An Experimental Study of" and "White" add extraneous words to your title. The second title is too general. A potential reader has only a vague idea about the focus of your study. The third example concisely conveys the essence of your study.

Place the title near the top of the title page, and center it between the left and right margins. If multiple lines are required, double-space them. Capitalize the

```
                                           The Aftereffects of

                                                    1




                     The Aftereffects of Prolonged Perception of Shape

                       Debra Cowart-Steckler and Robert H. Pollack

                                   University of Georgia
















                Running head:   PROLONGED PERCEPTION OF SHAPE
```

Figure 14-1. Sample title page (Cowart-Steckler & Pollack, 1982; reprinted with permission).

first letter of the first word, and of all subsequent words (except for articles and prepositions).

Author Name(s) and Affiliation(s). If you are the sole author of the paper, your name goes one double–spaced line beneath the title. Your name should include your given name, middle initial(s), and last name (in that order), centered between the margins. Do not include any titles (such as Mr., Ms., Dr.) or degrees (B.A., M.A., Ph.D., M.D., and so on).

Your affiliation is the organization that provided the local facilities and/or support for your research (usually a university or college). Its name appears one double-spaced line below yours on the title page, centered between the margins.

If there are two or more authors, how you organize the information depends on whether everyone has the same affiliation. Consult the APA style manual for details. In cases of multiple authorship, who gets listed first, second, and so forth becomes a matter of concern. Readers usually assume that the first author listed made the heaviest contribution to the paper, although this assumption is not always correct. If you conceived the study, designed it, and wrote major sections of the paper, your name should be first. If you ran the study under someone else's direction and wrote the method section, your name probably belongs farther down in the order. If the contributions of the authors are about equal, the authors usually agree on some fair method to assign the order.

Running Head. The *running head* is a shortened title, no more than 50 characters long (including letters, punctuation, and spaces between words) that appears at the top of each page of your published paper. Center it, in uppercase letters, at the bottom of the title page after the words "Running head:" (see Figure 14-1).

The Abstract

The **abstract** is a concise (50–150 words) summary of your paper in which you include the rationale for your study, your method, your results, and (if space permits) your conclusions. Figure 14-2 shows a sample abstract page.

Although short, the abstract is one of the most important parts of your manuscript. Abstracts of papers are reproduced in *Psychological Abstracts*, where readers use them to evaluate whether to obtain a complete copy of the report. If your abstract is poorly written, readers may fail to understand the significance of your research and may pass it by. Put some effort into writing a good abstract.

The abstract is the first substantive section of your paper, but you usually write it after you have completed the rest of the paper. Preparing a summary of a paper is much easier after your paper is written than before. After you have completed your paper, you have a clearer idea about what must be included in the abstract.

A few general guidelines will help you prepare your abstract. First, keep it short! An abstract for a report of empirical research should not exceed 100 words. For a theoretical paper, it should not exceed 150 words. Second, make sure all information in your abstract also appears in the body of your paper. You introduce no new information in the abstract. Third, make the abstract self-contained. Do not use any abbreviations or terms that cannot be understood from the abstract alone. Finally, unless you have compelling reasons to do so, do not include reference citations in an abstract (omitting them saves space). Include a citation only if it orients the reader with respect to some necessary fact; for

Observational Learning

2

Abstract

Following training to eat from the grain hopper, different groups of chickens were exposed to a positive correlation between keylight and food-hopper operation or to observation of another chicken (model) keypecking in response to the presentation of the keylight and grain. During the training phase, subjects were separated from the key and grain by a transparent partition. When given access to the key and grain, chickens that had observed the model responded earlier and more frequently than subjects that had only observed the correlation between stimuli or had no observational training. In addition, subjects that had observed the correlation of keylight and grain responded sooner and more often than did the group given no observational training. These results confirm that birds can learn through observation, and that observation of a conspecific model can enhance that learning.

Figure 14-2. Sample abstract page (Johnson, Hamm, & Leahey, 1986; reprinted with permission).

example, "The present experiment replicated and extended earlier work on short-term memory (Peterson & Peterson, 1959)."

When preparing your abstract, place it on a separate page. The word "Abstract" should appear centered at the top of the page, with the abstract itself beginning a double-spaced line beneath the title (see Figure 14-2).

The Introduction

The text of the paper begins with the introduction. The primary function of the **introduction** is to justify the study described in the report. To help the reader understand why the particular study was conducted, the introduction usually contains the following parts:

1. An introduction to the topic under study

2. A brief review of the research findings and theories related to the topic

3. A statement of the problem to be addressed by the research (identifying an area in which knowledge is incomplete)

4. A statement of the purpose of the present research (always to solve the problem identified, but perhaps only a specific aspect of it)

5. A brief description of the method, intended to establish the relationship between the question being addressed and the method used to address it

6. A description of any predictions about the outcome and of the hypotheses used to generate those predictions

To provide this information in a comprehensible way, the structure of the introduction proceeds from the general to the specific. The inverted triangle shown in Figure 14-3 illustrates this structure. In the opening paragraph of your introduction, discuss (in general terms) the issue you have chosen to study. Next, develop the underlying logic and rationale for your study in more specific terms by reviewing relevant research and integrating its findings. Then identify the problem addressed by your research and state the purpose of your study. Finally, show how your study addresses the question under study and state your specific hypotheses.

Students often have difficulty determining what should go into the review of previous findings. Should it include a comprehensive review of *all* relevant research, or be limited to a few papers that relate specifically to your research? The answer: "Try for something between these extremes."

You can assume your reader has some knowledge of the basic psychological concepts that underlie your study. Your job is to bring your reader up to date on the literature that most directly relates to your study. For example, if you investigated the effect of the amount of reinforcement on behavior modification of retarded children, you need not review all research on operant conditioning and reinforcement. You can assume your reader has some knowledge of the basic concepts of operant conditioning. Instead, focus on the important issues relating directly to using operant conditioning to modify the behavior of retarded persons.

Assume you have decided to focus your introduction on the important issues. You then head to the library and, to your shock and horror, you find 200 articles that relate in some way to your research topic. Just how many of these must be included in your literature review? Of course, you cannot hope to review them all.

In fact, such a comprehensive literature review is inappropriate for a research paper. Your review should focus on those issues that are most important for establishing the rationale of your study. Therefore, you should identify all of the

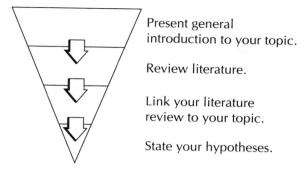

Present general
introduction to your topic.

Review literature.

Link your literature
review to your topic.

State your hypotheses.

Figure 14-3. General-to-specific organization of an APA-style introduction.

papers most directly relevant to the issues raised by your introduction. Within this narrower area, you can cite all relevant papers.

Formatting the Introduction. To follow APA style, you begin the introduction on a fresh page. Center the title of the paper at the top of the page and start the introduction immediately below the title. Do not type the heading "Introduction," as this is considered bad form by the guardians of APA style. Also, neither your name nor your affiliation appears on the first page of the introduction. Figure 14-4 shows a sample introduction. Notice how the authors followed the general-to-specific structure suggested in Figure 14-3 by beginning with a statement of the problem to study, followed by a review of relevant literature, and ending with a statement of the hypothesis to be tested.

The Method Section

After you have established the rationale of your study and stated your hypotheses in the introduction, you then must tell your reader exactly how your study was conducted. This is done in the **method section** of your paper. The method section describes in detail the characteristics of your subjects, materials, and apparatus used, as well as the procedures followed. The level of detail should be sufficient to allow another researcher to replicate your study.

The method section is usually divided into subsections to improve organization and readability. APA style permits considerable flexibility in how the divisions are made and labeled. The most commonly used format contains the following subsections: *subjects*, *apparatus* (or *materials*, if this descriptor is more appropriate), and *procedure*. If you consider it necessary, you may also include a *design* section in which you specify the design of your study. A design section

Yawning: Effects of Stimulus Interest

Yawning is characterized by gaping of the mouth
that is accompanied by a long inspiration followed by a
shorter expiration. Yawning is a behavior of the type
called "stereotyped" or "fixed" by ethologists and is
triggered by yet unspecified physiological states or
"released" by witnessing yawns or yawn-related stimuli
(Provine, 1986). Indeed, yawning may be the best
example of a stereotyped action pattern and stimulus
releaser in humans. Yawning is an obvious, common, and
probably universal human act that is performed
throughout the lifespan; however, there is much opinion
but little empirical evidence concerning why yawning
occurs, what function yawning serves, and what
environmental circumstances modulate yawning rate
(Barbizet, 1958; Heusner, 1946; Provine, 1986). For
example, the association of yawning with low levels of
arousal (Kataoka, 1975; Kishida, 1973; Sakai &
Takahashi, 1975) has led to speculation about the role
of yawning in increasing alertness. It also is commonly
believed that more yawning occurs while observing
uninteresting than interesting events. This may be the
basis for the recognition of the yawn as a
paralinguistic signal for boredom. The popular press
acknowledges that the yawn is a sign of boredom by

Figure 14-4. Sample introduction. (Provine & Hamernik, 1986; reprinted with permission.)

```
                                    Yawning:  Effects of

                                          4

referring to boring speeches and uninspiring artistic or

sports events as "yawners."

     The present study evaluated the hypothesis that

subjects yawn more while observing uninteresting than

while observing interesting stimuli by comparing the

yawns produced to two stimuli that differed in interest.

Subjects viewed either a 30-min videotape of rock

videos, an interesting and complex visual and auditory

stimulus for most college students, or a 30-min

videotape of an unchanging color-bar test pattern that

had no audio channel, a very uninteresting stimulus.
```

Figure 14-4. Sample introduction. (*continued*)

should only be included when your study uses an unconventional or complex design. You can also combine sections if this improves the clarity of the report. A description of each subsection follows.

Subjects. In the **subjects subsection**, you specify the nature and size of your subject sample. If animals were used as subjects, you must identify the species (rat, mouse, cat, and so on) and the strain (for example, Wistar rats). You must also specify the sex of the animals, the source for obtaining the animals, their ages at the time the study began, and important details of their care and housing (such as whether they were caged individually or as a group, whether they were given free or limited access to food and water, and the scheduling of light and darkness in the colony room). In this section you also specify the number of subjects assigned to each condition in your experiment and any other information (for example, special handling) that your reader would need to know in order to replicate your study.

Similar rules apply when you use humans in your research. Basic information must include the overall number of subjects, the number of subjects assigned to each condition, the sexes and approximate ages (or range of ages) of the subjects, how the subjects were obtained, and the details of any payment agreement. If you collected any *demographic information* (income or education, for example) or subject variables (IQ or personality variables, for example), include this information as well. Any special characteristics of your subjects such as mental retardation, psychopathology, or special abilities also should be included.

Apparatus. The equipment and other materials you used to measure behavior are described in the **apparatus subsection**. The level of detail necessary in your description depends on the nature of the equipment or materials you used.

If you used a commercial piece of laboratory equipment (for example, an operant chamber or a computer), you do not have to detail its characteristics. Instead, simply provide the name of the manufacturer and the model number of the equipment. Similarly, if you used a standardized test (such as the Stanford-Binet or the Bem Sex Roles Inventory), simply name the test (and the version, if relevant) and describe how it was obtained.

If you designed special equipment or developed a new measure, you must describe the equipment or measure in detail. If you designed a special operant chamber, for example, give its dimensions, materials of construction, and the types, characteristics, and locations of attached equipment (such as feeders, houselights, response levers, and sound sources). In short, provide any information your reader would need to reproduce your chamber in its essential details. Similarly, describe any measures you developed (for example, questionnaires).

Although you should provide enough information that another researcher could replicate your study, it is not feasible to reproduce extensive materials (such as a 250-item questionnaire or lengthy instructions) in your method section. If you used such materials, simply inform your reader where and how the materials can be obtained. Some journals may allow you to place such materials in an appendix.

Procedure. In the **procedure subsection**, tell your reader precisely what procedure was followed throughout the course of the study. Describe the conditions to which subjects were exposed or under which they were observed, what behaviors were recorded, how the behaviors were measured or scored, when the measures were taken, and any debriefing procedures. Provide enough information about the procedure that another researcher could reproduce its essential details.

If animal subjects were used, describe how the animals were handled, the length of the experimental sessions, any special deprivation schedules, and to what manipulations the subjects were exposed. If humans were used, include details about the instructions they received (if you cannot reproduce them, describe them in detail), informed consent procedures, procedures for assigning subjects to conditions, and how the experimental manipulations were introduced.

Combining Sections. You may find it convenient in some cases to combine the subjects and apparatus subsections, or the apparatus and procedure subsections. Do this if (and only if) combining the subsections makes the information easier to comprehend. For example, if different groups of subjects each were tested in different kinds of apparatus, it makes sense to describe each group and its apparatus together. Similarly, the presentation may be clearer if you describe each of several pieces of apparatus you used in the course of an experiment.

Formatting the Method Section. The method section begins immediately after the end of the introduction (do not necessarily start a new page). Center the word "Method." Now double-space, and type the word "Subjects" beginning at the left margin, and underline it. Again move down two lines, indent, and start the first paragraph of the subjects subsection. Follow the same format you used with the subjects subsection for the apparatus and procedure subsections. Figure 14–5 shows an example method section, with subjects, apparatus, and procedure subsections. Note how each subsection contributes to your understanding of the described experiment.

If you choose to combine subsections, use a combined heading. For example, a combined apparatus and procedure subsection would be given the heading "Apparatus and Procedure."

The Results Section

The major purpose of your **results section** is to report what you found. If your analysis is complex, you may want to provide an overview of your strategy for data analysis in the opening paragraph. Outline for the reader which statistical tests you applied, and in what order.

If you are using statistical tests that are not generally available, indicate to your reader where the test was found and how information about it can be obtained. Next, report the results of any tests used to establish that your data met the requirements of the applied statistical tests (for example, homogeneity of variance, normality). Report any data transformations you applied to your data.

After you have presented this preliminary information, you can report your results. Include values of any descriptive and/or inferential statistics you calculated, along with the relevant p values. Do not interpret or discuss your findings in the results section; that is done in the next section of your paper.

Formatting the Results Section. The results section begins immediately after the method section. Center the heading "Results," double-space, and indent to start the first paragraph. Figure 14–6 shows the first page of an example results section.

The results section is where you discuss any tables or figures that present data from your study. Although these will appear within the body of the *published* text, they do not appear there in the manuscript. Instead, you place a message in the manuscript at the approximate place where you want the figure or table to appear. The message for a figure states "Insert Figure X about here," where X is the number of the figure. Center the message and place a line above and below it, as in Figure 14–6. For a table, substitute the word "Table" for

Span of Apprehension

4

Method

<u>Subjects</u>

Volunteer psychology students (N = 68, with 17 of each sex/race combination--black, white, male, female) participated. They ranged in age from 18 to 27 years, with sex/race group mean ages of 19.5 to 22.3 years, and were in the sophomore or junior year.

<u>Apparatus</u>

A Kodak Carousel projector with collar-attached tachistoscopic shutter projected stimulus slides onto a standard screen; the slides showed two to eight random Arabic numerals. Each of 14 slides (2 each of two through eight digits) had a different combination of numbers. A single five-digit slide was used, open shutter, to familiarize the subjects with contrast, digit size, and screen placement. Data sheets identifying the 14 trials by letter (A-N) were used to record responses.

<u>Procedure</u>

The subjects were tested in random groups of 10 to 15, seated in an arc approximately 10 ft from the screen. Those needing glasses were asked to use them. Prior to testing, the subjects were told that the purpose of the experiment was to determine how much information the brain could assimilate with minimal

Figure 14-5. First page of a method section. (Buckalew & Hickey, 1984; reprinted with permission.)

Observational Learning

7

Results

Two measures of keypecking during the autoshaping transfer test were analyzed: number of trials until the first response and number of responses to the CS. Table 1 lists the trials to first response for individual subjects and also group medians. In order to test for

Insert Table 1 about here

group differences in the trials to first response, Mann-Whitney U tests were performed. The Mann-Whitney U tests revealed that the stimulus group responded earlier than did the control group, $U(6,6) = 5$, $p = .021$, that the model group responded earlier than did the control group, $U(6,6) = 0.5$, $p = .001$, and that the model group responded earlier than did the stimulus group, $U(6,6) = 1.5$, $p = .01$.

To show the different rates of response acquisition for each group, trials on the first transfer test day were divided into four blocks of 10 trials each, and the number of pecks emitted in each trial block was calculated (see Figure 1).

Insert Figure 1 about here

Figure 14-6. First page of a results section. (Johnson, Hamm, & Leahey, 1986; reprinted with permission.)

Table 14-1. Abbreviations for Statistical Symbols	
Abbreviation	Meaning
$\underline{df}$	Degrees of freedom
$\underline{F}$	F-ratio
$\underline{M}$	Arithmetic average (mean)
$\underline{N}$	Number of subjects in entire sample
$\underline{n}$	Number of subjects in limited portion of a sample
$\underline{p}$	p-value
$\underline{SD}$	Standard deviation
$\underline{t}$	t-statistic
$\underline{z}$	Results from z-test or a z-score
μ	Population mean (mu)
α	Alpha level
β	Beta

"Figure." (The placement of the figures and tables, and how to make them, is discussed later in this chapter.)

Presenting the results of a statistical analysis is a bit tricky, but not difficult once you get the hang of it. At one time, more complex analyses such as ANOVA were presented in detail within a table. All those numbers in the table, with their obscure labels (such as "Source of Variance"), looked so impressive that authors sometimes became overwhelmed with satisfaction and forgot to present the actual data! Today the results of statistical analyses are presented in less detail within the text of the results section, or simply appear as an asterisk or other symbol within a table of treatment means (indicating which differences were statistically significant at a specified level).

When you describe the results of a statistical analysis within the text, make them a part of a sentence. This sentence states what comparison is being evaluated, whether or not the difference is statistically significant, the critical statistic and its degrees of freedom, the value obtained for the statistic, and the level of significance achieved. Here's an example:

An analysis of variance indicated that the main effect of retention interval was significant, $\underline{F}$ (3,24) = 23.48, $\underline{p}$ <0.01.

Results from statistical tests are reported with underlined symbols, as shown. For example, an F-ratio is denoted with the symbol $\underline{F}$, the mean with $\underline{M}$, and a t-value with $\underline{t}$. Table 14-1 shows a partial list of some common statistical symbols.

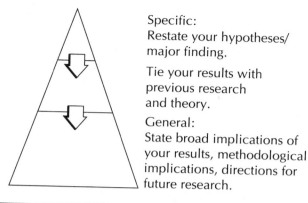

Specific:
Restate your hypotheses/
major finding.

Tie your results with
previous research
and theory.

General:
State broad implications of
your results, methodological
implications, directions for
future research.

Figure 14-7. Specific-to-general organization of an APA-style discussion section.

The Discussion Section

You interpret your results and draw conclusions in the **discussion section**. The structure of your discussion section reverses that used for the introduction. Instead of moving from the general to the specific, you move from the specific to the general. Begin with a summary of the important findings of your research, and then generalize your discussion to indicate how your results fit with previous research and theory. This strategy is shown in Figure 14-7. Notice that this time the triangle appears in its proper orientation. At the top is a focused discussion of your results, followed by the integration of your results with the broader theoretical and empirical issues.

Begin your discussion section with a brief restatement of your hypotheses. Next, briefly indicate whether your data were consistent with your pre-experimental hypotheses. Use the remainder of the discussion section to integrate your findings with previous research and theory. Discuss how consistent your findings are with previous work in the area.

If your study yielded results that are discrepant from previous work, you should speculate on why the discrepancies emerged. Also, point out any problems encountered during the course of your research that might temper any conclusions drawn from your study. Often methodological problems become evident only when you actually run your study, and these should be communicated to your reader. Finally, indicate what implications your research has for future research in the area. Point out any specific areas that need to be investigated further.

In the discussion section, you have license to speculate on the importance of your findings. Nevertheless, avoid the temptation to overstep the bounds of that

Yawning: Effects of

9

Discussion

The present analysis confirms the folk belief that people yawn more during uninteresting than interesting events. A positive correlation between yawning and the drowsiness experienced immediately before and after sleeping is reported elsewhere (Provine, Hamernick, & Curchack, 1986). Taken together, these results for stimulus interest and sleeping times provide empirical support for the recognition of the yawn as a paralinguistic signal for drowsiness, fatigue, disinterest, and boredom.

Yawning frequency and duration were both less in the interesting than in the uninteresting stimulus condition. As previously shown, yawns may be performed at rates ranging from zero to several yawns per minute (Provine, 1986). However, the yawn is a stereotyped action pattern that is performed at so-called "typical intensity"; extremely short or fractional yawns are seldom, if ever, produced (Provine, 1986). Although there are more constraints on the duration than the frequency of yawns, the present finding of shorter yawns by observers of interesting stimuli suggests that there is at least modest context-induced variability in yawn duration. A gender difference in yawn duration was also detected; males performed longer yawns than females.

Figure 14-8. First page of a discussion section. (Provine & Hamernik, 1986; reprinted with permission.)

license. Your interpretations must be based on your data, data from previous research, and/or established theory. Avoid the temptation to make unsubstantiated interpretations, even if they make intuitive sense to you.

Figure 14-8 shows an example of the first page of a discussion section. The authors of this paper followed the specific-to-general organization shown in Figure 14-7. Notice that the authors begin with a brief statement of what was found and follow by integrating their findings with those of other researchers in the area.

The Reference Section

The **reference section** provides a list of the bibliographical references cited in the report. Any articles or books you cited in the body of your paper *must* be listed in the reference section. Conversely, any references listed in the reference section *must* be cited in the paper. If you read hundreds of papers but only cited three of them, your reference section should contain only the three papers actually cited.

Formatting the Reference Section. Begin the reference section on a fresh page, and center the title "References" at the top. Then list your references in alphabetical order according to author. If you have more than one reference from the same author, order them alphabetically by second author, and so forth. Where authorship is identical, order the references by date of publication. Use a hanging indent format for each reference. That is, begin each reference entry at the left margin, but indent each subsequent line of the entry three spaces. Figure 14-9 shows a sample reference section page.

How to format each reference entry depends on the type of reference. Your references may include journal articles, books, book chapters from edited anthologies, papers presented at conventions, government publications, and so on. These references may be ascribed to a single author, multiple authors, or no author. The APA style manual shows you how to present each type of reference you are likely to encounter. However, most articles you cite will follow a fairly standard format. The general format for a journal article is as follows:

Last name, Initial of first name. Initial of middle name. (Date of publication). Title of journal article. Name of Journal, volume, pages.

A specific reference entry looks like this:

Collins, W. A. (1970). Learning of media content: A developmental study. Child Development, 41, 1133–1142.

Table 14-2 summarizes some of the more commonly used reference formats. If you encounter a reference of a type not covered in the table, consult the APA style manual.

Observational Learning

10

References

Brown, P. L., & Jenkins, H. M. (1968). Auto-shaping of
    pigeon's key-peck. <u>Journal of the Experimental
    Analysis of Behavior</u>, <u>11</u>, 1-8.

Browne, M. P. (1976). The role of primary reinforcemen
    and overt movements in auto-shaping in the pigeon.
    <u>Animal Learning & Behavior</u>, <u>4</u>, 287-292.

Darby, C. L., & Riopelle, A. J. (1959). Observational
    learning in the rhesus monkey. <u>Journal of
    Comparative and Physiological Psychology</u>, <u>52</u>, 94-
    98.

Del Russo, J. E. (1975). Observational learning of
    discriminative avoidance in hooded rats. <u>Animal
    Learning & Behavior</u>, <u>3</u>, 76-80.

Denny, M. R., Bell, R. C., & Clos, C. (1983). Two-
    choice observational learning and reversal in the
    rat: S-S versus S-R effects. <u>Animal Learning &
    Behavior</u>, <u>11</u>, 223-228.

Kohn, B., & Dennis, M. (1972). Observation and
    discrimination learning in the rat: Specific and
    nonspecific effects. <u>Journal of Comparative and
    Physiological Psychology</u>, <u>78</u>, 292-296.

Oberdieck, F., Strong, R., & Cheney, C. (1979,
    November). <u>The effect of observing positive CS-US
    correlations on subsequent autoshaping</u>. Paper

Figure 14-9. First page of a reference section. (Johnson, Hamm, & Leahey, 1986; reprinted with permission.)

Table 14-2. Reference Entry Formats

Journal Article

Bandura, A. (1977). Toward a unifying theory of behavioral change. Psychological Bulletin, 84, 191–215.

Storms, M. D., & Nisbett, R. E. (1970). Insomnia and the attribution process. Journal of Personality and Social Psychology, 16, 319–328.

Tulving, E., McNulty, J. A., & Ozier, M. (1965). Vividness of words and learning to learn in free recall learning. Canadian Journal of Psychology, 19, 242–252.

Magazine Article

Kessen, W., & Cahan, E. D. (1986, November, December). A century of psychology: From subject to object to agent. American Scientist, pp. 640–649.

Books

Bransford, J. D. (1979). Human cognition: Learning, understanding and remembering. Belmont, CA: Wadsworth.

Sarafino, E. P., & Armstrong, J. W. (1986). Child and adolescent development (2nd ed.). St. Paul, MN: West.

Article in an Edited Book

Winkel, G. H., & Sasanoff, R. (1970). An approach to objective analysis of behavior in architectural space. In H. M. Proshansky, W. H. Ittelson, & L. G. Rivlin (Eds.), Environmental psychology: Man and his environment (pp. 619–630). New York: Holt, Rinehart & Winston.

Unpublished Paper Presented at a Meeting

Rosch, J. (1984, June). Processing criminal cases in Japan: Implications for debate about plea bargaining in the U.S. Paper presented at the meeting of the Law and Society Association. Boston, MA.

```
                                          Yawning:  Effects of

                                                    11

                      Author Notes
            We gratefully acknowledge the statistical

      assistance of Marilyn Demorest and the editorial

      comments of Theodore Dembroski.  Requests for reprints

      should be sent to Robert R. Provine and the Department

      of Psychology, University of Maryland Baltimore County,

      Catonsville, MD 21228.
```

Figure 14-10. Sample author notes page. (Provine & Hamernik, 1986; reprinted with permission.)

Other Optional Information

Although the reference section is the last formal section of the report, additional information and materials follow it. This information may include author notes, footnotes, tables, figure captions, and figures. In the published report, each of these appears within the body of the report, but they all go at the end of the manuscript.

Author Notes. When published, most journal articles include a small footnote at the bottom of the first page. This footnote indicates where readers can write for a reprint of the article, what grant (if any) supported the project, the sponsoring agency, and additional information (if relevant) concerning the conditions under which the project was undertaken (for example, to partially fulfill the requirements of a master's or doctoral degree). The information is provided within the manuscript on a separate page entitled "Author Notes" (centered at the top of the page). Figure 14–10 shows an example author notes page.

Footnotes. Occasionally you may wish to present information in order to clarify a point made in the text of the paper or to provide additional details, but find that such information detracts from the flow of your discussion at that point. Such information can be placed in a footnote. At the point in the text where the reader should consult the footnote, simply place a superscript number (beginning with [1] for the first footnote), as in the following example:

An Experimental Investigation

8

Footnotes

[1]A more complete description of the trial may be found in Horowitz and Bordens (1988).

[2]This trial was adapted from an actual case (<u>Wilhoite v. Olin Corp.</u>, 1985). While the names of the various participants and locations were fictitious, the trial scenario in this study was taken from the above case.

Figure 14-11. Sample footnotes page.

The trial, used previously (Horowitz & Bordens, 1988), consisted of a 4-hour audiotape.[1]

The footnote itself appears in the manuscript on a separate page entitled "Footnotes." Figure 14-11 shows how each footnote is numbered and presented.

Tables. Tables are used to present complex information that cannot be easily summarized in the body of your paper. Tables can be used to illustrate the design of your study and materials, and to present data in the results section. Tables are somewhat time-consuming to make and expensive to reproduce. Use a table only when it is impractical to fully describe information in the text of your paper.

Tables prepared according to APA specifications include a title, a number, headings, a body, and, if necessary, notes. Figure 14-12 shows an example of an APA-style table. As shown in the figure, the title and number of a table are placed at the top of the page. This is in contrast to a figure, where neither the title nor the number appear on the figure itself. The headings of your table should clearly tell your reader what information is included in your table. In the body of the table, include the information you want your reader to see. Finally, use notes to explain the meaning of symbols in the table or to provide information not included in the table itself.

Figure Captions. Figure captions, unlike table captions, appear on a page separate from the figures to which they refer. Center the words "Figure Captions" at the top of the page. Underneath, beginning at the left margin, type "Figure 1."

Observational Learning

12

Table 1

Trials to First Response for Subjects in Each Group

Subject Number	Model Group	Stimulus Group	Control Group
1	6	47	26
2	2	15	24
3	1	5	22
4	1	2	26
5	1	10	17
6	1	9	75
Median	1	9.5	25

Figure 14-12. Sample table. (Johnson, Hamm, & Leahey, 1986; reprinted with permission).

and leave two spaces; then type the caption for Figure 1. Follow the same format for each subsequent figure. Figure 14–13 shows a sample figure captions page.

Figures. Like tables, *figures* are used in your paper to provide a graphic illustration of complex material or relationships that cannot be adequately described in text. Although they are most often described in the results section of your paper, they can also appear in any other section. For example, a figure may be used to illustrate the materials used in your study, or to show an important theoretical relationship in your introduction. Because figures are difficult to prepare and expensive to reproduce in journals, don't include a figure that represents a simple linear relationship between variables.

Graphs, drawings, and photographs are three commonly used types of figures. Graphs are used to illustrate complex relationships among variables. Drawings and photographs are used to illustrate equipment, materials, or stimuli that were used in a study. Photographs might also be used to convey aspects of results

```
                                    Observational Learning

                                                    13
                        Figure Captions
              Figure 1.  Mean responses of the three groups over
         the four 10-trial blocks that comprised the first
         session during the autoshaping transfer test.
              Figure 2.  Mean responses of the three groups over
         the four 10-trial blocks that comprised the seocnd
         session of the autoshaping transfer test.
```

Figure 14-13. Sample figure captions page. (Johnson, Hamm, & Leahey, 1986; reprinted with permission.)

that cannot be adequately described in the text of your paper. For example, in an article about physiological psychology, photographs of histological sections are often presented to show the location of a lesion or stimulating electrode in the brain.

A simple rule to follow when preparing graphs is to make them simple and accurate. A visually confusing graph adds little to your paper. An inaccurately drawn graph can confuse your reader or make small, albeit statistically significant, effects look unnaturally large. Carefully plan and draw your graphs.

On a graph, levels of the independent variable are represented on the X axis (the horizontal axis), and levels of the dependent variable on the Y axis (the vertical axis). The length of the Y axis should be about two–thirds the length of the X axis. Each axis must be clearly labeled as to what the axis represents. Tick marks are used to demarcate the units of measurement. Too much space between tick marks on either axis (or both axes) may distort your data. Panel A of Figure 14-14 shows this condition. Notice that the tick marks for the dependent variable are placed far apart. This makes the differences appear to be large when, in fact, the differences are really less than one unit. Panel B of Figure 14-14 shows the same data graphed correctly. The small differences among means are represented fairly, and your reader is not misled.

In some cases you may find it necessary to break an axis to fit all your data on a graph. For example, if values of the dependent variable can range from 0 to 100, but subjects only used numbers between 0 and 10, and 70 and 100, you

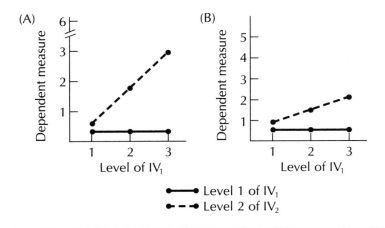

Figure 14-14. (A) Graph that inaccurately depicts a relationship. (B) Graph that accurately depicts a relationship.

may want to show the data on a graph similar to the one shown in Figure 14–15. Notice that the Y axis is broken by slash marks in the middle. This shows your reader that a range of values along the Y axis has been skipped over. You should also break any lines within the graph that cross the broken part of an axis. The bottom line in Figure 14–15 illustrates how this is done.

Each graph you prepare must include a *legend*. The legend tells your reader what each of the points and lines on your graph means. Look back at Figure 14–15. The legend at the top of the graph tells the reader that the solid line represents data from Level 1 of IV2, whereas the broken line represents data from Level 2 of IV2.

Citing References in Your Report

In some writing styles, citations in the body of your paper are indicated with footnotes. In APA style, however, citations are made by providing the name(s) of the author(s), the publication date of the source, and (when needed) specific pages within the source.

The format of a citation in the text depends on how you choose to write a sentence that includes the citation. If the citation is included as an integral part of the sentence, you give the last name(s) of the author(s) and, in parentheses, the year in which the work was published. Here is an example with two authors:

According to Smith and Jones (1982), memory for meaningful information is much better than memory for meaningless material.

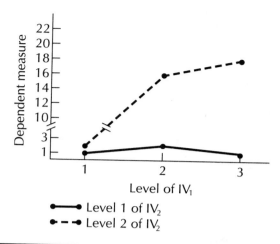

Figure 14-15. Graph showing a broken axis.

If the citation is "tacked on" to the sentence, enclose the entire citation in parentheses, as follows:

Memory for meaningful information tends to be much better than memory for meaningless information (Smith & Jones, 1982).

The two examples just provided are *multiple-author citations*. Notice that when you cite the names of two authors in the sentence itself (the first example), you use the word *and* to connect the authors' names. When the names are used in parentheses (as in the second example), you use an ampersand (&) to connect them.

When you have more than two authors, the citation takes the following form:

According to Smith, Jones, and Harris (1982), memory for meaningful information is better than memory for meaningless information.

or

Memory for meaningful information is better than memory for meaningless information (Smith, Jones, & Harris, 1982).

If you must cite an article with three or more authors several times in your paper, writing each name repeatedly becomes tedious. To avoid this problem, after the first author's name you can use "et al." (Latin for "and others") for the second and subsequent citations of the same article. Here is an example:

Memory for meaningful information is much better than memory for meaningless information (Smith, Jones, & Harris, 1982). . . . Smith et al. also point out that . . .

Although the "et al." format can be convenient, it can also be abused. If you cite the same multiple-author paper at widely separated points in your paper, your reader may not remember who is included in "et al." In such cases, spell out the names of all the authors.

However, if a paper you cite has an unreasonable number of authors (perhaps 10 authors), use "et al." even for the first citation. Provide the full reference in the reference list at the end of your paper.

Whenever you directly quote or paraphrase a source, you must acknowledge the source in a citation. As with citations, the form to follow depends on the sentence structure. For example,

Although research does suggest that television has the potential to aid in the socialization of children, there is still reason to be cautious. In fact, according to Liebert, Sprafkin, and Davidson (1982, p. 209), "Although most studies suggest that prosocial television can have desired effects, our ability to magnify these effects and minimize undesirable ones is in its infancy."

or

Even though research does suggest that television has the potential to aid in the socialization of children "our ability to magnify these effects and minimize undesirable ones is in its infancy" (Liebert, Sprafkin, & Davidson, 1982, p. 209).

These examples cited a direct quotation. Even when you simply paraphrase the ideas of Liebert et al., however, you still cite the source. This issue is discussed in greater detail later in this chapter in the section on plagiarism.

Finally, several special in-text citations are sometimes used. These are summarized in Table 14-3.

Using Numbers in the Text

In APA style, numbers lower than 10 are spelled out, whereas numbers 10 and higher are expressed numerically. A few exceptions to this rule are as follows:

1. When you start a sentence with a number greater than 10, write the number out (for example, "Twenty subjects were assigned to each group").

2. Use numerals for numbers less than 10 when they are included in a range statement ("Numbers on the scale ranged from 1 to 100").

3. Use numerals when you refer to a unit of measurement, even if the number is less than 10 ("Each rat received a 5-milligram injection of Valium").

Table 14-3. APA-Style, In-Text Citations

APPLICATION	CITATION FORMAT
Single Author	
Author named in sentence	
One article:	Jones (1985)
Two articles (same year):	Jones (1985a, 1985b)
Two articles (different years):	Jones (1982, 1985)
Personal communication:	Smith (personal communication, July 15, 1982)[a]
Author named in parenthesis	
One article:	(Jones, 1982)
Two articles (same year):	(Jones, 1985a, 1985b)
Two articles (different years):	(Jones, 1982, 1985)
Personal communication:	(Key, personal communication, July 15, 1982)[a]
Multiple Authors[b]	
Authors named in sentence	
Two authors:	Smith and Jones (1978)
More than two authors:	Smith, Jones, and Key (1982)
Authors named in parenthesis	
Two authors:	(Smith & Jones, 1978)
More than two authors:	(Smith, Jones, & Key, 1982)
Multiple citation for same idea:	(Smith & Jones, 1982; Harris, 1978; Jones, 1985)
Special Citations	
Legal Citations	
Litigants named in sentence:	Ballew v. Georgia (1976)
Litigants named in parenthesis:	(Ballew v. Georgia, 1976)

[a]Personal communication items are *not* placed in the reference list.
[b]Format for multiple articles follows that for single authors.

SOURCE: Information compiled from American Psychological Association, 1983.

4. Use numerals to refer to times, dates, ages, and so forth (6:45, December 15, 1953, 5 years old).

5. Write out numbers when they do not refer to specific measurements and are not grouped with other numbers lower than 10 ("Subjects were exposed to stimuli five times within a 30-second period")

6. Write out numbers when they are in a hyphenated expression ("second-level calculation," "ten-point scale").

For other exceptions to the general rule about numbers, see the APA style manual.

Avoiding Biased Language

Sometimes in our writing we inadvertently use language that presupposes that one group is preferred over another. According to the APA manual, for example, when we use the pronoun *he* to express our ideas we are falling into the trap of sexist writing. The manual cites two major areas in which biased writing occurs. These are designation and evaluation, each having two subtypes: (1) *ambiguity of referent*, when it is not clear whether you are referring to one or both sexes (American Psychological Association [APA], p. 44); and (2) *stereotyping*, when your writing suggests biased ideas about sex or ethnic group identity (APA, 1983, p. 44).

As an example of biased writing, consider the following short paragraph describing a survey:

Questionnaires were sent to all doctors in the state of Ohio and their wives. Each subject was instructed to complete and return his questionnaire separately.

These two sentences display sexist writing. In the first sentence, referring to "doctors and their wives" presumes that all doctors are male (or, at best, that being a doctor is a typically male role). In the second sentence the pronoun "his" refers to all subjects in the sample, despite the fact that some subjects in the sample are female. The paragraph can be quite easily rewritten to eliminate the obvious bias:

Questionnaires were sent to all doctors in the state of Ohio and their spouses. Subjects were instructed to complete and return their questionnaires separately.

Notice how a few minor changes have eliminated sex bias. Using the neutral word "spouse" is not only more accurate but also removes the presumption that the doctor role is typically male. Changing "his" to "their" removes the inaccurate reference.

Biased writing is not limited to sexist language use. You should also be sensitive to issues of race and ethnic group bias. For example, if you conducted a study using subjects of different races, avoid consistently placing one group first, or over another. For example,

> The subject sample consisted of 200 white and 200 black college students. . . . It was found that white college students were less interested in minority issues than were black college students.

In these two sentences, "white" is consistently placed before "black." This subtly places whites over blacks. The solution to this problem is simple: alternate the order of reference. For example,

> The subject sample consisted of 200 white and 200 black college students. . . . It was found that black college students were more interested in minority issues than were white college students.

The ways we use biased language are too numerous to list here. Biased writing occurs because we enter our own world views into our writing. Usually, we write what enters our minds most easily. Unfortunately, what results is writing slanted in the favor of our own reference groups (for example, sex and race). Avoid biased writing by giving extra thought to the sentences you write. After writing your paper, go back over it and eliminate any statements that seem biased. For more information on and examples of biased writing, see the *Publication Manual of the American Psychological Association* (third edition), pages 44–49.

Clarity of Expression, Organization, and Style

The previous sections explained the general conventions to be followed when writing an APA-style paper. Unfortunately, merely knowing about subsections and citation formats does not guarantee that you will write a quality paper. You must also know how to present your ideas in a clear and organized way. Although this chapter cannot teach you to be a good writer, it can help you to avoid some of the common pitfalls. This section points out some of the flaws commonly found in student papers.

Perhaps the most common flaws in student papers are poorly expressed ideas, unorganized presentation of ideas, and sloppy presentation style. You can have a good handle on your research topic, procedures, and results but still be unable to communicate them well to your readers. Important points become obscured by unclear writing and a disorganized presentation.

Clarity of Expression

Clarity of expression is the clear, concise communication of ideas to your reader. Three elements of clear expression are grammatical correctness, proper word choice, and economy of expression (APA, 1983). First, consider grammatical correctness.

Grammatical Correctness. Students often do not pay close enough attention to the grammatical structure of their sentences. A good illustration is the following ambiguous sentence:

> The experimenter recorded how fast each rat ran the maze with a stopwatch.

In this example, the intention was to say that the experimenter used a stopwatch to time the rat's running speed. Instead, you get the image of a rat running the maze while holding a stopwatch! The problem here is that the modifier "with a stopwatch" is misplaced in such a way that it refers to the rat, not to the experimenter. The following sentence is unambiguous, and consequently much clearer:

> Using a stopwatch, the experimenter timed each rat's running speed.

Here, the modifier is properly attached to the experimenter.

Another common grammatical error is disagreement between subject and verb. In the following incorrect sentence, the verb goes with the word "one" and not "records":

> Only one of the subject's *records were* included in the analysis.

This sentence should be corrected as follows:

> Only *one* of the subject's records *was* included in the analysis.

This chapter cannot explore all the common grammatical errors. Make an effort to reduce grammatical errors in your writing. Some good guides that may help you are Crews (1980); Hall (1979); Leggett, Mead, and Charvat (1978); and Strunk and White (1979).

Proper Word Choice. Proper word choice is the second aspect of clear writing. Make sure that your selected words convey your ideas as intended. For example, in general writing the words "belief" and "value" are used interchangeably. In scientific writing, however, they may mean very different things (APA, 1983). Choose the word that most accurately conveys your meaning. If you mean "value," then say "value."

Unnecessary qualifiers also tend to obscure clarity of expression. Phrases such as "approximately equal" and "particularly strong" are imprecise and may be interpreted differently by different readers. Be specific when referring to quantity estimates. And be careful about using pronouns in place of nouns, especially in long sentences. Following a sentence that has many "they's," "it's," and so on is difficult.

Also, avoid using complex words when a simple word would suffice. For example, don't say "masticate" when you mean "chew," or "cogitate" when you mean "think" (Hall, 1979, p. 84). And never utilize the word "utilize"—use "use" instead. Constant use of fancy words becomes tedious to read. Base your choice on how well a word conveys your meaning, not on how intelligent you think it makes you sound. If a complex word best conveys your meaning (for example, "clandestine" implies much more than "secret") by all means use it. In other cases, use the preferred simple word.

Economy of Expression. The third aspect of clear writing is *economy of expression.* Your sentences should be concise. A concise sentence expresses your meaning by using relatively few words. Overly long sentences can be unclear at best and confusing at worst. Consider the following examples:

Too Long: "The experimenter read subjects the experimental instructions and then let subjects listen to the audiotaped trials, which were recorded by a male graduate student."

Better: "Subjects listened to an audiotaped summary of a trial immediately after being instructed."

In the first example, too much information is packed into a single sentence. The second example works better because the sentence focuses on a single idea. Another sentence, more appropriately placed (that is, placed in the materials section) could point out that the voice on the tape was that of a male graduate student.

By the way, did you notice any ambiguity in the first example? The sentence was intended to say that the voice on the tape was that of a male graduate student. However, it could be interpreted as saying that the male graduate student operated the tape recorder. Lengthy sentences often become confusing through ambiguity.

Organization

Whereas clarity of expression relates most closely to the structure of sentences, organization relates to how those sentences are organized into paragraphs, and how paragraphs are woven into an entire paper. You can write the most beautiful, grammatically correct sentences, yet fail to clearly convey your ideas. A paragraph is more than a collection of grammatically correct sentences. Those sentences must be woven into a coherent, unified entity that clearly conveys information to your readers.

Paragraphs can include four types of sentences (Crews, 1980). These are *theme sentences*, *support sentences*, *limiting sentences*, and *transitional sentences*. The theme sentence, which is usually the first sentence in a paragraph, conveys to your reader the topic of the paragraph. Support sentences follow the theme sentence and support and elaborate the theme. Limiting sentences point out possible limits to the assertion made in the theme sentence. Finally, transitional sentences are used to shift smoothly from one idea to another within a paragraph. These four types of sentences should be combined to achieve unity.

Crews (1980) suggests four general rules to help you attain unity within paragraphs:

1. Make only one major point within a paragraph.

2. Your theme sentence should be the most general sentence within a paragraph. All subsequent sentences should focus on the theme stated in the theme sentence.

3. Stick to the theme stated at the outset of the paragraph. Unity is disrupted when you stray from the point.

4. Use complete sequences of limiting or supporting sentences. That is, if you have something positive to say about a topic, list all the positive elements before turning to the negative.

In addition to unity, a paragraph should have coherence. Coherence is disrupted when sentences that relate only tangentially to a topic are included in a paragraph (Hall, 1979, p. 193). Two problematic sentences are underlined in the following paragraph. The first disrupts unity, and the second disrupts coherence.

Methodological problems were apparent in the Jones and Smith (1978) experiment. Smith was only a graduate student at the time of the study. The methodological problems stemmed from outdated equipment that was used. Some of the equipment was so old that it could hardly be kept working. This equipment did not have the sensitivity to accurately record the subtle changes in the subjects' behavior.

The first underlined sentence is irrelevant to the topic introduced at the beginning of the paragraph. The second underlined sentence, although tangentially related, is not necessary. It serves only to break up the important points in the previous and subsequent sentences (points that should be linked directly). The two underlined sentences together add little to the discussion and disrupt the unity of the paragraph.

Without these two unnecessary statements, the paragraph still conveys the important idea that the Jones and Smith study was flawed because of archaic equipment:

Methodological problems were apparent in the Jones and Smith (1978) experiment. The methodological problems stemmed from outdated equipment that was used. This equipment did not have the sensitivity to accurately record the subtle changes in the subjects' behavior.

Paragraphs can become confusing when they become too long. Each paragraph should deal with a particular aspect of a topic. Several relatively short paragraphs are better than one long paragraph. Weave together paragraphs to create a unified and consistent narrative. Avoid confusing the reader with too much information packed into too little space.

Each section of your paper should be organized into units. For example, your introduction might be organized into three subsections (even if they are not labeled as such). In the first subsection, you introduce your topic (using perhaps two paragraphs). In the second subsection, you might review relevant literature (five paragraphs). Finally, in the third subsection, you might summarize the research you reviewed and state your hypotheses (three paragraphs). Information in your method, results, and discussion sections should be organized in a similar fashion.

The best way to avoid disorganization is to make an outline of your paper before you begin writing and then stick to the outline. Indicate the main sections (introduction, method, and so forth), and identify the subtopics to be handled within the major sections.

Style. Your final paper is a reflection of you as well as your work. A paper can be well organized and clearly written, yet still make a negative impression on your reader because of sloppy presentation. Frequent misspellings, misused words, and typographical errors detract significantly from your paper. Work to eliminate them.

Misspellings can best be avoided by using a dictionary (we recommend Webster's [ninth edition] or Webster's Third International Edition). If you have difficulty with spelling (as many of us do), have your paper read by a good speller. If you plan to use a computer to write your paper, look for a word processing program that includes a spelling checker (or purchase a stand-alone spelling checker). Although these programs may not correct all spelling errors, they do a good job of flagging errors. Once flagged, these words can be looked up in the dictionary and corrected. To help you flag your own spelling errors, Table 14-4 shows a list of commonly misspelled words (Rosnow & Rosnow, 1986).

Misused words also detract from your paper. For example, "affect" and "effect" are commonly confused. As a verb, "affect" means "to act on" and "effect" means "to bring about." Avoiding these errors involves acquiring a good vocabulary. If you have trouble in this area, have your paper read by someone who has a good vocabulary. If you use a word processor, you might also consider using one of the many style analyzers (such as RightWriter). Some of these catch and flag misused words. Table 14-5 lists some commonly misused words.

Frequent typographical errors (including crossed-out words, penciled-in words, and mistyping) also detract from your work. Careful proofreading is essential. Correct any errors you find before you submit your work. These corrections should be made on your typewriter or word processor, not penciled in on the manuscript.

A word processor can be invaluable for making corrections. Many students hand in sloppy papers because it is too much trouble to make a correction (especially if it means retyping an entire page). A word processor allows you to insert, delete, or move words or even whole paragraphs quickly and easily. You can fix errors, make stylistic changes, or improve organization without retyping sections of the manuscript.

Making It Work. A goal you should strive to achieve is to produce a well-written report of your results that is clear, organized, and visually pleasing. Most writers,

Table 14-4. Commonly Misspelled Words

abnormality	audiovisual	competition	discrimination
absence	authoritarianism	comprehensive	disease
accommodation	autistic	compulsion	displacement
accreditation	autokinetic	compulsory	dissonance
accuracy	autonomy	conceptualization	dominance
achievement	baccalaureate	conditioning	efficiency
adjustment	behaviorism	consciousness	elementary
administrator	benefited	conservatism	emotional
adolescence	bureaucracy	consistent	empathize
advancement	busing	contiguity	empiricism
advisory	calendar	contingencies	enrollment
affiliation	catastrophe	continuous	environmental
aggression	centralization	continuum	epistemology
aggressiveness	changing	cooperation	equilibrium
alcoholism	characteristic	correlation	equivalence
alienation	checklist	cost-effectiveness	eugenics
a lot (two words)	chi-square	counseling	exceed
altruistic	chimpanzee	counselor	exceptional
ambiguity	chromosome	criticism	existence
ambivalence	chronic	cross-cultural	existential
amnesia	chronological	curriculum	expectancy
analogy	circadian	curvilinear	extinction
analysis	classification	cyclical	extracurricular
analytical	coefficient	defensive	extrasensory
androgyny	cognitive	deficiency	extraversion
anomaly	colloquium	delusion	facilitation
antisocial	commission	democracy	feedback
anomie	commitment	depression	fetishism
anxiety	committed	descriptive	flexibility
apparatus	committee	desensitization	frequency
apprehension	commodity	determinant	frustration
archetype	communication	develop	gender
assimilation	comparative	diagnosis	generalization
attitude	comparison	dialogue	genetic
attribution	compensatory	dilemmas	government
attrition	competence	discipline	grammar

Table 14-4. Commonly Misspelled Words *(continued)*

guard	knowledge	parallel	respondent
guidance	liaison	paralysis	rhetoric
guideline	libido	parameter	satisfactorily
hallucination	linguistic	paranoid	self-actualization
handicapped	longitudinal	pedagogy	separate
helplessness	luminosity	perceive	schizophrenia
hereditary	maintenance	perceptual	scientific
heterogeneous	masochism	persistent	senior
heuristic	measurement	pertinent	sensitivity
hierarchical	meta-analysis	phenomenology	separation
holistic	metatheory	physiological	significance
homeostasis	methodology	precede	socialization
homogeneous	milieu	predominantly	spontaneity
hormone	mnemonics	probability	statistical
hypnotism	multidimensional	proceed	stereotype
hypothesis	multivariate	professional	succeed
hysterical	narcissistic	programmed	superego
idiographic	nature–nurture	prophecy	symptomatology
idiosyncratic	negativism	psychiatric	syndrome
illiteracy	neonatal	psychoanalysis	synthesis
illusion	neurosis	psycholinguistics	taboo
implement	nomothetic	psychopathology	tachistoscope
indefinite	nonverbal	psychosomatic	taxonomy
individual	obsessive	psychotic	technological
ingenious	obsessive-compulsive	puberty	testability
inhibition	occasion	qualitative	theoretical
intelligence	occurrence	quasi-experimental	therapeutic
intentionality	oedipal	questionnaire	threshold
interdisciplinary	operant	randomized	two-tailed
introversion	operationalism	rationalization	two–way
irradiation	optimum	receive	unconscious
judgment	organismic	recommendation	validity
juvenile	orientation	regression	variability
kindergarten	oriented	reinforcement	violence
kinesthesis	overreaction	resistance	voluntary

SOURCE: Rosnow & Rosnow, 1986; reprinted with permission.

Table 14-5. Commonly Misused Words

Words	True Meanings and Comments
affect/effect	*affect*: to influence *effect*: the result of; to implement
accept/except	*accept*: to take willingly *except*: excluding; to exclude
among/between	*among*: used when you refer to more than two *between*: used when you refer to only two
amount/number	*amount*: refers to quantity *number*: refers to countable elements
analysis/analyses	*analysis*: singular form *analyses*: plural form
cite/site	*cite*: make reference to *site*: location
datum/data	*datum*: singular form *data*: plural form
every one/everyone	*every one*: each one *everyone*: everybody
few/little	*few*: refers to number *little*: refers to amount
its/it's	*its*: possessive pronoun *it's*: contraction of "it is"
many/much	*many*: refers to countable elements *much*: refers to quantity
principle/principal	*principle*: strongly held belief *principal*: foremost
than/then	*than*: conjunction used when making a comparison *then*: refers to the past in time
that/which	*that*: used to specify a crucial aspect of something: "the study that was conducted by Smith (1984)" *which*: used to offer a qualification that is not crucial to something: "the study, which was published in 1984" (note that *which* is always preceded by a comma; *that* takes no comma)
there/their/they're	*there*: refers to a place *their*: possessive pronoun *they're*: contraction of "they are"
whose/who's	*whose:* the possessive of "who" *who's*: contraction of "who is"
your/you're	*your*: possessive pronoun *you're*: contraction of "you are"

SOURCE: Compiled from Crews, 1980; Hall, 1979; Leggett, Mead, & Charvat, 1978; and Strunk & White, 1979.

even professionals, cannot produce a "finished product" after only a single writing. The best way to approach writing a paper (especially in the early stages of your writing career) is to prepare a rough draft and then make careful revisions.

During the revision process, look for three major things. First, read through your paper, paragraph by paragraph, and check for unity, coherence, and proper word usage. Second, read your paper for organization between paragraphs and sections. Finally, carefully comb your paper for typographical errors, misused words, and other stylistic errors. Only after you have completed several cycles of writing and revising should you submit your paper to your instructor or to a journal.

Avoiding Plagiarism and Lazy Writing

Reference citations must be included in your paper to give credit to another person or persons who have published or presented ideas. If you use someone else's words or ideas without proper citation, you are guilty of **plagiarism**, which is at best unethical, and at worst illegal. Penalties for plagiarism can range from a failing grade on an assignment, to civil litigation (if plagiarized work is published).

A broad rule of thumb to avoid plagiarism is to provide a citation whenever another person's work influenced your thinking. Of course, this means citing more than direct quotations and paraphrases of someone else's writing. If an idea you present in your paper is not originally yours, then you must cite the source.

A writing deficiency closely related to plagiarism is **lazy writing** (Rosnow & Rosnow, 1986). In lazy writing, an individual simply lifts paragraph after paragraph out of one or more sources and presents them as a paper. The difference between plagiarism and lazy writing is that in lazy writing, the individual properly cites the source of the material.

Although lazy writing is technically not plagiarism, few instructors will accept a paper that relies heavily on quoted material. To avoid lazy writing, keep the amount of directly quoted material to a minimum. Quotations should be used only when you consider them important to your ideas. Quotations should be used to *support* ideas you develop, not to form the core of your paper.

Submitting a Paper for Publication

If you decide to pursue a career as a psychologist, you will probably need to submit your research to a journal for publication. Once you have prepared your APA-style paper, you must make a few decisions about publication. One decision is where to send your paper. If your paper has a highly specific focus (such as treating retarded children), you should consider sending your paper to a specialized journal (for this example, perhaps the *Journal of Abnormal Psychology*). If your paper is less focused, you might send it to a less specialized journal. For example, if you conducted a study of the attributions made by schizophrenic patients, you might send your paper to the *Journal of Personality and Social Psychology*. Refer to Chapter 2 for a list of some of the major psychological journals.

A second decision is whether to send your paper to a refereed or nonrefereed journal. As stated in Chapter 2, papers sent to a refereed journal are reviewed before publication, but those sent to a nonrefereed journal are not reviewed. Select a refereed journal because work published in a refereed journal usually receives more serious attention by the scientific community.

After your paper has been submitted to a refereed journal, it goes through a standard procedure for review and publication. Figure 14-16 outlines this procedure. First, your paper is sent out for review. After the initial review, you receive a decision about acceptance or rejection. The editor of the journal may unconditionally accept or reject your paper. In many cases, however, papers are given a *provisional acceptance*. The editor then asks you to revise and resubmit your paper. After resubmission, the paper may be sent out for another review if the revisions are extensive.

Once accepted, your paper goes to a *copy editor*, who makes sure the paper conforms to the style and requirements of the journal. Finally, you receive *galley proofs*, which are copies of your paper as it will appear in the journal. You read these proofs to be sure they agree with your manuscript and then send them back (together with any corrections) to the journal.

The cycle of submission-review-revision and resubmission-acceptance-publication is a relatively long one. After your initial submission to a refereed journal, two months or more may pass before you receive your first feedback. After revision, another two months or more may pass (depending on whether your paper was sent out for a second review). The entire process (from submission to publication) may take a year or more. Chapter 17 discusses this and other publication-related issues in greater detail.

Paper Presentations

In addition to publication, you can communicate your research results through a **paper presentation**. Paper presentations can range from class presentations, to more formal seminars, to presentations at professional meetings. Two methods of presenting the results of your research are used at professional meetings. You can deliver a talk or an *oral presentation* before an audience, or you can present your findings in a *poster session*.

Oral Presentations

For an *oral presentation*, you are usually given a limited amount of time to present your information. At paper sessions at professional meetings, for example, you

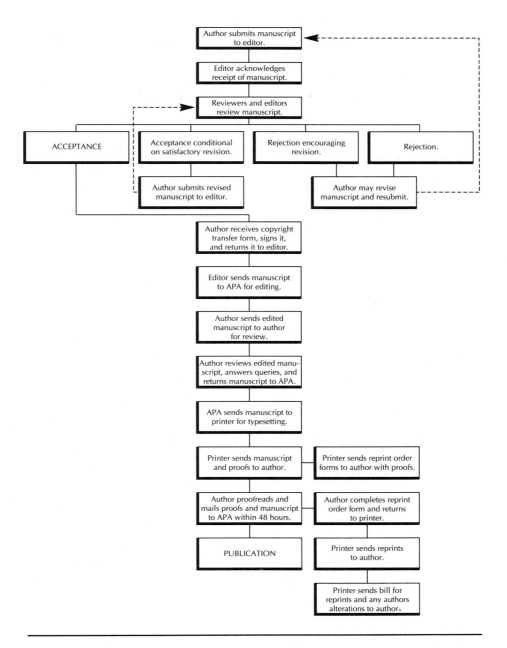

Figure 14-16. Diagram showing review and revision cycle for a refereed journal. (*Publication Manual of the American Psychological Association,* p. 171. Reprinted with permission.)

are given 15 minutes. In that brief period of time you must communicate to your audience the rationale behind your study, your methods, results, and conclusions.

When preparing for an oral presentation, follow a few general rules. First, organize your talk. Do not go before a room full of professionals (or even other students) and try to "wing it." Instead, develop an outline of your talk and stick to it. Second, do not read your paper. Store what you want to say in your head. Use your notes only as a guide. Third, use appropriate visual aids whenever possible. Slides, overhead projector transparencies, and printed handouts provide quick, easy ways to present complex methods and results. Rather than waste precious time describing methods and complex results, refer to your visual aids and restrict your discussion to the most important aspects of your research.

A common mistake during oral presentations is giving an overly detailed account of the methods and procedures. These complexities are not well communicated verbally. Listeners can retain only so much information and may become lost if you try to give too much. Try to boil down a complex method to its essential elements. To understand your study, listeners may need to know that you tested rats in an operant chamber. They may become lost in the details if you try to explain that the rats were Long-Evans females weighing between 250 and 350 grams and housed individually in $7 \times 7 \times 14$-inch wire cages, and that the chamber was $25 \times 25 \times 30$ cm, constructed from aluminum sheet, and fitted with a floor consisting of 0.8-cm diameter stainless steel bars spaced 1.2 cm apart. If your procedure is complicated, diagram it and present it on a slide or handout rather than attempting to explain it all verbally.

A final rule to follow is to avoid being pedantic and pompous. Some presenters are so consumed with self-importance that they consider it necessary to bore the audience with unnecessary details of their lives and research. Pomposity is manifested when the presenter is 13 minutes into his or her presentation and has yet to say anything about the methods and results of the study. Your audience will appreciate your presentation more and get more out of it if you focus your presentation on central issues of the research being reported.

Poster Sessions

In a *poster session*, you prepare a poster that outlines the rationale behind your study and your hypotheses, method, results, and conclusions. Unlike the oral presentation, you are not limited to 15 minutes. Poster sessions may last as long as an hour or more. Several related papers are presented within each session.

The main advantage of a poster session is that you can engage in meaningful conversations with other people who are doing research in your area. During oral presentations, interaction with the audience may be limited to a few questions immediately following your presentation or a few minutes after the paper session. In a poster session, an interested person can take time to read your poster and perhaps formulate more meaningful questions and input.

Poster sessions usually require more time and effort on your part than do oral presentations. Posters are time-consuming to make and sometimes difficult

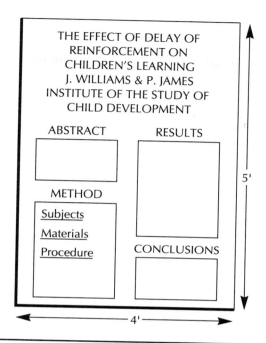

Figure 14-17. Sample format for a poster session presentation. (Adapted from Poppen, 1980.)

to transport. However, in some ways the poster format is superior to the oral presentation. It allows you greater freedom of presentation, more time for discussion, and less superficial interactions with other researchers in your area.

The guidelines for preparation of a poster vary somewhat from convention to convention. The guidelines for the Midwestern Psychological Association (MPA) are fairly representative of how a poster should be prepared.

A poster includes a title, author names and affiliations, an abstract, and procedure, results, and conclusions sections. All this information is placed on a poster board (5 × 4 feet). Figure 14-17 shows how a poster should be laid out.

Because your poster will be read from a distance, the lettering on your poster should be large. The MPA guidelines for lettering size are as follows:

Title:	1.5-inch letters
Author names:	1-inch letters
Affiliations:	1-inch letters
Section headings:	1-inch letters
Text:	No smaller than 0.25 inch

The lettering used for the text must be at least 0.25-inch high. To achieve this letter size, you must use a special typeface, such as IBM's Orator. An ordinary typeface, even if it is all capital letters, is not sufficient.

Figures and tables may be included in your poster. They should be professionally prepared, as should your entire poster. Remember, the quality of your poster is a reflection on you. Make the effort to prepare a professional-looking poster.

Summary

After you have designed and conducted a study, and have analyzed your data, you then prepare a report of your results. Two ways of reporting your results are the written report and presentation. The written report establishes a permanent record of your results that is less susceptible to misunderstanding and misinterpretation than is a presentation. The presentation format gives a forum to disseminate results quickly.

Psychological research is reported using APA style (or a close variant of it), which specifies how a paper must be prepared. An APA-style paper consists of a title page, an abstract, an introduction, a method section, a results section, a discussion section, and a reference list, plus additional pages for author notes, footnotes, tables, and figures.

The title page of your paper includes the title of your paper, your name, institutional affiliation, and a short running head. The abstract is a brief, but concise, summary of your research and is the last part of your paper that you write. The introduction of your paper introduces your topic, reviews relevant research, and states your hypotheses. It begins with a general discussion of issues and then moves to a specific discussion of your research. Its major purpose is to provide a logical justification for the study being reported.

The method section describes exactly how your study was conducted. Separate subsections provide information about subjects, apparatus or materials, and procedures. The goal of the method section is to provide enough information that another researcher could replicate your study in all its essential details.

Your results are presented in the results section, which provides a detailed report of the findings (illustrated if necessary with tables and figures) and the results of any statistical analyses of the data.

The results are discussed in the discussion section. The section usually begins with a brief summary of the results about to be discussed and a restatement of any hypotheses bearing on these results. The discussion indicates whether these hypotheses were supported by the results. The findings are then related to previous knowledge in the field and conclusions are drawn.

Figures and tables are used to communicate complex information about methods or results that cannot be adequately described verbally. Graphs of relationships must be carefully drawn to avoid misleading the reader. Graphs that make small, albeit statistically significant, effects look large should not be drawn. Clear legends and captions, listed on a separate figure captions page, must also be included. Tables, like figures, can help summarize complex information. Each table consists of a number, a title, a body, and (if needed) notes describing the table. Because figures and tables are time-consuming to prepare and expensive to reproduce in journals, they should only be used to illustrate complex materials or relationships.

Certain conventions are followed when you prepare an APA-style paper. References in the body of your paper are not footnoted. Instead, the author(s) of a reference are included in the text, along with the date of publication of the reference. Each reference cited in the body of your paper should be listed in expanded format in your reference section.

In a well-prepared paper, ideas must be clearly expressed, organized, and presented in a visually pleasing way. Clarity of expression requires sentences that are grammatically correct, properly chosen words, and economical expression. Ideas can be obscured by poorly constructed sentences (that is, ambiguous sentences), poorly chosen words, and wordy sentences.

Poor organization, like unclear expression, can obscure important points in your paper. Organization can be enhanced by developing and sticking to an outline.

Finally, a paper can be well written and organized, yet still make a bad impression on the reader. Frequent misspellings, typographical errors, and improper word usage makes your paper appear poor to your reader. Have someone proofread your paper to identify spelling and grammatical errors. Make corrections professionally by retyping, rather than penciling in or crossing out, information.

Plagiarism is using the words or ideas of another person without giving credit to the source. Plagiarism is considered extremely bad form and, in a published work, may result in legal action against you. Lazy writing is writing that consists primarily of quoted (although properly cited) material. Although lazy writing is not as serious a problem as plagiarism, it is still inappropriate. To avoid both, make sure your paper consists mainly of your own writing and ideas. Use quoted material and reference citations to support your ideas, not to present them.

After you have prepared your APA-style paper, you may want to submit it to a journal for publication. If you submit your paper to a refereed journal, it will be reviewed by outside reviewers. The editor of the journal can decide (based on the reviews) to unconditionally accept or reject a paper, or ask you to revise and resubmit your paper. If you revise and resubmit your paper, it may be sent out for a second review. Typically, the entire cycle of initial review, second review, acceptance, and publication takes almost a year.

Finally, you can also communicate your research findings through a presentation. In an oral presentation, you stand before an audience and present your results. In a poster session, you prepare a poster and answer questions about your work. The poster session affords more time and deeper communication with others in your field than does an oral presentation.

Key Terms

Abstract

Introduction

Method section

Subjects subsection

Apparatus subsection

Procedure subsection

Results section

Discussion section

Reference section

Plagiarism

Lazy writing

Paper presentation

15

Using Multivariate Design
and Analysis

DURING DISCUSSIONS OF EXPERIMENTAL and nonexperimental design, previous chapters assumed that only one dependent variable was included in a design, or that multiple dependent variables were treated separately in any statistical tests. This approach to analysis is called a **univariate strategy**. Although many research questions can be addressed with a univariate strategy, others are best addressed by considering variables together in a single analysis. When you include two or more dependent measures in a single analysis, you are using a **multivariate strategy**.

This chapter introduces the major multivariate analysis techniques. Keep in mind that providing an in-depth introduction to these techniques in the confines of one chapter is impossible. Such a task is better suited to an entire book. Also, the complex and laborious calculations needed to compute multivariate statistics are better left to computers. Consequently, this chapter does not discuss the mathematics behind these statistical tests, except for those cases where some mathematical analysis is required to understand the issues. Instead, this chapter focuses on practical issues: applications of the various statistics, the assumptions that must be met, and interpretation of results. If you want to use any of the statistics discussed in this chapter, read *Using Multivariate Statistics* (Tabachnick & Fidell, 1989), or one of the many monographs published by Sage Publications (such as Asher, 1976, or Levine, 1977).

Experimental and Correlational Multivariate Designs

Multivariate design and analysis applies to both experimental and correlational research studies. The following sections describe some of the available multivariate statistical tests.

Correlational Multivariate Design

If you include multiple measures in a correlational study, one strategy you could use to evaluate the degree of relationship among dependent measures is to calculate bivariate correlations (for example, Pearson correlations) for all possible pairs of measures. Or you might choose a *multivariate correlational analysis* in which you include all your measures in a single analysis.

Several analyses are designed to assess complex correlational relationships among multiple dependent variables. For example, the goal of **multiple regression** is to explain the variation in one variable (the dependent or *criterion variable*) based on variation in a set of others (the *predictor variables*). You measure several variables, one of which serves as the criterion variable in the analysis and the others as predictors. Precisely what constitutes a "predictor" and what constitutes a "criterion variable" is not related to anything inherent in the variable itself. Rather, you decide which variables to use as predictors based on your research question. Relevant previous research, theory, or practical experience should guide your decision about which variables should be measured and what role each variable should play in your analysis.

Two other multivariate techniques used to evaluate relationships in a correlational study are **discriminant analysis** and **canonical correlation**. Discriminant analysis is a variation of multiple regression in which your criterion variable is measured nominally (for example, yes/no). Canonical correlation allows you to evaluate the relationship between two *sets* of variables, one of which may be identified as a predictor set and the other as the criterion variable set.

In some research situations (questionnaire and test construction, for example), you may reduce a large set of variables to smaller sets that consist of variables relating to one another. **Factor analysis** is used for this purpose. In this analysis, several dependent variables are analyzed to find out if any of them constitute common underlying dimensions called *factors*. You examine the dependent variables that make up the factors to identify the dimension that those variables represent.

Experimental Multivariate Design

The logic of univariate experimental design applies to multivariate design. That is, you manipulate one or more independent variable(s) and look for changes in the value of your dependent variables. The major difference between a univariate experimental strategy and a multivariate experimental strategy is how dependent variables are handled. When you use a univariate strategy, multiple dependent measures are analyzed separately with multiple statistical tests. In contrast, when you use a multivariate strategy, multiple dependent variables are combined statistically (based on the correlations among them) and analyzed with a single statistical test.

Implied in your choice of a multivariate design over a univariate design is that your dependent measures are correlated. Typically, you include multiple dependent measures because you have some reason to believe that those measures are important to the phenomenon under study and that those measures relate in some way to one another. Multivariate statistical techniques take into account the correlations among your dependent measures and, in most cases, use them to your advantage.

Multivariate Statistical Tests. The two multivariate statistics most widely used to analyze multiple dependent variables in an experimental design are **multivariate analysis of variance (MANOVA)** and *multivariate analysis of covariance (MANCOVA)*. As with univariate statistics, these tests help you to evaluate the reliability of the relationship between your independent variable (or variables) and your dependent variables.

Advantages of the Experimental Multivariate Strategy. A multivariate experimental strategy has several advantages over a univariate strategy. First, collecting several dependent measures and treating them as a correlated set may reveal relationships that might be missed if a traditional univariate approach were taken. Because multivariate statistical tests consider the correlations among dependent variables, they tend to be more powerful than separate univariate tests of those same dependent variables. Second, because all your dependent variables are handled in a single analysis, complex relationships among variables can be studied with less chance of making a type I error than when using multiple univariate tests (Bray & Maxwell, 1982).

A third advantage of the multivariate strategy is realized when you have used a within-subjects design. A fairly restrictive set of assumptions underlies the univariate within-subjects ANOVA that are often difficult to satisfy. Using MANOVA allows you to analyze your data with less concern over these restrictive assumptions.

Advantages of the Correlational Multivariate Strategy. Single multivariate analysis has two major advantages over separate bivariate analyses. First, if you conduct a large number of independent bivariate correlation analyses, you may find a strong relationship merely by chance. Multivariate statistics allow you to look at complex relationships while controlling statistical errors. Second, independent univariate analyses only allow you to evaluate relationships between *pairs* of variables. You may discover Variable X correlates highly with Variable Y. However, what you do not know is whether this high correlation will persist when you consider a third variable, Z. It may be that X is correlated with Y only because Z is highly correlated with X. Multivariate statistics provide the information needed to evaluate the importance of a predictor variable for explaining variability in the criterion variable, given the effects of other predictor variables.

Causal Inference

Multivariate techniques enable you to draw some tentative causal inferences from correlational data. Path analysis applies multiple-regression analysis to the investigation of causal relationships among variables.

Path analysis begins with a theory (or model) specifying a causal chain of events that involves several variables and a behavior. For example, a model may suggest a consumer's buying behavior will not occur until the consumer first finds out about a product, then generates positive ideas about the product, and finally forms an intention to buy the product. You could obtain measures on the degree to which the consumer was familiar with the product, had positive ideas about it, and intended to buy it. You could then enter the measures into a series of multiple regression analyses. Based on the results, you could test the validity of your theory or model and begin to form some tentative conclusions about possible causal relationships among your variables.

To summarize, multivariate analysis is a family of analytic techniques designed to analyze research in which multiple dependent measures are used. These analytic techniques can be used with experiments or correlational studies that have multiple dependent measures. All the multivariate statistical tests make use of the correlations among your dependent measures. In most cases, using a multivariate analysis is more informative than using several univariate analyses.

Assumptions and Requirements of Multivariate Statistics

Before using multivariate statistics, you must check to see that your data meet the assumptions and requirements underlying the statistic to be used. These assumptions include linearity, normality, and homoscedasticity. In addition, you must evaluate your data for the presence of outliers, measurement error, and sample size.

Linearity

An assumption underlying bivariate correlational statistics is that the relationship between continuously measured variables is linear (see Chapter 11 for a more complete discussion). Violation of this assumption leads to an underestimation of the degree of relationship between variables. Multivariate statistics, which are all based on correlations (even MANOVA), also assume the relationships among continuously measured variables are linear. You check for linearity by visually inspecting scattergrams of pairs of variables. If your data are linear, then all the points should follow a straight line. Nonlinear data, in contrast, will show a horseshoe-shaped function (Tabachnick & Fidell, 1989).

Whereas mild deviations from linearity probably will not lead to a serious underestimation of a relationship by multivariate statistics, moderate-to-serious deviations may. If your data are nonlinear, you may be able to correct the problem by transforming your data. You may have to transform both offending variables in order to restore linearity. After any transformation, you should again inspect the scattergrams to see if the transformation had its intended effect.

Outliers

Bivariate correlational statistics work by fitting the best straight line to the data. This *regression line* minimizes the distance of the data points from the line according to some statistical criterion (usually a least squares criterion). If your data set has extreme scores or *outliers*, how the regression line fits the data may not represent the trend shown by the majority of scores. Outliers change the slope of the regression line calculated from your data. They also affect both the magnitude and sign of the calculated correlation. (See Chapter 11 for a more complete discussion.)

Identifying Outliers. Two types of outliers that must be considered in multivariate statistics are *univariate outliers* and *multivariate outliers*. A univariate outlier is a deviant score on one measure from a given source (for example, from a single subject), whereas a multivariate outlier is a deviant score on a combination of variables from a single source.

Univariate outliers may be detected by converting raw scores to z-scores. If the z-score is very deviant (such as ± 3), then that raw score is considered to be a univariate outlier, especially with a large sample (Tabachnick & Fidell, 1989). Another way to look for outliers is to evaluate the amount of skewness in your data. If your data are skewed, then outliers probably exist. However, note that measures of skewness (see Chapter 11) detect skewness if outliers exist only in one tail of your distribution.

Dealing with Outliers. You can use several strategies to deal with outliers if you discover them in your data. To normalize the distribution, Tabachnick and Fidell (1989), suggested using one of several transformations on the data from the offending variable. Data with a moderate positive skew should be transformed with a square-root transformation. You should use a logarithmic transformation if your data have a more serious positive skew. Again, transformations such as these reduce the impact of outliers if they are found only in one tail of your distribution. If outliers exist in both tails, transformations may not help (Tabach-nick & Fidell, 1989).

If your data are negatively skewed, you use a *reflecting strategy*. The first step in reflecting is to transform your data so that they are positively skewed. You accomplish this by subtracting each score from the highest score in the distribution and adding 1. The resulting positively skewed data are then transformed with either a square root or log transformation, depending on the degree of skewness.

Another way to deal with outliers is to delete from the analysis either all data from the subject with the outlying scores or the entire variable. The disadvantage to this procedure is that you lose data. If you start with a relatively small sample, the loss of data may preclude using multivariate statistics.

Finally, you should check for transcription and other data entry errors. Sometimes outliers are caused by entering the wrong numbers or by telling the computer to look for data in the wrong positions. Any erroneous data should be corrected.

Of all the requirements of multivariate statistics, the detection of outliers is probably the most important. The presence of just a single multivariate outlier can change the results of your analysis and affect your conclusions. Consequently, you should check and correct for both univariate and multivariate outliers.

Normality and Homoscedasticity

As is the case with bivariate statistics, multivariate statistics assume that the population distribution underlying your sample distribution is normal. This is the assumption of *normality*. Transform skewed data with one of the indicated transformations, in order to normalize the distributions, before using any multivariate statistic.

Homoscedasticity is related to normality. Figure 15-1 shows two scattergrams of two hypothetical variables. Panel A shows the pattern of data indicating homoscedasticity. Notice the shape of the scattergram created by the data points is elliptical. If both variables are normally distributed, homoscedasticity results.

Contrast the scattergram shown in Panel B of Figure 15-1 with the one shown in Panel A. Notice how the shape of the scattergram has changed from elliptical to conical. The conical pattern of data points indicates that *heteroscedasticity* is present. Heteroscedasticity usually occurs because the distribution of one or more variable(s) included in the analysis is skewed. Apply one of the data transformations previously discussed to eliminate heteroscedasticity.

Multicollinearity

Multicollinearity results when variables in your analysis are highly correlated (Tabachnick & Fidell, 1989). The impact of multicollinearity is complex and beyond the scope of this chapter. If two variables are highly correlated, one of

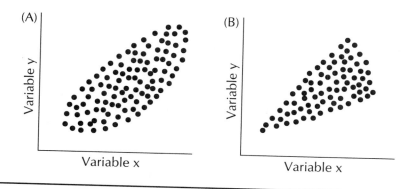

Figure 15-1. Homoscedasticity and heteroscedasticity: (A) homoscedasticity between two variables; (B) heteroscedasticity between two variables.

them should be eliminated from the analysis. The high correlation means the two variables are measuring essentially the same thing, so little is lost by eliminating one of them.

Error of Measurement

The heart of the research process is identifying important variables to study, measuring those variables, establishing relationships among variables, and drawing conclusions about behavior based on those relationships. Drawing valid conclusions about the behavior under study requires that your variables be accurately measured. Inaccurate measurement may lead to an inordinate number of type II errors. For example, you may conclude that a theoretical model is invalid when, in fact, the reason for rejecting the model was an inaccurate measurement of variables.

In a perfectly ordered world with perfect measuring devices, you could obtain the *true value* of your dependent variable. Unfortunately, we do not live in a perfectly ordered world, nor do we have perfect measuring devices. Consequently, the best you can do is to *estimate* the true value of a variable by obtaining an *observed value*. The difference between the true value of a variable and your observed value is the *error of measurement*. Figure 15-2 shows the relationship between a variable's true value, observed value, and measurement error. Notice the observed value is a function of both the true value of the variable and measurement error (Asher, 1976).

Error of measurement is a problem for both multivariate and univariate research. But it is particularly troublesome when you adopt a multivariate strategy because it leads to an underestimation of the correlations among variables that are used to compute the various multivariate statistics (Hunter, 1987; Asher, 1976). This leads to type II errors.

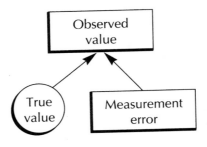

Figure 15-2. The observed value of any variable (top) is a function of the true value of that variable and measurement error (bottom).

Measurement error can arise from many sources, including incomplete, inaccurate, or biased sources of information. For example, if you were interested in studying the relationship between three predictor variables (sex, socioeconomic status, and education level) and crime rate, you need a good source for each of these four variables. Consider the crime rate. You could obtain records of crimes reported to the police. But this source may not be complete because many crimes go unreported. The best way to avoid this source of measurement error is to use multiple sources of information.

Another source of measurement error is inaccurate or invalid measurement devices. Defects in mechanical recording devices, poorly designed rating scales, and the like all contribute to measurement error. To avoid this source of error, be sure that your equipment is in working order and that you have adequately pretested your measures.

Sample Size

Fairly large sample sizes are needed for multivariate analyses. The large sample size is necessary because the correlations used to calculate these statistics are not very stable when based on small samples. A multivariate analysis that uses a small sample may result in an unacceptable type II error rate. This occurs because unstable correlations tend to provide less accurate estimates of the degree of relationship among your variables.

The sample size required for a multivariate analysis varies according to the statistic. Tabachnick and Fidell (1989) suggested an appropriate number for several types. For multiple regression, the ideal number of subjects is 20 times the number of predictor variables. If you have 10 predictors, for example, ideally you want to have at least 200 subjects in your sample. The minimum number of subjects required for multiple regression is somewhere around four to five times the number of subjects as variables. For factor analysis, 200 subjects is considered to be "fair," 300 "good," 500 "very good," and 1,000 "excellent."

In many cases, especially when you have a homogeneous population (for example, lawyers, engineers, and teachers), 100–200 may be sufficient for factor analysis. None of the multivariate statistics will yield valid results if the number of variables exceeds the number of subjects.

To summarize, several factors should be considered before using multivariate statistics. Make sure that your data meet the assumptions of the test you are going to use (that is, normality, linearity, and homoscedasticity); that you have removed any outliers or minimized their effects through transformation; that you have considered error of measurement; and that you have gathered a sufficiently large sample. If you violate the assumptions of the test, or fail to take into account the other important factors, the results you obtain may not be valid.

Multivariate Statistical Tests

Now that you are familiar with the general logic behind multivariate statistics and understand the assumptions and requirements of these tests, you can explore some of the more popular multivariate data analysis techniques. This discussion begins with an examination of factor analysis, then examines the techniques commonly applied to correlational designs, and finally discusses MANOVA.

Factor Analysis

Assume that for a class research project you decided to investigate the "attractiveness stereotype" that suggests physically attractive individuals are perceived more positively than less attractive individuals. After reviewing the literature, you find the stereotype does not always hold. That is, some studies show an attractive individual is actually downrated compared to a less attractive individual. You decide to investigate the nature of the stereotype by having subjects rate the behavior of either an attractive or unattractive individual (targets). With an eye toward investigating what factors make up the stereotype, you decide to include 15 rating scales on which your targets will be rated.

After running all your subjects, you now face the task of determining the underlying nature of the attractiveness stereotype from the 15 rating scales you included in your study. One question that interests you is whether all of your 15 rating scales measure a single dimension (such as beauty) or several dimensions (such as beauty, social desirability, and competence). Your search for the dimensions underlying the attractiveness stereotype lends itself perfectly to factor analysis.

Factor analysis operates by extracting as many significant factors from your data as possible, based on the bivariate correlations between your measures. A *factor* is a dimension that consists of any number of variables. In your study of the attractiveness stereotype, for example, you may find that your 15 measurement scales actually measure three underlying dimensions (for example, beauty,

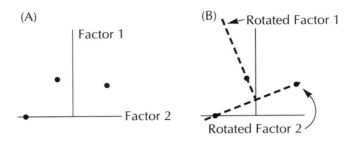

Figure 15-3. Factor rotation. (A) factor loadings, represented by large black dots before rotation; (B) the same loadings after rotation of the axis.

social desirability, and competence). Factor analysis involves extracting one factor (such as beauty) and then evaluating your data for the existence of other factors.

The successive factors extracted in factor analysis are not of equal strength. Each successive factor accounts for less and less variance. Typically, the first two or three factors will be the strongest (that is, account for the most variance). The strength of a factor is indicated by its *eigenvalue* (for a more complete discussion of eigenvalues, see Tatsuoka, 1971, or Tabachnick & Fidell, 1989). Factors with eigenvalues less than 1 usually are not interpreted.

Factor Loadings. In order to determine the dependent variables constituting a common factor, *factor loadings* are computed (usually with a computer because the calculations are laborious, even for only a few measures). Each factor loading is the correlation between a measure and the underlying factor. A positive factor loading means that a variable positively correlates with the underlying dimension extracted, whereas a negative loading means that a negative correlation exists. By convention, loadings are interpreted only if they are equal to or exceed plus or minus 0.30.

Rotation of Factors. After you have obtained your factor loadings, you must interpret them. The factor loadings computed initially are often difficult to interpret because they are somewhat ambiguous. *Factor rotation* is used to make the factors distinct. Figure 15-3 shows a plot of some factor loadings. The factor loadings for each variable are used as coordinates on the graph. Panel A of Figure 15-3 shows the plot of the unrotated factor loadings. Rotation means that the axes of the graph are rotated so that they better represent the points on the graph. Panel B of Figure 15-3 shows the axes after rotation.

Two types of rotation are *orthogonal rotation* and *oblique rotation*. In orthogonal rotation, the axes remain perpendicular. In oblique rotation, the angle between

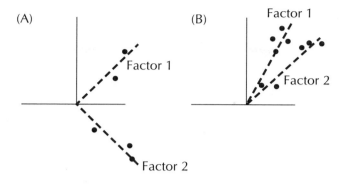

Figure 15-4. Orthogonal and oblique factor rotation. In orthogonal rotation (A), the rotated axes remain at right angles. In oblique rotation (B), the angle of the axes changes.

the axes, as well as the orientation of the axes in space, may change. Figure 15-4 illustrates the difference between the two rotation strategies. Panel A shows orthogonal rotation, whereas Panel B shows oblique rotation. Generally, orthogonal rotation is preferred over oblique rotation because the results are easier to interpret. The most popular orthogonal rotation method is varimax.

Principal Components and Principal Factors Analysis. Two types of factor analysis are principal components analysis and principal factors analysis. Panel A of Table 15-1 shows a standard three-variable correlation matrix. Remember, such correlations are used to calculate factor loadings. Panel B shows the same correlation matrix completed by filling in the correlations missing from the matrix in Panel A. Notice that the values on the diagonal of the matrix are all 1's. In principal components analysis, the diagonal of the completed correlation matrix is filled with 1's. In contrast, principal factors analysis completes the correlation matrix by entering *communalities* along the diagonal.

Essentially, a communality is a measure of a variable's reliability, and is fairly easy to obtain after factor analysis. In practice, however, you need these values before analysis. Various techniques have been proposed for estimating communalities (see Bennett & Bowers, 1976), none of which is much better than any other.

Your choice between principal components and factor analysis rests on the goals of the analysis. Tabachnick and Fidell (1989) suggested that principal components could be used first to extract as many significant factors as possible. Then you could perform a factor analysis by experimenting with different communality values, numbers of factors extracted, and rotation methods. This experimenting could be done until you reach a satisfactory solution. Given the

Table 15-1. Two Correlation Matrices for Three Variables

(A) HYPOTHETICAL CORRELATION MATRIX

	Variable 1	Variable 2	Variable 3
Variable 1			
Variable 2	0.71		
Variable 3	0.61	0.74	

(B) COMPLETED CORRELATION MATRIX

	Variable 1	Variable 2	Variable 3
Variable 1	1.00	0.71	0.61
Variable 2	0.71	1.00	0.74
Variable 3	0.61	0.74	1.00

absence of any clear information on which technique is best, you should probably use principal components in those situations where you do not have any empirical or theoretical guidance on the values of the communalities.

An Example of Factor Analysis. Consider the previous example of testing the dimensions underlying the attractiveness stereotype. Such an investigation was actually carried out by Bassili (1981). Bassili presented subjects with a photograph of either an attractive or unattractive female and a description of an event in which the female was involved (an end–of–the–year party where the female target got drunk and behaved badly). The dependent measures were 13 items from a standard social desirability index (Dion, Berscheid, & Walster, 1972), along with 4 items evaluating the target's behavior at the party.

The data from the social desirability index were analyzed with a principal components factor analysis with a varimax rotation applied. Bassili reported three factors were extracted (in the first of two experiments). These were interpersonal goodness, social vitality, and personal strength. Table 15-2 shows these three factors along with the rotated factor loadings, eigenvalues, and percentage of variance accounted for.

Bassili's results can illustrate how to name and interpret factors. First, notice how the eigenvalue associated with each factor decreases as you progress from the first to the third factor (5.87, 2.3, and 1.35). Also note that the percentage of variance accounted for by each factor progressively decreases from Factor 1 to Factor 3 (32.61, 12.76, and 7.49, respectively). Because all of the eigenvalues are greater than 1, however, all three factors can be interpreted.

Table 15.2. Rotated Factor Loadings from Bassili's (1981) Study of the Physical Attractiveness Stereotype

		FACTORS			
Interpersonal Goodness		Social Vitality		Personal Strength	
Measure	*Loading*	*Measure*	*Loading*	*Measure*	*Loading*
Kind	0.815	Exciting	0.757	Independent	0.786
Polite	0.779	Sexually warm	0.747	Strong	0.687
Sensitive	0.701	Interesting	0.689	Self-assertive	0.598
Refined	0.699	Warm	0.604		
Well mannered	0.685	Poised	0.592		
Sincere	0.619	Sociable	0.563		
Sophisticated	0.619				
Genuine	0.497				
Eigenvalue	5.87		2.30		1.35
Percent Variance	32.61		12.76		7.49

Next, look at the variables and factor loadings constituting the interpersonal goodness factor. High loadings (plus or minus 0.30) appear on measures relating to interpersonal concern (kind, sensitive, sincere, genuine), and proper etiquette (polite, refined, well mannered, sophisticated) (Bassili, 1981). The fact that all the loadings are positive indicates that each variable positively correlates with interpersonal goodness. That is, a person who is "interpersonally good" tends to be kind, polite, sensitive, refined, and so on. Similarly, the positive loadings found for the remaining factors indicate that the variables constituting them are positively related to the underlying factors extracted.

Based on the factor analysis and subsequent analyses of variance, Bassili concluded that the social desirability index developed by Dion et al. represented several dimensions rather than a single one, and that the most important dimension underlying the attractiveness stereotype was social vitality.

Partial and Part Correlations

Sometimes two variables are both influenced by a third variable. If this third variable was not held constant when the data were collected, it can affect the apparent relationship between the two variables of interest. However, if you have recorded the values of the third variable along with the other two, you can statistically evaluate the impact of the third variable. Partial correlation and part correlation (also called the *semipartial correlation*) are two statistics that determine the correlation between two variables while statistically controlling for the effect of a third.

Partial Correlation. **Partial correlation** allows you to examine the relationship between two variables with the effect of a third variable *removed* from both of these variables. For example, suppose you are interested in the factors relating to performance on the Scholastic Aptitude Test (SAT). You obtain the SAT scores from 500 high school seniors as well as their grade-point averages (GPA). You also collect data on the parent's educational level (PE) in the belief that the parent's educational level may affect SAT scores. Specifically, you are interested in the relationship between GPA and SAT scores, but are concerned that parental education may confound the relationship between GPA and SAT. You want to look at the relationship between GPA and SAT with any effect of PE removed. This problem calls for a partial correlation.

Imagine a causal relationship exists between parental education and grade-point average. In that case variations in parental education would induce variations in GPA. Imagine a causal relationship also exists between parental education and SAT scores. In that case, variations in parental education would also induce variations in SAT scores. If these were both direct relationships, then SAT scores and GPA would tend to rise and fall together as parental education rose and fell. In other words, SAT scores and GPA would be positively correlated. This positive correlation would emerge even if there were no direct causal connection between SAT scores and GPA.

Would a correlation remain if you could somehow remove the common influence parental education has on SAT scores and GPA? This is what partial correlation attempts to determine, as shown in Figure 15-5. Panel A shows a scattergram of the relationship between PE and GPA. The straight line through the points represents the trend relating changes in GPA to changes in PE. If you could remove this trend, the GPA scores would show less variability, and they would show no systematic change as PE changed.

In fact, you *can* remove this trend statistically by calculating a *residual score* for each data point. This residual score is the distance from the point to the line, measured (in this case) in terms of GPA. Panel B in Figure 15-5 plots the residual scores as a function of PE. Note the trend relating PE to GPA is now flat. The changes in GPA induced by changes in PE have been statistically removed.

The same process of statistically removing the effect of PE is also applied to the SAT scores. Panels C and D of Figure 15-5 show the relationship before and after this removal. The partial correlation is then determined by correlating the residual GPA scores (Panel B) with the residual SAT scores (Panel D). This is the correlation of GPA and SAT with the effect of PE removed from both.

Fortunately, there is an easier way to compute the partial correlation than by graphing and subtracting. First, you find the simple correlations between your three variables. Then these correlation coefficients are entered into a special partial correlation formula (see Appendix II).

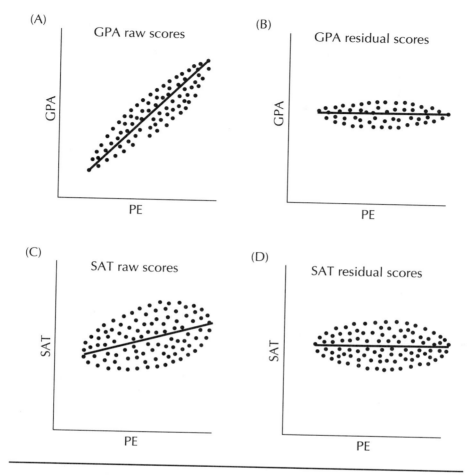

Figure 15-5. Four figures showing the logic behind partial correlation.

Partial correlation is not limited to three-variable cases. You can examine the relationship between two variables with the effects of several others removed. You can learn more about these more complex partial correlations in Thorndike (1978).

Part Correlation. In some cases you may want to examine the relationship between two variables where the influence of a third is removed only from *one* of these variables. The **part correlation** is used in this situation.

Conceptually, the part correlation is similar to the partial correlation. As with the partial correlation, the relationship between one variable (such as SAT) and the variable to be removed (such as PE) is determined and residual scores are calculated. This yields an SAT score for each subject with the effect of parental education held constant (Thorndike, 1978). These residual scores are then correlated with the *raw* scores of the other variable (GPA) to yield the part correlation coefficient (Thorndike, 1978).

In practice, the part correlation is computed by using a formula similar to that used for the partial correlation. This formula can also be found in Appendix II.

Multiple Regression

Assume you are interested in studying the variables correlating with ratings of a college instructor. You design a study in which you provide subjects with several pieces of information (cues) and ask them to rate the desirability of an instructor based on the nature of those cues. Multiple-regression analysis is the best statistic for this type of problem.

The Multiple-Regression Equation. Chapter 11 discussed bivariate linear regression and provided the linear equation for that analysis. The logic developed for the bivariate case can be easily extended to the multivariate case. The linear equation for multiple regression is

$$y' = B_1X_1 + B_2X_2 + B_3X_3 + B_4X_4 + B_5X_5 + constant$$

where y' is the predicted criterion score; B_1, B_2, B_3, B_4, and B_5 are the regression weights associated with the predictors; X_1, X_2, X_3, X_4, and X_5 are the values of the predictors; and *constant* is the y-intercept.

Types of Regression Analysis. The several types of regression analysis include *simple*, *hierarchical*, and *stepwise* analyses. The major difference between these types is how your predictor variables are entered into the regression equation, which may affect the regression solution.

In *simple regression analysis* (the type used in the example to follow), all variables are entered together. Each predictor variable is assessed as if it had been entered after each of the other predictors had been entered (Tabachnick & Fidell, 1989). In *hierarchical regression*, you specify the order in which your variables are entered into the regression equation. You use hierarchical regression if you have a well-developed theory or model suggesting a certain causal order. In *stepwise regression*, the order in which variables are entered is based on a statistical decision, and not on a theory.

When you enter variables into a stepwise regression analysis, the order in which predictors are entered is determined by the qualities of the sample data. The first variable entered is the one accounting for the most variance in the dependent measure. The next variable entered is the one that adds most to the ability of the regression equation to account for the variance in the dependent

Attribute	Rating
Interest	5
Communication	3
Workload	2
Knowledge of subject	7
Enthusiasm	2

Figure 15-6. Sample profile from instructor-rating study.

variable (that is, increases R-square the most). Variables are entered one at a time until none of the remaining variables add significantly to R-square.

Your choice of regression strategies should be based on your research questions or underlying theory. If you have a theoretical model suggesting a particular order of entry, use hierarchical regression. In the absence of any well-specified theory, you should usually choose simple regression. Stepwise regression is used infrequently because it tends to capitalize on chance. Sampling and measurement error tend to make unstable correlations among variables in stepwise regression. Thus the statistical decisions used to determine order of entry may vary considerably from sample to sample. The resulting regression equation may be unique to a particular sample.

An Example of Multiple Regression. The mathematics needed to calculate the regression weights and y-intercept are too complex to describe here. If you are interested in these details, consult Tabachnick and Fidell (1989) or Roscoe (1975). An example is presented to show how to use multiple regression analysis.

Recall the previously mentioned study of the factors correlating with ratings of college instructors. Such a study was conducted as an exercise by students in a research methods lab. Subjects rated the desirability of fictitious instructors on a seven-point scale. These ratings were based on "instructor" profiles that attached values to five variables: interest (X_1), communication skills (X_2), knowledge of subject (X_3), workload (X_4), and enthusiasm (X_5). Each subject rated 200 separate profiles. Figure 15-6 shows a sample profile.

The data from each subject were analyzed separately with a multiple-regression analysis. In effect, the 200 cases judged were the "subjects" in the analysis. The five variables listed in each profile were the predictor variables, and the rating of the instructor was the dependent variable.

The first step in a regression analysis is to evaluate the data to see whether they meet the assumptions of the test. Descriptive statistics were calculated for each variable (including a measure of skewness) to identify any univariate outliers. None were found. Next, the data were evaluated for multivariate outliers, normality, and homoscedasticity. A scattergram of residuals (the differences between the predicted Y scores and observed Y scores) was used to evaluate normality and homoscedasticity, whereas a Mahalanobis Distance was used to look for multivariate outliers. Visual inspection of the scattergram showed normality and homoscedasticity. The test for outliers revealed one outlying case, which was subsequently deleted. A second search for outliers showed no other outliers, and the regression analysis was then conducted on the remaining 199 cases.

The results of the analysis are shown in Table 15-3. The top portion of the table shows the multiple R, R-square, adjusted R-square, and standard error. Also shown is a test of significance associated with the analysis.

Multiple **R** *and* **R-***Square*. **Multiple** *R* is the correlation between the predicted values of Y (Y') and the observed values of Y. **R-square** is simply the square of multiple R and provides an index of the amount of variability in the dependent variable accounted for by the predictor variables (Roscoe, 1975). Notice in Table 15-3 the value labeled "Adjusted R-Square." R-square tends to overestimate the variance accounted for because of sampling error, especially with small samples (Tabachnick & Fidell, 1989). The adjusted R-square compensates for this overestimation. You should use the adjusted R-square as a measure of variance accounted for rather than the unadjusted R-square. Finally, the standard error gives you an indication of how much variability there is about the calculated regression line. The lower the value, the better.

Regression Weights. The bottom portion of Table 15-3 shows the regression weights (raw and standardized), along with the standard error of the raw weights, t-values, and significance levels of t. For each predictor variable, the table provides a raw regression weight (B) and a standardized regression weight (beta) calculated after the values of your measures have been standardized. The t-value and significance level tell you whether the regression weight is significant.

For most applications in psychological research, you should use the standardized regression weights (**beta weights**) because they can be directly compared, even if the variables to which they apply were measured on very different scales. For example, the beta weights given to variables such as intelligence, grade-point average, and socioeconomic status (which are all measured on different nonequivalent scales) can be directly compared, whereas the B weights cannot. Only when your variables are measured on the same standard scale should you use the raw score regression weights.

Interpretation of Regression Weights. If your regression analysis is significant, you may want to know how much of the variability in the criterion variable can

Table 15-3. Partial SPSS-X Output for a Multiple-Regression Analysis

Multiple R	.88398					
R-Square	.78143					
Adjusted R-Square	.77577					
Standard Error	.57109					

ANALYSIS OF VARIANCE

	df	Sum of Squares	Mean Square
Regression	5	225.04348	45.00870
Residual	193	62.94647	.32615

$F = 138.00103$ Signif $F = .0000$

VARIABLES IN THE EQUATION

Variable	B	SE B	Beta	T	Sig T	sr^2
KNOW	.578097	.023863	.823707	24.226	.0000	.66
COMM	.161711	.022762	.241419	7.104	.0000	.06
ENTHU	.157090	.023814	.223077	6.597	.0000	.05
INT	.144716	.023753	.206837	6.092	.0000	.04
WORK	.120692	.024247	.168359	4.978	.0000	.03
(Constant)	−.716986	.222439		−3.223	.0015	

be accounted for by variation in each predictor. Avoid using the beta weights for this. A beta weight is not an index of the *unique* contribution of a given predictor to variability in the dependent variable.

A beta weight for a given predictor variable may be high because the predictor *directly* produces most of the variance in the dependent variable, or because it is merely *correlated* with another effective predictor variable (Tabachnick & Fidell, 1989). Similarly, a beta weight for a given predictor variable may be low, and yet, the predictor may have a strong causal influence on the dependent variable. This situation can occur when other predictor variables in the analysis correlate with the effective variable. The analysis may then mistakenly assign weight to the correlated variables instead of to the effective one. In such cases, the correlated variables are termed "suppressor variables" because they mask (or suppress) the effect of the effective variable.

Rather than using beta weights to determine the unique contribution of each predictor, use the *squared semipartial correlation* (Tabachnick & Fidell, 1989). This correlation can be obtained indirectly from SPSS-X by including a "STATIS-TICS = ZPP" command in your program. This will yield part correlations, which are then squared to obtain the squared semipartial correlations. Alternatively, they can be calculated by hand with a simple formula (see Appendix II for this formula).

The squared semipartial correlations need not sum to R-square. If the sum of the semipartial correlations is less than R-square, then the difference between the two numbers represents the shared variance (Tabachnick & Fidell, 1989). In some cases, the sum of the squared semipartial correlations can be larger than R-square.

The interpretation of the regression analysis in the instructor-rating example is clear. An instructor's knowledge of the subject is the most important variable contributing to desirability (accounting for 66 percent of the variance in desirability). The remaining variables have little effect.

Discriminant Analysis

Imagine you are a budding psychologist with a strong interest in art. On a trip to a museum, you overhear several individuals giving opinions of different painting styles. After listening to a few of these amateur critics, you begin to wonder what dimensions underlie the perception of paintings in general, and more specifically whether or not different dimensions underlie the perception of different painting styles (for example, abstract and impressionistic).

You develop a study in which subjects judge several abstract and impressionistic paintings on 20 bipolar adjectives. The first question about the dimensions that underlie subjective perceptions of art can be addressed with factor analysis. The second question, concerning how perceptions of different painting styles differ, can be addressed using discriminant analysis.

Discriminant analysis is a special case of multiple regression. It is used when your dependent variable is categorical (for example, male/female or Democrat/Republican/Independent) and you have several predictor variables. Discriminant analysis allows you to predict membership in a group (one of the discrete categories of your dependent variable) based on knowledge of a set of predictor variables. You can use discriminant analysis to identify a simple rule for classifying subjects into groups, or to determine which of your predictor variables contributes most heavily to the separation of groups.

The analysis works by forming *discriminant functions*. For each dependent variable group, a discriminant function score is calculated according to the following formula (Tabachnick & Fidell, 1989):

$$D_i = d_{i1}z_1 + d_{i2}z_2 + \ldots + d_{in}z_n$$

where D_i is the discriminant function score calculated for each subject, d_i is the regression weight, and z_i is the standardized raw score on a particular predictor. In discriminant analysis, a new variable (D_i) is calculated for each subject. This variable is the best linear combination of predictor variables, just as in multiple regression. When the discriminant function scores have been calculated for each group, a *centroid* can then be determined. The centroid is simply the average of the discriminant function scores within a group.

More than one discriminant function can link your predictors with your dependent variable. However, the number of functions is limited to the number of predictors or to the number of levels of the dependent variable minus 1, whichever is smaller. For example, if you had seven predictors and three levels of the dependent variable, the number of possible functions is 2 (or 3 − 1). Each discriminant function represents a different linkage between the predictors and dependent variable. The first one calculated maximizes the separation between levels of the dependent variable. Subsequent functions represent progressively weaker linkages between the predictors and the dependent variable.

Because the computations needed to perform a discriminant analysis are complex, you will probably use a computer program to conduct a discriminant analysis. SPSS-X conducts a discriminant analysis within its MANOVA subprogram. The output of the SPSS-X analysis gives you several important pieces of information. First, the output will indicate the number of discriminant functions extracted, along with tests of statistical significance. Second, you can request several other statistics needed to interpret your results. These include the standardized discriminant function coefficients (analogous to beta weights), and pooled within-groups correlations between the discriminant functions and predictor variables (structure correlations).

You can use a discriminant analysis in two ways. First, you can evaluate the amount of variability accounted for by each function. SPSS-X (through the MANOVA subprogram) provides a dimension reduction analysis (if requested) that provides a canonical correlation coefficient and significance tests for each function. The squared canonical correlation coefficient provides a measure of the amount of variance in the dependent variable accounted for by a specific function. By looking at the dimension reduction analysis, you can determine the significance of each function and the amount of variance accounted for by each function.

The second way you can use the discriminant analysis is to evaluate the degree of contribution of each predictor (within a function) to the separation of groups. One strategy is to look at the standardized discriminant function coefficients. However, these weights (like beta weights) do not reveal how much each individual predictor contributes to variation in the dependent variable. Another strategy is to look at the structure correlations, which can be interpreted much like factor loadings. By convention, you typically consider those structure correlations that exceed 0.30. The structure correlations can help you determine what each discriminant function represents. However, they are not good indicators of the predictor's degree of unique contribution to discriminating among dependent variable groups (Tabachnick & Fidell, 1989).

Rather than looking at beta weights or structure correlations, you could conduct a set of specific contrasts in which each dependent variable group is contrasted with all others. You then look for which predictor variables separate a particular group from the rest (Tabachnick & Fidell, 1989). This procedure is too complex to fully describe here. (See Tabachnick & Fidell, 1989, pp. 321–326 for details.)

An Example of Discriminant Analysis. Clemmer and Bordens (1986) investigated the relationship between several cognitive variables and ratings of abstract and impressionist art. Subjects judged 16 paintings (eight by abstract artists and eight by impressionists). Each painting was rated by using a set of 24 semantic differential scales (for example, good-bad).

The first step in the analysis was to conduct a principal components factor analysis to identify which semantic differential scales measured the same underlying dimension. Next, factor scores were computed based on the results from the factor analysis (factor scores are similar to the predicted scores computed in multiple regression). These new scores were entered as predictors in a discriminant analysis, with painting type (abstract or impressionistic) defined as the dependent variable.

Table 15-4 shows a partial output from the discriminant analysis produced by SPSS-X. The top part of the table shows that the discriminant function was significant (chi-square is 489.9, $p < 0.001$), and that 64 percent of the variance was accounted for (simply the squared canonical correlation). The bottom part of Table 15-4 shows the structure correlation matrix and group centroids. The pattern of the structure correlations suggests that impressionist paintings are rated as more positive (on the good-bad factor) and more peaceful (on the peacefulness factor) than are abstract paintings.

Canonical Correlation

Multiple regression determines the relationship between a set of variables (predictors) and a *single* dependent variable. To determine the relationship between a set of predictors and a *set* of dependent variables, you use canonical correlation. Canonical correlation works by creating two new variables for each subject called *canonical variates*. A canonical variate is computed both for the dependent and predictor sets. The canonical variate is simply the score predicted from a regression equation based on the variables within a set. The correlation between the two canonical variates is the *canonical correlation*.

Canonical correlation does not appear much in published psychological literature because at this point in its development it is a purely descriptive strategy (Tabachnick & Fidell, 1989). It can be used to describe the relationship between two sets of variables, but it cannot be used to infer causal relationships. Consequently, this technique is not discussed further. If you want to know more about the technique, see Tabachnick and Fidell (1989) and Levine (1977).

Multivariate Analysis of Variance

Assume that you are required to conduct an experiment for a senior thesis. Your major area of interest is in the development of a concept of death among school-

Table 15-4. Simplified SPSS-X Output from a Discriminant Analysis

CHI-SQUARE	df	p	CANONICAL CORRELATION	WILK'S LAMBDA
489.9	5	.001	.80	.36

Structure Correlations

ARTFAC1	0.52418
ARTFAC2	0.48015
ARTFAC5	0.09096
ARTFAC4	0.03413
ARTFAC3	−0.03050

Group Centroids

GROUP	FUNC 1
1	1.33954
2	−1.33954

aged children. You have reviewed the literature and have found most of the current research to be correlational. You decide there is room for some experimental work in the area, but also decide to draw on the existing correlational research to help you develop your measures. You find that the previous research suggests several important measures should be applied to assessing children's concepts of death. So you decide to include three measures in your experiment.

The existing literature suggests that a child's concept of death can be accelerated by exposure to experience with the concept of death. So you decide to conduct a single-factor experiment with three groups. The first group is simply exposed to a film about a character who dies. The second group role-plays a dying animal. The third group, a control group, receives no special treatment.

After running your experiment, you are faced with the problem of how to analyze your three dependent measures. Of course, you could simply conduct three separate one-factor ANOVAs. You are uncomfortable with this strategy because the existing literature indicates your three chosen measures are correlated. You might miss some important relationships among your variables if you simply use a series of univariate tests. In this situation, a viable alternative is to use a MANOVA to analyze your data.

Like canonical correlation and discriminant analysis, MANOVA operates by forming a new linear combination of dependent variables for each effect in your design. For example, for a two-factor between-subjects design, a different linear combination of scores is formed for each of the two main effects and for the interaction.

Table 15-5. Data from Hypothetical Experiment on Developing a Concept of Death

Subject	FILM			ROLE PLAYING			CONTROL		
	X_1	X_2	X_3	X_1	X_2	X_3	X_1	X_2	X_3
1	6	3	5	8	7	9	1	2	1
2	5	5	3	7	9	5	2	2	4
3	6	4	2	9	9	7	1	1	2
4	4	2	2	6	8	8	3	3	3
5	3	2	6	7	8	9	4	1	2

Note: X_1, X_2, and X_3 refer to the three dependent measures listed in the text.

An Example of MANOVA. Suppose you conducted the one-factor experiment looking at the effect of a training program on children's concepts of death. Your measure of the concept of death consisted of a questionnaire containing several important questions concerning death (for example, "What happens when you die?" "What can you do to bring something dead back to life?" and "Do dead people feel pain?"). Children simply answered the questions. Independent raters then indicated how mature the concept of death was in each response. Because your measures were related to the same concept, you decide to use a MANOVA rather than separate ANOVAs to analyze the data.

Table 15-5 shows some hypothetical data that might be generated from such a study. Table 15-6 shows part of the output from an SPSS-X MANOVA analysis of these data. The top part of Table 15-6 shows the multivariate tests of significance. Although the results from a number of such tests are shown, you decide to use the Wilk's test (the reasons why you choose one test over another are not important here because in most cases there will be little difference among them). The Wilk's test indicates that the effect of the treatment was significant, $F (6,20) = 13.14$, $p < 0.001$. This tells you that your independent variable significantly affected the value of the linear dependent variable created in the MANOVA.

When you conduct a single-factor MANOVA, you get essentially the same analysis as a canonical correlation analysis. As in canonical correlation, SPSS-X MANOVA extracts as many discriminant functions as possible (two in this case). The second section of Table 15-6 shows the statistics relevant to the discriminant functions extracted. Here the canonical correlations are presented ("Canon Cor.") along with the percentage of variance accounted for ("Pct.") and the

Table 15-6. Partial SPSS-X Output for Hypothetical Experiment on Developing a Concept of Death

MULTIVARIATE TESTS OF SIGNIFICANCE ($S = 2$, $M = 0$, $N = 4$)

Test Name	Value	Approx. F	Hypoth. df	Error df	Sig. of F
Pillais	1.21442	5.66832	6.00	22.00	.001
Hotellings	17.82643	26.73964	6.00	18.00	.000
Wilk's	.03962	13.41251	6.00	20.00	.000
Roys	.94583				

Note: F statistic for Wilk's Lambda is exact.

EIGENVALUES AND CANONICAL CORRELATIONS

Root No.	Eigenvalue	Pct.	Cum. Pct.	Canon Cor.
1	17.459	97.940	97.940	.973
2	.367	2.060	100.000	.518

DIMENSION REDUCTION ANALYSIS

Roots	Wilk's L.	F Hypoth.	df	Error df	Sig. of F
1 TO 2	.03962	13.41251	6.00	20.00	.000
2 TO 2	.73140	2.01981	2.00	11.00	.179

ROY-BARGMAN STEPDOWN F-TESTS

Variable	Hypoth. MS	Error MS	Step-down	F Hypoth df	Error df	Sig. of F
DIE	33.80000	1.56667	21.57447	2	12	.000
LIFE	13.73684	1.06132	12.94322	2	11	.001
FEEL	7.89738	2.47695	3.18835	2	10	.085

EFFECT . . . COND (CONT.)

CORRELATIONS BETWEEN DEPENDENT AND CANONICAL VARIABLES

	Canonical	Variable
Variable	*1*	*2*
DIE	−.436	.870
LIFE	−.735	−.198
FEEL	−.376	−.025

associated eigenvalues. Eigenvalues are not discussed here. See Tabachnick and Fidell (1989) for a discussion of these values.

The third section of Table 15-6 presents the results of a dimension reduction analysis. This analysis reveals that only the first function was significant ($p < 0.001$).

The significant F-ratio in the multivariate test indicates a reliable effect of the training program on concepts of death. As a next step, you assess each dependent variable's contribution to this significant effect. There are several ways to do this. You could simply look at the univariate F-tests produced by SPSS-X. This strategy has some important limitations (see Tabachnick & Fidell, 1989, p. 253). Or you could examine the *Roy-Bargman stepdown analysis* shown in the bottom section of Table 15-6.

In the Roy-Bargman stepdown analysis, the first dependent variable is entered and tested for significance. Then the second variable is entered and the first variable is treated as a covariate. This test tells you whether each dependent variable explains variability over and above the variability already explained by those previously entered (Tabachnick & Fidell, 1989). The Roy-Bargman stepdown analysis is similar in concept to hierarchical regression. The main drawback to this analysis is that it can only be used when you can specify the order in which variables are entered. In the absence of a theoretically or empirically based order of entry, the Roy-Bargman test should not be used.

Finally, you could also look at the structure correlations shown at the bottom of Table 15-6 (labeled "Correlations Between DEPENDENT and Canonical Variables"). The structure correlations are similar to factor loadings and can be interpreted as such.

In addition to these analyses, you might want to conduct some *post-hoc* analyses to determine the specific effect of the independent variable on the dependent variables. These tests are similar to those used in univariate ANOVA, but more complex. The specifics are not discussed here (see Tabachnick & Fidell, 1989, pp. 250–252).

Using MANOVA for Within-Subjects Designs. Chapters 9 and 12 discussed within-subjects designs and analyses. Each subject in a within-subjects design is exposed to all levels of your independent variable. Chapter 12 indicated that a repeated measures ANOVA can be used to analyze data from this design. Data from within-subjects (and mixed) designs can also be analyzed with MANOVA.

The within-subjects ANOVA assumes homogeneity of both within-cell variances and within-cell covariances. The first assumption states that variance should be homogenous across treatments. This assumption is common between the between-subjects and within-subjects analyses. However, the assumption of homogeneity of covariance is special to the within-subjects ANOVA. The following example illustrates the idea of homogeneity of covariances.

Figure 15-7 shows a simple one-factor within-subjects design. Notice that the behavior of each subject is evaluated under each level of the independent variable. This being the case, you can form pairs of conditions and subtract the

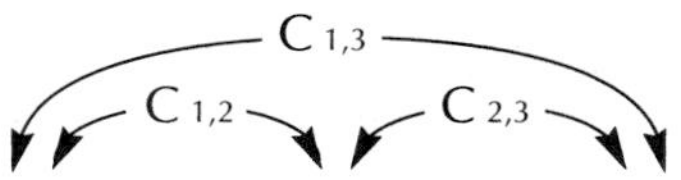

Subject	Level 1	Level 2	Level 3
1	$X_{1,1}$	$X_{2,1}$	$X_{3,1}$
2	$X_{1,2}$	$X_{2,2}$	$X_{3,2}$
3	$X_{1,3}$	$X_{2,3}$	$X_{3,3}$
4	$X_{1,4}$	$X_{2,4}$	$X_{3,4}$
5	$X_{1,5}$	$X_{2,5}$	$X_{3,5}$

Note: $X_{i,j}$ represents a subject's score where i = the level of the independent variable, and j = the subject number. $C_{i,j}$ indicates the covariances that could be calculated where i and j are the levels of the independent variables.

Figure 15-7. Three-treatment within-subjects design showing covariances.

scores associated with each subject within those two conditions (Keppel, 1982). You can then obtain variance based on the resulting difference scores. This variance is called *covariance*. In the design illustrated in Figure 15-7, you can form three pairs of conditions (C_1 with C_2, C_2 with C_3, and C_1 with C_3) and three concomitant covariances. If the covariances are not homogeneous, then the homogeneity of covariance assumption has been violated.

In a between-subjects ANOVA, mild to moderate violations of the homogeneity assumption do not significantly affect the validity of the statistical test. In a within-subjects ANOVA, however, violations of the homogeneity assumption lead to a serious positive bias: rejecting the null hypothesis more often than you should at a given alpha level. Thus, you are making more type I errors than is acceptable.

Another problem with the univariate within-subjects analysis is that when you add a second independent variable, the analysis becomes somewhat controversial. The controversy surrounds selecting an error term appropriate to test the main effects and interactions. You can select a "pooled" error term and use this same term for all the within-subjects factors, or you can use separate error terms for each. Unfortunately, the two choices may lead to different outcomes of the statistical analysis, and there is little agreement on which choice is best.

Because MANOVA circumvents the problems with the homogeneity assumptions and error-term selection, it has been suggested as an alternative to a standard within-subjects ANOVA (Tabachnick & Fidell, 1989; O'Brien &

Kaiser, 1985). In the MANOVA, the repeated measures taken on each subject are treated as correlated dependent variables and analyzed accordingly. Rather than assuming homogeneity of covariance, MANOVA takes into account the covariances actually present in the data. For information on using MANOVA to analyze within-subjects designs, see O'Brien and Kaiser (1985).

Loglinear Analysis

Most of the powerful inferential statistics discussed in this chapter and in Chapter 12 require that your variables be measured along at least an interval scale. However, there are research situations in which you may want to measure or manipulate categorical variables (for example, sex of subject). Statistics such as ANOVA, MANOVA, and multiple regression are not appropriate to analyze such data. For these cases, **loglinear analysis** is an alternative.

Loglinear analysis is analogous to chi-square (see Chapter 12) in that you use observed and expected frequencies to evaluate the statistical significance of your data. An important difference between chi-square and loglinear analysis is that loglinear analysis can be easily applied to experimental research designs that include more than two independent variables, whereas chi-square is normally limited to the two-variable case.

Applications of Loglinear Analysis. Loglinear analysis has a wide range of applications. You can use loglinear analysis if you conducted a correlational study with several categorical variables. Loglinear analysis is well suited to this task. You can also use loglinear analysis if you conducted an experiment including a categorical dependent variable (for example, guilty/not guilty), even if your independent variables were quantitative.

Loglinear analysis is also a useful tool for testing and building theoretical models. In this application, you specify how variables should be entered into the analysis for the models you wish to test. Loglinear analysis is then used to test the relative adequacy of each model.

Finally, because loglinear analysis is a nonparametric statistic, you can use it if your data violate the assumptions of parametric statistics (such as ANOVA). In this instance, you can use loglinear analysis even if your dependent variable was measured along an interval or ordinal scale (Tabachnick & Fidell, 1989). However, one important requirement must still be met.

Like chi-square, loglinear analysis uses observed and expected cell frequencies to compute your test statistic. In order to obtain valid results, your cell expected frequencies must be relatively large. Tabachnick and Fidell (1989) recommend having five times as many subjects as cells to ensure adequate expected frequencies. So, for example, if you have a $2 \times 2 \times 2$ design you should have $2 \times 2 \times 2 \times 5$ subjects (40 subjects) to ensure sufficiently large expected cell frequencies.

How Loglinear Analysis Works. When you use ANOVA or multiple regression to analyze your data, your analysis uses group means as a basis for analysis.

When you have categorical data, however, you must deal with proportions instead of means. For example, if you used a three-factor design with a categorical dependent variable (yes/no), you would summarize your data according to the proportion of subjects falling into each category.

In a standard analysis of proportional data from a two-factor experiment, where you are interested in a single relationship between two variables, chi-square is used to evaluate that relationship. However, when evaluating more than one relationship (that is, two main effects and an interaction), chi-square is not the best test statistic because the component chi-squares do not sum to the total chi-square (Tabachnick & Fidell, 1989). In this case a likelihood ratio (G^2) is used in place of chi-square. Although similar to chi-square (in that cell expected and observed frequencies are compared), G^2 involves taking the natural log (ln) of the ratio of observed cell frequency to the expected cell frequency, according to the following formula (Tabachnick & Fidell, 1989):

$$G^2 = 2 \ (f_0) \ \ln(f_0/f_e)$$

where f_0 is the observed cell frequency, and f_e is the expected cell frequency. A G^2 is computed for each main effect and interaction in your design and is interpreted in the same way as chi-square (using the chi-square tables to establish statistical significance).

Space limitations here preclude a detailed description of all the applications of loglinear analysis or how loglinear analysis is used. If you need to use loglinear analysis, detailed discussions can be found in Agresti and Finlay (1986) and Tabachnick and Fidell (1989).

Path Analysis

Path analysis applies multiple-regression techniques to causal modeling. For example, suppose you are interested in determining how attitudes and behaviors relate to one another. You have reviewed the literature and have come across the "theory of reasoned action" by Fishbein and Ajzen (1975). This theory postulates that attitudes are evaluative dimensions that, along with subjective norms (such as knowing what your friends are going to do), mediate between other variables (such as sex) and behavioral intentions (that is, what you specifically intend to do). According to the theory, behavioral intentions, in turn, determine behavior.

You decide to test the limits of the Fishbein and Ajzen theory by measuring each of the important components of the theory with a questionnaire. The topic you have chosen is the relationship between attitudes toward college and actual college attendance. In order to test the theory, you collect data on attitudes toward attending college, subjective norms about college, a specific intention to attend college, and actual college attendance behavior.

After you have collected your data, you now face the task of analyzing them. Whereas you could simply compute bivariate correlation coefficients between all variables, the disadvantages of this approach have been discussed. Besides, simple correlational analyses will not allow you to evaluate possible causal relationships among your variables. As an alternative, consider using path analysis.

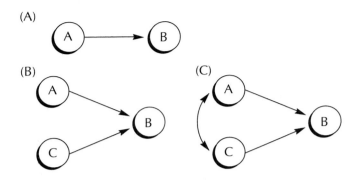

Figure 15-8. Three possible causal relationships: (A) Variable A causes changes in B; (B) Uncorrelated Variables A and C contribute to changes in the value of B; (C) Correlated Variables A and C cause changes in the value of B.

Unlike the other analytic techniques already discussed, path analysis is not a statistical procedure in and of itself. Rather, it is an application of multiple-regression techniques to the testing of causal models. Path analysis allows you to test a model specifying the causal links among variables, by applying simple multiple-regression techniques.

Always remember that path analysis is designed to test causal models, not to sift through data for interesting relationships among variables. Developing a clearly articulated causal model is crucial in path analysis. The model should not rest on flimsy ideas and unsupported conjecture. Instead, the causal relationships proposed in the model should rest on a strong theoretical or empirical base.

Translating theoretical propositions into a clearly defined path model can be tricky. You always are tempted to determine how to measure your variables first and then derive the model. This method may not be the best. It may limit the possible causal relationships within your model and consequently may not allow you to adequately test your theory. Instead, first develop a list of the causal links among variables as suggested by your theory (Hunter & Gerbing, 1982). Then show these links among variables in a *path diagram*. After developing the path model and diagram, you can then decide how to measure your variables.

Causal Relationships. The heart of path analysis is developing a causal model and identifying causal relationships. Causal relationships among variables can take many forms. The simplest of these is shown in Panel A of Figure 15-8, where Variable A (independent variable) causes changes in Variable B (dependent variable).

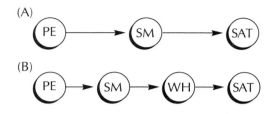

Figure 15-9. Three-variable causal chain (A) and a four-variable causal chain (B).

Another possible causal relationship is shown in Panel B. Here two variables impinge on Variable B. This model suggests variation in the dependent variable has multiple causes. These causal variables can be either uncorrelated (as shown in Panel B) or correlated.

Panel C shows a situation in which two variables believed to cause changes in the dependent variable are correlated. In Figure 15-8 (and in path analysis, in general), straight arrows denote causal relationships and are called *paths*. Curved, double-headed arrows denote correlational relationships.

The simple causal relationships just described can be combined to form more complex causal models. One such model is the *causal chain*, in which a sequence of events leads ultimately to variation in the dependent variable. To illustrate a simple causal chain, consider a modification of a previous example in which you were trying to determine what variables correlated with SAT scores.

Suppose you believe parental education (PE) and student motivation (SM) relate to variation in SAT scores. You have reason to believe a causal relationship exists. So you develop a causal model like the one illustrated in Panel A of Figure 15-9. Your model suggests PE causes changes in SM, which then causes changes in SAT scores. Notice you are proposing that PE does not directly cause changes in SAT, but rather it operates through SM.

When developing simple causal chains (and more complex causal models), keep in mind that the validity of your causal model depends on how well you have done your homework and conceptualized your model. Perhaps SM does not directly cause changes in SAT scores as conjectured, but rather operates through yet another variable, such as working hard (WH) in class. Panel B of Figure 15-9 shows a causal chain including WH. If you excluded WH from your model, the causal relationships and the model you develop may not be valid.

You can progress from simple causal chains to more complex models quite easily. Figure 15-10 shows three examples of more complex causal models. In Panel A, the causal model suggests Variables A and B are correlated (indicated with the curved arrow). Variable A is believed to exert a causal influence on Variable C, and B on D. Variable D is hypothesized to cause changes in C, and both D and C are believed to cause changes in E.

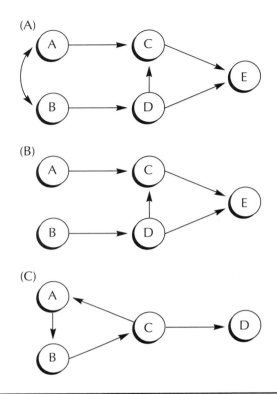

Figure 15-10. Three complex causal models.

Types of Variables and Causal Models. Variables A and B in Panel A of Figure 15-10 are called *exogenous variables*. Exogenous variables begin the causal sequence. Notice that no causal paths lead to Variables A or B. All the other variables in the model shown in Panel A are *endogenous variables*. These variables are internal to the model and changes in them are believed to be caused by other variables. Variables C, D, and E are all endogenous variables. Panel B of Figure 15-10 shows essentially the same model as Panel A, except that the two exogenous variables are not correlated in Panel B.

The models in Panels A and B are both known as *recursive models*. Notice that there are no loops of variables. That is, causal relationships run in only one direction (for example, D causes C, but C does not cause D). In contrast, Panel C of Figure 15-10 shows a *nonrecursive model,* which has a causal loop. In this case, Variable A is believed to be a cause of C (operating through B), but C can also cause A. In general, recursive models are much easier to deal with conceptually and statistically (Asher, 1976).

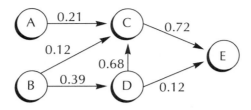

Figure 15-11. Path diagram showing path coefficients.

Estimating the Degree of Causality. After you have developed your causal models and measured your variables, you then obtain estimates of the causal relationships among your variables. These estimates are called *path coefficients*. Figure 15-11 shows a causal model with the path coefficients indicated for each causal path.

Path coefficients are determined by using a series of multiple regression analyses. Each endogenous variable is used as a dependent variable in the regression analysis. All the variables in the model that are assumed to impinge on the dependent variable are used as predictors. For example, the path coefficients for A–C and D–C in Figure 15-11 are obtained by using C as the dependent variable and A, B, and D as predictors. The path coefficients are the standardized regression weights (beta weights) from these analyses.

Interpreting Path Analysis. Path analysis is used to test the validity of a presumed causal model. To that end, you look at the path coefficients and determine whether the pattern expected by the model has emerged. In addition to looking at the path coefficients (which give you estimates of the direct effects of variables on other variables), you also decompose the paths into indirect effects. Decomposition can be done according to *Wright's rules* (cited in Asher, 1976).

Wright's rules state that the correlation between any two variables can be broken down into simple and compound paths. The compound path is the product of the simple paths that it comprises (Asher, 1976). The simple path is the direct link between the two variables, and the compound path consists of all indirect routes from one variable to another. The following are three general instructions given by Wright to guide the decomposition of a path (Asher, 1976, p. 33):

1. No path may pass through the same variable more than once.
2. No path may go backward on (against the direction of) an arrow after the path has gone forward on a different arrow.
3. No path may pass through a double-headed curved arrow . . . more than once in any single path.

Table 15-7. Decomposition of Path Model Shown in Figure 15-11

Path	Direct Effect	Indirect Effect
B → E	None	0.32
A → E	None	0.15
B → C	0.12	0.27
A → C	0.21	None

In Figure 15-11, the relationship between Variables B and C consists of the simple path linking B with C, plus the product of the path coefficients linking B, D, and C. Table 15-7 shows the decomposition of the model shown in Figure 15-11.

Interpretation of the path coefficients themselves can be tricky. In most cases, the beta weights cannot be interpreted as representing the unique contribution of one variable to variance in another. Remember that a beta weight not only has components of the degree of relationship between two variables, but also includes components of any other predictors. For example, in Figure 15-11 the path coefficient linking Variables C and E does not represent the unique contribution of C to E. Rather, Variables A, B, and D also contribute to E, and these contributions may be reflected in the C to E path coefficient.

There is no easy way around this conceptual difficulty. One possible solution is to use semipartial correlation coefficients in place of beta weights. As we indicated, these can be obtained indirectly from SPSS-X or calculated easily by hand (Tabachnick & Fidell, 1989). These semipartial correlations provide a better estimate of the degree of impact of one variable on another (with others held constant) than do the beta weights.

An Example of Path Analysis. Harrison, Thompson, and Rodgers (1985) tested the theory of reasoned action by Fishbein and Ajzen (1975). In the Harrison et al. study, subjects responded to a questionnaire concerning their attitudes toward attending college, subjective norms, intentions about attending college, and actual college attendance. The attitudes of subjects toward college attendance were assessed by asking subjects, "What would you like to do after high school?" Subjective norms were evaluated by asking subjects whether their friends were planning to attend college, and the extent to which subjects had discussed college with teachers and their parents. The intentions of the subjects about college attendance were evaluated by asking them if they planned to attend college after high school. The measure of college attendance was simply whether or not a subject actually attended college. Finally, Harrison et al. measured two demographic variables (sex of subject and father's education).

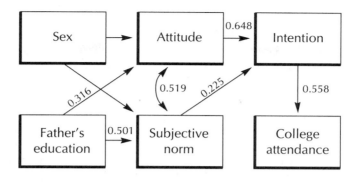

Figure 15-12. A path model. (Harrison, Thompson, & Rodgers, 1985; reprinted with permission.)

Figure 15-12 shows the path model followed by Harrison et al. (1985) and the significant standardized path coefficients. Recall that the theory of reasoned action predicts that attitudes and subjective norms mediate between other variables, and that intentions directly underlie behavior. The high path coefficients linking attitudes and intentions (0.648), and intention with college attendance (0.558), lend support to the approach by Fishbein and Ajzen (1975). The results also show exogenous variables (such as father's education) are mediated by attitudes (a finding that is also consistent with the theory).

Multivariate Analysis: A Cautionary Note

The bare bones overview of the major multivariate techniques in this chapter could not provide a detailed discussion of the controversies surrounding the use of these tests. Although some researchers characterize multivariate statistics such as MANOVA as "a powerful and rich methodology to characterize group difference" (Bray & Maxwell, 1982), others advocate extreme caution in applying multivariate statistics (Hunter, 1987). In our experience, caution is called for when multivariate statistics are used.

The computer can analyze multivariate data quickly and efficiently. In fact, the computer has made multivariate statistical techniques readily available to most researchers. With such easy access inevitably comes misapplication. The computer can grind out pages and pages of output in an amazingly short period of time. It cannot interpret the results for you, however. Much of the controversy over the use of multivariate statistics lies in the area of interpretation.

In multiple regression, for example, is it really better to use the standardized regression weights or the unstandardized weights to interpret the data? Or should you heed the advice of Tabachnick and Fidell (1989) to calculate semipartial correlations? In discriminant analysis, should you use the standardized coefficients or the structure correlations? In factor analysis, should you use orthogonal or oblique rotation? Unfortunately, there are no universally agreed-on answers to these and other major questions concerning multivariate analyses.

This chapter has discussed some of the advantages of multivariate statistics over univariate statistics. Unfortunately, multivariate statistics are not simple substitutions for univariate statistics. In a univariate ANOVA, for example, the effect of an independent variable on a dependent variable is evaluated by determining if the observed means change as a function of changes in the independent variable. Fine-grained analyses are then conducted to determine which means differ significantly. MANOVA, however, produces results that are more difficult to interpret. Instead of performing simple fine-grained analyses to localize significant effects, you set up contrasts with discriminant analyses. In short, interpreting results from a MANOVA is more complex than interpreting results from univariate ANOVAs.

The most prudent thing you can do at this point is to spend some time learning about the intricacies of these tests so you can identify and avoid these hidden traps. Thoroughly familiarize yourself with the assumptions of multivariate statistics and with how these statistics operate before attempting to use them.

Also, pay close attention to how you design your study. In many cases, failure to uncover relationships with a multivariate test is caused by faulty logic more during the design phase than during the analysis phase (Asher, 1976). Multivariate statistics cannot make sense out of poorly conceptualized and measured variables. There is no substitute for a carefully designed multivariate study that has a sound theoretical or empirical base and a well-defined measurement model.

Summary

Whenever you include several related measures in the same study, you are using a multivariate design. Analysis of your data is then done with one of the many multivariate statistical tests. There are multivariate tests for experiments with multiple dependent measures (MANOVA and MANCOVA) and tests for correlational designs (multiple regression, canonical correlation, discriminant analysis, and factor analysis). These tests allow you to identify complex relationships while controlling statistical errors.

Like univariate and bivariate statistics, multivariate statistics make assumptions that must be met. Your variables must be linearly related and normally distributed. Violations of these assumptions may lead to invalid conclusions. In addition, you must identify and deal with both univariate and multivariate outliers, because outliers can drastically affect the correlations used to compute multivariate statistics. Outliers can be handled by either deleting cases or variables, or by using an appropriate data transformation. Also, make an effort to develop a sound measurement model to avoid the problem of error of measurement. Error of measurement can lead to an unacceptable number of type II errors.

Factor analysis is used either to reduce a large set of variables to a smaller set, or to confirm that certain variables measure the same underlying factor. Two types of factor analysis are principal components and principal factors. The difference between the two is found in the values placed on the diagonal of the correlation matrix used to extract factors. In principal components analysis, ones are placed on the diagonal. In principal factors analysis, communalities are placed on the diagonal. These communalities are difficult to derive before factor analysis. Principal components analysis is therefore more popular.

Factor analysis extracts as many significant factors as possible. For each factor, a variable will have a certain loading. These loadings are the correlations between the original variable and the factor extracted. You should rotate the factors before interpreting the loadings. The most popular rotation method is varimax.

Partial and part correlation analyses are used when you want to evaluate the relationship between two variables while controlling for a third. Partial correlation evaluates the relationship between two variables with the effect of a third variable removed from both of the variables being correlated. A part correlation (also known as a *semipartial correlation*) evaluates the relationship between two variables with the effect of a third removed from only one of them.

Multiple regression is used when you have identified a single, continuously measured dependent variable and several predictor variables. The analysis operates by determining regression weights based on the correlations among your variables. Two types of regression weights are raw and standardized weights. In general, you should use the standardized weights to help interpret your results. Unfortunately, the standardized weights do not tell you how much each variable contributes to explaining variability in your dependent variable. To do this you should calculate the squared semipartial correlations. These correlations can then be used to determine the degree to which each variable independently contributes to variation in the dependent variable.

Discriminant analysis is an extension of canonical correlation. It is used when your dependent variable is categorical. Essentially, you are trying to predict group membership based on knowledge of your predictor variables. Interpretation is made by examining the amount of variability accounted for by each of the extracted discriminant functions, and by setting up contrasts between your dependent variable groups. The former tells you how important each function is, and the latter how important each variable is to the solution.

In situations where you have two sets of variables, the analysis of choice is canonical correlation. One set of variables may be identified as the dependent variable set, and the other the predictor variable set. Canonical correlation computes for each set a new variable called a *canonical variate*. The correlation between the canonical variates is the canonical correlation. Interpretation of a canonical analysis can be made by looking at the structure correlations. These can be interpreted much like factor loadings in factor analysis.

MANOVA is used when you have an experiment with several related dependent measures. The analysis is essentially an extension of discriminant analysis to experimental data. Interpretation is based on the significance of the discriminant functions extracted for each effect, the Roy-Bargman stepdown test, and the structure correlations.

MANOVA can also be used to analyze data from a within-subjects design. Because of the restrictive assumptions of the univariate within-subjects ANOVA, and the controversy surrounding error term selection for that analysis, MANOVA should be considered as an alternative. In MANOVA, the repeated measures taken from each subject are treated as correlated dependent variables. Using MANOVA in this capacity circumvents many of the problems associated with the traditional within-subjects ANOVA.

Loglinear analysis is a nonparametric multivariate statistic with a variety of applications. It can be used to analyze categorical data from an experiment or categorical variables from a correlational study. It can also be used on interval or ratio data in instances where your data do not meet the assumptions of the analysis of variance.

Path analysis is used to test a clearly specified causal model. Using a theory, you develop a causal model, measure your variables, and then use a series of simple multiple-regression analyses to derive path coefficients. The path coefficients are used as estimates of the magnitude of causal relationships among variables. Interpretation is facilitated by looking at both direct and indirect effects of variables.

Causal models can be of several types. Simple causal chains propose that there is a linear path from one variable to another. More complex models can involve complex path linkages. Models can be either recursive (which contain no causal loops) or nonrecursive (which contain causal loops). Conceptually, recursive models are easier to analyze and interpret.

Finally, multivariate analyses are complex and tricky to use. Don't try to use them until you have a sound understanding of how they work, what assumptions they make, and how results can be interpreted.

Key Terms

Univariate strategy

Multivariate strategy

Multiple regression

Discriminant analysis

Canonical correlation

Factor analysis

Multivariate analysis of variance (MANOVA)

Partial correlation

Part correlation

Multiple *R*

R-square

Beta weight

Loglinear analysis

Path analysis

16

Using Theory

THE FIRST FIFTEEN CHAPTERS OF THIS BOOK have discussed conducting a research study. Thus far, this text has explored the processes involved in finding a research question, adopting a strategy with which to pursue the question, gathering data, identifying relationships in the data, and determining the reliability of the data. The discussion has focused on those aspects of the research process that allow you to develop a sound research study. However, the discussion has not focused on the broader issues concerning how research results fit into the general framework of science. This chapter and Chapter 17 explore some of these issues.

At various points in this text, discussions have referred to theory. For example, Chapter 2 said that a theory is often used to help identify interesting research questions. This chapter focuses on theories by defining what a theory is, exploring what role theory plays in science and how theories are developed and evaluated.

What Is a Theory?

Defining what a **theory** is has always been hazardous, because the term is so often used in a variety of contexts. For example, a detective in a mystery novel is said to develop a "theory" of who committed a crime. In this context, the word *theory* is used as a synonym for *hypothesis*. That is, the detective has an idea about who is guilty, an idea that he or she will then test. The word has also been used to describe ideas that are developed about unverifiable events. For example, many ideas exist about how the miracles recounted in the Bible actually occurred. In this context, a "theory" is used to provide the final explanation for a phenomenon. Finally, the term is often applied in our everyday lives. How often have you said, "I have a theory about how that happened"?

As used in science, the term *theory* means something more than it does in everyday usage. A **scientific theory** is one that goes beyond the level of a simple hypothesis, deals with potentially verifiable phenomena, and is highly ordered and structured. This discussion adopts and extends the definition of theory provided by Martin (1985). According to Martin, a theory is a partially verified statement of a scientific relationship that cannot be directly observed. If the theory is stated formally, this statement consists of a set of interrelated propositions (and corollaries to those propositions) that attempt to specify the relationship between a variable (or set of variables) and some behavior. Not all scientific theories are expressed this way, but most could be.

A good example of a psychological theory with a clearly defined set of propositions and corollaries is "equity theory" (Walster, Walster, & Berscheid, 1978). Equity theory was developed to explain how individuals behave when placed in an interpersonal exchange situation, such as employer-employee relations or friendships. Table 16-1 presents the major propositions of equity theory and one corollary (other corollaries are outlined by Walster et al.). Notice that the first set of propositions make a general statement about how interpersonal exchanges are perceived. The later propositions and corollaries specify how a set of variables (such as inputs and outputs) should affect the perception of equity within a relationship.

A deeper exploration of the definition of "theory" shows that a scientific theory has several important characteristics. First, a scientific theory describes a scientific relationship — one established through observation and logic — that indicates how variables interact within the system to which the theory applies.

Second, the described relationship cannot be observed directly. Its existence must be *inferred* from the data. (If you could observe the relationship directly, there would be no need for a theory.) Third, the statement is only partially verified. This means that the theory has passed some tests, but not all relevant tests have been conducted.

Colloquial use of the term *theory* leads to confusion over what a theory really is. Confusion can also be found within the scientific community over the term. Even in scientific writing, "theory," "hypothesis," "law," and "model" are often used interchangeably. Nevertheless, these terms can be distinguished, as described in the next sections.

Theory Versus Hypothesis

Students often confuse theory with hypothesis, and even professionals sometimes use these terms interchangeably. However, as usually defined, theories are

---

Table 16-1. Propositions and Corollaries of Equity Theory

1. In an interpersonal relationship, a person will try to maximize his or her outcomes (where outcome = rewards − costs).

    Corollary: As long as a person believes that he or she can maximize outcomes by behaving equitably, he or she will. If a person believes that inequitable behavior is more likely to maximize outcomes, inequitable behavior will be used.

2a. By developing systems whereby resources can be equitably distributed among members, groups can maximize the probability of equitable behavior among their members.

2b. A group will reward members who behave equitably toward others and punish those who do not.

3. Inequitable relationships are stressful for those within them. The greater the inequity, the greater the distress.

4. A person in an inequitable relationship will take steps to reduce the distress aroused by restoring equity. The more distress felt, the harder the person will try to restore equity.

SOURCE: Based on Walster, Walster, & Berscheid, 1978.

---

more complex than hypotheses. For example, if you observe that more crime occurs during the period of full moon than during other times of the month, you might hypothesize that the observed relationship is caused by the illumination that the moon provides for nighttime burglary. You could then test this hypothesis by comparing crime rates during periods of full moon that were clear with crime rates during periods of full moon that were cloudy.

In contrast to the simple one-variable account provided by this hypothesis, a theory would account for changes in crime rate by specifying the action and interaction of a *system* of variables. Because of the complexity of the system involved, no single observation could substantiate the theory in its entirety.

Theory Versus Law

A theory that has been substantially verified is sometimes called a **law**. However, most laws do not derive from theories in this way. Laws are usually empirically verified, quantitative relationships between two or more variables, and thus are not normally subject to the disconfirmation that theories are. Such laws may idealize real-world relationships, as in Boyle's law, which relates change in temperature to change in pressure of a confined ideal gas. Because there are no ideal gases, the relationship described by Boyle's law is not directly observable. But as a description of the behavior of real gases, it holds well enough for most purposes. To an approximation, it represents a verified empirical relationship and is thus unlikely to be overthrown.

Such empirical laws are not theories grown solid through verification. They are relationships that must be explained by theory. For example, a theory to explain Boyle's law would specify the underlying mechanisms at the molecular or even atomic and subatomic levels that give rise to the relationship Boyle's law describes.

Theory Versus Model

Like *theory*, the term **model** can refer to a range of concepts. In some cases, it is simply used as a synonym for *theory*. However, in most cases *model* refers to a specific implementation of a more general theoretical view. For example, the Rescorla-Wagner model of classical conditioning formalizes a more general associative theory of conditioning (Rescorla & Wagner, 1972). This model specifies how the associative strength of a conditional stimulus (CS) is to be calculated following each of a series of trials in which the CS is presented alone or in conjunction with other stimuli. Where the general associative theory simply states that the strength of the stimulus will increase each time the CS is paired with an unconditional stimulus (US), the Rescorla-Wagner model supplies a set of assumptions that mathematically specify how characteristics of the stimuli interact on each trial.

Rescorla and Wagner made it clear when they presented their model that the assumptions were simply starting points. For example, they assumed that the associative strength of a compound stimulus (two or more stimuli presented together) would equal the sum of the strengths of the individual stimuli. If the learning curves resulting from this assumption proved not to fit the curves obtained from experiment, then the assumption would be modified.

Rescorla and Wagner could have chosen to try several rules for combining stimulus strengths. Each variation would represent a somewhat different model of classical conditioning, although all would derive from a common associative view of the conditioning process.

In a related sense, a model can represent an application of a general theory to a specific situation. In the case of the Rescorla-Wagner model, the assumptions of the model can be applied to generate predictions for reinforcement of a simple CS, for reinforcement of a compound CS, for inhibitory conditioning, for extinction, and for discrimination learning (to name a few). The assumptions of the model remain the same across all these cases, but the set of equations required to make the predictions changes from case to case. You might then say that each set of equations represents a different model: a model of simple conditioning, a model of compound conditioning, a model of differential conditioning, and so on. However, all the models would share the same assumptions of the Rescorla-Wagner model of conditioning.

This chapter uses the term *model* in all the ways just discussed. At times, a model will simply be a theory. At other times a model will be a specific version of a less well-specified theory or a particular application of a theory to a specific situation. The context will tell you which meaning applies.

Types of Theory

Theories may be classified in several ways. This section classifies theories along three dimensions: (1) quantitative or qualitative aspect, (2) level of description, and (3) scope (or domain) of the theory.

Quantitative Versus Qualitative Theory

The first dimension along which a theory can be classified is whether the theory is quantitative or qualitative. Some theories are expressed in mathematical terms, whereas others are stated in verbal terms. The next sections describe these two types of theories.

Quantitative Theory. A **quantitative theory** is expressed in mathematical terms. It specifies the variables and constants with which it deals numerically, and relates the numerical states of these variables and constants to one another. Given specific numerical inputs, the quantitative theory generates specific numerical outputs. The relationships thus described can then be tested by setting up the specified conditions and observing whether the outputs take on the specified values (within the error of measurement).

A good example of a quantitative theory in psychology is an information integration theory by Norman Anderson (1968). Anderson's theory attempts to explain how diverse sources of information are integrated into an overall impression. The theory proposes that each item of information used in an impression formation task is assigned both a weight and scale value. The weights and scale values are then combined according to the following formula:

$$J = \frac{\Sigma\,(W_i \times S_i)}{\Sigma W_i}$$

where W_i is the weight assigned to each item of information and S_i is the scale value assigned to each item of information. According to this theory, your final judgment (J) about a stimulus (for example, whether you describe a person as warm or cold, caring or uncaring, honest or dishonest) will be the result of a mathematical combination of the weights and scale values assigned to each piece of information.

Qualitative Theory. A **qualitative theory** is any theory that is not quantitative. Qualitative theories tend to be stated in verbal, rather than mathematical, terms. These theories state which variables are important and, loosely, how those variables interact.

The relationships described by qualitative theories may be quantitative, but if so, the quantities will be measured on no higher than an ordinal scale. For example, a theory of drug addiction may state that craving for the drug will increase with the time since the last administration and that this craving will be intensified by emotional stress. Note that the predictions of the theory specify only ordinal relationships. They state that craving will be greater under some conditions than under others, but they do not state by how much.

A good example of a qualitative theory in psychology is a theory of language acquisition by Noam Chomsky (1965). This theory states that a child acquires language by analyzing the language that he or she hears. The language heard by the child is processed, according to Chomsky, and the rules of language are extracted. The child then formulates hypotheses about how language works and then tests those hypotheses against reality. No attempt is made in the theory to quantify the parameters of language acquisition. Instead, the theory specifies verbally the important variables that contribute to language acquisition.

Level of Description

The second dimension along which theories may be categorized is according to the level of description the theory provides. Some theories are primarily designed to describe a phenomenon, whereas others attempt to explain relationships among variables that control a phenomenon. The following sections describe theories that deal with phenomena at different levels.

Descriptive Theories. At the lowest level, a theory may simply describe how certain variables are related, without providing an explanation for that relationship. A theory that merely describes a relationship is termed a **descriptive theory**.

An excellent example of a descriptive theory was provided by Johannes Kepler, who, in 1596, first developed equations that accurately described the motions of the planets around the sun. In essence, the theory stated that the planets follow elliptical orbits with the sun as one focus of the ellipse. Although this was an important advance (scientists had previously assumed that the planets moved along a series of circular orbits-on-orbits called *epicycles*), it did not explain *why* the planets moved in this way.

Most descriptive theories are simply proposed generalizations from observation. For example, arousal theory states that task performance increases with arousal up to some optimal arousal value, then deteriorates with further increases in arousal. The proposed relationship thus follows an inverted U-shaped function. Arousal and task performance are both classes of variables that can be operationally defined a number of ways. Arousal and task performance are general concepts rather than specific variables. The proposed relationship is thus not directly observable, but must be inferred from observation of many specific variables representative of each concept. Note also that the theory describes the relationship, but offers no real explanation for it.

A potential trap you can fall into when constructing a descriptive theory is to think you have explained a phenomenon when you have only given it a name. This problem became particularly acute during the heyday of functionalism, when nearly every animal behavior was being "explained" as the product of an instinct. For example, if a female mouse took care of her newborn offspring, it was because she had a "mothering instinct." But how do you know that the mouse had a mothering instinct? You know simply because she took care of her offspring. The concept of mothering instinct as used here is nothing more than a name for the observed behaviors. It says only that the mouse mothered because she had a tendency to mother.

Analogical Theories. At the next level are **analogical theories**, which explain a relationship through analogy. Such theories borrow from well–understood models (usually of physical systems) by suggesting that the system to be explained behaves in a fashion similar to that described by the well–understood model.

To develop an analogical theory, you equate each variable in the physical system with a variable in the behavioral system to be modeled. You then plug in values for the new variables and apply the rules of the original theory in order to generate predictions.

An example of an analogical theory was provided by Konrad Lorenz in 1950. Lorenz wanted to explain some relationships he had observed between the occurrence of a specific behavioral pattern (called a *fixed action pattern*, or FAP), a triggering stimulus (called a *sign* or *releaser stimulus*), and the time since last occurrence of the FAP. For example, chickens scan the ground and then direct pecks at any seeds they find there. Here the visual characteristics of the seeds act as a releaser stimulus, and the directed pecking at the seeds is the FAP. Lorenz had observed that the FAP could be elicited more easily by a sign stimulus as the time increased since the last appearance of the FAP. In fact, with enough time, the behavior became so primed that it sometimes occurred in the absence of any identifiable sign stimulus. However, if the behavior had just occurred, the sign stimulus usually was unable to elicit the FAP again.

Let's return to the chicken example. Chickens at first peck only at seeds. With increasing hunger, however, they begin to peck at pencil marks on a paper and other such stimuli that only remotely resemble seeds. With further deprivation, they even peck at a blank paper.

To explain this relationship, Lorenz imagined that the motivation to perform the FAP was like the pressure of water at the bottom of a tank that was being continuously filled (see Figure 16-1). As time went on, the water in the tank became deeper and the pressure greater. Lorenz pictured a pressure-sensitive valve at the bottom of the tank. This valve could be opened by depressing a lever, but the pressure required to open it became less as the pressure inside the

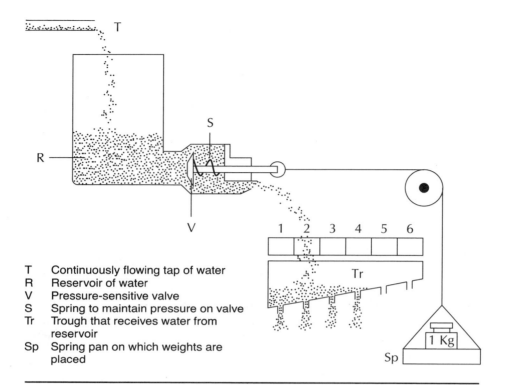

Figure 16-1. Lorenz's hydraulic model of motivation. (Lorenz, 1950; legend adapted from Dewsbury, 1978; reprinted with permission.)

tank rose. In Lorenz's conception, the lever was normally "pressed" by the appearance of the sign stimulus.

Notice the analogies in Lorenz's model. Motivation to perform the FAP is analogous to water pressure. Engaging in the FAP is analogous to water rushing out the open valve. And perception of the sign stimulus is analogous to pressing the lever to open the valve.

Now put the model into action. Motivation to perform the FAP builds as time passes (the tank fills). If a sign stimulus appears after the tank has partially filled, the valve opens and the FAP occurs. However, if the sign stimulus does not occur for a long time, the tank overfills and the pressure triggers the valve to open spontaneously (the FAP occurs without the sign stimulus). Finally, if the FAP has just occurred (the valve has just opened), there is no motivation to perform the FAP (the tank is empty) and the sign stimulus is ineffective. The model thus nicely accounts for the observed facts.

Lorenz's hydraulic model of motivation eventually gave way to more sophisticated theories when new data revealed its limitations. In general, analogical theories can only be pushed so far. At some point the analogy breaks down. After all, motivation is *not* quite the same thing as water pressure in a tank and may vary in ways quite unexpected for water pressure. Nevertheless, analogical theories can provide conceptual organization for the data and may predict relationships that otherwise would be unexpected.

Fundamental Theories. At the highest level are theories created *de novo* to explain phenomena within a particular area of research. These theories do not depend on analogy to provide their basic structures. Instead, they propose a new structure that directly relates the variables and constants of the system. This structure includes entities and processes not directly observable but invented to account for the observed relationships. Thus, these entities and processes go beyond descriptive theories, which simply describe relationships among observable variables. Since these theories have no accepted name, we'll call them **fundamental theories**, to distinguish them from the more superficial descriptive and analogical types. Such theories seek to model an underlying reality that produces the observed relationships among variables. In this sense, they propose a more fundamental description of reality than the analogical theory.

Newton's laws of motion derive from such a fundamental theory. By assuming the presence of an underlying attractive force between bodies (gravity), assuming certain relationships between the strength of this force and other variables (masses of the bodies, distance between the bodies), and adding other assumptions (motion of bodies undisturbed by forces), Newton was able to account for the orbits of the planets. Newton was able to explain both why their orbits approximate ellipses and why there are deviations from those ellipses (attraction of the planets to the sun and their mutual attraction to each other). In addition, the same principles could be applied with success to describe the motions of objects on Earth, such as pendulums and projectiles. Newton's theory provided a fundamental insight into these motions that Kepler's earlier descriptive theory of planetary motions had not.

Fundamental theories are disturbingly rare in psychology. Part of the reason for this rarity is that psychology is still a relatively new science, but this is probably only a small part. Mostly this rarity is because of the complexity of the system being studied and because of the extreme difficulty in controlling the relevant variables well enough to clearly reveal the true relationships among them (or even to measure them properly). The physicist can expect every electron to behave exactly like every other. The psychologist cannot even hope that his or her subjects will be this interchangeable. Nevertheless, some attempts at fundamental theorizing have been made. One of the most famous fundamental theories is the *cognitive dissonance theory* proposed by Festinger (1957).

Much like gravity in Newton's system, dissonance is the fundamental process in cognitive dissonance theory. According to the theory, whenever two (or more) attitudes or behaviors are inconsistent, a negative psychological state called *cognitive dissonance* is aroused. The arousal of dissonance motivates the individual to reduce dissonance. This can be done by changing behavior or by changing attitudes. Festinger's theory thus described how dissonance leads to behavioral or attitude change.

Another example of fundamental theory in psychology is the scalar timing theory proposed by John Gibbon (1977) to account for the patterns of responding that develop under various schedules of reinforcement. The central idea of Gibbon's theory is that well-trained subjects are able to estimate time to reinforcement by means of a "scalar timing" process. With scalar timing, the subject is able to adjust to changes in the time constant of a schedule by simply rescaling the estimated time distribution to fit the new constant. Estimates of time to reinforcement (together with the size and attractiveness of the reinforcer) determine the "expectancy" of reward, which in turn determines the probability of a response through a well-defined mechanism. Gibbon described how the assumption of scalar timing produces a better fit to data from a variety of paradigms than do other assumptions (such as timing based on a Poisson process).

Domain of a Theory

The third dimension along which theories differ is **domain** or *scope*. This dimension refers to the range of situations to which the theory may be legitimately applied. A theory with a wide scope can be applied to a wider range of situations than can a theory with a more limited scope.

Gibbon's scalar timing theory is an example of a theory with a relatively limited scope. It provided an explanation for behavioral patterns that emerge under a wide variety of reinforcement schedules, but it did not attempt to account for all behavior. Cognitive consistency theory, such as Festinger's (1957) theory of cognitive dissonance, is an example of a theory with a wider scope. It has been applied beyond attitude change (for which it was developed) to help explain motivational processes in other contexts.

A notable attempt to build a theory with broad scope in psychology was made in the 1940s and early 1950s by Clark Hull and Kenneth Spence. Based almost entirely on data from rat subjects, this theory provided a model for learning and performance in mazes, elevated runways, and (it was hoped) in natural environments. This attempt at theory building is discussed in detail later in the chapter. For now, simply note that the attempt eventually had to be abandoned. In the years since, most theories in psychology have been relatively limited in scope and have attempted to account for a small range of phenomena within a highly circumscribed research area.

The chances of dealing adequately with a range of phenomena are better for a small area of behavior than they are for a large area. On the negative side, however, concepts invented to deal with one area may have no relationship to those invented to deal with others, even though the behaviors may be mediated by partly overlapping (or even identical) mechanisms.

Roles of Theory in Science

Theories have several roles to play in science. These roles include providing an understanding of the phenomena for which they account, providing a basis for prediction, and guiding the direction of research.

Understanding

At the highest level, theories represent a particular way to understand the phenomena with which they deal. To the degree that a theory models an underlying reality, this understanding can be deep and powerful. For example, Jean Piaget's (1952) theory of development provided a deep insight into the thought processes of children and helped us better understand how the thought processes of children changed with age and experience. Piaget provided a broad description of the behaviors that are characteristic of children at various ages. Within the theory, he also proposed mechanisms (organization, adaptation, and equilibration) to explain why development takes place.

Prediction

Even when theories do not provide a fundamental insight into the mechanisms of a behaving system (as descriptive theories do not), they can at least provide a way to predict the behavior of the system under different values of its controlling variables. The descriptive theory will specify which variables need to be considered and how they interact to determine the behavior to be explained. If it is a good theory, the predictions will match the empirical outcome with a reasonable degree of precision.

The Ptolemaic system of astronomy (which held that Earth lay unmoving at the center of the universe, with the sun, moon, and planets revolving about it) had the fundamental relationships wrong. As a fundamental theory of planetary motion, it was a failure. Nevertheless, in its most highly refined form, the Ptolemaic system could predict the apparent positions of the known planets (as seen from Earth) with a precision not equaled by the sun-centered Newtonian system even today (the complexities of orbital perturbations induced by mutual attractions of bodies at constantly changing distances from one another limit the accuracy of calculations). The system thus provided an excellent means of prediction, even though it failed to correctly describe planetary movement.

Organizing and Interpreting Research Results

A theory can provide a sound framework for organizing and interpreting research results. For example, the results of an experiment designed to test Piaget's theory will be organized within the existing structure of confirmatory and disconfirmatory results. This organization is preferable to having a loose conglomeration of results on a topic.

In addition to being organized by theory, research results can be interpreted in the light of a theory. This is true even if your research was not specifically designed to test a particular theory. For example, results of a study of decision making may be interpreted in the light of cognitive dissonance theory, even though you did not specifically set out to test dissonance theory.

Generating Research

Finally, theories are valuable because they often provide ideas for new research. This is known as the *heuristic value* of a theory. The heuristic value of a theory is often independent of its validity. A theory can have heuristic value despite the fact that it is not supported by empirical research. Such a theory may implicate certain variables in a particular phenomenon, variables that had not been previously suspected of being important. Researchers may then design experiments or collect observations to examine the role of these variables. Often such variables turn out to be significant, although the theory that emphasized them may eventually be proven wrong.

A theory specifies the variables that need to be examined, the conditions under which they are to be observed, and may even state how they are to be measured. It provides a framework within which certain research questions make sense and others become irrelevant or even nonsensical. To take another example from the physical sciences, an early theory of chemical reactions stated that when things burn, they give off a substance called *phlogiston*. Under this theory, determining the properties of phlogiston (such as its specific gravity) was a focus of research efforts. When the phlogiston theory was replaced by a theory of latent heat, such research became not merely irrelevant, but actually nonsensical (Kuhn, 1970).

Within psychology, Gall's phrenology provides another example of how a theory guides research and determines which questions will be considered important. Gall was a nineteenth-century surgeon who became convinced that a person's abilities, traits, and personality were determined by specific areas of the cerebral cortex. If a part of the brain were highly developed, Gall believed, a person would have a higher degree of the particular trait or ability associated with that area than if that same part of the brain was less highly developed. In addition, Gall reasoned, the more highly developed area would require more volume of cortex. Consequently, the part of the skull covering this area would bulge outward and create a "bump" on the person's head (Fancher, 1979).

In the context of Gall's theory, the important research problems were to identify which parts of the cortex represented which traits or abilities, and to relate individual differences in the topography of the skull (its characteristic bumps and valleys) to personality variables. Special instruments were developed to measure the skull. Thousands of hours were devoted to making measurements and collecting profiles of mental abilities and personality traits.

Phrenology never gained acceptance within the scientific community and was severely damaged by evidence (provided by Pierre Flourens and other Gall contemporaries) showing rather conclusively that at least some of the brain areas identified as the seat of a particular trait had entirely different functions (Fancher, 1979). With the discrediting of phrenology, interest in measuring the skull and in correlating these measurements with traits and abilities went with it.

Both the phlogiston and phrenological theories provided a framework for research within which certain problems and questions became important. When these views were displaced, much of the work conducted under them became irrelevant. This loss of relevance is a serious concern. If data collected under a particular theory become worthless when the theory dies, then researchers working within a particular framework face the possibility that the gold they mine will turn to dross in the future.

This possibility has led some researchers to suggest that perhaps theories should be avoided, at least in the early stages of research. Speaking at a time when the Hull-Spence learning theory was still a force within the psychology of learning, B. F. Skinner (1949) asked in his presidential address to the Midwestern Psychological Association, "Are theories of learning necessary?" In this address, Skinner disputed the claim that theories are necessary to organize and guide research. Research should be guided, Skinner said, not by theory, but by the search for functional relationships and for orderly changes in data that follow the manipulation of effective independent variables. Such clearly established relationships have enduring value. These relationships become the data with which any adequate theory must deal.

Skinner's point has a great deal of merit, and it is discussed later in this chapter. However, for now you should not get the idea that theory is useless or, even worse, wasteful. Even theories that are eventually overthrown do provide a standard against which to judge new developments. New developments that do not fit the existing theory become anomalies, and anomalies generate further research in an effort to show that they result from measurement error or some other problem unrelated to the content of the theory. The accumulation of serious anomalies can destroy a theory. But in the process, the intense focus on the problem areas may bring new insights and rapid progress within the field. Because anomalies are unexpected findings, they exist only in the context of expectation — expectation provided by theory. Thus, even in failing, a theory can have heuristic value.

Characteristics of a Good Theory

In the history of psychology, many theories have been advanced to explain behavioral phenomena. Some of these theories have stood the test of time, whereas others have fallen by the wayside. Whether or not a theory endures depends on several factors, including the following.

Ability to Account for Data

To be of any value, a theory must account for most of the existing data within its domain. Note that the amount of data is "most" rather than "all" because at least some of the data may, in fact, be unreliable. A theory can be excused for failing to account for erroneous data. However, a theory that fails to account for well-established facts within its domain is in serious trouble. The phrase "within its domain" is crucial. If the theory is designed to explain the habituation of responses, it can hardly be criticized for its failure to account for schizophrenia. Such an account clearly would be beyond the scope of the theory.

Explanatory Relevance

A theory must also meet the criterion of *explanatory relevance* (Hempel, 1966). That is, the explanation for a phenomenon provided by a theory must offer good grounds for believing that the phenomenon would occur under the specified conditions. If a theory meets this criterion, you should find yourself saying, "Ah, but of course! That was indeed to be expected under the circumstances!" (Hempel, 1966). If someone were to suggest that the rough sleep you had last night was caused by the color of your socks, you would probably reject this theory on the grounds that it lacks explanatory relevance. There is simply no good reason to believe that wearing a particular color of socks would affect your sleep. To be adequate, the theory must define some logical link between socks and sleep.

Testability

Another condition that a good theory must meet is *testability*. A theory is testable if it is capable of failing some empirical test. That is, the theory specifies outcomes under particular conditions, and if these outcomes do not occur, then the theory is rejected.

The criterion of testability is a major problem for Freud's psychodynamic theory of personality. Freud's theory provides explanations for a number of personality traits and disorders, but it is too complex and loosely specified to make specific, testable predictions. For example, if a person is observed to be stingy and obstinate, Freudian theory points to unsuccessful resolution of the anal stage of psychosexual development. Yet diametrically opposite traits can also be accounted for with the same explanation. There is no mechanism within the theory to specify which will develop in any particular case. When a theory can provide a seemingly reasonable explanation no matter what the outcome of an observation, you are probably dealing with an untestable theory.

Prediction of Novel Events

A good theory should predict new phenomena. Within its domain, a good theory should predict phenomena beyond those for which the theory was originally designed. Strictly speaking, such predicted phenomena do not have to be new in the sense of not yet observed. Rather, they must be new in the sense that they were not taken into account in the formulation of the theory.

As an example, consider Einstein's theory of relativity. This theory accounted for the same data and produced the same predictions for a wide range of phenomena as did Newtonian mechanics. However, Einstein's theory went beyond Newton's to predict new phenomena not expected to occur from Newton's point of view. One implication of the relativistic view was that if two totally accurate clocks were set to the same time, and one of the clocks was shot into orbit while the other remained on Earth, then the clock in orbit would appear to lose time relative to the one on Earth. This experiment was actually conducted using superaccurate atomic clocks, and the predicted loss of time was, in fact, detected.

Parsimony

Einstein's view eventually replaced Newton's because the former proved better able to predict and to account for new data. In some cases, however, two theories appear to do an equally good job. In this case scientists generally prefer the theory that makes the fewest assumptions. A theory that makes relatively few assumptions is said to be a *parsimonious theory*.

When the Copernican and Ptolemaic systems of celestial mechanics were vying for acceptance, the Copernican system won partly on grounds of parsimony. The Ptolemaic system required numerous assumptions concerning the existence of epicycles on epicycles, and the relative orbital speeds and diameters (all of which had to be inferred from the very data the system was attempting to account for). But the Copernican system required only the assumption of planetary orbits and orbital speeds. Whereas the Ptolemaic system was confusingly complex, the Copernican system was elegantly simple.

In psychology, the collapse of interest in the Hull-Spence model of learning occurred primarily because the theory had been modified so many times to account for anomalous data (and had in the process gained so many *ad hoc* assumptions) that it was no longer parsimonious. Researchers could not bring themselves to believe that learning could be *that* complicated. In addition, as in the Ptolemaic system, so many parameters had to be estimated from the data that application of the theory became little more than an exercise in curve fitting.

Developing Theories

Developing a good theory is no easy task. There are no "cookbook" solutions, no established path to take. Nevertheless, you should follow some well-defined steps to develop a reasonably good theory. The following sections take you through the steps involved in developing a sound scientific theory.

Step 1: Defining the Scope of Your Theory

The first step is usually (in a sense) taken for you: defining the domain or scope of the theory. Usually you want to formulate a theory because you are faced with a perplexing set of data that seem to defy simple explanation. You hope to develop a theory that will provide a satisfactory explanation for the observed relationships. At least in the beginning, the scope of the theory will be limited to the relationships of which you are trying to make sense. Thus, your theory may be designed to account for the pattern of response generated by fixed interval schedules of reinforcement, for the serial position curve in list learning, or for the overgeneralization of the rules for forming plurals by young children learning to speak. You have a specific problem for which your theory will present a solution.

Step 2: Knowing the Literature

Once you have decided on the scope and nature of the theory you wish to develop, you should next become *thoroughly* familiar with the current and past research in the area the theory will cover. You must know the phenomena with which the theory will be expected to deal. In particular, you should know what lawful relationships have been discovered and proven reliable. If your theory does not explain these relationships, it will be a failure from the start. It is also a good idea to be familiar with the theory and research in other research areas.

An excellent example of the value of knowing the literature is the model proposed by Zajonc (1965) to account for discrepancies in the social facilitation literature. In the early part of this century, social psychologists were investigating the impact of an audience on the performance of individual subjects. Some of the research showed that the presence of others facilitated performance (thus the term *social facilitation*), whereas other research showed the presence of others inhibited performance. Because of the seemingly hopeless discrepancies in the literature, social psychologists partially abandoned social facilitation as a viable research area.

This state of affairs continued until 1965, when Robert Zajonc proposed a simple, yet elegant, solution to the discrepancies found in the social facilitation literature. Zajonc drew on his knowledge of Clark Hull's drive theory of learning. Blending that theory with the literature on social facilitation, Zajonc developed the idea that whether or not performance is facilitated by the presence of others depends on the dominance of the behavior being performed.

According to this view, if a person is asked to perform a task with which he or she is familiar, performance should be facilitated by the presence of others. However, if the task is not well learned, performance should be inhibited. For the most part, Zajonc's solution has been found to be valid.

Step 3: Formulating Your Theory

Formulating a theory is an act of creation, equivalent to composing a painting or inventing a good story plot. It requires effort, insight, inspiration, and luck.

In creating a good theory, you will be proposing a unique solution to a puzzle, one that makes the apparently random pieces neatly fit together to reveal a coherent picture where formerly there was only confusion. This is challenging, difficult work. To do it well, you must be patient and must be able to tolerate considerable frustration. If you succeed, you will be rewarded by the thrill of seeing your account neatly organize the data and explain what formerly appeared inexplicable. The intensity of emotional response that success can generate was immortalized in the account of a solution by Archimedes to a problem that had been vexing him for weeks.

Archimedes had been given the task of discovering a method to determine whether the gold in the king's crown had been diluted with a cheaper metal by an unscrupulous jeweler. As he stepped out of a bathtub, Archimedes noticed that the water level fell. He reasoned that the presence of an alloy in the king's crown could be detected by immersing equal amounts of pure gold and gold mixed with an alloy in separate containers of water and noting any difference in the amount of water displaced. Hitting on the solution while relaxing in the public bath, Archimedes bolted from the pool and ran through the streets of Athens yelling "Eureka, I've found it!"

If you succeed in developing a good theory, you may not run through the streets announcing your success. However, successful solution of a theoretical puzzle (as success in any difficult task) brings with it a wonderful feeling of accomplishment. Scientists are willing to work long, lonely hours to achieve it.

Although theories are unique solutions to empirical puzzles, they do not emerge in a vacuum. The successful theorist makes full use of information available and his or her own insight. In the course of theory construction, three processes may be used by the theorist: preparation, analogy, and introspection.

Preparedness. Perhaps the most important element required for successful theory construction is *preparedness*. Often you will hear a scientist state that the solution to a problem occurred almost by accident. For Archimedes, it happened when he chanced to notice that the level of water in the bath fell as he stepped out of it. Yet had Archimedes not grappled with the problem, had he not spent hours trying to identify the physical, observable differences between pure metals and their alloys, his chance observation in the bath would have meant nothing to him. The more familiar you are with the problem, with the relationships among the observed variables, with the apparently anomalous findings, and with solutions to related problems, the better the position you will be in to develop an adequate theory.

Using Analogy. Ideas for a theory may derive from knowledge of other, well-understood systems that behave in ways similar to the system you are trying to understand. By defining analogous variables in the two systems, you may be able to develop an analogical theory to account for the behaviors. Broadbent (1958) developed such a model when he was trying to account for certain results obtained from a series of experiments in dichotic listening. Dichotic listening involves listening to different words or messages being presented simultaneously or in quick succession to different ears (through stereo headphones).

In one experiment, subjects heard a series of six numbers presented two at a time, one to each ear. Each pair of numbers was presented simultaneously. After the numbers had been presented, the subject repeated the numbers back to the experimenter. Interestingly, subjects reported all three numbers received in one ear, then the three received in the other ear.

In a variation of the same experiment, subjects were asked to report the numbers in their correct pairs. Subjects had difficulty with the task and often were not able to recall all six numbers.

To account for these and other data, Broadbent pictured the numbers as balls being dropped into the mouths of two cylinders that came together at the bottom to form a "Y" (see Figure 16-2). A plate suspended from the place where the cylinders joined could swing left or right to block one or the other arm of the Y. This plate represented the attentional mechanism that would allow the subject to receive information (balls) from either the left ear (left cylinder) or right ear (right cylinder).

This mechanical model could account for the results of the first experiment by assuming that the subject first attended to the left ear. In the model, the plate would be swung to the right, allowing all three balls in the left tube to fall through. Then subjects would attend to the right ear, retrieving the information from echoic (auditory) memory. This would be represented in the model by swinging the plate to the left, allowing the remaining three balls in the right cylinder to fall through. Because the plate had to swing only twice, the time required to retrieve all the information (let all the balls through) would be short.

The second experiment could be represented in the model by assuming that, in order to recall the numbers in their proper pairs, attention would have to be switched back and forth repeatedly. That is, the plate would first have to swing right to admit one ball from the left cylinder, then left to admit one ball from the right cylinder, and so on. The additional time required to switch would allow some of the last numbers to fade from echoic memory before they could be delivered.

Using Introspection. Broadbent's model illuminates a second source of ideas for psychological theories: *introspection*. At least when dealing with your own behavior, you have access to private information concerning your perceptions, problem-solving strategies, memories, and so forth. In trying to divide attention between two sources of information (such as two people speaking to you), most people report difficulty in recalling what one person said while they were "listening" to the other person. "Listening" appears in quotation marks because, after all, your ears pick up the information from both sources. Listening appears to be a process controlled more centrally in the brain. This process is called *attention*, and it is attention Broadbent was modeling in his analogical theory.

Although introspection can be a useful source of ideas for theories, you should be aware of several potential traps when using introspection. First, important aspects of the system you are trying to understand may not produce any

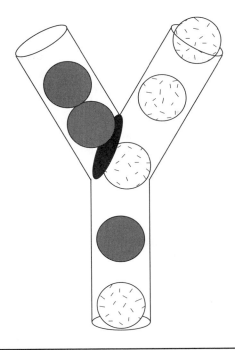

Figure 16-2. Broadbent's mechanical model of selective attention.

activity of which you are conscious. Memory processes are a prominent example. When you try to remember a particular fact, you are not aware of most of the activity by which your brain locates and retrieves the information. The fact simply comes to mind, or it doesn't. If your theory includes only the operations of which you are conscious, it will probably be incomplete.

Another trap when relying on introspective information is that the act of attempting to examine one's own mental processes may interfere with those processes and change their characters. You can never be sure that the information gleaned from introspection truly reflects what usually goes on.

A further problem is that the observable mental events may have no causal role in the operation of the system. John Watson, the founder of behaviorism, argued that such events are a sort of by-product of brain operation and have nothing directly to do with the observable external relationships between environmental events and behavior. Coming at a time when introspection was considered a primary source of psychological data, Watson's denial of the usefulness of introspective data led some to suggest that Watson had "lost his mind." Although using introspective data is again becoming respectable, Watson's warning still has force and suggests that introspectively derived concepts should be used cautiously.

A final problem with using introspection appears when theories are intended to explain the behavior of organisms other than human beings. To generalize human feelings, perceptions, thought processes, and motivations to other species is clearly dangerous. This activity is called *anthropomorphizing* — literally, "to make like a human." As both psychologists and ethologists have repeatedly demonstrated, many behaviors in nonhuman animals that appear to be directed by logical deduction or human-like motivations, turn out (on close examination) to be highly automated, stimulus-bound behaviors.

Lorenz and Tinbergen (1938, cited in Tinbergen, 1951) provided a classic example in the egg-retrieving behavior of the greylag goose. If an egg rolls out of the nest, the goose places its bill on the far side of the egg and, using a complex series of back-and-forth movements, carefully rolls the egg back to the nest and tucks it securely under her body. Obviously, on seeing the runaway egg the goose thinks, "Oh, no, my poor egg! I had better retrieve it before it gets cold! Let's see — ah, yes, I can just reach it with my bill . . . now if I can just scoop it back . . . oh, oh, it's rolling off to the left, better move my bill to the side . . . there, that's got it! Now to tuck Junior under and warm him up!"

This rather fanciful description of the goose's thought processes *could* be a reasonable approximation, minus the actual language content, don't you think? Well, if so, what do you make of the following facts? If you remove the egg after the goose starts to retrieve it, the goose will continue to "roll the egg," clear up to the point of standing up and tucking the (absent) "egg" underneath her. Also, if you place an object about the size of a goose egg (or better yet, an object larger than a goose egg) near the nest, the goose will retrieve it just as she would her own egg! A beer bottle works well. Only after she is actually sitting on the beer bottle will she then stand back up, examine the bottle, and toss it out. Do these facts change your mind about the goose's mental processes?

The lesson here, of course, is that anthropomorphizing is dangerous and probably leads to incorrect theories of animal behavior. If an animal seems to behave in ways that are similar to the ways a human would behave in the same situation, do not jump to the conclusion that the animal's behavior is guided by the same processes that guide the human's. It may be, but then again it may not.

Step 4: Establishing Predictive Validity

When you have developed a theory in its initial form, check the theory's predictions against existing data. In a sense, this step involves establishing the predictive validity of your theory. Your theory should be adequate to account for the relationships already discovered. If some predictions do not appear to fit the data very well, you have the choice of attempting to modify the theory or ignoring the discrepancies.

Ignoring the discrepancies may sound unscientific, but in practice there are many reasons why the data may not agree with prediction. Any theory provides an idealized view of the world, and the world is not ideal. Real springs do not vibrate exactly as would the ideal springs described by physics (owing to frictional losses). Real human beings do not behave exactly as theory would predict, because real human beings are sensitive to more variables than any theory is likely to contain.

Another reason why theory and data may disagree is that the experimental conditions only approximate the conditions specified by the theory. For example, the theory may assume that performance has reached asymptotic levels, yet the data may represent preasymptotic performance. Again the data may depart from theoretical values, but for reasons unrelated to the adequacy of the theory.

Whether to trust the data or not when theory and data disagree is thus a matter of judgment. You will have to weigh in such factors as the amount of the discrepancy, the degree to which the findings are supported by other data, and the success your theory has had in accounting for other phenomena.

If the theory seems to account adequately for the data on which the theory was originally based, the next step is to evaluate the theory against other data. These data may be existing data not used to develop the theory, or new data from experiments or observations specifically designed to test the theory's implications.

Step 5: Testing Your Theory Empirically

A worthwhile theory not only provides an account of the important phenomena within its domain, but also identifies conditions under which new, unsuspected phenomena will arise as a result of the interaction of the theory's variables. Testing the theory then involves setting up the specified conditions (or finding examples where the conditions occur naturally) and observing whether the outcome agrees (within reasonable limits) with the predictions.

Confirmation and Disconfirmation of Theories

A major theme developed in the preceding sections is that a good scientific theory must be testable with empirical methods. In fact, the final step in the business of theory construction is to subject the propositions of your theory to rigorous empirical scrutiny. This section explores what happens when a theory is put to the test.

Confirmation of Theories

If the relationships predicted by a theory are observed in empirical data, then your theory has been supported. When a theory is supported, you simply have more confidence in the ability of your theory to explain and predict the phenomena within its domain. It does *not* mean, however, that the theory has been *proven* correct. In fact, there is no logical way to prove a theory correct.

In the context of inferential statistics, it is a logical fallacy to try to prove the null hypothesis. This is so because the null hypothesis is a general statement. Generally speaking, it is extremely difficult, if not impossible, to prove a general statement.

The same logic can be extended to the notion of a theory. Inference involves going from specific observation to general statements. For example, you may have noticed that the sun rises every morning. From this fact you may infer that the sun will always rise in the morning. Furthermore, having seen the sun rise every morning throughout your life, you may have great confidence in this "theory." But what if the sun burns out tonight, or the universe comes to an end? You cannot prove that either of these events will not happen tonight, even if you are extremely confident that they will not. For exactly the same reason, you can never be sure that new data will not come along to destroy a theory, even if the theory has received strong support in the past.

Despite this problem, you should have more confidence in a theory if it has been tested many times under many conditions and each time has passed the test. Also, you should be more impressed with the results of a given test (it increases your confidence more) if the prediction was precise and/or the outcome was unexpected from the point of view of other existing theories.

One piece of evidence that provided strong support to Einstein's theory of relativity over Newtonian mechanics came when astronomers observed the apparent positions of stars "near" the sun (as seen from Earth) during a total eclipse of the sun. Einstein's view predicted that the gravitational field of the sun would bend the light rays passing near the sun on their way to Earth from distant stars. This bending would produce an apparent shift in the positions of those stars, compared to their positions as seen during another part of the year when the sun was no longer between the stars and Earth. This bending was not predicted by Newtonian mechanics. Furthermore, Einstein's view gave a precise figure for the amount of apparent shift.

Observation revealed the shift, and its amount agreed with the prediction within the estimated experimental error. The finding was both unexpected from the otherwise strongly supported Newtonian view and in exact agreement with the predicted shift. Einstein's view generated predictions identical with Newton's for the cases that had previously offered such strong support for Newton's view. For these reasons, the finding had a strong impact on confidence.

Although you can never prove a theory correct (witness the fate of Newtonian mechanics), you *can* logically prove a theory wrong. If a theory predicts a certain outcome under specified conditions, and that outcome does not occur, then (assuming nothing is wrong with the data) the theory (or some part of it) is wrong. The failure of Newtonian mechanics to predict the shift in apparent star positions is a case in point.

Disconfirmation of Theories

What happens to a theory when it fails a test? The answer to that question depends on many factors. Ideally, the theory is either scrapped or some way is found to modify the theory so that it now can account for the new findings. In practice, the theory may continue to be promoted. The theory's supporters may refuse to accept the test as valid, especially if there is no clearly defined way to operationalize the terms of the theory. For example, consider a theory that predicts a change in anxiety level of subjects following the introduction of a stressor. The supporters of the theory may claim that anxiety was not appropriately measured or that the stressor was not really stressful in the sense intended by the theory. However, unless the supporters can provide clear methods to operationalize the theory's terms, such excuses simply reveal that the theory in its present form is essentially untestable.

A theory may also continue to be promoted despite negative evidence if the theory provides organization to the literature and directions for research, and no better theory is available. Everyone in the field may agree that the theory is wrong, yet it remains useful. In addition, theories seem to acquire lives of their own if they seem to mesh with common sense or to fit the current zeitgeist. Information-processing views of behavior are popular at present. One view proposed to account for some data in operant conditioning experiments holds that subjects are motivated to acquire information about biologically relevant events, even if the information is bad news ("you are about to get a shock"). This hypothesis has failed in almost every test, yet it continues to be offered as a viable alternative for further testing.

One reason theories tend to be difficult to dislodge is that they are the intellectual "children" of their creator. Inventing a good theory is difficult work that not everyone can do well. If a theory survives initial scrutiny and captures the attention of researchers in the field, its inventor gains prominence and prestige. The theorist then has a personal stake in the further success or failure of the theory.

This commitment to the theory on the part of its creator is not necessarily bad. If the theory is to be adequately tested, it is important that it continue to be defended and explored well beyond the failure of a few predictions (which may have occurred through improper analysis of the theory's implications or other problems not related to the theory's essence). However, at some point the theory's supporters must be willing to "throw in the towel."

Strategies for Testing Theories

The usual picture of progress in science is that theories are subjected to testing and then gradually modified as the need arises. The theory evolves through a succession of tests and modifications until it can handle all extant data with a high degree of precision. This view of science has been challenged by Thomas Kuhn (1970). According to Kuhn, the history of science reveals that most theories continue to be defended and elaborated by their supporters even after convincing evidence to the contrary has been amassed. People who have spent their professional careers developing a theoretical view have too much invested to give up the view. When a more adequate view appears, the supporters of the old view find ways to rationalize the failures of their view and the successes of the new one. Kuhn concluded that the new view takes hold only after the supporters of the old view actually die off or retire from the profession. Then a new generation of researchers without investment in either theory objectively evaluates the evidence and makes its choice.

Strong Inference. Commitment to a theoretical position well beyond the point where it is objectively no longer viable is wasteful of time, money, and talent. Years may be spent evaluating and defending a view, with nothing to show for the investment. According to John Platt (1964), this trap can be avoided. Platt stated that the way to progress in science is to develop several alternative explanations for a phenomenon. Each of these alternatives should give rise to testable predictions. To test the alternatives, you try to devise experiments whose outcomes can support only one or a few alternatives while ruling out the others.

When the initial experiment has been conducted, some of the alternatives will have been ruled out. You then design the next experiment to decide among the remaining alternatives. You continue this process until only one alternative remains. Platt called this process **strong inference**.

Strong inference can work only if the alternative explanations generate well-defined predictions. In biochemistry (the field that Platt uses to exemplify the method), strong inference is a viable procedure because of the degree of control scientists have over variables and the precision of their measures. The procedure tends to break down when the necessary degree of control is absent (so that the data become equivocal) or when the alternatives do not specify outcomes with sufficient precision to discriminate them. Unfortunately, in most areas of psychology the degree of control is not sufficient and the theories (usually loosely stated verbalizations) generally predict little more than the fact that one group mean will be different from another.

Nevertheless, Platt's approach can often be applied to test specific assumptions within the context of a particular view. In this case, applying strong inference means developing alternative models of the theory and then identifying areas where clear differences emerge in predicted outcomes. The appropriate test can then be performed to decide which assumptions to discard and which to submit to further testing.

If several theories have been applied to the same set of phenomena, and these theories have been specified in sufficient detail to make predictions possible, you may also be able to use the method of strong inference if the theories make opposing predictions for a particular situation. The outcome of the experiment, if it is clear, will lend support to one or more of the theories while damaging others. This procedure is much more efficient than separately testing each theory, and you should adopt it wherever possible.

Following a Confirmational Strategy. A theory is usually tested by identifying implications of the theory for a specific situation not yet examined, then setting up the situation and observing whether the predicted effects occur. If the predicted effects are observed, the theory is said to be supported by the results and your confidence in the theory increases. If the predicted effects do not occur, then the theory is not supported and your confidence in it weakens.

When you test the implications of a theory in this way, you are following what is called a **confirmational strategy** (that is, a strategy of looking for confirmation of the theory's predictions). A positive outcome supports the theory.

Looking for confirmation is an important part of theory testing, but it does have an important limitation. Although the theory must find confirmation if it is to survive (too many failures would kill it), you can find confirmation until doomsday and the theory may still be wrong.

To see why this is so, consider how the confirmational strategy works. The logic is as follows. If A is true (if the theory is correct), then B is true (a predicted observation will be confirmed). Now, if B is false (the predicted observation is *not* confirmed), then A is false (the theory is defective). So far, so good. However, if B is true (the predicted observation is confirmed) this does not mean that A is true (the theory is correct). For example, if all swans are white, this implies that if an animal is not white, it is not a swan. However, if the animal *is* white, you cannot legitimately conclude that it is a swan. It could be a white rat or a white horse or any other white animal. To draw the conclusion that the animal must be a swan is to make a logical error known as *affirming the consequent*.

Spurious confirmations are particularly likely to happen when the prediction only loosely specifies an outcome. For example, in an experiment with two groups, if a theory predicts that Group A will score higher on the dependent measure than Group B, only three outcomes are possible at this level of precision: A may be greater than B, B may be greater than A, or A and B may be equal. Thus, the theory has about a one-in-three chance of being supported by a lucky coincidence.

Such coincidental support becomes less likely as the predictions of the theory become more precise. For example, if the theory predicts that Group A will score 25, plus or minus 2, points higher than Group B, it is fairly unlikely that a difference in this direction and within this range will occur by coincidence. Because of this relationship, confirmation of a theory's predictions has a much greater impact on your confidence in the theory when the predictions are precisely stated than when they are loosely stated.

Following a Disconfirmational Strategy. Even when a theory's predictions are relatively precise, many alternative theories could potentially be constructed that would make the same predictions within the stated margin of error. Because of this fact, following a confirmational strategy is not enough. To test a theory requires more than simply finding out if its predictions are confirmed. You must also determine whether outcomes *not* expected, according to the theory, do or do not occur.

This strategy follows this form: if A is true (the theory is correct), then B will not be true (a certain outcome will not occur); thus, if B is true (the outcome does happen), then A is false (the theory is erroneous). Because a positive result will *disconfirm* (rather than confirm) the prediction, this way of testing a theory is called a **disconfirmational strategy**.

The results of a kind of game invented by Mynatt, Doherty, and Tweney (1977, 1978) illustrate the difference between a confirmational and disconfirmational strategy. In the game (actually part of an experiment), subjects saw part of a "universe" presented on the screen of a computer. The universe contained only a few simple objects (circles, squares, and triangles). These objects came in three sizes and in three degrees of brightness. Using the computer keyboard, the subjects could move a "pointer" around the screen and point it in various directions. Pressing a certain key then caused the pointer to fire a "projectile" in the direction of aim.

As the projectile moved across the screen, it sometimes went straight and sometimes deflected. The object of the game was to discover the rules that determine when, where, and by how much the particle would be deflected.

Subjects usually began by moving more or less randomly around the "universe," aiming the pointer, and firing projectiles. By observing the result of each test, they began to develop hypotheses concerning the underlying rules. They then proceeded to test these hypotheses by identifying and testing specific predictions of the hypotheses. That is, they begin to follow a confirmational strategy.

Perhaps the hypothesis under test at one point was this: The particle is deflected by an invisible field surrounding all bright circles. Using a confirmational strategy, a subject would search for all examples of bright circles and test whether the beam was deflected by them. As it happens, a deflection would be observed near every bright circle. The subject would then conclude from this evidence that he or she had discovered one of the rules.

In actual fact, this was not one of the rules. Had the subject aimed the pointer at another object (a dim square, for example), he or she would have discovered that the particle was deflected in its vicinity as well. The subject's hypothesis would predict no deflection here. Thus, aiming the pointer at a dim or noncircular object follows a disconfirmational strategy.

Using Confirmational and Disconfirmational Strategies Together. Adequately testing a theory requires using both confirmational and disconfirmational strategies. Usually you will pursue a confirmational strategy when a theory is fresh and relatively untested. The object during this phase of testing is to determine whether the theory is able to predict or explain the phenomena within its domain with reasonable precision.

If the theory survives these tests, you will eventually want to pursue a disconfirmational strategy. The objective during this phase of testing is to determine whether outcomes that are unexpected from the point of view of the theory nevertheless happen. If unexpected outcomes do occur, it means that the theory is, at best, incomplete. It will have to be developed further so that it can account for the previously unexpected outcome, or it will have to be replaced by a better theory.

You now should have clear ideas about how to recognize, develop, and test adequate theories. However, an important question remains to be addressed: Should research be directed primarily toward testing theories or toward discovering empirical relationships?

Theory-Driven Versus Data-Driven Research

At one time in the not-too-distant history of psychology, research efforts in one field centered on developing a theory of learning. This theory would organize and explain data obtained from many experiments involving white laboratory rats running down straight alleys, learning discrimination tasks, and finding their ways through mazes. Ultimately this was to be a mathematical theory, complete with equations relating theoretical entities to each other and to observable variables.

The task of developing such a theory was taken up by Clark Hull at Iowa State University and by Hull's student, Kenneth Spence. Hull's approach to theory development was to follow the "hypothetico-deductive method," which consisted of adopting specific assumptions about the processes involved in learning, deriving predictions, submitting these predictions to experimental test, and then (as required) modifying one or more assumptions in the light of new evidence. Applied at a time when very little data was, in fact, available, the method was remarkably successful in producing an account that handled the relevant observations. This initial success galvanized researchers in the field and soon it seemed that nearly everyone was conducting experiments to test the Hull-Spence theory.

The new data quickly revealed discrepancies between prediction and outcome. Some researchers, such as Edwin Tolman, rejected some of the key assumptions of the Hull-Spence theory and proposed alternative views. But they were never able to develop their positions completely enough to provide a really viable theory of equivalent scope and testability. Besides, every time Tolman and others would find an outcome incompatible with the Hull-Spence view, Hull and Spence would find a way to modify the theory in such a way that it would now account for the new data. The theory evolved with each new challenge.

These were exciting times for researchers in the field of learning. The development of a truly powerful, grand theory of learning seemed just around the corner. Then, gradually, things began to come apart. Hull died in 1952. Even before his death, discontent was beginning to set in, and even the continued efforts of Spence were not enough to hold researchers' interest in the theory.

Interest in the Hull-Spence theory collapsed for a number of reasons. Probably the most significant reason was that it had simply become too complex, with too many assumptions and too many variables whose values had to be extracted from the very data the theory was meant to explain. Like the Ptolemaic theory of planetary motion, the system could predict nearly any observation (after the fact) once the right constants were plugged in. But it had lost much of its true predictive power, its parsimony, and its elegance.

With the loss of interest in the Hull-Spence theory went the relevance of much of the research that had been conducted to test it. Particularly vulnerable were those experiments that manipulated some set of variables in a complex fashion in order to check on some implication of the theory. These experiments demonstrated no clear functional relationship among simple variables, and the results were therefore of little interest except within the context of the theory. Viewed outside this context, the research seemed a waste of time and effort.

It was a tough lesson for many researchers. Much of the time and effort spent theorizing, tracing implications of the theory, developing experimental tests, and conducting observations was lost. This experience raises several questions concerning the use of theory in psychology. Should you attempt to develop theories? If you should develop theories, at what point should you begin? Should you focus your research efforts on testing the theories you do develop?

The answer to the first question is definitely yes, you should attempt to develop theories. The history of science is littered with failed theories: the Ptolemaic system of astronomy, the phlogiston theory of heat, Gall's phrenology—the list goes on. In each case, much of the theorizing and testing became irrelevant when the theory was discarded. However, in each case the attempt to grapple with the observations (particularly the anomalous ones) eventually led to the development of a more adequate theory. In this sense, the earlier efforts were not wasted.

Furthermore, it is the business of science to organize the available observations and to provide a framework within which the observations can be understood. At some point, theories must be developed if psychology is to progress.

The real question is not whether you should develop theories, but when. The major problem with the Hull-Spence theory is probably that it was premature. The attempt was made to develop a theory of broad scope before there was an adequate empirical data base on which to formulate it. As a result, the requirements of the theory were not sufficiently constrained. The assumptions had to be repeatedly modified as new data became available, making some tests obsolete even before they could be published.

To avoid this problem, a theory that is more than a simple hypothesis should await the development of an adequate observational base. A sufficient number of well-established phenomena and functional relationships should be available to guide theory development and demonstrate the power of the resulting formulation.

The third question asked to what extent you should focus your research efforts on testing the theories you do develop. There is no general agreement on the answer to this question. For one side of the issue, consider the letter written to *Science* by Bernard Forscher (1963) entitled "Chaos in the Brickyard."

Forscher's letter presented an allegory in which scientists were compared to builders of brick edifices. The bricks were facts (observations) and the edifices were theories. According to the story Forscher developed, at one time the builders made their own bricks. This was a slow process and the demand for bricks was always ahead of the supply. Still, the bricks were made to order, guided in their manufacture by a blueprint called a *theory* or *hypothesis*.

To speed the process, a new trade of brickmaking was developed, with the brickmakers producing bricks according to specifications given by the builders. With time, however, the brickmakers became obsessed with making bricks, and began to create them without direction from the builders. When reminded that the goal was to create edifices, not bricks, the brickmakers replied that when enough bricks had been made, the builders could select the ones they needed.

Thus it came to pass that the land was flooded with bricks. For the builders, constructing an edifice became impossible. They had to examine hundreds of bricks to find a suitable one, and it was difficult to find a clear spot of ground on which to build. Worst of all, little effort was made to maintain the distinction between an edifice and a pile of bricks.

Forscher's message was that experimentation conducted without the guidance of theory produces a significant amount of irrelevant information that is likely to obscure the important observations. From the infinite number of potential observations you could make, you need to select just those observations that will contribute most to progress in understanding. Theory provides one rationale for making that selection.

But theory does not provide the only guide to choosing what observations to make. Observation can also be guided by the systematic exploration of functional relationships within a well-defined domain. This empirical approach was forcefully defended by B. F. Skinner in his 1949 address to the Midwestern Psychological Association.

Much of the research conducted in psychology has followed this program. A systematic study of memory by Ebbinghaus (1885/1964), and the work that followed it, provides a case in point. Ebbinghaus invented a nearly meaningless unit to memorize (the CVC trigram) and several methods to measure the strength of memory for the CVCs. He then systematically explored the effects of many variables in a series of parametric experiments. These variables included the amount of practice, spacing of practice, length of the retention interval, and serial position of the CVC within the list. The resulting functional relationships between these variables and retention were subsequently shown to be highly reliable phenomena.

The data from such observations provide the reliable phenomena that any subsequently developed theory must explain. As Skinner and others have indicated, these data stand independent of any particular theoretical view. Thus, if an experiment is designed to clearly illuminate simple functional relationships among variables — even when the experiment is conducted mainly for the purpose of testing theory — then the data will retain their values even if the theory is later discarded.

What conclusions can you draw from this discussion? First, the choice of observations to make can be guided both by theory and by a plan of systematic exploration. Second, guidance by theory is more likely to be of value when sufficient observations already have been conducted to construct a reasonably powerful theory. Third, even when theory testing is the major goal of the research, designing the study to illuminate simple functional relationships among the variables, if possible, ensures that the resulting observations will continue to have value beyond the usefulness of the theory.

Chapter 1 indicated that a science is an organized and systematic way of acquiring knowledge. Science is best advanced when results from research endeavors can be organized within some kind of framework. In many cases, results from both basic and applied research can be understood best when organized within a theory. Keep in mind, however, that not all research *must* be organized within a theoretical framework. Some purely applied research, for example, may best be organized with other research that was also geared toward the solution of a specific problem. Nevertheless, theory plays a central role in advancing science.

Summary

Theory is a partially verified statement concerning the relationship among variables. A theory usually consists of a set of interrelated propositions and corollaries that specify how variables relate to the phenomenon to be explained. Hypothesis, law, and model are all terms that are often used as synonyms for theory. There are, however, important differences among them. A hypothesis is a specific statement about a relationship that is subjected to direct empirical test. A law is a relationship that has received substantial support and is not usually subjected to disconfirmation as theories are. A model is a specific implementation of a more general theoretical perspective. Models, therefore, usually have a more limited domain than do theories.

Theories vary along at least three dimensions. Some theories are quantitative in that they express relationships among variables in mathematical terms. Anderson's integration theory and the Rescorla-Wagner model of classical conditioning are examples of quantitative theories. Qualitative theories verbally express relationships among variables. No attempt is made to mathematically specify the nature of the relationships. Chomsky's theory of language acquisition is an example of a qualitative theory. Theories also differ according to level of analysis. At the lowest level, descriptive theories simply seek to describe a phenomenon. At the next level, analogical theories try to explain phenomena by drawing parallels between known systems and the phenomenon of interest. At the highest level, fundamental theories represent new ways of explaining a phenomenon. These theories tend to provide a more fundamental look at a phenomenon than do descriptive or analogical theories. Finally, theories differ according to domain. A theory with a large domain accounts for more phenomena than does a theory with a more limited domain.

Theories play an important role in science. They help us to better understand a phenomenon, allow us to predict relationships, help us to organize and interpret our data, and, in many cases, help generate new research. This latter role is often independent from the correctness of the theory. Some theories, even though they are not correct, have led to important research and new discoveries that greatly advanced science.

A theory must meet certain criteria before it can be accepted as a good theory. A theory must be able to account for most of the data within its domain. A theory that does not do this is of little value. A good theory must also meet the criterion of explanatory relevance, which means that a theory must offer good grounds for believing that the phenomenon would occur under the specified conditions. An important criterion that any good theory must meet is that the theory be testable. The propositions stated in, and the predictions made by, a theory must be testable with empirical methods. Theories that are not testable, such as Freudian psychodynamics, cannot be classified as valid scientific theories. A theory must also be able to account for novel events within its domain. Finally, a good theory should be parsimonious. That is, it should explain a phenomenon with the fewest number of propositions possible.

Developing good theories is an art that requires a great deal of time and effort. You should go through several steps when developing a scientific theory. First, you must define the domain of your theory. This is usually done for you when you choose the phenomenon to be explained by your theory. Second, you should become intimately familiar with the literature relating to the phenomenon of interest. It is also very helpful to be familiar with literature from other areas of science. In some cases, new solutions to existing problems come from an integration of ideas across fields of science. Third, you formulate your theory. You must be prepared in the sense that you have dealt with the issues within the scope of your theory on some level. Theories can sometimes be developed by using analogy and introspection. Introspection is a valuable tool in theory construction. However, it does have drawbacks such as the danger of anthropomorphizing. The final steps of theory construction involve establishing whether your theory accounts for the data that already exist within the theory's domain and subjecting your theory to empirical testing.

Theories that are subjected to empirical tests can be confirmed or disconfirmed. Confirmation of a theory means that you have more confidence in the theory than before confirmation. Unfortunately, it is logically impossible to prove that a theory is absolutely correct. Theories that are disconfirmed may be modified or discarded entirely, although many disconfirmed theories are adhered to for a variety of reasons.

In the course of testing a theory, various strategies can be used. Strong inference involves developing testable alternative explanations for a phenomenon and subjecting them simultaneously to an empirical test. The empirical test should be one that will unambiguously show which alternative is best. One way to test a theory is to use a confirmational strategy. That is, you design tests that will confirm the predictions made by the theory under test. When predictions are confirmed, then your confidence in the theory increases. Unfortunately, you may find confirming evidence even though the theory is wrong. Another approach is to adopt a disconfirmational strategy. In this case you look for evidence that does not support the predictions made by a theory. Often the best strategy to adopt is to use both confirmational and disconfirmational strategies together.

Finally, a controversy exists over the role a theory should play in driving research. Some scientists believe that research should be data driven, whereas others believe that research should be theory driven. Strong arguments have been made for each position and no simple solution to the controversy exists.

Key Terms

Theory

Scientific theory

Law

Model

Quantitative theory

Qualitative theory

Descriptive theory

Analogical theory

Fundamental theory

Domain

Strong inference

Confirmational strategy

Disconfirmational strategy

17

Making Sense of Research

DURING THE COURSE OF THIS BOOK, science and research have been characterized as preferred methods for acquiring knowledge. Science has been presented in its pure form, with emphasis on sound methodology and honesty in collecting, analyzing, and reporting data. This is how science *should* be conducted, but the ideal is rarely realized.

The scientific method comes closer than perhaps any other method to providing information free from the wishes and biases of those who collect and interpret it. Science is nevertheless subject to the same human faults and limitations that people bring to any endeavor. The social and psychological forces bearing down on researchers, theorists, reviewers, and journal editors inevitably distort the scientific process. This leads to bias in the published literature, both in the topics that get addressed and in the results that receive the stamp of approval.

If you are aware of these forces, however, you can take steps to avoid bias in your own work and to compensate for it as you evaluate the published literature. This chapter examines the forces that determine what research gets done and which findings get published. This chapter discusses how these pressures affect the archival literature, and describes techniques for dealing with conflicting findings and bias. This information can help you to make sense of published research findings. The discussion begins by examining the publication practices of journals.

Publication Practices

You have conducted what you feel is an important piece of research, prepared a manuscript, and submitted the manuscript to one of the leading journals dealing with the kind of research your manuscript describes. The editor of the journal receives your manuscript, assigns it a number, removes the title page (the only place where your name appears), and sends the manuscript to two reviewers for blind review. These reviewers are selected by the editor for their presumed expertise in the field. Therefore, you probably expect a competent, unbiased assessment of your work. But reviewers are people, too, and carry with them their own biases. Even if the reviewers were unbiased, you must contend with editorial policy. How bias and policy may affect the assessment of your paper (and everyone else's) is the subject of the next section.

Criteria for Acceptance of a Manuscript

Journals are intended to provide information that advances understanding. Given the limited space each journal has in which to publish articles, only those papers that offer significant contributions to understanding can be accepted. Thus, to determine which papers merit publication, editorial boards must define standards of acceptability. The paper must offer new information, not merely replicate old findings. These new findings must be reliable, as shown by replication within the study or (more commonly) by rejection of the null hypothesis at an appropriate alpha level (0.05 or 0.01). It must derive from acceptable methodology (free of confounding and other serious methodological problems that might create artifactual results or make interpretation problematic) and the information must contribute significantly to the field. Finally, editors of journals sometimes explicitly state those research areas from which research is most likely to be published.

The criteria just listed are intended to exclude papers whose contributions to progress are minimal, absent, or negative. Findings that derive from poor methods, merely replow old ground, or fail to meet standards of reliability should not become part of the archives. Yet these same criteria may at times delay understanding or create an impression of reliability in data that are, in fact, unreliable. Consider the following ways in which these publication practices affect the published research literature.

Statistical Significance. One case where criteria intended to exclude poor studies leads to bias in the published literature is the effect of employing minimum criteria for statistical significance. In most journals, editors are reluctant to accept papers in which results fail to achieve the accepted minimum alpha level of 0.05. The reason, of course, is that such results stand a relatively high chance of being attributable to random factors rather than to the effect of the independent variable. Researchers are aware of the requirement for statistical significance and, therefore, usually do not report the results of studies that fail to meet it.

If the investigator is convinced that an effect is there, despite the lack of statistical significance, he or she may elect to repeat the study while using better controls or different parameters. Nothing is inherently wrong with such a strategy. If the effect is there, better control over extraneous variables and selection of more favorable parameters are likely to reveal it. If the effect is *not* there, however, repeated attempts to demonstrate the effect eventually lead to obtaining statistically significant results by chance. Through probability pyramiding (see Chapter 12), the likelihood that this will happen is much greater than the stated alpha level would suggest.

The failures to obtain significant results generally wind up in someone's file drawer, forgotten and buried. In most cases, only those attempts that were successful in obtaining significant results are submitted for publication. Yet, because of probability pyramiding, the published results are more likely to have been significant because of chance than the stated alpha would lead us to believe. This effect is known as the **file drawer phenomenon** (Rosenthal, 1979, 1984). To the extent that the file drawer phenomenon operates, published findings as a group may be far less reliable than they seem. Later, this chapter shows you how to estimate the magnitude of the file drawer phenomenon.

Although chance effects may be published because the results are statistically significant, the failure to obtain statistical significance makes a study difficult to get published, even if the failure is because of a real lack of effect of the variable being investigated. The main reason for this is that, even when variables *are* effective, the failure to obtain an effect can occur readily through using poor methodology. For example, failing to exert sufficient control over variables can produce enough random variability in the data to obscure a relationship that is actually present. Reviewers and editors want proof that a failure to observe a significant relationship among variables is not the fault of improper procedures. Even when provided with such proof, they tend to remain skeptical.

The problem of negative findings is serious. The failure to obtain an expected relationship can be as important for understanding and for advancement of theory as confirmation. Yet this information is difficult to disseminate to the scientific community. Laboratories may independently and needlessly duplicate each other's negative findings simply because they are unaware of each other's negative results.

Consistency with Previous Knowledge. Another criterion used to assess a research paper's acceptability is the consistency of its findings with previous knowledge. Most findings are expected to build on the existing structure of knowledge in the field — to add new information, to demonstrate the applicability of known principles in new areas, to show the limits of conditions within which a phenomenon holds. Findings that do not make sense within the currently accepted framework are suspect.

When the currently accepted framework has deep support, then such anomalous findings call into question the study that generated them, rather than the framework itself. Reviewers and editors are likely to give the paper an especially critical appraisal in an attempt to identify faults in the logic and implementation of the design that may have led to the anomalous results. Ultimately, some reason may be found for rejecting the paper.

An excellent example in which this process operated was the initial work by John Garcia (1966) on learned taste aversions. Garcia exposed thirsty rats to a solution of water that had been given a flavor unfamiliar to the rats. Some of the rats were then injected with lithium chloride, and the rest of the group was given a placebo injection of saline solution. The rats injected with lithium chloride became ill from the injection about six hours later. The rats were allowed to recover, and then were given a choice between drinking plain water or the flavored water. Rats injected with the saline solution showed no preference between the two, but rats injected with lithium chloride avoided the novel flavor.

From this evidence, Garcia concluded that the rats injected with lithium chloride had formed, in a single "trial," an association between the novel flavor and the illness. In other words, classical conditioning had occurred between a conditioned stimulus (the flavor) and an unconditioned stimulus (the illness) across a six-hour interstimulus interval.

This was a striking finding. Classical conditioning had been extensively researched by Pavlov and others. It was well known that interstimulus intervals beyond a few *minutes* were completely ineffective in establishing a conditioned response, even when hundreds of trials were conducted. To reviewers and editors looking at Garcia's manuscript, something was fishy. Garcia's finding was a fluke, or some unreported aspect of methodology was introducing a confounding factor. The results simply couldn't be correct. The paper was repeatedly rejected by reviewers.

It was not until others heard of Garcia's findings "through the grapevine" and successfully replicated his results that the phenomenon of learned taste aversions gained credibility among reviewers. Only then did papers on the topic begin to be accepted in the established refereed journals. Once accepted, Garcia's discovery and other similarly anomalous findings became the basis for new theories concerning the nature and limits of laws of learning (such as Seligman & Hager, 1972).

In refusing to publish Garcia's findings, reviewers and editors delayed progress, but ultimately the new findings surfaced to challenge established thinking. Kuhn (1970) proposed that science frequently operates this way. According to Kuhn, workers within a given field conduct their research within a particular **paradigm** that defines the important questions to be addressed and prescribes the acceptable methods. Work within the paradigm consists of extending the organized body of knowledge along the lines delineated by the paradigm. Kuhn termed such work **normal science**.

However, as normal science continues, findings such as Garcia's come to light that do not fit. These anomalies at first are discounted or ignored, but as more of them surface, and attempts to "explain them away" fail to be supported, a crisis develops in which workers lose confidence in the paradigm. If, at this time, a new paradigm is developed that can reorganize the data to account satisfactorily both for the original findings and for the anomalies (so that they are no longer seen as anomalous), then the new paradigm is embraced. According to Kuhn, a **paradigm shift** occurs. Following the paradigm shift, workers return to doing "normal science," but now under the new paradigm.

Although paradigm shifts can bring progress toward understanding within a field, abandonment of established conclusions should not be done precipitously. Anomalous findings can result from improper conduct of studies and from statistical error. If every report of anomalous findings occasioned an immediate scrapping of accepted conclusions, the result would be chaos. However, refusal to accept methodologically sound results simply because they are anomalous may delay the surfacing of crucial information needed to achieve progress in understanding.

Editors and reviewers are thus in a tough position. To function effectively, they must be conservative in accepting papers that report anomalous findings. Yet they must be open-minded enough to avoid simply assuming that such findings *must* result from methodological flaws. Later this chapter examines just how successful editors and reviewers have been at maintaining this balance.

Significance of the Contribution. When determining whether to accept or reject a paper for publication, editors and reviewers must assess the degree to which the findings described in the paper contribute to the advancement of knowledge. At one time, papers were considered acceptable even if they reported only a single experiment involving simply an experimental and a control group. A researcher could publish a number of papers in a relatively short time, but each contributed little new information.

Today, journals usually insist that a paper report a series of experiments, or at least a parametric study involving several levels of two or more variables. For example, a paper might report a first experiment that demonstrates a relationship between two variables. Several follow-up experiments might then appear that trace the effective range of the independent variable and test various alternative explanations for the relationship. Such a paper provides a fair amount of information about the phenomenon under investigation and, in pursuing the phenomenon through several experiments, also demonstrates the phenomenon's reliability through immediate systematic replication.

Although these are important advantages, insisting on multiple experiments or studies within a paper can also have a negative side. Although the study provides more information, the information contained in the study cannot see the light of day until the entire series of experiments or observations has been completed. The resulting paper is more time-consuming to review and evaluate. Reviewers have more opportunities to find defects that may require modification of the manuscript. The result is delay in getting what may be an important finding out to the scientific community.

Fortunately there are ways to get around this difficulty. Early results of studies are frequently reported at scientific meetings. Such reports give others in the scientific community an opportunity to learn of interesting new findings and, if they wish, to begin their own explorations. The findings are not widely available, however, as only those attending the convention or receiving a copy of the program can learn of them. Or a researcher wanting to get some information published quickly can elect to publish in one of the journals specializing in quick publication of brief articles. For example, members of the Psychonomic Society can get brief reports (not exceeding four journal pages) published in the *Bulletin of the Psychonomic Society*.

Another problem with multiple-study papers is that the individual experiments or studies they contain may not be of equal quality. In one example, a paper offered a series of related experiments. Two experiments employed 30 subjects each and used essentially the same procedure with a minor variation. The results of the two experiments were identical. A third experiment addressed the same question as the first two, but the procedure and conditions of the test were significantly different.

Among other differences in procedure, the third experiment used only six subjects (three per group), a number that usually would be considered statistically unacceptable. This number is even more remarkable when you consider the relatively large number of subjects employed in the first two experiments. Nevertheless, the reviewers accepted the experiment (probably because its results appeared to agree with those of the preceding experiments). However, the procedure was, in fact, sufficiently different to suggest that a different outcome might be obtained. This possibility was supported when a subsequent attempt by another investigator to replicate this experiment yielded results that were actually opposite to those originally reported.

Editorial Policy. Frequently in the research process an area of research becomes hot, resulting in a flood of articles on a given topic. Researchers latch onto a particular research problem (for example, helping or eyewitness identification) and investigate it to the exclusion of other important research problems. When this occurs, a journal editor may take steps to restore a degree of balance.

An excellent example is the present focus on investigating various factors that affect the accuracy of testimony by an eyewitness and the juror's perceptions of that testimony in court. Because of its strong basic and applied research overtones, eyewitness accuracy and testimony has become one of the hottest research areas in the field of psychology and the law. Researchers have concentrated their efforts on discovering the factors that affect the accuracy of eyewitness identifications in criminal cases. This has led, predictably, to a plethora of published articles on the topic. In fact, two issues of *Law and Human Behavior* (the premier journal in psychology and law) devoted almost 43 percent of its editorial space (three out of seven articles) to the problem of eyewitness testimony. Those issues also included a "note/discussion" and a "presidential address" dealing with eyewitness testimony. No two other articles in these issues were on the same topic.

The 1986 volume of *Law and Human Behavior* was published under the guidance of a new editor (Michael Saks), who undoubtedly inherited various manuscripts from the previous editor for publication in 1986. In an eloquent message to researchers hoping to publish in *Law and Human Behavior*, Saks (1986) set a new editorial policy:

> I am struck by the limited range of topics they [the articles submitted to the journal] address. I want to sound a warning and extend an invitation. . . . I have received many papers devoted to the study of eyewitness phenomena; more, in fact, than any other category. Yet the subject of eyewitnesses will occupy at the most only a few hours of a law student's academic life. . . . [In the future,] greater weight will be given to manuscripts that are creative and groundbreaking, venturing into new legal domains.

Saks then listed several areas in law and psychology he felt needed to be researched. In his message to the readers of *Law and Human Behavior*, Saks clearly established an editorial policy that may affect the course of research in the area of psychology and law.

To summarize, sources of bias that arise from editorial policy exist in published literature. Editorial policies of journals (which are intended to screen out deficient reports and ensure the quality of the archival literature) may paradoxically lead to bias in the literature by encouraging the file drawer phenomenon. This phenomenon has prevented publication of important negative findings, delayed publication of interesting new findings, and allowed poorer experiments or observational studies to appear amid a series of otherwise good research.

But editorial policy is not the only source of bias. The next section discusses reviewer bias. Such bias not only affects what gets published and where, but also (when operating within the peer review system used for approving research grants) whether the research is undertaken at all.

Pernicious Problems of Peer Review

Peer Review. When your research paper is sent out for review, the journal editor sends the paper to reviewers (usually two) who are presumed to be experts in the field of research to which the paper relates. These are fellow scientists who, like yourself, have been conducting studies in the same general area. Reviewers are expected to be familiar with recent findings, accepted methodologies, opposing theoretical views, and current controversies. This process is known as **peer review** because those who review your work are your peers in the research community.

Peer reviewers are expected to carefully read your manuscript and then impartially judge its merits based on the information contained in the manuscript and the relationship of this information to the current state of research in the field. The journal editor uses the reviewers' comments, together with his or her own impressions of the manuscript, to judge whether to publish the study. Thus, the fate of your manuscript hinges on the judgments of your peers.

Sometimes these judgments will be negative. To ensure that reviewers can make such negative judgments without fear of reprisals by outraged authors, the identities of the reviewers are not made known to the authors. Given the severe limitations of space in most psychological journals, most papers must be rejected (rejection rates average about 80 percent). Anonymous review, by making negative judgments easier to render, helps editors to winnow the manuscripts to an acceptable number.

Problems with Peer Review. Anonymous peer review may be necessary, but it is not without its problems. Although you hope that your colleagues in research are honest and fair in their appraisals of your work, someone with a personal dislike for you or your ideas could sabotage your efforts. Even in the absence of malice, the reviewer may judge your manuscript unfairly because of a lack of knowledge, a bias against your general approach to research, or misreading.

The extent to which such factors operate within the peer review system has been the subject of research and debate over the past decade. For example, Mahoney (1977) investigated the influence of several properties of a research manuscript on its acceptance for publication by reviewers. With the approval of the editor, Mahoney sent manuscripts describing a fictitious experiment to 75 reviewers working for the *Journal of Applied Behavior Analysis*. Five randomly constituted groups of reviewers received different versions of the manuscript that varied according to their results and interpretations of those results. Mahoney found that the paper was consistently rated higher if its results supported the reviewer's theoretical bias and lower if they did not. How the results were interpreted had little impact. Similarly, the recommendation to accept or reject the paper for publication was strongly influenced by the direction of the data. If the data supported the reviewer's theoretical leanings, the reviewer usually recommended acceptance. If the data argued against those leanings, the reviewer usually recommended rejection or major revision.

Mahoney's findings showed that results favorable or unfavorable to the reviewer's point of view affect how the reviewer receives the manuscript. If the results are favorable, the reviewer is likely to believe that the results are valid and that the methodology was adequate. If the results are unfavorable, however, the reviewer is likely to believe that the study must be defective. The reviewer will search diligently for flaws in the design or execution of the study and use even minor problems as reasons for rejection.

Partly because of such sources of bias, estimates of interreviewer reliability in the social sciences have tended to be low. Fiske and Fogg (1990) examined 402 reviews of 153 papers and found almost no agreement among reviewers, not because the reviewers overtly disagreed, but because the reviewers found different aspects of the papers to criticize. It was as if they had read different papers! Lindsey (1978), in his book *The Scientific Publication System in Social Science*, noted that empirical studies have consistently found reliabilities of around 0.25 (the correlation between reviewer judgments). Whether both reviewers will agree that your paper is publishable is thus very nearly a chance affair.

The unreliability of the peer review system was highlighted by a study conducted by Peters and Ceci (1982). Peters and Ceci identified 12 *published* articles that had appeared in different major psychology journals. Each article was authored by at least one individual from a "prestige" institution and had appeared between 18 and 32 months earlier. The names of the original authors and their institutional affiliations were removed and replaced by fictitious names and affiliations. In addition, the titles, abstracts, and introductions were cosmetically altered (without changing the content) to reduce the chances that the articles would be recognized. Retyped as manuscripts, the articles were then resubmitted *to the same journals that had originally published them* (and in most cases, to the same editor).

The results were dramatic. Only 3 of the 12 articles were identified as resubmissions and rejected for this reason. The remaining 9 were undetected. Of those 9, *8 were rejected for publication.* Even more amazing, in every case both reviewers agreed and the editor concurred.

Because the articles had appeared before, the reviewers might have rejected the papers because they remembered the earlier data (although not the articles themselves) and thus viewed the information they contained as contributing nothing new. If this were the case, however, no hint of this was given in the reasons cited by the reviewers. According to Peters and Ceci, the reasons given for rejecting the papers usually concerned major flaws in the methodology. Thus, papers that had already been accepted into the archival literature only months earlier were subsequently seen as too methodologically flawed to merit publication.

Peters and Ceci offered two possible reasons for the new attitude toward the papers. The change in authorship and affiliation from prestigious to unknown may have had a negative influence on the evaluation. Or, because of the approximately 80 percent rejection rate, peer review may have been so unreliable that the chances of getting positive evaluations were just too low to expect acceptance the second time. This latter view assumes that getting a positive evaluation is essentially a matter of chance for manuscripts that cannot be rejected out of hand for obvious fatal flaws.

Whether either or both possibilities are true, the implication is that acceptance of your paper (given that it is reasonably good) depends to a large extent on factors that are not under your control.

Playing the Publication Game

If the discussion about the perils of publication leaves you with the feeling that the cards are stacked against you in the publication game, take heart. You can do several things to improve your chances:

1. *Do good research.* Although even well-designed and well-conducted research is difficult to get published, poorly designed and poorly conducted research is almost impossible to get published. Reviewers may

differ in their knowledge of the applicable literature, but most are experts at detecting serious design flaws. A serious deficiency will sink your paper before it gets away from the dock.

2. *Tackle important questions.* Although judgments may differ as to which questions are important, those whose answers clarify the effects of strong variables, settle theoretical debates, or provide a foundation for practical application are likely to be considered important (especially if you point out these applications in your manuscript). Your research is likely to be seen as especially important if it tackles questions that are currently "hot." Therefore, be aware of current trends and fads in research.

3. *Write clearly.* If reviewers cannot understand what you did, why you did it, or what you found, they will tend to judge your manuscript negatively. Keep your manuscript concise and to the point.

4. *Do not attack your colleagues.* If you must disagree with their ideas, methods, or findings, try to find a way that does not impugn their integrity or ability. *Ad hominem* attacks (arguing that an idea or finding must be bad simply because it came from so-and-so) are out of place in scientific writing.

5. *Submit a neat, clean manuscript.* A carefully prepared manuscript cleanly printed on heavy white paper, with an attractive type font, free of erasures, spelling errors, punctuation errors, and corrections, can give an initial favorable impression of your manuscript that can improve its chances for acceptance. Such a manuscript conveys a carefulness and attention to detail that suggest the way in which you conduct your research. If your manuscript is littered with mistakes and slop, the reviewers may assume that your research contains the same defects.

6. *If the reviews are unfavorable, and you feel that your paper has been criticized unfairly, write to the editor asking for reconsideration.* Identify the deficiencies in the reviews and clearly document where and how the reviewers erred. Also, acknowledge where the criticisms have been valid and explain how you intend to correct them. Editors have been known to reverse their decisions when given proof that a reviewer's negative decision was based on misunderstanding or ignorance.

7. *If the paper is rejected and the rejection is final, use the reviewer's comments constructively to improve the study.* This may entail adding controls (or other additional manipulations) and collecting additional data. Then resubmit the revised manuscript to the same journal or elsewhere. Unless you firmly believe in the worth of the paper as it stands, do not simply resubmit the same paper elsewhere. If your field is small, you would probably get at least one of the original reviewers.

There is another set of authors' "rules to increase likelihood and speed of acceptance of their manuscripts" offered somewhat tongue in cheek by Armstrong (1982). According to Armstrong's review of research on scientific journals, authors should (1) *not* pick an important problem, (2) *not* challenge existing beliefs, (3) *not* obtain surprising results, (4) *not* use simple methods, (5) *not* provide full disclosure, and (6) *not* write clearly. Armstrong says the last rule is particularly important, as it can offset potential damage caused by failing to follow the first five. Armstrong (1982) advocates checking your clarity of writing with the Gunning fog index, or G. The formula for G is as follows: $G = 0.4(S + W)$, where S is the average sentence length and W the percentage of words with three or more syllables (not including prefixes or suffixes). To meet Armstrong's Rule 6, the Gunning fog index should be about 18 or greater.

Armstrong's rules suggest that articles whose contents threaten established beliefs may be more difficult to get published than those whose contents support and reinforce those beliefs. Important problems (Rule 1) may be just those on which opinions (existing beliefs, Rule 2) are strongly held. Surprising results (Rule 3) are therefore likely to threaten those beliefs. One can attenuate the effects of these results to some extent by making the method too complex (Rule 4) to comprehend (and therefore to criticize with authority) or too muddy to understand (Rule 6).

Armstrong's rules are offered here not because they should be followed, but because they offer some insight into the problems faced by authors of scientific manuscripts. If your results conflict with established scientific belief or with the dominant theory in your field, you can expect your manuscript to face an uphill battle. Armstrong's rules, if followed, may (or may not) improve a manuscript's chances for acceptance, but they do not promote good science. We hope you *will* tackle important problems, *will* challenge existing beliefs if necessary, *will* attempt to publish surprising results if you believe them to be valid and reliable, *will* use the simplest, cleanest methods to test your hypotheses, and *will* write clearly. Then be prepared to defend your work.

Fads in Research

If you scan the issues of any particular journal across a number of years, you may discern a pattern in which certain research areas appear and then grow in popularity until a fairly large number of articles devoted to the topic grace the pages of the journal. Finally, interest wanes and the number of articles on the topic diminishes to a trickle. This section examines such fads in research. Understanding fads will help you to make sense of research.

Webster's dictionary defines a "fad" as a "custom, hobby, style, etc., adopted and pursued by many people for a time, with undue zeal; a passing fashion. . . ." Just as in other aspects of human activity, fads in research are "hot" topics toward which everyone within a particular specialty seems to be flocking. Fads are similar in some ways to trends in research but differ in other ways.

Fads Versus Trends in Research

Research fads must be distinguished from **research trends**. A research trend represents a sustained effort that, as knowledge accumulates, gradually changes the focus of research in an area. In contrast, fads explode onto the scene, show intense activity for a time, and then fade to a trickle of interest. Sometimes fads become trends and vice versa. Whereas an important difference exists between fads and trends, many important findings come out of research fads. Just because a research area comes and goes quickly does not necessarily mean that it produces useless data.

Sometimes fads can be identified within research trends. For example, from the mid-1960s to the present, the interest in research connecting psychology and the law has increased. At least two fads can be identified within that research trend. In the early years of research, an area of major concern was how defendant characteristics affected juror decisions. At the present time there seems to be a fad involving eyewitness research. Hence, within a research area (which may be relatively enduring) certain topics become hot (generating much research) and eventually cool off.

Why Fads Emerge and Die

Fads in research often emerge from a pioneering study that first identifies an interesting new phenomenon or first shows how a previously difficult topic may be studied. Suddenly there is new gold to mine, or a new way to mine old gold, and those looking for something new stake a claim and go to work. An aura of excitement pervades the research community. New variables are introduced and manipulated, and new hypotheses are created to explain the relationships discovered. Opposing theoretical camps develop, and a lively debate ensues in the literature over which explanation has more empirical support.

Eventually most of the "easy gold" is found. The obvious variables have been examined and some consensus develops concerning which findings are reliable and which interpretations are sound. Research and progress in the area become more difficult and findings begin to crop up that cannot be handled readily by the prevailing theories. At this point, those researchers with a continuing interest in the phenomenon settle down to parametric studies — to the "pick and shovel work" that Kuhn (1970) described as "normal" science. Other researchers, however, may become discouraged by the apparent slowing of progress. These workers may abandon the area to search for new, more promising frontiers. Research reports on the phenomenon dwindle to a trickle. The fad is over.

Reasons for Increased Popularity of a Research Area

Beyond research fads, many reasons explain why interest in certain research areas (and theories) waxes and wanes. Addressing these reasons for social psychology, Brigham (1986) drew on the work of Jones (1985) and Cartwright (1961) to develop the information presented in Table 17-1.

Table 17-1. Why Do Research and Theoretical Areas Gain and Lose Popularity?

Reasons for Increased Popularity of a Research Area	Reasons for Decreased Popularity of a Research Area
1. Research interests fit the "spirit of the times."	1. Researchers feel that the important aspects of the problem are already solved.
2. A particular theory appears to have great theoretical power.	2. Research appears to lead to an empirical dead end.
3. Appropriate research instruments and methodology are already available.	3. Research in the area is shown to be flawed by artifacts and poor methodology.
4. Prestigious, widely respected researchers are working in the area.	4. Changes in prevailing ethical standards make further research untenable.
5. There is strong financial support for research grants in the area.	5. There is decreased funding for research in the area.
6. An area is on the frontier of unexplored scientific territory.	

SOURCE: Brigham, 1986; reprinted with permission.

The table lists six reasons for increased popularity of a research area and five reasons for decreased popularity. Although developed for social psychology, the table probably applies equally well to all areas of psychological research. The following sections examine each of the reasons given in Table 17-1 and provide a few recent illustrations.

Research Interests Fit the "Spirit of the Times." Brigham (1986) provided several examples from social psychology in which the research meshed with the "social and political zeitgeist" (spirit of the times). One example was Milgram's (1963) obedience studies that stemmed from reactions to the Nazi extermination campaign against Jews and others (in which many apparently decent individuals carried out atrocities when the Nazis told them to do so). Another example was the concern with urban alienation (highlighted by the Kitty Genovese murder case, in which dozens of neighbors did not intervene for over a half hour while an assailant slashed Genovese to death in plain view) that sparked interest in researching bystander apathy.

In animal research, the zeitgeist seems to be swinging away from a strict behaviorist view of animal behavior toward a view that takes account of innately organized behavior patterns. In some ways this trend marks a return to ideas prevalent at the turn of the century as represented by the functionalists.

A Particular Theory Appears to Have Great Theoretical Power. For a time in psychology, the learning theory proposed by Clark Hull (1943) dominated the field of animal learning. The Hullian view was stated as a set of propositions that were complete enough to yield clear predictions. Considerable energy was expended setting up the appropriate experimental conditions to test these predictions. At about the same time, information theory, which developed out of the work of Shannon and Weaver (1949) on communication, began to revolutionize thinking about human information processing. Application of information-processing principles was epitomized by George Miller's (1956) well-known paper, "The Magical Number Seven, Plus or Minus Two."

Appropriate Research Instruments and Methodology Are Already Available. Often a potentially fruitful area of research lays dormant until the appropriate instruments or methodology are developed. As an example, instruments for detecting and displaying electrical activity of the cortex have been available for years. But only recently were techniques developed to extract reliable patterns from the mixtures of waveforms that precede and follow a stimulus presentation. These techniques have enabled researchers to identify these patterns (called *evoked potentials*) and to study the variables that affect them. In psychobiology, the discovery of natural opioid (morphinelike) substances in the brain and of blocking agents for those opioids led to a huge outpouring of research that investigated the behavioral effects of these substances.

Prestigious, Widely Respected Researchers Are Working in the Area. Having the "big guns" working in an area confers on it an aura of legitimacy and importance. The research conducted by these individuals receives considerable attention. These researchers are likely to be the ones asked to contribute chapters to anthologies and to describe their work in invited lectures and symposia. Following graduation, students of these researchers are likely to continue along the path set out by their mentors, thus yielding a high publication rate for the research data.

There Is Strong Financial Support for Research Grants in the Area. Researchers quickly learn where the money is for research. Granting agencies such as the National Science Foundation (NSF) and National Institute of Mental Health (NIMH) often initiate programs intended to encourage research in areas of interest to the government. Recently, for example, research into the psychology of aging was sought because the government became concerned with the growing numbers (both absolutely and proportionately) of elderly people in the population. Support for research on animal learning and motivation has become scarce in recent years, and many researchers in these areas have shifted to the better-supported areas of psychobiology, which require similar experimental skills.

An Area Is on the Frontier of Unexplored Scientific Territory. Researchers are frequently attracted to a new area because it is "wide open" to new research. A new finding can galvanize activity in an area if the finding appears sufficiently interesting. Garcia's research on learned taste aversions, once accepted, became a hot new area and continues to be vigorously pursued. The learned helplessness phenomenon (Overmeier & Seligman, 1967), the "matching law" (Herrnstein, 1961), and the discovery of REM (rapid eye movement) sleep (Aserinsky & Kleitman, 1953) provide additional examples of phenomena whose discovery sparked intense research interest.

Reasons for Decreased Popularity of a Research Area

As shown in Table 17-1, a research area loses popularity for almost as many reasons as it had for becoming popular in the first place.

Feelings That the Important Aspects of the Problem Are Already Solved. Interest in conducting research on the cognitive dissonance theory of Festinger (1957) has dropped dramatically (Jones, 1985). In the years immediately following the proposal of dissonance theory, researchers flocked to the theory and conducted many experiments to test the limits of the theory. As a mountain of information about dissonance theory grew, many of its important propositions were confirmed (or disconfirmed). Eventually, there were few new stones to turn, and interest in dissonance research waned (Jones, 1985).

Figure 17-1 clearly shows the downward trend in dissonance research. A review of the *Psychological Abstracts* from 1969 to 1984 shows a decline in dissonance research from between 64 and 94 articles in 1969–1972, to between 16 and 26 in 1980–1984.

Research Appears to Lead to an Empirical Dead End. Perhaps the classic case is the demise of interest in Hullian learning theory. As researchers continued testing the theory, it became evident that many of the hotly debated issues surrounding it (such as whether learning was fundamentally incremental, or all or none) could not be resolved empirically. Research aimed at testing the theory was not producing any new fundamental insights into the learning process, and interest evaporated.

Research in the Area Is Shown to Be Flawed by Artifacts and Poor Methodology. Brigham (1986) suggested that the "risky shift" phenomenon provides an example in this category. Early studies seemed to show that groups tended to make riskier decisions than its members would make individually (thus showing a shift toward greater risk). Later research showed that, in fact, groups tend to shift toward more extreme positions in either direction, depending on the direction in which individuals were leaning initially. Subjects who initially lean toward risk show a risky shift, whereas subjects who initially lean toward conservatism show a conservative shift.

Changes in Prevailing Ethical Standards Make Further Research Untenable. One of the serious problems in conducting psychological research is that many

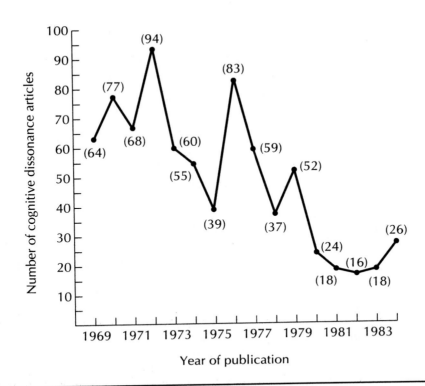

Figure 17-1. Decline in number of articles published on cognitive dissonance theory between 1969 and 1984.

important problems cannot be studied ethically in humans through the use of experimental methodology. For example, it is not possible to conduct studies that induce strong emotional distress or manipulate variables that may play a role in the genesis of psychopathology. To study these areas, researchers must rely on uncontrolled studies of naturally occurring situations, or use innocuous levels of these variables that probably do not provide much insight into the mechanisms that come into play at higher levels.

Heightened awareness of ethical issues (see Chapter 5) has made even some formerly acceptable manipulations taboo. Milgram's (1963) research on obedience to authority won Milgram an award at the time of its publication, but it probably would not be approved by an IRB (institutional review board) today. Similarly, tightening regulations on the use of animals in research have made it increasingly difficult to conduct meaningful studies on the effects of prolonged stress on the health and well-being of animals.

There Is Decreased Funding for Research in This Area. Just as increased funding for an area can stimulate research interest, decreased funding can induce researchers to move on to more lucrative fields. Consider the example of a very productive researcher in animal learning, who diverted his efforts to a secondary interest (human sleep research) when several attempts to obtain federal grants for the animal research met with no success. He has been having no trouble getting the sleep research funded. As funds for a research area dry up, money to support graduate students in that field declines and students find other areas to pursue. Thus, not only present research in the area, but also future productivity are affected.

Dealing with Fads in Research

Fads in research are not necessarily bad. They provide a periodic focus for research efforts that may lead to astonishingly rapid progress in the field. You can expect journal reviewers and editors to be familiar with the major findings, and your work will probably receive the attention of major figures in the field. Research money will probably be available. Thus, when you are starting your research career, working within an established area will probably be to your benefit.

However, one can become a slave to fads. Some researchers seem to jump into every new phenomenon that comes along. They conduct a few studies and then disappear, only to reappear in some other area.

Such a "flash-in-the-pan" strategy may keep the publications coming, but it is probably not a good strategy in the long run. Unless you have a phenomenal memory and an ability to speed-read, you will not be able to effectively keep up with the constant changing of fields. Your knowledge of an area will remain superficial, and your potential contribution to knowledge in any given area will remain small.

Most substantial contributions to psychology have come from people who single-mindedly pursued a topic with the dogged determination of a Sherlock Holmes. For example, Pavlov's research on classical conditioning continued from his discovery of the phenomenon just after the turn of the century, through the rest of his long career. Much of what is now known about the amazing complexities of bee behavior can be attributed to the patient, systematic studies of Von Frisch, begun around 1915 and extending more than 60 years. If you choose your topic well and then pursue it vigorously over the years, you will be astonished one day to look back and realize how much you have accomplished, how much better understood the phenomenon is than when you first took up its study.

As a second admonition, keep your eyes open for new discovery. Pavlov was not looking for classical conditioning when he discovered it during an experiment on the operation of the salivary glands. Yet he was able to recognize the potential importance of the new discovery, and dropped his studies of digestion (for which he had won the Nobel Prize in physiology) to focus his resources on the new area. New discoveries (especially those that cannot be accounted for by existing theory) are central to progress in science. And who knows? Perhaps you'll be able to start your own fad.

Making sense of research requires that you be aware of the biases and other sources of error that afflict research. Given the ubiquitous nature of these sources, it is not surprising that research findings within a given area often appear contradictory. The next section introduces a technique that permits you to assess the degree of confidence you should have in conclusions drawn from the literature. With this technique, even apparently contradictory findings sometimes can be shown to yield conclusions in which you can have a reasonable degree of confidence.

Meta-Analysis: A Tool for Comparing Results Across Studies

Imagine you are a researcher investigating the relationship between attitudes and memory. Specifically, you have been investigating whether or not subjects recall more attitude consistent information than attitude inconsistent information. After conducting several empirical investigations, you decide that a published literature review is needed to summarize and integrate the findings in the area. Consequently, you decide to conduct a literature review and to write a review article.

One strategy for this task is to conduct a **traditional literature review**. With this strategy, you read the relevant research in your area and then write an article. In your review, you may choose to summarize the major methods used to research the attitude-memory link, report the results of the major studies found, and draw conclusions about the variables that affect the relationship of interest.

In the traditional approach to literature review, you simply summarize what you find and draw conclusions about the state of the literature in a given area. For example, you might conclude that a certain variable is important (such as the length of a persuasive communication to which an individual is exposed), whereas others are less important (such as incidental versus intentional learning). However, the conclusions you draw are mostly subjective, based on your critical evaluation of the literature. The possibility exists that your subjective conclusion may not accurately reflect the actual strength of the relationships handled in your review.

You can reduce this possibility by adding a meta-analysis to your review. A **meta-analysis** is a set of statistical procedures that allow you to combine or compare the results from different studies. These procedures allow you to make statistically guided decisions about the strength of observed effects and reliability of results across a set of studies.

To conduct a meta-analysis, you must follow three steps: (1) identify relevant variables, (2) locate relevant research to review, and (3) conduct the meta-analysis proper.

Table 17-2. Sample of Factors to Include When Meta-Analyzing Literature

Full reference citation

Names and addresses of authors

Sex of experimenter

Sex of subjects used in each experiment

Characteristics of subject sample (such as how obtained, number)

Task required of subjects and other details about the dependent variable

Design of the study (including any unusual features)

Control groups and procedures included to reduce confoundings

Results from statistical tests that bear directly on the issue being considered in the meta-analysis (effect sizes, values of inferential statistics, p-values)

SOURCE: Adapted from Rosenthal, 1984.

Step 1: Identifying Relevant Variables

Before you can hope to conduct a meta-analysis, you must identify the variables to be analyzed. This may sound easy enough. However, you will find that in practice it is somewhat difficult, especially in a research area where there is a wide body of research. Generally, the rules that apply to developing testable research questions (see Chapter 2) apply to meta-analysis. It is not enough to say, "I want to do a meta-analysis of the memory literature." Such a broad, general analysis would be extremely difficult to do. The same is true even in less extensive research areas.

Much as in any research endeavor, your question to be evaluated must be sufficiently focused to allow for a reasonable meta-analysis. The unit of analysis in a meta-analysis should be the impact of Variable X on Variable Y (Rosenthal, 1984). Therefore, focus only on those variables that relate to your specific question. For example, you might choose to meta-analyze the impact of imagery on memory. Here you are limiting yourself to a small segment of the memory literature.

After you have narrowed the scope of your analysis, you must decide what variables to record (such as sex of subject, independent variables) as you review each study. Your decision will be driven by your research question. Table 17-2 shows a list of information that might be included in a meta-analysis.

In addition to recording the variables in each study, you should also record (for each study) the full reference (author or authors, title of the study, date, journal, issue, and page numbers), as well as the nature of the subject sample and procedures (Rosenthal, 1984).

The heart of meta-analysis is the statistical combination of results across studies. Consequently, you must record information about the findings from the results sections of the papers you review. What information is needed depends on the meta-analytic technique you use. To be safe, record the values of any statistics given (for example, t's, F's) along with the p-values (such as 0.05, 0.01). Later these values will be used as the "scores" in your meta-analysis. Data should be collected that help you to evaluate your specific research questions. You do not have to record the results from overall ANOVAs. Focus instead on the results of statistical tests that evaluate the specific relationships among the variables of interest (Rosenthal, 1984).

Step 2: Locating Relevant Research to Review

One of the most important steps in a meta-analysis is locating relevant research to review. In meta-analysis, you want to draw conclusions about the potency of a set of variables in a particular research area. To accomplish this end, you must thoroughly search the literature. Chapter 2 discussed doing a literature search, so the topic is not examined here.

Recall the previously discussed file drawer phenomenon, in which studies that do not achieve statistically reliable findings fail to reach publication (Rosenthal, 1979, 1984). The problem posed by the file drawer phenomenon is potentially serious for meta-analysis because it results in a biased sample. This bias inflates the probability of making a type I error (concluding that a variable has an effect when it does not). Studies that failed to be published because the investigated variables did not show statistically significant effects are not available to include in the meta-analysis. Meta-analytic techniques ultimately lead to a decision based on statistical information, so make allowances for the file drawer phenomenon.

There are two ways of dealing with the file drawer problem. First, you can attempt to uncover those studies that never reach print. This can be done by identifying as many researchers as possible in the research area you are covering. You then send each researcher a questionnaire, asking if any unpublished research on the issue of interest exists. Second, Rosenthal (1979, 1984) suggested estimating the extent of the impact of the file drawer phenomenon on your analysis. This is done by determining the number of studies that must be in the file drawer before serious biasing takes place (see Rosenthal, 1979; or Rosenthal, 1984, pp. 107–110, for details on how to estimate this). For example, if you determine (based on your analysis) that at least 3,000 studies must be in the file drawer before biasing of your results takes place, then you can be reasonably sure that the file drawer phenomenon is not a serious source of bias.

Step 3: Doing the Meta-Analysis

When you have located relevant literature and collected your data, you are ready to apply one of the many available meta-analytic statistical techniques. Table 17-3

Table 17-3. Meta-Analytic Techniques for Comparing and Combining Two Studies

Technique	Comments
Comparing Studies	Used to determine if two studies produce significantly different results.
Significance Testing	Record p-values from research and convert them to exact p-values (such as a finding reported at $p < 0.05$ may actually be $p = 0.036$). Used when information is not available to allow for evaluation of effect sizes.
Effect-Size Estimation	Record values of inferential statistics (F, t, for example) along with associated degrees of freedom. Estimate effect sizes from these statistics. Preferred over significance testing.
Combining Studies	Used when you want to determine the potency of a variable across studies.
Significance Testing	Can be used after comparing studies to arrive at an overall estimate of the probability of obtaining the two p-values under the null hypothesis (there is no causal relationship between the analyzed variables).
Effect-Size Estimation	Can be used after comparing studies to evaluate the average impact across studies of an independent variable on the dependent variable.

SOURCE: Adapted from Rosenthal, 1984.

illustrates meta-analytic techniques that can be applied to the situation where you have two studies. The first technique shows that you can compare studies. This comparison is made when you want to determine whether two studies produce significantly different effects. The second technique shows that you can also combine studies to determine the average effect of a variable across studies. Looking at the columns, you can evaluate studies by comparing or combining either p-values (significance testing, Rosenthal, 1984) or effect sizes.

Comparison of effect sizes of two studies generally is more desirable than simply looking at p-values (Rosenthal, 1984). This is because effect sizes provide a better estimate of the degree of impact of a variable than does the p-value. (Remember, all the p-value tells you is the likelihood of making a type I error.) The p-values are used when the information needed to analyze effect sizes is not included in the studies reviewed. The following discussion thus focuses on meta-analytic techniques that look at effect sizes. For simplicity, only the case involving two studies is discussed. The techniques discussed here can be easily applied to the situation where you have three or more studies. For more information, see Rosenthal (1979, 1984) and Mullen and Rosenthal (1985).

Comparing Studies. Imagine you are interested in comparing two one-factor experiments that investigated the impact of the credibility of a communicator on persuasion. In the results sections of the two studies, you found the following information concerning the effect of credibility on persuasion:

$Study\ 1$: $F(1,20) = 6.59$, $p < 0.01$, $n = 22$

$Study\ 2$: $F(1,40) = 4.89$, $p < 0.05$, $n = 42$

The first thing you must do is to determine the size of the effect of communicator credibility in both studies. Unfortunately, neither study provides that information (you will rarely find such information). So you must estimate the effect size based on the available statistical information. Of the many estimates of effect size, Rosenthal (1984) suggested using r, as defined by the formulas shown in Table 17-4. For the present analysis, use the formula shown for use with the F-statistic. Using this formula gives the following results:

$Study\ 1$: $r = \sqrt{6.59/(6.59 + 20)} = 0.50$

$Study\ 2$: $r = \sqrt{4.89/(4.89 + 40)} = 0.33$

The next step in the analysis is to convert the r-values into z-scores. This is necessary because the distribution of r becomes skewed as the population value of r deviates from zero. Converting r to z corrects for this skew (Rosenthal, 1984). A table for the conversion of r to z is provided in Table I-7 in Appendix I. For the r-values previously calculated, the z-values are 0.55 and 0.34, respectively.

When you have found the respective z-scores, you test for the difference between the two z-scores with the following formula:

$$Z = \frac{z_1 - z_2}{\sqrt{\frac{1}{(n_1 - 3)} + \frac{1}{(n_2 - 3)}}}$$

In the example, you have

$$Z = \frac{0.55 - 0.34}{\sqrt{\frac{1}{19} + \frac{1}{39}}} = \frac{0.21}{0.279} = 0.75$$

This z-score is then evaluated for statistical significance by using a table of areas under the normal curve (see Table I-5 of Appendix I). As it turns out, 0.75 is not significant beyond $p < .05$. Consequently, you would conclude that the effect sizes produced by the two evaluated studies do not differ significantly.

A significant difference would have been obtained had the F-values observed in each study been at least 85.69 and 4.08, respectively. For these values, the observed z-value would have been 2.22, which is significant beyond $p < .05$. In such a case, even though both studies produce significant effects, you would conclude that Study 1 produced a larger effect than did Study 2.

**Table 17-4. Effect-Size Formulas
for Selected Statistics**

Statistic	Effect-Size Formula
t	$r = \sqrt{t^2/(t^2 + df)}$
F	$r = \sqrt{F_{(1,n)}/(F_{(1,n)} + df_{(error)})}$
χ^2	$\phi = \sqrt{(\chi^2_{(1)}/N)}$

SOURCE: Formulas from Rosenthal, 1984.

If you do find a significant difference between effect sizes, the next question you should ask is why the difference exists. You might look at the methods, materials, and procedures used in each study. For example, you may find that one of the studies used more divergent values of the independent variable than the other.

Combining Studies. In some cases, you may want to determine the average size of an effect across studies. For example, you may want to determine whether a particular independent variable has produced a sufficiently large effect to warrant further investigation. In such a case, a variety of techniques is available. The technique suggested by Rosenthal (1984) again makes use of r and z.

The first step to take when combining the effect sizes of two studies is to calculate r for each and convert each r-value into corresponding z-scores. Next you enter the z scores into the following formula:

$$\overline{Z} = (z_1 + z_2)/2$$

Using the data from this example, you have

$$\overline{Z} = (0.55 + 0.34)/2 = 0.45$$

The r-value associated with this average z-score is 0.26. Hence, you now know that the average effect size across these two studies is 0.26.

Keep in mind a couple of factors when combining the results from two studies. First, always compare the studies before combining them. If the effect sizes of the two studies differ significantly, it makes little sense to average their effect sizes. This is especially true if the results from the studies are in opposite directions (for example, one study shows a positive effect of the independent variable, while the second shows a negative effect). Second, there is no established criterion to judge whether or not the combined effect size is significant or, for that matter, important. As a way around this second problem, Rosenthal (1984) and Rosenthal and Rubin (1982) suggested using the binomial effect size display (BESD).

Table 17-5. Difference Between Groups Associated with an Independent Variable Accounting for 10 Percent of the Variability in the Dependent Variable

	DEPENDENT VARIABLE	
Condition	Alive	Dead
Experimental	66	34
Control	34	66

SOURCE: Data from Rosenthal & Rubin, 1982; reprinted with permission.

Binomial Effect Size Display (BESD)

The **binomial effect size display**, or **BESD**, is a method of evaluating data against effect sizes to determine the amount of change in a measure to be expected across groups. Table 17-5 shows the size of the difference between groups when the effect size is only 0.10 (that is, when the independent variable accounts for only 10 percent of the variability in the dependent variable). Notice a total reversal occurs across the two groups. Rosenthal and Rubin pointed out that sometimes small effect sizes are, in fact, associated with large, perhaps important, differences between groups. They also maintained that you can easily dichotomize a continuous dependent variable and use the BESD with little loss of power. For more details on how to use the BESD, see Rosenthal and Rubin (1982) and Rosenthal (1984).

Comparing and Combining More Than Two Studies

Although the discussion in this chapter has focused on comparing or combining only two studies, you will probably want to compare more than two studies. Fortunately, meta-analytic techniques are available that follow the logic developed. Multiple studies can either be combined or contrasted with significance testing or effect-size estimation, as is the case with two studies. However, the tests in the multistudy meta-analysis can be either diffuse or focused. Diffuse tests simply tell you whether several studies in a set differ significantly (this is analogous to what you find with an overall F-test in an experiment). Focused tests are used to localize differences between specific studies (much like *post hoc* or planned comparisons after an overall F-test). The focused tests allow you to determine whether different levels of a particular variable (such as long versus short persuasive communication) produce different levels of significance across several studies.

The mathematical formulas used to meta-analyze several studies are a bit more complex than those used in the two-study case. However, the general logic applied to the two-study case applies to the multistudy case. The formulas for comparing and combining more than two studies can be found in Rosenthal (1984). Mullen and Rosenthal (1985) provide several computer programs that do most of the tedious calculations needed to perform such meta-analyses.

An Example of Meta-Analysis

The beginning of this section presented a research review issue that lends itself to meta-analysis: what is the relationship between attitudes and memory? A meta-analysis was undertaken on this topic by Roberts (1985).

Roberts began his meta-analysis by locating as much of the published research on the attitude-memory relationship as possible. To accomplish this, Roberts used the cumulative subject index and the subject index of *Psychological Abstracts* for the years 1935 to 1984. Social psychology texts were also searched for additional sources. All articles found were checked for additional references. Only those articles that dealt specifically with the memory-attitude relationship and those that included sufficient statistical information were included in this meta-analysis. In all, Roberts analyzed 38 studies.

Before reviewing the literature, Roberts identified several empirical issues to investigate. These were immediate versus delayed recall testing, incidental versus intentional learning, length of persuasive communication, and recall versus recognition testing. The strategy followed by Roberts was to block studies according to these issues. For example, Roberts compared the effect sizes for immediate recall against those for delayed recall, and compared studies using recall measures against those using recognition measures.

Roberts found that using an immediate versus delayed test of attitudes was the only factor that seemed to produce a significant difference between effect sizes. In addition, Roberts evaluated the file drawer problem and determined that 362 studies would have to be conducted with null results before a bias in the results would occur. Overall, the results of the meta-analysis show that, contrary to previous belief (based on qualitative reviews of the literature), a moderate relationship exists between attitudes and memory (Roberts, 1985).

Drawbacks to Meta-Analysis

Meta-analysis can be a powerful tool to evaluate results across studies. Even though many researchers have embraced the concept of meta-analysis, others question its usefulness on several grounds. This section explores some of the drawbacks to meta-analysis and presents some of the solutions suggested to overcome those drawbacks.

Assessing the Quality of the Research Reviewed. Chapter 2 pointed out that not all journals are created equal. The quality of the research found in a journal depends on its editorial policy. Some journals have rigorous publication standards, whereas others have less rigorous standards. This means that the quality of published research may vary considerably from journal to journal.

One problem facing the meta-analyst is how to deal with uneven research quality. For example, should an article published in a nonrefereed journal be given as much consideration as an article published in a refereed journal? Unfortunately, there is no simple answer to this question. Rosenthal (1984) suggested weighting articles according to quality.

There is no agreement as to the dimensions along which research should be weighted. The refereed/nonrefereed dimension is one possibility. Caution should be exercised with this dimension because whether or not a journal is refereed is not a reliable indicator of the quality of published research. Research in a new area, using new methods, is sometimes rejected from refereed journals even though it is methodologically sound and of high quality. Similarly, publication in a refereed journal is no guarantee that the research is of high quality.

A second dimension along which research could be weighted is according to the soundness of methodology, regardless of journal quality. Rosenthal (1984) suggested having several experts on methodology rate each study for its quality (perhaps on a zero to 10 scale). Quality ratings would be made twice—once after reading the method section alone, and once after reading the method and results sections together (Rosenthal, 1984). The ratings would then be checked for interrater reliability and used to weight the degree of contribution of each study to the meta-analysis.

Combining and Comparing Studies Using Different Methods. A frequent criticism of meta-analysis is that it is difficult to understand how studies with widely varying materials, measures, and methods can be compared. This is commonly referred to as the "apples versus oranges argument" (Glass, 1978).

Although common, this criticism of meta-analysis is not valid. Rosenthal (1984) and Glass (1978) suggested that comparing results from different studies is no different from averaging across heterogenous subjects in an ordinary experiment. If you are willing to accept averaging across subjects, you can also accept averaging across heterogenous studies (Rosenthal, 1984; Glass, 1978).

The core issue is not whether averaging should be done across heterogenous studies, but rather whether or not differing methods are related to different effect sizes. In this vein, Rosenthal pointed out that when a subject variable becomes a problem in research, you often "block" on that subject variable to determine how it relates to the differences that emerge. Similarly, if methodological differences appear to be related to the outcome of research, studies in a meta-analysis could be blocked on methodology (Rosenthal, 1984) to determine its effects.

Practical Problems. The task facing a meta-analyst is a formidable one. Experiments on the same issue may use widely different methods and statistical techniques. Also, some studies may not provide the necessary information to conduct a meta-analysis. For example, Roberts (1985) was able to include only 38 studies in his meta-analysis of the attitude-memory relationship. Some studies had to be eliminated because sufficient information was not provided. Also, Roberts reported that when an article said that F was less than 1 (as articles often do), he assigned F a value of zero. The problem of insufficient or imprecise information (along with the file drawer problem) may result in a nonrepresentative sample of research being included in your meta-analysis. Admittedly, the bias may be small, but it may nevertheless exist.

Do the Results of Meta-Analysis Differ from Those of Traditional Reviews? A valid question is whether or not traditional reviews produce results that differ qualitatively from those of a meta-analysis. To answer this question, Cooper and Rosenthal (1980) directly compared the two methods. Graduate students and professors were randomly assigned to conduct either a meta-analysis or a traditional review of seven articles dealing with the impact of the sex of subject on persistence on a task. Two of the studies showed that females were more persistent than males, whereas the other five either presented no statistical data or showed no significant effect.

The results of this study showed that subjects using the meta-analysis were more likely to conclude that there was an effect of sex on persistence than were subjects using the traditional method. Moreover, subjects doing the traditional review believed that the effect of sex on persistence was smaller than did subjects doing the meta-analysis. Overall, 68 percent of the meta-analysts were prepared to conclude that sex had an effect on persistence, whereas only 27 percent of subjects using the traditional method were so inclined. In statistical terms, the meta-analysts were more willing than the traditional reviewers to reject the null hypothesis that sex had no effect. It may be, then, that using meta-analysis to evaluate research will lead to a reduction in type II decision errors (Cooper & Rosenthal, 1980).

Finally, Cooper and Rosenthal reported that there were no differences between meta-analysis and traditional review groups in their abilities to evaluate the methodology of the studies reviewed. Also, there was no difference between the two groups in their recommendations about future research in the area. Most subjects believed research in the area should continue.

Summary

Science is a method used to acquire knowledge about some phenomenon. Like any other human endeavor, however, it is subject to influence by a variety of sources. Personal biases, interpersonal conflict, and the desire to succeed can all affect the validity of scientific findings.

Publication practices are one source of bias in scientific findings. Criteria for publication of a manuscript in a scientific journal include statistical significance of the results, consistency of results with previous findings, and editorial policy.

Each of these can affect which manuscripts are eventually accepted for publication. The result is that published articles are only those that meet subjective, and somewhat strict, publication criteria.

The peer review process is intended to ensure the quality of the product in scientific journals. Peer review involves an editor of a journal sending your manuscript to two (perhaps more) experts in your research field. The reviewers are expected to read your work and pass judgment. Unfortunately, peer reviewers are affected by personal bias. For example, reviewers are more likely to find fault with a manuscript if the reported results do not agree with their personal views on the issue studied.

You can do several things to maximize the chances that your manuscript will be published: (1) do good research; (2) tackle important problems; (3) write clearly; (4) avoid attacking colleagues; (5) submit a clean-looking manuscript; (6) contact the editor and ask for reconsideration; and (7) revise and resubmit a rejected manuscript to a second journal.

Sometimes research areas appear, generate intense interest, and fade quickly. Areas that follow this pattern are called research fads. Fads come and go frequently in research. Fads emerge because researchers see an opportunity to discover new findings, create new theories, and engage in new debates. After the major questions have been addressed, however, interest in a fad research area wanes relatively quickly. In contrast, a research trend involves a gradual evolution of thinking in a research area and is more enduring than a fad.

Interest in certain research areas waxes and wanes for many reasons. Research areas become popular because the particular research fits with the current "spirit of the times," a powerful theory generates much interest, new methods or instruments allow researchers to investigate phenomena, widely respected researchers are working in the area, funding is available, or there is an unexplored research frontier. Interest in a research area also wanes for many reasons. These include feeling that the important aspects of a problem have been solved, that the research leads to a dead end, and that the research suffers from flawed methods.

Meta-analysis is a family of statistical techniques that can help you evaluate results from a number of studies in a given research area. In contrast to a traditional literature review (in which subjective evaluations rule), meta-analysis involves statistically combining the results from a number of studies. Meta-analytic techniques tend to be more objective than traditional literature review techniques.

The three steps involved in conducting a meta-analysis are (1) identifying relevant variables to study; (2) locating relevant research to review; and (3) actually doing the meta-analysis (comparing or combining results across studies). Although meta-analysis has advantages over traditional literature reviews, there are some drawbacks. First, it is sometimes difficult to evaluate the quality of the research reviewed. Second, studies in a research area may use vastly different methods, making comparison of results suspect. Third, the information in published articles may be incomplete, eliminating potentially important studies from the analysis.

Key Terms

File drawer phenomenon
Paradigm
Normal science
Paradigm shift
Peer review

Research fad
Research trend
Traditional literature review
Meta–analysis
Binomial effect size display (BESD)

Appendix I
Statistical Tables

Table I-1A. Table of 1,000 Six-digit Random Numbers (first 500)

1	2	3	4	5	6	7	8	9	10
192805	905642	577821	582703	418793	921234	423676	926116	359852	611072
696843	580817	915407	920290	587586	090028	592469	094911	428558	679779
459327	255992	252995	257878	756380	258822	761262	263704	528645	779865
706608	962545	590582	595465	925173	427615	930056	432498	597352	848572
603541	637720	928169	933052	093968	596408	098850	601291	697438	948659
469093	312895	265757	270640	262761	765202	267644	770085	766145	017367
283598	988069	634724	639607	431554	933995	436437	938878	866232	117453
716374	663244	972311	977194	600348	102790	605231	107673	934939	186160
180530	338419	309899	314782	769141	271583	774024	276466	035026	286247
613306	044973	647486	652369	937935	440377	942818	445260	103733	354954
046083	720147	985073	989956	106729	609170	111612	614053	203820	455040
478858	395322	322661	327543	275523	777964	280406	782847	272527	523747
561285	070497	660248	665130	475696	978137	480579	983020	372613	623834
293364	745671	997834	002718	644490	146932	649372	151814	441320	692541
025442	420846	335422	340305	813283	315725	818166	320608	541407	792627
726139	127400	673009	677892	982077	484518	986959	489401	610114	861334
458218	802574	010597	015480	150871	653312	155754	658195	710200	961421
190296	477749	348184	353067	319664	822105	324547	826988	778907	030128
890993	152924	717151	722034	488458	990899	493341	995782	878994	130215
623072	828098	054739	059622	657251	159693	662134	164576	947700	198922
323770	503273	392326	397209	826045	328487	830928	333370	047788	299009
055848	209827	729913	734796	994838	497280	999721	502163	116495	367715
787926	885001	067501	072383	163633	666074	168516	670956	216582	467802
488624	560176	405088	409970	332426	834867	337309	839750	285288	536509
220702	235351	742675	747557	501220	003662	506103	008544	385375	636596
571051	910525	080262	085145	670013	172455	674896	177338	485462	736682
952780	585700	417849	422732	838807	341249	843689	346131	554169	805389
303129	260874	755436	760319	007601	510042	012484	514925	654255	905476
653478	967428	093024	097907	176395	678835	181277	683718	722962	974182
035208	642603	430611	435494	345188	847629	350071	852512	823049	074270
385556	317778	768198	773081	513981	016423	518864	021306	891755	142977
735905	992952	137166	142049	682775	185217	687658	190100	991842	243064
117635	668127	474753	479636	851568	354010	856451	358893	060550	311770
467983	343301	812340	817223	020363	522804	025246	527687	160637	411857
818332	049856	149928	154810	189156	691597	194039	696480	229343	480564
200062	725030	487515	492397	357950	860391	362833	865273	329430	580651
550410	400205	825102	829984	526743	029185	531626	034068	398137	649357
900759	075380	162689	167572	726917	229359	731799	234241	498224	749444
251109	750554	500276	505159	895710	398152	900593	403035	566930	818151
632837	425728	837863	842746	064505	566945	069387	571828	667017	918237
983186	132283	175451	180334	233298	735739	238181	740622	735724	986944
333536	807457	513038	517921	402091	904532	406974	909415	835810	087032
715264	482632	850625	855508	570885	073327	575768	078210	904517	155739
065614	157807	219593	224476	739678	242120	744561	247003	004605	255825
415963	832980	557180	562063	908472	410914	913355	415797	073312	324532
797691	508155	894767	899650	077266	579707	082149	584590	173398	424619
148041	214710	232355	237237	246060	748501	250943	753383	242105	493326
498390	889884	569942	574824	414853	917294	419736	922177	342192	593412
880118	565059	907529	912411	583647	086089	588529	090971	410899	662119
230468	240234	245116	249999	752440	254882	757323	259765	510985	762206

Table I-1A. Table of 1,000 Six-digit Random Numbers (second 500)

1	2	3	4	5	6	7	8	9	10
869354	895876	568055	572938	409027	911468	413910	916351	350086	601306
687077	571051	905642	910525	577821	080262	582703	085145	418793	670013
449562	246226	243230	248113	746614	249056	751497	253939	518879	770100
696843	952780	580817	585700	915407	417849	920290	422732	587586	838807
593775	627955	918404	923286	084202	586643	089085	591526	687673	938893
459327	303129	255992	260874	252995	755436	457878	760319	756380	007601
273833	978303	624958	629841	421789	924230	426672	929113	856466	107688
706608	653478	962545	967428	590582	093024	595465	097907	925173	176395
170765	328653	300133	305016	759376	261818	764259	266701	025261	276481
603541	035208	637720	642603	928169	430611	933052	435494	093968	345188
036317	710382	975307	980190	096964	599405	101847	604287	194054	445275
469093	385556	312895	317778	265757	768198	270640	773081	262761	513981
551520	060731	650482	655365	465931	968371	470813	973254	362848	614068
283598	735905	988069	992952	634724	137166	639607	142049	431554	682775
015676	411080	325657	330540	803517	305959	808400	310842	531641	782862
716374	117635	663244	668127	972311	474753	977194	479636	600348	851568
448452	792809	000832	005714	141105	643546	145988	648429	700435	951655
180530	467983	338419	343301	309899	812340	314782	817223	769141	020363
881228	143158	707385	712268	478692	981133	483575	986016	869228	120450
613306	818332	044973	049856	647486	149928	652369	154810	937935	189156
314005	493507	382560	387443	816279	318721	821162	323604	038023	289243
046083	200062	720147	725030	985073	487515	989956	492397	106729	357950
778160	875236	057735	062618	153867	656308	158750	661191	206816	458036
478858	550410	395322	400205	322661	825102	327543	829984	275523	526743
210937	225585	732909	737792	491454	993895	496337	998778	375609	626830
561285	900759	070497	075380	660248	162689	665130	167572	475696	726917
943014	575934	408084	412967	829041	331483	833924	336366	544403	795623
293364	251109	745671	750554	997834	500276	002718	505159	644490	895710
643712	957663	083259	088141	166629	669070	171512	673953	713196	964417
025442	632837	420846	425728	335422	837863	340305	842746	813283	064505
375791	308012	758432	763315	504216	006658	509099	011541	881990	133211
726139	983186	127400	132283	673009	175451	677892	180334	982077	233298
107869	658361	464987	469870	841803	344245	846686	349127	050784	302005
458218	333536	802574	807457	010597	513038	015480	517921	150871	402091
808566	040090	140162	145045	179391	681832	184274	686714	219578	470798
190296	715264	477749	482632	348184	850625	353067	855508	319664	570885
540645	390439	815336	820219	516978	019420	521860	024302	388371	639592
890993	065614	152924	157807	717151	219593	722034	224476	488458	739678
241343	740788	490511	495394	855944	388386	890827	393269	557165	808385
623072	415963	828098	832980	054739	557180	059622	562063	657251	908472
973420	122517	165686	170568	223532	725973	228415	730856	725958	977179
323770	797691	503273	508155	392326	894767	397209	899650	826045	077266
705499	472866	840859	845742	561119	063561	566002	068444	894752	145973
055848	148041	209827	214710	729913	232355	734796	237237	994838	246060
406197	823215	547414	552297	898706	401148	903589	406031	063546	314767
787926	498390	885001	889884	067501	569942	072383	574824	163633	414853
138275	204944	222589	227472	236294	738735	241177	743618	232340	483560
488624	880118	560176	565059	405088	907529	409970	912411	332426	583647
870353	555293	897763	902646	573881	076323	578764	081206	401133	652353
220702	230468	235351	240234	742675	245116	747557	249999	501220	752440

NOTE: This table was generated with a computer program written in BASIC.

Table I-1B. Random Orderings of the Numbers 1–30

1	2	3	4	5	6	7	8	9	10	11	12	13	14	15	16	17	18	19	20
25	15	25	30	20	14	25	3	21	2	20	27	19	26	17	30	22	4	6	10
14	26	17	7	2	9	14	13	6	20	29	16	13	19	9	17	14	16	22	20
17	11	2	17	21	13	3	24	23	21	12	24	24	2	3	25	6	17	25	29
5	4	18	18	23	20	16	20	26	14	1	7	26	21	22	9	26	13	27	22
3	16	12	19	16	22	10	7	13	7	21	20	29	11	24	20	27	8	12	15
19	20	5	11	11	26	6	21	16	22	23	21	20	7	16	22	20	22	17	25
22	6	23	21	24	17	19	22	29	25	10	4	6	22	13	5	19	24	29	26
10	22	24	24	18	1	21	23	19	23	24	23	22	25	26	23	30	26	20	19
23	23	16	14	17	19	11	16	2	15	27	9	3	16	27	15	21	28	1	28
24	13	28	25	30	5	26	26	20	26	16	25	23	27	21	28	2	3	23	21
16	28	27	28	19	21	15	28	3	28	30	26	11	28	2	27	23	21	3	3
27	29	1	2	5	10	2	30	22	29	22	18	25	30	4	19	10	5	24	4
28	3	21	5	9	23	4	1	10	30	4	28	16	4	23	29	25	23	10	23
29	21	4	22	22	25	20	6	24	4	6	29	27	24	5	2	15	10	26	11
30	5	7	9	14	16	9	25	15	10	25	30	28	10	25	7	28	27	16	27
4	10	26	26	25	27	24	12	27	27	14	1	2	15	15	26	1	14	30	16
8	27	13	15	1	30	13	27	1	19	28	5	5	29	28	12	3	29	2	1
13	14	29	1	3	3	27	17	4	1	18	13	9	18	30	16	9	30	4	7
2	30	30	4	7	6	30	2	8	3	2	17	15	5	19	4	11	20	8	8
21	19	20	8	13	12	17	4	11	8	7	2	1	8	7	6	29	6	28	14
6	9	6	12	15	15	7	9	28	12	13	6	4	14	11	10	18	11	13	2
11	12	9	29	4	4	22	15	17	18	17	11	8	1	1	13	4	1	21	5
1	2	14	16	8	7	23	19	5	5	5	14	12	20	20	3	8	19	5	9
20	17	3	6	12	24	1	5	9	9	8	3	30	9	6	21	12	7	9	12
7	7	22	23	26	2	18	10	12	11	11	22	18	12	10	11	16	12	14	30
12	24	10	13	28	18	8	14	30	16	15	10	21	17	14	14	5	15	19	18
15	1	15	3	29	8	12	18	18	6	19	15	10	6	18	18	24	18	7	6
18	18	19	20	6	11	28	8	7	24	9	19	14	23	8	8	13	9	11	24
9	8	8	10	10	28	29	11	25	13	26	8	17	13	12	24	17	25	15	13
26	25	11	27	27	29	5	29	14	17	3	12	7	3	29	1	7	2	18	17

Table I-1B (continued).

21	22	23	24	25	26	27	28	29	30	31	32	33	34	35	36	37	38	39	40
19	19	29	5	19	15	15	21	18	8	11	6	6	11	30	25	16	20	19	11
26	12	21	17	30	11	8	9	7	14	3	17	18	24	16	13	23	26	15	12
11	21	5	24	11	24	20	22	16	23	15	19	13	21	6	18	28	8	26	27
8	24	24	19	4	28	25	25	24	28	20	10	11	15	20	1	20	3	30	22
21	27	17	8	24	17	27	19	26	17	19	15	21	2	22	4	13	24	22	17
17	30	10	22	22	22	28	16	20	20	6	20	25	16	12	21	2	16	23	1
13	22	25	16	9	4	22	27	19	3	26	23	27	5	23	22	21	15	5	20
28	5	27	12	27	21	1	29	6	18	24	25	28	19	26	8	5	27	24	3
29	23	19	25	25	6	23	20	22	7	25	27	1	20	18	23	22	30	9	21
18	15	30	28	17	23	4	3	13	21	18	3	22	8	27	24	10	29	25	7
2	25	23	30	28	12	24	5	23	11	28	22	3	23	28	15	25	21	18	23
6	18	2	1	1	25	12	23	17	24	29	7	24	13	2	27	27	23	27	24
22	28	9	3	23	27	26	12	25	27	30	24	8	26	4	28	19	7	28	15
10	29	26	23	2	16	17	26	2	15	5	14	26	29	25	30	29	11	2	29
27	2	14	7	6	29	29	17	3	29	9	26	17	1	9	2	30	28	4	30
15	7	28	26	26	30	30	28	21	30	27	16	30	4	13	6	4	19	8	2
30	11	18	15	15	5	2	1	10	5	16	4	2	7	29	11	7	1	13	4
3	16	3	29	29	7	6	7	14	10	1	9	4	25	19	29	12	4	1	9
5	1	7	18	21	14	11	11	1	13	22	13	9	12	5	17	15	9	3	28
9	4	13	6	3	1	16	15	4	1	8	1	29	30	10	3	3	14	6	14
12	9	1	9	7	19	3	2	9	4	12	5	16	17	15	5	6	2	11	19
16	13	20	13	12	9	5	6	11	22	2	21	20	6	3	10	11	5	29	6
7	17	8	2	18	13	9	10	15	12	21	11	7	9	21	14	14	25	16	10
23	6	11	20	5	3	13	13	5	2	10	2	10	27	11	20	17	12	21	13
25	8	15	11	8	18	19	30	8	19	13	18	14	28	14	7	8	18	7	18
14	26	4	14	13	8	7	18	12	9	17	8	5	3	17	12	24	6	12	8
4	3	22	4	16	26	10	8	27	25	7	12	23	22	8	16	1	10	17	25
20	20	12	21	20	2	14	24	28	26	23	28	12	10	24	19	18	13	20	26
24	10	16	10	10	20	18	14	29	16	14	29	15	14	1	9	9	17	10	16
1	14	6	27	14	10	21	4	30	6	4	30	19	18	7	26	26	22	14	5

Table I-1B (continued).

41	42	43	44	45	46	47	48	49	50
20	15	25	25	12	7	16	17	7	1
16	19	21	20	30	27	8	30	15	17
9	3	1	3	17	15	25	20	28	18
26	11	22	21	7	23	28	23	25	14
23	21	13	13	19	3	23	9	16	3
24	23	9	7	22	18	20	26	3	20
18	18	23	22	11	21	1	24	19	10
28	17	24	23	24	5	21	13	22	11
29	24	18	16	25	22	5	29	5	21
22	26	26	26	16	12	24	28	24	24
4	30	28	28	28	24	13	19	11	27
7	6	29	30	18	25	26	21	26	28
25	22	30	1	1	17	27	3	27	2
14	10	3	6	5	28	18	6	18	4
27	14	5	24	8	29	29	11	29	22
19	27	27	12	26	30	30	27	30	7
2	1	14	27	15	4	2	18	4	26
5	4	20	17	29	11	6	1	10	13
11	7	2	2	3	14	10	8	14	29
15	12	6	4	21	1	17	10	1	30
3	28	10	9	9	19	3	16	21	19
6	16	17	15	13	8	7	2	8	9
10	5	4	19	2	13	11	7	12	12
13	8	7	5	6	16	14	25	2	16
30	25	11	10	23	6	4	14	20	5
17	2	15	14	14	9	22	5	9	8
21	20	19	18	4	26	12	22	13	25
12	9	8	8	20	2	15	12	17	15
1	13	12	11	10	20	19	15	6	6
8	29	16	29	27	10	9	4	23	23

NOTE: These random orders were derived with a computer program written in BASIC.

Table I-2. Table of Critical Values of *t*

	ALPHA LEVEL (TWO-TAILED TEST)									
	.8	.5	.2	.1	.05	.02	.01	.005	.002	.001
1	0.325	1.000	3.078	6.314	12.706	31.821	63.657	127.32	318.31	636.62
2	.289	0.816	1.886	2.920	4.303	6.965	9.925	14.089	22.327	31.598
3	.277	.765	1.638	2.353	3.182	4.541	5.841	7.453	10.214	12.924
4	.271	.741	1.533	2.132	2.776	3.747	4.604	5.598	7.173	8.610
5	0.267	0.727	1.476	2.015	2.571	3.365	4.032	4.773	5.893	6.869
6	.265	.718	1.440	1.943	2.447	3.143	3.707	4.317	5.208	5.959
7	.263	.711	1.415	1.895	2.365	2.998	3.499	4.029	4.785	5.408
8	.262	.706	1.397	1.860	2.306	2.896	3.355	3.833	4.501	5.041
9	.261	.703	1.383	1.833	2.262	2.821	3.250	3.690	4.297	4.781
10	0.260	0.700	1.372	1.812	2.228	2.764	3.169	3.581	4.144	4.587
11	.260	.697	1.363	1.796	2.201	2.718	3.106	3.497	4.025	4.437
12	.259	.695	1.356	1.782	2.179	2.681	3.055	3.428	3.930	4.318
13	.259	.694	1.350	1.771	2.160	2.650	3.012	3.372	3.852	4.221
14	.258	.692	1.345	1.761	2.145	2.624	2.977	3.326	3.787	4.140
15	0.258	0.691	1.341	1.753	2.131	2.602	2.947	3.286	3.733	4.073
16	.258	.690	1.337	1.746	2.120	2.583	2.921	3.252	3.686	4.015
17	.257	.689	1.333	1.740	2.110	2.567	2.898	3.222	3.646	3.965
18	.257	.688	1.330	1.734	2.101	2.552	2.878	3.197	3.610	3.922
19	.257	.688	1.328	1.729	2.093	2.539	2.861	3.174	3.579	3.883
20	0.257	0.687	1.325	1.725	2.086	2.528	2.845	3.153	3.552	3.850
21	.257	.686	1.323	1.721	2.080	2.518	2.831	3.135	3.527	3.819
22	.256	.686	1.321	1.717	2.074	2.508	2.819	3.119	3.505	3.792
23	.256	.685	1.319	1.714	2.069	2.500	2.807	3.104	3.485	3.767
24	.256	.685	1.318	1.711	2.064	2.492	2.797	3.091	3.467	3.745
25	0.256	0.684	1.316	1.708	2.060	2.485	2.787	3.078	3.450	3.725
26	.256	.684	1.315	1.706	2.056	2.479	2.779	3.067	3.435	3.707
27	.256	.684	1.314	1.703	2.052	2.473	2.771	3.057	3.421	3.690
28	.256	.683	1.313	1.701	2.048	2.467	2.763	3.047	3.408	3.674
29	.256	.683	1.311	1.699	2.045	2.462	2.756	3.038	3.396	3.659
30	0.256	0.683	1.310	1.697	2.042	2.457	2.750	3.030	3.385	3.646
40	.255	.681	1.303	1.684	2.021	2.423	2.704	2.971	3.307	3.551
60	.254	.679	1.296	1.671	2.000	2.390	2.660	2.915	3.232	3.460
120	.254	.677	1.289	1.658	1.980	2.358	2.617	2.860	3.160	3.373
∞	.253	.674	1.282	1.645	1.960	2.326	2.576	2.807	3.090	3.291

DEGREES OF FREEDOM

NOTE: To obtain one-tailed alpha levels, simply divide the two-tailed alpha by two (for example, $p < 0.05$ for a one-tailed test is 0.1/2 = 0.05).

SOURCE: Adapted from Table 12, *Biometrika: Tables for Statisticians* (Vol. 1, 3rd ed.), 1966, by E. S. Pearson and H. O. Hartley; reprinted with permission.

Table I-3A. Table of Critical Values of F ($p < 0.05$)

		DEGREES OF FREEDOM IN THE NUMERATOR							
	1	**2**	**3**	**4**	**5**	**6**	**7**	**8**	**9**
1	161.4	199.5	215.7	224.6	230.2	234.0	236.8	238.9	240.5
2	18.51	19.00	19.16	19.25	19.30	19.33	19.35	19.37	19.38
3	10.13	9.55	9.28	9.12	9.01	8.94	8.89	8.85	8.81
4	7.71	6.94	6.59	6.39	6.26	6.16	6.09	6.04	6.00
5	6.61	5.79	5.41	5.19	5.05	4.95	4.88	4.82	4.77
6	5.99	5.14	4.76	4.53	4.39	4.28	4.21	4.15	4.10
7	5.59	4.74	4.35	4.12	3.97	3.87	3.79	3.73	3.68
8	5.32	4.46	4.07	3.84	3.69	3.58	3.50	3.44	3.39
9	5.12	4.26	3.86	3.63	3.48	3.37	3.29	3.23	3.18
10	4.96	4.10	3.71	3.48	3.33	3.22	3.14	3.07	3.02
11	4.84	3.98	3.59	3.36	3.20	3.09	3.01	2.95	2.90
12	4.75	3.89	3.49	3.26	3.11	3.00	2.91	2.85	2.80
13	4.67	3.81	3.41	3.18	3.03	2.92	2.83	2.77	2.71
14	4.60	3.74	3.34	3.11	2.96	2.85	2.76	2.70	2.65
15	4.54	3.68	3.29	3.06	2.90	2.79	2.71	2.64	2.59
16	4.49	3.63	3.24	3.01	2.85	2.74	2.66	2.59	2.54
17	4.45	3.59	3.20	2.96	2.81	2.70	2.61	2.55	2.49
18	4.41	3.55	3.16	2.93	2.77	2.66	2.58	2.51	2.46
19	4.38	3.52	3.13	2.90	2.74	2.63	2.54	2.48	2.42
20	4.35	3.49	3.10	2.87	2.71	2.60	2.51	2.45	2.39
21	4.32	3.47	3.07	2.84	2.68	2.57	2.49	2.42	2.37
22	4.30	3.44	3.05	2.82	2.66	2.55	2.46	2.40	2.34
23	4.28	3.42	3.03	2.80	2.64	2.53	2.44	2.37	2.32
24	4.26	3.40	3.01	2.78	2.62	2.51	2.42	2.36	2.30
25	4.24	3.39	2.99	2.76	2.60	2.49	2.40	2.34	2.28
26	4.23	3.37	2.98	2.74	2.59	2.47	2.39	2.32	2.27
27	4.21	3.35	2.96	2.73	2.57	2.46	2.37	2.31	2.25
28	4.20	3.34	2.95	2.71	2.56	2.45	2.36	2.29	2.24
29	4.18	3.33	2.93	2.70	2.55	2.43	2.35	2.28	2.22
30	4.17	3.32	2.92	2.69	2.53	2.42	2.33	2.27	2.21
40	4.08	3.23	2.84	2.61	2.45	2.34	2.25	2.18	2.12
60	4.00	3.15	2.76	2.53	2.37	2.25	2.17	2.10	2.04
120	3.92	3.07	2.68	2.45	2.29	2.17	2.09	2.02	1.96
∞	3.84	3.00	2.60	2.37	2.21	2.10	2.01	1.94	1.88

DEGREES OF FREEDOM IN THE DENOMINATOR

SOURCE: Adapted from Table 18, *Biometrika: Tables for Statisticians* (Vol. 1, 3rd ed.), 1966, by E. S. Pearson and H. O. Hartley; reprinted with permission.

Table I-3A (continued). Table of Critical Values of F ($p < 0.05$)

	DEGREES OF FREEDOM IN THE NUMERATOR									
	10	12	15	20	24	30	40	60	120	∞
1	241.9	243.9	245.9	248.0	249.1	250.1	251.1	252.2	253.3	254.3
2	19.40	19.41	19.43	19.45	19.45	19.46	19.47	19.48	19.49	19.50
3	8.79	8.74	8.70	8.66	8.64	8.62	8.59	8.57	8.55	8.53
4	5.96	5.91	5.86	5.80	5.77	5.75	5.72	5.69	5.66	5.63
5	4.74	4.68	4.62	4.56	4.53	4.50	4.46	4.43	4.40	4.36
6	4.06	4.00	3.94	3.87	3.84	3.81	3.77	3.74	3.70	3.67
7	3.64	3.57	3.51	3.44	3.41	3.38	3.34	3.30	3.27	3.23
8	3.35	3.28	3.22	3.15	3.12	3.08	3.04	3.01	2.97	2.93
9	3.14	3.07	3.01	2.94	2.90	2.86	2.83	2.79	2.75	2.71
10	2.98	2.91	2.85	2.77	2.74	2.70	2.66	2.62	2.58	2.54
11	2.85	2.79	2.72	2.65	2.61	2.57	2.53	2.49	2.45	2.40
12	2.75	2.69	2.62	2.54	2.51	2.47	2.43	2.38	2.34	2.30
13	2.67	2.60	2.53	2.46	2.42	2.38	2.34	2.30	2.25	2.21
14	2.60	2.53	2.46	2.39	2.35	2.31	2.27	2.22	2.18	2.13
15	2.54	2.48	2.40	2.33	2.29	2.25	2.20	2.16	2.11	2.07
16	2.49	2.42	2.35	2.28	2.24	2.19	2.15	2.11	2.06	2.01
17	2.45	2.38	2.31	2.23	2.19	2.15	2.10	2.06	2.01	1.96
18	2.41	2.34	2.27	2.19	2.15	2.11	2.06	2.02	1.97	1.92
19	2.38	2.31	2.23	2.16	2.11	2.07	2.03	1.98	1.93	1.88
20	2.35	2.28	2.20	2.12	2.08	2.04	1.99	1.95	1.90	1.84
21	2.32	2.25	2.18	2.10	2.05	2.01	1.96	1.92	1.87	1.81
22	2.30	2.23	2.15	2.07	2.03	1.98	1.94	1.89	1.84	1.78
23	2.27	2.20	2.13	2.05	2.01	1.96	1.91	1.86	1.81	1.76
24	2.25	2.18	2.11	2.03	1.98	1.94	1.89	1.84	1.79	1.73
25	2.24	2.16	2.09	2.01	1.96	1.92	1.87	1.82	1.77	1.71
26	2.22	2.15	2.07	1.99	1.95	1.90	1.85	1.80	1.75	1.69
27	2.20	2.13	2.06	1.97	1.93	1.88	1.84	1.79	1.73	1.67
28	2.19	2.12	2.04	1.96	1.91	1.87	1.82	1.77	1.71	1.65
29	2.18	2.10	2.03	1.94	1.90	1.85	1.81	1.75	1.70	1.64
30	2.16	2.09	2.01	1.93	1.89	1.84	1.79	1.74	1.68	1.62
40	2.08	2.00	1.92	1.84	1.79	1.74	1.69	1.64	1.58	1.51
60	1.99	1.92	1.84	1.75	1.70	1.65	1.59	1.53	1.47	1.39
120	1.91	1.83	1.75	1.66	1.61	1.55	1.50	1.43	1.35	1.25
∞	1.83	1.75	1.67	1.57	1.52	1.46	1.39	1.32	1.22	1.00

DEGREES OF FREEDOM IN THE DENOMINATOR

Table I-3B. Table of Critical Values of F ($p < 0.01$)

	DEGREES OF FREEDOM IN THE NUMERATOR								
	1	2	3	4	5	6	7	8	9
1	4052	4999.5	5403	5625	5764	5859	5928	5981	6022
2	98.50	99.00	99.17	99.25	99.30	99.33	99.36	99.37	99.39
3	34.12	30.82	29.46	28.71	28.24	27.91	27.67	27.49	27.35
4	21.20	18.00	16.69	15.98	15.52	15.21	14.98	14.80	14.66
5	16.26	13.27	12.06	11.39	10.97	10.67	10.46	10.29	10.16
6	13.75	10.92	9.78	9.15	8.75	8.47	8.26	8.10	7.98
7	12.25	9.55	8.45	7.85	7.46	7.19	6.99	6.84	6.72
8	11.26	8.65	7.59	7.01	6.63	6.37	6.18	6.03	5.91
9	10.56	8.02	6.99	6.42	6.06	5.80	5.61	5.47	5.35
10	10.04	7.56	6.55	5.99	5.64	5.39	5.20	5.06	4.94
11	9.65	7.21	6.22	5.67	5.32	5.07	4.89	4.74	4.63
12	9.33	6.93	5.95	5.41	5.06	4.82	4.64	4.50	4.39
13	9.07	6.70	5.74	5.21	4.86	4.62	4.44	4.30	4.19
14	8.86	6.51	5.56	5.04	4.69	4.46	4.28	4.14	4.03
15	8.68	6.36	5.42	4.89	4.56	4.32	4.14	4.00	3.89
16	8.53	6.23	5.29	4.77	4.44	4.20	4.03	3.89	3.78
17	8.40	6.11	5.18	4.67	4.34	4.10	3.93	3.79	3.68
18	8.29	6.01	5.09	4.58	4.25	4.01	3.84	3.71	3.60
19	8.18	5.93	5.01	4.50	4.17	3.94	3.77	3.63	3.52
20	8.10	5.85	4.94	4.43	4.10	3.87	3.70	3.56	3.46
21	8.02	5.78	4.87	4.37	4.04	3.81	3.64	3.51	3.40
22	7.95	5.72	4.82	4.31	3.99	3.76	3.59	3.45	3.35
23	7.88	5.66	4.76	4.26	3.94	3.71	3.54	3.41	3.30
24	7.82	5.61	4.72	4.22	3.90	3.67	3.50	3.36	3.26
25	7.77	5.57	4.68	4.18	3.85	3.63	3.46	3.32	3.22
26	7.72	5.53	4.64	4.14	3.82	3.59	3.42	3.29	3.18
27	7.68	5.49	4.60	4.11	3.78	3.56	3.39	3.26	3.15
28	7.64	5.45	4.57	4.07	3.75	3.53	3.36	3.23	3.12
29	7.60	5.42	4.54	4.04	3.73	3.50	3.33	3.20	3.09
30	7.56	5.39	4.51	4.02	3.70	3.47	3.30	3.17	3.07
40	7.31	5.18	4.31	3.83	3.51	3.29	3.12	2.99	2.89
60	7.08	4.98	4.13	3.65	3.34	3.12	2.95	2.82	2.72
120	6.85	4.79	3.95	3.48	3.17	2.96	2.79	2.66	2.56
∞	6.63	4.61	3.78	3.32	3.02	2.80	2.64	2.51	2.41

DEGREES OF FREEDOM IN THE DENOMINATOR

SOURCE: Adapted from Table 18, *Biometrika: Tables for Statisticians* (Vol. 1, 3rd ed.), 1966, by E. S. Pearson and H. O. Hartley; reprinted with permission.

Table I-3B (continued). Table of Critical Values of F ($p < 0.01$)

	DEGREES OF FREEDOM IN THE NUMERATOR									
	10	12	15	20	24	30	40	60	120	∞
1	6056	6106	6157	6209	6235	6261	6287	6313	6339	6366
2	99.40	99.42	99.43	99.45	99.46	99.47	99.47	99.48	99.49	99.50
3	27.23	27.05	26.87	26.69	26.60	26.50	26.41	26.32	26.22	26.13
4	14.55	14.37	14.20	14.02	13.93	13.84	13.75	13.65	13.56	13.46
5	10.05	9.89	9.72	9.55	9.47	9.38	9.29	9.20	9.11	9.02
6	7.87	7.72	7.56	7.40	7.31	7.23	7.14	7.06	6.97	6.88
7	6.62	6.47	6.31	6.16	6.07	5.99	5.91	5.82	5.74	5.65
8	5.81	5.67	5.52	5.36	5.28	5.20	5.12	5.03	4.95	4.86
9	5.26	5.11	4.96	4.81	4.73	4.65	4.57	4.48	4.40	4.31
10	4.85	4.71	4.56	4.41	4.33	4.25	4.17	4.08	4.00	3.91
11	4.54	4.40	4.25	4.10	4.02	3.94	3.86	3.78	3.69	3.60
12	4.30	4.16	4.01	3.86	3.78	3.70	3.62	3.54	3.45	3.36
13	4.10	3.96	3.82	3.66	3.59	3.51	3.43	3.34	3.25	3.17
14	3.94	3.80	3.66	3.51	3.43	3.35	3.27	3.18	3.09	3.00
15	3.80	3.67	3.52	3.37	3.29	3.21	3.13	3.05	2.96	2.87
16	3.69	3.55	3.41	3.26	3.18	3.10	3.02	2.93	2.84	2.75
17	3.59	3.46	3.31	3.16	3.08	3.00	2.92	2.83	2.75	2.65
18	3.51	3.37	3.23	3.08	3.00	2.92	2.84	2.75	2.66	2.57
19	3.43	3.30	3.15	3.00	2.92	2.84	2.76	2.67	2.58	2.49
20	3.37	3.23	3.09	2.94	2.86	2.78	2.69	2.61	2.52	2.42
21	3.31	3.17	3.03	2.88	2.80	2.72	2.64	2.55	2.46	2.36
22	3.26	3.12	2.98	2.83	2.75	2.67	2.58	2.50	2.40	2.31
23	3.21	3.07	2.93	2.78	2.70	2.62	2.54	2.45	2.35	2.26
24	3.17	3.03	2.89	2.74	2.66	2.58	2.49	2.40	2.31	2.21
25	3.13	2.99	2.85	2.70	2.62	2.54	2.45	2.36	2.27	2.17
26	3.09	2.96	2.81	2.66	2.58	2.50	2.42	2.33	2.23	2.13
27	3.06	2.93	2.78	2.63	2.55	2.47	2.38	2.29	2.20	2.10
28	3.03	2.90	2.75	2.60	2.52	2.44	2.35	2.26	2.17	2.06
29	3.00	2.87	2.73	2.57	2.49	2.41	2.33	2.23	2.14	2.03
30	2.98	2.84	2.70	2.55	2.47	2.39	2.30	2.21	2.11	2.01
40	2.80	2.66	2.52	2.37	2.29	2.20	2.11	2.02	1.92	1.80
60	2.63	2.50	2.35	2.20	2.12	2.03	1.94	1.84	1.73	1.60
120	2.47	2.34	2.19	2.03	1.95	1.86	1.76	1.66	1.53	1.38
∞	2.32	2.18	2.04	1.88	1.79	1.70	1.59	1.47	1.32	1.00

DEGREES OF FREEDOM IN THE DENOMINATOR

Table I-4A. Table of Critical Values of the Mann-Whitney *U*-Test

	\(p < 0.05\) (TWO-TAILED TEST)																			
	n																			
m	1	2	3	4	5	6	7	8	9	10	11	12	13	14	15	16	17	18	19	20
1	—																			
2	—	—																		
3	—	—	—																	
4	—	—	—	0																
5	—	—	0	1	2															
6	—	—	1	2	3	5														
7	—	—	1	3	5	6	8													
8	—	0	2	4	6	8	10	13												
9	—	0	2	4	7	10	12	15	17											
10	—	0	3	5	8	11	14	17	20	23										
11	—	0	3	6	9	13	16	19	23	26	30									
12	—	1	4	7	11	14	18	22	26	29	33	37								
13	—	1	4	8	12	16	20	24	28	33	37	41	45							
14	—	1	5	9	13	17	22	26	31	36	40	45	50	55						
15	—	1	5	10	14	19	24	29	34	39	44	49	54	59	64					
16	—	1	6	11	15	21	26	31	37	42	47	53	59	64	70	75				
17	—	2	6	11	17	22	28	34	39	45	51	57	63	69	75	81	87			
18	—	2	7	12	18	24	30	36	42	48	55	61	67	74	80	86	93	99		
19	—	2	7	13	19	25	32	38	45	52	58	65	72	78	85	92	99	106	113	
20	—	2	8	14	20	27	34	41	48	55	62	69	76	83	90	98	105	112	119	127
21	—	3	8	15	22	29	36	43	50	58	65	73	80	88	96	103	111	119	126	134
22	—	3	9	16	23	30	38	45	53	61	69	77	85	93	101	109	117	125	133	141
23	—	3	9	17	24	32	40	48	56	64	73	81	89	98	106	115	123	132	140	149
24	—	3	10	17	25	33	42	50	59	67	76	85	94	102	111	120	129	138	147	156
25	—	3	10	18	27	35	44	53	62	71	80	89	98	107	117	126	135	145	154	163
26	—	4	11	19	28	37	46	55	64	74	83	93	102	112	122	132	141	151	161	171
27	—	4	11	20	29	38	48	57	67	77	87	97	107	117	127	137	147	158	168	178
28	—	4	12	21	30	40	50	60	70	80	90	101	111	122	132	143	154	164	175	186
29	—	4	13	22	32	42	52	62	73	83	94	105	116	127	138	149	160	171	182	193
30	—	5	13	23	33	43	54	65	76	87	98	109	120	131	143	154	166	177	189	200
31	—	5	14	24	34	45	56	67	78	90	101	113	125	136	148	160	172	184	196	208
32	—	5	14	24	35	46	58	69	81	93	105	117	129	141	153	166	178	190	203	215
33	—	5	15	25	37	48	60	72	84	96	108	121	133	146	159	171	184	197	210	222
34	—	5	15	26	38	50	62	74	87	99	112	125	138	151	164	177	190	203	217	230
35	—	6	16	27	39	51	64	77	89	103	116	129	142	156	169	183	196	210	224	237
36	—	6	16	28	40	53	66	79	92	106	119	133	147	161	174	188	202	216	231	245
37	—	6	17	29	41	55	68	81	95	109	123	137	151	165	180	194	209	223	238	252
38	—	6	17	30	43	56	70	84	98	112	127	141	156	170	185	200	215	230	245	259
39	0	7	18	31	44	58	72	86	101	115	130	145	160	175	190	206	221	236	252	267
40	0	7	18	31	45	59	74	89	103	119	134	149	165	180	196	211	227	243	258	274

SOURCE: Reprinted from R. C. Milton (1964), An extended table of critical values for the Mann–Whitney (Wilcoxon) two–sample statistic, *Journal of the American Statistical Association, 59,* 925–934.

Table I-4B. Table of Critical Values of the Mann-Whitney U-Test

										$p < 0.01$ (TWO-TAILED TEST)										
										n										
m	1	2	3	4	5	6	7	8	9	10	11	12	13	14	15	16	17	18	19	20
1	—																			
2	—	—																		
3	—	—	—																	
4	—	—	—	—																
5	—	—	—	—	0															
6	—	—	—	0	1	2														
7	—	—	—	0	1	2	4													
8	—	—	—	1	2	4	6	7												
9	—	—	0	1	3	5	7	9	11											
10	—	—	0	2	4	6	9	11	13	16										
11	—	—	0	2	5	7	10	13	16	18	21									
12	—	—	1	3	6	9	12	15	18	21	24	27								
13	—	—	1	3	7	10	13	17	20	24	27	31	34							
14	—	—	1	4	7	11	15	18	22	26	30	34	38	42						
15	—	—	2	5	8	12	16	20	24	29	33	37	42	46	51					
16	—	—	2	5	9	13	18	22	27	31	36	41	45	50	55	60				
17	—	—	2	6	10	15	19	24	29	34	39	44	49	54	60	65	70			
18	—	—	2	6	11	16	21	26	31	37	42	47	53	58	64	70	75	81		
19	—	0	3	7	12	17	22	28	33	39	45	51	57	63	69	74	81	87	93	
20	—	0	3	8	13	18	24	30	36	42	48	54	60	67	73	79	86	92	99	105
21	—	0	3	8	14	19	25	32	38	44	51	58	64	71	78	84	91	98	105	112
22	—	0	4	9	14	21	27	34	40	47	54	61	68	75	82	89	96	104	111	118
23	—	0	4	9	15	22	29	35	43	50	57	64	72	79	87	94	102	109	117	125
24	—	0	4	10	16	23	30	37	45	52	60	68	75	83	91	99	107	115	123	131
25	—	0	5	10	17	24	32	39	47	55	63	71	79	87	96	104	112	121	129	138
26	—	0	5	11	18	25	33	41	49	58	66	74	83	92	100	109	118	127	135	144
27	—	1	5	12	19	27	35	43	52	60	69	78	87	96	105	114	123	132	142	151
28	—	1	5	12	20	28	36	45	54	63	72	81	91	100	109	119	128	138	148	157
29	—	1	6	13	21	29	38	47	56	66	75	85	94	104	114	124	134	144	154	164
30	—	1	6	13	22	30	40	49	58	68	78	88	98	108	119	129	139	150	160	170
31	—	1	6	14	22	32	41	51	61	71	81	92	102	113	123	134	145	155	166	177
32	—	1	7	14	23	33	43	53	63	74	84	95	106	117	128	139	150	161	172	184
33	—	1	7	15	24	34	44	55	65	76	87	98	110	121	132	144	155	167	179	190
34	—	1	7	16	25	35	46	57	68	79	90	102	113	125	137	149	161	173	185	197
35	—	1	8	16	26	37	47	59	70	82	93	105	117	129	142	154	166	179	191	203
36	—	1	8	17	27	38	49	60	72	84	96	109	121	134	146	159	172	184	197	210
37	—	1	8	17	28	39	51	62	75	87	99	112	125	138	151	164	177	190	203	217
38	—	1	9	18	29	40	52	64	77	90	102	116	129	142	155	169	182	196	210	223
39	—	2	9	19	30	41	54	66	79	92	106	119	133	146	160	174	188	202	216	230
40	—	2	9	19	31	43	55	68	81	95	109	122	136	150	165	179	193	208	222	237

SOURCE: Reprinted from R. C. Milton (1964), An extended table of critical values for the Mann-Whitney (Wilcoxon) two-sample statistic, *Journal of the American Statistical Association, 59*, 925–934.

Table I-5. Table of Areas Under the Normal Curve

z	HUNDREDTHS VALUE OF z									
	.00	.01	.02	.03	.04	.05	.06	.07	.08	.09
0.0	.0000	.0040	.0080	.0120	.0160	.0199	.0239	.0279	.0319	.0359
0.1	.0398	.0438	.0478	.0517	.0557	.0596	.0636	.0675	.0714	.0753
0.2	.0793	.0832	.0871	.0910	.0948	.0987	.1026	.1064	.1103	.1141
0.3	.1179	.1217	.1255	.1293	.1331	.1368	.1406	.1443	.1480	.1517
0.4	.1554	.1591	.1628	.1664	.1700	.1736	.1772	.1808	.1844	.1879
0.5	.1915	.1950	.1985	.2019	.2054	.2088	.2123	.2157	.2190	.2224
0.6	.2257	.2291	.2324	.2357	.2389	.2422	.2454	.2486	.2517	.2549
0.7	.2580	.2611	.2642	.2673	.2704	.2734	.2764	.2794	.2823	.2852
0.8	.2881	.2910	.2939	.2967	.2995	.3023	.3051	.3078	.3106	.3133
0.9	.3159	.3186	.3212	.3238	.3264	.3289	.3315	.3340	.3365	.3389
1.0	.3413	.3438	.3461	.3485	.3508	.3531	.3554	.3577	.3599	.3621
1.1	.3643	.3665	.3686	.3708	.3729	.3749	.3770	.3790	.3810	.3830
1.2	.3849	.3869	.3888	.3907	.3925	.3944	.3962	.3980	.3997	.4015
1.3	.4032	.4049	.4066	.4082	.4099	.4115	.4131	.4147	.4162	.4177
1.4	.4192	.4207	.4222	.4236	.4251	.4265	.4279	.4292	.4306	.4319
1.5	.4332	.4345	.4357	.4370	.4382	.4394	.4406	.4418	.4429	.4441
1.6	.4452	.4463	.4474	.4484	.4495	.4505	.4515	.4525	.4535	.4545
1.7	.4554	.4564	.4573	.4582	.4591	.4599	.4608	.4616	.4625	.4633
1.8	.4641	.4649	.4656	.4664	.4671	.4678	.4686	.4693	.4699	.4706
1.9	.4713	.4719	.4726	.4732	.4738	.4744	.4750	.4756	.4761	.4767
2.0	.4772	.4778	.4783	.4788	.4793	.4798	.4803	.4808	.4812	.4817
2.1	.4821	.4826	.4830	.4834	.4838	.4842	.4846	.4850	.4854	.4857
2.2	.4861	.4864	.4868	.4871	.4875	.4878	.4881	.4884	.4887	.4890
2.3	.4893	.4896	.4898	.4901	.4904	.4906	.4909	.4911	.4913	.4916
2.4	.4918	.4920	.4922	.4925	.4927	.4929	.4931	.4932	.4934	.4936
2.5	.4938	.4940	.4941	.4943	.4945	.4946	.4948	.4949	.4951	.4952
2.6	.4953	.4955	.4956	.4957	.4959	.4960	.4961	.4962	.4963	.4964
2.7	.4965	.4966	.4967	.4968	.4969	.4970	.4971	.4972	.4973	.4974
2.8	.4974	.4975	.4976	.4977	.4977	.4978	.4979	.4979	.4980	.4981
2.9	.4981	.4982	.4982	.4983	.4984	.4984	.4985	.4985	.4986	.4986
3.0	.4987	.4987	.4987	.4988	.4988	.4989	.4989	.4989	.4990	.4990
3.1	.49903									
3.2	.49931									
3.3	.49952									
3.4	.49966									
3.5	.49977									
3.6	.49984									
3.7	.49989									
3.8	.49993									
3.9	.49995									
4.0	.50000									

ONES AND TENTHS VALUE OF z

SOURCE: Reprinted with permission from *Computational Handbook of Statistics,* by J. L. Bruning & B. L. Kintz. Copyright © 1987, 1977, 1968 by Scott, Foresman & Company.

Table I-6. Table of Critical Values of Chi-square

				p VALUE			
DEGREES OF FREEDOM	.25	.10	.05	.025	.01	.005	.001
1	1.32330	2.70554	3.84146	5.02389	6.63490	7.87944	10.828
2	2.77259	4.60517	5.99146	7.37776	9.21034	10.5966	13.816
3	4.10834	6.25139	7.81473	9.34840	11.3449	12.8382	16.266
4	5.38527	7.77944	9.48773	11.1433	13.2767	14.8603	18.467
5	6.62568	9.23636	11.0705	12.8325	15.0863	16.7496	20.515
6	7.84080	10.6446	12.5916	14.4494	16.8119	18.5476	22.458
7	9.03715	12.0170	14.0671	16.0128	18.4753	20.2777	24.322
8	10.2189	13.3616	15.5073	17.5345	20.0902	21.9550	26.125
9	11.3888	14.6837	16.9190	19.0228	21.6660	23.5894	27.877
10	12.5489	15.9872	18.3070	20.4832	23.2093	25.1882	29.588
11	13.7007	17.2750	19.6751	21.9200	24.7250	26.7568	31.264
12	14.8454	18.5493	21.0261	23.3367	26.2170	28.2995	32.909
13	15.9839	19.8119	22.3620	24.7356	27.6882	29.8195	34.528
14	17.1169	21.0641	23.6848	26.1189	29.1412	31.3194	36.123
15	18.2451	22.3071	24.9958	27.4884	30.5779	32.8013	37.697
16	19.3689	23.5418	26.2962	28.8454	31.9999	34.2672	39.252
17	20.4887	24.7690	27.5871	30.1910	33.4087	35.7185	40.790
18	21.6049	25.9894	28.8693	31.5264	34.8053	37.1565	42.312
19	22.7178	27.2036	30.1435	32.8523	36.1909	38.5823	43.820
20	23.8277	28.4120	31.4104	34.1696	37.5662	39.9968	45.315
21	24.9348	29.6151	32.6706	35.4789	38.9322	41.4011	46.797
22	26.0393	30.8133	33.9244	36.7807	40.2894	42.7957	48.268
23	27.1413	32.0069	35.1725	38.0756	41.6384	44.1813	49.728
24	28.2412	33.1962	36.4150	39.3641	42.9798	45.5585	51.179
25	29.3389	34.3816	37.6525	40.6465	44.3141	46.9279	52.618
26	30.4346	35.5632	38.8851	41.9232	45.6417	48.2899	54.052
27	31.5284	36.7412	40.1133	43.1945	46.9629	49.6449	55.476
28	32.6205	37.9159	41.3371	44.4608	48.2782	50.9934	56.892
29	33.7109	39.0875	42.5570	45.7223	49.5879	52.3356	58.301
30	34.7997	40.2560	43.7730	46.9792	50.8922	53.6720	59.703
40	45.6160	51.8051	55.7585	59.3417	63.6907	66.7660	73.402
50	56.3336	63.1671	67.5048	71.4202	76.1539	79.4900	86.661
60	66.9815	74.3970	79.0819	83.2977	88.3794	91.9517	99.607
70	77.5767	85.5270	90.5312	95.0232	100.425	104.215	112.317
80	88.1303	96.5782	101.879	106.629	112.329	116.321	124.839
90	98.6499	107.565	113.145	118.136	124.116	218.299	137.208
100	109.141	118.498	124.342	129.561	135.807	140.169	149.449

SOURCE: Adapted from Table 8, *Biometrika: Tables for Statisticians* (Vol. 1, 3rd ed.), 1966, by E. S. Pearson and H. O. Hartley; reprinted with permission.

Table I-7. Table of Conversion of r to z

r	z	r	z	r	z	r	z	r	z
.000	.000	.200	.203	.400	.424	.600	.693	.800	1.099
.005	.005	.205	.208	.405	.430	.605	.701	.805	1.113
.010	.010	.210	.213	.410	.436	.610	.709	.810	1.127
.015	.015	.215	.218	.415	.442	.615	.717	.815	1.142
.020	.020	.220	.224	.420	.448	.620	.725	.820	1.157
.025	.025	.225	.229	.425	.454	.625	.733	.825	1.172
.030	.030	.230	.234	.430	.460	.630	.741	.830	1.188
.035	.035	.235	.239	.435	.466	.635	.750	.835	1.204
.040	.040	.240	.245	.440	.472	.640	.758	.840	1.221
.045	.045	.245	.250	.445	.478	.645	.767	.845	1.238
.050	.050	.250	.255	.450	.485	.650	.775	.850	1.256
.055	.055	.255	.261	.455	.491	.655	.784	.855	1.274
.060	.060	.260	.266	.460	.497	.660	.793	.860	1.293
.065	.065	.265	.271	.465	.504	.665	.802	.865	1.313
.070	.070	.270	.277	.470	.510	.670	.811	.870	1.333
.075	.075	.275	.282	.475	.517	.675	.820	.875	1.354
.080	.080	.280	.288	.480	.523	.680	.829	.880	1.376
.085	.085	.285	.293	.485	.530	.685	.838	.885	1.398
.090	.090	.290	.299	.490	.536	.690	.848	.890	1.422
.095	.095	.295	.304	.495	.543	.695	.858	.895	1.447
.100	.100	.300	.310	.500	.549	.700	.867	.900	1.472
.105	.105	.305	.315	.505	.556	.705	.877	.905	1.499
.110	.110	.310	.321	.510	.563	.710	.887	.910	1.528
.115	.116	.315	.326	.515	.570	.715	.897	.915	1.557
.120	.121	.320	.332	.520	.576	.720	.908	.920	1.589
.125	.126	.325	.337	.525	.583	.725	.918	.925	1.623
.130	.131	.330	.343	.530	.590	.730	.929	.930	1.658
.135	.136	.335	.348	.535	.597	.735	.940	.935	1.697
.140	.141	.340	.354	.540	.604	.740	.950	.940	1.738
.145	.146	.345	.360	.545	.611	.745	.962	.945	1.783
.150	.151	.350	.365	.550	.618	.750	.973	.950	1.832
.155	.156	.355	.371	.555	.626	.755	.984	.955	1.886
.160	.161	.360	.377	.560	.633	.760	.996	.960	1.946
.165	.167	.365	.383	.565	.640	.765	1.008	.965	2.014
.170	.172	.370	.388	.570	.648	.770	1.020	.970	2.092
.175	.177	.375	.394	.575	.655	.775	1.033	.975	2.185
.180	.182	.380	.400	.580	.662	.780	1.045	.980	2.298
.185	.187	.385	.406	.585	.670	.785	1.058	.985	2.443
.190	.192	.390	.412	.590	.678	.790	1.071	.990	2.647
.195	.198	.395	.418	.595	.685	.795	1.085	.995	2.994

SOURCE: Reprinted with permission from A. L. Edwards (1985), *Experimental Design in Psychological Research* (5th ed.).

Appendix II
Formulas and
Worked Examples

(I) Sum of Squares
(Gravetter & Wallnau, 1990)

$$SS = \sum X^2 - \frac{\left(\sum X\right)^2}{N}$$

Example:

X	X²
3	9
5	25
8	64
9	81
6	36
2	4
$\sum$ = 33	219

$$SS = 219 - \left(\frac{1089}{6}\right) = 37.5$$

(II) Standard Deviation (Using SS Formula)

$$S = \sqrt{\frac{SS}{(N-1)}}$$

$$\sigma = \sqrt{\frac{SS}{N}}$$

$$S = \sqrt{\frac{37.5}{5}} = 2.74$$

$$\sigma = \sqrt{\frac{37.5}{6}} = 2.50$$

(III) Pearson Correlation Coefficient
(Gravetter & Wallnau, 1990)

$$r = \frac{SP}{\sqrt{SS_x SS_y}}$$

where

$$SP = \Sigma XY - \frac{(\Sigma X)(\Sigma Y)}{N}$$

$$SS_x = \Sigma X^2 - \frac{(\Sigma X)^2}{N}$$

$$SS_y = \Sigma Y^2 - \frac{(\Sigma Y)^2}{N}$$

Example:

X	Y	ΣXY
6	5	30
4	6	24
6	7	42
7	9	63
5	4	20
Σ = 28	31	179

$$\Sigma X^2 = 162 \qquad \Sigma Y^2 = 207$$

$$SP = 179 - \frac{28 \times 31}{5} = 179 - 173.6 = 5.4$$

$$SS_x = 162 - \left(\frac{784}{5}\right) = 5.2$$

$$SS_y = 207 - \left(\frac{961}{5}\right) = 14.8$$

$$r = \frac{5.4}{\sqrt{(5.2)(14.8)}} = \frac{5.4}{8.77} = 0.62$$

(IV) Spearman Rank Order Correlation
(Gravetter & Wallnau, 1990)

$$r_s = \frac{SP}{\sqrt{SS_x SS_y}}$$

where

$$SP = \sum XY - \frac{\left(\sum X\right)\left(\sum Y\right)}{N}$$

SS_x and SS_y = the sums of squares for X and Y, respectively (see above for formula)

$\sum X$ and $\sum Y$ = the sums of the ranks for X and Y, respectively (see below)

Example:

X	Y	Rank X	Rank Y	XY
3	4	2	1	2
5	8	3	5	15
6	5	4	2	8
2	7	1	4	4
8	9	6	6	36
7	6	5	3	15

$\sum X$ and $\sum Y$		21	21	80
$\sum X^2$ and $\sum Y^2$		91	91	

$$SP = 80 - \frac{(21)(21)}{6} = 6.5$$

$$SS_x \text{ and } SS_y = 91 - \left(\frac{21^2}{6}\right) = 17.5$$

$$r_s = \frac{6.5}{\sqrt{(17.5)(17.5)}} = 0.37$$

(V) Point–Biserial Correlation
(Roscoe, 1975)

$$r_{pb} = \frac{M_1 - M_0}{\sigma_x} \sqrt{pq}$$

where

M_1 = mean of the subjects on the continuous variable for subjects falling into Category 1 of the dichotomous variable

M_0 = mean of the subjects on the continuous variable for subjects falling into Category 2 of the dichotomous variable

σ_x = standard deviation of the continuous variable

p = proportion of all subjects falling into Category 1

q = proportion of all subjects falling into Category 2

Example:

X	Y
6	1
7	1
5	0
4	0
8	1
2	0

$$M_1 = \frac{6 + 7 + 8}{3} = 7$$

$$M_0 = \frac{5 + 4 + 2}{3} = 3.67$$

$$\sigma_x = 1.97$$

$$p = 0.5$$

$$q = 0.5$$

$$r_{pb} = \frac{7 - 3.67}{1.97} \sqrt{(0.5)(0.5)} = 0.85$$

(VI) Partial Correlation
(Thorndike, 1978)

$$r_{12 \cdot 3} = \frac{r_{12} - r_{13}r_{23}}{\sqrt{1 - r_{13}^2}\ \sqrt{1 - r_{23}^2}}$$

Example:

$$r_{12} = 0.67$$

$$r_{13} = 0.55$$

$$r_{23} = 0.71$$

$$r_{12 \cdot 3} = \frac{(0.67 - [0.55] [0.71])}{\sqrt{1 - 0.55^2} \ \sqrt{1 - 0.71^2}} = 0.47$$

(VII) Part Correlation (Semipartial Correlation)
(Thorndike, 1978)

$$r_{1_{(2 \cdot 3)}} = \frac{r_{12} - r_{13}r_{23}}{\sqrt{1 - r_{23}^2}}$$

Example (using previous correlations):

$$r_{1_{(2 \cdot 3)}} = \frac{.67 - (.55)(.71)}{\sqrt{1 - .72^2}} = .40$$

(VIII) One–Factor Between–Subjects ANOVA
(Keppel, 1982)

Preliminary Calculations

$$[A] = \frac{\Sigma Ai^2}{s} \qquad [T] = \frac{T^2}{as} \qquad [AS] = \Sigma(AS^2)$$

where

A_i = each treatment sum

T = total of all scores

s = number of subjects in each treatment group

a = number of levels of the independent variable

$\Sigma(AS)^2$ = sum of the squared scores

Calculation of Sum of Squares (SS), Degrees of Freedom (df), Mean Squares (MS), and *F*-ratio

$$SS_A = [A] - [T], \ \ SS_{S/A} = [AS] - [A]$$

$$df_A = (a - 1), \ \ df_{S/A} = a(s - 1)$$

$$MS_A = \frac{SS_A}{df_A}, \ \ MS_{S/A} = \frac{SS_{S/A}}{df_{S/A}}$$

$$F = \frac{MS_A}{MS_{S/A}}$$

Example:

	Group 1	Group 2	Group 3
	3	5	10
	2	6	9
	1	8	10
	3	7	9
	4	8	8
ΣX	13	34	46
ΣX^2	39	238	426
M	2.6	6.8	9.2

$$[T] = \frac{(93)^2}{3(5)} = 576.6 \qquad [A] = \frac{(13)^2 + (34)^2 + (46)^2}{5} = 688.2$$

$$[AS] = (3)^2 + (2)^2 + \cdots + (9)^2 + (8)^2 = 703$$

$$SS_A = [A] - [T] = 688.2 - 576.6 = 111.6; \quad df_A = (3 - 1) = 2$$

$$SS_{S/A} = [AS] - [A] = 703 - 688.2 = 14.8; \quad df_{S/A} = 3(5 - 1) = 12$$

$$MS_A = \frac{111.6}{2} = 55.8$$

$$MS_{S/A} = \frac{14.8}{12} = 1.23$$

$$F_A = \frac{55.8}{1.23} = 45.36$$

(IX) One–Factor Within–Subjects ANOVA
(Keppel, 1982)

Preliminary Calculations

$$[A] = \frac{\Sigma A_i^2}{s}, \quad [T] = \frac{T^2}{as}, \quad [S] = \frac{\Sigma S_i^2}{a}, \quad [AS] = \Sigma (AS)^2$$

where

A_i = each treatment sum

s = number of subjects in each treatment group

T = total of all scores

a = number of levels of the independent variable

S_i = sum across levels of the independent variable for each subject

$\Sigma(AS)^2$ = sum of the squared scores

Calculation of Sum of Squares (SS), Degrees of Freedom (df), Mean Squares (MS), and F-ratio

$$SS_A = [A] - [T], \quad SS_S = [S] - [T], \quad SS_{AS} = [AS] - [A] - [S] + [T]$$

$$df_A = (a - 1), \quad df_S = (s - 1), \quad df_{AS} = (a - 1)(s - 1)$$

$$MS_A = \frac{SS_A}{df_A}, \quad MS_S = \frac{SS_S}{df_S}, \quad MS_{AS} = \frac{SS_{AS}}{df_{AS}}$$

$$F_A = \frac{MS_A}{MS_{AS}}, \quad F_S = \frac{MS_S}{MS_{AS}}$$

Example:

	Group 1	Group 2	Group 3	Sum
	3	5	10	18
	2	6	9	17
	1	8	10	19
	3	7	9	19
	4	8	8	20
$\sum X$	13	34	46	93
$\sum X^2$	39	238	426	
M	2.6	6.8	9.2	

$$[T] = \frac{(93)^2}{3(5)} = 576.6 \qquad [A] = \frac{(13)^2 + (34)^2 + (46)^2}{5} = 688.2$$

$$[S] = \frac{(18)^2 + (17)^2 + (19)^2 + (19)^2 + (20)^2}{3} = 578.33$$

$$[AS] = (3)^2 + (2)^2 + \cdots + (9)^2 + (8)^2 = 703$$

$$SS_A = [A] - [T] = 688.2 - 576.6 = 111.6; \quad df_A = (3 - 1) = 2$$

$$SS_S = [S] - [T] = 578.33 - 576.6 = 1.73; \quad df_S = (5 - 1) = 4$$

$$SS_{AS} = [AS] - [A] - [S] + [T] = 703 - 688.2 - 578.33 + 576.6$$

$$= 13.07; \quad df_{AS} = (3 - 1)(5 - 1) = 8$$

$$MS_A = \frac{111.6}{2} = 55.8$$

$$MS_S = \frac{1.73}{4} = 0.44$$

$$MS_{AS} = \frac{13.07}{8} = 1.63$$

$$F_A = \frac{55.8}{1.63} = 34.23$$

$$F_S = \frac{0.44}{1.63} < 1$$

(X) Two-Factor Between-Subjects ANOVA
(Keppel, 1982)

Preliminary Calculations

$$[A] = \frac{\sum A_i^2}{bs}, \quad [B] = \frac{\sum B_i^2}{as}, \quad [AB] = \frac{\sum (AB_{ij})^2}{s},$$

$$[T] = \frac{T^2}{abs}, \quad [ABS] = \sum (ABS)^2$$

where

$$a = \text{number of levels of Factor } a$$
$$b = \text{number of levels of Factor } b$$
$$s = \text{number of subjects per group}$$
$$A_i = \text{each treatment sum for Factor } A$$
$$B_j = \text{each treatment sum for Factor } B$$
$$AB_{ij} = \text{sum of the scores in each cell}$$
$$s = \text{number of subjects in each group}$$
$$T = \text{total of all scores}$$
$$\sum (ABS)^2 = \text{sum of the squared scores}$$

Calculation of Sum of Squares (SS), Degrees of Freedom (df), Mean Squares (MS), and F-ratio

$$\text{SS}_A = [A] - [T], \quad \text{SS}_B = [B] - [T],$$
$$\text{SS}_{AB} = [AB] - [A] - [B] + [T], \quad \text{SS}_{S/AB} = [ABS] - [AB]$$
$$\text{df}_A = (a-1), \ \text{df}_B = (b-1), \ \text{df}_{AB} = (a-1)(b-1), \ \text{df}_{S/AB} = ab(s-1)$$
$$\text{MS}_A = \frac{\text{SS}_A}{\text{df}_A}, \quad \text{MS}_B = \frac{\text{SS}_B}{\text{df}_B}, \quad \text{MS}_{AB} = \frac{\text{SS}_{AB}}{\text{df}_{AB}}, \quad \text{MS}_{S/AB} = \frac{\text{SS}_{S/AB}}{\text{df}_{S/AB}}$$
$$F_A = \frac{\text{MS}_A}{\text{MS}_{S/AB}}, \quad F_B = \frac{\text{MS}_B}{\text{MS}_{S/AB}}, \quad F_{AB} = \frac{\text{MS}_{AB}}{\text{MS}_{S/AB}}$$

Example:

	A_1		A_2	
	B_1	B_2	B_1	B_2
	2	1	3	10
	3	2	3	10
	0	1	2	9
	1	5	1	9
	4	3	4	10
$\sum X =$	10	12	13	48
$\sum X^2 =$	30	40	39	462
$M =$	2	2.4	2.6	9.6

$$[T] = \frac{(83)^2}{(2)(2)(5)} = 344.45 \qquad [A] = \frac{(22)^2 + (61)^2}{2(5)} = 420.5$$

$$[B] = \frac{(23)^2 + (60)^2}{2(5)} = 412.9$$

$$[AB] = \frac{(10)^2 + (13)^2 + (12)^2 + (48)^2}{5} = 543.4$$

$$[ABS] = (2)^2 + (3)^2 + \cdots + (9)^2 + (10)^2 = 571$$

$$SS_A = [A] - [T] = 420.5 - 344.45 = 76.05; \quad df_A = (2 - 1) = 1$$

$$SS_B = [B] - [T] = 412.9 - 344.45 = 68.45; \quad df_B = (2 - 1) = 1$$

$$SS_{AB} = [AB] - [A] - [B] + [T] = 543.4 - 420.5 - 412.9 + 344.5 = 54.5$$

$$df_{AB} = (2 - 1)(2 - 1) = 1$$

$$SS_{S/AB} = [ABS] - [AB] = 571 - 543.4 = 27.6$$

$$df_{S/AB} = (2)(2)(5 - 1) = 16$$

$$MS_A = \frac{76.05}{1} = 76.05 \qquad F_A = 43.96$$

$$MS_B = \frac{68.45}{1} = 68.45 \qquad F_B = 39.56$$

$$MS_{AB} = \frac{54.5}{1} = 54.5 \qquad F_{AB} = 31.5$$

$$MS_{S/AB} = \frac{27.6}{16} = 1.73$$

(XI) z-Test for Two Proportions
(Glassnap & Poggio, 1985)

$$z = \frac{P_1 - P_2}{\sqrt{P_p(1 - P_p)\left(\dfrac{1}{n_1} + \dfrac{1}{n_2}\right)}}$$

where

P_1 and P_2 = the two proportions

n_1 and n_2 = number of subjects in each group

P_p = a calculation from the observed frequency (f) in each group with the following formula:

$$P_p = \frac{f_1 + f_2}{n_1 + n_2}$$

where
f_1 = frequency of the observed response in Group 1
f_2 = frequency of the observed response in Group 2
n_1 and n_2 = number of subjects in each group

Example:

$$P_1 = 0.80$$
$$P_2 = 0.30$$
$$n_1 = n_2 = 10$$
$$P_p = \frac{(8 + 3)}{(10 + 10)} = 0.55$$
$$z = \frac{(0.8 - 0.3)}{\sqrt{0.55(1 - 0.55)\left(\frac{1}{10} + \frac{1}{10}\right)}} = 2.24$$

(XII) Formula for Squared Semipartial Correlation
(Tabachnik & Fidell, 1989)

$$sr^2_i = \frac{F}{df_{residual}}(1 - R^2)$$

Note: If the program you are using provides t values rather than F-ratios, simply square t (t^2) and substitute that value for F in the formula.

(XIII) Chi-square for a Two-Way Contingency Table
(Roscoe, 1975)

$$\chi^2 = \Sigma \frac{(O_{ij} - E_{ij})^2}{E_{ij}}$$

where
O_{ij} = observed frequency within a cell
E_{ij} = expected frequency within a cell, defined as

$$E_{ij} = \frac{R_i \times C_j}{N}$$

where
R_i = the appropriate row sum
C_j = the appropriate column sum
N = the total frequency count over all cells

Example:

Table of Observed Frequencies

	C_1	C_2	Row Sum
R_1	25	12	37
R_2	14	35	49
Column Sum	39	47	86

Expected Frequencies:

$$E_{1,1} = \frac{39 \times 37}{86} = 16.8$$

$$E_{1,2} = \frac{47 \times 37}{86} = 20.2$$

$$E_{2,1} = \frac{39 \times 49}{86} = 22.2$$

$$E_{2,2} = \frac{47 \times 49}{86} = 26.8$$

$$\chi^2 = \frac{(25 - 16.8)^2}{16.8} + \frac{(12 - 20.2)^2}{20.2} + \frac{(14 - 22.2)^2}{22.2} + \frac{(35 - 26.8)^2}{26.8} = 12.87$$

(XIV) Mann–Whitney U-test
(Roscoe, 1975)

$$U_a = n_a n_b + \frac{n_b(n_b + 1)}{2} - \Sigma R_b$$

$$U_b = n_a n_b + \frac{n_a(n_a + 1)}{2} - \Sigma R_a$$

where

n_a = the number of subjects in Group a

n_b = the number of subjects in Group b

R_a and R_b are the sums of the ranks for Groups a and b, respectively

Example:

Group a	Group b
23	14
32	21
15	33
39	18
22	16

Distribution of Ordered Scores

Scores and (group)	Rank	Group a Ranks	Group b Ranks
14 (b)	1		1
15 (a)	2	2	
16 (b)	3		3
18 (b)	4		4
21 (b)	5		5
22 (a)	6	6	
23 (a)	7	7	
32 (a)	8	8	
33 (b)	9		9
39 (a)	10	10	
Sum of Ranks		33	22

$n_a = 5$
$n_b = 5$

$$U_a = 5 \times 5 + \frac{5(5 + 1)}{2} - 22 = 18$$

$$U_b = 5 \times 5 + \frac{5(5 + 1)}{2} - 33 = 7$$

(XV) *t*-test for Independent Samples
(Roscoe, 1975)

$$t = \frac{M_t - M_c}{S_{M_t - M_c}}$$

where

M_t = mean for the group receiving the treatment

M_c = mean for the control group

$S_{M_t - M_c}$ = the standard error defined as:

$$S_{M_t - M_c} = \sqrt{\frac{SS_t + SS_c}{(n_t + n_c) - 2}\left(\frac{1}{n_t} + \frac{1}{n_c}\right)}$$

Example:

Treatment (t)	Control (c)
9	3
8	2
7	2
7	1
6	3
8	4
9	2
10	1
7	5
8	3
$M = 7.9$	2.6

$$S_{M_t - M_c} = \sqrt{\frac{12.6 + 14.4}{(10 + 10) - 2}\left(\frac{1}{10} + \frac{1}{10}\right)} = .551$$

$$t = \frac{7.9 - 2.6}{.551} = 9.62$$

(XVI) *t*-test for Correlated Samples
Roscoe (1975)

$$t = \frac{\overline{D}}{S_{\overline{D}}}$$

where $\overline{D}$ = the average of the difference scores between pairs of scores (treatment − control). In the equations that follow, "D" refers to a difference score.

$S_{\overline{D}}$ = the standard error of d defined as:

$$S_{\overline{D}} = \sqrt{\frac{\Sigma d^2}{N(N-1)}}$$

where

$$\Sigma d^2 = \Sigma D^2 - \frac{(\Sigma D)^2}{N}$$

Example:

Treatment (t)	Control (c)	D	D²
9	3	6	36
8	2	6	36
7	2	5	25
7	1	6	36
6	3	3	9
8	4	4	16
9	2	7	49
10	1	9	81
7	5	2	4
8	3	5	25
		$\Sigma D = 53$	$\Sigma D_2 = 317$
		$\overline{D} = 5.3$	

$$\Sigma d^2 = 317 - \frac{53^2}{10} = 36.1$$

$$S_{\overline{D}} = \sqrt{\frac{36.1}{10(9)}} = .633$$

$$t = \frac{5.3}{.633} = 8.37$$

Glossary

ABAB design In a single-subject baseline design, the baseline (A) and intervention (B) phases are each repeated to provide an immediate intrasubject replication.

ABA design In a single-subject baseline design, the baseline phase (A) is run before and after the intervention phase (B).

Abstract A concise (50–150 words) summary of an APA-style manuscript that includes a brief description of the rationale for the study, methods, results, and conclusions.

Accurate measure A measure whose values agree with an established standard.

Alpha level (α) The probability that an observed difference between means occurred because of sampling error (chance). By convention, the maximum acceptable alpha level is 0.05.

Alternative hypothesis In inferential statistics, any statistical hypothesis other than the null hypothesis; for example, the hypothesis that Mean A is greater than Mean B in the population.

Analogical theory A theory that explains a relationship through analogy to a well-understood model.

Analysis of covariance (ANCOVA) Variant of the analysis of variance used to analyze data from experiments that include a correlational variable (covariate).

Analysis of variance (ANOVA) An inferential statistic used to evaluate data from experiments with more than two levels of an independent variable or data from multifactor experiments. Versions are available for between-subjects and within-subjects designs.

APA style Writing style specified by the APA (American Psychological Association); the style used when preparing manuscripts for most psychological journals.

Apparatus subsection Subsection of the method section of an APA-style manuscript in which any equipment, materials, and measures are described in detail. Sometimes called the "materials" subsection.

Applied research Research carried out to investigate a real-world problem.

Archival research A nonexperimental research strategy in which you make use of existing records as your basic source for data.

Baseline design A single-subject experimental design in which subjects are observed under each of several treatment conditions. Observations made during baseline periods (no treatment) are compared with observations made during intervention periods (treatment introduced).

Baseline phase Phase of a single-subject, baseline design in which you establish the level of performance on the dependent measure before introducing the treatment.

Basic research Research carried out primarily to test a theory or empirical issues.

Behavioral baseline Level of behavior under the baseline and intervention phases of a single-subject, baseline design. It is used to determine the amount of uncontrolled variability in the data.

Behavioral category The general and specific classes of behavior to be observed in an observational study.

Behavioral measure A measure of a subject's activity in a situation; for example, the number of times a rat presses a lever (frequency of responding).

Belief-based explanation An explanation for behavior that is accepted without evidence because it comes from a trusted source or fits within a larger framework of belief.

Beta weight Standardized regression weight used to interpret the results of a linear regression analysis. A beta weight can be interpreted as a partial correlation coefficient.

Between-subjects design An experimental design in which different groups of subjects are exposed to the various levels of the independent variable.

Biased sample A sample that is not representative of the population it is supposed to represent.

Binomial effect size display (BESD) A meta-analytic method of evaluating data against effect sizes to determine the amount of change in a measure to be expected across groups.

Canonical correlation Multivariate statistical techniques used to correlate two sets of variables.

Carryover effect A problem associated with within-subjects designs in which exposure to one level of the independent variable alters the behavior observed under subsequent levels.

Case history A nonexperimental research technique in which an individual case is studied intensively to uncover its history (for example, a patient in therapy).

Casual relationship A relationship in which changes in the value of one variable *cause* changes in the value of another.

Chi-square (χ^2) Nonparametric inferential statistic used to evaluate the relationship between variables measured on a nominal scale.

Circular explanation When a behavior is explained by reference to factors whose only proof of existence is the behavior they are being called on to explain.

Cluster sampling A sampling technique in which naturally occurring groups (such as students in an elementary school class) are randomly selected for inclusion in a sample.

Coefficient of determination A statistic, computed by squaring a correlation coefficient, that tells you the amount of variance shared by two variables.

Cohort-sequential design A developmental design including cross-sectional and longitudinal components.

Combined design A research design that combines design types (for example, experimental and correlational).

Commonsense explanation Loose explanations for behavior that are based on what we believe to be true about the world.

Confirmational strategy A strategy for testing a theory that involves finding evidence that confirms the predictions made by the theory.

Confounding variable An uncontrolled variable that varies with an independent variable in such a way that its effects cannot be separated from those of the independent variable.

Constant Any characteristic or quantity whose value is fixed.

Content analysis A nonexperimental research technique that is used to analyze a written or spoken record for the occurrence of specific categories of events.

Control group A group of subjects in an experiment that does not receive the experimental treatment. The data from the control group are used as a baseline against which data from the experimental group are compared.

Correlational relationship A relationship in which the value of one variable changes systematically with the value of a second variable.

Correlational research Research in which no independent variables are manipulated. Instead, two or more dependent variables are measured to identify possible correlational relationships.

Counterbalancing A technique used to combat carryover effects in within-subjects designs. Counterbalancing involves assigning the various treatments of an experiment in a different order for different subjects.

Covariate A correlational variable (usually a characteristic of the subject) included in an experiment to help reduce the error variance in statistical tests.

Critical region Portion of the sampling distribution of a statistic within which observed values of the statistic are considered to be statistically significant. Usually the 5 percent of cases found in the upper and/or lower tail(s) of the distribution.

Cross-sectional design A developmental design in which subjects from two or more age groups are measured at about the same time. Comparisons are made across age groups to investigate age-related changes in behavior.

Data file A computer file, usually stored on disk, containing the data of a study.

Data transformation Mathematical operation applied to raw data such as taking the square root or arc sine of the original scores in a distribution. Often applied to data that violate the assumptions of parametric statistical tests, to help them meet those assumptions.

Debriefing A session, conducted after an experimental session, in which subjects are informed of any deception used and the reasons for the deception.

Deception A research technique in which subjects are misinformed about the true nature and purpose of a study. Deception is ethical if the researcher can demonstrate that important results cannot be obtained in any other way.

Deductive reasoning Reasoning that goes from the general to the specific. Forms the foundation of the rational method of inquiry.

Degrees of freedom (df) The number of scores that are free to vary in a distribution of a given size having a known mean.

Demand characteristics Cues inadvertently provided by the researcher or research context concerning the purposes of a study or the behavior expected from subjects.

Demonstration A nonexperimental technique in which some phenomenon is demonstrated. No control group is used.

Dependent variable The variable measured in a study. Its value is determined by the behavior of the subject and may depend on the value of the independent variable.

Descriptive theory A theory that simply describes the relationship among variables without attempting to explain the relationship.

Design The plan of a study specifying the levels of the independent variables or the predictor variables to be included, as well as the procedures and measures.

Directionality problem A problem that interferes with drawing causal inferences from correlational results that involves not being able to clearly specify the direction of causality between variables.

Direct replication Exactly replicating an experiment. No new variables are included in the replication.

Disconfirmational strategy A method of testing a theory that involves conducting research to provide evidence that disconfirms the predictions made by the theory.

Discrete trials design A single-subject experimental design in which subjects receive each treatment condition dozens or hundreds of times. Each trial (exposure to a treatment) produces one data point, and data points are averaged across trials to provide stable estimates of behavior.

Discriminant analysis Multivariate statistical technique used when you have multiple predictor variables and a categorical criterion variable.

Discussion section The section of an APA-style manuscript that includes the author's interpretation of the findings of a study and conclusions drawn from the data.

Distribution A collection of scores arranged by size in which the number of scores of each size is tabulated.

Domain The range of situations to which a theory applies. Also called the *scope* of a theory.

Dummy-coding In a data file, using numbers to stand for category values; for example, 0 = male, 1 = female.

Empirical question A question that can be answered through objective observation.

Equivalent time samples design A variation of the time series design in which a treatment is administered repeatedly, with each administration followed by an observation period.

Error variance Variability in the value of the dependent variable that is related to extraneous variables and not to the variability in the independent variable.

Expectancy effect When a researcher's preconceived ideas about how subjects should behave are subtly communicated to subjects and, in turn, affect the subjects' behavior.

Experimental group A group of subjects in an experiment that receives a nonzero level of the independent variable.

Experimental research Research in which independent variables are manipulated and is behavior measured while extraneous variables are controlled.

Experimenter bias When the behavior of the researcher influences the results of a study. Experimenter bias stems from two sources: expectancy effects and uneven treatment of subjects across treatments.

External validity The extent to which the results of a study extend beyond the limited sample used in the study.

Extraneous variable Any variable that is not systematically manipulated in an experiment but that still may affect the behavior being observed.

Factor analysis Multivariate statistical technique that uses correlations between variables to determine the underlying dimensions (factors) represented by the variables.

Factorial design An experimental design in which every level of one independent variable is combined with every level of every other independent variable.

Familywise error The likelihood of making at least one type I error across a number of comparisons.

File drawer phenomenon A problem associated with publication practices and meta-analysis that occurs because results that fail to achieve statistical significance often fail to be published (that is, get relegated to the researcher's file drawer).

F-ratio The test statistic computed when using an analysis of variance. It is the ratio of the between-groups variance to within-groups variance.

Frequency distribution See *Distribution.*

Fundamental theory A theory that proposes a new structure or underlying process to explain how variables and constants relate.

Generality, *or* Generalization The extent to which results from a study based on a sample apply to the population as a whole.

Higher-order factorial design Experimental design that includes more than two independent variables (factors).

Histogram (bar graph) A graph on which data from groups of subjects are represented by bars of differing heights tied to the value of the dependent variable for the group.

Hypothesis A tentative statement, subject to empirical test, about the expected relationship between variables.

Independent variable The variable that is manipulated in an experiment. Its value is determined by the experimenter, not by the subject.

Informed consent The research requirement that subjects must be informed of and agree to the procedures of a study before their participation, and must be given the opportunity to decline or withdraw their participation without penalty.

Institutional review board (IRB) A committee that screens proposals for research using human subjects for adherence to ethical standards.

Interaction When the effect of one independent variable on the dependent variable in a factorial design changes over the levels of another independent variable.

Internal validity The extent to which a study evaluates the intended hypotheses.

Interrater reliability The degree to which multiple observers agree in their classification or quantification of behavior.

Interrupted time series design A variation of the time series design in which changes in behavior are charted as a function of time before and after some naturally occurring event.

Intersubject replication The behaviors of multiple subjects used in a single-subject design are compared to establish the reliability of results.

Interval scale A measurement scale in which the spacing between values along the scale is known. The zero point of an interval scale is arbitrary.

Intervention phase Phase of a single-subject, baseline design in which the treatment is introduced and the dependent measure evaluated.

Interview Method of administering a questionnaire that involves face-to-face interaction with the subject. Two types are the structured and unstructured interview.

Intrasubject replication In a single-subject experiment, each treatment is repeated at least once for each subject and behavior is measured. This helps establish the reliability of the results obtained from a single-subject experiment.

Introduction The first major section of an APA-style manuscript, which includes the rationale for the study, a literature review, and usually a statement of the hypothesis to be tested.

Latin square design A counterbalanced design assuring that each treatment appears an equal number of times at each ordinal position across subjects.

Law A relationship that has been substantially verified through empirical test.

Lazy writing Flaw in writing, closely related to plagiarism, that involves using too much quoted (albeit properly cited) material in a manuscript.

Least squares regression line Straight line, fit to data, that minimizes the sum of the squared distances between each data point and the line.

Linear regression Statistical technique used to determine the straight line that best fits a set of data.

Line graph A graph on which data relating the variables are plotted as points connected by lines.

Literature review A review of relevant research and theory conducted during the early stages of the research process to identify important variables and accepted methods, and to establish a rationale for research hypotheses.

Loglinear analysis A nonparametric, multivariate statistical technique used primarily to evaluate data from multifactor research with a nominal dependent variable. It can also be used on interval or ratio data that violate the assumptions of the analysis of variance.

Longitudinal design A developmental design in which a single group of subjects is followed over a specified period of time and measured at regular intervals.

Mail survey Method of administering a survey that involves mailing questionnaires to subjects. Nonresponse bias may be a problem.

Main effect The independent effect of one independent variable in a factorial design on the dependent variable. There are as many main effects as there are independent variables.

Manipulation check Measures included in an experiment to test the effectiveness of the independent variables.

Mann-Whitney _U_-test Nonparametric inferential statistic used to evaluate data from a two-group experiment where the dependent variable was measured along at least an ordinal scale. It can also be used on interval or ratio data if the data do not meet the assumptions of the _t_-test.

Matched-groups design Between-subjects experimental design in which matched sets of subjects are distributed, at random, one per group across groups of the experiment.

Matched-pairs design A two-group matched-groups design.

Mean The arithmetic average of the scores in a distribution. The most frequently reported measure of central tendency.

Measure of central tendency A single score, computed from a data set, that represents the general magnitude of the scores in the distribution.

Median The middle score in an ordered distribution.

Meta-analysis A statistics-based method of reviewing literature in a field that involves comparing or combining the results of related studies. See also _Traditional review_.

Method of authority Relying on authoritative sources (for example, books, journals, scholars) for information.

Method section The section of an APA-style manuscript in which the methods used in a study are described in detail. The subjects, apparatus, and procedure subsections are included within the method section.

Misplaced data error Error committed while transcribing data in which a value is placed in the wrong column, causing the computer to misread the value.

Mixed design An experimental design that includes between-subjects as well as within-subjects factors. Also called a *split-plot design*.

Mode The most frequent score in a distribution. The least informative measure of central tendency.

Model Specific application of a general theoretical view. The term *model* is sometimes used as a synonym for *theory*.

Multiple-baseline design Simultaneously sampling several behaviors in a single-subject, baseline design to provide multiple baselines of behavior. Used if your independent variable produces irreversible changes in the dependent variable.

Multiple control group design Single-factor, experimental design that includes two or more control groups.

Multiple *R* The correlation between the best linear combination of predictor variables entered into a multiple-regression analysis and the dependent variable.

Multiple regression Multivariate linear regression analysis used when you have a single criterion variable and multiple predictor variables.

Multistage sampling A variant of cluster sampling in which naturally occurring groups of subjects are identified and randomly sampled. Individual subjects are then randomly sampled from the groups chosen.

Multivariate analysis of variance (MANOVA) Multivariate analog to the analysis of variance used to analyze data from an experimental design with multiple dependent variables.

Multivariate design A research design in which multiple dependent or predictor variables are included. Multivariate designs can be between-subjects, within-subjects, or mixed.

Multivariate strategy A data analysis strategy in which multiple dependent measures are analyzed with a single, multivariate statistical test.

Naturalistic observation Observational research technique in which subjects are observed in their natural environments. The observers remain unobtrusive so that they do not interfere with the natural behaviors of the subjects being observed.

Negative skewness A skewed frequency distribution in which most of the scores fall into the higher response categories.

Nested design An experimental design with a within-subjects factor in which different levels of one independent variable are included under each level of a between-subjects factor.

Nominal scale A measurement scale that involves categorizing cases into two or more distinct categories. This scale yields the least information.

Nonequivalent control group design A time series experiment that includes a control group that is not exposed to the experimental treatment.

Nonparametric design Experimental research design in which levels of the independent variable are represented by different categories rather than differing amounts.

Nonparametric statistic A statistic that makes no assumptions about the population underlying a sample.

Nonrefereed journal A journal in which articles do not undergo prepublication editorial review.

Nonresponse bias A problem associated with survey research, caused by some subjects not returning a questionnaire, resulting in a biased sample.

Normal distribution A specific type of frequency distribution in which most scores fall around the middle category. Scores become less frequent as you move from the middle category. Also referred to as a *bell-shaped curve*.

Normal science The situation in which researchers working within a paradigm produce findings that extend the organized body of knowledge along the lines delineated by the paradigm.

Null hypothesis In inferential statistics, the hypothesis that population values do not differ (most often applied to population means).

Open-ended item Questionnaire item that allows the subject to fill in a response rather than selecting a response from provided alternatives.

Operational definition A definition of a variable in terms of the operations used to measure it.

Ordinal scale A measurement scale in which cases are ordered along some dimension (for example, large, medium, or small). The distances between scale values are unknown.

Paper session A meeting at a scientific convention where the most up-to-date research results are presented. A paper session may involve disseminating data by reading a paper or presenting a poster.

Paradigm A general view used by scientists to direct research. A paradigm defines the important questions to be addressed and prescribes the acceptable methods for research.

Paradigm shift A situation in which, when existing paradigms fail to provide adequate explanations for new findings, a new paradigm may emerge that explains original findings and new ones.

Parametric design An experimental design in which the amount of the independent variable is systematically varied across several levels.

Parametric statistic A statistic that makes assumptions about the nature of an underlying population (for example, that scores are normally distributed).

Parsimony The ability of an explanation or theory to explain a relationship using relatively few assumptions.

Part correlation (semipartial correlation) Multivariate correlational statistic used to examine the relationship between two variables with the effects of a third variable removed from only one of them.

Partial correlation Multivariate correlational statistic used to examine the relationship between two variables with the effect of a third variable removed from both of them.

Partially open-ended item Questionnaire item that provides subjects with response categories but includes an "other" response category with a space for subjects to define the category.

Participant observation An observational research technique in which a researcher insinuates him- or herself into a group to be studied.

Path analysis An application of multiple regression used to develop and test causal models using correlational data.

Pearson product moment correlation (Pearson *r*) The most popular measure of correlation. Indicates the magnitude and direction of a correlational relationship between variables.

Peer review Process of editorial review used by refereed journals. Manuscripts are usually sent out to at least two reviewers who screen the research for quality and importance.

Per-comparison error The alpha level for each of any multiple comparisons made among means.

Personal communication Information obtained privately from another researcher (for example, by letter or phone).

***Phi* (φ) coefficient** Measure of correlation used when both variables can take on only two values.

Physiological measure A measure of a bodily function of subjects in a study (for example, heart rate).

Pie chart Type of graph in which a circle is divided into segments. Each segment represents the proportion or percentage of responses falling in a given category of the dependent variable.

Pilot study A small, scaled-down version of a study used to test the validity of experimental procedures and measures.

Plagiarism A serious flaw in writing that involves using another person's words or ideas without properly citing the source. See also *Lazy writing*.

Planned comparison Hypothesis-directed statistical tests made after finding statistical significance with an overall statistical test (such as ANOVA).

Point-biserial correlation A variation of the Pearson correlation used when one variable can take on only two values.

Population All possible individuals making up a group of interest in a study. For example, all U.S. women constitute a population. A small proportion of the population is selected for inclusion in a study (see *Sample*).

Positive skewness A skewed frequency distribution in which most of the scores fall into the lower response categories.

Power The ability of an experimental design or inferential statistic to detect an effect of a variable when one is present.

Pretest-posttest design A research design that involves measuring a dependent variable (pretest), then introducing the treatment, and then measuring the dependent variable a second time (posttest).

Primary source A reference source that contains the original, full report of a study. It includes all the details needed to replicate and interpret the study.

Principle 9 of the Ethical Principles of Psychologists The principle of the APA ethical code that specifies the rules for using human subjects in research.

Principle 10 of the Ethical Principles of Psychologists The principle of the APA ethical code that specifies the rules for using animal subjects in research.

Procedure subsection The subsection of the method section of an APA-style manuscript that provides a detailed description of the procedures used in a study.

Proportionate sampling A variation of stratified sampling in which the proportion of subjects sampled from each stratum is matched to the proportion of subjects in each stratum in the population.

Pseudoexplanation An explanation proposed for a phenomenon that simply relabels the phenomenon without really explaining it.

***p*-value** In a statistical test, the probability, estimated from the data, that an observed difference in sample values arose through sampling error. p must be less than or equal to the chosen alpha level for the difference to be statistically significant.

Qualitative theory A theory in which terms are expressed verbally rather than mathematically.

Quantitative theory A theory in which terms are expressed mathematically rather than verbally.

Quasi-independent variable A variable resembling the independent variable in an experiment, whose levels are not assigned to subjects at random (the subject's age, for example).

Randomized two-group design A between-subjects design in which subjects are assigned to groups randomly.

Random sample A sample drawn from the population such that every member of the population has an equal opportunity to be included in the sample.

Range The least informative measure of variability; the difference between the lowest and highest score in a distribution.

Range effect A problem in which a variable being observed reaches an upper limit (ceiling effect) or lower limit (floor effect).

Rational method Developing explanations through a process of deductive reasoning.

Ratio scale Highest scale of measurement; it has all of the characteristics of an interval scale plus an absolute zero point.

Refereed journal A journal whose articles have undergone prepublication editorial review by a panel of experts in the relevant field.

Reference section The section of an APA-style manuscript in which all citations used in the manuscript are listed alphabetically.

Regression weight Value computed in a linear regression analysis that provides the slope of the least squares regression line. See also *Beta weight.*

Reliable measure A measure that produces highly similar results when used repeatedly in identical circumstances.

Replication Repeating a study in order to determine whether its results are reproducible.

Representative sample A sample of subjects in which the characteristics of the population are adequately represented.

Research fad When research in an area becomes extremely popular for a short period of time, resulting in a rush of studies in that area.

Research trend A sustained effort to accumulate knowledge in a particular area in which changes in the focus of research are gradual.

Restricted item Questionnaire item that provides subjects with response alternatives from which the subject selects an answer.

Results section The section of an APA-style manuscript that contains a description of the findings of a study. The section normally reports the values of descriptive and inferential statistics obtained.

Reversal strategy Running a second baseline phase after the intervention phase in a single-subject, baseline design.

Role playing Alternative to deceptive research that involves having subjects act as though they had been exposed to a certain treatment.

***R*-square** The square of the multiple *R* in a multiple-regression analysis. Provides a measure of the amount of variability in the dependent measure accounted for by the best linear combination of predictor variables.

Sample A relatively small number of individuals drawn from a population for inclusion in a study. See also *Population.*

Sampling distribution The distribution of a sample statistic when all possible samples of a given size are taken from the population. Sampling distributions have been determined for a wide range of statistics (such as t and F) and are used to evaluate the probability of observing a given value of that statistic.

Scattergram A graph used to display correlational data from two measures. Each point represents the two scores provided by each subject, one for each measure, plotted against one another.

Scientific explanation A tentative explanation for a phenomenon, based on objective observation and logic, and subject to empirical test.

Scientific method The method of inquiry preferred by scientists. It involves developing hypotheses, empirically testing the hypotheses, and refining and revising hypotheses.

Scientific theory A theory that goes beyond simple hypothesis, deals with verifiable phenomena, and is highly ordered and structured.

Secondary source A reference source that summarizes information from a primary source and includes research reviews and theoretical articles.

Self-report measure A measure that requires subjects to report on their past, present, or future behavior.

Semi-interquartile range A measure of variability in which an ordered distribution of scores is divided into four groups. The score separating the lower 25 percent is subtracted from the score separating the upper 25 percent. The resulting difference is divided by 2.

Simple random sampling A sampling technique in which every member of a population has an equal chance of being selected for a sample and the sampling is done on a purely random basis.

Simulation A laboratory research technique in which you attempt to recreate as closely as possible a real-world phenomenon.

Single-blind technique A technique used to combat experimenter bias in which the experimenter is not informed of the hypotheses being evaluated and does not know to which condition a subject has been assigned.

Single-factor multigroup design A between-subjects experimental design that includes only one independent variable with more than two levels.

Single-subject design An experimental design that focuses on the behavior of an individual subject rather than groups of subjects.

Skewed distribution A frequency distribution in which most scores fall into categories above or below the middle category.

Solomon four-group design An expansion of the pretest-posttest design that includes control groups to evaluate the effects of administering a pretest on your experimental treatment.

Spearman rank order correlation (*rho*) A measure of correlation used when variables are measured on at least an ordinal scale.

Split-plot design An experimental design that includes both between-subjects and within-subjects factors. Also called a *mixed design*.

Stability criterion Criterion used to establish when a baseline in a single-subject, baseline design no longer shows any systematic trends. Once the criterion is reached, the subject is placed in the next phase of the experiment.

Standard deviation The most frequently reported measure of variability. The square root of the variance.

Standard error of estimate A measure of the accuracy of prediction in a linear regression analysis. It is a measure of the distance between the observed data points and the least squares regression line.

Standard error of the mean An estimate of the amount of variability in expected sample means across a series of samples. It provides an estimate of the deviation between a sample mean and the underlying population mean.

Stratified sampling A sampling technique designed to ensure a representative sample that involves dividing the population into segments (strata) and randomly sampling from each stratum.

Strong inference A strategy for testing a theory in which a sequence of research studies are systematically carried out to rule out

alternative explanations for a phenomenon.

Systematic replication Conducting a replication of an experiment while adding new variables for investigation.

Systematic sampling A sampling technique in which every *k*th element is sampled after a randomly determined start.

Systematic variance Variability in the value of the dependent variable that is caused by variation in the independent variable.

Telephone survey Method of conducting a survey that involves calling subjects on the telephone and asking them questions from a prepared questionnaire.

Theory A set of assumptions about the causes for behavior and the rules that specify how the causes operate. A theory is subjected to empirical test and retained, modified, or rejected.

Third-variable problem A problem that interferes with drawing causal inferences from correlational results. A third, unmeasured variable affects both measured variables, causing the latter to appear correlated even though neither variable influences the other.

Time series design A research design in which behavior of subjects in naturally occurring groups is measured periodically both before and after introduction of a treatment.

Traditional review A literature review that involves reading, summarizing, and interpreting research in a given field. See also *Meta-analysis*.

Transcription error Accidentally changing a value when copying data from one place to another.

t-**test** An inferential statistic used to evaluate the reliability of a difference between two means. Versions exist for between-subjects and within-subjects designs, and for evaluating a difference between a sample mean and a population mean.

Type I error Deciding to reject the null hypothesis when, in fact, the null hypothesis is true. Also referred to as an *alpha error*.

Type II error Deciding not to reject the null hypothesis when, in fact, the null hypothesis is false. Also referred to as a *beta error*.

Univariate strategy A data analysis strategy in which multiple dependent measures are analyzed independently with separate statistical tests.

Unplanned comparison Comparison between means that is not directed by your hypothesis and is made after finding statistical significance with an overall statistical test (such as ANOVA).

Validity The extent to which a measuring instrument measures what it was designed to measure.

Valid measure A measure that actually measures what it is intended to measure.

Variable Any quantity or quality that can take on a range of values.

Variance A measure of variability. The averaged square deviation from the mean.

Volunteer bias Bias in a sample that results from using volunteer subjects exclusively.

Within-subjects design An experimental design in which each subject is exposed to all levels of an independent variable.

References

Abbott, B., & Badia, P. (1979). Choice for signaled over unsignaled shock as a function of signal length. *Journal of the Experimental Analysis of Behavior, 32,* 409–417.

Abrams, D. B., & Wilson, G. T. (1983). Alcohol, sexual arousal, and self-control. *Journal of Personality and Social Psychology, 45,* 188–198.

Ackerman, B. P. (1982). Retrieval variability: The efficient use of retrieval cues by young children. *Journal of Experimental Child Psychology, 33,* 413–428.

Adair, J. G. (1973). *The human subject: The social psychology of the psychological experiment.* Boston: Little, Brown.

Agresti, A., & Finlay, B. (1986). *Statistical Methods for the Social Sciences.* San Francisco: Dullen.

Allport, G. W., & Postman, L. (1945). The basic psychology of rumor. *Transactions of the New York Academy of Sciences, 11,* 61–81.

American Psychological Association. (1973). *Ethical principles in the conduct of research with human participants.* Washington, DC: American Psychological Association.

American Psychological Association. (1983). *Publication manual of the American Psychological Association* (3rd ed.). Washington, DC: American Psychological Association.

American Psychological Association (APA). (1990). Ethical principles of psychologists. *American Psychologist, 45,* 390–395.

Anastasi, A. (1976). *Psychological testing* (4th ed.). New York: Macmillan.

Anderson, J. F., & Berdie, D. R. (1975). Effects on response rates of formal and informal questionnaire follow-up techniques. *Journal of Applied Psychology, 60,* 255–257.

Anderson, N. (1968). A simple model for information integration. In R. P. Abelson, E. Aronson, W. J. McGuire, T. M. Newcomb, M. J. Rosenberg, & P. Tannenbaum (Eds.), *Theories of cognitive consistency: A sourcebook* (pp. 731–743). Chicago: Rand McNally.

Applebaum, M. I., & McCall, R. B. (1983). Design and analysis in developmental psychology. In P. H. Mussen & W. Kessen (Eds.), *Handbook of child psychology*, Vol. 1: *History, theory, and methods* (pp. 415–476). New York: Wiley.

Armstrong, J. S. (1982). Barriers to scientific contributions: The author's formula. *The Behavioral and Brain Sciences, 5,* 197–199.

Arnett, B., & Rikli, R. (1981). Effects of method of subject selection and treatment variable on motor performance. *Research Quarterly for Exercise and Sport, 52,* 433–440.

Aronson, E., & Carlsmith, J. M. (1968). Experimentation in social psychology. In G. Lindzey & E. Aronson (Eds.), *Handbook of social psychology* (Vol. 1, pp. 1–79). Reading, MA: Addison-Wesley.

Aserinski, E., & Kleitman, N. (1953). Regularly occurring periods of rapid eye motility and concomitant phenomena during sleep. *Science, 118,* 273.

Asher, H. B. (1976). *Causal modeling.* Sage University Paper Series on Quantitative Applications in the Social Sciences. Series number 07-003. Beverly Hills, CA: Sage.

Badia, P., & Culbertson, S. (1972). The relative aversiveness of signalled vs. unsignalled escapable and inescapable shock. *Journal of the Experimental Analysis of Behavior, 17,* 463–471.

Badia, P., Harsh, J., & Abbott, B. (1979). Choosing between predictable and unpredictable shock conditions: Data and theory. *Psychological Bulletin, 86,* 1107–1131.

Bakeman, R., & Gottman, J. M. (1989). *Observing Interaction: An Introduction to Sequential Analysis.* Cambridge, England: Cambridge University Press.

Bassili, J. N. (1981). The attractiveness stereotype: Goodness or glamour? *Basic and Applied Social Psychology, 2,* 235–252.

Baumrind, D. (1964). Some thoughts on the ethics of research: After reading Milgram's "Behavioral study of obedience." *American Psychologist, 26,* 887–896.

Belsky, J., & Rovine, M. J. (1988). Nonmaternal care in the first year of life and the security of infant-parent attachment. *Child Development, 59,* 157–167.

Bennett, S., & Bowers, D. (1976). *An introduction to multivariate techniques for social and behavioral sciences.* New York: Wiley.

Berkowitz, L. (1970). The contagion of violence: An S-R mediational analysis of some effects of observed aggression. *Nebraska Symposium on Motivation, 18,* 95–136.

Bolles, R. C., & Fanselow, M. S. (1980). A perceptual-defensive-recuperative model of fear and pain. *Behavioral and Brain Sciences, 3,* 291–301.

Bolt, M., & Myers, D. G. (1983). *Teacher's resource and test manual to accompany Social Psychology.* New York: McGraw-Hill.

Bordens, K. S. (1984). The effects of likelihood of conviction, threatened punishment, and assumed role on mock plea bargain decisions. *Basic and Applied Social Psychology, 5,* 59–74.

Bordens, K. S., & Horowitz, I. A. (1983). Information processing in joined and severed trials. *Journal of Applied Social Psychology, 13,* 351–370.

Bouchard, T. J. (1972). A comparison of two group brainstorming procedures. *Journal of Applied Psychology, 56,* 418–421.

Braithwaite, R. B. (1953). *Scientific Explanation.* New York: Harper & Row.

Bray, J. H., & Maxwell, S. E. (1982). Analyzing and interpreting significant MANOVAs. *Review of Educational Research, 52,* 340–367.

Bray, R. M., & Kerr, N. L. (1982). Methodological considerations in the study of the psychology of the courtroom. In N. L. Kerr & R. M. Bray (Eds.), *The psychology of the courtroom* (pp. 287–324). New York: Academic Press.

Brigham, J. C. (1986). *Social psychology.* Boston: Little, Brown.

Broadbent, D. E. (1958). *Perception and communication.* London: Pergamon.

Brown, R. (1965). *Social psychology.* New York: Free Press.

Bruning, J. L., & Kintz, B. L. (1987). *Computational handbook of statistics* (3rd ed.). Glenview, IL: Scott, Foresman.

Buckalew, L. W., & Hickey, R. S. (1984). Subject and stimulus variables in short-term recall and span of apprehension. *Bulletin of the Psychonomic Society, 22,* 37–39.

Buckhout, R. (1974). Eyewitness testimony. *Scientific American, 231,* 23–31.

Campbell, D. T. (1969). Prospective: Artifact and control. In R. Rosenthal and R. L. Rosnow (Eds.), *Artifact in behavioral research* (pp. 351–382). New York: Academic Press.

Campbell, D. T., & Stanley, J. C. (1963). *Experimental and quasi-experimental designs for research.* Chicago: Rand McNally.

Cartwright, D. (1961). A decade of social psychology. In W. Dennis (Ed.), *Current trends in psychological theory: A bicentennial program* (pp. 9–30). Pittsburgh: University of Pittsburgh Press.

Chassan, J. B. (1967). *Research design in clinical psychology and psychiatry.* New York: Appleton-Century-Crofts.

Chomsky, N. (1965). *Aspects of a theory of syntax.* Cambridge, MA: MIT Press.

Clemmer, E. J., & Bordens, K. S. (1986). Perception of abstract and impressionistic art. Unpublished manuscript, Emerson College, Boston, MA.

Conrad, E., & Maul, T. (1981). *Introduction to experimental psychology.* New York: Wiley.

Cooper, H. M., & Rosenthal, R. (1980). Statistical versus traditional methods for summarizing research findings. *Psychological Bulletin, 87,* 442–449.

Cooperman, E. (1980). Voluntary subjects' participation in research: Cognitive style as a possible biasing factor. *Perceptual and Motor Skills, 50,* 542.

Cowart-Steckler, D., & Pollack, R. H. (1982). The aftereffects of prolonged perception of shape. *Bulletin of the Psychonomic Society, 20,* 239–241.

Craik, F. I. M., & Tulving, E. (1975). Depth of processing and the retention of words in episodic memory. *Journal of Experimental Psychology: General, 104,* 268–294.

Crano, W. D., & Brewer, M. B. (1986). *Principles and methods of social research.* Boston: Allyn & Bacon.

Crespi, L. (1942). Quantitative variation of incentive and performance in the white rat. *American Journal of Psychology, 55,* 467–517.

Crews, F. (1980). *The Random House handbook* (3rd ed.). New York: Random House.

Davis, A. J. (1984). Sex-differentiated bias in nonsexist picture books. *Sex Roles: A Journal of Research, 11,* 1–16.

Deni, R. (1986). *Programming microcomputers for psychology experiments.* Belmont, CA: Wadsworth.

Dewsbury, D. A. (1978). *Comparative animal behavior.* New York: McGraw-Hill.

Dillman, D. A. (1978). *Mail and telephone surveys: The total design method.* New York: Wiley.

Dion, K. K., Berscheid, E., & Walster, E. (1972). What is beautiful is good. *Journal of Personality and Social Psychology, 24,* 285–290.

Donnerstein, E., & Donnerstein, M. (1973). Variables in interracial aggression: Potential ingroup censure. *Journal of Personality and Social Psychology, 27,* 143–150.

Ebbinghaus, H. E. (1885/1964). *Memory: A Contribution to Experimental Psychology.* New York: Dover.

Edwards, A. L. (1953). *Techniques of attitude scale construction.* New York: Appleton-Century-Crofts.

Edwards, A. L. (1985). *Experimental design in psychological research* (5th ed.). New York: Harper & Row.

Eron, L. (1963). Relationship of TV viewing habits and aggressive behavior in children. *Journal of Abnormal and Social Psychology, 67,* 193–196.

Fancher, R. E. (1979). *Pioneers of psychology.* New York: Norton.

Fancher, R. E. (1985). *The intelligence men: Makers of the IQ controversy.* New York: Norton.

Feild, H. S., & Barnett, N. J. (1978). Students vs. "real" people as jurors. *Journal of Social Psychology, 104,* 287–293.

Festinger, L. (1957). *A theory of cognitive dissonance.* Stanford, CA: Stanford University Press.

Festinger, L., Riecken, H. W., & Schacter, S. (1982). When prophecy fails. In A. Pines & C. Maslach (Eds.), *Experiencing social psychology: Readings and projects* (2nd ed., pp. 69–75). New York: Knopf.

Fiedler, F. E., Bell, C. H., Chemers, M. M., & Patrick, D. (1984). Increasing mine productivity and safety through management training and organization development: A comparative study. *Basic and Applied Social Psychology, 5,* 1–18.

Fishbein, M., & Ajzen, I. (1975). *Belief, attitude, intention and behavior: An introduction to theory and research*. Reading, MA: Addison-Wesley.

Fiske, D. W., & Fogg, L. (1990). But the reviewers are making different criticisms of my paper! *American Psychologist, 45*, 591–598.

Forscher, B. K. (1963). Chaos in the brickyard. *Science, 42*, 339.

Freedman, J. L. (1969). Role playing: Psychology by consensus. *Journal of Personality and Social Psychology, 13*, 107–114.

Friedrich, L. K., & Stein, A. H. (1973). Aggressive and prosocial television programs and the natural behavior of preschool children. *Monographs for the Society for Research on Child Development, 38*.

Gamson, W. A., Fireman, B., & Rytina, S. (1982). *Encounters with unjust authority*. Homewood, IL: Dorsey Press.

Gibbon, J. (1977). Scalar expectancy theory and Weber's law in animal timing. *Psychological Review, 84*, 279–325.

Glass, D. C., Singer, J. E., & Friedman, L. N. (1969). Psychic cost of adaptation to an environmental stressor. *Journal of Personality and Social Psychology, 12*, 200–210.

Glass, G. V. (1978). In defense of generalization. *The Behavioral and Brain Sciences, 1*(3), 394–395.

Glassnap, D. R., & Poggio, J. P. (1985). *Essentials of statistical analysis for the behavioral sciences*. Columbus, OH: Merrill.

Gold, P. E. (1987). Sweet memories. *American Scientist, 75*, 151–155.

Goldiamond, I. (1965). Stuttering and fluency as manipulable operant response classes. In L. Krasner & L. P. Ullman (Eds.), *Research in behavior modification* (pp. 106–156). New York: Holt, Rinehart & Winston.

Goldstein, J. H., Rosnow, R. L., Goodstadt, B. E., & Suls, J. E. (1972). The good subject in verbal operant conditioning research. *Journal of Experimental Research in Personality, 28*, 29–33.

Gravetter, F. J., & Wallnau, L. B. (1990). *Statistics for the behavioral sciences* (2nd ed.). St. Paul, MN: West.

Greenberg, B. S. (1980). *Life on television: Current analyses of U.S. TV drama*. Norwood, NJ: Ablex.

Greene, E., & Loftus, E. F. (1984). What's in the news? The influence of well-publicized news events on psychological research and courtroom trials. *Basic and Applied Social Psychology, 5*, 211–221.

Grice, G. R. (1966). Dependence of empirical laws upon the source of experimental variation. *Psychological Bulletin, 66*, 488–498.

Hall, D. (1979). *Writing well*. Boston: Little, Brown.

Hall, R. V., Lund, D., & Jackson, D. (1968). Effects of teacher attention on study behavior. *Journal of Applied Behavior Analysis, 1*, 1–12.

Haney, C. (1984). On the selection of capital juries. *Law and Human Behavior, 8*, 121–132.

Haney, C., Banks, C., & Zimbardo, P. (1973). Interpersonal dynamics in a simulated prison. *International Journal of Criminology and Penology, 1*, 69–87.

Harari, H., Harari, O., & White, R. V. (1985). The reaction to rape by American male bystanders. *Journal of Social Psychology, 125,* 653–668.

Harrison, W., Thompson, V. D., & Rodgers, J. L. (1985). Robustness, and sufficiency of the theory of reasoned action in longitudinal prediction. *Basic and Applied Social Psychology, 6,* 25–40.

Hempel, C. G. (1966). *Philosophy of natural science.* Englewood Cliffs, NJ: Prentice-Hall.

Herrnstein, R. J. (1961). Relative and absolute strength of response as a function of frequency of reinforcement. *Journal of the Experimental Analysis of Behavior, 4,* 267–272.

Higbee, K. L., Millard, R. J., & Folkman, J. R. (1982). Social psychology research during the 1970s: Predominance of experimentation and college students. *Personality and Social Psychology Bulletin, 8,* 182–183.

Hite, S. (1976). *The Hite report: A nationwide study on female sexuality.* New York: Macmillan.

Hite, S., (1983). *The Hite report on male sexuality.* New York: Ballantine Books.

Holmes, D. S. (1976a). Debriefing after psychological experiments I: Effectiveness of postdeception dehoaxing. *American Psychologist, 31,* 858–867.

Holmes, D. S. (1976b). Debriefing after psychological experiments II: Effectiveness of postdeception desensitizing. *American Psychologist, 31,* 868–875.

Holsti, O. R. (1969). *Content analysis for the social sciences and humanities.* Reading, MA: Addison-Wesley.

Hooke, R. (1983). *How to tell the liars from the statisticians.* New York: Dekker.

Hornik, J. (1982). Impact of pre-call on response to a mail questionnaire. *Journal of Marketing Research, 19,* 144–151.

Horowitz, I. A. (1969). The effects of volunteering, fear arousal, and number of communications on attitude change. *Journal of Personality and Social Psychology, 11,* 34–37.

Horowitz, I. A. (1985). The effects of jury nullification instructions on verdicts and jury functioning in criminal trials. *Law and Human Behavior, 9,* 25–36.

Horowitz, I. A., Bordens, K. S., & Feldman, M. S. (1980). A comparison of verdicts obtained in severed and joined criminal trials. *Journal of Applied Social Psychology, 10,* 444–456.

Horowitz, I. A., & Rothschild, B. H. (1970). Conformity as a function of deception and role playing. *Journal of Personality and Social Psychology, 14,* 224–226.

Huck, S. W., & Sandler, H. M. (1979). *Rival hypotheses: Alternative explanations of data based conclusions.* New York: Harper & Row.

Hull, C. L. (1943). *Principles of behavior.* Englewood Cliffs, NJ: Prentice-Hall.

Humphreys, A. P., & Smith, P. K. (1987). Rough and tumble, friendship, and dominance in school children: Evidence for continuity and change with age. *Child Development, 58,* 201–212.

Hunter, J. E. (1987). Multiple dependent variables in program evaluation. In M. M. Mark & R. L. Shotland (Eds.), *Multiple methods.* San Francisco: Jossey-Bass.

Hunter, J. E., & Gerbing, D. W. (1982). Unidimensional measurement, second-order factor analysis and causal models. *Research in Organizational Behavior, 4,* 267–320.

Jaccard, J., & Becker, M. A. (1990). *Statistics for the Behavioral Sciences* (2nd ed.). Belmont, CA: Wadsworth.

Janis, I., & Mann, L. (1965). Effectiveness of emotional role playing in modifying smoking habits and attitudes. *Journal of Experimental Research in Personality, 1,* 84–90.

Johnson, S. B., Hamm, R. J., & Leahey, T. H. (1986). Observational learning in gallus gallus domesticus with and without a conspecific model. *Bulletin of the Psychonomic Society, 24,* 237–239.

Jones, E. E. (1985). Major developments in social psychology in the past five decades. In G. Lindzey & E. Aronson (Eds.), *Handbook of social psychology* (Vol. 1, pp. 47–107). New York: Random House.

Kanuk, L., & Berenson, C. (1975). Mail surveys and response rates: A literature review. *Journal of Marketing Research, 12,* 440–453.

Katz, J. (1972). *Experimentation with human beings.* New York: Russell Sage Foundation.

Kazdin, A. E. (1976). Statistical analyses for single-case experimental designs. In M. Hersen & D. H. Barlow (Eds.), *Single-case experimental designs: Strategies for studying behavior change* (pp. 265–316). New York: Pergamon Press.

Kelly, G. (1963). *A theory of personality: The psychology of personal constructs.* New York: Norton.

Kelman, H. C. (1967). The use of human subjects: The problem of deception in social psychological experiments. *Psychological Bulletin, 67,* 1–11.

Keppel, G. (1973). *Design and analysis: A researcher's handbook.* Englewood Cliffs, NJ: Prentice-Hall.

Keppel, G. (1982). *Design and analysis: A researcher's handbook* (2nd ed.). Englewood Cliffs, NJ: Prentice-Hall.

Key, W. B. (1973). *Subliminal seduction.* New York: Signet.

Kish, L. (1965). *Survey sampling.* New York: Wiley.

Kuhn, T. S. (1970). *The structure of scientific revolutions* (2nd ed., enlarged). Chicago: University of Chicago Press.

Landy, E., & Aronson, E. (1969). The influence of the character of the criminal and his victim on the decisions of simulated jurors. *Journal of Experimental Social Psychology, 5,* 141–152.

Leaton, R. N., & Borszcz, G. S. (1985). Potentiated startle: Its relation to freezing and shock intensity in rats. *Journal of Experimental Psychology: Animal Behavior Processes, 11,* 421–428.

Leggett, G., Mead, C. D., & Charvat, W. (1978). *Prentice-Hall handbook for writers* (7th ed.). Englewood Cliffs, NJ: Prentice-Hall.

Levine, M. S. (1977). *Canonical analysis and factor comparison.* Sage University Paper Series on Quantitative Applications in the Social Sciences. Series number 07-006. Beverly Hills, CA: Sage.

Liberman, R. P., & Smith, V. (1972). Multiple baseline study of systematic desensitization in a patient with multiple phobias. *Behavior Therapy, 3,* 597–603.

Lindsey, D. (1978). *The scientific publication system in social science.* San Francisco: Jossey-Bass.

Loftus, E. F. (1979). *Eyewitness testimony.* Cambridge, MA: Harvard University Press.

Loftus, E. F., Greene, E., & Smith, K. H. (1980). How deep is the meaning of life? *Bulletin of the Psychonomic Society, 15,* 282–284.

Lorenz, K. (1950). The comparative method in studying innate behavior patterns. *Symposium of the Society for Experimental Biology, 4,* 221–268.

Lorenz, K., & Tinbergen, N. (1957). Taxis and instinctive action in egg-retrieving behavior of the gray lag goose. In C. H. Schiller (Ed.), *Instinctive behavior* (pp. 176–208). New York: International Universities Press.

Lorge, I. (1930). Influence of regularly interpolated time intervals on subsequent learning. *College Contributions to Education, 438,* 1–57.

Macaulay, D. (1979). *Motel of the mysteries.* Boston: Houghton Mifflin.

Mahoney, M. J. (1977). Publication prejudices: An experimental study of confirmatory bias in the peer review system. *Cognitive Therapy and Research, 1,* 161–175.

Martin, E. (1985). *Doing psychology experiments* (2nd ed.). Monterey, CA: Brooks/Cole.

Mayo, C., & LaFrance, M. (1977). *Evaluating research in social psychology.* Monterey, CA: Brooks/Cole.

McDonnell, J. D. (1968). Effect of pricing on perception of product quality. *Journal of Applied Psychology, 52,* 331–334.

McFarland, S. (1981). Effects of question order on survey responses. *Public Opinion Quarterly, 48,* 208–215.

McNemar, Q. (1946). Opinion-attitude methodology. *Psychological Bulletin, 43,* 289–374.

Milgram, S. (1963). Behavioral study of obedience. *Journal of Abnormal and Social Psychology, 67,* 371–378.

Milgram, S. (1974). *Obedience to authority.* New York: Harper & Row.

Miller, G. A. (1956). The magical number seven, plus or minus two: Some limits on our capacity for processing information. *Psychological Review, 63,* 81–97.

Milton, R. C. (1964). Extended tables for the Mann-Whitney (Wilcoxon) two-sample test. *Journal of the American Statistical Association, 59,* 925–934.

Mintz, A. (1951). Nonadaptive group behavior. *Journal of Abnormal and Social Psychology, 46,* 150–159.

Moser, C. A., & Kalton, G. (1972). *Survey methods in social investigation.* New York: Basic Books.

Mullen, B., & Rosenthal, R. (1985). *Basic meta-analysis: Procedures and programs.* Hillsdale, NJ: Lawrence Erlbaum Associates.

Myers, D. G. (1983). *Social psychology*. New York: McGraw-Hill.

Mynatt, C. R., Doherty, M. E., & Tweney, R. D. (1978). Consequences of confirmation and disconfirmation in a simulated research environment. *Quarterly Journal of Experimental Psychology, 30,* 395–406.

Neisser, U. (1976). *Cognition and reality: Principles and implications for cognitive psychology.* San Francisco: Freeman.

Nunnally, J. C. (1967). *Psychometric theory.* New York: McGraw-Hill.

O'Brien, R. G., & Kaiser, M. K. (1985). MANOVA method for analyzing repeated measures designs: An extensive primer. *Psychological Bulletin, 97,* 316–333.

Orne, M. T. (1962). On the social psychology of the psychological experiment with particular reference to demand characteristics and their implications. *American Psychologist, 17,* 776–783.

Overmeier, J. B., & Seligman, M. E. P. (1967). Effects of inescapable shock upon subsequent escape and avoidance learning. *Journal of Comparative and Physiological Psychology, 63,* 28–33.

Pagano, R. R. (1986). *Understanding statistics in the behavioral sciences* (2nd ed.). St. Paul, MN: West.

Panksepp, J., Normansell, L., Siviy, S., Rossi, J., & Zolovick, A. J. (1983). Casomorphins reduce separation distress in chicks. *Peptides, 5,* 829–831.

Pearson, E. S., & Hartley, H. O. (Eds.). (1966). *Biometrika: Tables for statisticians.* London: Cambridge University Press.

Peters, D. P., & Ceci, S. J. (1982). Peer-review practices of psychological journals: The fate of published articles submitted again. *The Behavioral and Brain Sciences, 5,* 187–255.

Peterson, L. R., & Peterson, M. J. (1959). Short-term retention of individual verbal items. *Journal of Experimental Psychology, 58,* 193–198.

Piaget, J. (1952). *The origins of intelligence in children.* New York: Norton.

Piliavin, J. A., & Piliavin, I. (1972). Effects of blood on reactions to a victim. *Journal of Personality and Social Psychology, 23,* 353–361.

Platt, J. R. (1964). Strong inference. *Science, 146,* 347–353.

Poppen, R. (1980). *How to construct and present a poster.* Available from the Midwestern Psychological Association.

Pressley, M. M., & Tullar, W. L. (1977). A factor interactive investigation of mail survey response rates from a commercial sample. *Journal of Marketing Research, 14,* 108–111.

Provine, R. P., & Hamernik, H. B. (1986). Yawning: Effects of stimulus interest. *Bulletin of the Psychonomic Society, 24,* 437–438.

Rauh, V. A., Achenbach, T. M., Nurcomb, B., Howell, C. T., & Teti, D. M. (1988). Minimizing adverse effects of low birthweight: Four-year results of an early intervention program. *Child Development, 59,* 544–553.

Rescorla, R. A., & Wagner, A. R. (1972). A theory of Pavlovian conditioning: Variations in the effectiveness of reinforcement and nonreinforcement. In A. H. Black & W. F. Prokosy (Eds.), *Classical conditioning II: Current research and theory* (pp. 64–99). New York: Appleton-Century-Crofts.

Resnick, J. H., & Schwartz, T. (1973). Ethical standards as an independent variable in psychological research. *American Psychologist, 28,* 134–139.

Reynolds, G. S. (1961). Attention in the pigeon. *Journal of the Experimental Analysis of Behavior, 4,* 203–208.

Roberts, J. V. (1985). The attitude–memory relationship after 40 years: A meta-analysis of the literature. *Basic and Applied Social Psychology, 6,* 221–242.

Roscoe, J. T. (1975). *Fundamental statistics for the behavioral sciences* (2nd ed.). New York: Holt, Rinehart & Winston.

Rosenthal, R. (1976). *Experimenter effects in behavioral research* (enlarged ed.). New York: Irvington.

Rosenthal, R. (1979). The "file drawer problem" and tolerance for null results. *Psychological Bulletin, 86,* 638–641.

Rosenthal, R. (1984). *Meta-analytic procedures for social research.* Applied Social Research Methods, Vol. 6. Beverly Hills, CA: Sage.

Rosenthal, R., & Rosnow, R. L. (1975). *The volunteer subject.* New York: Wiley.

Rosenthal, R., & Rubin, D. B. (1982). A simple, general purpose display of magnitude of experimental effect. *Journal of Educational Psychology, 74,* 166–169.

Rosnow, R. L., & Rosnow, M. (1986). *Writing psychology papers.* Monterey, CA: Brooks/Cole.

Ross, L., Lepper, M. R., & Hubbard, M. (1975). Perseverance in self-perception and social perception: Biased attributional processes in debriefing paradigms. *Journal of Personality and Social Psychology, 32,* 880–892.

Runyon, R. P., & Haber, A. (1984). *Fundamentals of behavioral statistics.* Reading, MA: Addison-Wesley.

Saks, M. J. (1986). The law does not live by eyewitness testimony alone. *Law and Human Behavior, 10,* 279–280.

Saunders, D. R. (1980). Definition of stroop interference in volunteers and nonvolunteers. *Perceptual and Motor Skills, 51,* 343–354.

Schachter, S. (1971). *Emotion, obesity, and crime.* New York: Academic Press.

Schaie, K. W. (1965). A general model for the study of developmental problems. *Psychological Bulletin, 64,* 92–107.

Schuler, H. (1982). *Ethical problems in psychological research.* New York: Academic Press.

Seligman, M. E. P. (1970). On the generality of the laws of learning. *Psychological Review, 77,* 406–418.

Seligman, M. E. P., & Haber, J. L. (1972). *Biological boundaries of learning.* New York: Appleton-Century-Crofts.

Shaffer, D. (1985). *Developmental psychology: Theory, research, and applications.* Monterey, CA: Brooks/Cole.

Shannon, C. E., & Weaver, W. (1949). *The mathematical model of communication.* Urbana, IL: University of Illinois Press.

Sharp, L. M., & Frankel, J. (1983). Respondent burden: A test of some common assumptions. *Public Opinion Quarterly, 47,* 36–53.

Sheridan, C. E. (1979). *Methods of experimental psychology.* New York: Holt, Rinehart & Winston.

Sidman, M. (1953). Two temporal parameters of the maintenance of avoidance behavior by the white rat. *Journal of Comparative and Physiological Psychology, 46,* 253–261.

Sidman, M. (1960). *Tactics of scientific research: Evaluating experimental data in psychology.* New York: Basic Books.

Siegel, S., & Castellan, N. J. (1988). *Nonparametric statistics for the behavioral sciences* (2nd ed.). New York: McGraw-Hill.

Sigelman, L. (1981). Question order effects on presidential popularity. *Public Opinion Quarterly, 45,* 199–207.

Silverman, I., Schulman, A. D., & Weisenthal, D. L. (1970). Effects of deceiving and debriefing psychological subjects on performance in later experiments. *Journal of Personality and Social Psychology, 14,* 203–212.

Singer, E., Frankel, M. R., & Glassman, M. B. (1983). The effect of interviewer characteristics on responses. *Public Opinion Quarterly, 47,* 68–73.

Singer, P. (1975). *Animal liberation: A new ethics for our treatment of animals.* New York: Avon Books.

Skinner, B. F. (1949). Are theories of learning necessary? *Psychological Review, 57,* 193–216.

Slovic, P., & Fischoff, B. (1977). On the psychology of experimental surprise. *Journal of Experimental Psychology: Human Perception and Performance, 3,* 544–551.

Smith, S. S., & Richardson, D. (1983). Amelioration of deception and harm in psychological research: The important role of debriefing. *Journal of Personality and Social Psychology, 44,* 1075–1082.

Snowdon, C. T. (1983). Ethology, comparative psychology, and animal behavior. *Annual Review of Psychology, 34,* 63–94.

Strunk, W., & White, E. B. (1979). *The elements of style* (3rd ed.). New York: Macmillan.

Tabachnick, B. G., & Fidell, L. S. (1989). *Using multivariate statistics* (2nd ed.). New York: Harper & Row.

Tanford, S. L. (1984). Decision making processes in joined criminal trials. Unpublished doctoral dissertation, University of Wisconsin, Madison.

Tanner, W. P., Jr., Swets, J. A., & Green, D. M. (1956). *Some general properties of the hearing mechanism* (Tech. Rep. No. 30). Ann Arbor: University of Michigan, Electronic Defense Group.

Tatsuoka, M. M. (1971). *Multivariate analysis: Techniques for educational and psychological research.* New York: Wiley.

Thorndike, R. M. (1978). *Correlational procedures for research.* New York: Gardner Press.

Tinbergen, N. (1951). *The study of instinct.* Oxford: Clarendon Press.

Treadway, M., & McCloskey, M. (1987). Cite unseen: Distortions of Allport and Postman's rumor study in the eyewitness testimony literature. *Law and Human Behavior, 11,* 19–26.

Ullman, D., & Jackson, T. (1982). Researchers' ethical concerns: Debriefing from 1960–1980. *American Psychologist, 37*, 972–973.

U.S. Department of Health and Human Services. (1982). Protection of human subjects. HHS Document 4.108:45, Pt. 46. Washington, DC: Author.

Vinacke, W. (1954). Deceiving experimental subjects. *American Psychologist, 9*, 155.

Wadsworth, B. J. (1971). *Piaget's theory of cognitive development.* New York: McKay.

Walster, E., Berscheid, E., Abrahams, D., & Aronson, E. (1967). Effectiveness of debriefing after deception experiments. *Journal of Personality and Social Psychology, 6*, 371–380.

Walster, E., Walster, G. W., & Berscheid, E. (1978). *Equity theory and research.* Boston: Allyn & Bacon.

Warner, J. L., Berman, J. J., Weyant, J. M., & Ciarlo, J. A. (1983). Assessing mental health program effectiveness: A comparison of three client follow-up methods. *Evaluation Review, 7*, 635–658.

Wexley, K. N., & Thornton, C. L. (1972). Effect of verbal feedback of test results on learning. *Journal of Educational Research, 66*, 665–666.

Williams, C. D. (1959). The elimination of tantrum behavior by extinction procedures. *Journal of Abnormal and Social Psychology, 59*, 269.

Wilson, D. W., & Donnerstein, E. (1977). Guilty or not guilty? A look at the simulated jury paradigm. *Journal of Applied Social Psychology, 7*, 175–190.

Winer, B. J. (1971). *Statistical principles in experimental design* (2nd ed.). New York: McGraw-Hill.

Winkel, G. H., & Sasanoff, R. (1970). An approach to objective analysis of behavior in architectural space. In H. M. Proshansky, W. H. Ittelson, & L. G. Rivlin (Eds.), *Environmental psychology: Man and his environment* (pp. 619–630). New York: Holt, Rinehart & Winston.

Wood, C. (1979). The I-knew-it-all-along effect. *Journal of Experimental Psychology: Human Perception and Performance, 43*, 345–353.

Yaremko, R. M., Harari, H., Harrison, R. C., & Lynn, E. (1982). *Reference handbook of research and statistical methods.* New York: Harper & Row.

Zajonc, R. B. (1965). Social facilitation. *Science, 149*, 269–274.

Text Credits

Name Index

Subject Index